NORTON ANTHOLOGY OF
WESTERN MUSIC

VOLUME 2: CLASSIC TO TWENTIETH CENTURY

FIFTH EDITION

NORTON ANTHOLOGY OF
WESTERN MUSIC

VOLUME 2: CLASSIC TO TWENTIETH CENTURY

FIFTH EDITION

Edited by

J. Peter Burkholder

and

Claude V. Palisca

W. W. NORTON & COMPANY

NEW YORK LONDON

Copyright © 2006, 2001, 1996, 1988, 1980 by W. W. Norton & Company, Inc.

ISBN 0-393-92562-5 (pbk.)

W. W. Norton & Company, Inc., 500 Fifth Avenue, New York, N.Y. 10110
    www.wwnorton.com

W. W. Norton & Company Ltd., Castle House, 75/76 Wells Street, London W1T 3QT

7 8 9 0

CONTENTS

THE NINETEENTH CENTURY

Revolution and Change

The Romantic Generation: Song and Piano Music

Romanticism in Classic Forms: Orchestral, Chamber, and Choral Music

Romantic Opera and Musical Theater to Midcentury

MAKING CONNECTIONS:
HOW TO USE THIS ANTHOLOGY

The *Norton Anthology of Western Music* (NAWM) is a companion to *A History of Western Music*, Seventh Edition (HWM), and *Concise History of Western Music*, Third Edition. It is also designed to stand by itself as a collection representing the most significant traditions, trends, genres, national schools, innovations, and historical developments in the history of music in Europe and the Americas.

The editions of the scores are the best available for which permission could be secured, including several new editions especially prepared for NAWM. Where no publication or editor is cited, Claude V. Palisca or I have edited the music from the original source. Each selection is followed by a new, detailed commentary, separate from the discussion of the piece in HWM, that describes the piece's origins, points out its important features and stylistic traits, and addresses issues of performance practice, including any unusual aspects of notation. All foreign-language texts are accompanied by English translations by one or both coeditors, except where another translator is credited. These are literal to a fault, corresponding to the original line by line, often word for word, to facilitate understanding of the ways the composer has set the text.

An anthology of musical scores is greatly enhanced by recordings. Excellent, authoritative recordings of all the items in NAWM are included on the *Norton Recorded Anthology of Western Music*. Many are new to this edition. For music composed prior to the nineteenth century, the performers on the recordings use period instruments and seek to reflect the performance practice of the time, to the extent that we understand it today. The recordings also include performances with period instruments for several works composed during the nineteenth century: symphonies of Beethoven and Berlioz, Clara Schumann's Piano Trio, an oratorio by Mendelssohn, and songs by Bishop and Foster. The ragtime and jazz recordings all feature the original artists. In many periods and genres, musicians were expected to improvise, embellish, or otherwise alter the written music; when these or other discrepancies occur between score and recording, we have provided an explanation in the commentary.

To make listening easier, compact disc numbers and track numbers have been added to the scores—in notched rectangles for the complete 12-CD set and in plain rectangles for the 6-CD Concise set. The boxes are shaded a light gray to make them stand out on the page. The CD number is located in the running head at the top of the page, and the track numbers are placed in the score itself. Tracks are positioned not only at the beginning of each selection or movement but also to mark major sections, themes, and other events in the music, especially those pointed out in the commentaries.

Why These Pieces?

We have aimed to include outstanding works that represent their makers, genres, and times. But because only a small fraction of the music worthy of attention could be included, it is incumbent on us to explain why we chose the pieces we did. Knowing our thinking will help students and teachers make the best use of this collection.

The title *Norton Anthology of Western Music* (NAWM) needs one important qualifier: this is a *historical* anthology of the Western musical tradition. Rather than serve up great works to be studied in splendid isolation, this anthology seeks to place each piece in a historical context, relating it to the society from which it came and to other music that the composer used as model or inspiration. Studying music in its contexts can illuminate the choices composers made, the values of the society they lived in, and the meanings of the pieces themselves. Just as composers did not create in a musical void, standing aloof from their predecessors and contemporaries, so the historically oriented listener must have access to the primary material in order to establish connections. This anthology invites students and teachers to make such connections.

Breadth of Repertoire

Making connections depends on having a wide range of examples. The repertoire covered in this edition of NAWM is broader than ever before. Women composers are represented across the centuries—in the twelfth century by Hildegard of Bingen (7) and Beatriz de Dia (9); in the seventeenth by Barbara Strozzi (69) and Elisabeth-Claude Jacquet de la Guerre (78); in the nineteenth by Clara Schumann (123); and in the twentieth by Amy Cheney Beach (134), Bessie Smith (149), Ruth Crawford Seeger (156), Ellen Taaffe Zwilich (169), and Sofia Gubaidulina (171). Music of Spain is covered more fully, and Latin America is now included as well, represented by a medieval cantiga (12), a Renaissance secular villancico (48), works for vihuela (60), a South American Christmas villancico (81), the first opera composed and staged in the New World (80), and a symphonic picture of an Afro-Cuban ritual by Mexico's Silvestre Revueltas (155). The African-American traditions of ragtime, blues, and jazz are included for the first time, with a Joplin rag (136), Bessie Smith's *Back Water Blues* (149), Louis Armstrong's rendition of *West End Blues* (150), Ellington's *Cotton Tail* (152), and Parker and Gillespie's *Anthropology* (159). Also here for the first time are classics of band literature, from Sousa (135) to Husa (167). Coverage of music in the United States and Eastern Europe has been increased, adding pieces by Billings (97), Foster (115), Gottschalk (120), Rachmaninov (139), Gershwin (151), Barber (162), Penderecki (165), Cage (166), Pärt (170), and Sheng (172), who is the first Asian-born composer to be included in any edition of NAWM.

Breadth of repertoire is matched by depth. Several composers are represented by more than one work to permit comparison of early and later styles (for example, Du Fay, Monteverdi, Beethoven, Schubert, Schoenberg, and Stravinsky) and to show distinct approaches by a single composer to diverse genres (for example, Adam de la Halle, Machaut, Josquin, Byrd, Bach, Handel, Haydn, Mozart, and Mendelssohn). Instead of relying solely on excerpts to give a taste of multimovement genres, NAWM includes complete examples of a Gregorian chant Mass,

Baroque keyboard suite, Corelli trio sonata, Vivaldi concerto, Bach cantata, and Haydn symphony, to show how such works are constructed and what types of movement they contain. In the same spirit, complete scenes from operas by Monteverdi, Rameau, Handel, Mozart, Rossini, Weber, and Verdi demonstrate how differently these composers construct a scene.

Styles and Genres

Perhaps the primary role of a historical anthology is to present examples of the most important styles and genres in music history and to trace their development through time. The generally chronological organization of the book, which follows the order in which these selections are discussed in HWM, highlights changes in both style and genre from ancient Greece (NAWM 1–2), medieval monophony (3–13), and early polyphony (14–23) through the fourteenth century (24–30); the first, middle, and later generations of Renaissance composers (31–36, 37–41, and 42–62); the early, middle, and late Baroque period (63–76, 77–84, and 85–92); the Classic era (93–107); the first and second halves of the nineteenth century (108–126 and 127–135); and the twentieth century before (136–158) and after (159–172) World War II.

Genres, styles, conventions, and forms develop only because composers pick up ideas from each other and replicate or build on them in their own music, a process that can be observed again and again through the pieces in this anthology. The monophonic songs of the troubadours in southern France (8–9), for example, inspired those of the trouvères in the north (10), Minnesinger in Germany (11), and cantiga composers in Spain (12). Later generations of poet-musicians, active in the fourteenth century, wrote polyphonic secular songs and codified standard forms for them, notably the French rondeau (26 and 33), virelai (27), and ballade (34), and the Italian madrigal, caccia, and ballata (28–30). In the Renaissance, new forms and styles of secular song emerged, including the Spanish villancico (48), German Lied (38), Italian frottola and madrigal (49–53), and new types of French chanson (54–55) and songs in English (56–58). A similar path can be traced from the creation of opera in Italy (65–68) through its diffusion to other lands and the many changes of style through the nineteenth (125–131) and twentieth centuries (143 and 161), or in religious music from Gregorian chant (3–5) to the modern style of Pärt (170).

Musicians frequently use an old word to mean new things, so that the very nature of a genre may change. For example, the motet began as a work that added text to existing music (21a), then became a new piece based on chant in the bottom voice (21c), which could be secular, like Adam de la Halle's (22). In the Renaissance, from Dunstable (32) to Lasso (47), the motet was redefined as a polyphonic Latin sacred work with equal voices, and in the seventeenth century it came to include solo works with accompaniment by Grandi (70) and others. Exploring and explaining such changes is a central theme of this anthology and of HWM.

Similar chains of development can be seen in instrumental music. Dance music in the Middle Ages (13) and Renaissance (59) led to stylized dances of many types: independent pieces for keyboard, including those by Byrd (61) and Chopin (117); keyboard dance suites in the Baroque period, such as those by Jacquet de la

Guerre (78) and François Couperin (86), a genre revived in the modern era by Schoenberg (142) and others; and dance movements in other works, including Corelli's trio sonatas (83d) and symphonies from Haydn (104c) to Shostakovich (154). In addition, dance rhythms infect many vocal and instrumental works, from the air in minuet rhythm in Lully's opera *Armide* (77) to the seguidilla from Bizet's *Carmen* (129).

The canzonas of Gabrieli (62) and others established a tradition of extended instrumental works in several sections with contrasting meters, tempos, and moods, leading to the sonatas of Marini (76) and the multimovement sonatas of Corelli (82) and later composers. Out of this tradition emerged the string quartet and other forms of chamber music, from Haydn (103) to Crumb (163). The symphony grew from its Italian beginnings, represented by Sammartini (100), to become the major instrumental genre of the late eighteenth and nineteenth centuries, dominated by Austrian and German composers such as Stamitz (101), Haydn (104), and Beethoven (109). Berlioz's *Symphonie fantastique* (121) and Brahms's Fourth Symphony (132) represent opposite sides of the nineteenth-century division between programmatic and absolute music. The symphony was a continuing presence in the twentieth century, represented here by Webern (144), Stravinsky (146), Shostakovich (154), Still (158), and Zwilich (169).

As suggested by these descriptions, almost every genre has roots in an earlier one. Here is where the evolutionary metaphor so often applied to music history seems most applicable, tracing lines of development both within and between genres. This anthology provides ample material for making these connections. The development of individual genres can be traced by using the Index of Forms and Genres at the back of each volume.

Techniques

In addition to genres, composers often learn techniques from their contemporaries or predecessors and extend them in new ways. Compositional practices that start in one genre or tradition often cross boundaries over time. To give just one example, imitative counterpoint, developed in the medieval canon (23) and caccia (29), became a structural principle in Renaissance vocal music from the late fifteenth century, illustrated by Josquin's motet *Ave maria . . . virgo serena* (39), through the early seventeenth century, as in Weelkes's madrigal *As Vesta was* (57). The technique was taken over into instrumental music through the canzona (62) and ricercare (75), and the latter developed into the fugue (see the fugues in 84 and 88). Fugal passages occur in many types of work, from oratorios (92c and 124) to the development sections of symphonies (104a and 109), and imitation remains a device learned by every student of Western music.

Forms morph into new forms or combine with others. Binary form, invented for dance music (59a and 78), was used for abstract sonata movements by Domenico Scarlatti (98) and others and developed into sonata form as used in Mozart's piano sonatas (105) and the first movements of symphonies (100, 101, 104a and d, and 109). A small binary form could also be expanded into a longer movement by serving as the theme for a movement in rondo form, as in the finale of Haydn's *Joke* String Quartet (103). The elements of sonata form could in turn be combined with ritornello form in a concerto first movement, as in the concertos by J. C. Bach (102) and Mozart (106), or with rondo form in a sonata-rondo, used for finales by Beethoven (108), Mendelssohn (122), and others.

Styles also cross genres and traditions. Vocal music served as the basis for early instrumental works, like the intabulations and variations of Narváez (60). Moreover, the styles and gestures of vocal music have been imitated by instrumental composers again and again, including recitative and vocal monody in Marini's violin sonata (76), singing styles in piano sonatas by C. P. E. Bach (99) and Mozart (105), and bel canto operatic style in Chopin's nocturnes (118). Musicians cannot afford to know only the literature for their own instrument, for composers are constantly borrowing ideas from other repertoires, and performers need to know how to reflect these allusions to other styles in their performances.

Several selections document the influence of vernacular and traditional music on art music. Medieval English singers improvised polyphony with parallel thirds and sixths, which entered notated music in the thirteenth-century *Sumer is icumen in* (23), fifteenth-century carols (31), and the works of English composer John Dunstable (32) and exercised a profound influence on Continental composers such as Binchois (33) and Du Fay (35). Debussy adapted the texture and melodic idiom of a Javanese gamelan to his own orchestral conception in *Nuages* (138). Stravinsky simulated folk polyphony in *The Rite of Spring* (145). Bartók borrowed elements of Serbo-Croatian song and Bulgarian dance styles in his *Music for Strings, Percussion and Celesta* (147). Still's *Afro-American Symphony* (158) incorporates the twelve-bar blues (149–150), the style of African-American spirituals, and instrumental sounds from jazz. Sheng makes the cellist imitate the sounds and playing styles of Chinese instruments in his *Seven Tunes Heard in China* (172).

Twentieth-century composers have introduced a constant stream of innovations, and this anthology includes a number of pioneering works. Notable are Schoenberg's *Pierrot lunaire* (141), his most famous atonal piece and the first to use *Sprechstimme*; his Piano Suite (142), the first complete twelve-tone work; Webern's Symphony (144), a model of *Klangfarbenmelodie* and pointillism; Stravinsky's *Rite of Spring* (145), whose block construction influenced so many later composers; Babbitt's *Philomel* (164), an early example of combining a live singer with electronic music on tape; Cage's *Music of Changes* (166), one of the first pieces composed using chance operations; Penderecki's *Threnody* (165), which produces novel clusters of sound from a string orchestra; and Adams's *Phrygian Gates* (168), which applies minimalist techniques to create a gradually changing canvas of sound.

Learning from History

Besides learning from their contemporaries and immediate predecessors, many composers have reached back across the centuries to revive old methods or genres, often producing something remarkably new in the process. Inspired by the ancient Greek idea of suiting music to the rhythm and mood of the words, illustrated here by the *Epitaph of Seikilos* (1), Renaissance composers sought to capture the accents and feelings of the text, evident in motets by Josquin (39) and Lasso (47), in the new genre of the madrigal (50–53), and in the *musique mesurée* of le Jeune (55). Among the tools Renaissance composers borrowed from ancient Greek music and music theory was chromaticism, found in Euripides's *Orestes* (2);

after madrigal composers like Rore (51), Marenzio (52), and Gesualdo (53) used it as an expressive device, it became a common feature in instrumental music as well, such as in Frescobaldi's chromatic ricercare (75), and later composers from Bach (89) to Wagner (128) made it an increasingly central part of the musical language. In a classic example of creating something new by reaching into the distant past, the attempt to revive the principles of ancient Greek tragedy led to the invention of opera and recitative in Peri's *Euridice* (65).

Romantic and modern composers have often sought to revive the spirit of earlier music. Recollections of Baroque music include Beethoven's fugue in his String Quartet in C-sharp minor (110a), Brahms's chaconne in the finale of his Fourth Symphony (132), and Schoenberg's passacaglia in *Nacht* from *Pierrot lunaire* (141a). Webern's Symphony (144) contains elaborate canons modeled on those of the Renaissance, and Hindemith's *Un cygne* (153) resurrects the Renaissance chanson in a modern harmonic language. Messiaen borrowed the isorhythmic techniques of Vitry (24) and Machaut (25) in his *Quartet for the End of Time* (160), and Barber echoed medieval chant, heterophony, and open-fifth harmonies in his picture of a medieval monk (162).

Reworkings

In addition to drawing on general styles, genres, and techniques, composers have often reworked particular compositions, a process that can be traced through numerous examples in this anthology. In one notable case, a single chant gave rise to a chain of polyphonic accretions. *Viderunt omnes* (3d) was elaborated by Léonin in an organum for two voices (17), which in turn was refreshed by his successors with new clausulae (18) that substituted for certain passages in Léonin's original. His younger colleague Pérotin wrote a four-voice organum on the same chant (19). Meanwhile, anonymous musicians fitted words to the upper parts of some of the clausulae, creating the new genre of the motet (21a). Later composers borrowed the tenor line of a clausula (21b) or a passage from the original *Viderunt omnes* chant (21c and 22) and added one, two, or three new voices to create ever more elaborate motets.

NAWM contains many other instances in which composers reworked existing music into new pieces, a recurring thread in music history. Anonymous medieval church musicians added monophonic tropes (6) to the chant *Puer natus* (3a) and developed early types of polyphony that add other voices to a chant (14–15). Machaut based the Kyrie of his *La Messe de Nostre Dame* (25) on the chant *Kyrie Cunctipotens Genitor* (3b). Many Renaissance composers wrote masses that rework existing models, including Du Fay's cantus-firmus mass based on his own polyphonic ballade *Se la face ay pale* (36); Ockeghem's mass (37) on Binchois's rondeau *De plus en plus* (33); Josquin's paraphrase mass on the chant hymn *Pange lingua* (40); and Victoria's imitation mass on his own motet *O magnum mysterium* (46). Du Fay elaborated a Gregorian hymn in fauxbourdon style (35), and Luther recast another (42a) as a Reformation chorale (42b), later used by J. S. Bach as the basis for a cantata (90).

Such elaborations of existing material are not confined to religious music. Narváez's *Cancion Milles regres* (60a) is a reworking for vihuela of Josquin's chanson *Mille regretz* (41), and Byrd's *Pavana Lachrymae* (61) recasts Dowland's lute song *Flow my tears* (58) into an idiomatic keyboard piece. Gottschalk's *Souvenir de Porto Rico* (120) uses a melody of Puerto Rican street musicians. Both Berlioz's *Symphonie fantastique* (121) and Crumb's *Black Angels* (163) borrow phrases from the chant *Dies irae*. The Coronation scene from Musorgsky's *Boris Godunov* (130) incorporates a Russian folk song, and Ives's *General William Booth Enters into Heaven* (148) is based on a hymn tune. The theme of the finale of Beach's Piano Quintet (134) is modeled on a theme from Brahms's Piano Quintet. Both Ellington's *Cotton Tail* (152) and Parker and Gillespie's *Anthropology* (159) borrow the harmonic progression from the chorus of Gershwin's song *I Got Rhythm* (151). Copland's *Appalachian Spring* (157) includes variations on a Shaker hymn, Husa's *Music for Prague* (167) derives much of its material from a Czech hymn, and the first movement of Sheng's *Seven Tunes Heard in China* (172) varies the melody of a Chinese song.

Improvisation

Improvisation has been part of the Western tradition since ancient times. Eleventh-century organum (15) was an improvisatory practice before it was a written one. Singers and instrumentalists from the Renaissance to the early nineteenth century often improvised ornaments and embellishments to decorate the written music, as represented on many of the recordings that accompany this anthology. Lutenists and keyboard players demonstrated their skill through elaborate improvisations, exploring a mode or introducing another work; from these developed the written tradition of the toccata and prelude, represented by examples from Frescobaldi (74), Jacquet de la Guerre (78a), Buxtehude (84), and J. S. Bach (88). Part of the individuality of the keyboard music of C. P. E. Bach (99), Schumann (116), Chopin (118), Liszt (119), Rachmaninov (139), and Scriabin (140) derives from textures or passages that sound improvisatory, however carefully calculated they may be. The invention of sound recording has made possible the preservation of improvisations themselves, which are a fundamental part of the blues and jazz tradition, represented here in the recordings of Jelly Roll Morton (playing Joplin's *Maple Leaf Rag*, 136b), Bessie Smith (149), Louis Armstrong (150b), Ben Webster (soloing in Ellington's *Cotton Tail*, 152), and Charlie Parker (159).

Reception

Certain pieces won a place in this anthology because contemporary critics or the composers themselves singled them out. A legend developed that when some Catholic leaders sought to ban polyphonic music from church services, Palestrina saved it by composing his *Pope Marcellus Mass* (45). Giovanni Maria Artusi dismembered Monteverdi's *Cruda Amarilli* (63) in his dialogue of 1600, which contains both a critique and a defense of Monteverdi's innovations. Caccini wrote that *Vedrò 'l mio sol* (64) was one of his pioneering attempts to write a new type of solo song. Cesti's *Intorno all'idol mio* (68b) was one of the most frequently cited arias of the mid-seventeenth century. Athanasius Kircher praised the scene of Carissimi's *Jephte* (71) as a triumph of the powers of musical expression. Jean-Jacques Rousseau roundly criticized and Jean le Rond d'Alembert carefully analyzed Lully's monologue in *Armide, Enfin il est en ma puissance* (77b). The first movement of Beethoven's *Eroica Symphony* (109) and Stravinsky's *The Rite of Spring* (145) were both objects of critical uproars after their premieres. Britten's *Peter Grimes* (161) became the first English opera to win international acclaim in over two centuries, and Zwilich's Symphony No. 1 (169) earned her the first Pulitzer Prize awarded to a woman. The reactions to these compositions are exemplars of "reception history," a field that has attracted considerable attention among teachers and historians.

Relation to Politics

Finally, musical influences are not the only connections that can be made between these pieces. For example, many grew out of a specific political context, and studying the ways those links are reflected in the music can be illuminating. Walther von der Vogelweide's *Palästinalied* (11) is a crusade song, celebrating the Christian warriors from Western Europe who sought to wrest the Holy Land from the Muslims. *Fole acostumance/Dominus* (21b) attacks hypocrisy and deception in the church and in French politics. Lully's operas (77) were part of a political program intended to glorify King Louis XIV of France and centralize his power through the arts. Schütz's *Kleine geistliche Konzerte* (72) were written for reduced forces in response to the Thirty Years' War. Gay's *The Beggar's Opera* (95) spoofed social norms by taking a criminal as its hero. Political commentary is a recurrent theme in twentieth-century music, including Berg's appeal for better treatment of the poor in *Wozzeck* (143), Britten's condemnation of social ostracism in *Peter Grimes* (161), Crumb's reflections on the Vietnam War in *Black Angels* (163), Penderecki's memorial for the first victims of nuclear war (165), and Husa's protest against the Soviet invasion of Czechoslovakia in *Music for Prague 1968* (167).

Your Turn

All of these and many other potential connections can be made through the works in this anthology. But they remain unrealized until you, the reader, make them real for yourself. We invite you to study each piece for what it shares with others here as well as for its own distinctive qualities. You will encounter much that is unfamiliar, perhaps including pieces you will grow to love and others that may never suit your tastes. At the end, the goal is to understand as much as possible why those who created this music made the choices they did, and how each piece represents a trend, genre, style, and time that played an important role in our long and ever-changing tradition of Western music.

ACKNOWLEDGMENTS

Any book is a collaborative effort, and teaching materials are especially so. There are many people to thank.

I am indebted first of all to Claude V. Palisca, who devised NAWM as a companion to HWM and compiled its first four editions. Most of the selections and translations are his, and I have incorporated material from his commentaries for those works. I regret that his untimely death kept us from collaborating more closely.

The creative efforts of many others are represented in these pages. W. W. Norton and I appreciate the individuals and publishers cited in the source notes who granted permission to reprint or adapt material under copyright. I am especially grateful to Edward H. Roesner for his edition of Léonin's *Viderunt omnes* and to Rebecca A. Baltzer for her editions of *Factum est salutare/Dominus* and *Fole acostumance/Dominus* and her editorial revisions of Adam de la Halle's *De ma dame vient/Dieus, comment porroie/Omnes*, which were prepared specifically for NAWM. Thomas J. Mathiesen kindly provided phonetic transliterations of the Greek poetry and new engravings of the music for NAWM 1 and 2. Ann Shaffer assisted with the re-editing and typesetting of NAWM 55, 60b, and 72. David Budmen elegantly typeset the other new items that were not reproduced from existing editions. Several experts offered guidance on translations, including Rex Sprouse for Walther von der Vogelweide and Martin Luther, Luis Dávila for the *Cantigas de Santa Maria*, James Franklin for early Latin polyphonic works, and Andrew Dell'Antonio for Latin and Italian selections. I had assistance in writing several of the commentaries, from Patrick Warfield (NAWM 135), Felicia Miyakawa (149–152 and 159), and Roger Hickman (153–154, 163, 165, 168, 170, and 172). Alison Trego helped to assemble scores and researched the backgrounds of dozens of pieces, and Felix O. Cox also offered research support. Thanks to all of them for their assistance.

Members of the Editorial Advisory Board for HWM, especially Jane A. Bernstein, Geoffrey Block, Michael Broyles, Matthew Dirst, Melanie Lowe, Roberta Montemorra Marvin, Kevin N. Moll, Margaret Murata, Larry Starr, and Neal Zaslaw, reviewed the proposed contents and made very helpful suggestions. Russell E. Murray advised on the choice of repertoire and helped to find alternatives. My colleagues at Indiana University offered advice and suggestions, especially David Baker, Halina Goldberg, Jeffrey Magee, and Daniel Melamed. So did former students, notably John Anderies, Felicia Miyakawa, Scott Stewart, and Patrick Warfield. The staff of the Cook Music Library at Indiana University offered every possible assistance. Andrew Dell'Antonio, Claudia Macdonald, Richard Crawford, and Larry Starr reviewed the commentaries, helping me to refine my thinking and writing, clarify important issues, and avoid pitfalls. Edward Swenson also offered helpful suggestions. I appreciate their advice, which has made this a far better book.

Assembling the recordings was an especially complex task, and I am deeply grateful to everyone who contributed. I began with an initial list, matching editions to recordings wherever possible. Russell E. Murray did extensive research to find the high-quality recordings of musical performances that complement the commentary and scores in NAWM. He also worked with Ronnie Thomas from Naxos to ensure that the mastering of each CD was precise. Russell meticulously checked and rechecked each of the disks, and Ronnie carefully mastered the CDs. Justyn Baker, licensing and production manager for Naxos, oversaw the production of the CD sets, and along with Diamond Time, Ltd., negotiated the licensing for each track—a laborious and complicated effort. Luis Lange assisted Justyn in coordinating the licensing and production of the project and obtained all of the source recordings. Their enthusiastic work brought the recording set to fruition, and I greatly appreciate their efforts.

For many works and for the new editions, no satisfactory recordings were available, and Maribeth Anderson Payne energetically located performers and commissioned new recordings. Paul Elliott organized, directed, and sang in several excellent new performances from medieval chant to nineteenth-century parlor songs, collaborating with Concentus, Nigel North, Matthew Leese, Wolodymyr Smishkewych, and Yonit Lea Kosovske. Konrad Strauss and his staff produced the recordings, and Indiana University School of Music generously offered the performing space. New recordings were also contributed by Tonus Peregrinus, under the direction of Antony Pitts; Ellen Hargis with Paul O'Dette; and Mark Rimple, David Douglass, and Mary Springfels of the Newberry Consort. Their wonderful performances have made the set of recordings better and more complete, and I gratefully thank them all.

It has been a pleasure to work with the staff at W. W. Norton. Allison Benter oversaw and coordinated the entire NAWM project, facilitating communication between all of the project's contributors and cheerfully handling every difficulty that came along. She also copyedited the entire manuscript, offered encouragement, and gently nudged me to completion. Kathy Talalay, Michael Ochs, and Courtney Fitch assisted with the copyediting. Courtney also secured permissions and drafted the appendices and indexes. Maribeth Anderson Payne, music editor, has been a constant source of ideas and enthusiasm for NAWM as well as HWM. JoAnn Simony oversaw production, contributed the beautiful design and attractive layout, and found ways to make the schedule work when I fell behind. I cannot thank them all enough for their skill, dedication, care, and counsel.

Thanks finally but most of all to my family, especially Donald and Jean Burkholder, who introduced me to the love of music; Bill, Joanne, and Sylvie Burkholder, whose enthusiasm renewed my own; and P. Douglas McKinney, whose patient support made this book possible. I look forward to sharing the music in this anthology with them, and with all who use and enjoy it.

—*J. Peter Burkholder*
June 2005

RECORDINGS

Recordings accompanying this anthology are available under the titles *Norton Recorded Anthology of Western Music* (12 CDs containing all of the pieces in the two volumes) and *Concise Norton Recorded Anthology of Western Music* (6 CDs containing 92 of the pieces in the two volumes). The corresponding CD numbers are indicated in the scores. Track numbers for both sets of CDs are indicated in the scores as follows:

12-CD set (tracks indicated in notched boxes):

CD 1: NAWM 1–18
CD 2: NAWM 19–37
CD 3: NAWM 38–57
CD 4: NAWM 58–70
CD 5: NAWM 71–82
CD 6: NAWM 83–92
CD 7: NAWM 93–102 and 104–105
CD 8: NAWM 103 and 106–118
CD 9: NAWM 119–128
CD 10: NAWM 129–140
CD 11: NAWM 141–157
CD 12: NAWM 158–172

6-CD set (tracks indicated in plain boxes):

CD 1: NAWM 1–46
CD 2: NAWM 47–73 and 77
CD 3: NAWM 74 and 78–103
CD 4: NAWM 104–119
CD 5: NAWM 121–138
CD 6: NAWM 141–172

PITCH DESIGNATIONS

In this book, a note referred to without regard to its octave register is designated by a capital letter (A). A note in a particular octave is designated in italics, using the following system:

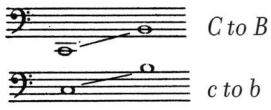 *C to B*

c to b

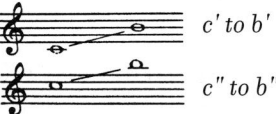 *c' to b'*

c" to b"

Giovanni Battista Pergolesi (1710–1736)

93

La serva padrona: Excerpt

Intermezzo

1733

(a) Recitative: *Ah, quanto mi sta male*

CD 7|1 CD 3|55

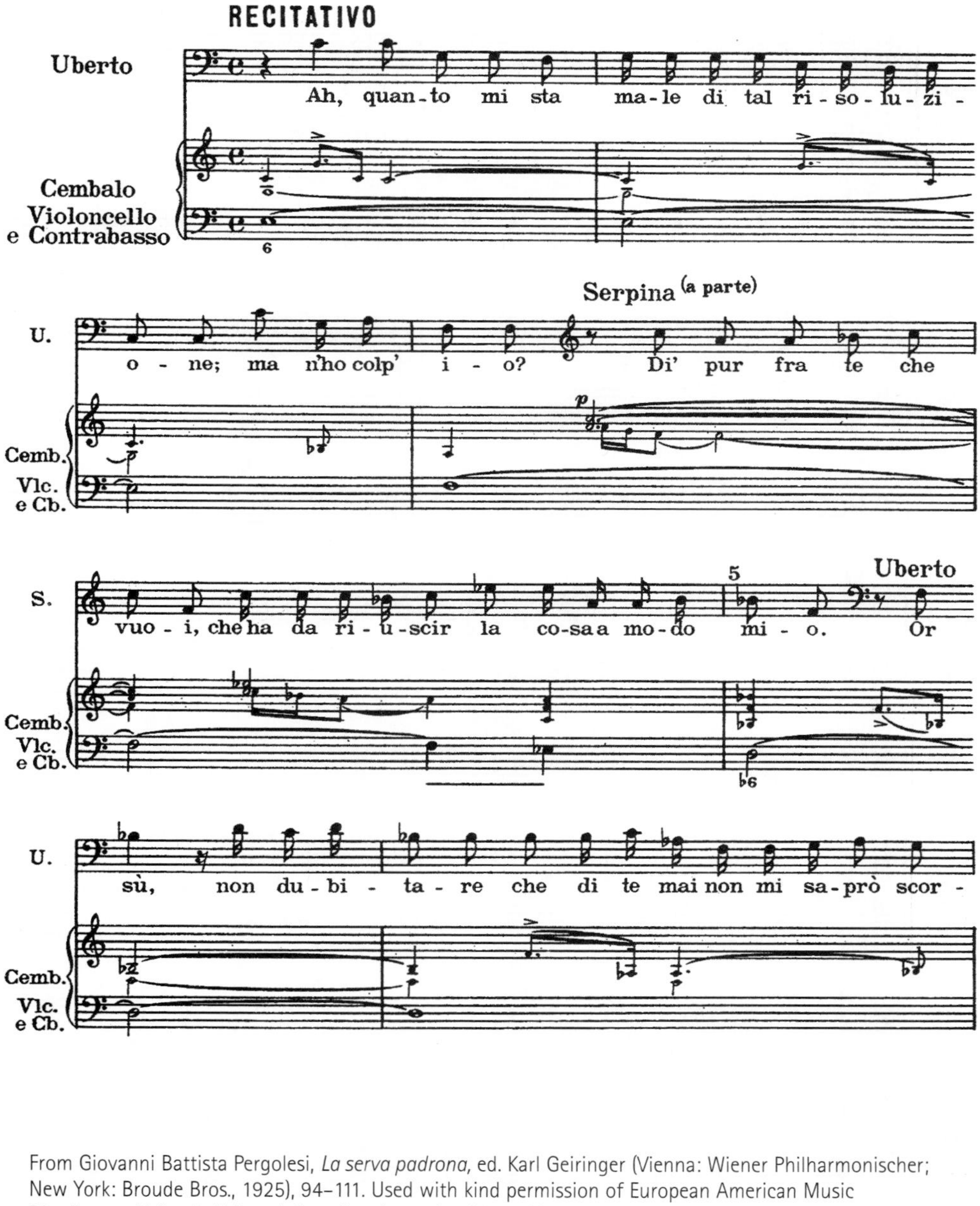

From Giovanni Battista Pergolesi, *La serva padrona*, ed. Karl Geiringer (Vienna: Wiener Philharmonischer; New York: Broude Bros., 1925), 94–111. Used with kind permission of European American Music Distributors LLC, sole U.S. and Canadian Agent for Schott Musik International.

(b) Aria: *Son imbrogliato io*

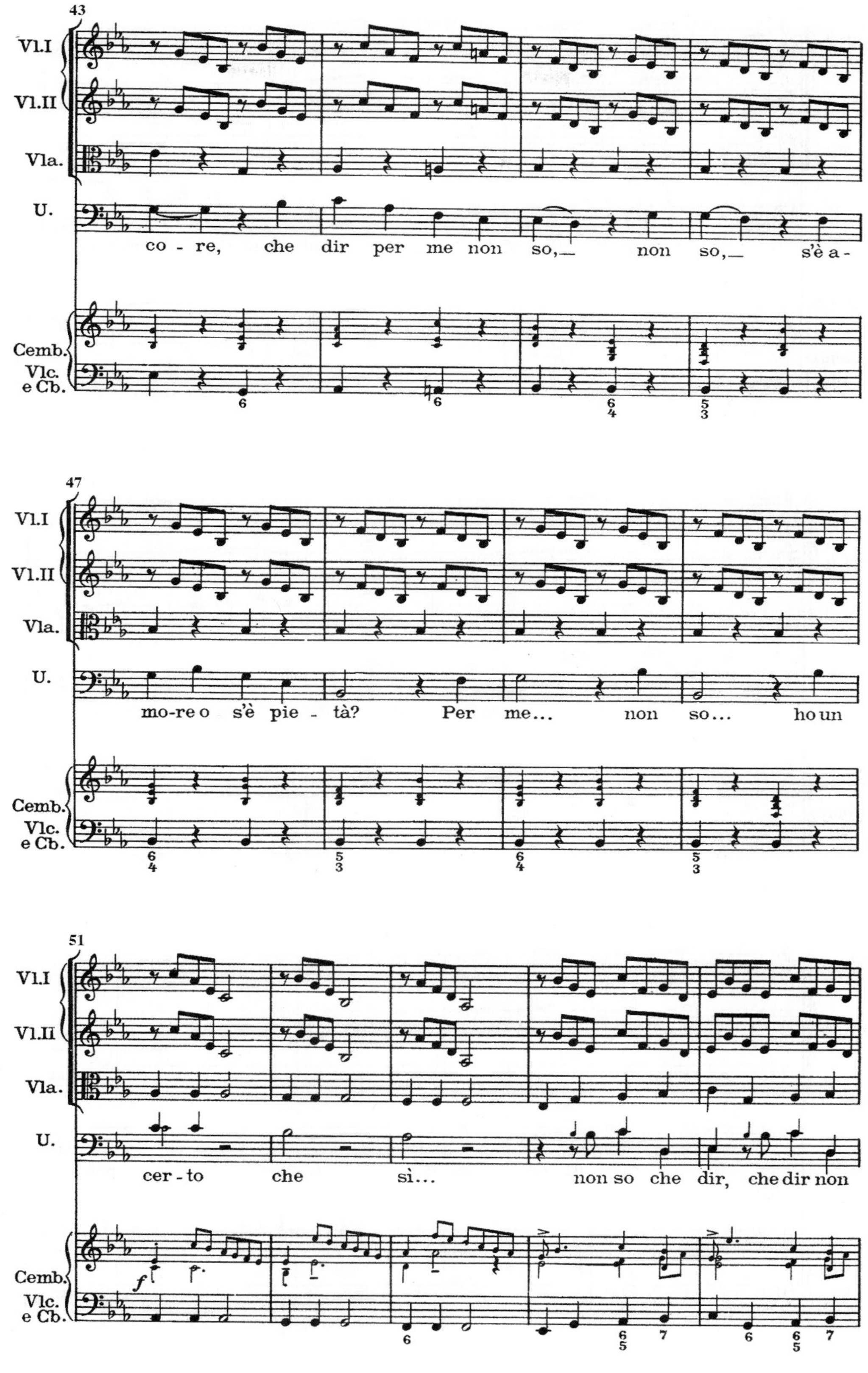
43
Vl.I
Vl.II
Vla.
U.
co - re, che dir per me non so, non so, s'è a -
Cemb.
Vlc. e Cb.
47
Vl.I
Vl.II
Vla.
U.
mo-re o s'è pie - tà? Per me... non so... ho un
Cemb.
Vlc. e Cb.
51
Vl.I
Vl.II
Vla.
U.
cer - to che sì... non so che dir, che dir non
Cemb.
Vlc. e Cb.

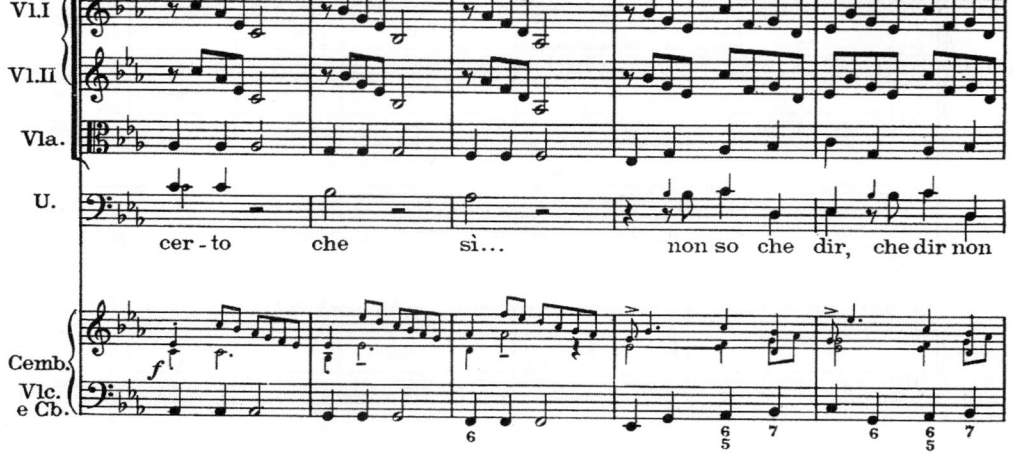

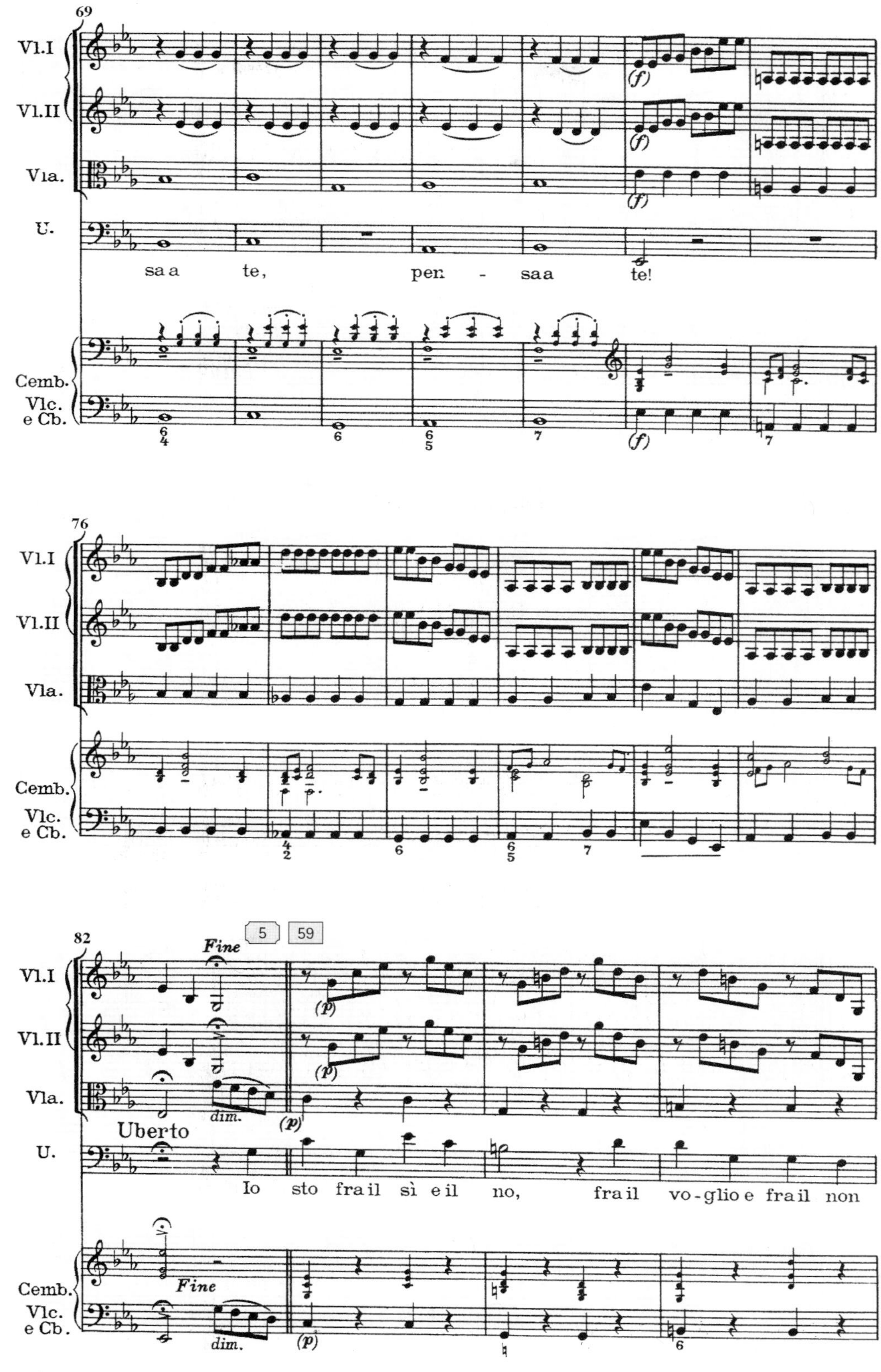
69
Vl.I
Vl.II
Vla.
U.
saa te, per - saa te!
Cemb.
Vlc. e Cb.
76
Vl.I
Vl.II
Vla.
Cemb.
Vlc. e Cb.
82
5
59
Fine
Vl.I
Vl.II
Vla.
dim.
Uberto
U.
Io sto fra il sì e il no, fra il vo-glio e fra il non
Fine
Cemb.
Vlc. e Cb.
dim.

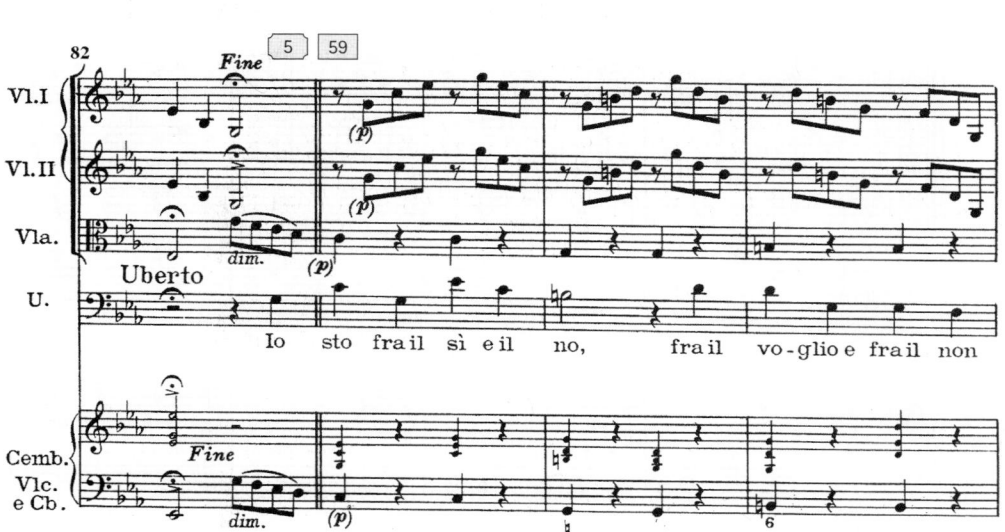

UBERTO (aside)

Ah, quanto mi sta male   Ah, it doesn't feel right—
Di tal risoluzione;   this resolution;
Ma n'ho colpa io?   but is it my fault?

SERPINA (aside)

Di' pur fra te che vuoi;   Tell yourself what you want,
Che ha da riuscir la cosa a modo mio   because this affair will end my way.

UBERTO

Orsù, non dubbitare   Come now, do not doubt
Che di te mai non mi saprò scordare.   that I could ever disagree with you.

SERPINA

Vuol vedere il mio sposo?   Do you want to see my groom?

UBERTO

Si, l'avrei caro.   Yes, I would love to.

SERPINA

Io mandarò per lui: I shall send for him.
Giù in strada ei si trattien.   He is waiting down in the street.

UBERTO

Va.   Go ahead.

SERPINA

Con licenza . . . *(parte)*   With your permission . . . *(leaves)*

UBERTO

Or indovino, chi sarà costui!	Now I can guess who it will be.
Forse la penitenza farà così.	This will be her penance perhaps.
Di quant'ella ha fatto al padrone;	He will do to her what she did to me.
S'è ver, come mi dice, un tal marito	If what she told me is true, a husband like that
La terrà fra la terra ed il bastone.	would keep her between the earth and a stick.
Ah, poveretta lei!	Poor thing, she is.

[Accompanied Recitative]

Per altro io penserei . . .	Otherwise I would think of . . .
Ma ella è serva . . .	but she is a servant . . .
Ma il primo non saresti . . .	but I would not be the first . . . .
Dunque, la sposeresti?	Would you marry her, then?
Basta . . . oh! no, no, non sia.	Enough . . . oh no, no, it cannot be.
Su, pensieri ribaldi, andate via!	Rascally thoughts, go away!
Piano, io me l'ho allevata:	Easy, I raised her for myself.
Sò poi com'ella è nata . . .	I know how she was born . . . .
Eh! Che sei matto!	How crazy you are!
Piano di grazia,	Easy now, please,
Eh non pensare affatto.	think no more about it.
Ma io ci ho passione, e pur . . .	Still, I feel a passion for her . . .
Quella meschina . . .	that wretched creature . . . .
Eh torna . . .	And yet . . . .
Oh Dio! . . . e siam da capo . . .	Oh God! . . . are we beginning all over?
Oh . . . che confusione!	Oh! . . . what confusion!

Aria

Son imbrogliato io già,	I am all mixed up.
Ho un certo chè nel core,	I have a certain something in my heart.
Che dir per me non so,	Truly, I cannot tell
S'è amore o s'è pietà.	whether it's love or pity.
Sent'un che poi mi dice:	I hear a voice that tells me:
Uberto, pensa a te.	Uberto, think of yourself.
Io sto fra il sì e 'l no,	I am between yes and no,
Fra il voglio e fra il non voglio,	between wanting and not wanting,
E sempre più m'imbroglio,	and I get more confused all the time,
Ah misero infelice,	unhappy fellow.
Che mai sarà di me!	What will ever become of me?

—G. A. FEDERICO

La serva padrona (The Maid as Mistress) is an *intermezzo,* a miniature type of Italian comic opera in two or three parts performed between the acts of a serious opera or play. Giovanni Battista Pergolesi wrote this intermezzo for performance with his own opera seria *Il prigionier superbo* (The Prideful Prisoner), and both were premiered at the Teatro San Bartolomeo in Naples on September 5, 1733.

Most intermezzi have only two singing roles, and *La serva padrona* is no exception. Uberto, a well-to-do bachelor, is attracted to his maid Serpina, but he hesitates to promise marriage. She tricks him into committing himself and proposing marriage by confronting him with a rival suitor, who is really his valet Vespone (a mute character) dressed up as a soldier. Clever servants and foolish masters are stock characters in intermezzi, and plots involving love and trickery are common. The servants' names reveal their cunning: Serpina means "little snake," and Vespone "large wasp."

This scene, containing a dialogue between Uberto and Serpina followed by a soliloquy by Uberto, shows Pergolesi's outstanding ability to convey the personalities and emotions of the characters through music. Having just announced that she has accepted a proposal of marriage, Serpina asks Uberto if he would like to meet her intended husband. He agrees, and she leaves to fetch the "groom." In accordance with conventions of both serious and comic opera, their dialogue is in simple recitative accompanied only by harpsichord and cello. After she leaves, Uberto continues in this style as he suggests that having a dominating husband would be fit penance for Serpina, considering all she has done to him. But then doubts overwhelm him, and he voices his own thoughts of marrying her. Each time he wavers, the orchestra interjects a comment, at first with broken chords, then excitedly with rushing scale figures. In serious opera, recitatives accompanied by orchestra were usually reserved for moments of high drama, so Pergolesi's use of the style here to illustrate mere confusion achieves an effect of comic exaggeration. Throughout both the simple and the accompanied recitatives, the harmony modulates constantly, as is typical of the intermezzo style. In this scene, the frequent shifts suggest the rapid flow of dialogue or of Uberto's thoughts.

Uberto's aria is in da capo form, the most common aria form at the time (see NAWM 82). As was customary, the A section includes two complete statements of a poetic text (measures 12 and 42), each framed by instrumental ritornellos. The contrasting B section (measure 83) sets a new text and explores new keys and musical ideas. The A section then repeats. Instead of developing one motive and projecting a single mood, as was customary in earlier Baroque opera, both the main sections and the middle section present a number of contrasting ideas, each conveying a different mood. The sudden juxtapositions are humorous but also meaningful, depicting Uberto's conflicting feelings as he experiences them.

He begins by expressing his confusion in a rapid patter style (measures 12–14). An angular motive shows his nervous indecision through unpredictable jumps and changes of direction. The same melodic idea repeats three times, reinforcing it for the listener and suggesting a paralyzed mental state. But then Uberto sings a slower, more lyrical line as he describes something moving in his heart, unsure whether it is love or pity (measures 15–25). Breaks in the melody remind us of his uncertainty. A brief pause leads to the expression of yet another feeling, one of caution, as an inner voice urges him to think of himself. The music here slows even further, with a brooding, drawn-out melody in F minor (measures 30–39). A short ritornello reaffirms F minor and leads to a review of earlier music in Uberto's second vocal statement, which modulates back to the tonic E♭. The orchestra repeats the opening music in the tonic (at measure 54), twisted from an authentic-cadence pattern into a deceptive one, but the opening words are withheld until they reinvoke Uberto's dark doubts (measure 58–60). The unusual shape of the second vocal statement, as if Uberto has gotten his words mixed up and forgot to sing his opening melody (leaving it to be played by the orchestra), further illustrates his confusion. The brooding melodic idea is transposed into the tonic (measures 66–74), and an abbreviated ritornello closes the first portion of the aria. The middle section (measures 83–100) transposes some of the musical motives from the first section into C minor and G minor, developing earlier material rather than presenting contrasting music. The slower rhythmic pace, the repetition of melodic figures, and the minor tonality in the middle section illustrate Uberto's paralyzed mental state. The first section of the aria is then repeated.

The instrumental forces used here were standard for early eighteenth-century Italian opera: a small four-part string orchestra (violins I and II, violas, and cellos doubled by contrabass) with continuo. In comic opera, humor and exaggerated characterizations were more important than beauty of vocal tone, and singers often approximated pitches and used scoops, glissandos, and other departures from the written music to convey the characters' personalities in comic style. Italian comic opera exploited the possibilities of the bass voice with particular success, both in straight comedy and in burlesque of other styles, and this is a classic scene for *basso buffo* (comic bass).

JOHANN ADOLF HASSE (1699–1783)

Cleofide: Act II, Scene 9, *Digli ch'io son fedele*

Opera seria

1731

Edited from Dresden, Sächsische Landesbibliothek, MS 2477-T-9a. Ornamented versions of the vocal line are published in Hellmuth Christian Wolff, *Original Vocal Improvisations from the 16th–18th Centuries* (Cologne: Arno Volk Verlag Hans Gerig, 1972), 143–68. Included there are a version created by or for Hasse's wife Faustina Bordoni, who was the first to sing the role of Cleofide, and a version sung by the Italian castrato Porporino and transcribed by Frederick II (the Great), King of Prussia.

cor, che non dis-pe — ri, che non__ dis-pe-ri an-cor, che

non__ dis-pe-ri an-cor. Di-gli ch'io son__ fe-

de — le, Di-gli ch'è il mio te-so-ro, Che m'a-mi, ch'io l'a-do-ro, che m'a —

che non ____ dis - pe - ri an cor,   che non ____ dis - pe - ri an -

Ob. *Fine*

Fine

cor.

Bsn.,Vcl.
Fine

di - gli che lo con - so - li in - tan - to L'i - ma - gi - ne di - quel - la

Che vi - ve nel suo cor, che vi - ve nel suo cor.

Adagio
Ob.
Ob.
Bsn., Vcl.
Dal segno al Fine

CLEOFIDE

Digli ch'io son fedele	Tell him that I am faithful,
Digli ch'è il mio tesoro:	tell him that he's my darling;
Che m'ami, ch'io l'adoro,	to love me; that I adore him;
Che non disperi ancor.	that he not yet despair.
Digli che la mia stella	Tell him that my star
Spero placar col pianto;	I hope to placate with weeping;
Che lo consoli intanto	that meanwhile let him be consoled
L'immagine di quella	by the image of her
Che vive nel suo cor.	who lives in his heart.

—PIETRO METASTASIO

Cleofide was premiered in Dresden on September 13, 1731, and was Johann Adolf Hasse's first opera after his appointment as *maestro di cappella* for the Elector of Saxony. Michelangelo Boccardi adapted the libretto from Pietro Metastasio's *Alessandro nell'Indie.* In the aria included here, the poetic text is unchanged from Metastasio's original drama. Cleofide, queen of India, expresses her faithful love for Poro, an Indian prince. She does not realize that Poro, disguised as his own general Gandarte (who is leading the battle against Alexander of Macedonia), is listening.

The first four lines of text are set in the first section of this da capo aria, and the next five lines are set in the middle section, after which the first section is repeated *dal segno*, omitting the ritornello. The opening ritornello introduces the main ideas that will appear in the first section, all in the tonic E major. The presentation of several different ideas in short phrases separated by rests distinguishes Hasse's early galant style from the more continuous style of Scarlatti (see NAWM 82b) or Bach (NAWM 90b and 90d).

At the first vocal entrance (measure 10), the identical rhythm and similar words of the first two lines allowed Hasse to construct parallel melodic phrases that capture both the natural rhythm of the words and the hopeful sentiment of Cleofide. The unstressed final syllables of the words *fedele, tesoro,* and *adoro* at the ends of the first three lines result in a type of syncopated cadence that was common at this time, in which an accented suspension on the downbeat (on the last stressed syllable) resolves on the following eighth note. In some cases, even when a line ends on a stressed syllable, as at *ancor,* Hasse softens it with an accented suspension (see measure 16). Further syncopations occur on the accented initial syllables of the words *m'a-mi* and *ch'i-o* in measure 15, through the so-called Scotch snap or Lombardic rhythm (an accented note with a short value followed by an unaccented note three times as long). The rhythmic figuration for the singer changes frequently, providing variety and opportunity for vocal display. In particular, there are long passages of *fioratura* (flowery singing) on the words "love" (*ami*) and "despair" (*disperi*), drawing the listener's attention and deepening the expression of feeling.

The first vocal statement modulates to the dominant, closing with the material that concluded the ritornello, now transposed to the new key. After a greatly abbreviated ritornello—just the first and last motive—in the dominant, the second vocal statement (measure 21) varies the first, repeating the text of the first stanza, further developing musical ideas already introduced, and modulating back to the tonic. The first section closes with a ritornello that is shorter than the opening statement but not so brief as the second. Except in the ritornellos, the orchestra remains subordinate, accompanying the singer with a steady pulsation or very light figuration.

The middle section offers a strong contrast. The text turns to images of weeping and consolation, and the music changes from E major to E minor and from slow duple meter to slightly faster triple meter. The simplicity of the music in this section may show a simpler side of the Indian queen or may suggest a private, tender passion that contrasts with the public display of power she conveys in the outer sections.

The role of Cleofide was first sung by Hasse's wife, Faustina Bordoni, who undoubtedly embellished the written vocal line. An ornamented version of the soprano part improvised by or composed for her survives, as do versions by other singers of the time. Embellishments were added particularly in the da capo repetition, but Bordoni and probably most singers held more strictly to the composer's notation the first time through. This approach to ornamentation may be heard in the recorded performance accompanying this anthology. Some embellishments are already written in by the composer. The grace notes (small notes slurred to regular notes, as in measures 16–17) are to be performed on the beat, decreasing the duration of the notes to which they are attached, and the trills begin one step above the written note.

JOHN GAY (1685–1732)

The Beggar's Opera: Excerpt from Scene 13

Ballad opera

1728

CD 7|12

POLLY: And are you as fond as ever, my dear?

MACHEATH: Suspect my honour, my courage, suspect anything but my love. May my pistols miss fire, and my mare slip her shoulder while I am pursu'd, if I ever forsake thee!

POLLY: Nay, my dear, I have no reason to doubt you, for I find in the Romance you lent me, none of the great Heroes were ever false in love.

Air XV

MACHEATH

My heart was so free,
It rov'd like the Bee,
'Till Polly my passon requited;
I sipt each flower,

Come Fair one be kind,
You never shall find,
A Fellow so fit for a Lover;
The World shall view,

Text and notes from *The Beggar's Opera by John Gay*, ed. Louis Kronenberger and Max Goberman (Larchmont: Argonaut Books, 1961), xxxii–xxxiv. The facsimiles here, taken from the third edition of Gay's *The Beggar's Opera* (London, 1729), present the melodies with basses that may be by Johann Christoph Pepusch.

I chang'd every hour,
But here ev'ry flower's united.

     —JOHN GAY

My Passion for you,
But never your Passion discover.

—PILLS TO PURGE MELANCHOLY,
VOL. 4

13

POLLY: Were you sentenc'd to Transportation, sure, my dear, you could not leave me behind you—could you?

MACHEATH: Is there any power, any force that could tear me from thee? You might sooner tear a pension out of the hands of a Courtier, a fee from a Lawyer, a pretty woman from a looking-glass, or any woman from Quadrille. But to tear me from thee is impossible!

Air XVI

MACHEATH
Were I laid on Greenland's coast,
And in my arms embrac'd my lass;
Warm amidst eternal frost,
Too soon the half year's night would pass.

Jockey was a bonny Lad,
And e'er was born in Scotland fair;
But now poor Jockey is run mad,
For Jenny causes his Despair;

POLLY
Were I sold on Indian soil,
Soon as the burning day was clos'd,
I could mock the sultry toil,
When on my charmer's breast repos'd.

Jockey was a Piper's Son,
And fell in Love while he was young:
But all the Tunes that he could play,
Was, o'er the Hills, and far away,

MACHEATH
And I would love you all the day,

'Tis o'er the Hills, and far away,

POLLY
Every night would kiss and play,

'Tis o'er the Hills, and far away,

MACHEATH
If with me you'd fondly stray

'Tis o'er the Hills, and far away,

POLLY
Over the hills and far away.

The wind has blown my Plad away.

—JOHN GAY

—PILLS TO PURGE MELANCHOLY,
VOL. 5

The Beggar's Opera was the first English ballad opera, and its success spawned many imitators. John Gay wrote the play and inserted sixty-nine songs with newly written texts set to folk, popular, or other familiar melodies. Although earlier English plays had often featured music, it was normally newly composed and reserved for only a few of the characters. Gay's play was the first in which all the characters sang, as in opera, and the music was all borrowed from sources well known to the listeners. Gay chose the tunes and wrote the new poetry, but the music was probably arranged by Johann Christoph Pepusch (1667–1752), who directed the first performance on January 29, 1728, at the Lincoln's Inn Fields theater in London.

The plot satirized the pretensions of London society and of serious opera by depicting thieves, prostitutes, and other contemporary low-life characters instead of the noble and mythic figures of antiquity that were typical in operas. In the scene excerpted here, the highwayman Macheath, in danger of execution, is fleeing the law and hiding in the room of Polly, whom he has secretly married. His song *My heart was so free / It roved like a bee* (Air XV) parodies the simile aria of the Baroque operas, in which a character's predicament is described through a comparison (for example, to a ship tossed in a storm) and illustrated with appropriate musical depiction. It is sung to the melody of *Come Fair one be kind,* a courting song in the meter of a jig. (Gay's words are reprinted here in the left-hand column after each song, with the original texts on the right.) After a brief dialogue, Macheath and Polly alternate strains as they pledge constancy to each other in *Were I laid on Greenland's coast.* The tune here is from *O'er the Hills, and far away,* whose text tells of a young man driven mad by despair over a young woman. Polly's brief mention of the original text reinforces the allusion, which adds an ironic twist for those who know the original song (as almost everyone in Gay's audience certainly did). Gay found both songs in Henry Playford's *Pills to Purge Melancholy,* an anthology of songs from theatrical productions, broadside ballads (so named for the large folios on which they were printed and circulated), and other sources. The first is a binary dance form in B♭ major, but the second is modal, in C Dorian, with the verse-refrain form of a traditional song.

Pay records show that an orchestra of about a dozen string players and a harpsichordist played for ballad operas, but the original accompaniments do not survive. The oldest surviving copies of *The Beggar's Opera* are the versions of the songs that were published for amateurs to use for singing at home, with the melodies over basses intended for basso continuo realization. The versions reprinted here are from the third edition of the songs from the opera, published in 1729. Modern productions often include preludes or accompaniments arranged for ensembles like those that performed in the eighteenth-century theaters. The characters were portrayed by actors who could sing in popular style, not by professionally trained singers. True to this tradition, a 1983 BBC-TV production featured Roger Daltrey of the rock band the Who in the role of Macheath.

CHRISTOPH WILLIBALD GLUCK (1714–1787)

Orfeo ed Euridice: Excerpt from Act II, Scene 1

Opera

1762

Christoph Willibald Gluck, *Sämtliche Werke*, ser. 1, vol. 1, ed. Anna Amelie Abert and Ludwig Finscher
(Kassel: Bärenreiter, 1963), 55–75. Reprinted by permission.

Coro

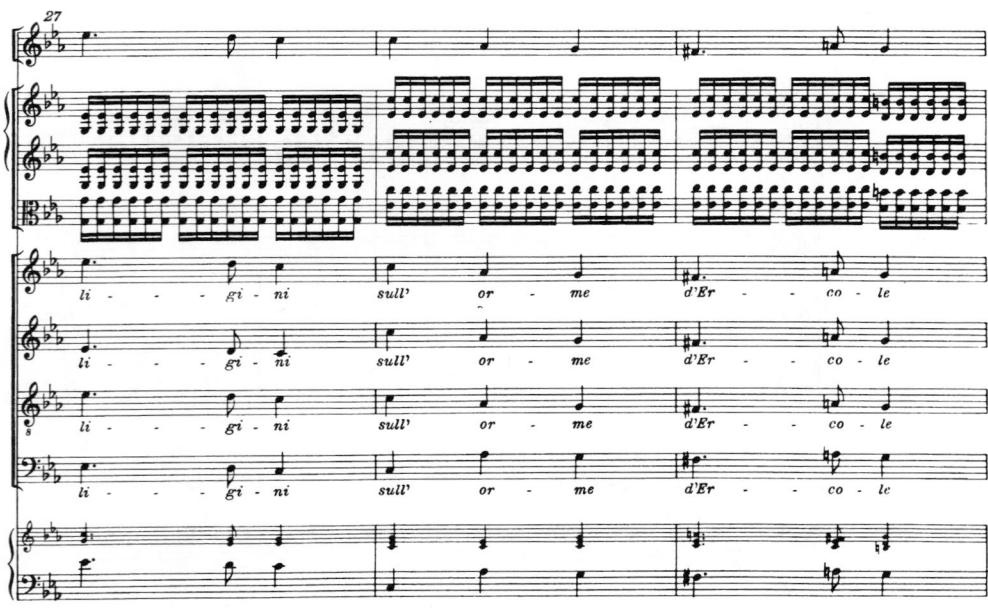

Ballo

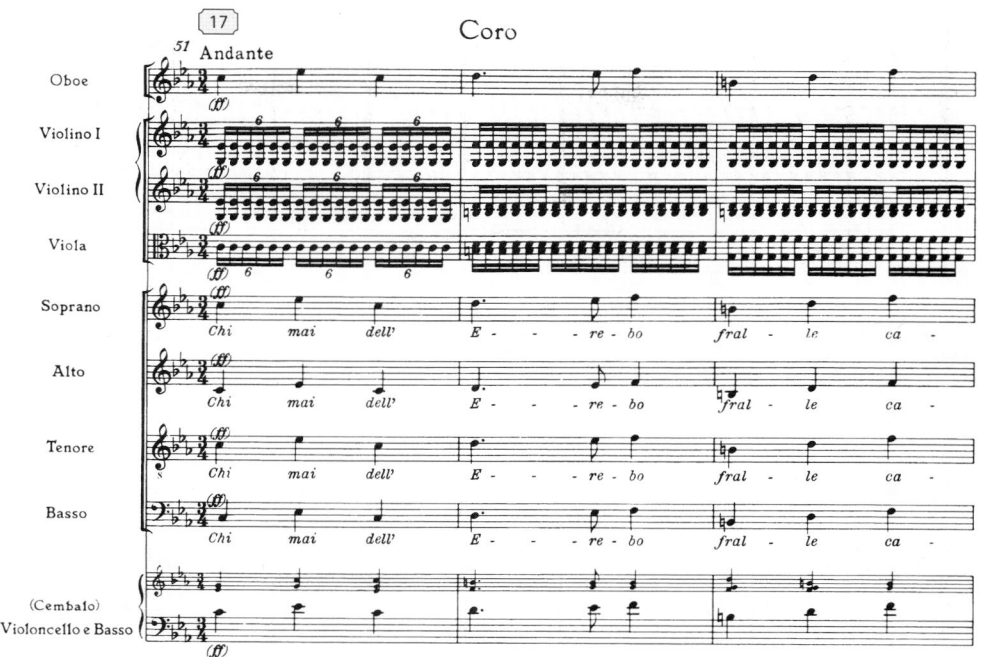

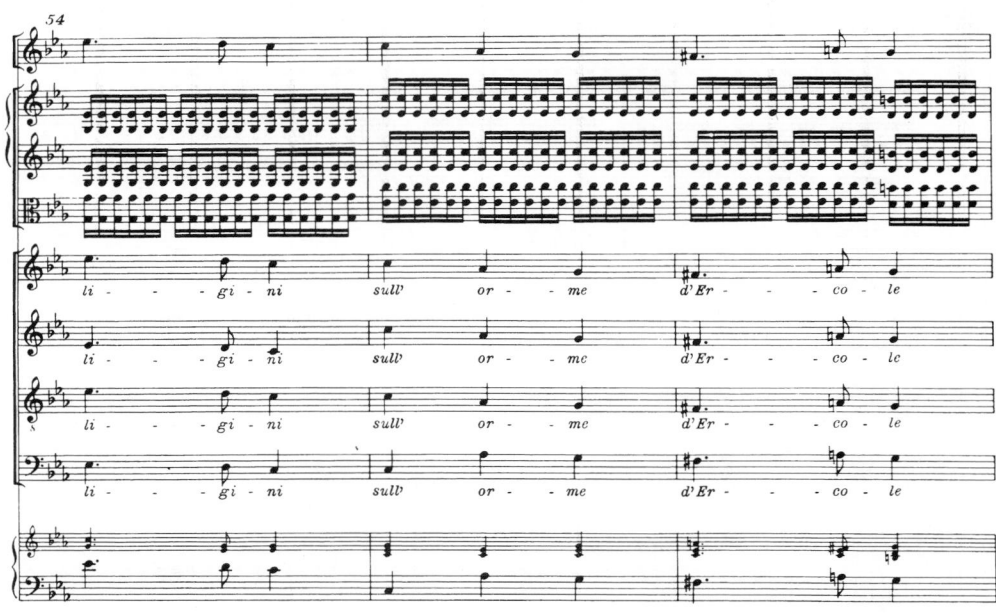

gli ur - li di Cer - be - ro, se un dio non è!

gli ur - li di Cer - be - ro, se un dio non è!

gli ur - li di Cer - be - ro, se un dio non è!

gli ur - li di Cer - be - ro, se un dio non è!

Segue il Ballo, girando intorno ad Orfeo per spaventarlo.

Ballo

ca - - te - vi   con   me,   Fu - rie,   lar - ve,

Nò!   Nò!

Nò!   Nò!

Nò!   Nò!

Nò!   Nò!

Call & response!

ren - da al - men   pie - to - se   il mio bar - ba - ro do - lor!   Fu - rie,

Nò!

Nò!

Nò!

Nò!

bar - ba - ro do - lor,   il_ mio bar - ba - ro   do - - lor!

Chorus

Chi mai dell'Erebo	Who from Erebus
Fralle caligini	through the dark mists,
Sull'orme d'Ercole	in the footsteps of Hercules
E di Piritoo	and of Peirithous
Conduce il piè?	would ever set forth?

D'orror l'ingombrino	He would be blocked with horror
Le fiere Eumenidi,	by the fierce Eumenides
E lo spaventino	and frightened by
Gli urli di Cerbero,	the shrieks of Cerberus,
Se un dio non è.	unless he were a god.

(The Furies dance, circling around Orfeo to frighten him.)

ORFEO

Deh, placatevi con me.	Please, be gentle with me.
Furie, Larve, Ombre sdegnose!	Furies, specters, scornful phantoms!

CHORUS

No! . . . No! . . .	No! . . . No! . . .

ORFEO

Vi renda almen pietose	Let it at least make you merciful,
Il mio barbaro dolor!	my cruel pain!

—RANIERO DE CALZABIGI

Orfeo ed Euridice, produced in Vienna in 1762, was the first of three operas on which Christoph Willibald Gluck and the poet Raniero de Calzabigi (1714–1795) collaborated in an effort to reform Italian opera. As Gluck stated some years later in the preface to his French opera *Alceste* (1769), he aimed "to confine music to its true function of serving the poetry by expressing feelings and the situations of the story."

The impressive choral scene included here takes place in the cavernous spaces of the underworld, obscured by thick dark smoke and illumined only by flames. Orfeo (Orpheus) has traveled there in search of his bride Euridice, but he is stopped by the Furies. There are two orchestras. The first, with two oboes, two horns, strings, and harpsichord, later joined by cornetto and two trombones, accompanies the ballet and chorus sections in which the menacing Furies try to obstruct Orfeo's passage. The second orchestra accompanies Orfeo and includes only plucked strings—harp, pizzicato strings, and harpsichord—to imitate Orfeo's playing on the lyre as he attempts to calm the Furies with his song. Gluck marshaled the powerful new resources of the symphony orchestra, calculated key relationships, and unprepared diminished and dominant seventh chords in different inversions to contrive a terrifying and suspenseful theatrical experience.

The first ballet of the Furies begins with emphatic unisons on E♭, the key in which Orfeo later begins his pleading, but it quickly modulates through chromaticism and dissonance to C minor, the key in which the chorus of Furies then sings as it blocks Orfeo's path to Euridice. The Furies express their menace in three ballets and two choruses before Orfeo begins his song, which is punctuated with unison exclamations by the chorus. Gluck uses a variety of means to make the

Furies seem threatening: suddenly loud dynamics, tremolos in the strings, chromatic motion, dissonant chords (including diminished seventh chords at the ends of phrases, as at measure 90), and blasts from the brass (as at measures 116–17). Unlike the divertissements of Lully's operas, in which dance and choral music were used for decoration, this scene features a ballet and chorus that are integrated with the central action of the drama.

Gluck prided himself on the simplicity of his melodies, sparseness of embellishment, and economy of melodic and text repetition, all of which are illustrated in Orfeo's song to the Furies. His song proceeds in the balanced two- and four-measure phrases of the contemporary Italian style, but with a more limited range and with very simple melodic ornamentation—mostly sighing appoggiaturas—that would not have offended French tastes. Characteristic of Gluck, this scene combines Italian style with French elements, including the chorus (marked "coro" in the score), dances (marked "ballo"), and evocative use of instrumental timbre.

The role of Orfeo was written for a castrato, as was typical of heroic male roles in Italian operas of the eighteenth century. In Gluck's later French adaptation of the opera for performance in Paris, Orfeo (now Orphée) was recast as a tenor because castrati were not in fashion on the French stage. Since the modern revival of historical performance practice has not extended to the creation of castratos, the part of Orfeo is now normally sung by either by a male countertenor or a female mezzo-soprano. As was typical in Gluck's time, the singer on the recording accompanying this anthology adds some improvised embellishment to the melody, especially in the final phrase.

WILLIAM BILLINGS (1746–1800)

Creation, from *The Continental Harmony*

Fuging tune

CA. 1794

From *The Complete Works of William Billings,* vol. 4, *The Continental Harmony (1794),* ed. Karl Kroeger
(Boston: The American Musicological Society and The Colonial Society of Massachusetts, 1990), 67–71.

54

keep in Tune so long, should keep in Tune so long,

long, should keep in Tune so long, _____ so long,

keep in Tune _ so _ long, _____

Strings, Should keep _ in _ Tune, should keep in Tune so long,

58

Strange! that a Harp, of thou- sand Strings, Should keep in Tune so long.

Strange! that a Harp, of thou- sand Strings, Should keep in Tune so long.

Strange! that a Harp, of thou- sand Strings, Should _ keep in Tune so long.

Strange! that a Harp, of thou- sand Strings, Should keep in Tune so long.

When I with pleasing Wonder stand,
And all my Frame survey,
Lord, 'tis thy Work, I own; thy Hand
Thus built my humble Clay.

Our Life contains a thousand Springs,
And dies, if one be gone:
Strange! that a Harp, of thousand Strings,
Should keep in Tune so long.

William Billings learned to sing and read music in singing schools (institutions that were common in New England during the late eighteenth century), and he later became a renowned singing master in Boston and the surrounding areas.

Apparently self-taught as a composer, Billings wrote over 340 pieces for use in singing schools and churches, and between 1770 and 1794, he published them in six collections. Almost all his compositions were sacred works for unaccompanied four-part choir. Most were *plain tunes* (hymn tunes harmonized in four parts), but he also wrote about fifty anthems (longer works in the Anglican tradition) and 51 *fuging tunes*, which include some imitative counterpoint.

Creation is a fuging tune from Billings's last collection, *The Continental Harmony*. As in most fuging tunes, roughly the first half of the piece is homophonic and mostly syllabic, and the second half features freely imitative polyphony (the "fugue-ing" section) before returning to homophony at the end. In *Creation*, the form of the text, in two rhymed quatrains, is reflected in the music. The first two lines of text in both quatrains are set to variants of the same music (compare measures 1–8 and 23–30). The last two lines of the first quatrain are set twice, the second time in a faster triple meter (measures 16–22). The change from homophony to imitative polyphony begins with the third line of the second quatrain. As is typical in fuging tunes by Billings, the imitation is quite free. For example, the opening figure (in the bass at measure 31) is slightly different almost every time it enters, and some imitation is disguised (such as the soprano in measure 33, echoing the alto in the previous measure). There is word-painting in this section: the word "long" is held on long notes, then treated in long melismas (bass and alto, measures 41–44, then tenor and soprano, measures 48–53). The two final lines of text repeat in four-part homophony to close out the piece.

Billings typically wrote the tenor melody first, giving it the main tune. He added the bass to form consonant counterpoint with the tenor, then worked out the soprano and finally the alto, making each voice consonant with those already written. At times an upper voice forms parallel octaves or fifths with another voice (for example, alto and tenor in measures 3 and 12; soprano and bass in measure 4, 19–20, and 25–26; and soprano and alto in measures 20–21 and 26–27). Such parallel perfect intervals, considered unacceptable by composers since the Renaissance, are signs of Billings's lack of formal training in music theory. Together with the open fifth chords that begin or end some phrases (as in measures 1, 15, and 61), the parallel octaves and fifths give the music a rustic, resonant quality that Billings and his admirers found appealing.

Since the tune was in the tenor, Billings often advised that some soprano voices sing the tenor an octave higher and some tenors sing the soprano part an octave lower. He seldom included dynamic markings, implying that the piece should be performed at a comfortably full dynamic level throughout, as was standard for congregational singing.

DOMENICO SCARLATTI (1685–1757)

Sonata in D Major, K. 119

Keyboard sonata

CA. 1740s

23   62

il primo tempo

Domenico Scarlatti composed most of his harpsichord sonatas while he was in the
service of Maria Barbara, daughter of King John V of Portugal and later the wife of

King Ferdinand VI of Spain. At her instigation, in the 1740s and 1750s, near the end of his life, he compiled several volumes of his sonatas. Among the works he included is this one-movement sonata, written probably in the 1740s and numbered 119 in Ralph Kirkpatrick's catalogue.

Like virtually all of Scarlatti's sonatas, this one is in binary form, with two repeated sections. (The repetitions are omitted on the recording that accompanies this anthology.) The first section presents a remarkable number of different ideas, most immediately restated. This self-parroting, common in Scarlatti's music, resembles the practice in comic opera of reiterating phrases to make the most of especially witty lines. It may also reflect the function of the keyboard sonatas as learning exercises for the player, or it may have been used simply to provide balance and grace. Most of the ideas are harmonically stable, designed to project the key clearly. The initial series of figures asserts the tonic D major through broken chords (measure 1–6), scales (measure 6–14), a cadential figure (measures 14–18), and a repeated-note figure over leaping octaves (measures 18–27). A cadence on the dominant of the dominant is highlighted with a scalar flourish. Then a new set of ideas begins in the key of the dominant, first minor, then major. The figures here include a winding, syncopated melody above pulsing chords (at measure 36), a passage with dense chords and trills (measure 56), a new cadential figure (measure 65), the repeated-note figure again (marking the return to the major mode), and then brilliant passagework with arpeggios and hand-crossing to close the section.

After the first section modulates from tonic to dominant, the second works its way back home to the tonic. The ideas that opened the movement are absent here. Instead, Scarlatti varies elements from later in the first section by modulating through nearby keys and back to the tonic. The latter part of the first section, from the winding melody to the end, returns in varied form at measure 143, transposed from the dominant into the tonic. This restatement creates *rounded binary form*, in which both halves end with the same material, although in different keys.

Several of the figures in this sonata are especially characteristic of Scarlatti, including the large leaps, rushing scales, and rapid arpeggios that together create a brilliant effect. Forcing the keyboardist to cross hands, using the left to play high notes (as in measures 81–83) or the right to play low ones (as in measures 87–90), is a trick that Scarlatti frequently employed, and it must have amused his audiences as well as the pupils who played his music. Some elements seem to reflect his surroundings in Spain, including the castanet-like rhythms of the repeated figure in measures 19–27 and the dense chords in measures 56–65, which resemble an effect heard in guitar music when an unchanging open string is strummed along with changing chords fingered on the other strings.

The diversity of figuration and the rapid passagework give the player quite a workout, which was surely intentional; when Scarlatti published a set of thirty sonatas in 1738 he called them *Essercizi per il gravicembalo* (Exercises for the Harpsichord). Although they were originally written for harpsichord, Scarlatti's sonatas have become favorites of pianists, who enjoy the crisp brilliance of his style.

CARL PHILIPP EMANUEL BACH (1714–1788)

99

Sonata in A Major, H. 186, Wq. 55/4: Second movement, Poco adagio

Keyboard sonata

1765

CD 7|26   CD 3|65

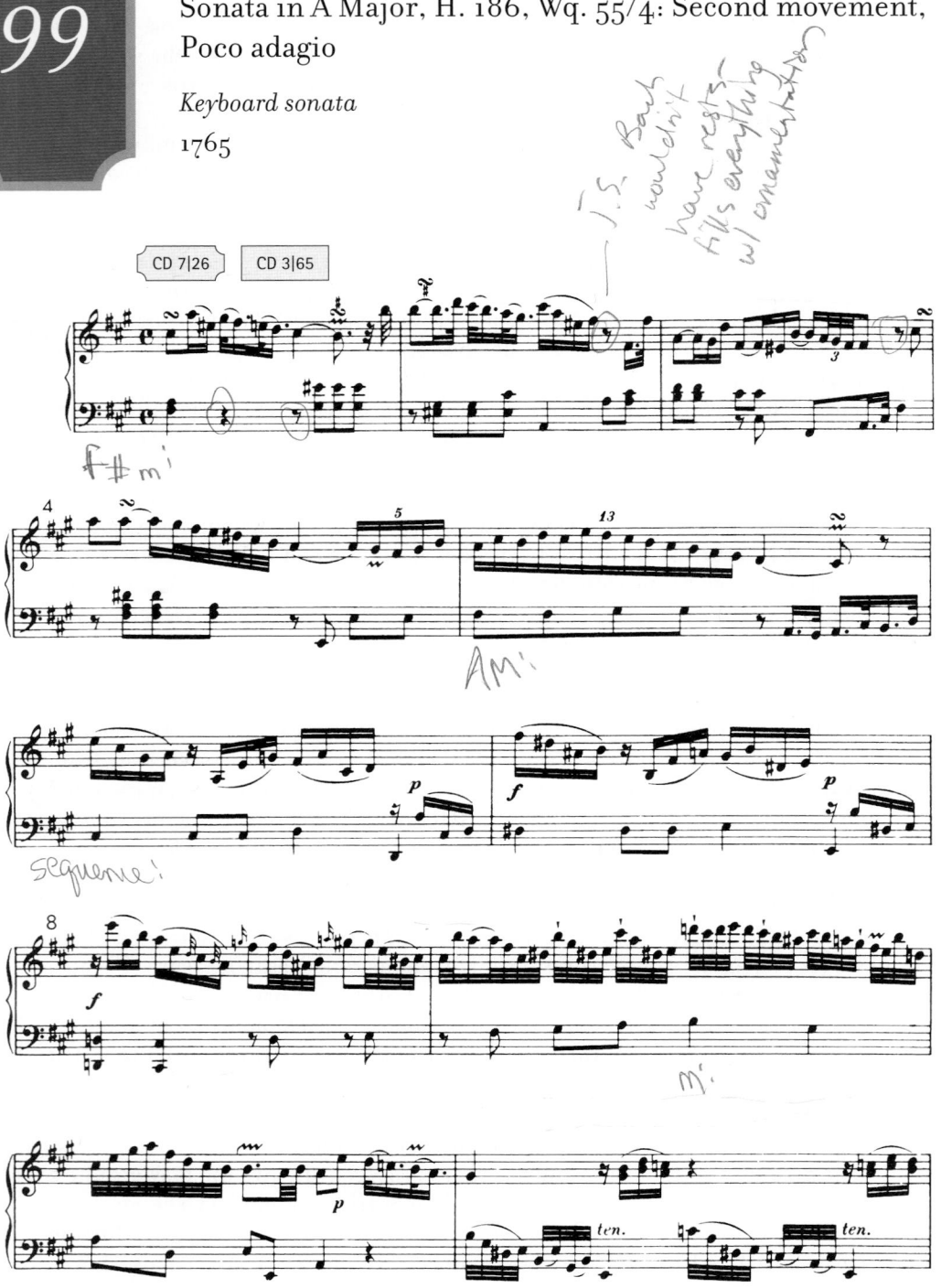

Carl Philipp Emanuel Bach, *Sechs Clavier-Sonaten für Kenner und Liebhaber* (Leipzig, 1779). Reprinted from Carl Philipp Emanuel Bach, *Die Sechs Sammlungen von Sonaten, freien Fantasien und Rondos für Kenner und Liebhaber,* ed. Carl Krebs, rev. ed. Lothar Hoffmann-Erbrecht, vol. 1, *Sechs Clavier-Sonaten* (Leipzig: Breitkopf & Härtel, 1954), 24–36. Used by permission. This sonata is no. 186 in Eugene E. Helm, *Thematic Catalog of the Works of Carl Philipp Emanuel Bach* (New Haven: Yale University Press, 1989) and no. 55/4 in Alfred Wotquenne, *Thematisches Verzeichnis der Werke von Carl Philipp Emanuel Bach (1714–1788)* (Leipzig: Breitkopf & Härtel, 1905).

Carl Philipp Emanuel Bach composed this sonata in 1765 and published it in 1779 as the fourth in a collection called *Sechs Clavier-Sonaten für Kenner und Liebhaber* (Six Clavier Sonatas for Connoisseurs and Amateurs). Like most of his published keyboard music, these sonatas were written for amateurs to play for their own enjoyment. This collection sold well over three thousand copies, making it a best seller by contemporary standards and earning Bach a sum equivalent to several years' salary.

Bach was one of the leading exponents of the *empfindsam* (sentimental) style, a manner of conveying refined passion and melancholy. Typical traits of the style are especially evident in the sonata's second movement, Poco adagio. It begins with a singing line that leaps up, gradually descends, and ends with an appoggiatura that resolves on a weak beat, followed by a rest. This opening figure is embellished with turns, a chromatic neighbor figure, Scotch snaps, and a trill. Throughout this movement, ornamentation serves as a means of expression, not as mere decoration; here, the embellishments help to lend a wistful mood, as if the player is reluctant to move on without lingering on each detail. Throughout the movement, the rhythm is constantly changing, giving the music an unpredictable, restless quality. Typical of the empfindsam style, sequential repetition, nonharmonic tones—particularly appoggiaturas—and subtle chromatic changes convey suspense and excitement. Also typical are sudden changes in harmony, dynamic level, texture, or other elements, making use of the unexpected as a powerful means of expressing emotion.

This movement is distinct in style, but it shares many elements with other music of its time. As in the prevailing galant style, the texture is an expressive melody over light accompaniment, although here the left hand often fills in with figuration when the melody rests at the ends of phrases. Bach uses a type of binary form that has been described as sonata form without development. The first half of the movement presents an opening idea in the tonic, F♯ minor, modulates to the relative, A major (reached in measure 5), then confirms that key with new material. The A-major section turns from a singing melody with accompaniment to a pianistic display exploiting all the registers. The second half of the movement, beginning at measure 15, reprises the first half, but now the modulatory passage is altered to arrive back on the tonic, and the material originally in A major appears in the tonic (starting at measure 22). A brief coda brings the movement to a close.

On the accompanying recording, this movement is played on a reconstruction of an early piano, now often called a *fortepiano* to distinguish it from the modern piano. Early pianos were strung on wooden frames rather than iron ones, so the tension on the strings is not as high. For this and other reasons, the fortepiano sounds softer than the modern piano, and notes decay much more quickly after being struck. These differences can be viewed as advantages, especially for playing music of the late eighteenth century, because subtly fluctuating dynamic levels play a vital part in the music's expressivity. The recording was made with the microphone so close to the instrument that it picked up the sounds of the mechanism, the player's breathing, and other extraneous noises. Rather than representing a performance for an audience, the recording thus recreates how the piece would sound when played for one's own entertainment, which was the primary function of piano sonatas at the time.

GIOVANNI BATTISTA SAMMARTINI (CA. 1700–1775)

Symphony in F Major, No. 32: First movement, Presto

Symphony

CA. 1740

The symphonies are identified through the numbering in Newell Jenkins and Bathia Churgin, *Thematic Catalogue of the Works of Giovanni Battista Sammartini* (Cambridge, Mass.: Harvard University Press for the American Musicological Society, 1976). Reprinted by permission of the publisher from *The Symphonies of G. B. Sammartini*, vol. 2, ed. Bathia Churgin, Harvard Publications in Music 2 (Cambridge, Mass.: Harvard University Press, 1968), 95–97. © 1968 by the President and Fellows of Harvard College.

*m. 35: In mm. 35-36, the octave skips in the manuscript are reversed, starting with the upper octave and descending.

Giovanni Battista Sammartini was the most prominent of the early symphony composers active in the region around Milan in northern Italy. He composed this symphony by about 1740–44, when it was copied into a manuscript collection of three hundred instrumental works prepared for a French magistrate and music patron, Pierre Philibert de Blancheton.

The opening Presto follows the form typical for symphonic first movements at mid-century, as described by Heinrich Christoph Koch in the third volume of his *Introductory Essay on Composition* (1793). The overall structure is binary form, with two main sections that are each repeated. The first section contains a single period (a self-contained unit including at least two phrases and closed with a cadence) that opens in the tonic, modulates (measures 6–10), and closes on the dominant.

The second section has two periods, one that modulates back to the tonic key (measures 15–24) and another that presents a full recapitulation of the first section with the latter portions altered to close in the tonic. According to Koch's description, each period includes a series of phrases that may vary considerably in length, and the first section and the second period in the second section follow a set pattern of phrases, while the middle period is more variable. The following diagram shows how Koch's model fits this movement:

Music	Key	Measure
FIRST SECTION (ONE MAIN PERIOD)		
First and second phrases	I	1
Third phrase	modulate to V	6
Fourth phrase	V	11
Appendix	V	13
SECOND SECTION (TWO MAIN PERIODS)		
FIRST MAIN PERIOD		
Free	modulates	15
Preparation for return	on V	22
SECOND MAIN PERIOD		
First and second phrases	I	25
Third phrase	modulates	30
Fourth phrase	I	34
Appendix	I	37

This form later became known as *sonata form*, and the three periods were termed *exposition*, *development*, and *recapitulation*.

As is typical of Sammartini's symphonies, one idea follows another in rapid succession, each with a distinct rhythm and texture. The opening hammerlike blows in unisons and octaves were a favorite beginning gesture in early symphonies. Such a distinctive first idea captures the listener's attention and is readily remembered, making it easy to recognize when it returns and thus easy to follow the movement's form. Only one element, a rising line over a pulsing bass (measures 6–8), is reused before the double bar (measures 11–12), to bring the first section to a close. In the second period, the hammer blows are harmonized in the dominant, but almost immediately a B♭ in the bass thrusts the harmony toward the tonic. In the final period, after the return of the movement's opening material (measures 25–30), a new transition (measures 30–34) simulates a modulation to the subdominant but quickly leads back to the tonic. The material presented in the dominant at the end of the first section now appears in the tonic, and repeated tonic chords bring the second section to a close.

Like most early symphonies, this one is scored for strings in four parts—violins I and II, violas, and a bass line played by cellos, doubled an octave lower by bass viol—joined by a harpsichord for realizing the basso continuo. Orchestras of the time were usually small by modern standards, with perhaps ten to sixteen string players, including three to five on each violin part, one to four each on viola and cello, and one on bass viol.

JOHANN STAMITZ (1717–1757)

Sinfonia a 8 in E-flat Major, Op. 11, No. 3: First movement, Allegro assai

Symphony

MID-1750s

From *La melodia germanica*, Op. 11 (1758). Reprinted from *Denkmäler deutscher Tonkunst*, ser. 2, *Denkmäler der Tonkunst in Bayern*, year 7, vol. 2 (Leipzig, 1906), 1–12.

As director of instrumental music at the Mannheim court of the Elector Palatine, Johann Stamitz wrote orchestral and chamber music and directed the orchestra, which was famed for its precision and dramatic dynamic effects. This symphony was published in *La melodia germanica*, a collection of symphonies by several composers that was issued in Paris in 1758. Stamitz had died the previous year and presumably composed this work in the last few years of his life. Besides the opening movement, reprinted here, and an Andante slow movement, the symphony includes both a minuet and trio movement and a Prestissimo finale, comprising the set of four movements that became standard in later symphonies by Haydn (see NAWM 104) and other composers.

Comparing this first movement to that of Sammartini's Symphony in F Major (NAWM 100) is illuminating. The overall formal plan of three large periods is similar, but in the movement by Stamitz, the proportions are much expanded, and the repetitions of each section, which articulated the Sammartini movement, are omitted. The material presented in the first section of this and later symphonies tends to be more tuneful than the series of short, striking ideas presented by Sammartini, leading nineteenth-century analysts to describe the form in terms of themes rather than phrases. This later interpretation has become the most common for analyzing sonata form, but Koch's approach is still useful because it reminds us that eighteenth-century composers thought in terms of harmonic areas and phrases within an expanded binary form. Here, the two views are applied to the first section of Stamitz's first movement:

Koch's Model	Key	Measure	Nineteenth-Century Model
FIRST SECTION			EXPOSITION
First and second phrases	I	1	First theme
Third phrase	mod V	19	Transition
Fourth phrase	V	47	Second theme
Appendix	V	67	Closing theme

In the opening period, or exposition, the first theme area projects the tonic key through three different ideas: heavy tonic chords and unison arpeggios; a tuneful, soft violin melody suffused with sighing figures and a few dynamic surprises (measures 5–10); and a horn call (measures 11–18). The transition to the dominant (measures 19–46) includes two dramatic crescendos (measures 19–23 and 27–31), a Mannheim trademark, and recalls both the horn call and sighing melody of the first theme area. Stamitz was one of the first symphony composers to highlight the arrival of the dominant key with a contrasting theme, usually more lyrical to balance the dynamic, energetic opening section. Here, a graceful duet for two oboes (measures 47–66) provides a pleasant relief after the rather military and busy tonic section. The brief closing theme (measures 67–74) recalls part of the transition, including the horn call once again.

The second period, or development (beginning in measure 74), returns momentarily to the tonic before beginning to modulate through several closely related keys. The horn call and motives from the transition are briefly reworked before leading back to a repetition of the latter part of the transition, transposed into the tonic (compare measures 92–107 to 31–46).

What happens next is unusual. Instead of returning to the first theme at the beginning of the recapitulation and playing through the material from the first section in order, Stamitz skips the first theme. Having used the latter part of the transition at the end of the development, he proceeds directly to the second and closing themes, now transposed into the tonic (from measure 108). This constitutes the final period, a partial recapitulation. The movement closes triumphantly with elements from the first thematic area, presented in reverse order: the horn call (measures 132–38 parallel 11–17) and then the opening chords and unisons.

The key of this symphony, E♭ major, is often associated with the presence of horns, so that the key acquired associations with horn calls and thus hunting, heroism, the outdoors, nature, and the sublime. In addition to two violin sections, violas, cellos, and basses, Stamitz orchestrated the piece for two horns and two wind instruments, marked for oboes with the option of adding or substituting flutes or clarinets.

The horns are transposing instruments whose music is always notated in the key of C major, though they sound a major sixth lower, in E♭ major. (It is easy to follow their parts in the score by pretending they are in bass clef with a three-flat signature and then transposing up an octave.) Until the early nineteenth century, horns had no valves. Orchestral horn parts sounded primarily the notes of the natural overtone series, notated c–g–c'–e'–g'–bb'–c''–d''–e''–$f\#''$–g'', though horn players could obtain other notes by varying the position of their right hand in the bell of the horn (see for instance the written f below the staff in measures 13 and 17 and f'' on the top line of the staff in measures 74, 85, and 120–26).

The string parts are notable for the double, triple, and even quadruple stops in the violins, used to reinforce loud chords (see for example measures 1, 11, and 109), and for the tremolos marked with diagonal bars through the stem, used to suggest movement and energy (as in violin II and viola, measures 5–13).

JOHANN CHRISTIAN BACH (1735–1782)

102

Concerto for Harpsichord or Piano and Strings in E-flat Major, Op. 7, No. 5: First movement, Allegro di molto

Keyboard concerto

1770   — Double exposition

Violine I · Violine II · Violoncello · Cembalo oder Klavier

CD 7|36

Allegro di molto

Tutti! · *weak opening theme* · *A theme* · I

transitional (m.)
material (w/o modulating)

2nd theme (B)

Solo!

same theme but ornamented

Known as "the London Bach," Johann Christian Bach (J. S. Bach's youngest son and C. P. E. Bach's half brother) was a leading figure in musical life in the British capital for two decades. From 1765 to 1781, he and fellow composer Carl Friedrich Abel produced an annual series of public concerts. It was probably for these concerts that Bach wrote the six concertos for keyboard and strings published in 1770 as his Opus 7. However, the fact that he published them suggests that he also meant them to be performed by amateur keyboard players for making music at home, perhaps accompanied by only one player on each of the string parts.

The first movement of the Concerto in E♭ Major, Op. 7, No. 5, follows the form common to first movements of Classic-era concertos, a combination of the ritornello form of the Baroque concerto and the sonata form of symphonic first movements. As in a Vivaldi concerto (see NAWM 85), the movement is framed by ritornellos scored for the entire orchestra in alternation with episodes featuring the soloist. There are three main episodes that take the shape of the exposition, development, and recapitulation of a sonata form:

Section:	Ritornello				First Episode					Ritornello	Second Episode
Music:	1T	Tr	2T	CT	1T	Tr	NT	2T	CT	CT	new material
Key:	E♭				E♭	mod		B♭		B♭	mod
Measure:	1	12	25	31	44	59	71	85	91	106	115

Cadence	Third Episode				Cadenza	Ritornello
	1T	Tr	2T	CT		CT
on V of E♭	E♭					
144	146	161	171	177	191	192

The opening ritornello is the longest, presenting most of the movement's thematic material in the order of a sonata-form exposition but remaining in the tonic: a soft first theme (1T in the above diagram), a louder and more vigorous transition (Tr), a light second theme (2T), and a dynamic closing theme (CT). The first solo episode then restates this material in embellished form, joined occasionally by the orchestra. The first theme is imaginatively decorated, and the transition is embroidered with runs and turns (measures 59–70) and extended with new material (measures 71–84) that modulates to the dominant. Some analysts regard this new material as a new theme (marked NT in the diagram); its first four measures suggest the periodic phrasing of a theme, but it quickly returns to the sequences and modulating harmonies typical of transitional material. The second and closing themes (the latter much altered) now appear in the dominant, elaborated by solo and orchestra, completing the episode. According to some modern interpretations of concerto first-movement form, the opening ritornello and first solo episode are called "the orchestral exposition" and "the solo exposition" respectively, since they both present the main material. The key of the dominant is confirmed by the second ritornello, which repeats the closing theme in a form closer to its first appearance.

The second solo episode is similar to the development section of a sonata form. But here, instead of developing ideas already presented, Bach introduces a new idea in the keyboard part that modulates through several keys and ends back on the dominant. In lieu of a ritornello, the composer caps the episode with a *forte* cadence played by the full orchestra and embellished by the soloist.

The final solo episode constitutes the recapitulation, repeating the themes but changing the transition, omitting the new material, and remaining in the tonic for the second and closing themes. A cadential six-four chord announces the cadenza, an extended, unaccompanied, improvisatory display for the soloist that typically falls between the last episode and the closing ritornello. The final ritornello ends the movement with one last statement of the closing theme in the tonic.

Bach's singing themes, galant style, elegant figurations, and fluid keyboard writing all sound very much like Mozart to modern listeners. This is no coincidence, as Bach was a formative influence on Mozart, who spent over a year in London during 1764–65 (when he was eight and nine years old). The young prodigy came to know Bach well, learned a great deal from him, and imitated Bach's music in his own.

The concertos in Bach's Op. 7 can be played on either harpsichord or piano, but the latter seems better suited to the contrasts of *forte* and *piano* that help to articulate the form. The performance on the accompanying recording features a reconstruction of an eighteenth-century fortepiano. The score indicates that the soloist should play continuously, even accompanying the orchestra during the ritornellos, as was customary in Baroque concertos. In most later concertos, the soloist was expected to rest during the ritornellos, providing a greater contrast between solo and orchestral statements. Bach wrote out a lengthy cadenza for this movement, but in the accompanying performance, the soloist plays a relatively short cadenza based on excerpts from Bach's.

Joseph Haydn (1732–1809)

String Quartet in E-flat Major, Op. 33, No. 2 (*The Joke*), Hob. III:38: Fourth movement, Presto

String quartet

1781

From Joseph Haydn, *Quartet No. 38 in E-flat major*, Op. 33, No. 2, ed. Wilhelm Altmann, Edition Eulenburg 52 (London: Ernst Eulenburg, n.d.), 13–18.

Joseph Haydn wrote much of his music for his patron Prince Nikolaus Esterházy, but he also wrote pieces for sale to the public, including the six quartets of Op. 33. He composed them in the summer and fall of 1781 for the Viennese publisher Artaria and boasted in a letter that they were quartets of "a new and entirely special kind." Among the new features was his use of rondo form for the finales of Nos. 2, 3, and 4 (Haydn's earlier quartets do not contain rondo finales). The rondo finales of Op. 33 match the light and playful character of the entire set and follow the popular fashion for the rondo, which began in the 1770s.

A rondo alternates a theme, or refrain, with contrasting episodes, or *couplets.* The refrain almost always returns in the tonic, but the episodes may modulate to nearby keys. In this rondo, as in most of Haydn's, the refrain (measures 1–36) is a small binary form whose second section concludes with a complete restatement of the first. The first time the refrain is heard, each section is repeated, but the repeats are omitted when it returns at measure 72, after the first episode, and only the first section returns after the second episode. There are two episodes, creating an ABACA form, as was typical for Haydn:

Section:	Refrain	Episode	Refrain	Episode	Refrain	Coda
Music:	A ‖: a :‖: b a :‖	B	A a b a	C	A' a	Adagio a'
Key:	E♭	A♭ f	E♭			
Measure:	1 9 28	36 49	72 80 100	107	141	148 153

An effective rondo refrain is easily recognized yet maintains enough interest to withstand multiple repetitions. This theme meets these requirements. Its familiar balancing of two- and four-measure phrases and the frequent recurrences of the opening rhythm make it easy to recognize, yet each new phrase has a new melodic contour, combining variety with familiarity. The melody's short phrases and staccato notes are reminiscent of *opera buffa,* and its tendency to outrun its accompaniment, spilling over into the middle of the measure rather than stopping each phrase on the downbeat, has a comic effect. Including the obligatory repeats, we hear the first eight measures of the refrain seven times, yet the passage maintains its liveliness throughout the piece.

The two episodes do not introduce new material, as often occurs in rondos, but instead they develop figures from the theme. Episode B flirts with the subdominant and supertonic, while C (which starts with a four-measure recollection of B) remains in the tonic.

This quartet acquired the nickname *The Joke* because of the enigmatic rests at the end of the finale (see below), but humor pervades the whole movement, as

Haydn deliberately plays with the players' and listeners' expectations. The b section of the refrain builds suspense with repetitive figures over a pedal point that lead through a diminished chord to a dominant-seventh chord momentarily left unresolved. After a pause prolongs the drama, Haydn surprises us with a witty letdown—a simple return of the refrain's opening period. Haydn follows the same strategy at the end of each episode, so that each return of his comic opening melody is preceded by a disproportionately dramatic buildup.

In a major surprise at the end, a *pianissimo* statement of the refrain (measure 141) is cut off after the first section by a grand pause, making the listener wonder if the movement is finished. Instead, loud chords intrude, marking a change to Adagio tempo and duple meter, perhaps to mock all the formal rehashing. When the Presto returns, Haydn keeps the listener in doubt by isolating each two-measure phrase of the refrain's opening period with long pauses. After the fourth phrase, the piece seems to be over, but after an even longer pause, the opening motive of the refrain returns again, as if the refrain were going to repeat once more. Haydn seems to be poking fun at the redundant rondo, the beat-counting musicians, and the listeners wondering when to applaud.

Joseph Haydn (1732–1809)

Symphony No. 92 in G Major (*Oxford*), Hob. I:92

Symphony

1789

104

(a) First movement, Adagio—Allegro spiritoso

CD 7|51 CD 4|1

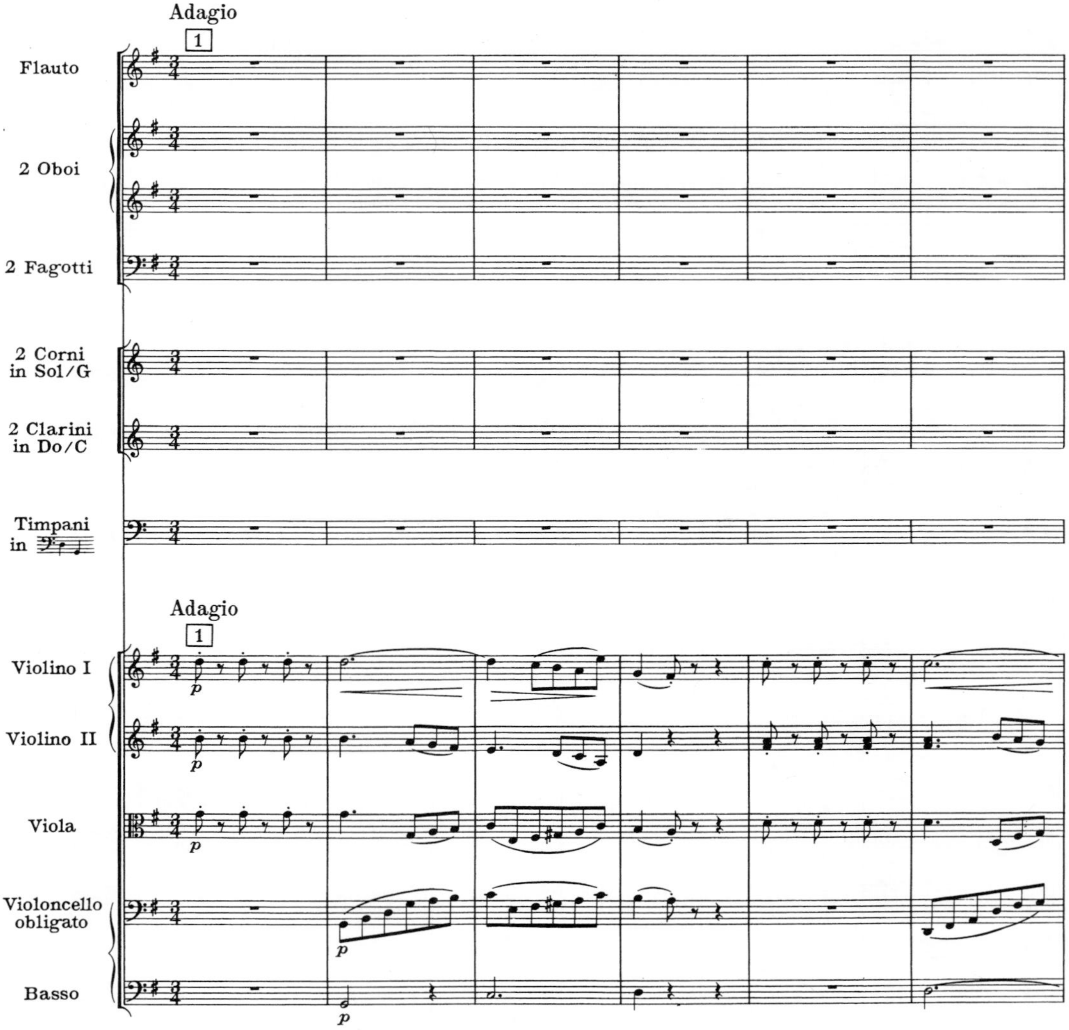

From *Joseph Haydn, Symphonies 88–92 in Full Score* (New York: Dover Publications, Inc.)

(b) Second movement, Adagio cantabile

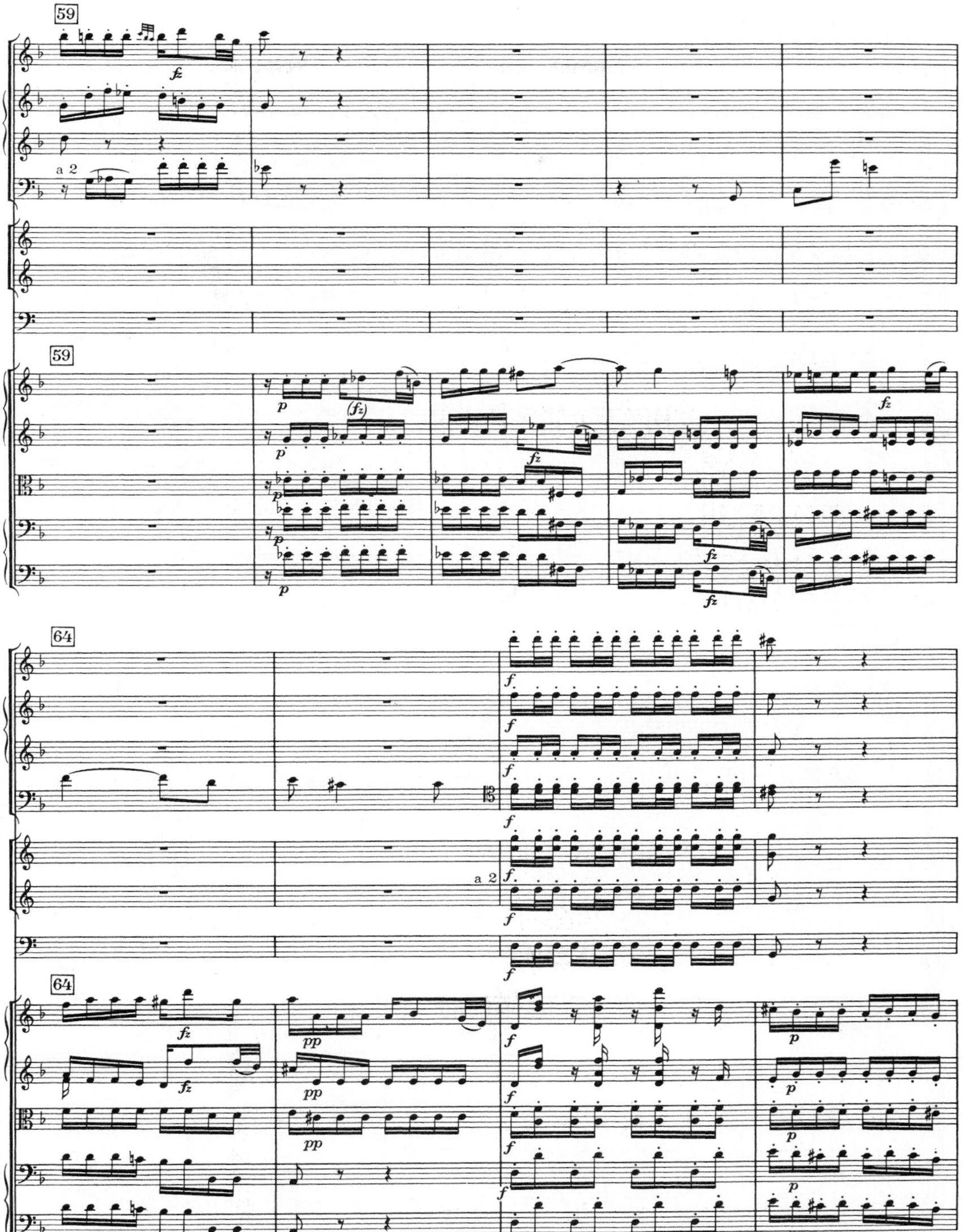
59
a 2
fz
59
p
(fz)
fz
64
f
a 2
pp
p

(c) Third movement, Menuetto, Allegretto

Menuetto da capo

(d) Fourth movement, Presto

transition V

Development

development of B theme

Fine

Symphony No. 92 in G Major is known as the *Oxford* Symphony because Haydn presented it to Oxford University when the institution awarded him an honorary Doctor of Music degree in 1791. However, he had written the piece two years earlier as the last of a set of three symphonies commissioned by the French Count d'Ogny. Like most of Haydn's mature symphonies, this one has four movements in the arrangement that became standard for the genre: a fast sonata-form movement, a slow movement, a minuet, and a fast finale.

The first movement (diagrammed below) begins with a slow introduction, as in many of Haydn's symphonies. After a sunny, serene beginning in the tonic G major, the Adagio introduction suddenly turns to chromaticism (measure 11) and the parallel minor, interjecting an element of dramatic pathos and closing on an augmented sixth chord. The Allegro spiritoso (measure 21) then begins on the dominant rather than the customary tonic chord. The first thematic area (1T in the diagram below) contains three highly contrasting ideas: (a) a quiet scalar figure on the dominant, like a giggle that breaks the solemn mood; (b) a suddenly loud, boisterous figure on the tonic that leaps up to a dotted quarter note on the second beat and then tumbles down in sixteenths; and (c) a repetitive cadential phrase. The first two of these ideas are elaborated in the following transition (Tr) to the dominant, which treats the ebullient sixteenth-note figures in a modulating sequence. As was Haydn's frequent practice, the second thematic area begins with the first idea from the first theme, now accompanied by a countermelody. A stormy minor-mode idea (d) marked by sforzando hammerstrokes introduces a moment of high drama. By contrast, the closing theme (e), is in a sweet, popular style with staccato notes and a turning figure. All the strong contrasts of style and mood delineate the form clearly and at the same time create a kaleidoscope of rapidly changing feelings, like an instrumental drama poised between seriousness and wit. There is something here for everybody—one reason this and other Haydn symphonies enjoyed such popular success.

Section:	Introduction	Exposition									Development
Music:		‖: 1T			Tr	2T		CT	:‖		e, a, b, d
		a	b	c	a, b	a'	d	e			
Key:	G	G			mod	D					mod
Measure:	1	21	25	32	41	57	61	72			83

Recapitulation							Coda			
1T			Tr	2T		CT				
a	b	c	a, new, e	a'	a, b	e	a	d	a, e, b
G										
125	129	137	145		166		191	200	212	220

The development modulates through several related keys, including the relative minor, while developing figures from the exposition and continuing the contrasts of loud and soft dynamics. After recalling the closing theme (at measure 83) and motive a from the first theme (at measure 89), Haydn combines them in counterpoint (measure 95), treats motive a in close imitation and inversion (measure 99), and then, astonishingly, converts it into a variant of motive b, the second element of the first theme (measure 104). With each new permutation, he increases the dramatic intensity through denser textures and offbeat sforzandos. The stormy idea from the second theme takes over (measure 110), then motive b returns (measure 115), leading to a dramatic pause. Throughout, Haydn finds fresh ways to rework and recombine his material, capitalizing on the open-ended quality of many of his musical ideas to string them together in new arrangements.

In the recapitulation, the first theme proceeds as before, now with motives a and b imitated in the flute. Although the transition only seems to modulate, returning to the home key so that the latter part of the exposition can appear in the tonic, Haydn makes it as dramatic and surprising as before and alters it to incorporate motive e from the closing theme. The second thematic area is greatly changed, and everything after motive a resembles further development of material from the first theme. This leaves the stormy hammerstrokes of motive d unresolved, so after the closing theme Haydn appends a substantial coda that transposes motive d into the tonic region and reviews the most significant motives one last time.

The slow movement, in ABA form, provides a period of calm after the energy and strong contrasts of the first movement. The songlike theme, begun by all the violins in unison and then continued by the first violins, is harmonized simply by the rest of the strings. Then flutes, bassoons, and horns subtly accent a restatement. The idyllic atmosphere is broken by the onset, *forte* and tutti, of the middle section in the parallel minor (measure 40), to which Haydn in a later revision added trumpets and timpani. Although its repeated chords sharply contrast with the character of the previous music, the *minore* (minor) interlude is built on a motive from the opening section. An abbreviated return of the *maggiore* (major) section is followed by an epilogue that features the winds.

As in most Haydn symphonies, the third movement is a minuet and trio. This type of movement combines two stylized minuets, repeating the first after the second (called the trio) to create an ABA form overall. Both minuet and trio are in binary form with repeats, although the repetitions are usually omitted when the minuet is heard a second time. Haydn's minuet and trio movements tend to be simpler in style, form, and texture and lighter in mood than the other movements in his symphonies. There are frequent touches of humor, especially in the rhythm and dynamics. Here, the phrases in the first section of the minuet are six measures long instead of four, which the listener might expect. As the second section begins (measure 13), sforzandos on the third beat of the measure and a surprising silence knock the listener off balance. The trio (measure 51) also uses six-measure phrases and sforzandos on the third beat. The sforzandos develop into a passage in which three contrapuntal voices each stress a different beat of the measure (beginning at measure 72), creating maximum metric confusion.

The finale, marked Presto, is in sonata form:

Section:	Exposition					Development			Recapitulation				Coda
Music:	‖: 1T	Tr	2T	CT	:‖	(1T)	(2T)	(1T)	1T	Tr	2T	CT	(1T)
Key:	G	mod	D			mod	C	to V	G				
Measure:	1	32	79	98		114	178	206	222	237	268	287	299

The playful first theme, embellished with chromaticism, is immediately repeated. Its signature opening motive returns frequently throughout the movement: in the middle of the transition before the second theme (measure 54), on the dominant and laced with countermelodies; at the beginning of the closing theme; in various guises throughout the development; leading into the dominant at the end of the development (measure 206); at the recapitulation, again just before the second theme (measure 258) and at the closing theme; and throughout the coda. The second theme appears in the development section (at measure 178) but is otherwise little heard. Yet it is very similar in character to the first theme, giving the entire movement an exuberant quality.

The performance on the accompanying recording uses an orchestra of the size and composition typical of Haydn's day. It includes a harpsichord playing the *basso continuo*, still used at the time in England (though not in Haydn's orchestra at Eszterháza) but omitted in most modern performances.

WOLFGANG AMADEUS MOZART (1756–1791)

Piano Sonata in F Major, K. 332 (300k): First movement, Allegro

Piano sonata

1781–83

From Wolfgang Amadeus Mozart, *Sonatas and Fantasies for the Piano,* ed. Nathan Broder, rev. ed. (Bryn Mawr: Theodore Presser, 1960), 167–73. Reprinted by permission of Theodore Presser. This sonata was item 332 in the thematic catalogue by Ludwig Köchel (*Chronologisch-thematisches Verzeichnis,* 1862) but is assigned the number 300k in the sixth edition, ed. Alfred Einstein (Wiesbaden: Breitkopf & Härtel, 1964), to reflect newer understanding of the chronology of Mozart's music.

The Sonata in F Major, K. 332, is one of three piano sonatas published in 1784 as Mozart's Op. 6. He wrote these sonatas either while visiting Munich in 1781 or during his first two years in Vienna.

The first movement of the Sonata in F Major clearly follows sonata form, with repeats marked for the exposition and for the development and recapitulation as a unit. What is perhaps most interesting is the way Mozart uses contrasts of style and figuration to delineate the parts of the form. Musicians and listeners of the late eighteenth century were familiar with many styles, from the lightly accompanied singing style of galant operas to the older learned style marked by counterpoint, and including styles associated with hunting, the military, dances, hymn-singing, and other diverse aspects of life. In this movement, Mozart used several of these styles in rapid succession.

In the first thematic area, the opening phrase presents a songlike melody over an Alberti bass. At measure 5, the singing style continues, but Mozart combines it with the imitation and counterpoint that exemplify the learned style. A new, more stepwise melody begins at measure 12, harmonized in hunting style, in which the left hand imitates a pair of natural horns, following the pitches of the harmonic series. The three segments of the first thematic area are linked by their emphasis on songlike melody, but players and listeners of Mozart's day would have recognized the references to three different styles, each with its own associations.

The transition at measure 22 is in *Sturm und Drang* (storm and stress) style, a dramatic, impassioned style characterized by minor mode, fast rhythms, loud dynamics, chromatic harmony, and strong dissonances like the diminished seventh chords in measures 25–26 and 29–30. The second theme (measure 41), in the dominant, is in galant style and is immediately restated in varied form (measure 49). The remaining elements of the exposition are also each set off with a distinctive figuration and style: a dramatic extension after the second theme (measure 56), a chordal, hymnlike or folklike closing theme (measure 71); and a series of cadential ideas.

As is often true of Mozart's sonatas, the development begins with a new melody (measure 94). Instead of varying the themes, the rest of the development focuses on the transitional passage between the second and closing themes in the exposition, developing it through strong dynamic contrasts into a passage of high drama. The storm then gradually quiets through undulating figures and expectant pauses. In the recapitulation, the first thematic area returns unchanged, the transition modulates to distant harmonies yet closes on the tonic, and the remainder of the exposition returns, transposed into the tonic.

The alternation between cheerful, songlike themes and minor-mode, turbulent or dramatic transitional and developmental sections creates a very satisfying emotional experience for both player and listener, embracing a wide range of feelings yet allowing the brighter moods to prevail. Emphasizing Mozart's references to diverse eighteenth-century styles can enrich a performance of this sonata. One important choice facing the pianist is whether to play the marked repeats. Playing both repeats stresses the similarity of sonata form to binary form, its direct ancestor, and thus leads to associations with dance and balance. Omitting the repetition of the development and recapitulation (and perhaps of the exposition as well) tends to create the feeling of a three-part form that may suggest a narrative—a story of departure, adventure, and return.

Another choice for the pianist is whether to play the piece on a modern piano or on a piano like those of Mozart's time. On the latter, sounds will fade more quickly, lending an emotional edge to sforzandos and sighing figures that may be missed on the more powerful modern instrument. Moreover, the typical piano of Mozart's day had a range of only five octaves, from *F'* an octave below the bass clef to *f'''* an octave above the treble clef, making clear that in this movement Mozart used almost the full range available to him, to heighten the drama and contrasts. Yet this sonata has been performed continuously since the early 1800s on a range of pianos modern for their time, from little spinets to ten-foot grands, and it is part of the very core of the piano repertoire. The choice of instrument must remain a personal one.

WOLFGANG AMADEUS MOZART (1756–1791)

Piano Concerto in A Major, K. 488: First movement, Allegro

Piano concerto

1786

From *Neue Mozart Ausgabe*, ser. 5, workgroup 15, vol. 7, ed. Hermann Beck (Kassel: Bärenreiter, 1959), 3–34. Baerenreiter Music Corporation. Used by permission.

Transition

Tutti | Solo | Tutti
A~B CL | A~B CL | CL
I – I | I — V | V

Transition to Cl

A (embellishing A theme)

Transition

Transition

B section

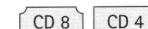

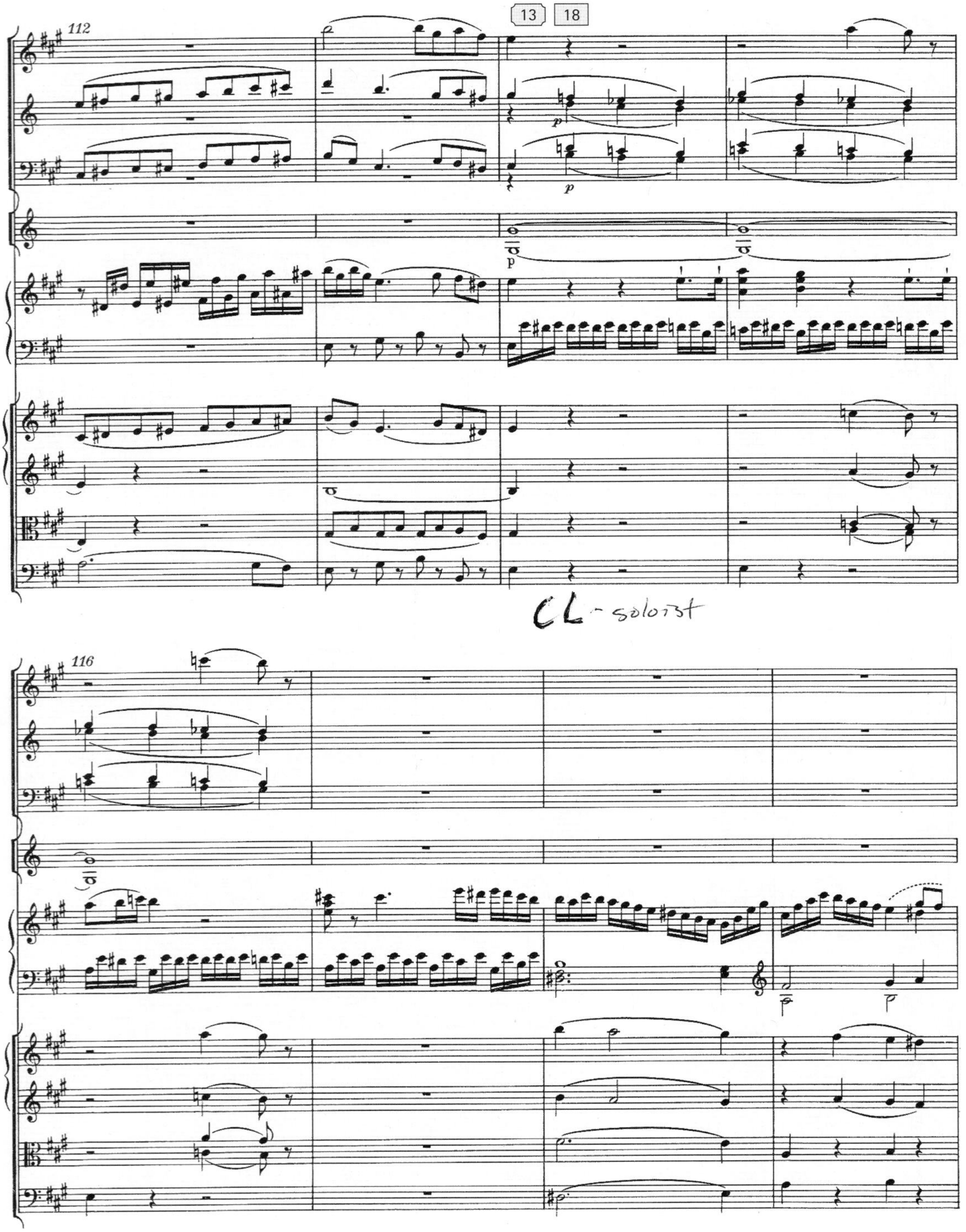

13
18
112
p
p
p
CL - soloist
116

Tutti

CL -Tutti

contrapuntal closing

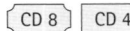

15 20

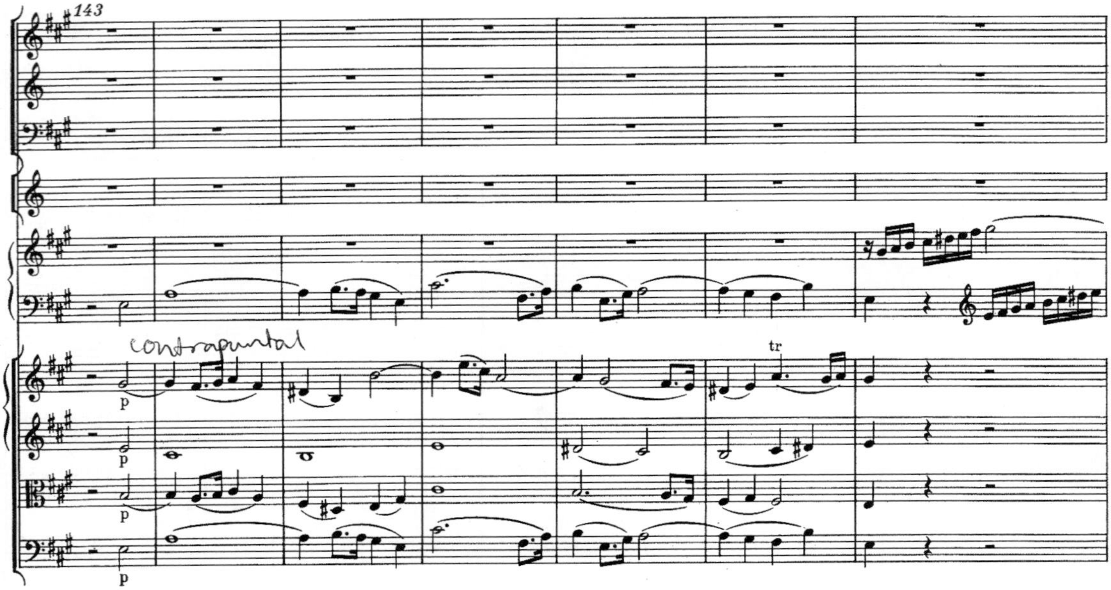
143
contrapuntal
tr
p

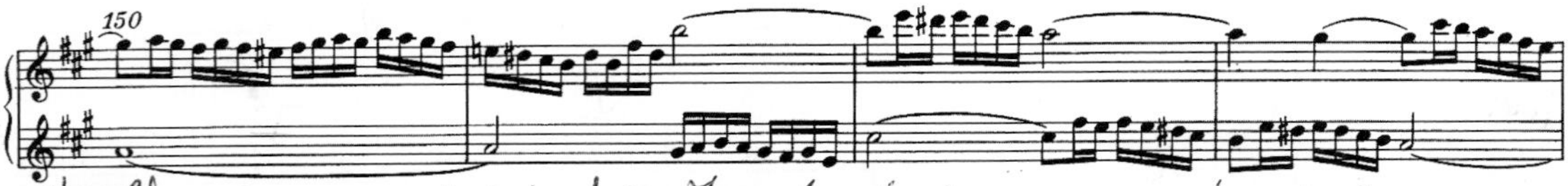
150

development — soloist does the developing in a classical concerto

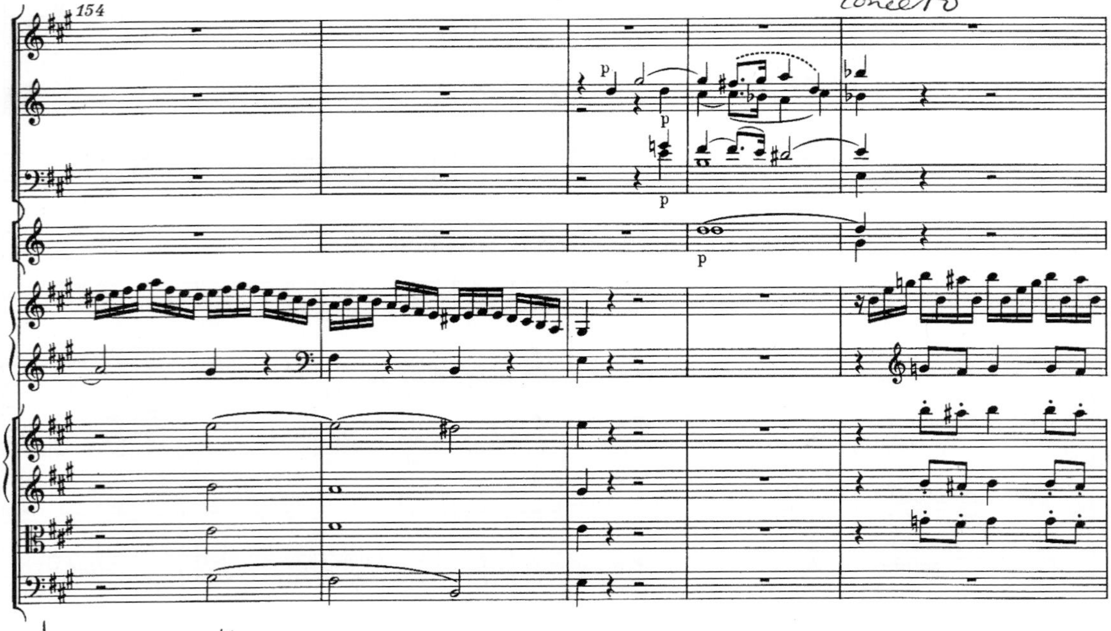
154
p

development

Sequene — show off

mini-cadenza

less simple→more tension

recapitulation

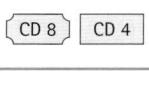

Mozart completed the Piano Concerto in A Major, K. 488, in March 1786 but apparently began composing it considerably earlier. He sold the work to Prince von Fürstenburg at Donaueschingen. The form of the first movement is comparable to that of the Concerto for Harpsichord or Piano and Strings in E♭ Major, Op. 7, No. 5 (NAWM 102), by J. C. Bach, whose keyboard concertos Mozart knew and emulated. Mozart followed a very similar pattern in this movement, combining aspects of sonata and ritornello form, yet introducing several unique elements:

Section:	Ritornello				First Episode				Ritornello		Second Episode	
Music:	1T	Tr	2T	CT	1T	Tr	2T	CT	TR	NT	NT	
Key:	A				A	mod	E		E		mod	on V
Measure:	1	18	30	46	67	82	98	114	137	143	149	178

Ritornello	Third Episode					Ritornello		Cadenza	Ritornello
1T	1T	Tr	2T	CT	NT	Tr	NT		CT
A									
198	206	213	228	244	261	284	290	297	298

The opening orchestral section of sixty-six measures displays both the thematic variety of a sonata-form exposition and several qualities of the Baroque concerto ritornello. Like a symphonic exposition, it presents a first theme, second theme, and closing theme and features contrasts of orchestral color, including extensive passages for winds alone. But like a Baroque ritornello, the section is in a single key, and parts of it return in various keys later in the movement. The first theme is built on a graceful, symmetrical eight-measure melody. A transition scored for full orchestra leads to an elegant second theme, still in the tonic, that alternates even and dotted rhythms. A stirring closing theme scored for the whole orchestra (measures 46–66) closes the opening ritornello (sometimes called the "orchestral exposition").

The first solo episode (or "solo exposition") follows the same sequence of events as the opening ritornello but modulates to the dominant. It begins with the pianist's exposition of the first theme, delicately ornamented and discreetly accompanied by the orchestra. The full orchestra initiates the transition, which is completed by modulatory figuration in the piano that leads to E major, the dominant key. Soloist and orchestra then engage in dialogue during the second and closing themes. As the first solo section ends, the orchestra returns with an abbreviated ritornello, just the transition transposed into the dominant, and then continues with six measures of new material (NT in the diagram, for "new theme").

The second solo episode (measure 149) is akin to the development section of a symphony. Here, instead of developing the ideas presented earlier, Mozart varies the new theme just introduced by the orchestra in a dialogue among the piano, the winds, and the strings. This section makes excursions into several remote keys, including E minor, C major, and F major, before culminating in a twenty-measure pedal point on the dominant.

Mozart lets the orchestra begin the recapitulation (measure 198), initiating the final large solo section. As in the first solo section, the full orchestra initiates the transition, and dialogue suffuses the second and closing themes, now in the tonic. After a surprising pause, soloist and orchestra reprise the new material that opened the second solo section and develop it further (measure 261).

The movement closes with a final orchestral ritornello (measure 284). This begins with the transition, back in the tonic, and continues with the new material from the development. The most suspenseful moment of the concerto arrives when the orchestra pauses dramatically on a tonic six-four chord that seems urgently in need of resolution. The soloist is then expected to decorate the cadence by playing an extended cadenza, either improvised or worked out in advance. Mozart's autograph cadenza for this concerto and a number of others survive, and many performers today choose to play Mozart's cadenza or one of many others written over the years by various performers and composers. Closing this movement, the passage for orchestra alone that ended the opening ritornello repeats, with the first several measures omitted.

Describing the form in terms of an orchestral exposition, solo exposition, development, and recapitulation emphasizes how this movement's structure resembles sonata form. But one could emphasize its similarities to Baroque ritornello form by noting the passages for full orchestra alone that act like ritornellos (measures 1–66, 137–49, 198–205, 284–97, 298–end). The genius of Classic-period concerto form is that it combines the strengths of both its relatives, creating increased coherence among the solo passages (in comparison with the Baroque concerto) and providing a wider variety of resources for color, drama, and dialogue (in comparison with the sonata).

The performance on the recording that accompanies this anthology features forces similar to those Mozart would have used: a small orchestra of twenty to thirty players and a fortepiano for the soloist. The fortepiano does not have the volume to compete with a full orchestra, so when the soloist and orchestra play together, the orchestra parts are more lightly scored. This and Mozart's other piano concertos are staples of the modern orchestral repertoire, and the soloists often play on large grand pianos. Despite their use of modern instruments, soloists often seek to emulate the light, crisp sound of the fortepianos of Mozart's time, and conductors often reduce the size of their orchestras.

Wolfgang Amadeus Mozart (1756–1791)

Don Giovanni: Act 1, Scenes 1–2

Opera (dramma giocoso)

1787

107

From *Neue Mozart Ausgabe,* ser. 2, workgroup 5, vol. 17, ed. Wolfgang Plath and Wolfgang Rehm (Kassel: Bärenreiter, 1968), 28–45. Baerenreiter Music Corporation. Used by permission.

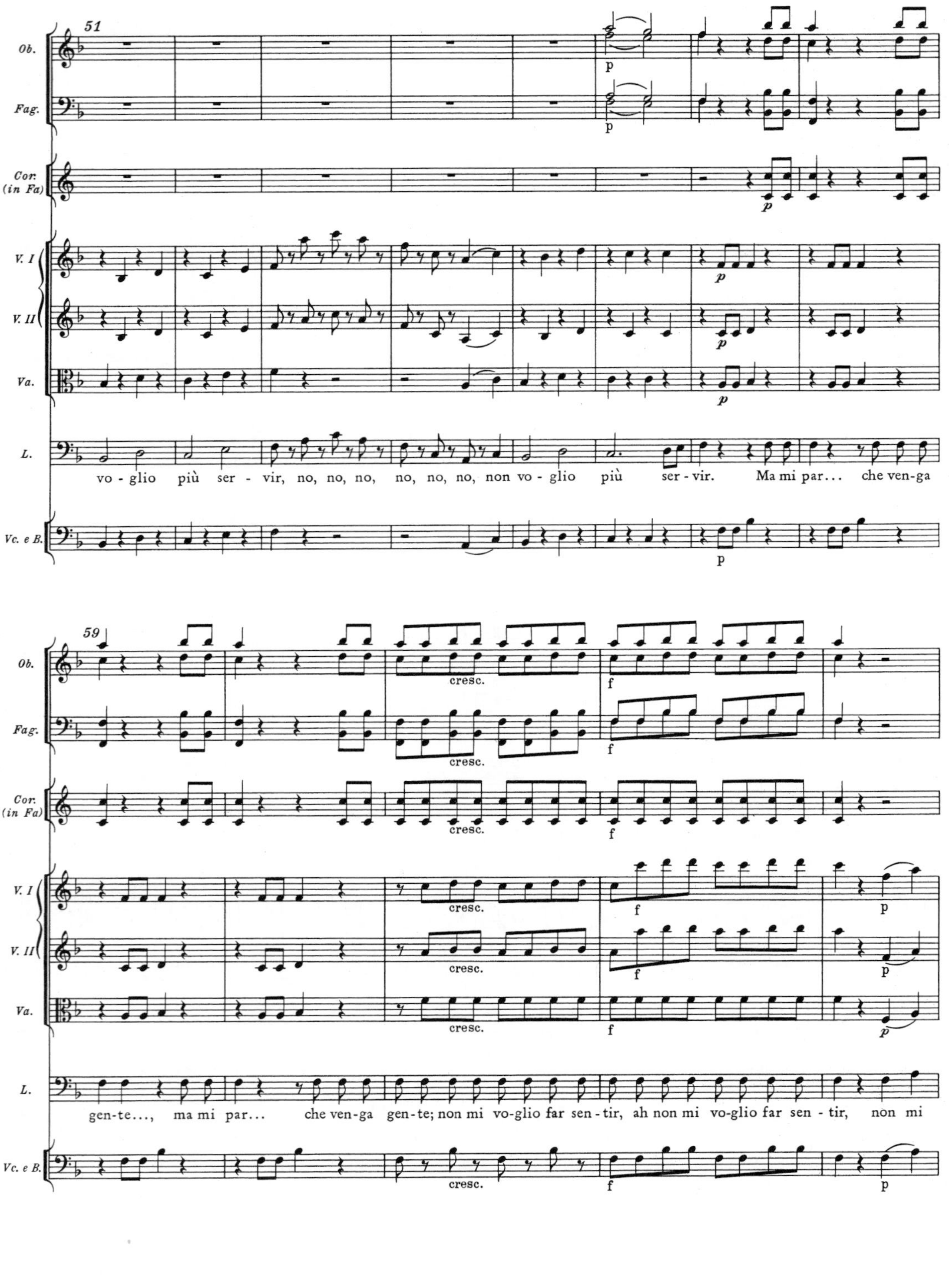

voglio più servir, no, no, no, no, no, no, non voglio più servir. Ma mi par... che venga

gente..., ma mi par... che venga gente; non mi voglio far sentir, ah non mi voglio far sentir, non mi

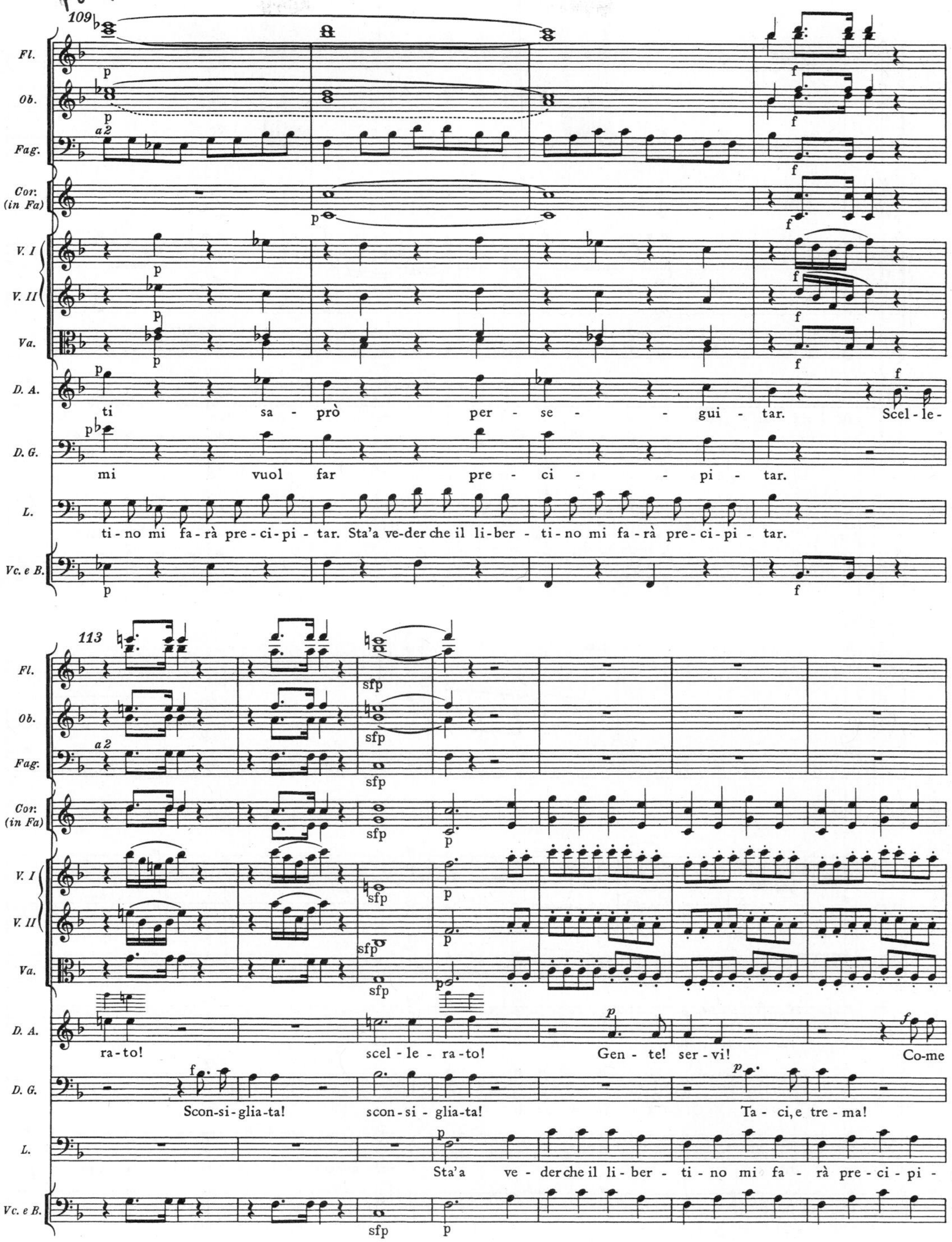
109
Fl.
Ob.
Fag.
Cor. (in Fa)
V. I
V. II
Va.
D. A.
ti sa - prò per - se - - gui - tar. Scel - le -
D. G.
mi vuol far pre - ci - - pi - tar.
L.
ti - no mi fa - rà pre - ci - pi - tar. Sta'a ve - der che il li - ber - ti - no mi fa - rà pre - ci - pi - tar.
Vc. e B.
113
ra - to! scel - le - ra - to! Gen - te! ser - vi! Co - me
Scon - si - glia - ta! scon - si - glia - ta! Ta - ci, e tre - ma!
Sta'a ve - der che il li - ber - ti - no mi fa - rà pre - ci - pi -

Patter

SCENE 1

LEPORELLO

Notte e giorno faticar	Night and day I toil hard
Per chi nulla sa gradir;	for one whom nothing can please;
Piova e vento sopportar,	rain and wind I suffer,

Mangiar male e mal dormir.	eating badly and sleeping poorly.
Voglio far il gentiluomo,	I would like to be the gentleman,
E non voglio più servir.	and no more be the servant.
Oh che caro galantuomo!	Oh what a dear and upright man!
Voi star dentro colla bella,	You are inside with a beautiful woman,
Ed io far la sentinella!	while I keep sentry duty out here!
Voglio far il gentiluomo,	I would like to be the gentleman,
E non voglio più servir.	and no more be the servant.
Ma mi par . . . che venga gente;	But I think . . . that someone's coming;
Non mi voglio far sentir.	I don't want to be discovered.

(Leporello hides as Don Giovanni rushes in, pursued by Donna Anna.)

DONNA ANNA
(holding tightly onto Don Giovanni's arm)

Non sperar, se non m'uccidi,	Do not hope, if you don't kill me,
Ch'io ti lasci fuggir mai.	that I'll ever let you flee.

DON GIOVANNI
(still trying to conceal himself)

Donna folle! Indarno gridi!	Crazy woman! You cry out in vain!
Chi son io tu non saprai.	Who I am you will never know.

LEPORELLO
(to himself)

Che tumulto! Oh ciel, che gridi!	What an uproar! Oh Heavens, what shouts!
Il padron in nuovi guai.	My master is in trouble again.

DONNA ANNA

Gente! Servi! Al traditore!	People! Servants! Get the traitor!

DON GIOVANNI

Taci, e trema al mio furore.	Be quiet, or fear my fury.

DONNA ANNA

Scellerato!	Wicked man!

DON GIOVANNI

Sconsigliata!	Rash woman!

LEPORELLO
(to himself)

Sta' a veder che il libertino	You're about to see that the libertine
Mi farà precipitar.	will cause my downfall.

DONNA ANNA

Come furia disperata	Like a desperate fury
Ti saprò perseguitar.	I will haunt you.

DON GIOVANNI
(to himself)

Questa furia disperata	This desperate fury
Mi vuol far precipitar.	wants to bring about my downfall.

(Hearing her father, the Commendatore, as he approaches,
Donna Anna lets Don Giovanni go and reenters the house.)

THE COMMENDATORE

Lasciala, indegno,	Let her go, unworthy man!
Battiti meco!	Fight with me!

DON GIOVANNI

Va', non mi degno	Go away, it would not be worthy of me
Di pugnar teco.	to fight with you.

THE COMMENDATORE

Così pretendi da me fuggir?	Is this how you plan to escape me?

LEPORELLO
(to himself)

(Potessi almeno di qua partir!)	If only I could get away!

DON GIOVANNI

Misero, attendi, se vuoi morir!	Wretch, wait then, if you want to die!

(They fight. The Commendatore is mortally wounded. The Commendatore,
Don Giovanni, and Leporello sing the following lines simultaneously.)

THE COMMENDATORE

Ah . . . soccorso! . . . son tradito! . . .	Ah . . . help! . . . I am betrayed! . . .
L'assassino . . . m'ha ferito . . .	The assassin . . . has wounded me . . .
E dal seno palpitante	And from my throbbing breast
Sento l'anima partir.	I feel my life ebbing away.

DON GIOVANNI
(to himself)

Ah . . . già cadde il sciagurato . . .	Ah . . . already falls the unfortunate man . . .
Affannosa e agonizzante	His breathing is labored, he is in mortal agony.
Già dal seno palpitante	Already from his throbbing breast
Veggo l'anima partir.	I see his life ebbing away.

LEPORELLO
(to himself)

Qual misfatto! Qual eccesso!	What a crime! What an excess!
Entro il sen, dallo spavento,	Within my breast, I feel my heart
Palpitar il cor mi sento.	Pounding with fright.
Io non sò che far, che dir.	I don't know what do to or what to say.

(The Commendatore dies.)

SCENE 2

DON GIOVANNI

Leporello, ove sei?   Leporello, where are you?

LEPORELLO

Son qui per mi disgrazia; e voi?   I'm here, unfortunately. And you?

DON GIOVANNI

Son qui.   I'm here.

LEPORELLO

Chi è morto, voi, o il vecchio?   Who's dead, you or the old man?

DON GIOVANNI

Che domanda da bestia! Il vecchio.   What a stupid question! The old man.

LEPORELLO

Bravo: due imprese leggiadre!   Well done! Two lovely exploits!
Sforzar la figlia, ed ammazzar il padre.   Forcing yourself on the daughter, and
                                           murdering the father.

DON GIOVANNI

L'ha voluto, suo danno.   He wished it, it's his loss.

LEPORELLO

Ma Donn' Anna, cosa ha voluto?   But Donna Anna, what did she wish?

DON GIOVANNI

Taci, non mi seccar, vien meco,   Be quiet, don't annoy me, and come with me
Se non vuoi qualche cosa ancor tu!   if you don't want something more yourself!

(Raises his hand to strike Leporello.)

LEPORELLO

Non vuo' nulla, Signor, non parlo più.   I don't want anything, Sir. I won't say
                                         another word.

(They exit.)

—LORENZO DA PONTE

Don Giovanni was commissioned by an impresario in Prague after *The Marriage of Figaro* enjoyed great success there in 1786–87. The librettist for *Figaro*, Lorenzo da Ponte, also wrote the libretto for *Don Giovanni*, and Mozart directed the first performances in Prague in October 1787. The new opera caused a sensation, leading to a second production in Vienna the following year with several changes and added numbers. Soon *Don Giovanni* was staged elsewhere, often in German translation, and it quickly became one of Mozart's most popular works. The standard editions and most modern performances draw on both the Prague and Vienna versions.

Few comedies begin with a murder on stage, but *Don Giovanni* does. What is most startling, and ultimately both amusing and deeply moving, about this opera is the way it constantly plays with our expectations. The plot and especially the music often surprise us, manipulating conventions and mixing genres and styles in ways that can be hilarious yet can also make us think about issues of class, morality, liberty, and responsibility.

As the opera opens, the scene is a garden at night, in front of the house of Donna Anna (Lady Anna). Leporello (the name translates roughly as "Little Rabbit") paces up and down, lamenting his lot as the servant of Don Giovanni (Don Juan, or Lord John). Leporello's aria follows the straightforward form ABCBDB' (B starts at measure 20, C at 32, D at 57). Every idea in the music is aptly attuned to the text. Leaping notes and quick scalar flourishes in bare octaves wonderfully depict Leporello's pacing and set a comic tone. When he declares that he would like to be a gentleman (measure 20), his melody suddenly becomes smooth and elegant, and he is joined by horns playing a figure that suggests the hunt, an activity normally restricted to gentlemen and aristocrats. But as he explains why he no longer wants to be a servant, he reverts back to the skipping melody, bass tones, and short notes typical of the opera buffa servant (measures 26–32), and when he is startled by approaching footsteps, he expresses his fright through rapid comic patter (measure 57).

Upward-rushing string tremolos, a crescendo, and a key change from F to B♭ announce a change to a more serious style (measure 70). A masked Don Giovanni rushes in pursued by Donna Anna, whom he has tried to seduce (whether by force or deceit, and whether he succeeded, we are left to guess). She holds his arm and tries to discover his identity. Throughout the opera, Donna Anna sings in the elevated, dramatic style of opera seria. Don Giovanni, true to his character as a duplicitous scoundrel, tends to communicate in the manner of whomever he is with, so here he matches her style. Leporello, always concerned about how events will affect him, frets from his hiding place in triadic, repetitive opera buffa style (as at measures 98 and 108). Mozart repeats words and has the characters sing simultaneously or in quick alternation to convey the confused situation more realistically. Despite the histrionics, the music unfolds in a perfectly controlled ABB form (with the B sections beginning at measures 90 and 112).

The music then becomes more tense, marked by tremolos and rushing scales in G minor as Donna Anna's father the Commendatore (commander, a military title) rushes in to protect her (measure 135). He challenges Don Giovanni to fight, and in a brilliant piece of musical representation we can hear their swords thrust and parry, depicted by rapid rising scales and leaping octaves (measure 167). The Commendatore falls mortally wounded. In a magnificent F minor trio, he pants out his final words, their syllables separated by longer and longer rests, while Don Giovanni and Leporello comment on the situation.

This powerful series of sections—aria, trio, dramatic action, and closing trio—unfolds without a break to depict the onrush of events. Yet Mozart uses coherent forms and a logical key scheme, beginning and ending in F with excursions to closely related keys. This combination of coherent musical framework with rapidly changing situations is typical of Mozart's ensemble scenes, including his famous finales, and it helps to explain why the events seem logical, even inevitable, when they occur.

Sinking chromatic lines depict the life ebbing from the Commendatore (measures 190–93), and the music pauses on a first-inversion G major triad, the dominant of the dominant. In perfect tune with the shock the audience feels at the unexpected turn to tragedy, the scene ends without a final cadence. Convention would call for applause after the opening scene, but because applause would interrupt the drama, Mozart does not give the audience the expected signals. Instead, he moves right on to a recitative in opera buffa style between Don Giovanni and Leporello. Here is a shock of a new sort: jesting right after a murder.

The singers adopt the performing style appropriate to their characters. Donna Anna and the Commendatore sing in the dramatic style of opera seria, Don Giovanni moves between seductive lyric baritone and comic style, and Leporello uses the bent tones and speech-like vowels of the opera buffa bass.

Ludwig van Beethoven (1770–1827)

Piano Sonata in C Minor, Op. 13 (*Pathétique*): Third movement, Rondo, Allegro

Piano sonata

1797–98

From Ludwig van Beethoven, *Sonatas for Piano,* ed. Carl Krebbs (New York, 1898; repr. Kalmus, n.d.), 131–36.

Beethoven composed the *Sonate pathétique* in 1797–98, and it was published in Vienna in 1799. "Pathétique" means emotionally moving, especially in the sense of arousing pity, grief, or tenderness. The sonata became very popular as soon as it was published. Beethoven thought that the work's name contributed to its success with the music-buying public, and indeed such evocative names were common tools for marketing music throughout the nineteenth century.

This finale is a sonata-rondo, which blends rondo form with aspects of sonata form. Rondos were traditionally cheerful, spirited, tuneful pieces in a major key, but this one does not fit that mold. Written in C minor, it recalls the intense, stormy mood of the sonata's first movement. The main theme, or refrain, twists and turns around the minor third and the semitones of the major scale. The episodes, or couplets, although in major keys, soon drift into minor. Even the coda feints toward major, then ends dramatically in minor. The constant reversion to minor mode helps to convey the pathos promised by the piece's title.

The refrain is not a small binary form, as in the rondo finale of Haydn's *Joke* Quartet (NAWM 103), but a simple period (measures 1–17). It returns three times, alternating with episodes to create the overall form ABACAB'A Coda. Typical of sonata-rondos, the refrain and first episode resemble the exposition of a sonata form, the refrain comprising the first theme and the episode the remainder: a modulatory transition (measure 18), second theme in a contrasting key (measure 25, in the relative major E♭), and closing theme (measure 43). When this material returns in the third episode, it is in the tonic C major or C minor, as it would be in a sonata-form recapitulation. Similar to a sonata development, the central episode (measure 78) in A♭ major presents a contrasting, contrapuntal idea. Beethoven develops this episode by adding to its opening motto a new countersubject that is presented in invertible counterpoint. The form may be summarized as follows:

Section:	Refrain	Episode 1			Refrain	Episode 2	Refrain	Episode 3			Refrain	Coda
Music:	A	Trans	B1	B2	A	C	A	Trans	B1	B2	A	Coda
Key:	c	mod	E♭		c	A♭	c	mod	C		c	c
Measure:	1	18	25	43	61	78	120	128	134	153	171	182

The form is readily audible because the sections are clearly set off by cadences or prepared by transitions. The return of the refrain in the tonic is twice announced by a *fortissimo* run cascading down two and a half octaves, followed by a long pause on the dominant seventh chord (measures 58–61 and 117–20). This figure makes two more dramatic appearances in the coda. Each time it occurs, it lends an aura of expectation and inevitability, adding to the pathos of the piece. The last two statements of the refrain are abbreviated.

Beethoven drew connections between this and the other movements of the sonata. The finale's refrain borrows the rhythm and opening intervals of the first movement's second theme:

Such thematic links between movements became frequent in the works of Beethoven and his nineteenth-century successors. Even more common were harmonic reminiscences. Here, the central episode in A♭ and a brief suggestion of that key just before the end (measures 202–6) allude back to the key of the sonata's middle movement.

109

Ludwig van Beethoven (1770–1827)

Symphony No. 3 in E-flat Major, Op. 55 (*Eroica*): First movement, Allegro con brio

Symphony

1803

CD 8|36 CD 4|41

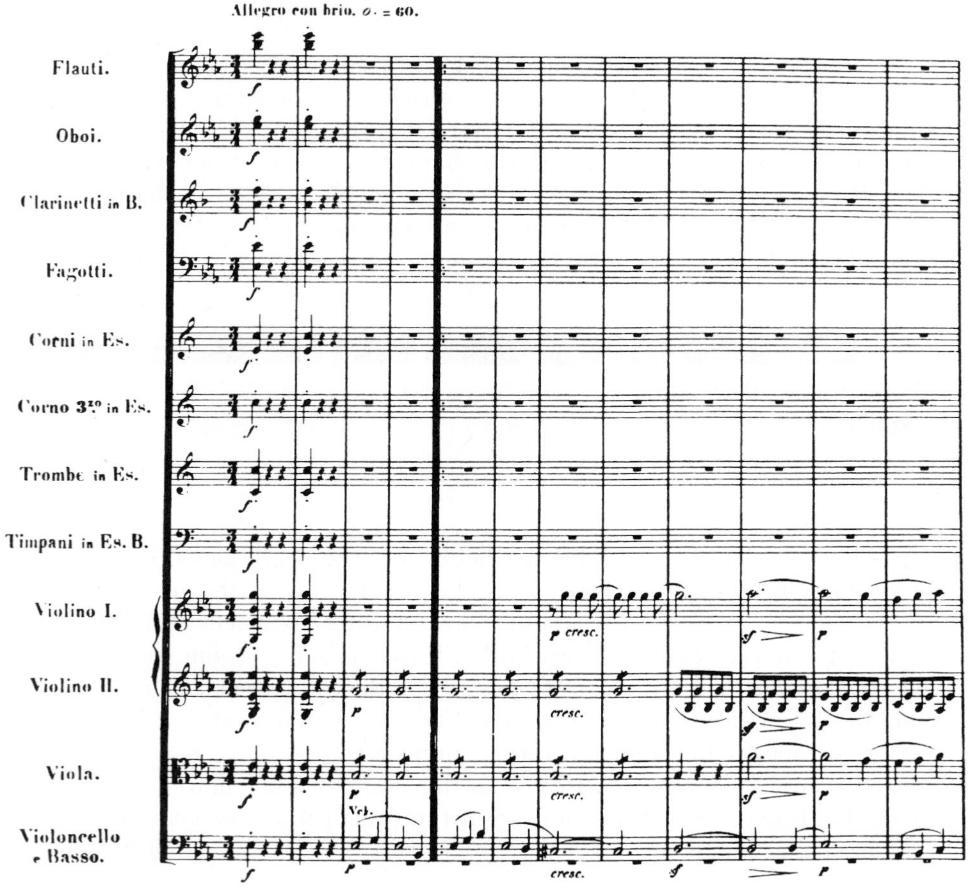

From *Ludwig van Beethovens Werke: Vollständige kritisch durchgesehene überall berechtigte Ausgabe*, ser. 1, vol. 1 (Leipzig: Breitkopf & Härtel, 1862–65), 113–45. Sketches reproduced from Gustav Nottebohm, *Ein Skizzenbuch von Beethoven aus dem Jahre 1803* (Leipzig, 1865).

Beethoven composed his Third Symphony mostly in 1803. It was played at a private concert in the summer of 1804 at the estate of his patron Prince Franz Joseph von Lobkowitz, then given its public premiere in Vienna on April 7, 1805. Its first audiences were divided between those who rated it a masterpiece and those who found it too long, difficult, and strange. All the movements departed in unexpected ways from Beethoven's previous symphonic writing, and the first movement alone was as long as entire symphonies from a generation earlier.

Some of the unusual features can best be explained by reference to the extramusical elements implied by its title. Beethoven originally called it "Bonaparte," in honor of Napoleon, his admired hero who promised to lead humanity into the new age of liberty, equality, and fraternity. But by the time of the symphony's publication in 1806, Beethoven was apparently disillusioned by Napoleon and had renamed it "Sinfonia Eroica . . . composta per festeggiare il sovvenire di un grand Uomo" (Heroic Symphony . . . composed to celebrate the memory of a great man). He dedicated it to Prince Lobkowitz, and it has been suggested that the "great man" was Lobkowitz's friend Prince Louis Ferdinand of Prussia, who was greatly taken with Beethoven's symphony when he heard it at Lobkowitz's palace and who died a hero in 1806. Of course, that happened well after the piece was written. Many scholars believe that the heroism celebrated in the piece was Beethoven's own courage in continuing to write music in spite of his growing deafness.

The first movement is particularly "heroic" in its expansive form, thematic richness, exciting climaxes, and forceful, obstinate assertion of individual imagination. Typical of symphonic first movements, the overall form is a sonata, with a first theme group, transition to the dominant, second theme (at measure 83), and closing theme (measure 109) in the exposition, followed by development (measure 154), recapitulation (measure 398), and coda (measure 551). Yet within this familiar structure, the principal motive is treated like a character in a drama, portrayed as striving, being opposed and subdued but triumphing in the end. It first appears in the cellos (measures 3–7) instead of the violins, an unusual placement that was an important precedent for later Romantic symphonists. It resembles a fanfare, suggesting a heroic character, but unexpectedly sinks down chromatically, hinting at an inner weakness. It reappears in various guises during the exposition, sometimes in sequence, but always eventually falling back. Then, in the development (starting at measure 154), it contends with various other elements from the exposition, especially a leaping figure associated with offbeat accents and syncopation (measures 25–35) and a motive from the transition (at measures 45–55). A *fugato*, or fugal passage, on the latter (at measure 236) leads into a development of the leaping figure (measures 248–71) and a peak of dissonance and rhythmic disruption (measure 272–79), spelling apparent defeat for the protagonist, the main motive. But the opening theme gradually reasserts itself, leading to the recapitulation. Near the end of the development (measures 338–41), the principal motive achieves an unalloyed heroic form, arpeggiating as before but remaining on its highest pitch, the fifth of the triad, rather than sinking down at the end. This new form is confirmed in the recapitulation (in the horn and flute at measures 408–23), then triumphantly asserted in the coda by horns, strings, and finally winds through a powerful crescendo (at measures 631–62).

Commentators and analysts from as early as Beethoven's time have pointed out certain peculiarities of the first movement.

1. The development section (244 measures) outweighs the exposition (153 measures) and recapitulation (153 measures), which are equal (although the exposition is repeated). The coda (141 measures) is nearly as long as the exposition.
2. The transition from the first theme group in the tonic to the second theme group in the dominant is very short, and the latter has a multiplicity of themes.
3. A new theme is presented in the middle of the development (measure 284).
4. There are disconcerting and abrupt changes of key, such as the succession E♭–F–D♭ within sixteen measures (measures 401–16) in the recapitulation, and E♭–D♭–C (measures 555–62) within eight measures of the coda.
5. Certain passages are insistently dissonant.
6. The French horn seems to state the main theme prematurely just before the recapitulation.

Points 1, 4, and 5 directly reflect the heroic character Beethoven sought to achieve. The piece is an adventure with the main motive as the protagonist, whose transformations over the course of the movement—especially in the long development and coda—convey a sense of a heroic struggle and final triumph, as suggested above. The striking changes of key, dissonant passages, and other unusual features evoke the surprises, confrontation, and violent opposition the hero encounters.

Points 2, 3, and 6 are debatable, and they prompt an investigation of what we can learn from Beethoven's sketches. Looking at the early drafts gives us some insight into his overall design and the function of these and other peculiarities.

Beethoven used sketches to determine how to give the music precisely the shape and effect that he wanted. We can use them to retrace his steps—to discern what he sought to accomplish and how he achieved it. After initial sketches, Beethoven would write out a "continuity draft" of an entire section or piece. Example 1 shows the first continuity draft of the exposition, and it exhibits some striking similarities to and differences from the final version. For example, the symphony opens with two short tonic chords on the downbeats, but the sketch opens with two dominant chords in a different rhythm; Beethoven clearly desired the effect of surprising, brief chords, but he changed the harmony and rhythm to create a more stable beginning. The draft includes the first theme (measures 3–23) in virtually its final form, but it lacks the striking leaping figure with its syncopated effect (measures 25–35) that becomes a major character in the ensuing drama.

Example 1. Continuity draft from MS Landsberg 6, p. 11, after Gustav Nottebohm, *Ein Skizzenbuch von Beethoven aus dem Jahre 1803* (Leipzig, 1865), pp. 6–7, over outline of parallel passages in published score, measures 1–129

The sketch may help us understand point 2 above, concerning the transition and second theme. Some analysts have interpreted measure 45 as the end of the transition and the beginning of the second theme group, with the first of many short thematic ideas. Others have interpreted measure 45 as the end of the first theme group and the beginning of the transition. Some of the latter regard the second theme as beginning at measure 57, where the key of B♭ (the dominant) first arrives, making for a disproportionately short transition and a sly entry of the second theme group.

Where the transition begins is a matter of definition. If Beethoven is following Haydn's frequent practice of launching the transition by reiterating the opening material and then steering the music in new directions, measure 37 is a logical candidate (though the parallel in the continuity draft, at measure 31 of the sketch, would already be on the dominant!). But the draft makes clear that the motive in measures 45–56 is a variant of the descending tail of the main theme (E♭–D–C♯, first heard in measures 6–7) and thus is part of the transition. Moreover, in the draft this passage is quite fragmentary, and neither it nor the motive at measure 57 has the balanced, articulated phrasing of a theme. It is quite clear in this sketch that the dramatic arrival on the dominant was to occur just before the theme at measure 83, suggesting that this was where Beethoven planned for the second theme to begin.

The entire section of this draft that later became measures 45–83 may be interpreted as part of the transition to and establishment of the dominant key, B♭. In this view, the length of the transition is in proportion to the dimensions of the movement, and the second theme (at measure 83) is a tonally stable and formal statement in balanced four-measure phrases.

A subsequent revision, shown in Example 2, elaborates on the ideas Beethoven had already sketched.

Example 2. Revision to the above draft of measures 45–56 from MS Landsberg 6, p. 10, after Nottebohm, pp. 8–9, over outline of parallel passages in published score

Although one might gain the impression that Beethoven's transition abounds in new material, actually it draws motives from the first theme section, in keeping with past symphonic practice. As Beethoven worked on his early drafts, the origin of some material became obscured by imaginative variation, including the three quite distinct motivic variants that appear in this transition: at measure 45, from the opening theme's descending tail; at measure 57, from the rising scale figures of measures 12–14; and at measure 65, elaborating the arpeggiated chords and leaping figures of measures 23–35. Some of these derivations can be seen more clearly in the sketches. In general, far from crowding the movement with a plethora of themes, Beethoven kept very much to the elemental ideas announced in the first thirty-six measures. Here, he preferred the unitary motivic concentration of Haydn to the melodic abundance of Mozart. Yet in the final version, each of these elements—at measures 45, 57, and 65—has become so different from the first-theme material from which Beethoven derived it that the lines between first theme, transition, and second theme are blurred. Both measure 45 and measure 57 offer lyrical ideas in the winds, as is common for second themes, and the dominant arrives at least temporarily at measure 57. Still, the more emphatic cadence in measures 75–83 and the four-bar phrasing and stable harmony at measure 83 make clear that this is the true second theme.

The "new theme" in the development (point 3 above) has also occasioned much comment. Here again the drafts are enlightening. The so-called new theme in E minor played by the oboe at measure 284 does not appear at that point in any of the drafts. Example 3 shows a relatively early draft in which Beethoven sketched a melody all but identical to what the cellos and second violins play at this point in the final version, showing that he considered this cello line to be the main melodic strand. The oboe "theme" is thus a counterpoint to the cello. It first appears in the draft eight measures later, where in the final version the bassoons repeat the cello melody in A minor. This cello melody itself is a variant of the primary theme, whose notes are marked with asterisks in the example—it follows the same contour (rising from tonic to third, falling through tonic to dominant, and rising again to tonic) while filling in all the skips and leaps with stepwise motion. The "new theme" reappears in E♭ minor at measure 322 and again in the coda at measure 581.

Example 3. Continuity draft from MS Landsberg 6, pp. 38–39, over outline of parallel passages in published score

Finally, just before the recapitulation, the horn softly states the first four notes of the main theme in measure 394 against a soft tremolo in the violins (point 6 above). Early listeners thought that the horn had entered too soon. Carl Czerny, Beethoven's pupil, thought this entrance should be eliminated, and even Berlioz thought it was a copyist's mistake. But the sketches show that Beethoven contemplated this clever ploy from the very first drafts.

Beethoven's *Eroica* Symphony is one of the best known in the orchestral repertoire, played by orchestras around the world. Much less familiar is the sound of the orchestras that played the symphony when it was first composed. On the recording that accompanies this anthology, the ensemble attempts to reconstruct that sound by using instruments from the period. The orchestra is small by modern standards, allowing the solo winds to be heard more easily over the whole orchestra. The string instruments use gut rather than wire strings, and the wind instruments have fewer keys than the modern versions (keys were added later in the nineteenth century to make tuning and intonation easier, but also reduced the interesting variations in timbre across each instrument's range). The timpani sound drier, more punchy than the modern drums. And the horns and trumpets have no valves or pistons to alter the pitch, requiring the players to play only notes from the harmonic series or to bend those pitches (trumpet players accomplish this by using their lips, and horn players do so by using their hands in the bell, which also changes the timbre and the volume). The recording also follows Beethoven's tempo marking, which is somewhat faster than conductors since his time have tended to go, and includes the repetition of the exposition, often omitted in modern performances. The perhaps paradoxical result is a fresh sounding rendition of a familiar work.

110

Ludwig van Beethoven (1770–1827)

String Quartet in C-sharp Minor, Op. 131: First and second movements

String quartet

1826

(a) First movement, Adagio ma non troppo e molto espressivo

CD 8|52 CD 4|57

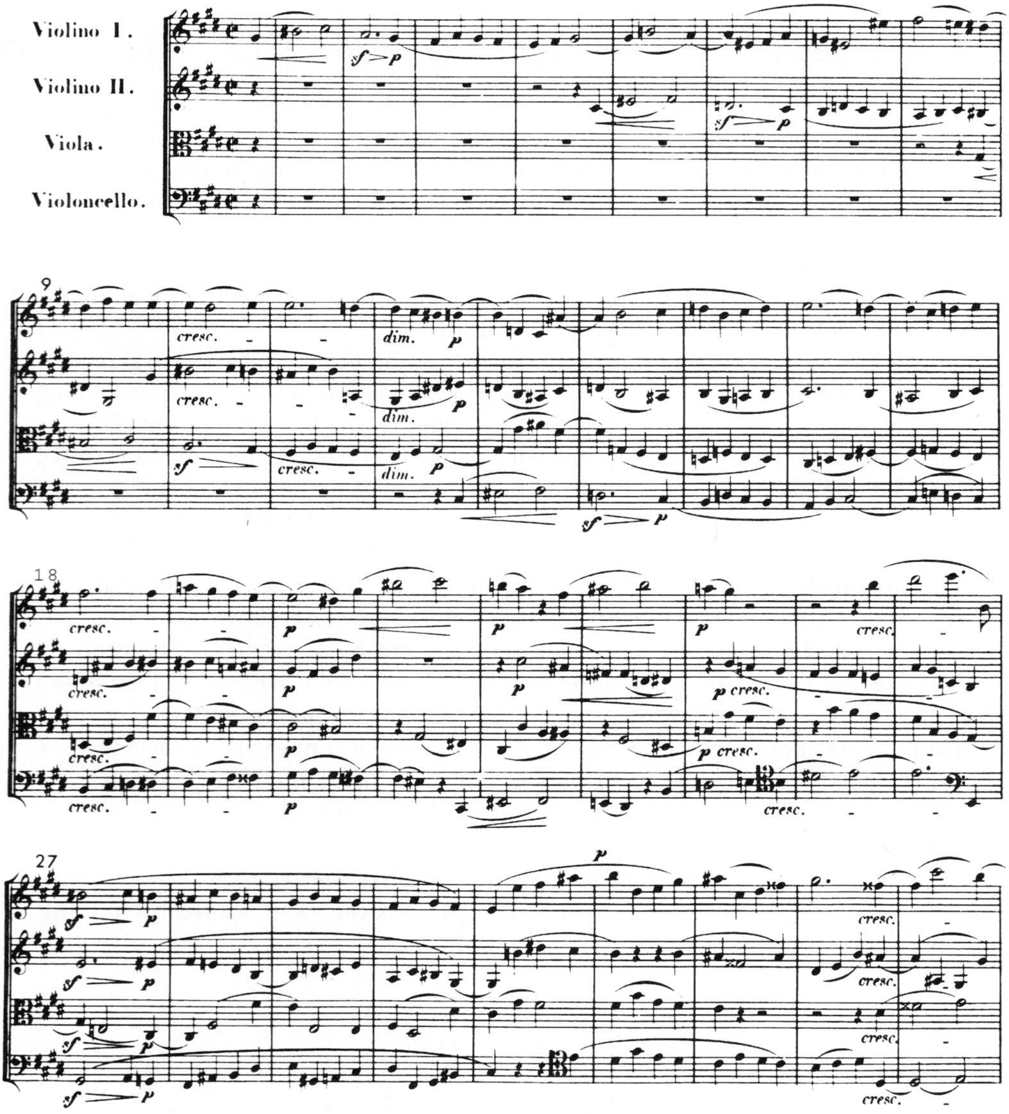

From *Ludwig van Beethovens Werke: Vollständige kritisch durchgesehene überall berechtigte Ausgabe*, ser. 6, vol. 2 (Leipzig: Breitkopf & Härtel, 1862–65), 119–26.

(b) Second movement, Allegro molto vivace

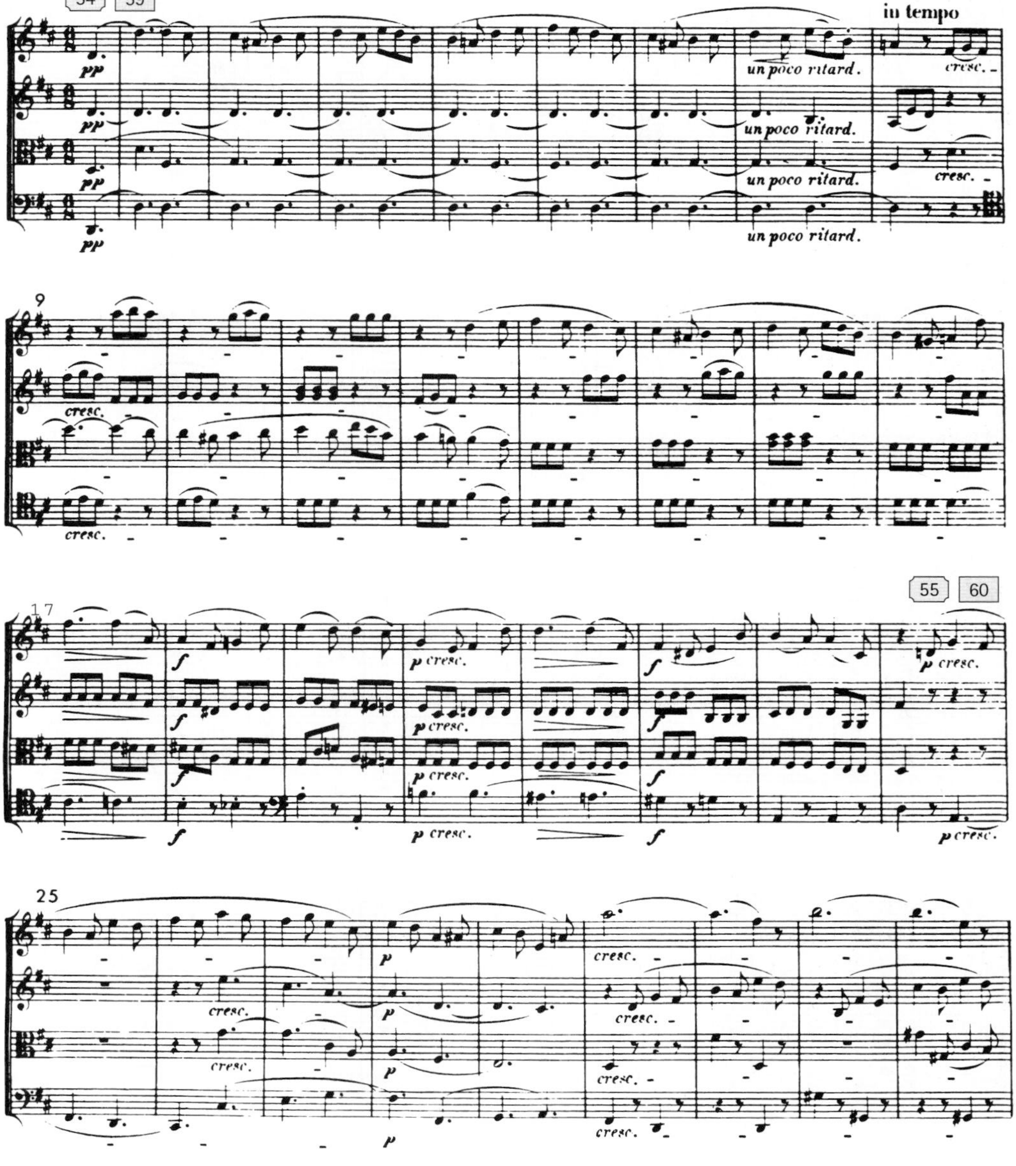

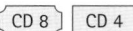

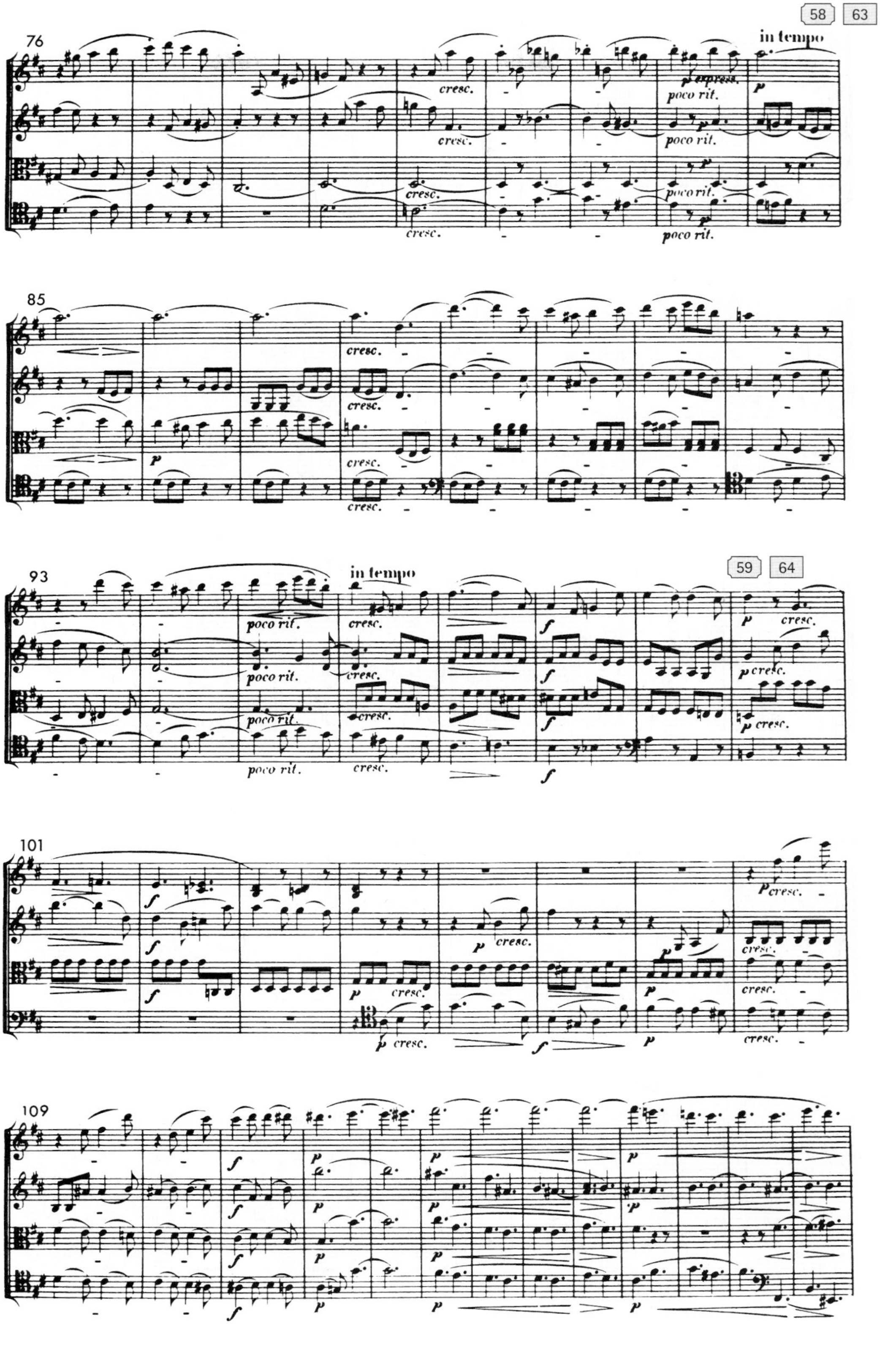
58 63
76
in tempo
cresc.
espress.
poco rit.
85
cresc.
93
in tempo
poco rit.
cresc.
59 64
101
cresc.
109

Beethoven composed his String Quartet in C-sharp Minor, Op. 131, in 1825–26. It was the fourth of five quartets that he composed during his last three years of life, and Beethoven himself thought it was his greatest work in the medium. He dedicated it to Baron Joseph von Stutterheim, leader of the army regiment in which his troubled nephew Karl (for whom Beethoven served as guardian) had recently enlisted.

This quartet is extraordinary in many ways. It is in seven movements that are played without pause. The traditional four movements of a string quartet—sonata form, slow movement, minuet or scherzo, and finale—are all present, but reordered and with additions. The first two movements, reprinted here, are a fugue and a sonata-rondo, both forms that might occur as finales but rarely if ever as first movements. A recitative-like third movement introduces the slow movement (in variation form), which is followed by the scherzo (in duple instead of the expected triple meter). The brief sixth movement serves as an introduction to the seventh, a sonata-form movement of a style and weight normally associated with first rather than last movements. The key structure is also unusual: the outer movements are in C♯ minor, but the second movement is in D major, the third movement starts in B minor, the slow movement is in A major, the scherzo in E, and the sixth movement in G♯ minor.

The most unusual movement is the first, a slow fugue—unusual because in string quartets first movements are almost always fast, and fugues appear only as fast finales. The subject is made up of two segments: a four-note opening motto ending with a surprising *sforzando* (measures 1–2), and a continuation in flowing quarter notes (measures 2–4). Only the opening exposition (measures 1–16) engages all four voices in playing the subject. After that, statements of the subject in fragmentary form or in diminution are separated by episodes that develop one or the other segment of the subject. In the final section (measures 91–121), the complete subject returns in C♯ minor (in the viola at measure 93, followed by a statement in the cello in augmentation at measure 99). All these devices are normal for a learned fugue.

What makes this fugue stand apart are its extreme emotionalism, its novel harmony, and its anticipation of the main key centers of later movements. The composer marked it "molto espressivo" (very expressive) and filled the score with precise indications of crescendos, *sforzandos, rinforzandos,* and diminuendos. The harmony includes augmented triads (as in measures 14 and 27) and some unusual progressions. Between the opening exposition and the return to the tonic, Beethoven takes us through a wide range of keys, including E major, G♯ minor, B major, A major, and D major—all of which will reappear as the keys of later movements. Another unusual feature is the statement of the fugal answer in the subdominant F♯ rather than the dominant. But this choice relates to the larger key scheme as well: the notes that are stressed in the subject and answer—the long, accented notes A and D, the low notes E and A, and the beginning notes G♯ and C♯—are precisely the notes that become the keys for later movements. Of course, the dominant G♯ and the relative major E are to be expected as keys in a quartet in C♯ minor, but A and D are unusual, and these are the notes that get the most emphasis in the subject and answer. These complex interrelationships, operating at many levels, are a sign that Beethoven intended the work to be studied and appreciated by connoisseurs.

The fugue ends on a sustained C♯-major chord, followed by bare rising octaves on C♯. This is immediately followed by octaves on D that begin the next movement, thus emphasizing the unusual key relationship. The second movement refers back to the first, specifically to the keys of its fugue subject and answer, through cadences on C♯ (measures 44–48) and F♯ (measures 122–26), both unusual in a movement in D major.

The form is a sonata-rondo, which blends aspects of rondo and sonata form:

Rondo:	Refrain	Episode 1	Refrain	Episode 2	Refrain	Episode 3		Refrain	Coda
	A	B	A	C	A	from B	C	A	from B
Sonata:	Exposition					Development	Recapitulation		Coda
	1T	Tr		2T	1T		2T	1T	
Key:	D	mod	E	A	D	mod	D	G, D	D
Measure:	1	24	48	60	84	100	133	157	169

The rondo refrain, parallel to the first theme in a sonata form, features a lilting melody in the violin that is immediately repeated in the viola. The first episode acts as a modulatory transition, and the second episode is like a second theme in a sonata, appearing in the dominant key and strongly contrasting with the first theme. After the refrain returns in the tonic, the third episode acts similarly to a development, drawing on the first theme and transition. The second episode and refrain then return in the tonic, as in a recapitulation in which the first and second themes appear in reversed order. Finally, a coda rounds out the movement.

Another way to view the movement is as a sonata without development, with the recapitulation beginning at measure 84. Yet every element leads back around to A, as in a rondo. What seems ultimately most important is that Beethoven evokes familiar formal schemes but then goes his own way to create a movement that is unique in form.

The contrasts in dynamics and in tempo are here more comic than dramatic, in tune with the light-hearted main theme. In both spirit and form, this movement is like a typical quartet finale, not like the usual first fast movement. By beginning the quartet with a slow fugue and a fast sonata-rondo in two keys a half step apart, Beethoven plays on the listener's expectations, posing problems of form and key relationship that will take the entire quartet to resolve.

FRANZ SCHUBERT (1797–1828)

Gretchen am Spinnrade, D. 118

Lied

1814

From *Franz Schuberts Werke: Kritisch durchgesehene Gesamtausgabe*, ser. 20, vol. 1 (Leipzig: Breitkopf & Härtel, 1884–97), 191–96.

300

Meine Ruh' ist hin,   My peace is gone,
Mein Herz ist schwer;   my heart is heavy;
Ich finde sie nimmer   I'll never find peace,
Und nimmermehr.   never again.

Wo ich ihn nicht hab'	Where I do not have him
Ist mir das Grab,	is to me like a tomb.
Die ganze Welt	The whole world
Ist mir vergällt.	is bitter to me.
Mein armer Kopf	My poor head
Ist mir verrückt,	is confused.
Mein armer Sinn	My poor mind
Ist mir zerstückt.	is torn apart.
Nach ihm nur schau' ich	For him alone do I look
Zum Fenster hinaus,	out the window.
Nach ihm nur geh' ich	For him alone do I go
Aus dem Haus.	out of the house.
Sein hoher Gang,	His lofty bearing,
Sein' edle Gestalt,	his noble figure,
Seines Mundes Lächeln,	the smile on his lips,
Seiner Augen Gewalt,	the strength of his gaze,
Und seiner Rede	and his conversation's
Zauberfluß,	magical flow,
Sein Händedruck,	the press of his hand,
Und, ach, sein Kuß!	and, ah, his kiss!
Mein Busen drängt	My heart pines
Sich nach ihm hin;	for him.
Ach, dürft' ich fassen	Ah, if I could seize him
Und halten ihn	and hold him
Und küssen ihn,	and kiss him
So wie ich wollt',	all I wanted,
An seinen Küssen	in his kisses
Vergehen sollt'!	I would be lost!

— JOHANN WOLFGANG
VON GOETHE

Franz Schubert wrote *Gretchen am Spinnrade* (Gretchen at the Spinning Wheel) in October 1814. He was just seventeen but had already composed more than forty *Lieder*, or songs, and was developing his mature style. *Gretchen* was his first Lied set to a text by the famous poet and dramatist Johann Wolfgang von Goethe (1749–1832), and it became one of his most famous, prized for its dramatic and empathetic portrayal of a young woman's first feelings of love. It was published in 1821 as his Opus 2.

In this scene from Goethe's drama *Faust*, Gretchen is alone, spinning thread and admitting to herself how much she has been affected by Faust, the handsome young man she has recently met. Schubert used the accompaniment both to set the scene and to portray Gretchen's emotions. The top line in the piano depicts the rapid rotations of the spinning wheel through a constantly rising and falling figuration. The rhythmic pattern in the middle of the texture, played by the left hand, imitates the action of the treadle, a pedal Gretchen must press repeatedly to keep the wheel in motion. At the same time, the unceasing motion suggests Gretchen's agitation as she thinks of her beloved.

The poem is strophic, but Schubert did not adopt the purely strophic setting that was common in Lieder at the time. Instead, he varied the setting of each strophe in order to convey the drama. He also repeated the first stanza after the third and sixth stanzas of the original poem (reprinted above) and began but left incomplete another statement at the end of the song (see the repetitions at measures 31, 73, and 114). Thus, he made the first stanza into a refrain, giving the song a rondo-like form and reminding us often of Gretchen's opening words, which tell of her anxious feelings and heavy heart.

The refrain builds from *pianissimo* to *forte*, representing Gretchen's turbulent emotions. Her restlessness is reflected in the harmony, which modulates without warning from D minor to C major with hints of C minor (measures 7–12). Each of the sections between refrains likewise explores new harmonic regions and builds to a climax that grows more impassioned with each verse, creating successive waves of increasing intensity. As Gretchen's complaints deepen in the second and third stanzas, the harmony modulates to A minor, E minor, and F major, and the vocal line reaches a new peak (in measure 26). When she describes her beloved in the fourth through sixth stanzas, the harmony goes still farther afield, touching G minor, A♭ major, and B♭ major. As she recalls his kiss, she is overcome by her feelings (measures 66–68): the accompanimental pattern stops, indicating that she has stopped the wheel, and two diminished seventh chords and a sustained high G embody her passion. Haltingly, she begins to spin again as she recovers her composure (measures 69–73). In the last two stanzas, a rising harmonic sequence dramatizes her desire to embrace her lover (measures 84–92). She then fantasizes about being lost in his kisses, twice reaching the highest note in the song (measures 93–112) as she repeats the final stanza. Schubert even takes liberties with Goethe's words, adding the line "o könnt' ich ihn küssen" (O if I could kiss him, measures 101–2) to show the strength of her yearning. Through all of these devices, Schubert turns the simple strophic poem into a deeply felt portrayal of Gretchen's complex emotions.

Schubert often performed his Lieder at informal gatherings of his friends, called Schubertiads. Lieder were primarily intended for amateurs to sing at home, but many of Schubert's songs later became staples in voice recitals. Although the piano part in this song carries much of the meaning, it remains an accompaniment and must never overpower the singer. Ornamentation is not part of the Lieder tradition. Rather, the performers are expected to reproduce the notes on the page. But the performers on the recording that accompanies this anthology use subtle changes in tempo, demarcating the ends of sections with slight ritardandos and at times suggesting Gretchen's motions or emotions by pressing forward or holding back. Such flexibility of tempo is a common feature of the Romantic performance tradition.

112

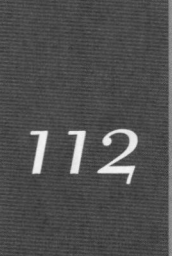

Franz Schubert (1797–1828)

Winterreise, D. 911: No. 5, *Der Lindenbaum*

Song cycle

1827

CD 8|68 CD 4|73

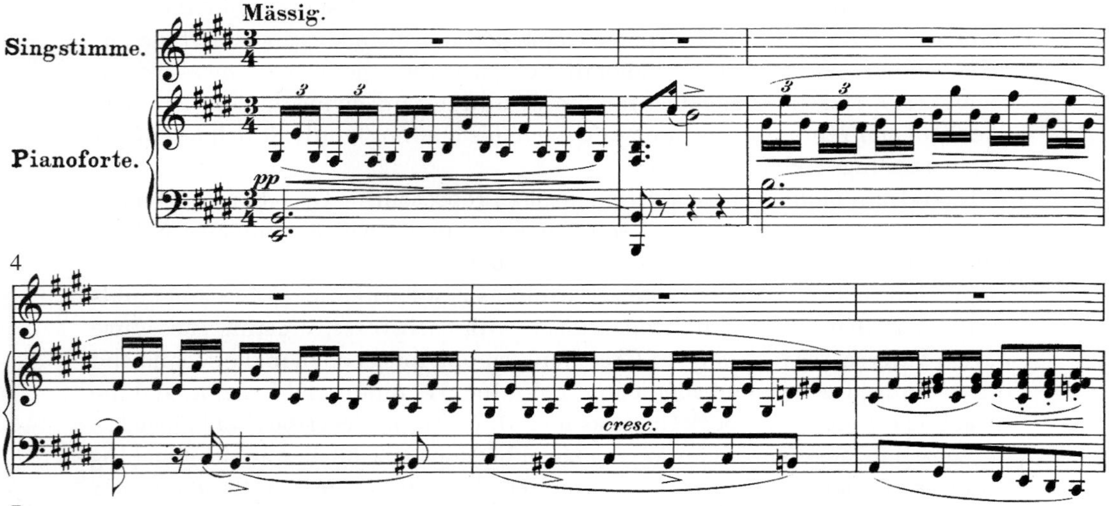

From *Franz Schuberts Werke: Kritisch durchgesehene Gesamtausgabe*, ser. 20, vol. 9 (Leipzig: Breitkopf & Härtel, 1884–97), 16–19.

manches liebe Wort; es zog in Freud' und Lei-de zu ihm_mich immer fort.

Ich musst' auch heu-te wan_dern vor-bei in tie-fer Nacht, da

hab' ich noch im Dun_kel die Au_gen zu_ge_macht. Und sei_ne Zweige

rausch_ten, als rie_fen sie mir zu: komm her zu mir, Ge_sel_le, hier

Am Brunnen vor dem Thore	At the well by the gate
Da steht ein Lindenbaum;	there stands a linden tree.
Ich träumt' in seinem Schatten	I dreamt in its shade
So manchen süssen Traum.	many a sweet dream.
Ich schnitt in seine Rinde	I carved into its bark
So manches liebe Wort;	many a word of love.
Es zog in Freud' und Leide	In joy and sorrow
Zu ihm mich immer fort.	I was always drawn to it.
Ich musst' auch heute wandern	Again today I had to walk
Vorbei in tiefer Nacht,	by it in the deep of night.
Da hab' ich noch im Dunkel	Even in the dark I
Die Augen zugemacht.	closed my eyes.
Und seine Zweige rauschten,	And its boughs rustled
Als riefen sie mir zu:	as if they called to me:
Komm her zu mir, Geselle,	"Come to me, companion,
Hier find'st du deine Ruh!	here you'll find your rest!"
Die kalten Winde blieben	The cold winds blew
Mir grad' in's Angesicht,	straight into my face.
Der Hut flog mir von Kopfe,	My hat flew off my head,
Ich wendete mich nicht.	I did not turn around.
Nun bin ich manche Stunde	Now I am some hours
Entfernt von jenem Ort,	away from that place,
Und immer hör' ich's rauschen:	and always I hear it rustle:
Du fändest Ruhe dort!	"You would find your rest there."

—WILHELM MÜLLER

In a song cycle, a composer sets a series of poems, usually by a single poet, that together tell or suggest a story. Schubert's *Winterreise* (Winter's Journey) consists of twenty-four poems by Wilhelm Müller that relate the story of a young man who in the cold of winter revisits places he remembers from the previous spring and summer, when he met and wooed a young woman who later spurned him. Schubert wrote the cycle in 1827, when he was growing increasingly sick from syphilis, and its gloom may have reflected his own feelings.

Der Lindenbaum (The Linden Tree), the fifth in the set, contrasts the young man's pleasant memories of a linden tree with its current reality. In warmer times, he lay dreaming beneath the tree and carved loving words in its bark, but now its leafless boughs rustle in an icy wind, calling him back to a rest that can only mean death.

Schubert uses a variety of musical ideas to convey the moods and images of the poem. A brief prelude in the piano introduces a fluttering triplet figuration that suggests the gentle breezes and whispering leaves of summer. But later this figure returns, altered with chromatic harmonies, to depict the cold wind and eerie rustling of the tree in winter (measures 45–56). This figure is also used as an interlude (measures 25–28) and postlude (measures 77–82), so that it serves as a frame for the verses in between. A horn-call figure that closes the prelude (measures 7–8) and returns before the last stanza (measures 57–58) evokes associations with nature and the outdoors, but also with distance (since hunting horns were often heard from afar) and thus separation from the beloved. The vocal melody is for the most part simple and folklike, well suited to express the simple pleasures that brought the young man happiness and now are only nostalgic memories.

The poem is strophic, but the song is in a modified strophic form with a contrasting section, for an overall form of AA'BA''. The A section (measures 9–24) sets the first two stanzas of the poem, which describe past joys. The folklike, major-mode melody in four-measure phrases is itself a little aabb' form and is accompanied by chordal harmony in horn-call style. The A' section (measures 29–44) repeats this melody for the next two stanzas but with a broken-chord accompaniment. The mode shifts to minor as the young man speaks of walking by the tree in the dark, then back to major for the rustling boughs that call him back— a truly uncanny shift in which the words make the major mode sound even spookier than the minor. In the fifth stanza, he describes a cold wind that seems to push him back to the tree; this is set in dramatic declamatory style over a variant of the fluttering triplet figuration. The last stanza is sung twice to the melody of the A section, back in the major mode and over an accompaniment like that of the A' section. The young man is safe, far from the linden tree, yet he still hears it calling. The recollection of both earlier sections nicely captures his ambivalence, nostalgic for the tree in summer yet spooked by it today.

As is true for many of Schubert's songs, the more one examines the poetry and how the music enhances its meaning, the more one finds. Such songs transcended the original function of Lieder as entertainment for the performers and their friends and family, and became recognized as art songs.

113

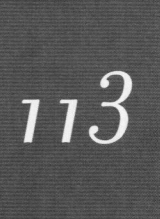

Robert Schumann (1810–1856)

Dichterliebe, Op. 48: No. 1, *Im wunderschönen Monat Mai*

Song cycle

1840

CD 8|72

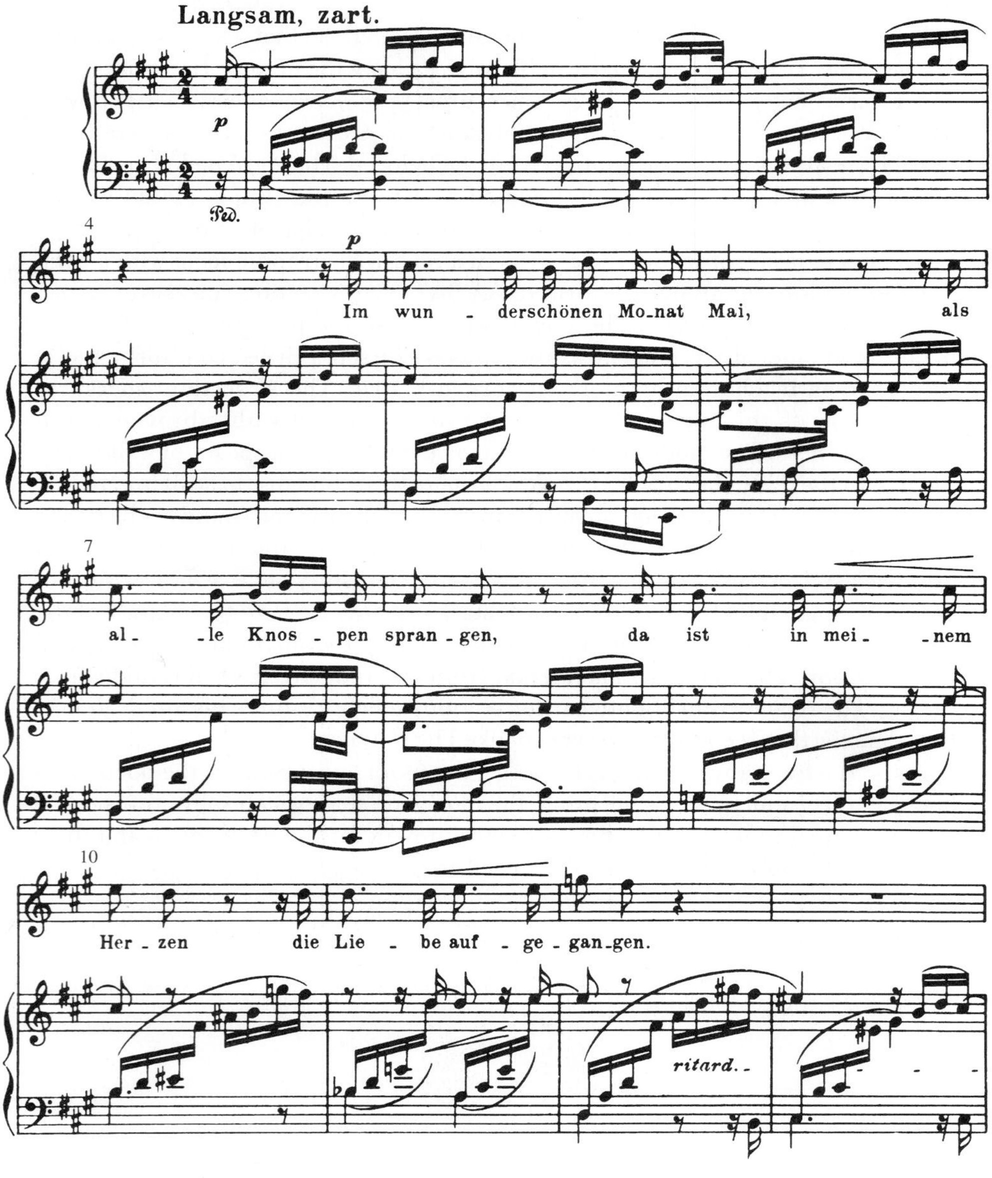

Langsam, zart.
p
Ped.
Im wun - derschönen Mo_nat Mai, als
al_ -le Knos - pen spran - gen, da ist in mei_ -nem
Her_zen die Lie - be auf - ge - gan_gen.
ritard.

From Robert Schumann, *Dichterliebe*, Op. 48, ed. Max Friedlaender (Leipzig: C. F. Peters, n.d.).

Im wunderschönen Monat Mai,	In the marvelous month of May,
Als alle Knospen sprangen,	when all the buds burst open,
Da ist in meinem Herzen	then in my heart
Die Liebe aufgegangen.	love broke out.
In wunderschönen Monat Mai,	In the marvelous month of May,
Als alle Vögel sangen,	as all the birds sang,
Da hab' ich ihr gestanden	then I confessed to her
Mein Sehnen und Verlangen.	my longing and desire.

—HEINRICH HEINE

Robert Schumann wrote the song cycle *Dichterliebe* (A Poet's Love) in May of 1840, his "Year of Song," during which he composed over 120 songs. *Dichterliebe* consists of sixteen songs set to poems selected from the more than sixty in Heinrich Heine's *Lyrisches Intermezzo* (Lyrical Intermezzo, 1823 and later editions; the poem in the song presented here was first published in Heine's *Minnelieder* in 1822). Schumann arranged the poems to suggest the course of a love affair, from initial longings to heartbreak and resignation. He composed the cycle four months before he and Clara Wieck were married, while he was in the midst of a nasty legal battle with her father, Friedrich Wieck, who was trying to prevent the marriage. It is not hard to hear in the cycle an expression of Schumann's yearning to be united with his beloved and of the pain he suffered during their forced separations.

The first song of the cycle, *Im wunderschönen Monat Mai,* sets two stanzas that each begin with the same line and contain the same rhymes. The parallelism of textual form and ideas prompts Schumann's setting in a written-out strophic form, framed by a piano prelude that returns as interlude and postlude. The poem happily describes springtime and a newly confessed love, but dissonances and tonal ambiguity give the music a sense of unfulfilled longing. The appoggiaturas and suspensions that begin almost every other measure, which Schumann added only in the final draft, reveal the bittersweet anxiety of the lover. Some suspensions in the piano are left unresolved (see the right-hand piano part in measures 9–12), adding to the tension as the vocal line builds to its climax. The key signature of three sharps would normally indicate that a piece is in either A major or F♯ minor, but the music in this song never commits to a tonality: the piano prelude twice states a half cadence in F♯ minor, the first two vocal lines cadence in A major, the next line moves to B minor, the stanza ends on D major, and then the prelude music returns, leaving the listener unsure of the tonic key. After a second cycle through the same sequence, the song closes on the unresolved dominant seventh of F♯, prolonging the feeling of "Sehnen und Verlangen" (longing and desire).

The lack of resolution at the end matches the mysterious beginning, away from the tonic chord (whatever that may be!) and in the midst of motion toward a cadence. Beginning with what sounds like a middle and ending without resolution, the song seems like a fragment, and the double cycle through a series of chords that never reach a final resolution suggests the possibility of circling around endlessly—a perfect musical metaphor for the seemingly unfulfillable longing of the lover. The fragment was a quintessentially Romantic idea that Schumann cultivated in many of his works. Of course, here in the song cycle, the open-ended first song leads smoothly into the next, which establishes A major more securely as its tonic.

The melodies in voice and piano are fragments too, for the true melody of the song is shared between them. Comparing the right-hand piano part with the vocal line in measures 4–13 shows that sometimes the piano takes the lead (as at the b'–d'' and a'–d'' pickup figures in measures 4 and 6 before the voice enters on $c\sharp''$), sometimes the voice takes the lead (as in measures 9–12), and at other times they move together. The opening idea in the prelude, with its striking figure of a rising sixth and falling steps, reappears in inversion at the end of the first full measure of the vocal line, further weaving voice and piano together into one unbroken melody. In this song, the piano is equal to the voice and is perhaps even the leading partner, since it contains the greater part of the musical fabric.

HENRY R. BISHOP (1786–1855)

Home! Sweet Home!

Theatrical song and drawing-room ballad (parlor song)
1823

From Home! Sweet Home!*, words by John Howard Payne, music composed and arranged by Henry R. Bishop (London: Goulding & D'Almaine, 1823).*

Perhaps the most famous song of the nineteenth century was *Home! Sweet Home!*, whose text extolled the sweet joys of home in an era when millions of people had moved away from their places of birth to pursue new opportunities in distant cities, foreign lands, or new territories such as the American West. By midcentury, it was known and sung across Europe and throughout the English-speaking world. Its composer, Henry R. Bishop, is remembered today almost entirely for this single song, but in the early nineteenth century he was renowned as England's most outstanding composer of music for the theater.

Many of Bishop's works were English-language "operas," which were spoken plays with overtures and numerous pieces of music interpolated into the scenes. One such opera was *Clari, or The Maid of Milan*, first performed on May 8, 1823, in

London at the Theatre Royal, Covent Garden, where Bishop was resident composer and music director. *Home! Sweet Home!* was sung by the title character Clari at the end of Act I, and it returned in varied forms at other points in the opera as a recurring theme. The words were by American poet John Howard Payne, but the music was recycled from a version of the tune that Bishop had written for a show in 1816 (*Who Wants a Wife?*) and included as a "Sicilian Air" in an 1821 collection he edited of *National Airs* (when he could not find a genuine melody from Sicily). The tremendous popularity of *Home! Sweet Home!*, rather than of the earlier versions, suggests that the combination of words and music was the secret of its success.

The song is in verse-refrain form, with two sixteen-measure verses and an eight-measure refrain. The piano begins with a brief prelude that anticipates the opening phrase of the vocal line and then continues with a decorated variant of the first phrase of the refrain (compare measures 5–8 with the vocal line of measures 26–29). The second phrase of the prelude later returns in decorated form as an interlude between the verses (measures 33–36).

The vocal melody is almost wholly diatonic and deceptively simple. The verse contains four four-measure phrases in AA'BB' form, suffused with lilting dotted rhythms. Each A phrase rises by step to the fifth scale degree *b'*, then floats slowly downward by skip and step; each B phrase leaps to the upper octave *e''*, then descends as before. In each pair, the first phrase closes on the third scale degree, and the second closes on the tonic. The refrain begins with a new phrase whose contour resembles A, then continues with a variant of B'. The second verse slightly alters the rhythms and notes to fit the new text. Thus, a small set of ideas is varied in constantly changing ways, combining simplicity with variety in a manner that helps to account for the song's appeal.

The words likewise articulate variations on a simple idea: home, however humble, is a unique place that is unmatched by the grandeur or pleasures encountered elsewhere. In the poet's view, home is sweet, sacred ("A charm from the skies seems to hallow us there"), an abode of peace, at one with nature ("The Birds singing gaily that came at my call"). This song encapsulated and thus helped to foster the nineteenth-century notions of the sanctity of home and nostalgia for the past.

The edition presented here is based on the first publication of *Home! Sweet Home!* in its arrangement for voice and piano, and it preserves the original accompaniment. As the song gained almost universal popularity in Europe and North America, it was often arranged with new accompaniments, as was traditional for popular songs and operatic excerpts (though not for art songs). But the original piano arrangement was well designed to illuminate the words. The simple arpeggiated figure under the first verse fills in the texture without detracting from the soloist. At the refrain, both piano and voice suddenly move more slowly, creating an atmosphere of reverence appropriate to the words "Home! Home! sweet sweet Home!" In the second verse, long trills appear in the right-hand piano part to suggest "The Birds singing gaily." At the refrain, the piano's reverent pauses are delayed to the ends of phrases, creating a fresh emotional effect when a simple repetition of the first refrain might have been cloying.

The dynamic markings in the piano part reflect those in the original orchestral score, with forceful punctuation at the cadences. On a modern piano, the *fortissimos* would sound excessive, but they strike the right conclusive tone on the nineteenth-century domestic square piano used in the accompanying recording. The sixteenth-note grace notes were most likely sung on the beat, as in Classic-era music. The small note in measure 29 indicates a *portamento*, or rapid glide, up from the B to high E. The fermata, trill, and small notes in measure 32 invite a brief cadenza, and the *ad lib.* in measure 59 allows a longer one, if desired. The cadenza reflects the song's original purpose as theatrical music, but also offers the parlor singer a chance to emote. At both these points, the piano is marked *colla voce* (with the voice), indicating that the player is to follow the singer's free rhythm.

STEPHEN FOSTER (1826–1865)

Jeanie with the Light Brown Hair

Parlor song

1854

CD 8|75

Moderato

I dream of Jea-nie with the light brown hair, Borne, like a va-por, on the sum-mer air; I

see her trip-ping where the bright streams play, Hap-py as the dai-sies that

dance on her way. Ma-ny were the wild notes her mer-ry voice would pour,

From Stephen C. Foster, *Jeanie with the Light Brown Hair* (New York: Firth, Pond, 1854).

fond hopes that die: Sigh-ing like the night wind and sob-bing like the rain,
cheered us and gone.   Now the nod-ding wild flowers may with-er on the shore

Wail-ing for the lost one that comes not a-gain: Oh!___ I long   for Jea-nie, and my
While her gen-tle fin-gers will cull them no more: Oh!___ I sigh   for Jea-nie with the

heart bows___ low,   Ne-ver more to find her where the bright   wa-ters flow.
light brown___ hair,   Float-ing, like a va-por, on the soft   sum-mer air.

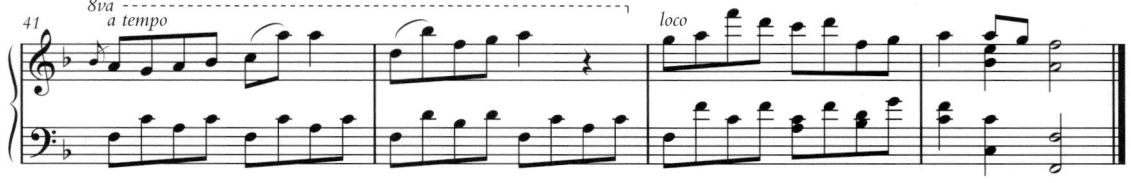

Stephen Foster grew up in Pittsburgh, Pennsylvania, hearing the music of German, Italian, and Scots-Irish immigrants, and in his parlor songs he combined elements of those styles with both British and American ballad traditions. After achieving tremendous success with the minstrel show song *Oh! Susanna*, he signed a contract with a New York publisher in 1849 and for the rest of his life made his living by writing songs for sale to the public. By 1854, when he wrote *Jeanie with the Light Brown Hair*, he had stopped writing minstrel songs and was concentrating his efforts on parlor songs. He was briefly separated from his wife Jane (also known as Jennie) in 1853–54, and Foster's brother Morrison once suggested that this song was written in an attempt to woo her back. Whatever its inspiration, it soon became one of Foster's most widely known songs.

The words, written by Foster himself, idealize Jeanie with images of nature: summer, air, streams, daisies, and birds. The second and third verses turn darker, with images of dying hopes, night winds, and sobbing rain, leading to the revelation that Jeanie is gone, never to return. The sentiments of love, loss, and regret, and the use of nature imagery to convey feelings, were common in nineteenth-century song traditions, from German Lieder to parlor songs and popular songs. So too were songs about a particular woman, which has remained a frequent topic throughout the ensuing two centuries.

Despite the change of mood from one stanza to the next, the song is strophic, framed by a brief piano prelude and a postlude after each stanza. The melody is laid out in four-measure phrases in an AA'BA" pattern, with each phrase setting a rhymed couplet. The first half of each phrase is harmonically static, then the second half changes chords every half-measure and then with each beat, leading to a cadence. All but the last phrase close on the dominant, sustaining the forward momentum until the final tonic cadence. The accompaniment is very simple, well within the abilities of amateur players or of a singer accompanying himself, yet Foster changes figuration every four measures to mark off the phrases.

Within this framework, subtle elements make the melody especially poignant and memorable. Segments of melody alternate between the diatonic and the purely pentatonic (as in measures 7–8), evoking the style of Irish folk songs popularly associated with themes of nostalgia and distance. The A phrases begin on an unharmonized D, the sixth degree of the scale, creating a sense of floating in midair. Surprising leaps at "like a vapor" (measures 7 and 19) add to the airy feeling. The very simplicity of the harmony highlights the frequent accented dissonances that suggest the lover's yearning or even intoxication (see the accented neighbor tones on "Jeanie," "like," "tripping," "daisies," "notes," "floating," and "summer"). A little cadenza before the last phrase (measure 16) adds an expressive touch from Italian opera.

Jeanie with the Light Brown Hair became so well known that many people learned the melody by ear, like a folk song. As was common in the tradition of popular music, it was often arranged with new accompaniments. But when first published,

143
83
84
sf
148
ff
f

(b) No. 3: *Warum?*

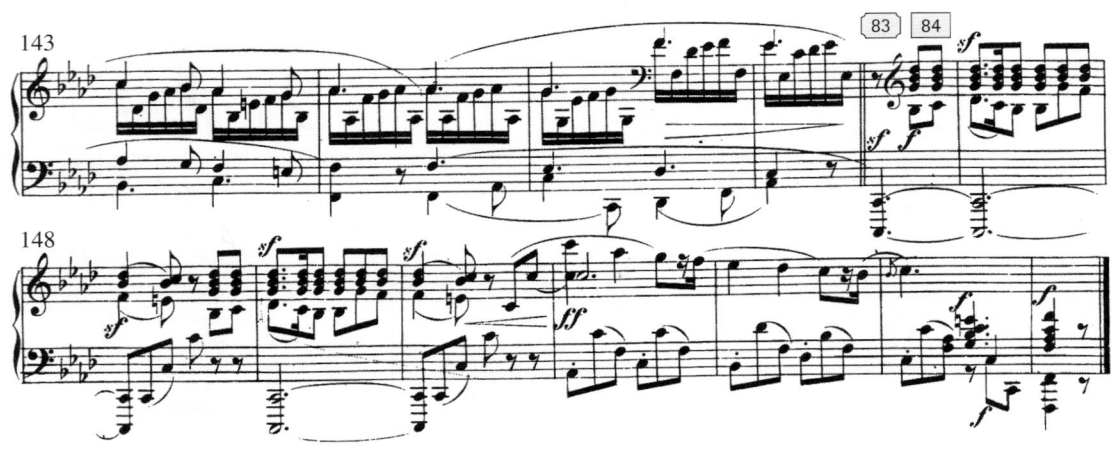

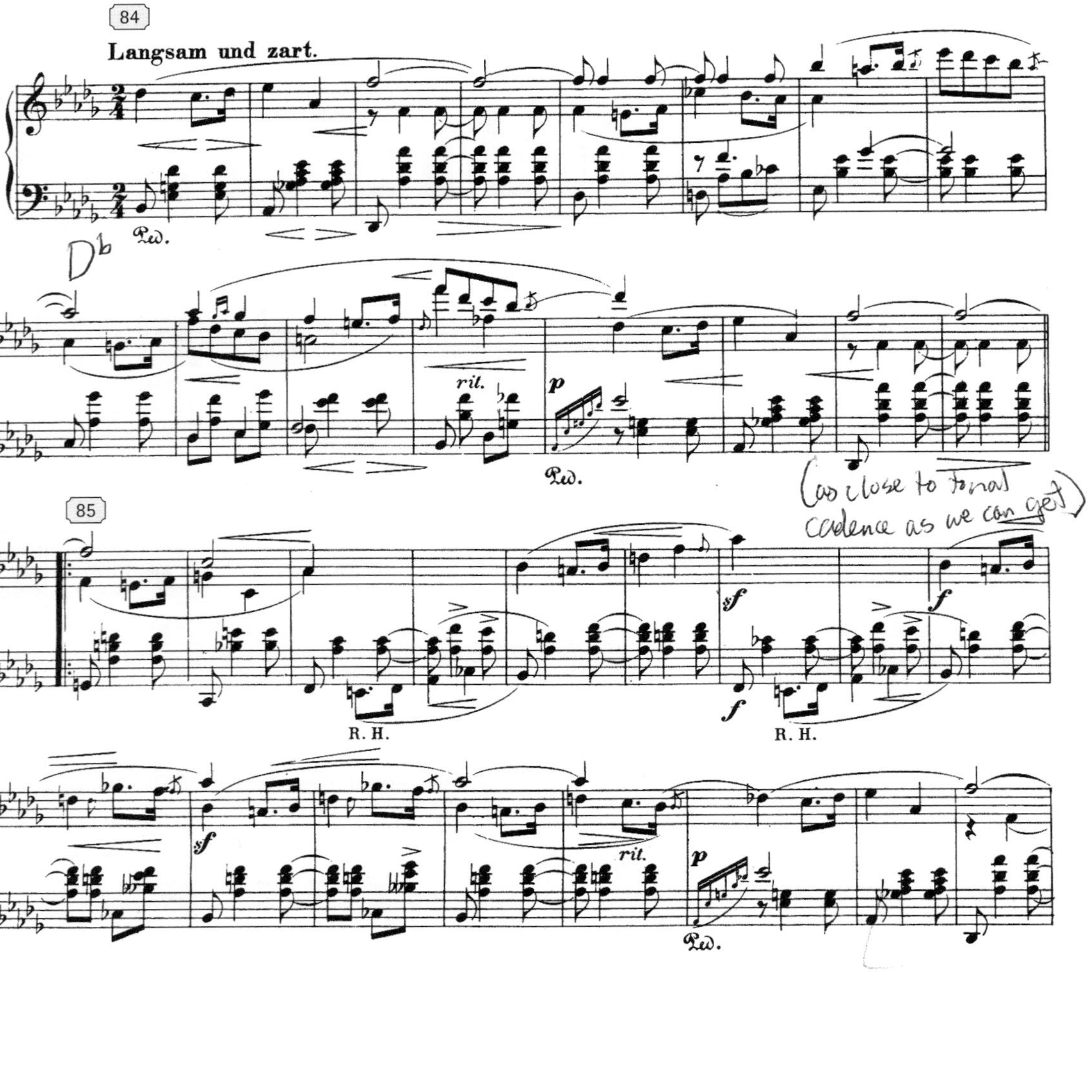
84
Langsam und zart.
9
rit.
p
85
17
R. H.
sf
f
26
rit.
p
D♭
(as close to tonal cadence as we can get)

Schumann wrote many sets of *character pieces* for piano, short pieces intended to capture a mood or suggest a scene or character. He was inspired to write his *Fantasiestücke* (Fantasy Pieces) in the summer of 1837 after meeting British pianist Anna Robena Laidlaw, to whom he dedicated them when they were published the next year as his Op. 12. He drew the title from *Fantasiestücke in Callots Manier,* by the Romantic writer E. T. A. Hoffmann, and the eight pieces in the set reflect the typically Romantic interest in representing what is original, individual, out of the ordinary, curious, evocative, and emotional.

Throughout many of his writings and compositions, Schumann personified two sides of his personality in the imaginary figures of Florestan, an impulsive revolutionary named after the imprisoned hero of Beethoven's opera *Fidelio*, and Eusebius, a contemplative dreamer named after St. Eusebius, a fourth-century pope. The opening pieces of *Fantasiestücke* alternate between the two characters. The second piece, *Aufschwung* (Soaring), shows Florestan at the height of his passion. The third, *Warum?* (Why?), can be interpreted as Eusebius's response to what he sees as Florestan's excesses.

Aufschwung presents four strongly contrasting ideas in a complex form with ternary (ABA') structures on three levels. There are three large sections, the third a varied reprise of the first. Each of those sections is in ternary form, and the middle portion of the outer sections is itself a small ternary form:

Section:	**I**					**II**				**I'**				
	A	B			A"	C	D	C	Trans	A	B			A"
		a	b	a'							a	b	a'	
Key:	f/A♭	D♭			f/b♭/f	B♭	mod	B♭	mod	f/A♭	A♭			f
Measure:	1	16	24	32	40	53	61	85	93	114	122	130	138	146

The first large section has two themes, each soaring in a different way. The A theme begins with a tense motive in the middle register that leads to a half cadence in the tonic F minor. This gesture repeats over sustained octaves on the lowest Cs on the piano, turning what in measure 1 could be heard as the subdominant chord (B♭ minor) into a very dissonant chord of the dominant minor ninth. Next, the music soars upward five octaves to the highest note in the A section, then cascades down through a buoyant scalar melody in hemiola rhythm to cadence on the relative major A♭. The whole theme then repeats for emphasis. The B theme, in D♭ major, is quieter but no less impulsive, with a stepwise melody in the right hand that again rises up and then floats down. It is accompanied by a rippling figure in the right hand and paralleled by an inner voice in the tenor range a thirteenth or tenth below. When the A section returns, it is made even more dramatic by a sudden turn to B♭ minor, the subdominant of F minor. The cadence on F minor (measure 52) is both unexpected and fleeting, as the music flows continuously into the middle section.

The C theme borrows a cadential figure from the A theme (compare measures 7–8 with measures 53–54) and extends it into a full eight-measure phrase. The next section, D, begins as if it will be a theme, with a melody above rising eighth-note scales in tenths (at measure 61), but it quickly becomes developmental. Rising and falling eighth-note figures take over as the harmony modulates, slowly moving chromatically upward. After the C theme returns, running eighth notes low in the bass begin a transition back to the first section. The opening gesture of the A theme appears in various transpositions, gradually rising from the depths (see measures 104–13). At the return, the A theme is thickened with added notes, the B theme is transposed to the relative major A♭, and the final statement of the A theme at last grants the definitive cadence on F minor that Schumann has withheld from the beginning of the piece.

Warum? also begins away from the tonic and then immediately cadences in D♭, the apparent key of the piece. This sets up a problem for the composer: if you begin with a cadence in the tonic, how do you continue? Schumann uses the opening melodic idea to create a dialogue between an inner voice and the upper line, changing the motive each time to lead to a new harmony and circling through a succession of harmonies until the opening phrase returns in original form (measures 13–16). The inner voice then initiates a new dialogue between bass and treble (measures 17–24) that seems to settle on the dominant seventh of E♭ minor (at measures 25–30). But instead of moving to that key, Schumann returns to the opening phrase, whose initial harmony of an E♭ dominant seventh follows smoothly. The middle voices twice feint toward G♭, but the opening phrase keeps repeating, reconfirming D♭. Yet the harmonic motion never sounds final because the melodic phrase always ends on F, the third degree of the scale, rather than the tonic, and every time we have heard this idea it has been followed by a progression that has led off in another direction. That happens yet again when the second half of the piece repeats. By the time D♭ returns, we are not sure whether to believe it is the tonic. Paradoxically, as the opening motive repeats three more times, it sounds less definitive than it did when we first heard it. The music just trails off, leaving the question unanswered. Thus Eusebius's endless contemplation counters Florestan's enthusiastic questing.

Schumann's piano writing poses interesting challenges for the performer. He meant the *Fantasiestücke* for amateurs, but several movements are technically demanding, including *Aufschwung*. At the beginning of both of these movements, the pedal marking under the first note indicates that the player is to press the damper pedal, which holds the dampers off the strings and lets them ring. This marking normally is used for passages in which the pedal is held down to sustain a chord under the melody notes and then is released at the asterisk to allow a change of chord, an unharmonized melody, or a staccato effect (as in measure 83 of *Aufschwung*). But the opening pedal marking in this piece is never canceled, leaving it up to the player to clear the pedal at each change of chord or to hold it to allow some expressive blurring. In *Aufschwung*, the left hand does some impressive leaping—as much as two octaves between notes (measure 8). When Schumann writes a span of more than an octave between simultaneous notes in one staff, he may intend the other hand to help out, as the left hand may do in playing the first six notes of the opening gesture and the right hand must do at measures 60–64. Alternatively, he may expect the pianist to arpeggiate, as in the left-hand chords at the end of measure 48. The B theme requires the pianist to emphasize the melody, marked with upward stems, and play the rest of the right-hand figuration more lightly. Throughout, the player is welcome to adjust the tempo by pulling back or pressing ahead slightly to emphasize cadences, climaxes, and expressive gestures.

117

Fryderyk Chopin (1810–1849)

Mazurka in B-flat Major, Op. 7, No. 1

Mazurka (dance)

CA. 1831

CD 8|86

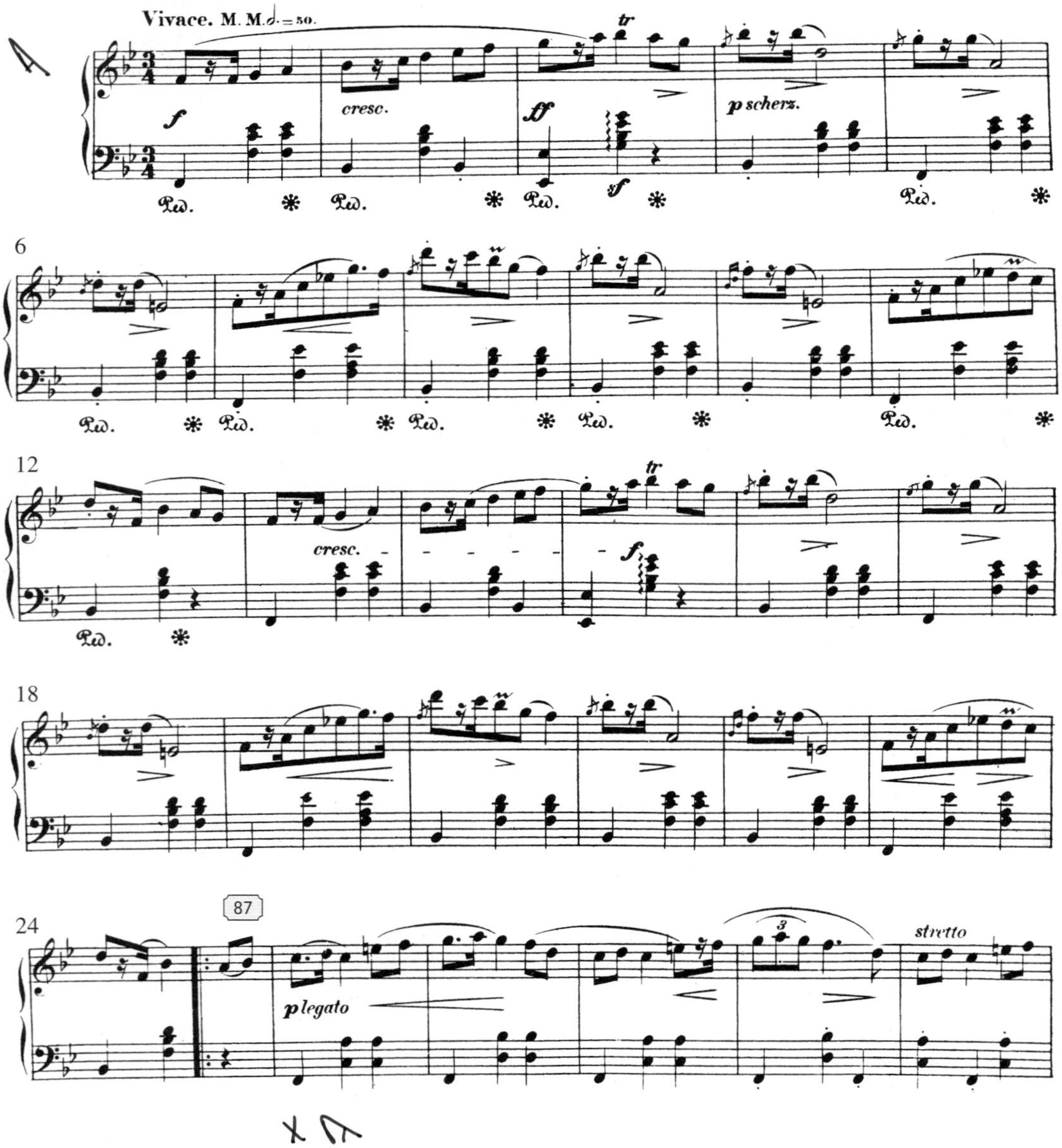

From Frédéric Chopin, *Fr. Chopin's Pianoforte-Werke,* ed. Carl Mikuli, vol. 1, *Mazurkas* (Leipzig: Fr. Kistner, n.d.; repr. New York: Dover, 1987), 10–11. Dover Publications, Inc.

This mazurka is one of several that Fryderyk Chopin wrote in 1830–31 while in Vienna seeking a career as pianist and composer. Unable to return to his home in Poland because of political repression caused by a failed revolution against

Russian rule, he next moved to Paris, where he quickly met success and lived for the rest of his life. The Vienna mazurkas were published in two sets in 1832, and Chopin dedicated the Op. 7 set to Paul Emil Johns, the American representative of the Pleyel publishing house.

The mazurka was a Polish couple dance from Mazovia, the region around Warsaw. Originally a folk dance, it had been introduced to courts in Poland, Germany, and Russia during the eighteenth century, and by Chopin's time it was popular in Polish and Parisian high society. Chopin undoubtedly heard folk mazurkas during his youth, but his sense of the genre was formed primarily by the mazurkas of aristocratic ballrooms and urban salons, which incorporated stylized evocations of folk elements as a way to assert Polish national identity. Chopin drew on this tradition in his own mazurkas, which were meant for playing, not dancing, but strongly evoke the physicality of the dance as well as its Polish trademarks.

A mazurka is in triple meter and features a basic rhythm with either two eighth notes or a dotted eighth and sixteenth on the downbeat followed by two quarter notes. These rhythms tend to accentuate the second or third beat of the measure. Both the rhythm and the shifted accent are evident in this Chopin mazurka, with stresses on beats two or three emphasized by dynamics (as in measure 3), long notes (measures 4–6), trills (measures 3, 8, and 11), and melodic high points (measures 3 and 7). Beyond these features of the dance itself, other stylized Polish elements include grace notes that are a leap or skip from the main note, instead of a step below or above it (as in measures 4–10); slurs that begin on the last sixteenth note of a beat, in imitation of folk bowing practices (measures 9–14); open fifths, imitating bagpipe drones (measures 45–51); and augmented seconds, which became a conventional Romantic emblem for the exotic (measure 45). In addition, large leaps and rapid crescendos and diminuendos (as in measures 4–10) evoke the playing style of a folk violinist. Whatever the actual similarity of these traits to Polish folk music, they are highly stylized in Chopin's music and are meant as stylistic markers notable for their divergence from the common musical language, not as authentic representations of real folk music. Through them, Chopin achieved a distinctive personal and national style, which was part of the appeal of his music to listeners and to amateurs who bought the music to play.

The dance character of the piece is clear in the oom-pah-pah accompaniment and in the four-measure phrases and repeating periods. The opening period (measures 1–12) contains three phrases in abb' form. The a phrase ends on the tonic but without a V–I cadence, making the repeated dominant-tonic motion of the b phrase a necessary and satisfying conclusion. The opening period repeats, then alternates with two contrasting eight-measure phrases, producing an overall form of AA‖:BA:‖:CA:‖. The A period begins on the dominant rather than the tonic, which has the effect at the outset of creating the sense of a rapid forward rush. The contrasting B and C phrases end on the dominant, so that the return of A serves as an appropriate completion for both. In these details, Chopin demonstrated his sophisticated mastery of form.

Knowing that this piece is based on a stylized dance can enhance a pianist's performance. On the accompanying CD, Vladimir Ashkenazy's performance is very uneven in tempo: he rushes through the opening ascent, mimicking the quick steps of a dancing couple, and then he lingers at the trill in measure 3 and at several other points, imitating the time it takes for a woman to execute a turn or for a man to lift his partner and set her back down. Through much of the piece, Chopin's pedal markings emphasize the lilt of the dance by connecting the notes in each measure but releasing the pedal before each downbeat. The *stretto* marking at measure 29 suggests faster motion, suited to the more rapid alternation there between bass note and chord in the left hand and heightening the whirling feel of the repeated motive over a pedal point. The pedal is held down through all of measures 45–51, enhancing the sound of the open fifth and the exotic-sounding melody, made even more mysterious and evocative by the soft dynamic and the marking *sotto voce* (literally, "in a low voice"). The *rubato* marking at measure 49 indicates a departure from the regular pulse, either in both hands at once or in the right hand over a steady accompaniment. Rubato was part of the Romantic pianist's expressive repertoire at almost all times, whether marked or not.

FRYDERYK CHOPIN (1810–1849)

Nocturne in D-flat Major, Op. 27, No. 2

Nocturne (character piece)

1835

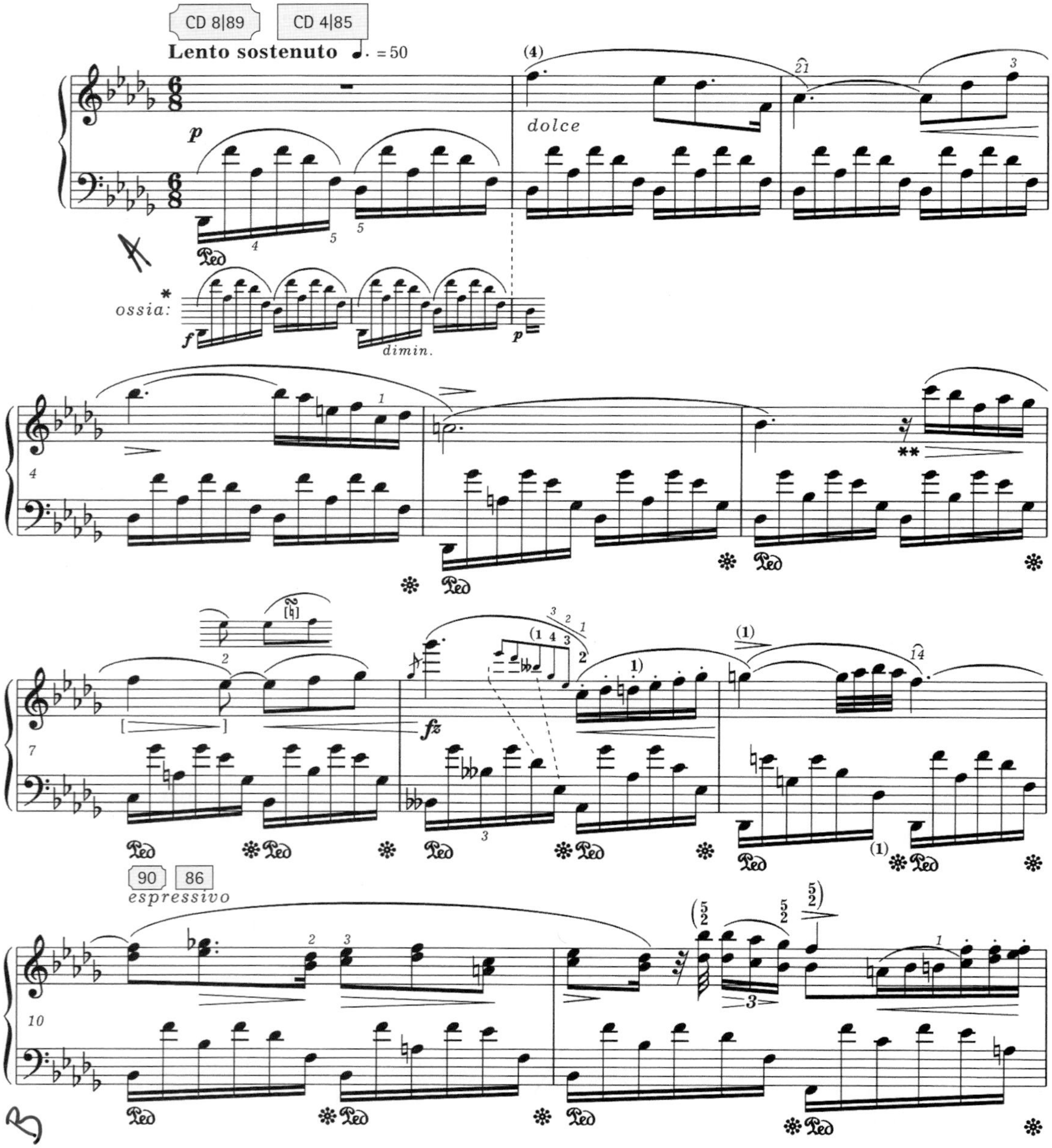

* Another reading of the variant - *vide Source Commentary.*   ** In one of the sources a change of uncertain authenticity from ⟶ to ⟵ .

From Fryderyk Chopin, *Nocturnes,* ed. Jan Ekier, National Edition, ser. A, vol. 5 (Krakow: Polskie Wydawnictwo Muzyczne, 2000), 54–59. Used by permission.

Coda

Chopin wrote eighteen nocturnes, spanning almost his entire career. He composed the nocturne included here and a companion in C♯ minor in 1835 and issued them the next year as his Op. 27, with a dedication to Countess Thérèse d'Apponyi, wife of the Austrian ambassador in Paris. Since there were few international copyright agreements in place at the time, Chopin arranged to have his music released simultaneously by publishers in Paris, Leipzig, and London in order to secure copyright in France, German-speaking lands, and Britain. He sometimes slightly adjusted the music after sending a piece off to one or more of the publishers, which resulted in small variants between the published versions. Several performance variants are included in the score reprinted here, marked *ossia* (Italian for "or rather").

While Chopin's mazurkas represent a Polish national tradition, his nocturnes represent a cosmopolitan one. He borrowed the name and the concept from Irish composer John Field, who published sixteen nocturnes between 1815 and 1836. Both Field and Chopin drew from the embellished singing style of Italian opera, so that the texture of a nocturne was essentially that of an ornamented song over arpeggiated accompaniment.

In this nocturne, the accompanimental figuration arches over two octaves and capitalizes on the piano's natural resonance by using wide spacing in the bass and closer spacing in the middle range. The melody also ranges widely, featuring large leaps and florid embellishments that are inspired by vocal coloratura but beyond the capacity of most voices, as in measures 8, 32, 45, and 60. These and other passages, especially the cadenza-like effusion in measures 51–52, bring elements of the virtuoso piano tradition into a genre more closely associated with the salon and the parlor than with the concert stage.

The structure of the piece is songlike, a modified strophic form in three "verses" with coda:

Music:	A	B		trans		A'	B'		trans	A"	B"	trans		Coda
Key:	D♭	b♭ e♭		on V of D♭		D♭	A	c♯	mod	D♭	e♭	to V of D♭	D♭	
	I	vi ii		V		I	♭VI	i	to V	I	ii	V		I
Measure:	1	10 14		18		26	34	38 42		46	54	58		62

The A theme unfolds unpredictably through constant variation, without internal repetitions. After an initial descent and ascent through the notes of the tonic chord, the first phrase is extended to five measures by long appoggiaturas (measures 4–5) that are echoed by another appogiatura at the end of the shorter second phrase (measure 9). This theme always returns in the tonic, with its first phrase largely unchanged (except for dynamics) but its second phrase intensified through rhythmic changes, denser textures, ornamentation, and chromaticism. The B theme provides a contrast of keys but is more regular than the A theme, featuring a two-measure unit in parallel thirds or sixths that is immediately varied and transposed. It is followed by a transition, different each time, that leads back to the dominant to prepare the return of A, often through intensely chromatic harmony (see measures 21–25 and 41–45). The coda recalls the chromaticism that has played such an important role in the work through parallel diminished seventh chords (measures 62–68) and melodic motion (measures 69–73), but neutralizes the potentially disruptive effects of chromaticism by remaining securely in D♭ major over a constantly reiterated D♭ pedal point in the bass.

Chopin accentuates the harmonic placidity at the beginning of his A theme by calling for the damper pedal to be held until the first chord change (measure 5), then indicating a release of the pedal after each new chord. The extent of the chromaticism in this piece is made plain by a passage in which the pianist is asked to play an A♮ and A♭ simultaneously in the same octave (measure 13), an effect so rare at the time that there is not even a standard notation for it. With the damper pedal held down, such chromaticism creates a slight blur when played on a piano of Chopin's time and a more noticeable one on the bigger, more resonant modern concert grands. The editor has used dotted lines to suggest placement for some of the grace notes (written in small notation) in relation to the regularly moving accompaniment (see measures 8 and 12 for examples).

119

FRANZ LISZT (1811–1886)

Trois études de concert (Three Concert Études): No. 3, *Un sospiro* (A Sigh)

Étude

1845–49

- Thematic transformation
- virtuosic
- passive listener

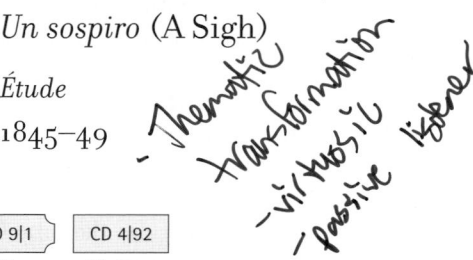

CD 9|1 CD 4|92

Allegro affettuoso.
armonioso
legatiss.
(p)
poco agitato
Ped.
A
D♭
3
cantando
*)
dolce con grazia
Ped.
5
sempre Pedale
7

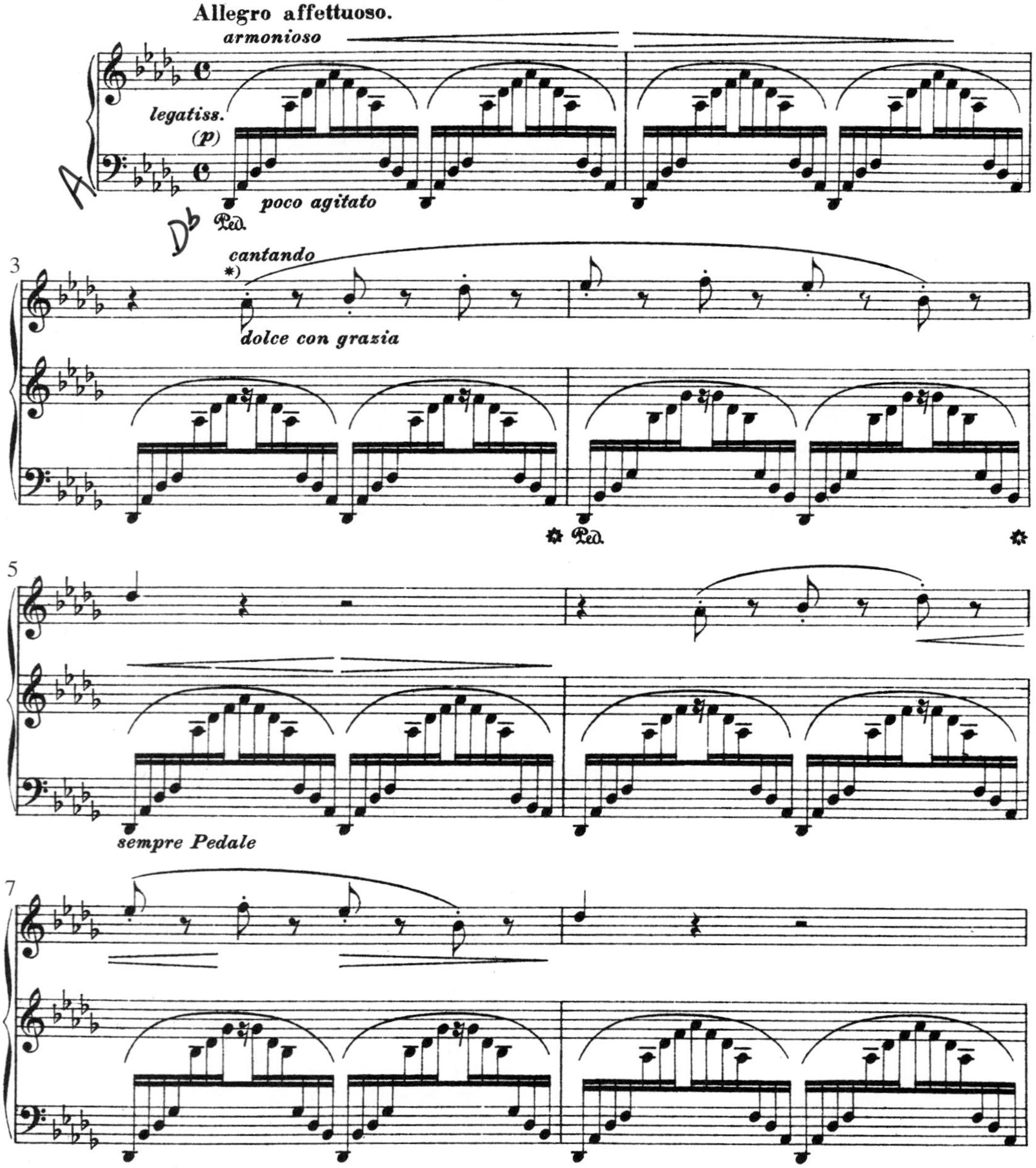

*) The notes with stems pointing downward are to be played with the left hand, and those with stems pointing upward, with the right hand.

From Franz Liszt, *Complete Études for Solo Piano*, Series II, ed. Ferruccio Busoni (New York: Dover, 1988), 160–68. Dover Publications, Inc.

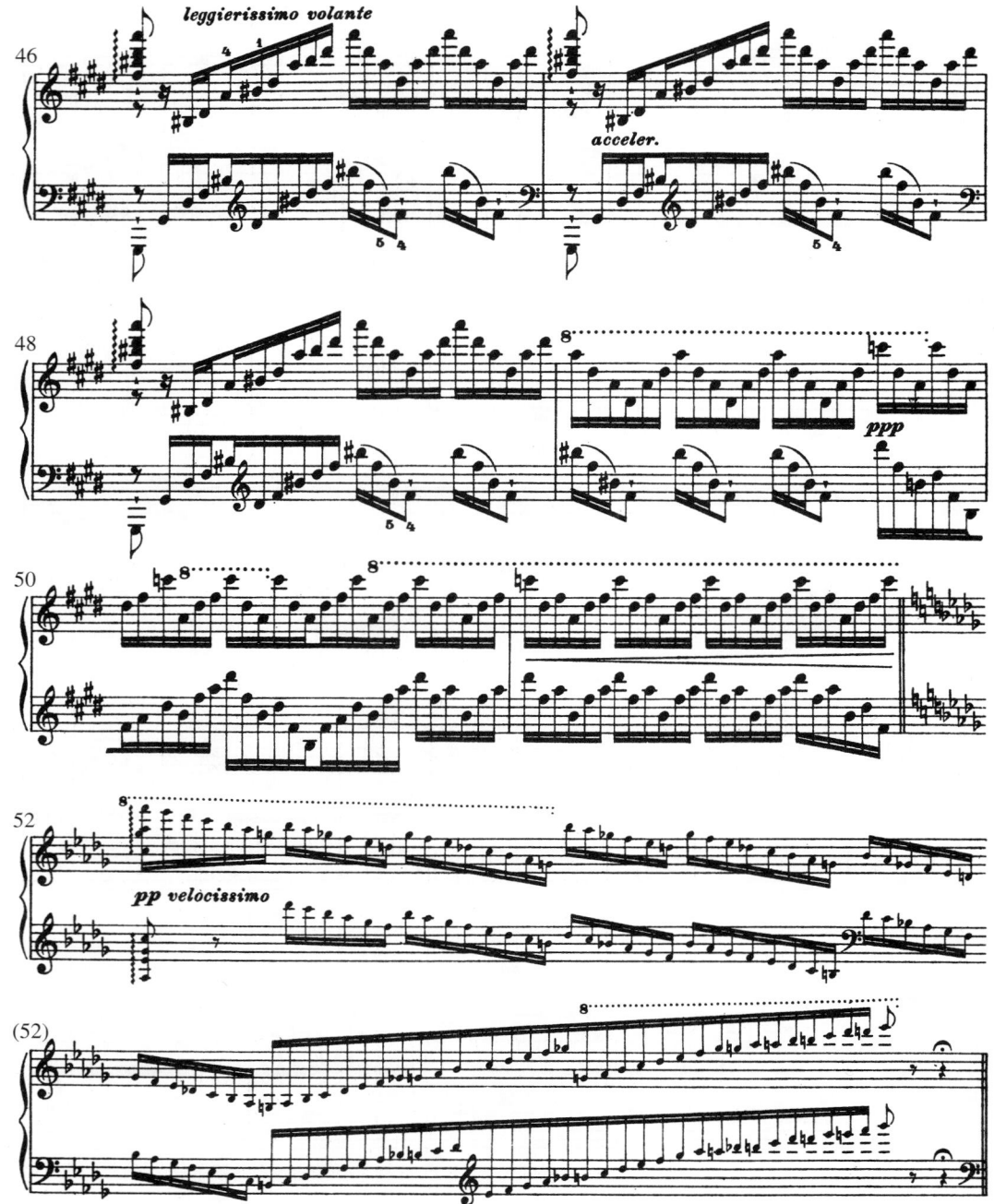

Coda

Franz Liszt wrote his *Three Concert Études* between 1845 and 1849 during his last years as a touring virtuoso and his first year as court music director at Weimar, where he was appointed in 1848. They were published in 1849 without the evocative names they later acquired (which were not given by the composer). In these and earlier études and concert works for piano, Liszt elicited new sounds and textures from the instrument and forced pianists to develop new techniques. Although more than just a display piece, *Un sospiro*, the étude included here, reflects the composer's superior skill as a pianist. Indeed, he was considered the most brilliant pianist of his time and perhaps has never been surpassed in virtuosity.

Études usually focus on particular technical challenges. In *Un sospiro*, the greatest challenge for the player is accentuating the slowly moving melody that occurs outside or within rapid broken-chord figuration. Holding the damper pedal down allows each arpeggiated chord to resonate while the two hands brave treacherous leaps over each other. The pianist must alternate between using the left and right hands to pick out a tune either above the figuration, as in measures 3–20, or within its compass, as in measures 53–61. Liszt chose the key of D♭ major and laid out the melody so that most of its notes are played on the black keys, which are easier to find and play without error while the hands leap around the keyboard.

In addition to differentiating the melody, the pianist faces several formidable obstacles as the piece unfolds. The simple notes of the melody change to rolled octaves in measures 13–21, forcing the hands to move even faster than before. At measures 30–34, the left hand must strike the notes of the melody in octaves and insert chords below them, while the right hand executes "impetuous" arpeggios periodically reinforced by thirds. Here, two hands must do the work of three. Cadenzas in parallel major sixths—the first marked *presto* (quickly, at measure 37) and the second marked *velocissimo* (very rapidly, at measure 52)—require both speed and accuracy. At the reprise of the main theme (measures 53–61), the accompaniment, earlier marked *legatissimo*, must now sound like a harp while the player accents the melodic notes nested in the arpeggiation.

Both the form and the key scheme are unusual:

Music:	A	A'		B	ext/cadenza	B'	ext/cadenza	B"	ext/cadenza	A"	B"'	Coda
Key:	D♭	D♭ → A		A	f	F	c♯		c♯ on V of c♯/D♭	D♭		
	I		♭VI	iii		III	i		V	I		
Measure:	1	13	19	22	27		30	35		38	46	53	62	66

The main theme, A, begins with a three-measure pentatonic phrase played twice over a D♭ pedal point. Arpeggios alternate between tonic and subdominant triads, with added sixths supplied by the melody. Here, the melody's lack of semitones, its undulating rise and fall, its three-measure phrases, and its immediate repetitions join with the oscillating harmony to create an unusual effect of stasis, or lack of movement, despite the rapid flow of the arpeggiations. In contrast, the answering phrase (measures 9–12) moves forcefully toward a cadence in D♭. The A theme then repeats in rolled octaves, with the answering phrase varied so it now modulates toward A major (enharmonically B♭♭), the lowered sixth degree.

Theme B is a variant of A, still pentatonic but now questing ever upward, instead of rising and falling, and trimmed to two-measure phrases, creating a much greater sense of forward movement. It appears three times, in A major, F major, and C♯ minor, each time followed by a new, longer, and more virtuosic extension and cadenza. The A theme then returns varied in the tonic D♭ followed by a variant of the B theme in the tonic and a coda that hints once more at the A theme (see the accented and highest notes in measures 70–73).

The form can be interpreted in several ways: as a series of variations on the opening idea; as an enlarged ternary form that presents A in the tonic, B in other keys, and A back in the tonic; or even as a relative of sonata form, with two themes presented in different keys, a development section (here focused on B), and a recapitulation of both themes in the tonic.

The harmonic plan, with three keys (and their parallel minors) separated by major thirds, reflects Liszt's fascination with equal divisions of the octave. Assuming the equivalence of enharmonically spelled notes (like C♯ and D♭), the octave can be divided into three major thirds or four minor thirds, and Liszt experimented with both. Division into major thirds produces the key scheme seen here and, on the level of individual chords, augmented triads like the one in measure 37. Division into minor thirds is reflected in diminished seventh chords and in the *octatonic scale*, which alternates whole and half steps in tracing a circle of minor thirds. As if to showcase the two possibilities, the coda features a descending octatonic scale in the bass (D♭–C♭–B♭–A♭–G–F–E–D–D♭ at measures 66–70) accompanied by the four major triads that can be derived from that scale (D♭, B♭, G, and E). The final chord progression (measures 73–77) highlights the D♭, B♭♭ (enharmonically A), and F major triads that formed the main key areas of the piece. Liszt's systematic exploration of these scales and chord progressions was novel at the time and profoundly influenced later composers, especially in Russia (see NAWM 130, 140, and 145–146).

Louis Moreau Gottschalk (1829–1869)

Souvenir de Porto Rico (Marche des Gibaros), Op. 31

Character piece

1857–58

From *Piano Music of Louis Moreau Gottschalk*, ed. Richard Jackson (New York: Dover, 1973), 176–85.
Dover Publications, Inc.

Louis Moreau Gottschalk, the first North American to win an international reputation as a pianist and composer, spent most of his career touring as a virtuoso
through Europe, the United States, Canada, the Caribbean, and Latin America. He
wrote *Souvenir de Porto Rico* in 1857–58 during a rest stop in Puerto Rico. The subtitle *Marche des Gibaros* (March of the Jibaros) refers to the rustic peasants called
Jibaros who farmed inland areas of the island and whose music Gottschalk incorporated into several pieces. Here, he uses a theme (measures 17–32) derived from
Si me dan pasteles, les dénmelos calientes (If you give me cakes, give them to me
hot), a Puerto Rican song performed by strolling bands of musicians during the
Christmas season.

The form of the piece suggests the sound of a band of musicians as they appear
in the distance, gradually approach, pass by, and march away. At first, only hints
of the music are heard—a few soft notes and a cadence to establish the key of E♭
minor. The borrowed theme enters quietly (at measure 17) and repeats, and then
a second idea marked *malinconico* (melancholy, measures 49–58) provides some
contrast with a brief turn to a higher register and major mode. Both themes are
accompanied by a traditional march rhythm (half note, half note, two quarter
notes, and half note in $\frac{2}{4}$ meter). There follow seven variations of the two themes,
which grow louder, denser, and more rhythmically complex until reaching a climax in the fifth variation and then returning to a softer and thinner texture before
finally fading away.

In several of the variations, Gottschalk uses Afro-Caribbean rhythms he had
learned in Cuba or heard in Puerto Rico. Shown below are the *tresillo*, a pattern of
three unequal notes in a measure; two forms of *cinquillo*, patterns of five unequal
notes; and the *habanera*, a dance rhythm from Havana.

These rhythms are used only in variations of the Puerto Rican song, shown as A in
the chart below. But some variations of A and all variations of the contrasting idea
B instead receive figurations typical of European virtuoso music, including chromatic scales and arpeggios, repeated-note figures, and a polonaise-like rhythm
(eighth, two sixteenths, and two eighths, in measures 165–70) marked *martellato*
(hammered). To lessen the predictability of the piece, B is sometimes trimmed
from ten to eight measures and is sometimes repeated. The climactic fifth variation is in the relative major (written enharmonically as F♯), and B is omitted to
make way for an exciting chromatic transition back to the tonic. This variation and
transition, incorporating all four of the Caribbean rhythms, reaches an unprece-
dented level of complexity in its syncopations. The last two variations borrow

from earlier ones, emphasizing the arch-like shape of the piece. The form can be charted as follows:

Measure	Section	Key	Rhythms and other elements
1	Intro	e♭	
17	Theme A		march rhythm
49	B		march rhythm
59	Var 1 A		tresillo, cinquillo 1
75	B		= Theme
85	Var 2 A		chromatic scales (later, cinquillo 1)
101	B		chromatic scales and arpeggios
117	Var 3 A		repeated-note figures
133	B		= Var 2
149	Var 4 A		habanera, cinquillo 1, tresillo
165	B	mod	martellato figure
173	Var 5 A	F♯ (G♭)	habanera, cinquillo 1, cinquillo 2, tresillo
202	Trans	mod	habanera, cinquillo 1, cinquillo 2, tresillo
220	Var 6 A	e♭	= Var 2
236	B		= Var 2
252	Var 7 A		tresillo, cinquillo 1, cinquillo 2
268	B		= Theme
278	Coda		

With an exotic subject, an extramusical program, virtuosic display, exciting rhythms, and a form that was intriguing but easy to follow, *Souvenir de Porto Rico* combined numerous elements that appealed to middle-class audiences and ambitious amateur performers. It also poses interesting problems for the player, from syncopated Caribbean rhythms to virtuoso touches. For example, the third variation requires both hands to fly across the keyboard as the right hand repeatedly leaps from four rapid sixteenth notes up two octaves to the highest register of the piano, requiring the left hand to share the melody (m.d. means *main droite*, or right hand, and m.g. means *main gauche*, or left hand). In the fourth variation, the large leaps in the left hand are so challenging that Gottschalk provided a simplified alternate version (measures 176–72, marked *facilité*) for those incapable of playing the original.

HECTOR BERLIOZ (1803–1869)

Symphonie fantastique: Fifth movement, "Dream of a Witches' Sabbath"

Program symphony

1830

[handwritten annotations:]
- exploits winds
- huge waves of sound thru crescendos
- and dynamic + tempo markings
- idée fix
- dies irae
- special effects - col legno
- uses idea of massive choruses

CD 9|16   CD 5|1

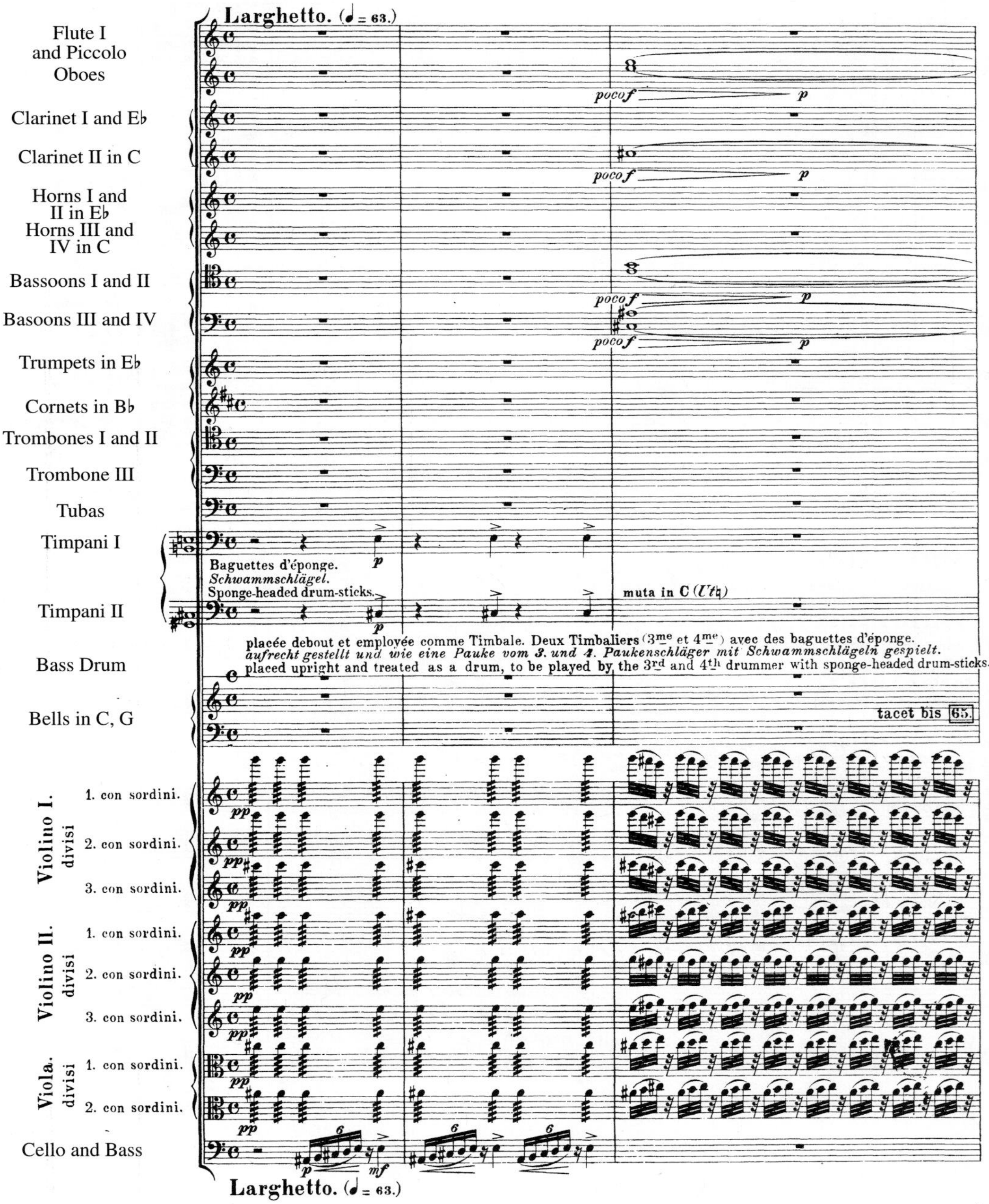

From Hector Berlioz, *Symphonie Fantastique and Harold in Italy in Full Score*, ed. Charles Malherbe and Felix Weingartner (Leipzig: Breitkopf & Härtel, 1900; repr. New York: Dover, 1984), 97–150. Dover Publications, Inc.

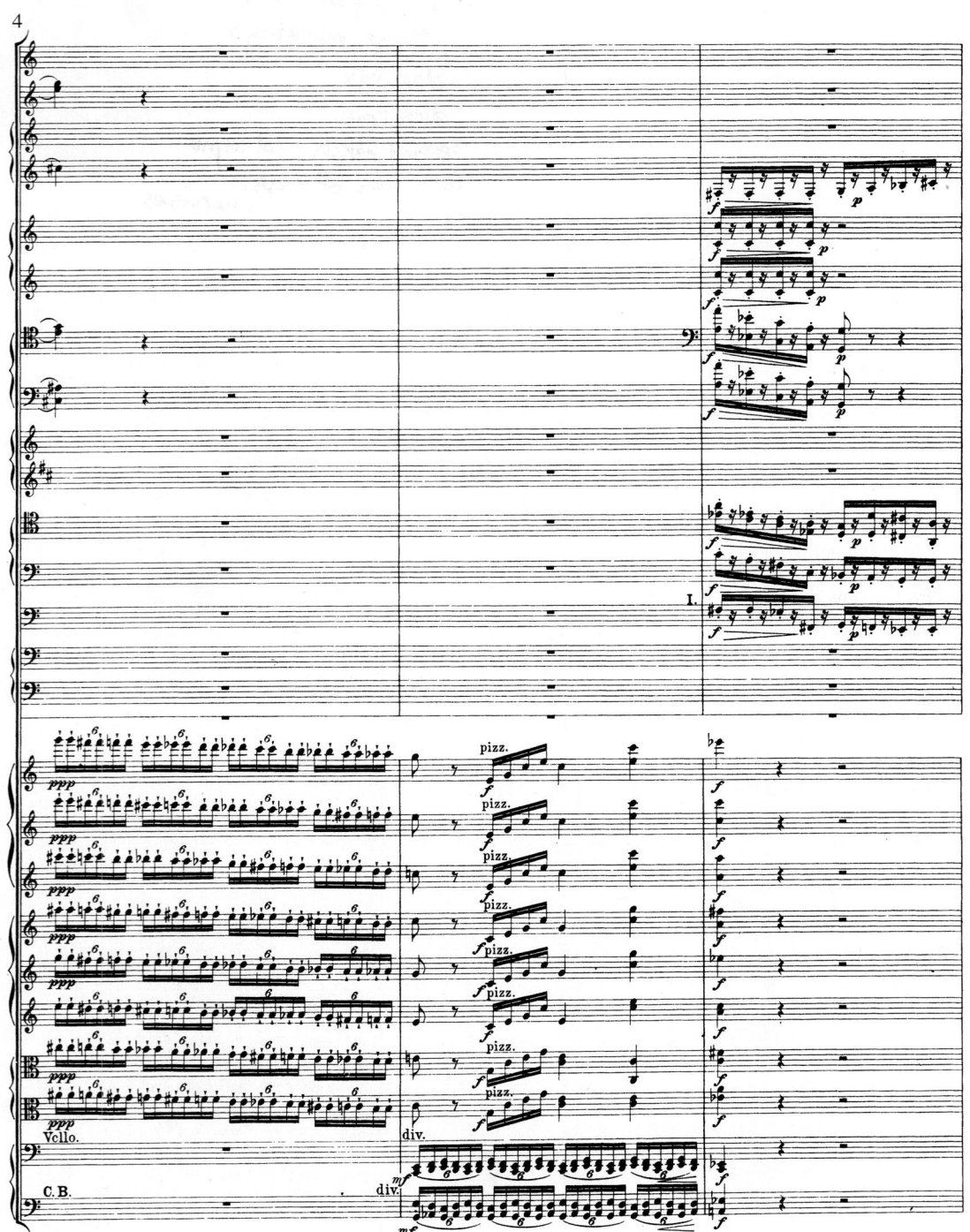

13

17 2
21
Allegro. (♩. = 112.)
Allegro assai. (𝅝 = 67.)
(lointain)
(entfernt)
(distant)
ppp
tr
cresc. poco a poco
senza sord.
a 2.
ff
I.
p cresc. poco a poco
p
cresc. poco a poco
cresc. poco a poco
senza sord.
senza sord.
senza sord.
senza sord.
senza sord.
senza sord.
senza sord.
senza sord.
Allegro. (♩. = 112.)
Allegro assai. (𝅝 = 67.)

67
Fl. I.
ff
Fl. picc.
Ob.
Clar.
a 2.
Cor.
Fag.
a 4.
Tr.
Ctti
Tromb.
Tuba I.
Timp.
Viol.

146

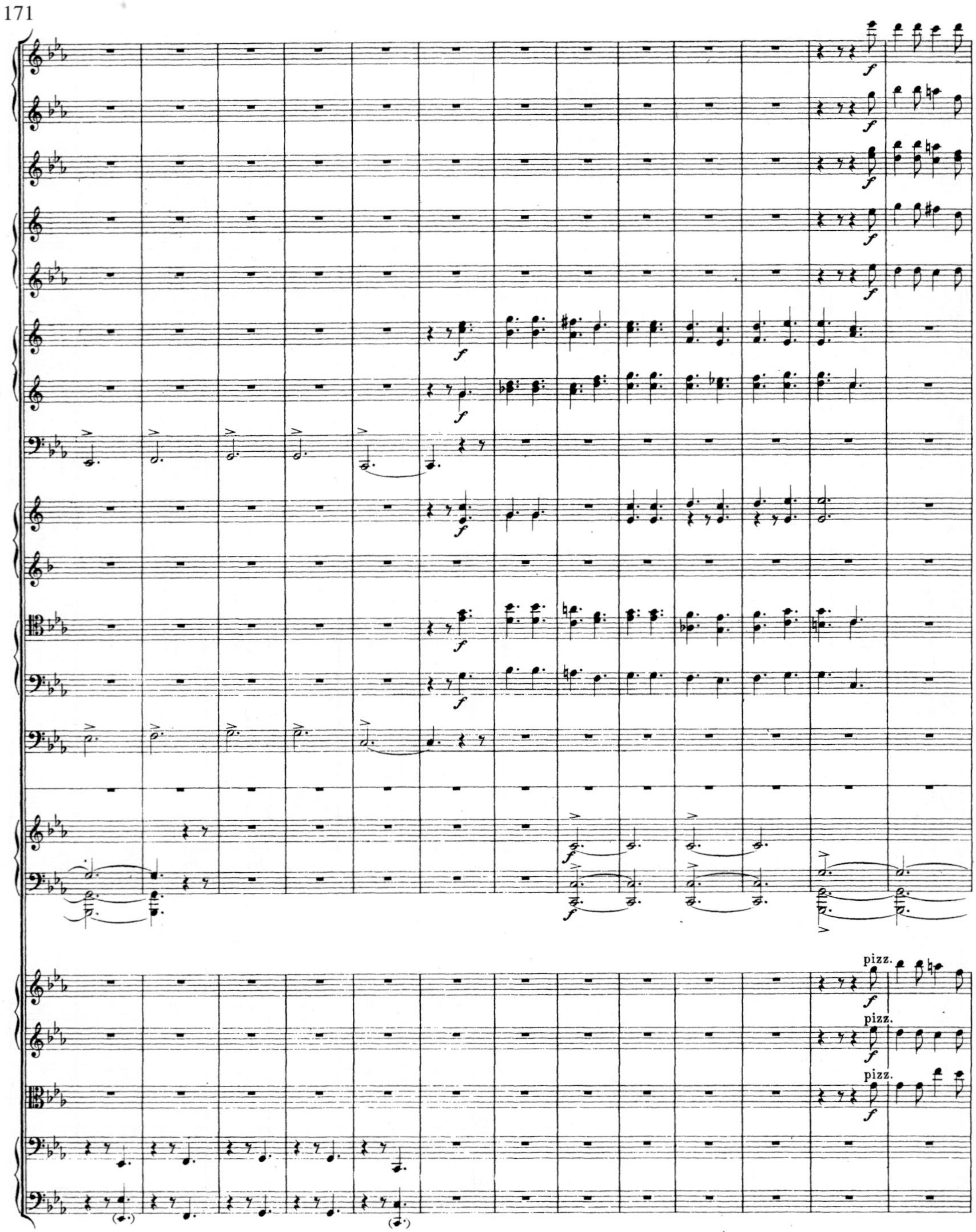
171
pizz.
pizz.
pizz.

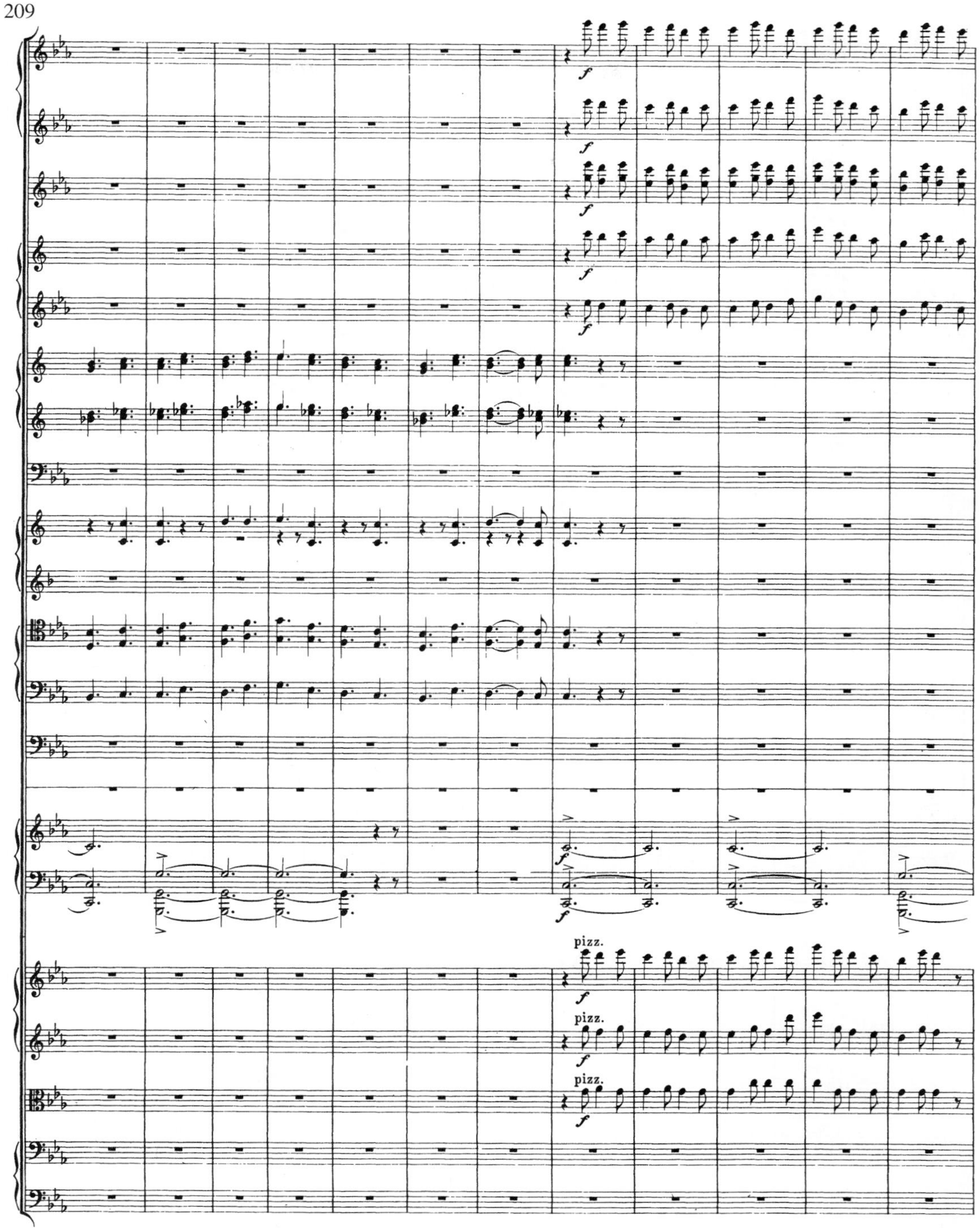
209
f
pizz.

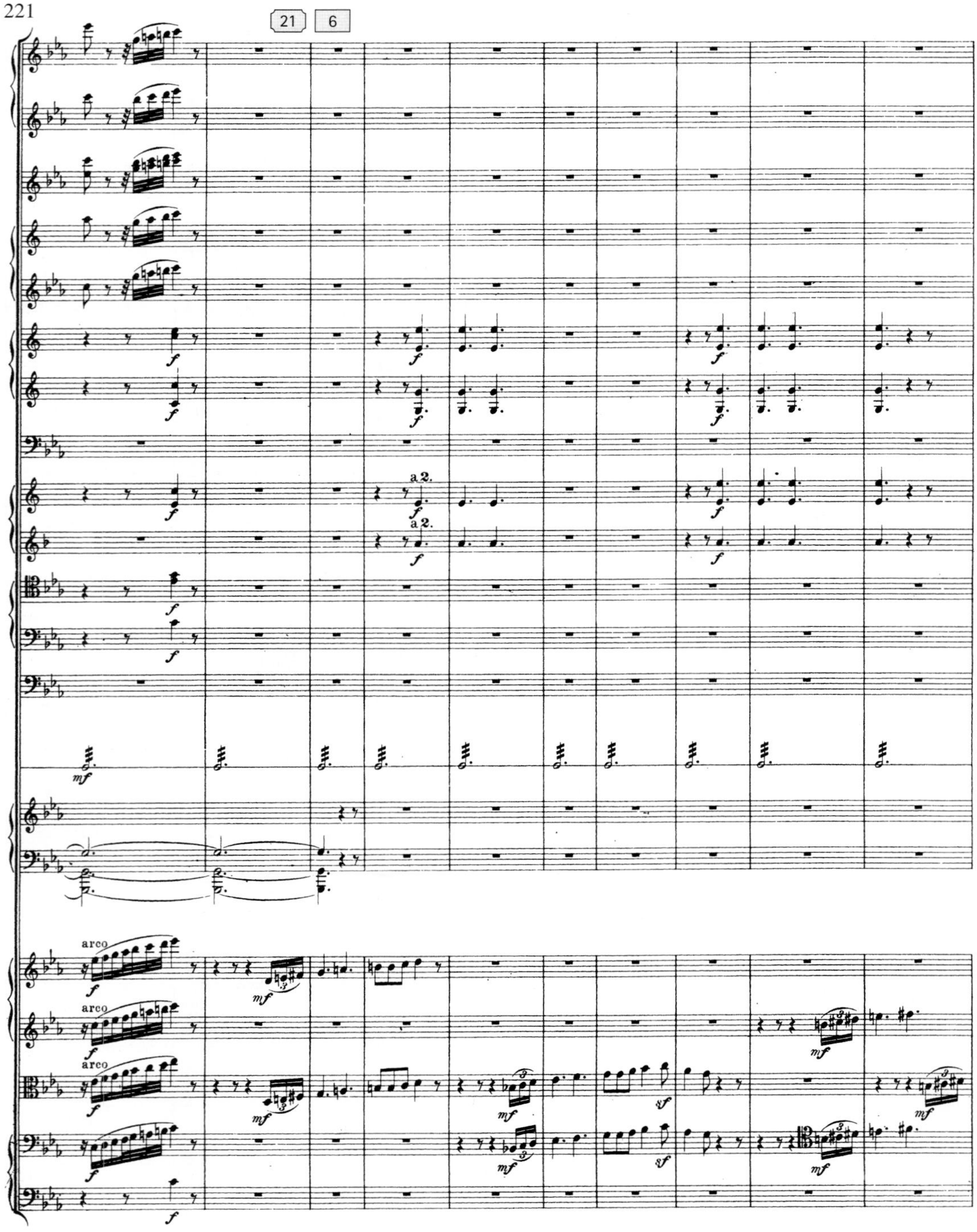
221
21
6
a 2.
a 2.
arco
arco
arco

Ronde du Sabbat.
Witches' round dance.
241   **Poco meno mosso.**

Poco meno mosso.

257

272

289

306

335

371

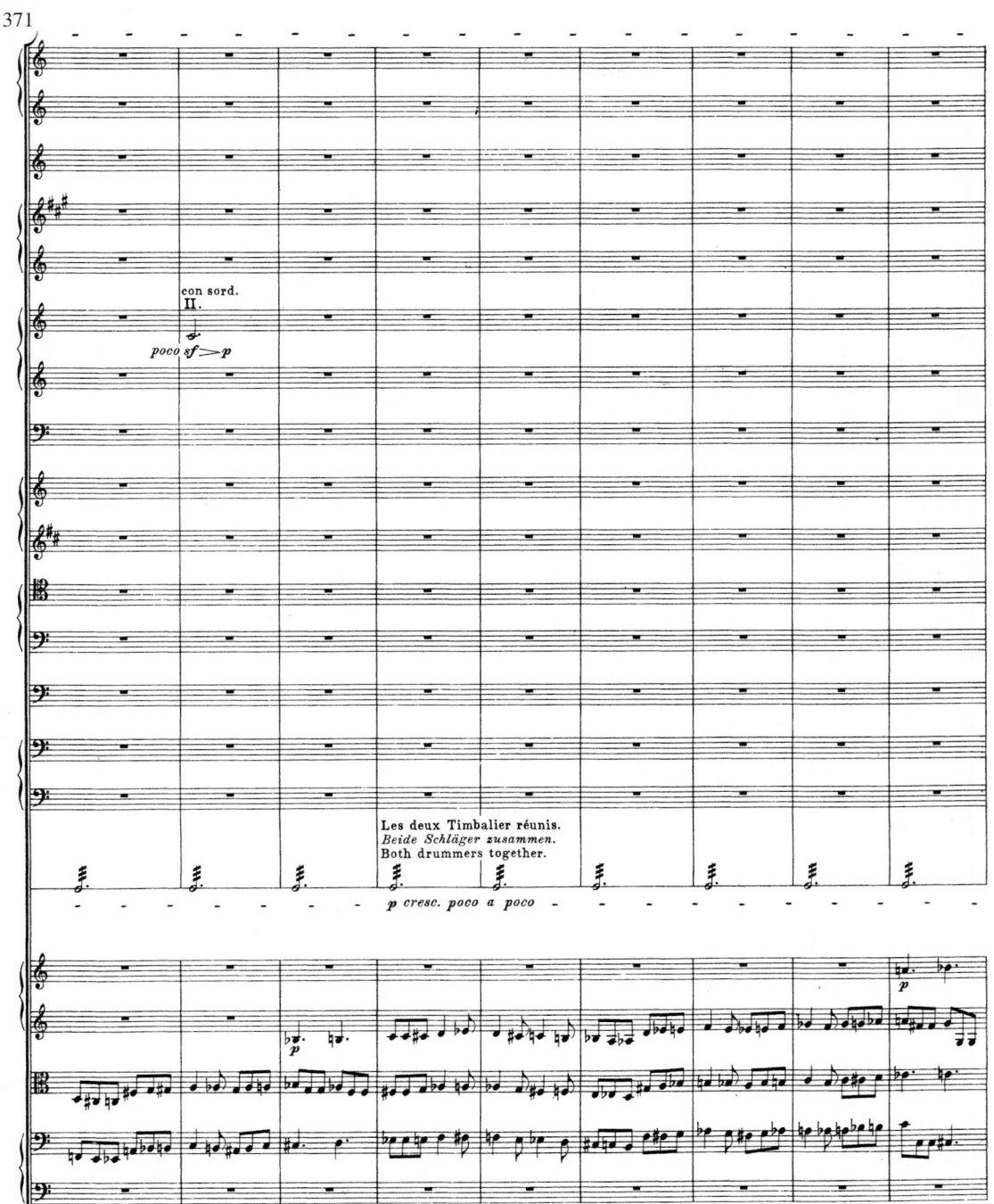

380
mf
I.
senza sord.
a 4.
cresc.
poco a poco
cresc. sempre
f cresc. sempre

27   12

414   Dies irae et Ronde du Sabbat (ensemble).
      Dies irae and witches' round dance (together).

423

429

435

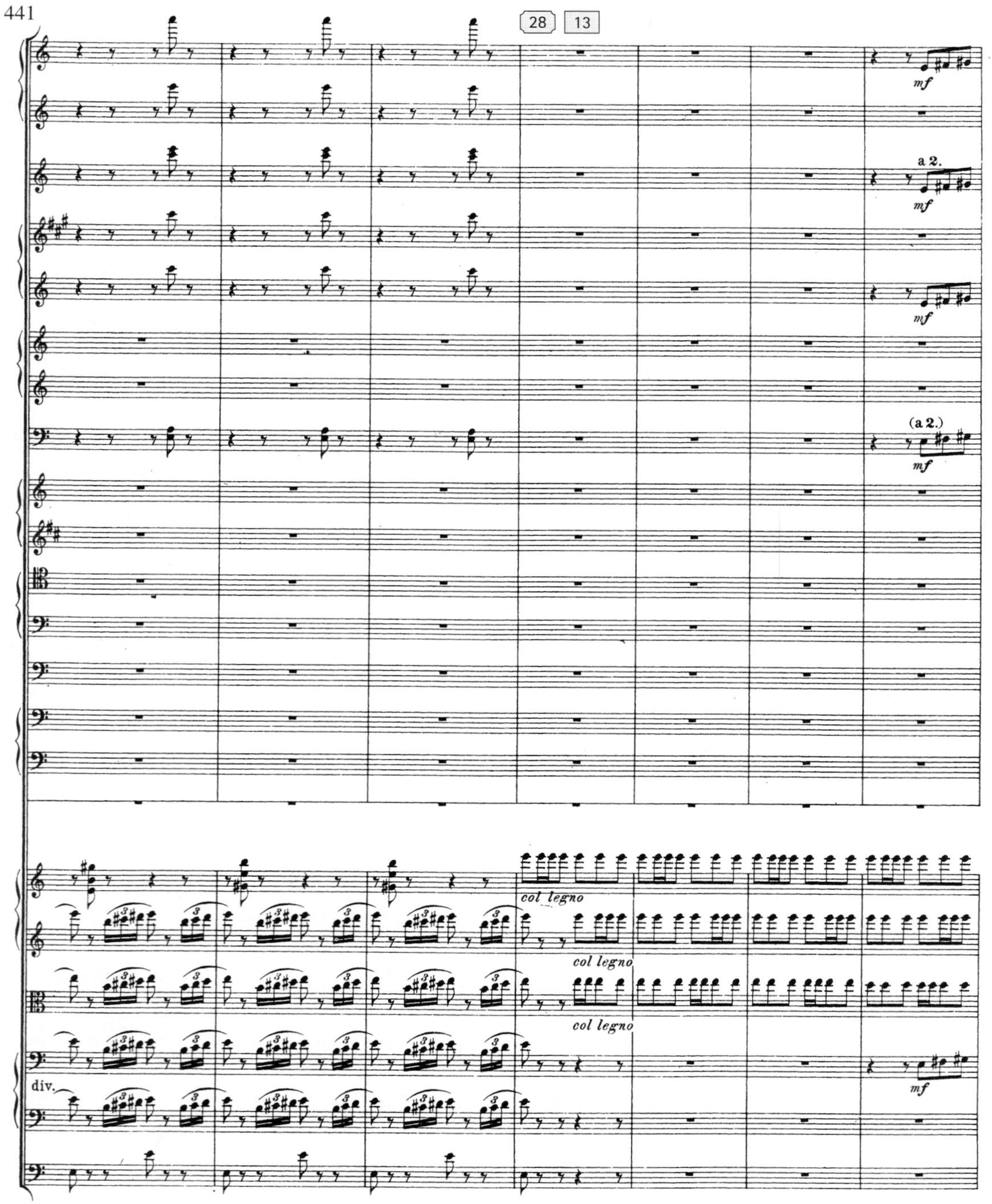
441
28
13
mf
a 2.
mf
mf
(a 2.)
mf
col legno
col legno
col legno
div.
mf

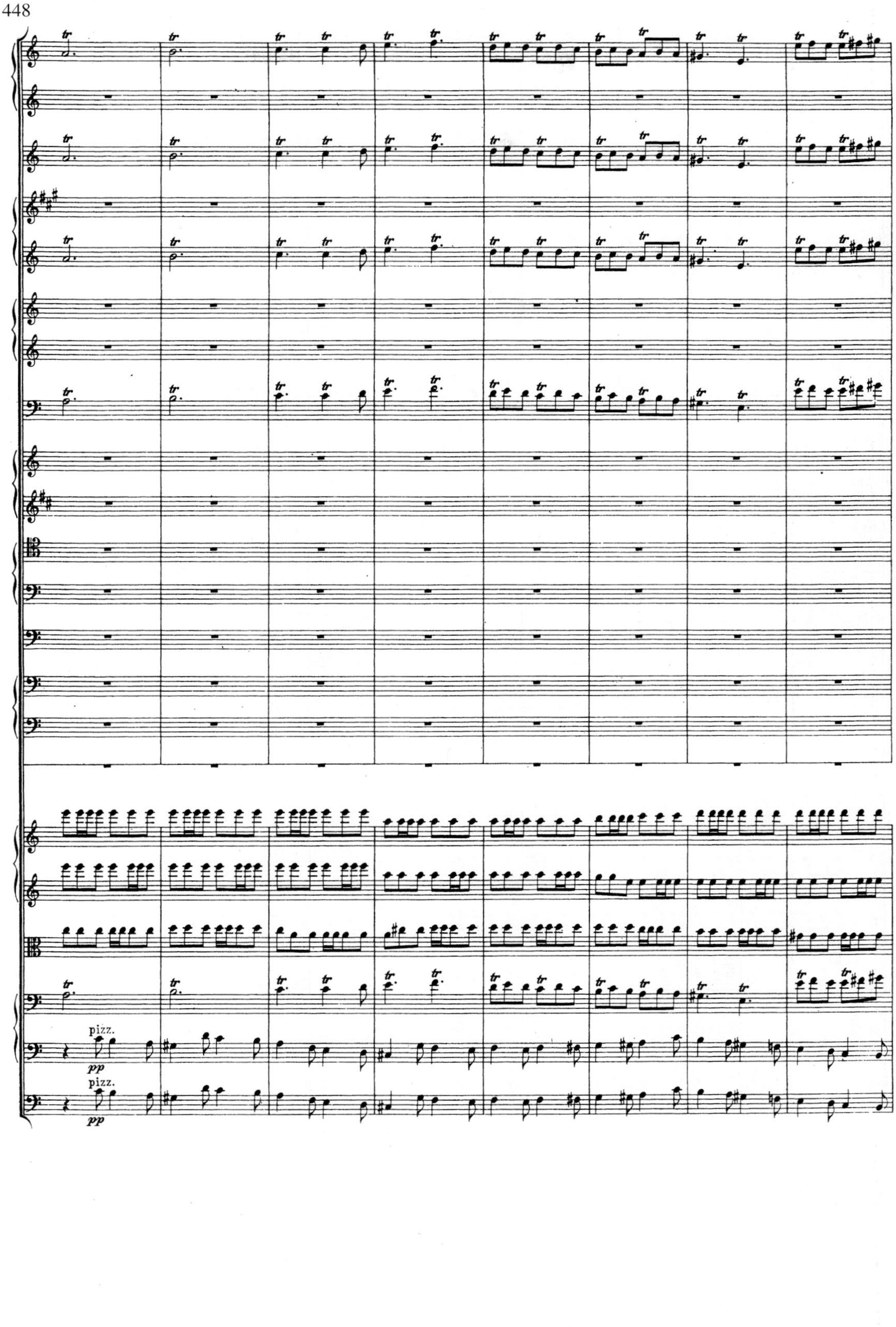
448
tr
pizz.
pp
pizz.
pp

456

474

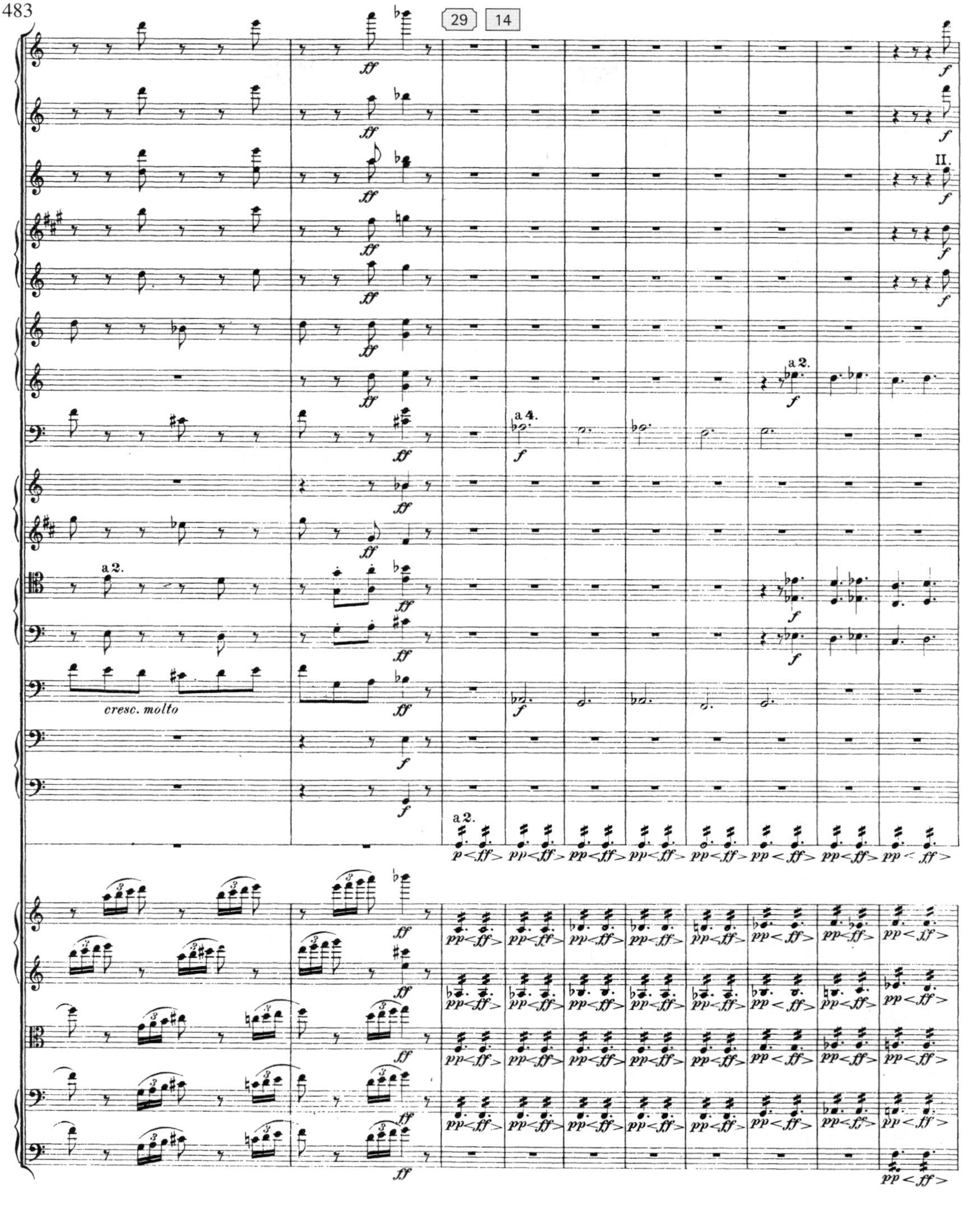
483
29
14
a 2.
II.
a 4.
cresc. molto
ff
f
pp < ff >

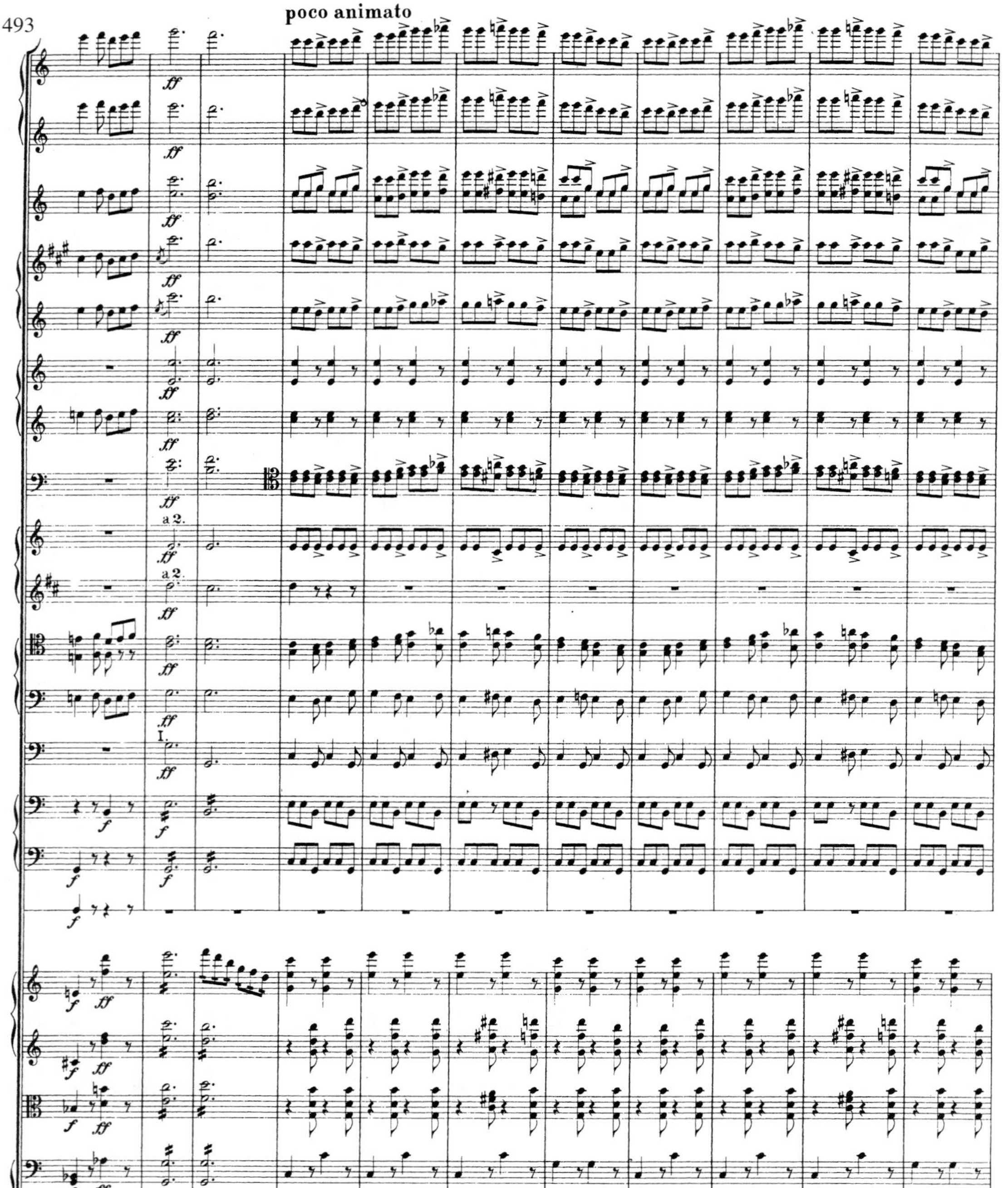
493
poco animato
ff
a 2.
a 2.
I.
f
poco animato

504

515

Coup frappé sur une Cymbale avec une baguette
couverte d'éponge ou un tampon.
*Schlag auf ein Becken mit einem Schwamm-
schlägel oder Klöppel.*
Struck on a cymbal with a sponge-headed
drum-stick.

Cinelli.

Hector Berlioz wrote his *Symphonie fantastique* in 1830, when he was only twenty-six. At that time he was deeply affected by German Romanticism, especially Goethe's *Faust* and Beethoven's symphonies. He originally called the symphony "An Episode in the Life of an Artist, Fantastic Symphony in Five Parts." The first performance was planned for May 1830 but had to be canceled after a disastrous rehearsal, because Berlioz had gathered an orchestra of 130 that was too large for the stage. The symphony was finally premiered on December 5, 1830, at the end of a concert that also featured other works by Berlioz, including an overture and the cantata that had won him the coveted Prix de Rome earlier that year.

The symphony has five movements: a fast sonata form with a long, slow introduction; a dance (a waltz instead of a minuet); a slow movement; a march; and a fast finale. Except for the march, this scheme resembles the standard four-movement plan of most symphonies.

Berlioz wrote the following detailed program for the symphony, which was distributed to the audience at the premiere and printed with the score, first published in 1845. The composer likened the program to the text of an opera, for it inspired and explained the symphony's music in the same way the libretto does for an opera. The story was inspired by his own infatuation with the English actress Harriet Smithson.

Note

The composer has aimed to develop, to the extent they can be rendered in music, various situations in the life of an artist. The plan of the instrumental drama, since it lacks the assistance of words, needs to be outlined in advance. Thus the following program* should be considered in the same way as the spoken words of an opera, serving to introduce the pieces of music, whose character and expression it motivates.

*Distribution of this program to the audience, in the concerts that include this symphony, is essential for complete understanding of the dramatic plan of the work.

First Part
Dreams and Passions

The author supposes that a young musician, affected by the moral malady that one celebrated writer calls the wave of passions, sees for the first time a woman who joins together all the charms of the ideal being of which his imagination has dreamed, and falls madly in love. By a peculiar quirk, the beloved image never appears in the artist's mind without being linked to a melody, in which he finds a certain character that is passionate, yet noble and shy, like that he ascribes to the object of his love.

This melodic reflection along with its model pursue him ceaselessly, like a double *idée fixe* [obsession]. Such is the reason for the constant appearance, in all the movements of the symphony, of the melody that begins the first Allegro. The passage from this state of melancholy reverie, interrupted by some unprovoked fits of joy, to that of a delirious passion, with its movements of fury, of jealousy, its returns to tenderness, its tears, its religious consolations, is the subject of the first movement.

Second Part
A Ball

The artist is placed in the most varied circumstances of life, in the middle of the tumult of a party, in the peaceful contemplation of the beauties of nature; but everywhere, in the city, in the country, the beloved image appears to him and sows confusion in his heart.

Third Part
Scene in the Country

Finding himself one evening in the country, he hears in the distance two shepherds who pipe back and forth a *ranz des vaches* [Swiss melody used to summon cows]. This pastoral duet, the scene, the light rustle of the trees gently agitated by the winds, some grounds for hope that he recently conceived, all converge to return to his heart an unaccustomed calm, to give a happier tinge to his ideas. He reflects on his isolation; he hopes soon to be no longer alone . . . But what if she misled him! . . . This mixture of hope and fear, these ideas of happiness disturbed by some dark presentiments, form the subject of the Adagio. At the end, one of the shepherd again takes up the *ranz des vaches;* the other does not respond . . . Distant noise of thunder . . . solitude . . . silence . . .

Fourth Part
March to the Scaffold

Having become certain that his love is ignored, the artist poisons himself with opium. The dose of the narcotic, too weak to grant him death, plunges him into a sleep accompanied by the strangest visions. He dreams that he has killed her whom he loves, that he is condemned and conducted to the scaffold, and that he is witnessing his own execution. The procession advances to the sounds of a march at times dark and savage, at times brilliant and solemn, in which a muffled sound of solemn steps is followed without transition by the noisiest clamor. At the end of the march, the first four measures of the *idée fixe* reappear like a last thought of love interrupted by the fatal blow.

Fifth Part
Dream of a Witches' Sabbath

He sees himself at a Witches' Sabbath, in the midst of a dreadful company of ghosts, sorcerers, and monsters of all kinds who have assembled for his funeral. Strange noises, moaning, bursts of laughter, distant cries to which other cries seem to respond. The beloved melody reappears once more, but it has lost its character of nobility and shyness; it is no more than a wretched, commonplace, and grotesque dance tune; it is she who comes to the Sabbath . . . Roars of joy at her arrival . . . She joins in the diabolical orgy . . . Funeral knell, burlesque parody of the *Dies irae*,** Witches' Sabbath round dance. The Sabbath round dance and the *Dies irae* together.

**Hymn sung in the funeral ceremonies of the Catholic Church.

The five movements of the symphony are linked both by the story and by the recurring melody, the *idée fixe*. At its first appearance, as the first theme of the sonata-form first movement, the melody is gracious, but full of signs of yearning: leaps, dynamic swells, and phrases that reach upward to ever higher peaks, then fall back down.

The idea recurs in varied form in all the later movements, often interrupting the other musical material, as Berlioz states in the program.

The finale closely follows the events described in the program. It begins slowly and mysteriously with muted strings playing a diminished seventh chord tremolo and tritones in the bass, both associated with the diabolical. Soft flutters in the strings and louder figures in the winds and brass suggest the convergence of the ghosts, wizards, and monsters described in the program. As if from a distance, and then gradually approaching, a clarinet begins a distorted, mocking version of the *idée fixe* in a fast ⁶⁄₈, embellished with grace notes and trills (measure 21); this represents the debauched beloved as she comes to the sabbath and is greeted by roars from the assembled demons (measure 29). The entire *idée fixe* then appears in the E♭ clarinet, whose tone has a particularly saucy sound (measure 40), and the other instruments gradually join in the revels.

In the following section, interwoven with hints of the coming round dance of the witches (measure 84), the orchestral bells ring the funeral knell three times (measure 102). As the bells continue, we hear phrases from *Dies irae*, the Gregorian chant sequence sung during the Mass for the Dead (measure 127). There are three excerpts from the chant, and each appears in three guises: in long notes in bassoons and tubas; twice as fast in parallel thirds in horns and trombones; and faster still in winds and pizzicato strings. The contrast of ponderous slow notes and quick dance-like rhythms comprise the "burlesque parody" of the chant mentioned in the program, as the ghastly crowd mocks the artist's death.

This passage inspired a tradition of using the *Dies irae*, especially its opening four or eight notes, as a symbol for death, the macabre, or the diabolical, carried on in countless works by Liszt, Saint-Saëns, Rachmaninov, and others.

Hints of the witches' round dance (measure 222) herald the dance itself (measure 241), which begins with fugal entrances suggesting the swirl of dancing witches and offbeat accents suggesting their lurching movements. Motives from the fugue subject are developed in an episode (measure 269), the subject appears in stretto (measure 289), and further developments ensue. Fragments of the *Dies irae* are heard again (measure 348), and after a long, intense *crescendo*, the round dance subject returns (measure 404) and round dance and *Dies irae* are heard together (measure 414). The coda includes stunning sound effects, such as the strings playing with the wood of the bow (*col legno*) to produce a dry, ghostly sound (measure 444), and rapid tremolo *crescendos* and *diminuendos* to accompany the last *Dies irae* before the demonic celebration roars to a close.

Berlioz was the first composer to score a piece for an orchestra of over a hundred, and many later composers followed his lead. He was also a master orchestrator and invented a number of new effects and devices. There are many innovative details worth noting besides those already mentioned: the strings divided into many sections (measure 1) and frequently alternating plucked (*pizzicato*) and bowed (*arco*) sounds; the large numbers of wind, brass, and percussion instruments; glissandos in winds and horn (measures 8–11); rapid passagework in the bassoon (measure 47); the four timpani that must be retuned during the movement and played with a variety of sticks (measures 232); the bass drum, played by two people (measure 374); the tubular bells used to imitate church bells; and much else.

The performance on the accompanying recording uses authentic nineteenth-century instruments (or reconstructions of them) to achieve a sound much like Berlioz intended. For example, the bass line of the brass section, indicated for tubas in the edition included here, was actually composed for ophicleide, an instrument with a brass mouthpiece, a shape somewhat resembling a bassoon, and a system of mechanical keys like that of the saxophone.

Felix Mendelssohn (1809–1847)

Violin Concerto in E Minor, Op. 64: Third movement, Allegretto non troppo—Allegro molto vivace

Violin concerto
1844

122

From *Mendelssohn Konzert für Violine und Orchester e-moll . . . op. 64* (Wiesbaden: Breitkopf & Härtel, n.d.; repr. New York: Dover, 1985), 101–19. Dover Publications, Inc.

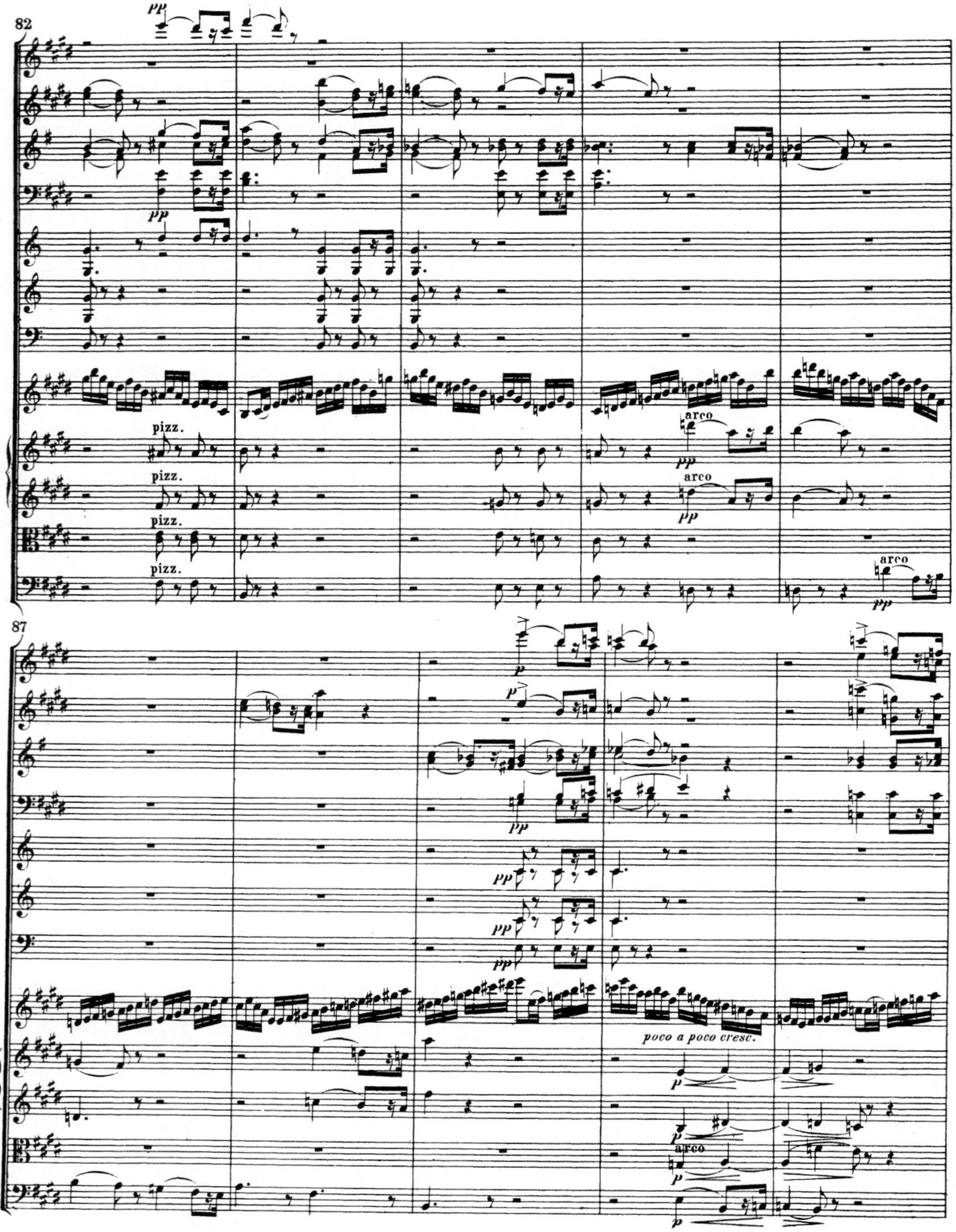

82
pp
pp
pizz.
pizz.
pizz.
pizz.
arco
pp
arco
pp
arco
pp
87
p
p
pp
pp
pp
pp
poco a poco cresc.
p
p
arco
p
p

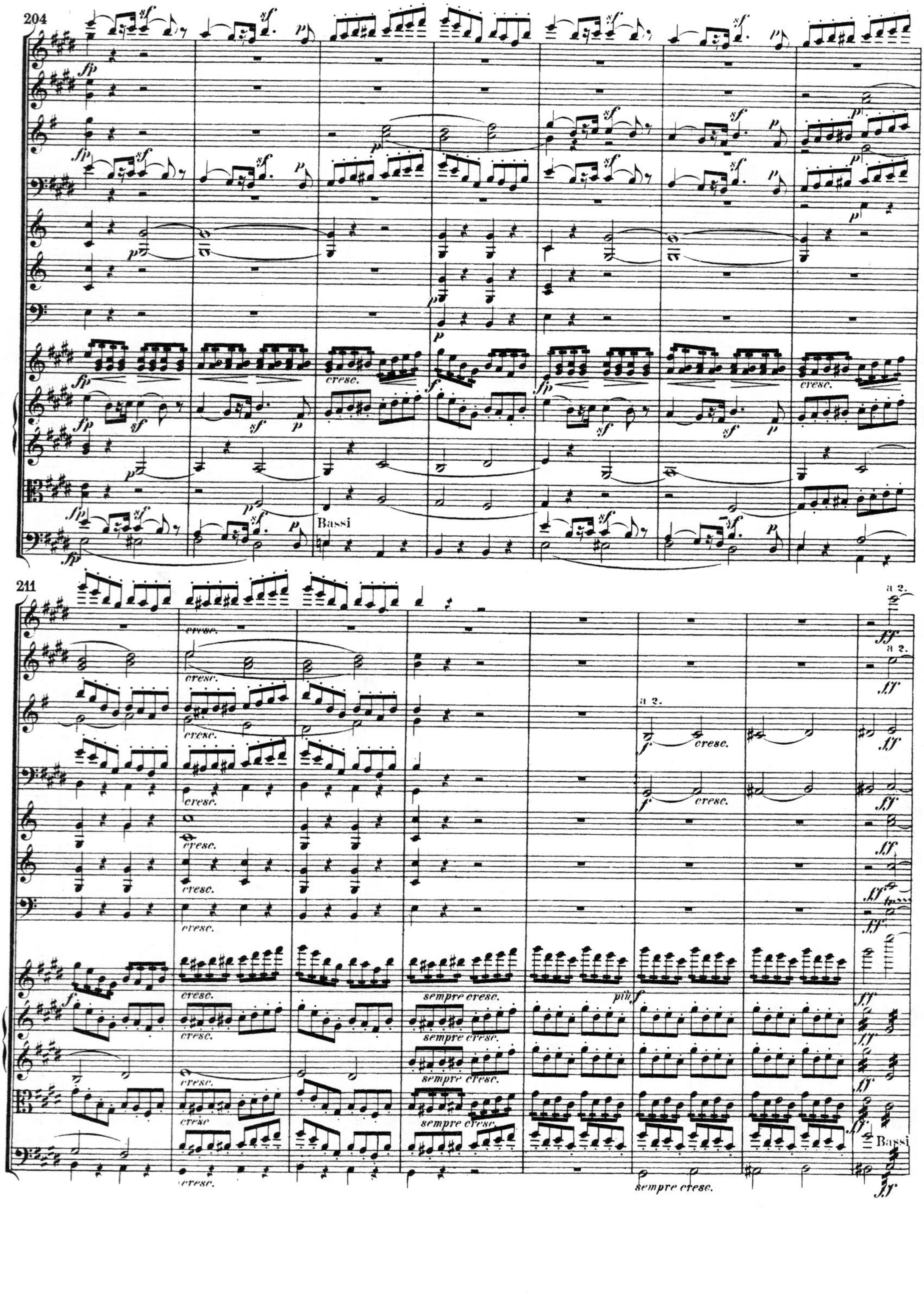
204
211
Bassi
cresc.
sempre cresc.
a 2.
più f
Bassi

Felix Mendelssohn's Violin Concerto in E Minor is one of the most popular of all concertos, and it is also a monument to a longstanding friendship. Mendelssohn and violinist Ferdinand David met and became friends when they were teenagers. When Mendelssohn became conductor of the Leipzig Gewandhaus Orchestra in 1835, he appointed his friend concertmaster (lead violinist), and eight years later he named David as the principal violin professor at his new conservatory in Leipzig. Since 1838 Mendelssohn had been intending to write a concerto for David, and in 1844 he set to work in earnest, often asking the violinist's advice on technical matters. At its premiere the next year, the work was a great success, prized for its formal innovations, its winning melodies, its profound expression, and the glittering virtuosity of the solo part. It is a concerto conceived in the same spirit as a symphony, in which the soloist's display of technique is subordinated to conveying the ideas of the composer.

The form of the concerto is innovative in two principal ways. First, the first movement is in sonata form instead of the blend of sonata and ritornello forms that had become standard for concertos in the Classic era (see NAWM 102 and 106). The first theme is presented at the outset by the soloist, and the cadenza— which Mendelssohn wrote out, rather than leaving to the discretion of the performer—is placed just before the recapitulation, the most dramatic moment in a sonata form, instead of just before the final ritornello, the most dramatic moment in a ritornello form. The second principal formal innovation is the connection of all three movements, which are bound together by linking passages that create a continuous flow of music.

The bridge between the second movement and the finale is a slow fourteen-measure passage, marked Allegretto non troppo, whose melody in the solo violin hints at the main theme of the first movement. The harmony here moves from A minor to a half-cadence in E major, linking the C-major tonality of the middle movement to the E-major tonality of the finale.

The finale is a fast sonata-rondo in a light, playful style that has been identified with Mendelssohn ever since the premiere of his *Midsummer Night's Dream Overture* in 1827. A standard pattern for sonata-rondos was ABACAB'A (see NAWM 108), with A serving as the first theme in a sonata; B as a second theme, presented in the dominant and recapitulated in the tonic; and C as the development. Mendelssohn follows this pattern, with some novel twists:

Section:	Intro	Refrain	Episode			Refrain	Episode		Refrain	Episode		Refrain	Coda
Music:	intro	A A'	trans	B	ext	A	C	C	A + C	B	ext	A	from B
Key:	on V	E	mod	B	mod	G	G	B	E	E	E	E	E
Measure:	1	9 26	41	55	81	101	107	118	133	150	168	190	198

After a brief, fanfare-like introduction, the soloist presents the sprightly refrain theme A, which is immediately repeated and varied. The first episode modulates to the dominant and then presents theme B, which alternates dotted rhythms in martial style with motives from the A theme. There follows a developmental extension that begins like a closing theme in a sonata form but then starts to modulate, as if to blur the line between exposition and development. Theme A then returns in G major, a key that played an important role in the first movement. Since the refrain in a rondo normally always returns in the tonic, the appearance of the A theme in G major has the effect of suggesting a moment in a sonata-form development when the first theme appears in some other key. Next, a new, lyrical theme C is introduced, first in the solo violin in G major and then in the orchestral strings in B major, the key of the dominant. It is accompanied both times by figuration derived from theme A, as development continues. At the next refrain (the equivalent of the recapitulation in a sonata form), theme A is back in the tonic in the solo violin, now joined by theme C as a countermelody in the orchestral strings. Theme B and its extension return in the tonic as expected, followed by a final recollection of the refrain, varied and abbreviated, and a coda based on motives from theme B.

Throughout, the concerto blends tradition with novelty and virtuosic display with musical substance. It is perhaps for this reason that the piece appeals to a wide variety of listeners. Particularly notable is the way the thematic material is shared between soloist and orchestra. The violin leads during the A theme but is always accompanied by the upper winds, which take over the theme at its last appearance. Theme B is first presented by the orchestra, then varied and completed by the violin. Theme C first appears in the violin over elements of A in the strings, then the two reverse roles. This way of presenting the themes integrates soloist and orchestra into a single vehicle for conveying the ideas and emotions intended by the composer.

The first entrance of the soloist is marked *scherzando* (jesting), and this quality continues throughout, calling for a light touch along with speed and skill. In several passages, rapid bow motions are required for a *bariolage* effect, alternating between a constantly repeating tone on an open string and a moving line on another string (as in measures 41–44), or for arpeggiating across all four strings, as in measures 49–52. At one striking moment (measures 93–95), the soloist alternates bowing across all four strings (*arco*) with plucking all four together (*pizzicato*). In contrast to Berlioz's *Symphonie fantastique* (see NAWM 121), the orchestra for this concerto is smaller in size, and Mendelssohn does not introduce any special effects.

123

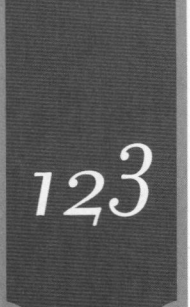

Clara Schumann (1819–1896)

Piano Trio in G Minor, Op. 17: Third movement, Andante

Piano Trio

1846

CD 9|41 CD 5|26

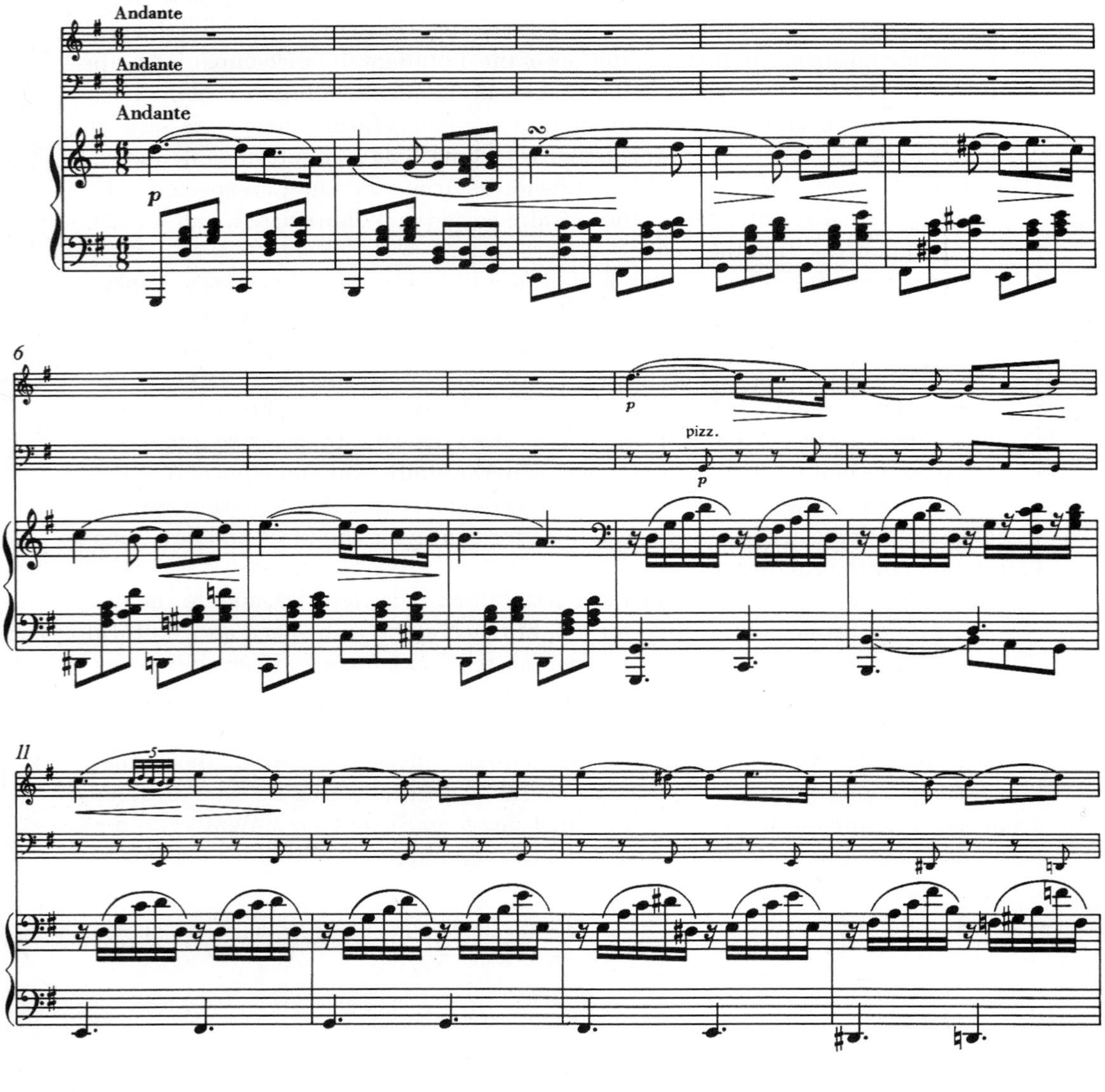

Clara Schumann wrote her Piano Trio in 1846, six years after her marriage to Robert Schumann, and it was published the following year as her Op. 17. An enlightened husband by the standards of the time, Robert encouraged her work as both a performer and a composer. Yet his work took precedence, and Clara sometimes had difficulty finding the time to practice or compose. She also had accepted the common contemporary belief that women were incapable of greatness as composers. She wrote about the Trio soon after completing it, "There is no greater joy than composing something oneself and then listening to it. There are some pretty passages in the Trio, and I believe it is also fairly successful as far as the form goes. Naturally, it is still only woman's work, which always lacks force and occasionally invention." Despite her self-doubt, the Trio is today regarded as her best composition.

The piano trio, scored for violin, cello, and piano, was first developed in the mid-eighteenth century as a genre for home music-making, but by the 1840s piano trios were frequently performed in concerts for the public. In Clara Schumann's Trio, instead of the usual fast-slow-fast sequence of three movements, there are four: two sonata-form outer movements, a scherzo, and a slow third movement. The slow movement, included here, is in modified ternary form (ABA') and in G major, the parallel major to the G minor key of the Trio.

The A section resembles a nocturne in texture and mood, with a songlike melody over resonant accompaniment. The piano begins alone with the first half of the melody, whose rhythms are simple yet remarkably varied from measure to measure, and whose frequent appoggiaturas contribute to a feeling of yearning or melancholy. The violin enters (measure 9) and repeats what has so far been heard of the melody, over new figuration in the piano and pizzicato notes in the cello. Then the rest of the melody is played by the cello in its high range, again suggesting Romantic yearning, joined by a countermelody in the violin and a new figuation in the piano (measure 17).

The contrasting middle section is in the relative E minor, with louder dynam-ics, more animated tempo, and more aggressive material featuring stark dotted rhythms. Here, as in the first section, all three instruments take the lead in turn (for example, see the violin at measure 25, the cello at measure 29, the piano at measure 45, and the exchange of material between violin and piano at measures 33 and 43).

At the return of the A section (measure 53), the cello varies the first half of the melody over a new accompaniment in the piano and pizzicatos in the violin. Then the violin varies the second half of the melody while the cello plays the counter-melody. In the coda (measure 68), the violin and piano trade a brief descending idea from the A theme, harking back to their initial dialogue while moving toward a restful close. The sharing back and forth of the leading melody and the frequent changes in the accompanimental figuration create a great variety of textures that sustain the interest of players and listeners alike.

The performers on the accompanying recording use instruments from Schumann's time. The strings on the violin and cello are made of gut rather than wire, and the piano is less tightly strung than modern ones. The resulting sound, less brilliant and penetrating than modern ears are accustomed to, is perhaps better suited to the rich blend of sonorities and the conversation among equal partners in this movement.

FELIX MENDELSSOHN (1809–1847)

Elijah, Op. 70: Chorus, *And then shall your light break forth*

Oratorio

1846, REV. 1847

Throughout the nineteenth century, one of the most popular types of music making was choral singing by amateurs, including church choirs, choruses sponsored by businesses or other groups, and independent choral societies. Across Britain, France, Germany, Austria, and North America, large festivals were held where singers—often in the hundreds, sometimes in the thousands—gathered to rehearse and perform choral works. Their repertoire ranged from the oratorios of Handel and Haydn to new pieces written in a similar spirit.

Among the most widely performed new choral works was Mendelssohn's oratorio *Elijah*, which was premiered at a festival in Birmingham, England, in August 1846 and which Mendelssohn revised before performances in other English cities the next spring. The score was published in 1847, Mendelssohn's last work put into print before his death. Like Haydn's oratorios, *Elijah* has both German and English texts, making it suitable for choruses in both linguistic regions, where the choral movement was especially strong. Mendelssohn originally set the music to the German text, but the English translation was used at the premiere and can be regarded as equally authentic.

Like most of Handel's oratorios, *Elijah* tells a story from the Old Testament—in this case, an account of the life of the prophet Elijah, taken from 1 Kings 17–21 and 2 Kings 1–2. Soloists play the important roles: Elijah; the widow who shelters him and whose son he revives from death; Ahab, king of Israel; and Ahab's wife Jezebel. The chorus comments on the story and its ramifications by singing chorales (an idea borrowed from Bach's Passions) and other texts. It also often plays a part in the drama—for instance, as the people of Israel pleading for relief from drought, and later as the priests of Baal, whose cry to their false god goes unanswered in one of the most dramatic contrasts of loudness and silence in all of choral literature.

The final chorus resembles that of a Handel oratorio (see NAWM 92c), alternating passages of homophony with fugal writing. It begins in the style of an accompanied recitative, punctuated by dramatic unison runs in the strings and featuring dissonances and harmonic surprises like those in recitatives by Bach or Handel. A brief imitative passage (measure 9) heralds "the glory of the Lord" and leads to a massive choral fugue in D major praising God. The fugal texture is maintained much longer than in a typical Handel fugue, showing Mendelssohn's equally important debt to Bach. After the initial four-voice exposition that begins over a long tonic pedal (measure 18), there is a stretto in all voices centered on F♯ minor (beginning measure 43). A rising sequence of entrances in the bass (measure 64) leads back to D major (altos, measure 76) over a dominant pedal. The fugue culminates with a homophonic statement of the subject in four-part harmony (measure 90) and a contrapuntal closing Amen, recalling procedures Handel used in *Messiah* and other oratorios.

Amid the evocations of the Baroque oratorio tradition are signs of Mendelssohn's own times. The tonal plan, moving a third away from the tonic to

F♯ minor rather than to the dominant, is typical of Romantic rather than Baroque harmony. So are some of the chromatic harmonies, although several of the most striking effects—like the three successive descending tritones in the bass at the beginning of the Amen (measures 113–118)—may have been inspired by Bach and Handel (compare the bass line in Bach's chorale prelude on *Durch Adams Fall*, NAWM 89).

As satisfying as it is to hear, this music was especially intended to be satisfying for amateurs to sing. Thus, each vocal line has an almost equal share in the melodic substance, with melodies that are interesting and challenging—but not too challenging. For the most part, the orchestra plays a supporting role, reinforcing the singers and providing punctuation between phrases.

GIOACHINO ROSSINI (1792–1868)

Il barbiere di Siviglia: Act I, No. 7, *Una voce poco fa*

Comic opera

1816

[handwritten notes:]
- quick write – lots of patter
- uses contemporary novels as plots
- 1st part is mock tragic = lots of dotted rhythms
- lots of written out coloratura
- slow, lyrical tempo then fast

CD 9|48

[handwritten: Cantabile]

[handwritten: orchestral intro]

From Gioachino Rossini, *The Barber of Seville* (New York: Broude Brothers, n.d.), 112–22.

move to
fast, showing
tempo

Cabaletta

car, fa _ rò gio _ car, fa _ rò gio _ car.

ROSINA

Una voce poco fa	A voice a short while ago
Qui nel cor mi risuonò.	here in my heart resounded.
Il mio cor ferito è già,	My heart is already wounded,
E Lindor fu che il piagò.	and Lindoro is the culprit.
Sì, Lindoro mio sarà,	Yes, Lindoro will be mine.
Lo giurai la vincerò.	I swore that I would win.
Il tutor ricuserò,	The guardian I shall refuse.
Io l'ingegno aguzzerò.	I shall sharpen my wits.
Alla fin s'accheterà,	In the end he will be appeased,
E contenta io resterò.	and I shall be happy.
Sì, Lindoro mio sarà,	Yes, Lindoro will be mine.
Lo giurai la vincerò.	I swore that I would win.
Io sono docile, son rispettosa,	I am docile, I am respectful,
Sono obbediente, dolce amorosa,	I am obedient, sweetly loving;
Mi lascio reggere, mi fo guidar.	I let myself be governed, be led.
Ma se mi toccano dov'è il mio debole,	But if they touch my weaker side,
Sarò una vipera, e cento trappole	I can be a viper, and a hundred tricks
Prima di cedere farò giocar!	I'll play before I give in!

—CESARE STERBINI

Gioachino Rossini signed the contract to compose *Il barbiere di Siviglia* (The Barber of Seville) for the Teatro Argentina in Rome on December 27, 1815, less than two months before the opera was to be premiered. He was accustomed to working fast, having composed sixteen operas over the previous four years, but a popular legend that he wrote the opera in thirteen days is probably an exaggeration. Cesare Sterbini wrote the libretto based on Pierre-Augustin Caron de Beaumarchais's *Le barbier de Séville* and on the libretto for Giovanni Paisiello's 1782 opera on the same play. The first performance of Rossini's version, on February 20, 1816, was a relative failure, perhaps because the production was hastily prepared or because it faced opposition from Paisiello's partisans. But the opera was a great success when it was revived at Bologna that summer. It quickly became Rossini's most famous comic opera, and many regard it as the best of all time.

In collaboration with his librettists, Rossini developed a standard pattern for solo scenes in operas. His format includes an orchestral introduction followed by an aria that expresses two or more contrasting moods in at least two sections: a slow *cantabile* (Italian for "singable") and a faster *cabaletta*. In most scenes, especially in dramatic (as opposed to comic) operas, a *scena* (scene) in recitative precedes the cantabile, and a *tempo di mezzo* (middle movement) appears between the cantabile and cabaletta, during which something happens that changes the situation or the character's mood. *Una voce poco fa* contains only a cantabile and cabaletta. This is an entrance aria (the aria a character sings on his or her first appearance), known as a *cavatina*. The librettist laid out the text in rhymed poetry, using seven-syllable lines for the cantabile and eleven-syllable lines for the cabaletta—the two most common line lengths in Italian poetry.

Rosina is the ward of old Dr. Bartolo, who strictly watches over her and wants to marry her. But she has also attracted the attention of a young Spanish nobleman named Count Almaviva, who plots to win her from her guardian. In *Una voce poco fa*, Rosina reveals her interest in her new suitor. In the cantabile, she recalls being serenaded by Lindoro, a poor young man who is actually Count Almaviva in disguise. The orchestral introduction announces rhythmic figures and motives that later appear during the cantabile. Although there is no separate recitative, Rossini sets the first six lines in a manner similar to accompanied recitative, with brief phrases, mostly syllabic text-setting, and only chordal accompaniment. This recitative-like style combines with the dotted rhythms to create an impression of tentativeness that nicely suits the text. Larger leaps (measures 18–21) and sudden effusions of *coloratura*, or florid figuration (measures 22–28), suggest Rosina's passion as she resolves to win Lindoro. When she declares that she will refuse to obey the wishes of her guardian (measure 30), she sings rapidly repeated notes as in a comic patter song, and the violins seem to wink at her with a lightly skipping figure and grace notes. The cantabile closes with a repetition of the section in which Rosina vows to make Lindoro her own.

The cabaletta begins with an orchestral statement (measure 43) followed by Rosina singing the same melody (measure 55). She claims to be docile, respectful, and obedient, but her music contradicts her text—her elaborate embellishments suggest a willful coquette. Her truer nature becomes clear as she boasts that when she is crossed, she stings like a viper (measure 60). The stings are evoked by accented high notes in the voice and pizzicatos in the orchestra, and the viper is illustrated by a quickly slithering descent in the vocal line. As she vows to play a hundred tricks before giving in, she first repeats a variant of the previous musical phrase (measure 70) and then introduces a new idea that contrasts pleading chromaticism (measures 74–76) with playful turns (measure 77) and dramatic scales (measures 81–82) that demonstrate the range of emotional tricks she can play. In measures 83–89, as Rosina begins to repeat the entire text of her cabaletta, Rossini introduces a type of passage that became closely identified with him: a crescendo on a constantly repeating figure, creating a rising wave of excitement. Here, the crescendo is humorously ironic: as Rosina vows that she is docile, obedient, and easily guided, the orchestra plays music better suited to a whirlwind. This leads to a repetition of the music set to the last three lines of the text (measure 90 repeats measure 66), followed by a rousing coda (measure 107). Such repetition of part or all of the cabaletta is typical for Rossini, as is the increase in energy toward the end of an aria.

The many contrasting musical ideas in both sections of the aria provide a well-rounded portrait of Rosina's character, combining attractive melodies, comic description, and vocal display. Given the close relationship between music and text, it may seem surprising that Rossini adapted the music from an aria to very different words, which he had composed the previous fall for Queen Elizabeth to sing in his opera *Elisabetta, regina d'Inghilterra* (Elizabeth, Queen of England), staged in

Naples. Rossini often borrowed from himself in this manner—especially when writing a new opera for a different city—but he always chose music that was well suited for the new text and dramatic situation, and reworked it to fit perfectly.

Except during introductions and interludes, the orchestra stays out of the way of the singer, offering light accompaniment. As was standard practice at the time, the singer in the accompanying recording freely adds embellishments, especially when a section of music repeats (as at measure 35–42 and measures 90–107), and takes opportunities for cadenzas at cadences (as in measure 114).

Handwritten annotations (top):
- avante garde
- big orchestration
- special effects orch
- in German
- not a strict form
- static harmonies

CARL MARIA VON WEBER (1786–1826)

Der Freischütz: Act II, Finale, Wolf's Glen Scene

126

Opera
1817–21

Handwritten annotations:
- lots of chromaticism
- winds used as affect for scary parts
- chorus of invisible spirits
- mythical, magical themes
- no cantabiles or cabalettas

Handwritten (left margin):
German recit is more melodic + "singy" Italian, but no certain melody

orchestra is unified — weeps piece together

CD 9|55

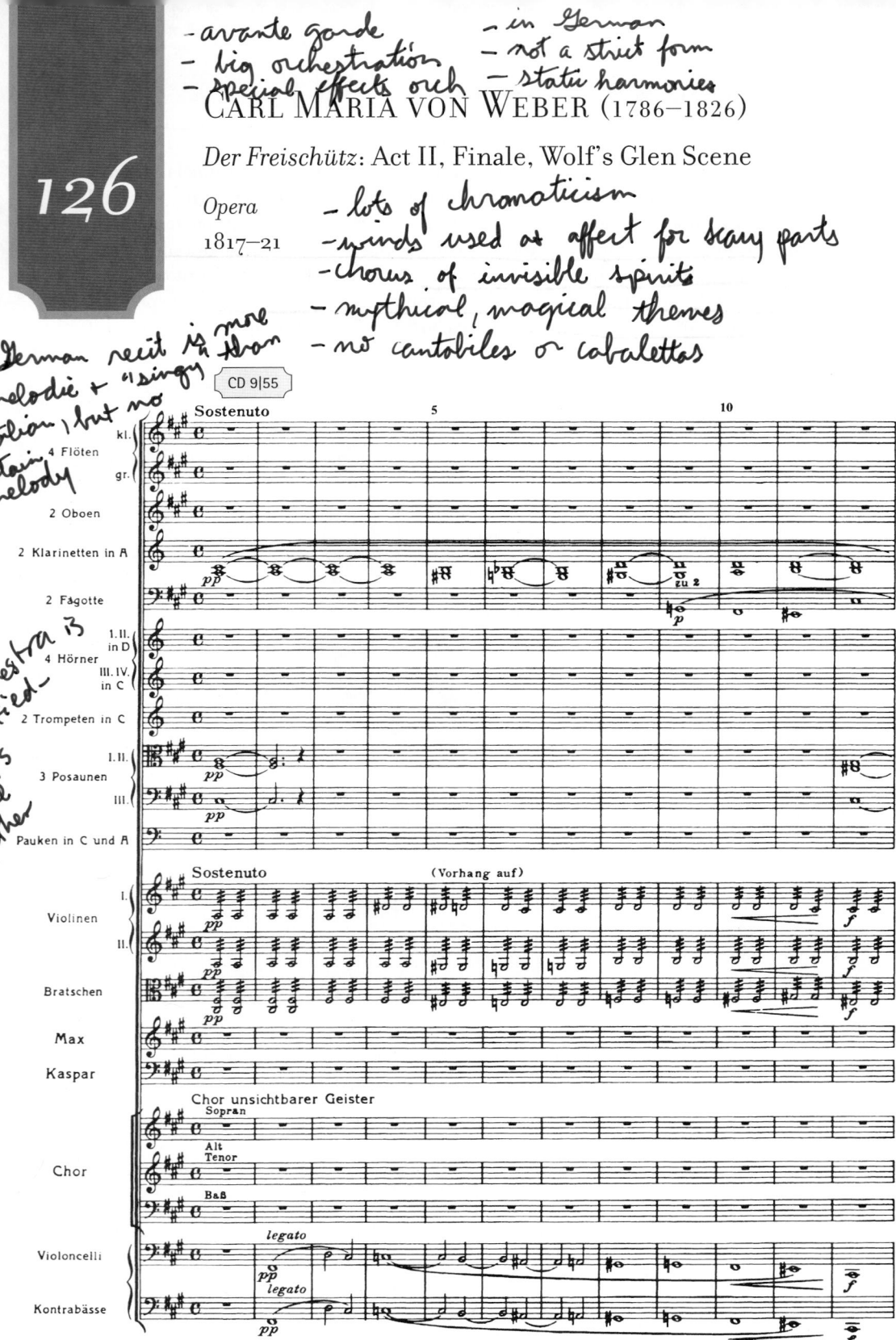

Reprinted from *Der Freischütz* (New York: Broude Brothers, n.d.).

58

(Kaspar richtet sich langsam und erschöpft auf und trocknet sich den Schweiß von der Stirn. Der Hirschfänger mit dem Toten-
kopf ist verschwunden, an dessen Stelle kommt ein kleiner Herd mit glimmenden Kohlen, dabei einige Reißbunde aus der Erde)

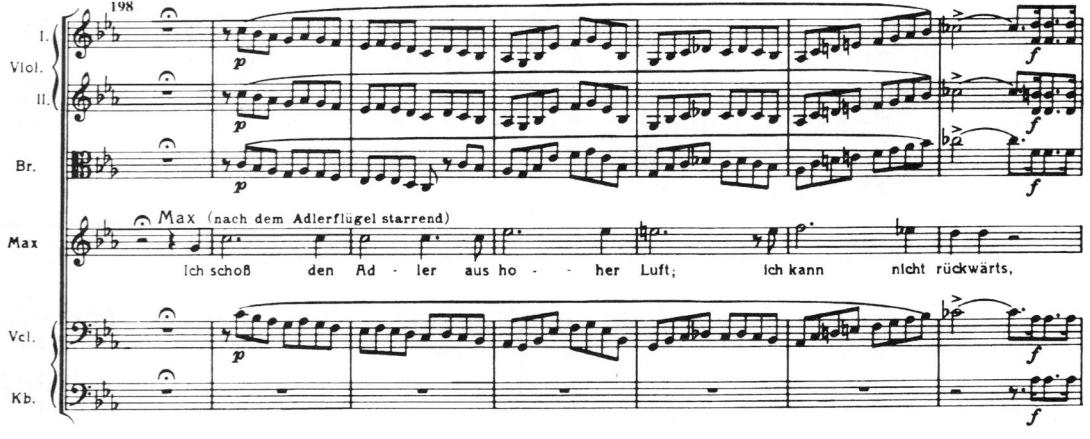

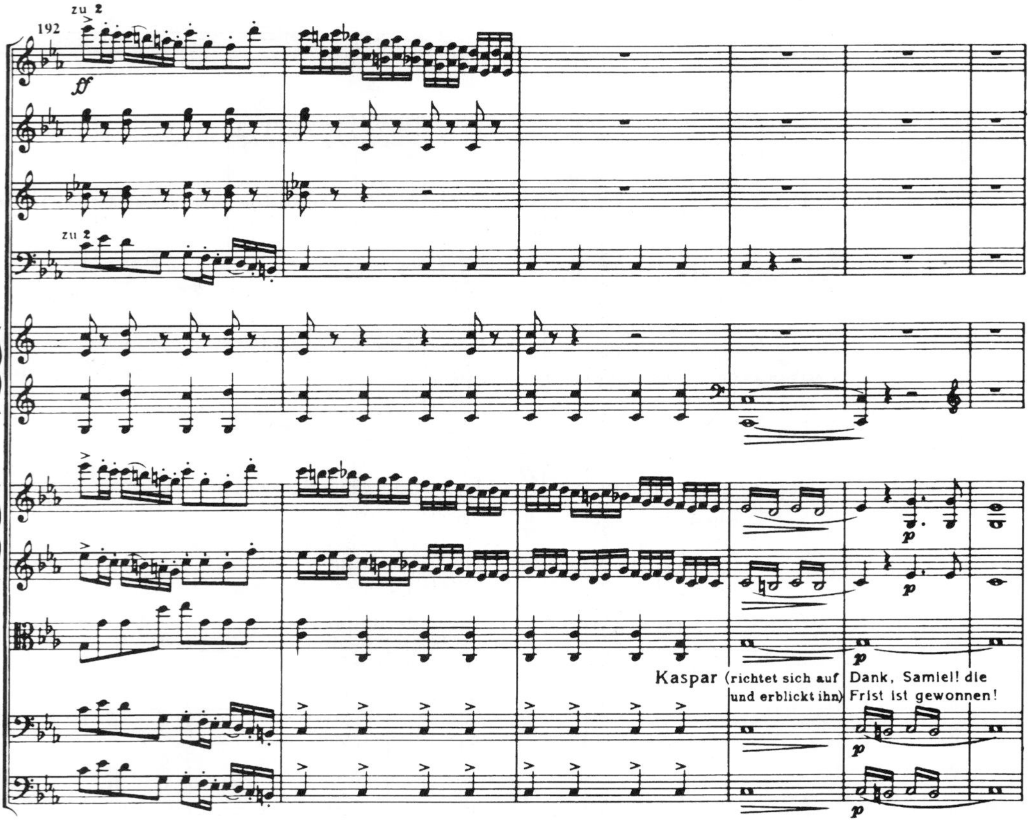
192
zu 2
Gr. Fl.
Ob.
Klar. in A
Fag.
I. II. in Es
Hr.
III. IV. in C
I.
Viol.
II.
Br.
Kaspar (richtet sich auf und erblickt ihn) Dank, Samiel! die Frist ist gewonnen!
Vcl.
Kb.

Kaspar (zu Max) Kommst du endlich, Kamerad? Ist das auch recht, mich so allein zu lassen? Siehst du nicht, wie mir's sauer wird? (Hat das Feuer mit dem Adlerflügel angefacht und erhebt diesen im Gespräch gegen Max)

198
I.
Viol.
II.
Br.
Max
Max (nach dem Adlerflügel starrend)
Ich schoß den Ad - ler aus ho - - her Luft; ich kann nicht rückwärts,
Vcl.
Kb.

NB. Diese beiden Wiederholungszeichen sind mit Bleistift im Autograph angegeben und werden nur ausgeführt, wenn Max nicht genug Zeit haben sollte.

Kaspar (wirft ihm die Jagdflasche zu,die Max weglegt).Zuerst trink einmal! Die Nachtluft ist kühl und feucht.Willst du selbst gießen?

Max. Nein, das ist wider die Abrede.

Kaspar. Nicht? So bleib außer dem Kreise, sonst kostet's dein Leben!

Max. Was hab ich zu tun, Hexenmeister?

Kaspar. Fasse Mut! Was du auch horen und sehen magst, verhalte dich ruhig.(Mit eigenem heimlichen Grauen.) Kame vielleicht ein Unbekannter, uns zu helfen,was kummert es dich? Kommt was anders, was tut's? So etwas sieht ein Gescheiter gar nicht!

Max. O, wie wird das enden!

Kaspar. Umsonst ist der Tod! Nicht ohne Widerstand schenken verborgene Naturen den Sterblichen ihre Schatze. Nur wenn du mich selbst zittern siehst, dann komme mir zu Hilfe und rufe,was ich rufen werde,sonst sind wir beide verloren.(Max macht eine Bewegung des Einwurfs) Still! Die Augenblicke sind kostbar!(Der Mond ist bis auf einen schmalen Streif verfinstert. Kaspar nimmt die Gießkelle.) Merk auf,was ich hineinwerfen werde,damit du die Kunst lernst! (Er nimmt die Ingredienzen aus der Jagdtasche und wirft sie nach und nach hinein.)

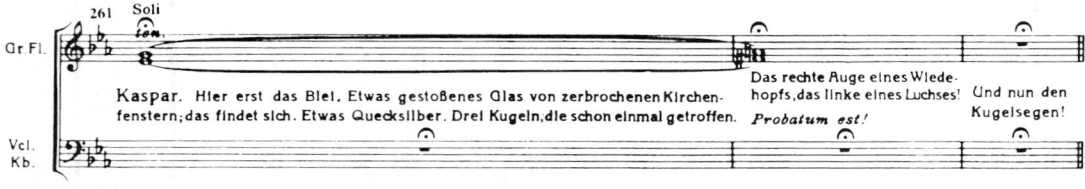

MELODRAM

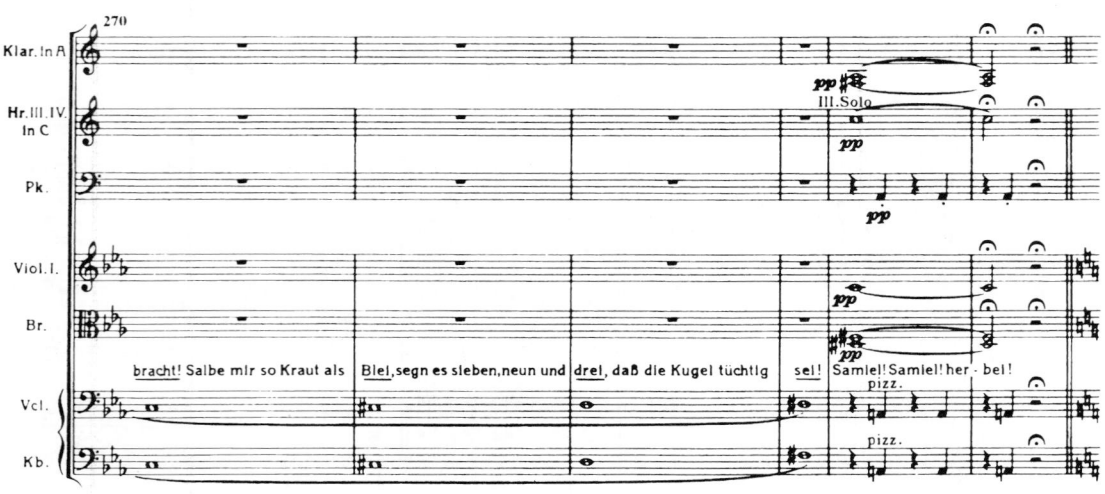

(Die Masse in der Gießkelle fängt an zu gähren und zu zischen und gibt einen grünlichweißen Schein. Eine Wolke läuft über den Mondstreif, daß die ganze Gegend nur noch von dem Herdfeuer, den Augen der Eule und dem faulen Holz des Baumes erleuchtet ist)

Kaspar (gießt, läßt die Kugel aus der Form fallen und ruft) Eins! Das Echo (wiederholt) Eins!

(Waldvögel kommen herunter, setzen sich um das Feuer, hüpfen und flattern.)   Kaspar (gießt und zählt) Zwei! Echo Zwei!

64

293 Poco più moto

Poco più moto

(Ein schwarzer Eber raschelt durchs Gebüsch und jagt wild vorüber)

Kaspar (zählt ängstlich) Vier! Echo Vier!

66

(Man hört Rasseln, Peitschengeknall und Pferdegetrappel. Vier feurige, funkenwerfende Räder rollen über die Bühne)

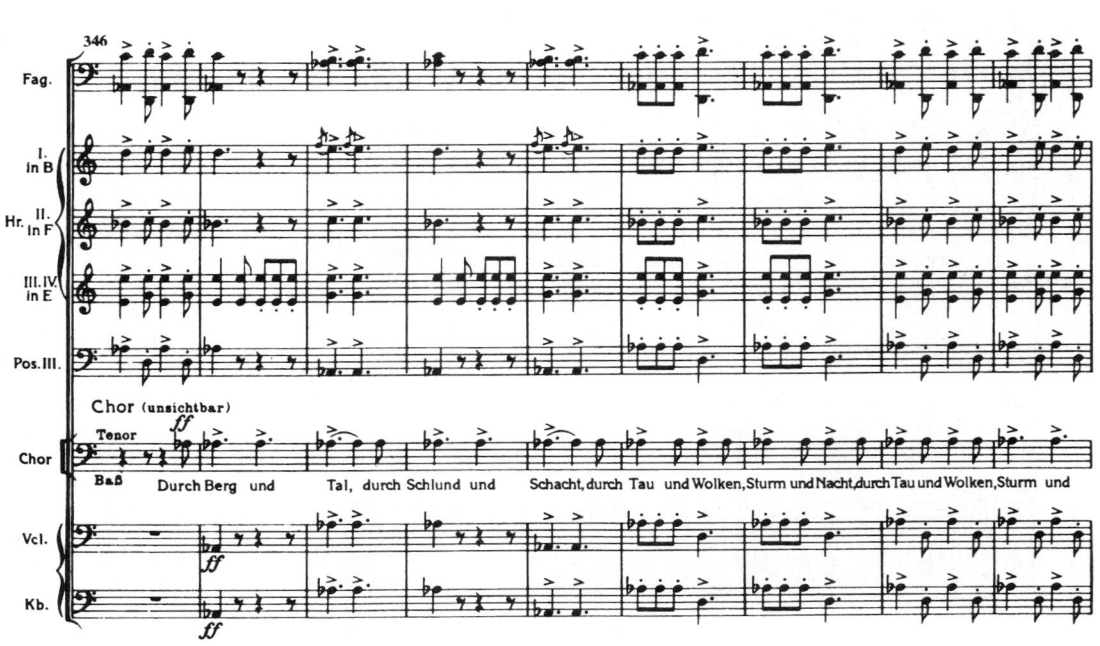

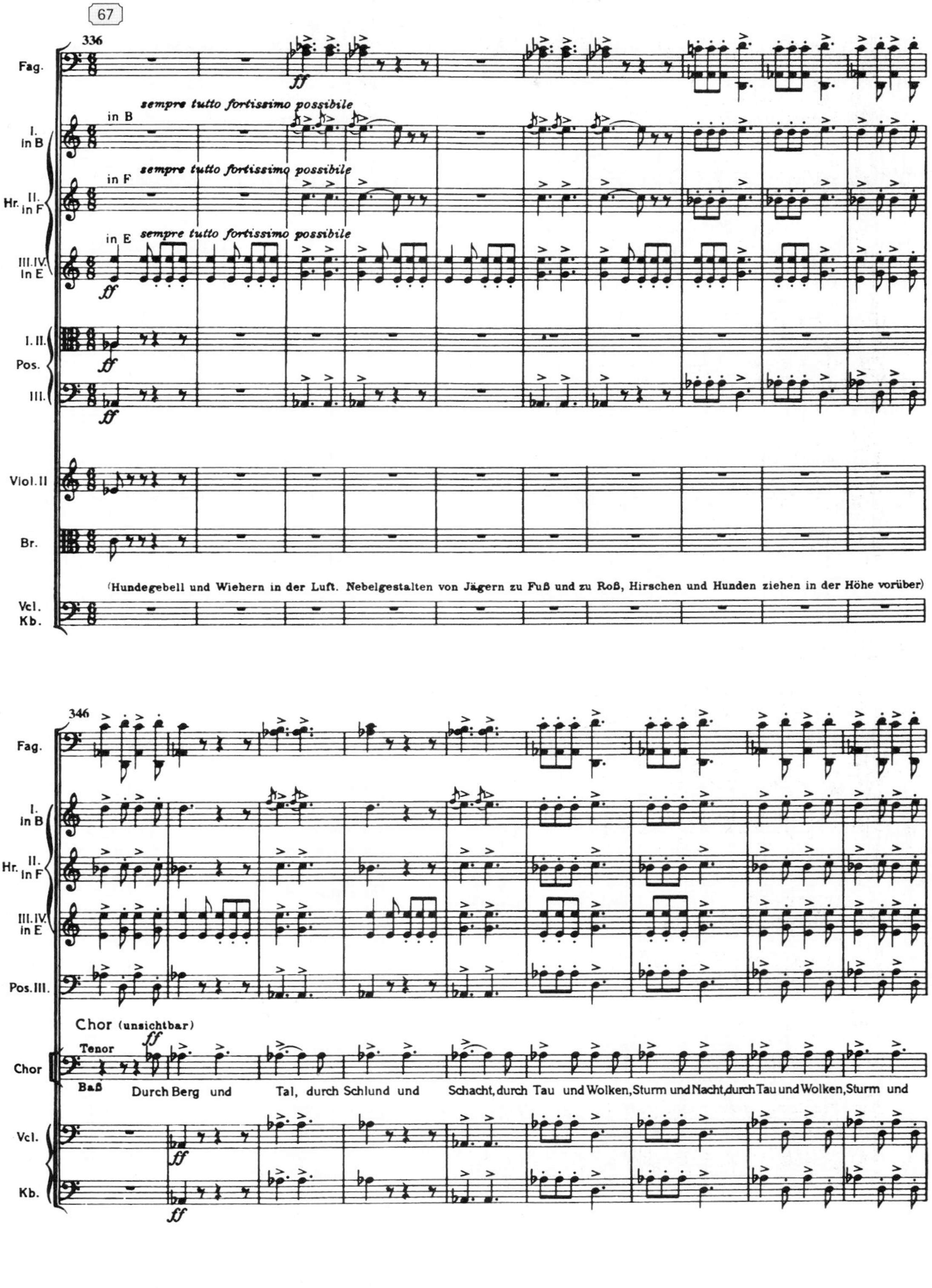
67
336
Fag.
sempre tutto fortissimo possibile
in B
I. in B
in F
Hr. II. in F
in E
III.IV. in E
ff
I. II.
Pos.
III.
Viol. II
Br.
(Hundegebell und Wiehern in der Luft. Nebelgestalten von Jägern zu Fuß und zu Roß, Hirschen und Hunden ziehen in der Höhe vorüber)
Vcl. Kb.
346
Pos. III.
Chor (unsichtbar)
Tenor
Baß
Chor
Durch Berg und Tal, durch Schlund und Schacht, durch Tau und Wolken, Sturm und Nacht, durch Tau und Wolken, Sturm und
Vcl.
Kb.

(Der ganze Himmel wird schwarze Nacht; die Gewitter treffen furchtbar zusammen. Flammen schlagen aus der Erde. Irrlichter

(Vorhang fällt)

zu Boden)

(Es schlägt eins. Plötzliche Stille. S a m i e l ist verschwunden. K a s p a r liegt noch mit dem Gesicht zu Boden. M a x richtet sich konvulsivisch auf.)

Ende des zweiten Aufzuges

*(A frightful glen with a waterfall. A pallid full moon. A storm is brewing.
In the foreground a withered tree shattered by lightning seems to glow. In other trees,
owls, ravens, and other wild birds. Caspar, without a hat or coat, but with hunting pouch
and knife, is laying out a circle of black fieldstones, in the center of which lies a skull.
A few steps away, a hacked-off eagle wing, a ladle, and bullet molds.)*

CHORUS OF INVISIBLE SPIRITS

Milch des Mondes fiel auf's Kraut,	The milk of the moon fell on the herbs,
Uhui! Uhui!	Uhui! Uhui!
Spinnweb' ist mit Blut bethaut!	Spider webs dabbed with blood!
Uhui! Uhui!	Uhui! Uhui!
Eh' noch wieder Abend graut,	Before another evening darkens,
Ist sie todt, die zarte Braut!	will she die, the lovely bride!
Eh' noch wieder sinkt die Nacht,	Before another night falls,
Ist das Opfer dargebracht!	will the sacrifice be offered!
Uhui! Uhui! Uhui!	Uhui! Uhui! Uhui!

(A clock in the distance strikes twelve. The circle of stones is completed.)

(Caspar violently pulls out the hunting knife and thrusts it into the middle of the skull.)

CASPAR
(lifts up the hunting knife with the skull, turns around three times, and calls)

Samiel! Samiel! erschein!	Samiel, Samiel, appear!
Bei des Zaub'rers Hirngebein!	By the wizard's skull-bone,
Samiel! Samiel! erschein!	Samiel, Samiel, appear!

(He puts both back in the middle of the circle.)

SAMIEL
(steps out of a rock)

Was rufst du?	Why do you call?

(Caspar throws himself at Samiel's feet.)

CASPAR
(groveling)

Du weisst, dass meine Frist	You know that my days of grace
Schier abgelaufen ist.	are coming to an end.

SAMIEL

Morgen!	Tomorrow!

CASPAR

Verläng're sie noch einmal mir!	Will you extend them once more?

SAMIEL

Nein!	No!

CASPAR

Ich bringe neue Opfer dir.	I bring you new sacrifices.

SAMIEL

Welche?

Which ones?

CASPAR

Mein Jagdgesell, er naht,
Er, der noch nie dein dunkles Reich betrat.

My hunting companion—he approaches—
he who has never before set foot in your dark
    kingdom.

SAMIEL

Was sein Begehr?

What does he want?

CASPAR

Freikugeln sind's, auf die er Hoffnung baut.

Magic bullets, in which he puts his hope.

SAMIEL

Sechse treffen, sieben äffen!

Six strike, seven deceive!

CASPAR

Die siebente sei dein:
Aus seinem Rohr lenk' sie nach seiner Braut!
Dies wird ihn der Verzweiflung weih'n,
Ihn und den Vater.

The seventh is yours:
From his own gun it will aim at his bride.
That will drive him to despair,
both him and his father.

SAMIEL

Noch hab' ich keinen Teil an ihr.

I side with neither party.

CASPAR
(afraid)

Genügt er dir allein?

Will he be sufficient for you?

SAMIEL

Das findet sich!

We'll see!

CASPAR

Doch schenkst du Frist,
Und wieder auf drei Jahr,
Bring' ich ihn dir zu Beute dar!

If you will grant me grace
for another three years,
I will bring him to you as prey!

SAMIEL

Es sei! Bei den Pforten der Hölle!
Morgen er oder du!

So be it! By the gates of hell!
Tomorrow: he or you!

(He disappears amid muffled thunder.)

*(Caspar stands up slowly, exhausted, and wipes the sweat off his brow.
The hunting knife and skull have disappeared, and in their place is a small fireplace
with glowing coals, and near it some bundles of kindling.)*

CASPAR
(sees them)

Trefflich bedient!	Splendidly served.

(He takes a drink from his canteen.)

Gesegn' es, Samiel!	Thank you, Samiel.

(drinks)

Er hat mir warm gemacht!	It warms my heart.
Aber wo bleibt denn Max?	But what is keeping Max?
Sollte er wortbrüchig werden?	Would he break his word?
Samiel, hilf!	Samiel, help!

(Caspar, not without anxiety, goes back and forth in the circle. The coals threaten to die out, and he kneels down, puts more wood on the fire, and blows on it. Owls and other birds flap their wings, as if they wanted to fan the fire. The fire smokes and crackles.)

(Max appears on top of a rock, opposite the waterfall, and looks down into the glen.)

MAX

Ha! Furchtbar gähnt	Ah, how frightful yawns
Der düst're Abgrund! Welch' ein Grau'n!	this gloomy abyss! How dreadful!
Das Auge wähnt	The eyes imagine [they are]
In einen Höllenpfuhl zu schau'n!	looking into a pool of hell!
Wie dort sich Wetterwolken ballen,	Behold the storm clouds forming.
Der Mond verliert von seinem Schein,	The moonlight is dimming.
Gespenst'ge Nebelbilder wallen,	Ghostly, misty apparitions float in.
Belebt ist das Gestein,	The stones appear alive,
Und hier, husch! husch!	And here, hush, hush,
Fliegt Nachtgevögel auf in Busch!	the nightbirds fly into the bush!
Rotgraue, narb'ge Zweige Strecken	Scarred red-gray boughs stretch
Nach mir die Riesenfaust!	their giant claws at me!
Nein! Ob das Herz auch graust	No! Even if the heart feels horror
Ich muss; ich trotze allen Schrecken.	I must [proceed], despite all the terrors.

(He clambers down several steps.)

CASPAR
(stands up and sees him)

Dank, Samiel! die Frist ist gewonnen.	Thanks, Samiel, the grace period is granted.

(to Max)

Kommst du endlich, Kamerad? Ist das	You have finally arrived, friend? Was it
auch recht, mich so allein zu lassen?	right to make me wait so long? Can't
Siehst du nicht, wie mir's sauer wird?	you see how painful it has been?

(He has fanned the fire with the eagle's wing and lifts it up while speaking to Max.)

MAX
(staring at the eagle's wing)

Ich schoss den Adler aus hoher Luft;	I shot the eagle at a high altitude;
Ich kann nicht rückwärts, mein Schicksal ruft!	I cannot go backward, my fate calls!

(He climbs a few steps, then stands still, gazing fixedly at the opposite rock.)

(The ghost of his mother appears in the rock.)

Weh mir!	Woe is me!

CASPAR

So komm doch, die Zeit eilt!	Come on, time flies!

MAX

Ich kann nicht hinab!	I can't go ahead.

CASPAR

Hasenherz! Klimmst ja sonst wie eine Gemse!	Coward! You always climbed like a mountain goat.

MAX

Sie dort hin, sieh!	See there, see!

(He points to the moonlit rock. A white, veiled figure becomes evident, raising her hand.)

Was dort sich weist, ist meiner Mutter Geist.	What you see there is my mother's ghost.
So lag sie im Sarg, so ruht sie im Grab.	She lies in the coffin, resting in the grave.
Sie fleht mit warnendem Blick,	She implores with a cautioning glimpse.
Sie winkt mir zurück!	She nods to me to return.

CASPAR
(to himself)

Hilf, Samiel!	Help, Samiel!

(aloud)

Alberne Fratzen! Ha! Ha! Ha!	Silly rascal! Ha! ha! ha!
Sieh noch einmal hin, damit du die	Look once more, and recognize
Folgen deiner feigen Torheit erkennst!	your faint-hearted folly.

(The veiled figure disappears. Agathe's form now is apparent, her hair disheveled and adorned with leaves and straw. She acts like a madwoman about to throw herself into the waterfall.)

MAX

Agathe! Sie springt in den Fluss!	Agathe! She is jumping into the river!
Hinab, hinab, ich muss!	I must go down!

(The apparition evaporates. Max climbs down all the way. The moon begins to darken.)

CASPAR
(jeering, to himself)

Ich denke wohl auch, du musst!   I think likewise, you must!

MAX
(forcefully to Caspar)

Hier bin ich! Was hab ich zu tun?   Here I am! What do I have to do?

CASPAR
(tosses him the canteen, which Max puts aside)

Zuerst trink' einmal! Die Nachtluft ist   First drink. The night air is cold
kühl und feucht. Willst du selbst giessen? and damp. Do you want to cast the
                                            bullets yourself?

MAX

Nein, das ist wider die Abrede.   No, that was not the agreement.

CASPAR

Nicht? So bleib' ausser dem Kreise,   No? Then stay outside of the circle,
sonst kostet's dein Leben!   or it will cost you your life!

MAX

Was hab' ich zu tun, Hexenmeister?   What must I do, Wizard?

CASPAR

Fasse Mut! Was du auch hören und   Courage! Whatever you may hear or see,
sehen magst, verhalte dich ruhig.   stay calm.

(with his own secret dread)

Käme vielleicht ein Unbekannter, uns zu   Should a stranger come to help us, don't
helfen, was kümmert es dich? Kommt   let it bother you. Whatever happens, fear
was anders, was tut's? So etwas sieht ein not. If you are wise, you will pay no
Gescheidter nicht.   attention.

MAX

O, wie wird das enden!   How will this ever end?

CASPAR

Umsonst ist der Tod! Nicht ohne   Death is in vain. Not without resistance
Widerstand schenken verborgene   will the invisible powers give up their
Naturen den Sterblichen ihre Schätze.   treasures. But when you see me falter,
Nur wenn du mich selbst zittern siehst, then come to my aid and repeat the call
dann komme mir zu Hülfe und rufe, was   that I make; otherwise we shall both be
ich rufen werde, sonst sind wir beide   lost.
verloren.

(Max stirs to raise an objection.)

Still! Die Augenblicke sind kostbar!   Be quiet. The moments are precious.

(The moon is barely visible except for a thin stripe. Caspar seizes the crucible.)

Merk' auf, was ich hineinwerfen werde,
damit du die Kunst lernst!

Now mark what I throw in, that you may learn the art!

(He takes the ingredients from his pouch and throws them in one by one.)

Hier erst das Blei. Etwas Glas von
zerbrochnen Kirchenfenstern, das findet
sich. Etwas Quecksilber. Drei Kugeln,
die schon einmal getroffen. Das rechte
Auge eines Wiedehopfs, das linke eines
Luchses! *Probatum est!* Und nun den
Kugelsegen!

Here first, the lead. Some glass from
broken church windows. Some mercury.
Three bullets that have already hit the
mark. The right eye of a lapwing, and
the left of a lynx. *Probatum est!* Now to
bless the bullets.

Melodrama

CASPAR

(pausing three times, bowing to the earth)

Schütze, der im Dunken wacht,
Samiel! Samiel! Hab' acht!
Steh mir bei in dieser Nacht,
Bis der Zauber ist vollbracht!
Salbe mir so Kraut als Blei,
Segn' es sieben, neun und drei,
Dass die Kugel tüchtig sei!
Samiel! Samiel! Herbei!

Hunter, who watches in the darkness,
Samiel! Samiel! Pay attention!
Stay with me through this night
until the magic is achieved.
Anoint for me the herbs and lead.
Bless the seven, nine and three,
so that the bullet will be skillful.
Samiel! Samiel! Come to me!

*(The material in the crucible begins to hiss and bubble, sending forth a greenish-white
flame. A cloud passes over the moon, so that the whole scene is lit only by the hearth fire,
the eyes of the owls, and the decomposing wood of the tree.)*

CASPAR
(pours, lets the first bullet fall out of the form, and calls)

Eins!   One!

ECHO

Eins!   One!

(Forest birds come down and crowd around the fire, fluttering and hopping about.)

CASPAR
(pours and counts)

Zwei!   Two!

ECHO

Zwei!   Two!

(A black boar rustles through the bushes and wildly races past.)

CASPAR
(seems to be startled, and counts)

Drei!   Three!

ECHO

Drei!   Three!

(A storm starts to rage, treetops bend and break, sparks shoot from the fire, and so forth.)

CASPAR
(counts anxiously)

Vier!   Four!

ECHO

Vier!   Four!

*(Rattling, cracking of whips, and the sound of galloping horses are heard.
Four fiery wheels roll across the stage, throwing off sparks.)*

CASPAR
(more and more alarmed, counts)

Fünf!   Five!

ECHO

Fünf!   Five!

*(Dogs barking and horses neighing, up in the air. Misty shapes of hunters on foot
and on horse, stags, and hounds pass by high above.)*

CHORUS
(invisible)

Durch Berg und Tal,	Through hill and dale,
Durch Schlund und Schacht,	through glen and mire,
Durch Tau und Wolken,	through dew and cloud,
Sturm und Nacht!	storm and night!
Durch Höhle, Sumpf und Erdenkluft,	Through marsh, swamp, and chasm,
Durch Feuer, Erde, See und Luft,	through fire, earth, sea, and air,
Jo ho! Wau wau! Jo ho! Wau wau!	Yo ho! Bow wow! Yo ho! Bow wow!
Jo ho ho ho ho ho ho ho!	Yo ho ho ho ho ho ho ho!

CASPAR

Wehe! Das wilde Heer! Sechs! Wehe!   Alas! The Devil's hunt! Six! Alas!

ECHO

Sechs! Wehe!   Six! Alas!

*(The whole sky turns to blackest night. The storm lashes with terrifying force.
Flames shoot up out of the ground. Will-o'-the-wisps appear on the mountains,
and so forth.)*

CASPAR
(jerking convulsively and crying out)

Samiel! Samiel!   Samiel! Samiel!

(He is thrown to the ground.)

Hilf! Sieben!   Help! Seven!

MAX
*(Also tossed about by the storm, he jumps out of the magic circle, grasps a branch
of the dead tree, and shouts.)*

Samiel!   Samiel!

*(In an instant the storm begins to die down. In place of the withered branch
stands the Black Huntsman, grasping Max's hand.)*

SAMIEL
(in a frightful voice)

Hier bin ich!   Here I am!

(Max makes the sign of the cross and falls to the ground.)

*(The clock strikes one. Sudden silence. Samiel has disappeared. Caspar remains
motionless, face to the ground. Max rises convulsively.)*

—LIBRETTO BY JOHANN FRIEDRICH KIND

The world of nature intertwines with supernatural incidents and human actions in Carl Maria von Weber's *Der Freischütz*, a pioneering work of German Romantic opera that was first performed in Berlin in 1821. Johann Friedrich Kind based the libretto on a story by Johann August Apel, who in turn drew on folklore and the model of Goethe's *Faust*. The story centers on the legend of a *Freikugel*, a magic bullet. The opera's name is difficult to translate succinctly; since *Schütze* means huntsman, marksman, or rifleman, *Der Freischütz* might be rendered "The Magic Rifleman."

Caspar and Max are assistant foresters who are both in love with Agathe, the daughter of the prince's head forester Kuno. Max has gained Agathe's affection, but according to tradition, he must win a test of marksmanship in order to earn Agathe's hand in marriage. If he wins, he will be Kuno's successor as head forester. Yet as the date for the test approaches, he is unable to hit anything at all. Caspar, who has sold his soul to the devil in the form of Samiel, the legendary Black Huntsman, convinces Max to use magic bullets for the competition. Caspar informs Max that the bullets will obey the marksman's wishes, but he does not reveal to Max that the last bullet fired will be controlled by Samiel. Caspar believes that the last bullet is destined for Agathe, but in the end, it is he whom it kills.

In the "Wolf's Glen" scene, included here, Caspar and Max meet in the eerie middle of the night to cast the magic bullets. The somber, diabolical forest serves as the background and is depicted through suggestive orchestration and a harmonic scheme that contrasts F♯ minor at the beginning and end of the scene with C minor, a tritone away, for much of the middle. The key of A minor, midway between them, also plays a role in some of the spookiest passages (see measures 236 and 276), and A appears in the timpani and pizzicato cellos and basses as the bass note in a diminished seventh chord whenever Caspar calls for Samiel (as at measure 43). E♭ major also appears, at Max's entrance (measure 57), completing a full complement of keys related by minor thirds and tritones. Weber's use of tritone-related and third-related harmonies, diminished seventh chords, and string tremolos to evoke mystery, danger, and the supernatural contributed to the establishment of these associations as conventions followed by countless Romantic composers and still used by composers for film and television.

The scene begins with soft tremolos and chromatic harmony laced with diminished seventh chords, leading to an invisible, ghostly chorus. The clock strikes midnight (measure 40), Caspar calls on Samiel over a diminished seventh chord, and the harmony suddenly shifts to C minor at Samiel's appearance (measure 50). In a deft touch of characterization, Samiel only speaks; his inability to sing indicates that he is devilish, neither human nor godly, beyond the reach of divine harmony. Almost seven centuries earlier, Hildegard of Bingen had used the same technique to characterize the Devil in her *Ordo virtutum* (NAWM 7).

Though he has already sold his soul, Caspar was given a period of grace, which expires in one day. Here, as he pleads for Samiel to take a new victim—Max—instead of himself (measure 51), the orchestra develops a single motive through many transformations and modulations, lending coherence to the music and excitement to the scene. The orchestra's obstinate insistence on this agitated, rhythmically pointed motive seems to depict the chains that ensnare Caspar. His vocal line, in a style between recitative and aria, tends to draw its tones from the orchestra rather than being accompanied by it, a technique later used by Verdi, Wagner, and many others (see NAWM 127 and 128). Samiel frequently interrupts Caspar to lay down the terms for granting the magic bullets, but he finally agrees to accept Max's soul and promptly disappears to the sound of thunder.

Caspar waits for Max, who when he finally enters is frightened by what he sees. The texture in this part of the scene (beginning at measure 110) is essentially that of accompanied recitative, but Caspar only speaks, either during rests in the music or as the music plays, and Max only sings, perhaps to indicate that he has not yet succumbed to the devil's power. The musical material changes often to reflect the happenings on stage. When Caspar takes a drink (measures 127–28), Weber briefly recalls a drinking song heard earlier in the opera. After Max enters (measure 157), some of his music recalls the previous scene with Agathe. Clambering down into the Glen, Max sees apparitions of his mother (measure 210) and of Agathe (measure 236), and each apparition is given highly descriptive music. Once Max arrives at the magic stone circle where Caspar will cast the bullets, he begins to speak as well (measure 259), and he sings no more during the rest of the scene. In the context of this scene, this is a sign that he has, at least temporarily, gone over to the dark side.

Particularly notable is Weber's use of *melodrama* as the bullets are being cast (measures 264–430). Melodrama was a genre in musical theater that featured spoken dialogue accompanied by music. Here, Caspar's lines are spoken over continuous music in the orchestra. Caspar invokes Samiel's aid and then casts each bullet in turn, calling out the number of bullets completed as the mountains echo his voice. After each bullet is cast, Weber paints a miniature tone-picture of the terrifying setting, the dark forest's wildlife, and the supernatural events that intensify with each bullet, joining music, lighting effects, and stage effects to create a series of spooky visions: after the first bullet, the greenish light of the fire and the fluttering of birds; after the second, a black boar running wild and startling Caspar; after the third, a storm brewing; after the fourth, galloping horses, cracking whips, and fiery wheels rolling across the stage; after the fifth, barking dogs and neighing horses. At this point, an unseen unison chorus of devilish hunters sings in a monotone accompanied by horns playing tritones. As Caspar shouts "Six!," the storm increases, the sky blackens, and flames shoot from the earth. Before the casting of the fatal seventh bullet, stormy music foreshadowed in the overture and in Max's Act I aria breaks in, above which Caspar shouts "Seven!" (measure 408). Max calls for Samiel, who appears and grasps his hand. Max crosses himself and falls. Suddenly there is silence, and the scene concludes with a return to the F# minor tremolos with which it began.

GIUSEPPE VERDI (1813–1901)

La traviata: Act III, Scene and Duet

Opera
1853

From *La Traviata* (Milan: G. Ricordi, n.d.; repr. New York: Dover, 1990), 366–403. Dover Publications, Inc.

539

tempo d'attaco

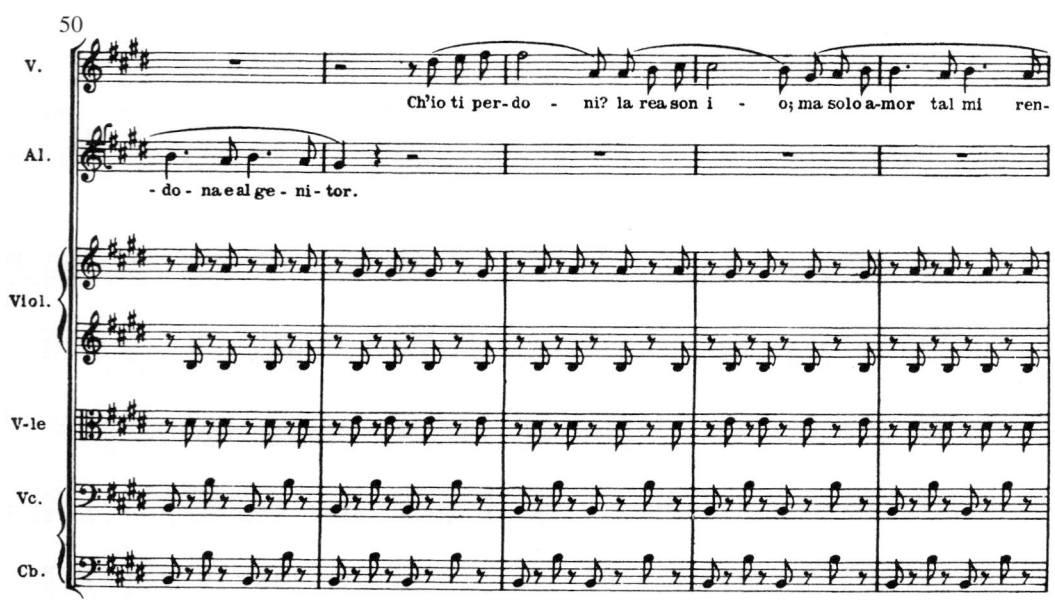

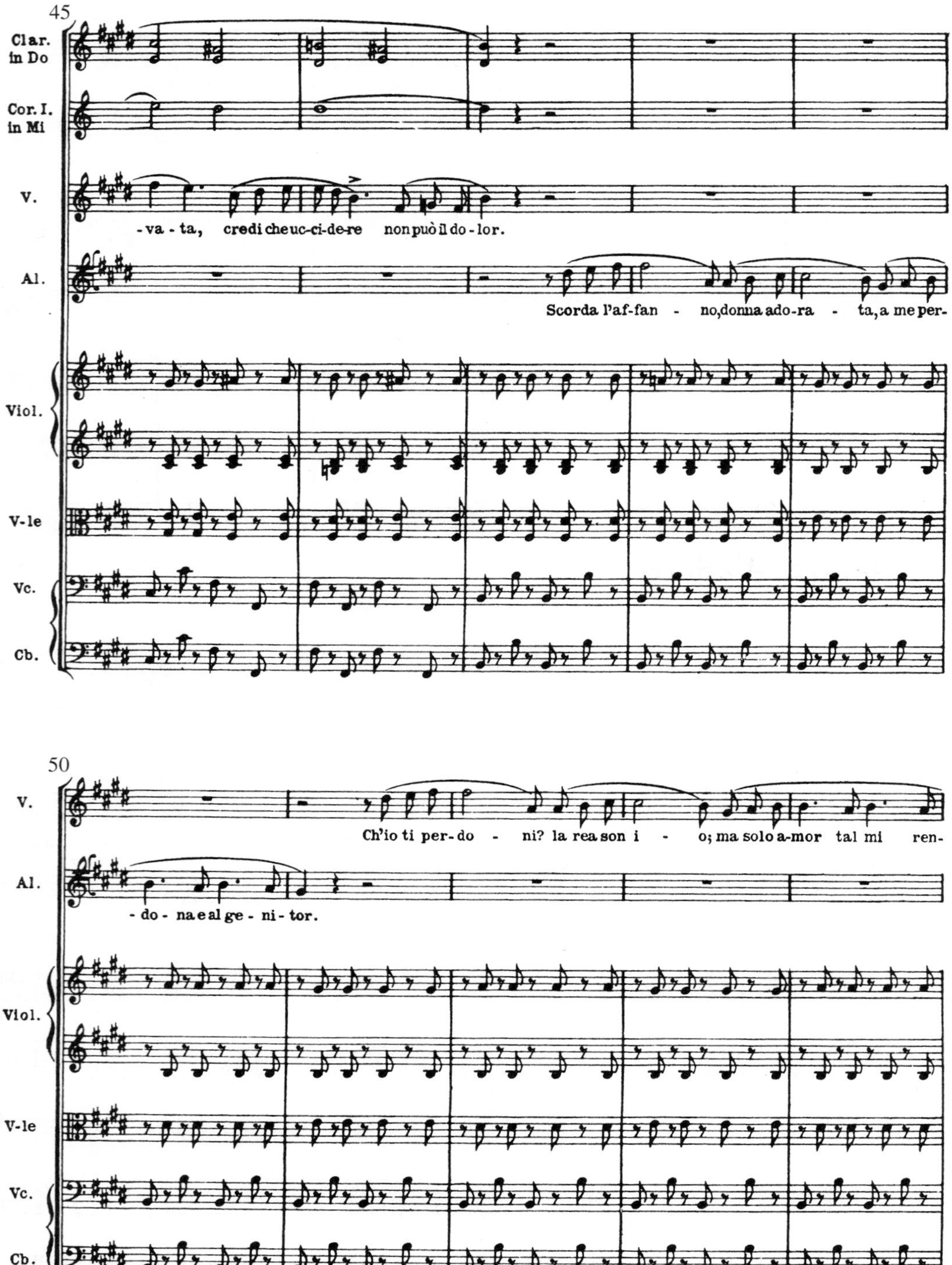
45
Clar. in Do
Cor. I. in Mi
V.
-va - ta, credi che uc-ci-de-re non può il do - lor.
Al.
Scorda l'af-fan - no, donna ado-ra - ta, a me per-
Viol.
V-le
Vc.
Cb.
50
V.
Ch'io ti per-do - ni? la rea son i - o; ma solo a-mor tal mi ren-
Al.
- do - na e al ge - ni - tor.
Viol.
V-le
Vc.
Cb.

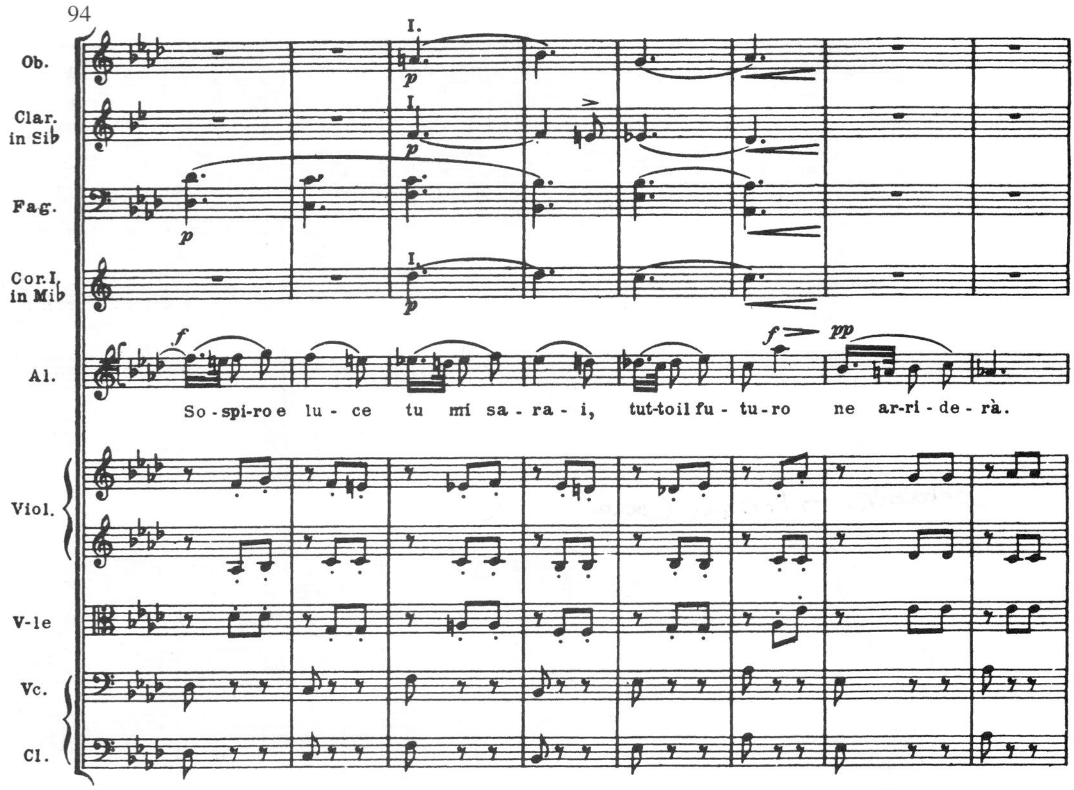
94
Ob.
Clar. in Sib
Fag.
Cor. I. in Mib
Al.
So-spi-ro e lu-ce tu mi sa-ra-i, tut-to il fu-tu-ro ne ar-ri-de-rà.
Viol.
V-le
Vc.
Cl.

Violetta *dolce a mezza voce*
102
Pa-ri-gi, o ca-ro, noi la-sce-re-mo, la vi-ta u-ni-ti tra-scor-re-re-mo...
Al.
Sì.
Viol.
V-le
Vc.
Cl.

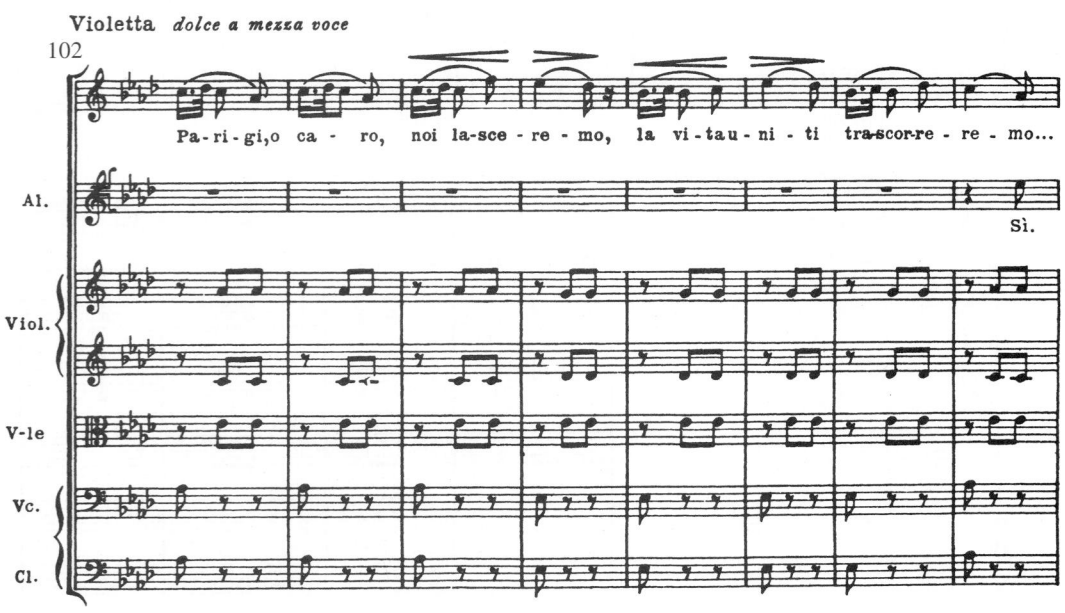

beginning of
CODA - lots of cadences

ter-mi-ne   ser-ba-to al nostro a-mor!   Oh! Al-

Vio-let-ta mia, deh! cal-ma-ti,   m'uc-ci-de il tuo do-lor. Ah! Vio-

big
diminished
harmonies

[Scena/Recitative]

ANNINA
(entering hastily and speaking hesitatingly)

Signora . . .	Madam . . .

VIOLETTA

Che t'accade?	What's happening?

ANNINA

Quest'oggi, è vero? vi sentite meglio?	Today, is it true? You're feeling better?

VIOLETTA

Sì, perche?	Yes, why?

ANNINA

D'esser calma promettete?	Do you promise to be calm?

VIOLETTA

Sì, che vuoi dirmi?	Yes, what do you want to tell me?

ANNINA

Prevenir vi volli	I want to warn you
Una gioia improvvisa.	of an unexpected joy.

VIOLETTA

Una gioia? dicesti?	A joy? you are saying?

ANNINA

Sì, o signora. . . .	Yes, madame. . . .

VIOLETTA

Alfredo! Ah tu il vedesti!	Alfredo! You saw him!

(Annina nods in affirmation and goes to open the door.)

(Alfredo appears.)

Ei vien! T'affretta. Alfredo?	He's coming! He hastens. Alfredo?

(They embrace.)

Amato Alfredo, oh gioia!	Beloved Alfredo, O joy!

ALFREDO

Oh mia Violetta, oh gioia!	O, my Violetta, O joy!

[Tempo d'attacco/Opening section]

ALFREDO

Colpevol sono. . . .   I am guilty. . . .
So tutto, o cara. . . .   I know everything, my dear. . . .

VIOLETTA

Io so che alfine   I know that you have finally
Reso mi sei!   been returned to me!

ALFREDO

Da questo palpito   From this throbbing heart
S'io t'ami impara,   you know that I love you.
Senza te esistere   Without you
Più non potrei.   I cannot exist anymore.

VIOLETTA

Ah s'anco in vita   Even though still alive
M'hai ritrovata,   you found me again,
Credi che uccidere   do you believe
Non può il dolor.   that sorrow cannot kill?

ALFREDO

Scorda l'affanno,   Forget the anxiety,
Donna adorata,   my adored woman.
A me perdona   Pardon me
E al genitor.   and my father.

VIOLETTA

Ch'io ti perdoni?   Pardon you?
La rea son io;   I am the guilty one;
Ma solo amor   but only love
Tal mi rende.   makes me so.

ALFREDO AND VIOLETTA

Null'uomo o demon,   No man or demon,
Angiol mio,   my angel,
Mai più dividermi   can ever separate me
Potrà da te.   from you again.

[Cantabile]

ALFREDO AND VIOLETTA

Parigi, o cara,   Paris, my dear,
Noi lasceremo,   we shall forsake;
La vita uniti   united, our life
Trascorreremo.   we shall pass together.
De' corsi affanni   For past anguish,
Compenso avrai,   you will be rewarded.
La tua (mia) salute   Your (my) health

Rifiorirà.	will flourish again.
Sospiro e luce	Breath and light
Tu mi sarai,	you will be to me.
Tutto il futuro	All the future
Ne arriderà.	will smile at us.

[Tempo di mezzo/Middle section]

VIOLETTA

Ah non più . . . a un tempio . . .	Ah, no more . . . to a church . . .
Alfredo, andiamo,	Alfredo, let's go,
Del tuo ritorno	for your return
Grazie rendiamo. . . .	let's render thanks. . . .

(She staggers.)

ALFREDO

Tu impallidisci! . . .	You're turning pale! . . .

VIOLETTA

È nulla, sai?	It's nothing, you know?
Gioia improvvisa	Sudden joy
Non entra mai,	never comes into
Senza turbarlo,	the sad heart
In mesto core . . .	without upsetting it . . .

ALFREDO
(frightened, supporting her)

Gran Dio! . . . Violetta! . . .	Great God! . . . Violetta! . . .

VIOLETTA
(She lets herself fall, worn out, onto a chair.)

È il mio malore! . . .	I am feeling faint! . . .

(forcing herself)

Fu debolezza. . . .	It was weakness. . . .
Ora son forte. . . .	Now I am strong. . . .
Vedi? sorrido. . . .	See? I'm smiling. . . .

ALFREDO
(distressed)

(Ahi, cruda sorte!)	(Ah! cruel fate!)

VIOLETTA

Fu nulla . . . Annina,	It was nothing . . . Annina,
Dammi a vestire.	bring me something to wear.

ALFREDO

Adesso? attendi . . .	Now? wait . . .

VIOLETTA
(standing up)

No! . . . voglio uscire.	No! . . . I want to go out.

(Annina gives Violetta a dress that she tries to put on, but hampered by weakness, she exclaims, with desperation:)

Gran Dio! . . . non posso!	Great God! . . . I can't!

(She flings away the dress in despair and falls back on the chair.)

ALFREDO

(Cielo! che vedo!)	(Heavens! what do I see!)

(to Annina)

Va pel dottore . . .	Go for the doctor . . .

VIOLETTA
(to Annina)

Ah! . . . digli . . .	Ah! . . . tell him . . .
Digli che Alfredo	tell him that Alfredo
È ritornato	has returned
All'amor mio.	to my love.
Digli che vivere	Tell him that
Ancor vogli'io . . .	again I want to live . . .

(Annina leaves.)

(to Alfredo)

Ma se tornando	But if your returning
Non m'hai salvato,	has not saved me,
A niuno in terra	to no one on Earth
Salvarmi è dato.	is it given to save me.

[Cabaletta]

VIOLETTA
(rising impetuously)

Ah!	Ah!
Gran Dio! morir sì giovane,	Great God! To die so young,
Io che penato ho tanto!	I who have suffered so much!
Morir sì presso a tergere	To die so close to wiping away
Il mio sì lungo pianto!	my tears of so many years!
Ah, dunque fu delirio	Ah, so the credulous hope
La credula speranza;	was delirium;
Invano di costanza	in vain with constancy
Armato avrò il mio cor!	did I arm my heart!

ALFREDO

Oh mio sospiro e palpito,	Oh my breath and heartthrob,
Diletto del cor mio!	darling of my heart!

Le mie colle tue lacrime	My tears with yours
Confondere degg'io!	I must mingle!
Ma più che mai, deh! credilo,	But more than ever, for pity's sake! believe it,
M'è d'uopo di costanza.	for me constancy is necessary.
Ah! tutto alla speranza	Ah! do not totally
Non chiudere il tuo cor!	close your heart to hope.

VIOLETTA

Oh! Alfredo, il crudo termine	Oh! Alfredo, the cruel end
Serbato al nostro amor!	remains despite our love!

ALFREDO

Ah! Violetta mia, deh! calmati,	Ah! My Violetta, for pity's sake, calm yourself,
M'uccide il tuo dolor.	your sorrow is killing me.

(Violetta collapses onto the sofa.)

—LIBRETTO BY FRANCESCO MARIA PIAVE

Giuseppe Verdi composed *La traviata* on a libretto that Francesco Maria Piave based on *La Dame aux camélias,* a play by Alexandre Dumas fils. The opera was first performed at Teatro La Fenice, Venice, on March 6, 1853. Most of Verdi's operas tell stories set in the historical past, but *La traviata* is set in his own time, the middle nineteenth century, and the realistic characters, situations, and emotions inspired some of his most impassioned music.

Violetta, the "traviata" (fallen woman) of the title, decides to give up her career as a courtesan and marry Alfredo, who has fallen in love with her. But Alfredo's father is concerned that Violetta's reputation will reflect badly on his family and ruin his daughter's chance to marry a respectable suitor. He persuades Violetta to leave Alfredo, and while Alfredo is away from the home they are sharing in the suburbs of Paris, Violetta packs her things and returns to the city, leaving him a note that does not explain the real reason she has left. That night, Alfredo finds her at a party with one of her old admirers, Baron Douphol. Alfredo insults Violetta and the Baron, and the two men fight a duel. Alfredo wounds the Baron and leaves the country.

As Act III begins, Alfredo's father has repented and told his son of Violetta's sacrifice. Alfredo returns to Paris to ask her forgiveness, and in this scene he arrives at her shabby apartment and finds her gravely ill with tuberculosis. Violetta is overjoyed to see Alfredo and agrees to leave Paris with him. But her illness has weakened her so much that she cannot even dress to leave the apartment. She is thrown into despair, and at the end of the act, she dies in his arms.

This scene follows the structure that was common for duets since it was developed by Rossini:

- a *scena* (scene) in recitative, accompanied by the orchestra;
- a *tempo d'attacco* (opening section) in which the characters trade phrases of melody in dialogue;
- a slow, lyrical *cantabile*, that expresses a relatively calm feeling such as sadness or hope;
- a *tempo di mezzo* (middle section), in which something happens to alter the situation or the characters' moods; and
- a fast *cabaletta* that expresses a more active emotion such as joy or anger.

Verdi fills out this conventional structure with a variety of contrasting styles and textures that delineate the plot and intensify the drama. He also introduces a harmonic plan that highlights the sharply different moods of the three main sections by focusing on three keys related by major thirds—E major for the *tempo d'attacco*, A♭ major for the *cantabile*, and C major for the *cabaletta*.

The opening dialogue between Violetta and her maid Annina is in blank verse of mixed seven- and eleven-syllable lines, with poetic lines often split between characters as they rapidly converse. (Note that in Italian poetry, successive vowels are elided as one syllable, even from one word to the next.) Instead of using the traditional style of accompanied recitative, Verdi sets the dialogue in short phrases above a continuous melodic fabric in the orchestra, whose skipping melody in four-measure phrases and throbbing accompaniment suggest Annina's excitement at having seen Alfredo. A Rossiniesque crescendo begins when Alfredo appears and builds to a climax as the lovers embrace, their reunion symbolized by the long melodic phrase they share in octaves (measure 28).

The ensuing dialogue between Alfredo and Violetta (measure 35) comprises the *tempo d'attacco*, featuring more tuneful melodies in the voices over simple accompaniment. Here, the poetry turns to rhyming pairs of five-syllable lines, which Verdi sets in balanced, four-measure phrases. Each character repeats the other's melodies in urgent rising or falling lines that convey their joy at being together again while also suggesting the pain and despair each has suffered.

A quick modulation from E major to A♭ major precedes the *cantabile*, "Parigi, o cara" (measure 75), in which the lovers vow that they will leave Paris to spend their life together and express hope that they will be rewarded with future happiness for their past suffering. The form is simple, AABB with coda. In the A section, first Alfredo and then Violetta sings a melody whose rhythm and accompaniment resemble a slow waltz and whose regular phrasing, limited range, and lack of embellishment make it as direct and appealing as a popular song. In the B section (measure 125), both characters repeat text from the A section, but Alfredo sings a grandiose, legato melody, and Violetta sings a chromatic, staccato line. At the end of the section, the characters join together to sing a cadenza-like coda (measures 169–76).

In the following *tempo di mezzo* (measure 177), hope gives way to despair as it becomes clear that Violetta's illness is too far advanced to allow for her to begin a new life with Alfredo. Verdi expresses the characters' emotional transformations through stark contrasts of style, including orchestral interjections, singing that varies from recitative to arioso, and even a lighthearted attempt at aria style as Violetta claims to be strong and smiling (measure 191). Instead of increasing during the scene as was customary, the momentum seems to collapse when Violetta acknowledges that she will not improve (measure 227). The cabaletta (measure 238) does not provide the usual rousing close, but expresses Violetta's desperation through plodding rhythms and quickly changing dynamics. The form is AABA' with coda. Alfredo responds to Violetta in the repetition of the A section (measure 254) and tries to calm her in the contrasting passage (measure 270). Finally, the coda (measure 300) builds to a climax of despair.

RICHARD WAGNER (1813–1883)

Tristan und Isolde: Excerpt from Act I, Scene 5

Opera (music drama)

1857–59

CD 9|78 CD 5|39

From Richard Wagner, *Tristan und Isolde,* ed. Felix Mottl (Frankfurt: Peters, 1914), 85–102.

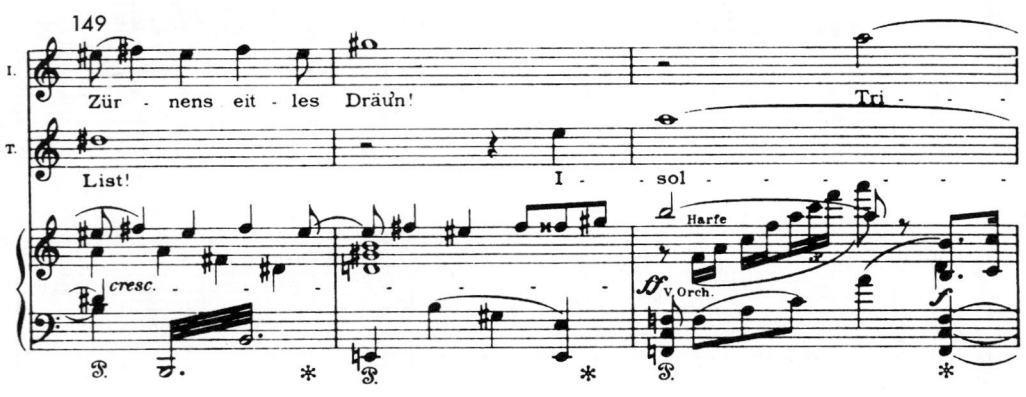

Glück - li-cher Held!

Heil Kö - nig Mar - ke!

Heil Kö - nig Mar - ke!

Mit

B. Vorwärts im Tempo

rei - chem Hof - ge - sin - de, dort auf Na - chen naht Herr Mar - ke.

Hei! wie die Fahrt ihn freut, daß er die Braut _____ sich

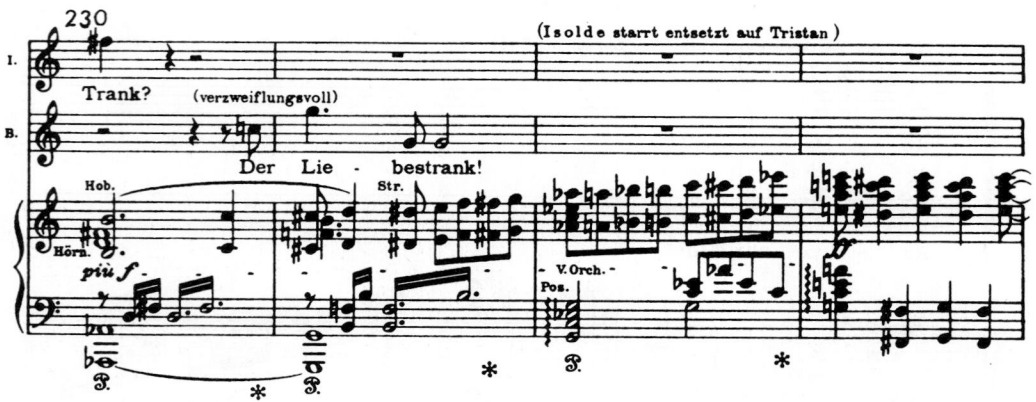

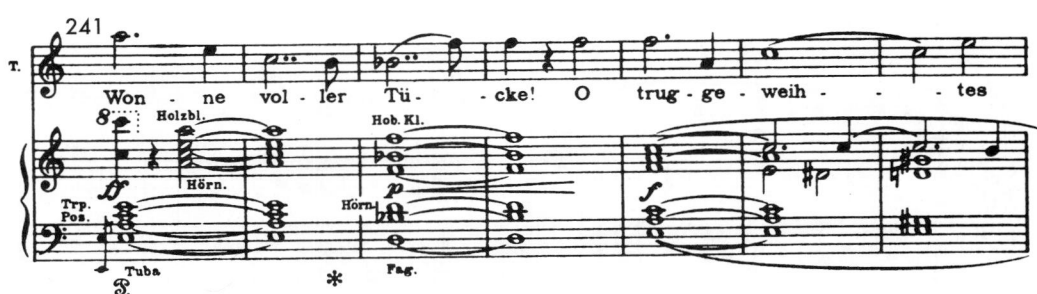

SAILORS
(outside)

Auf das Tau!	Haul the line!
Anker ab!	Drop the anchor!

TRISTAN
(starting wildly)

Los den Anker!	Drop the anchor!
Das Steuer dem Strom!	Stern to the current!
Den Winden Segel und Mast!	Sail and mast to the wind!

(He takes the cup from Isolde.)

Wohl kenn' ich Irlands	Well know I Ireland's
Königin,	Queen,
Und ihrer Künste	and her art's
Wunderkraft:	magic.
Den Balsam nützt' ich,	The balsam I used
Den sie bot:	that she brought.
Den Becher nehm' ich nun,	The goblet I now take
Dass ganz ich heut' genese.	so that I might altogether today recover.
Und achte auch	And heed also
Des Sühneeids,	the oath of atonement,
Den ich zum Dank dir sage!	which I in thanks made to you!
Tristans Ehre,	Tristan's honor,
Höchste Treu!	highest truth!
Tristans Elend,	Tristan's anguish,
Kühnster Trotz!	brave defiance!
Trug des Herzens!	Betrayal of the heart!
Traum der Ahnung!	Dream of presentiment!
Ew'ger Trauer	Eternal sorrow,
Einz'ger Trost:	unique solace:
Vergessens güt'ger Trank,	forgetting's kindly draught,
Dich trink' ich sonder Wank!	I drink without wavering!

(He sits and drinks.)

ISOLDE

Betrug auch hier?	Betrayed even in this?
Mein die Hälfte!	The half is mine!

(She wrests the cup from his hand.)

Verräter! Ich trink' sie dir!	Traitor, I drink to you!

*(She drinks, and then throws away the cup. Both, seized with shuddering, gaze
at each other with deepest agitation, still with stiff demeanor, as the expression
of defiance of death fades into a glow of passion. Trembling grips them.
They convulsively clutch their hearts and pass their hands over their brows.
Then they seek each other again with their eyes, sink into confusion, and once
more turn with renewed longing toward each other.)*

ISOLDE
(with wavering voice)

Tristan!   Tristan!

TRISTAN
(overwhelmed)

Isolde!   Isolde!

ISOLDE
(sinking on his chest)

Treuloser Holder!   Treacherous lover!

TRISTAN
(He embraces her with ardor.)

Seligste Frau!   Divine woman!

(They remain in silent embrace.)

ALL THE MEN
(outside)

Heil! König Marke Heil!   Hail! King Mark, hail!

*(Brangäne, who with averted face, full of confusion and horror, had leaned
over the side, turns to see the pair sunk into a love embrace, and hurls herself,
wringing her hands in desperation, into the foreground.)*

BRANGÄNE

Wehe! Weh!   Alas! Alas!
Unabwendbar   Inevitable,
Ew'ge Not   endless distress,
Für kurzen Tod!   instead of quick death!
Tör'ger Treue   Misleading loyalty,
Trugvolles Werk   deceitful work
Blüht nun jammernd empor!   now blossoms pitifully upward.

(Tristan and Isolde break from their embrace.)

TRISTAN
(bewildered)

Was träumte mir   What did I dream
Von Tristans Ehre?   of Tristan's honor?

ISOLDE

Was träumte mir   What did I dream
Von Isoldes Schmach?   of Isolde's disgrace?

TRISTAN

Du mir verloren?   Are you lost to me?

ISOLDE

Du mich verstossen?   Have you repulsed me?

TRISTAN

Trügenden Zaubers Tückische List?	False magic's nasty trick!

ISOLDE

Törigen Zürnes Eitles Dräu'n!	Foolish wrath's vain menace!

TRISTAN

Isolde! Süsseste Maid!	Isolde, sweetest maiden!

ISOLDE

Tristan! Trautester Mann!	Tristan; most beloved man!

BOTH

Wie sich die Herzen wogend erheben,	How our heaving hearts are uplifted!
Wie alle Sinne wonnig erbeben!	How all our senses blissfully quiver!
Sehnender Minne	Longing passion,
Schwellendes Blühen,	swelling bloom,
Schmachtender Liebe	languishing love,
Seliges Glühen!	blessed glow!
Jach in der Brust	Precipitate in the breast
Jauchzende Lust!	exulting desire!
Isolde! Tristan!	Isolde! Tristan!
Tristan! Isolde!	Tristan! Isolde!
Welten entronnen	Escaped from the world,
Du mir gewonnen!	you have won me.
Du mir einzig bewusst,	You, my only thought,
Höchste Liebeslust!	highest love's desire!

(The curtains are now drawn wide apart. The entire ship is filled with knights and sailors, who joyfully wave at the shore from aboard. Nearby is seen a cliff crowned by a castle. Tristan and Isolde remain lost in mutual contemplation, unaware of what is taking place)

BRANGÄNE
(to the women, who at her signal ascend from below)

Schnell den Mantel,	Quick, the cloak,
Den Königsschmuck!	the royal robe.

(rushing between Tristan and Isolde)

Unsel'ge! Auf!	Up, unfortunate pair! Up!
Hört, wo wir sind.	See where we are!

(She puts the royal cloak on Isolde, who does not notice anything.)

ALL THE MEN
(on the ship)

Heil! Heil!	Hail, hail!
Heil! König Marke Heil!	Hail! King Mark, hail!
Heil dem König!	Hail the king!

KURWENAL

(approaching cheerfully)

Heil, Tristan!	Hail, Tristan!
Glücklicher Held!	Fortunate hero!
Mit reichem Hofgesinde	With splendid courtiers
Dort auf Nachen	there in the skiff
Naht Herr Marke.	Mark approaches.
Heil! wie die Fahrt ihn freut,	Ah, how the ride delights him,
Dass er die Braut sich freit!	for soon he will be wooing the bride.

TRISTAN

(looking up, bewildered)

Wer naht?	Who comes?

KURWENAL

Der König!	The King.

TRISTAN

Welcher König?	Which King?

(Kurwenal points over the side. Tristan stares stupefied at the shore, until Isolde calls his name.)

ALL THE MEN

(waving their hats)

Heil! König Marke Heil!	Hail! King Mark, hail!

ISOLDE

(confused)

Was ist, Brangäne!	What is that, Brangäne?
Welcher Ruf?	What is the shouting?

BRANGÄNE

Isolde! Herrin!	Isolde! Mistress,
Fassung nur heut'!	get hold of yourself!

ISOLDE

Wo bin ich? Leb' ich?	Where am I? Am I alive?
Ha! Welcher Trank?	Oh, what drink was it?

BRANGÄNE

(despairingly)

Der Liebestrank!	The love potion!

(Isolde stares, horror-stricken, at Tristan.)

ISOLDE

Tristan!	Tristan!

TRISTAN

Isolde!	Isolde!

ISOLDE

Muss ich leben?   Must I live?

(She falls, fainting, upon his chest.)

BRANGÄNE
(to the women)

Helft der Herrin!   Help your mistress!

TRISTAN

O Wonne voller Tücke!   O rapture full of cunning!
O Truggeweihtes Glücke!   O fraudulently won good fortune!

ALL THE MEN
(in a general acclamation)

Kornwall Heil!   Cornwall, hail!

*(People have climbed over the ship's side, others have extended a bridge, and the
atmosphere is one of expectation of the arrival of those that have been awaited.
The curtain falls quickly.)*

Richard Wagner wrote his own libretto for his music drama *Tristan und Isolde*, based on a thirteenth-century romance by Gottfried von Strassburg. He first worked out a prose sketch, then a prose draft, and finally finished a version in verse in September 1857. Using some sketches he wrote the previous year, he then began to write the music and finished the work in 1859. The piano-vocal score and full score were both published in 1860, before the work was staged—unusual for an opera. Under the sponsorship of King Ludwig II of Bavaria, *Tristan und Isolde* was finally premiered in Munich on June 10, 1865. The opera was too novel and complex for most members of the audience, but through subsequent performances, it came to be regarded as one of the most important and influential operas ever composed.

The knight Tristan is bringing Isolde, daughter of the Irish king, on a ship to Cornwall to marry his uncle King Mark. Isolde is secretly in love with Tristan, but he has offended her. Skilled in the magical arts, she resolves to kill herself and Tristan with a poisoned drink before they reach land. She summons Tristan and offers to share with him a drink of atonement, claiming that through it she will forgive him for a wrong he had done to her in the past. As this excerpt begins, they drink the draught together. But Isolde's companion Brangäne, unwilling to go along with the plot, has substituted a love potion for the poison. Tristan and Isolde fall instantly in love and are oblivious to the excitement around them as the ship arrives and the crew hails the waiting king on shore. In Act II, Isolde and Tristan meet secretly and embrace in passionate love, despite her marriage to Mark, but they are discovered, and Tristan is wounded by another knight. In the final act,

Tristan lies dying at his castle in Brittany. Isolde arrives in response to his summons, but it is too late, and he dies in her arms. Having learned of the potion from Brangäne, Mark has followed Isolde and is willing to forgive both lovers. But Isolde has no will to live without Tristan and soon joins him in death.

The opera is not divided into separate numbers, as earlier operas were. Rather, the music continuously follows the action of the drama through each act. The orchestra maintains the continuity, and the characters sing in melodies that vary from speechlike to soaring and passionate. Much of the music, both vocal and orchestral, is woven from *leitmotives* (leading motives), that are associated with particular people, things, events, or ideas through the texts or situations with which they first appear.

At measure 38 of this excerpt, the leitmotive of Tristan's honor is introduced and identified by the sung text, "Tristans Ehre, höchste Treu!" (Tristan's honor, highest truth). It is developed through the rest of his speech in many permutations, some close to the original (as in the orchestra at measure 56) and others quite distant (for instance, in the voice at measure 46, which reorders the pitches). The motive of a rising sixth and two descending semitones at Isolde's "Ich trink' sie dir!" (I drink to you, measure 64), first heard at the very beginning of the opera, is associated with the love potion from here through the end of the opera. It is joined to the "Tristan chord" (measures 66–69), a striking sonority that is the first chord in the opera, and to a rising chromatic motive in the orchestra that symbolizes longing (measures 69–70). The "Tristan chord" and the motives symbolizing the potion and longing permeate the following passage, as the potion takes effect and the two fall hopelessly in love. Wagner laid out this section as a pantomime, prescribing particular gestures and actions to be performed by the two characters at specific points in the music.

A climax is reached at measure 102, when Isolde and Tristan stare longingly at each other, and the rising chromatic motive culminates in a deceptive cadence from a dominant seventh chord on E to an F-major harmony with a blistering B-natural appoggiatura (instead of the expected A minor). Such evasions of resolution continue throughout the scene and much of the opera, symbolizing the unfulfillable desire of the lovers. Indeed, the harmony is ever restless and the melodies constantly varied, creating the effect Wagner described as "endless melody."

A new melody then begins in the violas and cellos (measure 103), intermittently joined by the voices as Isolde and Tristan call to each other; this exemplifies Wagner's tendency to give the leading musical role to the orchestra and to extract the vocal lines from the orchestral texture. After interruptions by the crew hailing King Mark (measure 113) and Brangäne worrying about what she has done, the lovers' dialogue (starting at measure 132) builds on motives already introduced, often developing them into new variants that are then repeated and developed in turn. At the words "Sehnender Minne" (passionate love, at measure 160), a new leitmotive appears. All of these leitmotives are short, often two measures or less, and open-ended, so that they can be repeated in sequence or combined in different ways.

At measure 192, the music hailing the king begins to penetrate the lovers' consciousness, and Tristan's friend Kurwenal comes to summon them. Tristan and

Isolde realize what has happened but are powerless to change it, and the act draws to a close amid the crew's raucous celebration of returning home.

Wagner used such a large orchestra and gave it such a commanding role that he needed new, more powerful kinds of singers—a *Heldentenor* (hero-tenor) and a dramatic soprano—whose voices would not be drowned out. To sing such roles requires a heavier, more robust and penetrating voice than is needed to sing Italian opera (see NAWM 125 and 127). The vocal lines are almost entirely syllabic, a sign of how important the text had become. A recording offers only part of the experience Wagner sought to provide, which combined music, poetry, scenic design, staging, and action to form what he called a *Gesamtkunstwerk* (total or collective artwork).

GEORGES BIZET (1838–1875)

Carmen: Act I, No. 10, Seguidilla and Duet

Opera

1873–74

CD 10|1 CD 5|47

Allegretto.

Carmen.

Don José.

Allegretto. (♪=160.)

Piano.

pp

Carmen.

pp e leggiero.

Près   des   rem -
Near   to   the

parts   de Sé -   vil -   -le,   Chez   mon a -
walls   of Se -   vil -   -la,   With   my good

From Georges Bizet, *Carmen* (New York: G. Schirmer, 1895), 95–105. English singing translation by Theodore Baker. For a more literal translation, see pp. 622–24.

67

veut m'ai-mer? je l'ai - me - rai! | Qui veut mon
will love me? I will love him! | Who'll have my

a tempo.

70

portamento. portamento.

â - - -me? Elle est à pren-dre! | Vous ar - ri -
soul?___ 'Tis for the ask - ing! | Now some good

74

portamento. portamento.

vez___ au bon mo - ment! Je n'ai guè - re le temps d'at-
fair - y has sent you here! And my patience will bear no

78

ten - dre, Car a - vec mon nou - vel a - mant,___
task - ing, For, be - side my new lov - er dear,___

174

sempre f

nil - la:＿＿＿＿＿＿＿＿＿＿　tra la la la
nil - la:＿＿＿＿＿＿＿＿＿＿

p　*sf*

177

ff

la la la la la la la,＿＿＿＿＿＿＿＿＿　tra la

180

la la la la la la la la la la.

sf　*ff*

CARMEN

Près des remparts de Séville,
Chez mon ami Lillas Pastia
J'irai danser la Séguidille
Et boire du Manzanilla.
J'irai chez mon ami Lillas Pastia.

Near to the ramparts of Seville,
at the tavern of my friend Lillas Pastia
I'll go to dance the Seguidilla
and drink Manzanilla.
I'll go to the place of my friend Lillas
　　Pastia.

Oui, mais toute seule on s'ennuie,	Yes, but all alone one gets bored,
Et les vrais plaisirs sont à deux;	and the real pleasures are for two;
Donc, pour me tenir compagnie,	so, to keep me company,
J'emmènerai mon amoureux!	I will bring along my lover!
Mon amoureux il est au diable,	My lover has gone to the devil,
Je l'ai mis à la porte hier!	I threw him out yesterday!
Mon pauvre cœur très consolable,	My poor heart is very consolable,
Mon cœur est libre comme l'air!	my heart is as free as the air!
J'ai des galants à la douzaine,	I have beaux by the dozen,
Mais ils ne sont pas à mon gré.	but they are not to my taste.
Voici la fin de la semaine:	Here it is the end of the week:
Qui veut m'aimer? je l'aimerai!	who wants to love me? I will love him!
Qui veut mon âme? Elle est à prendre!	Who wants my soul? It's here for the taking!
Vous arrivez au bon moment!	You come at an opportune moment!
Je n'ai guère le temps d'attendre,	I hardly have the time to wait,
Car avec mon nouvel amant,	for with my new lover,
Près des remparts de Séville,	Near to the ramparts of Seville,
Chez mon ami Lillas Pastia	at the tavern of my friend Lillas Pastia
J'irai danser la Séguidille	I'll go to dance the Seguidilla
Et boire du Manzanilla.	and drink Manzanilla.
Oui, j'irai chez mon ami Lillas Pastia!	Yes, I'll go to the place of my friend Lillas Pastia!

DON JOSÉ

Tais-toi! je t'avais dit de ne pas me parler!	Quiet! I told you not to speak to me!

CARMEN

Je ne te parle pas, je chante pour moi-même!	I am not talking to you, I am singing for myself.
Et je pense! il n'est pas défendu de penser!	And I am thinking! It is not forbidden to think!
Je pense à certain officier,	I am thinking of a certain officer,
Qui m'aime	who loves me
Et qu'à mon tour,	and who in my turn,
Oui, qu'à mon tour, je pourrais bien aimer.	yes, who in my turn I could well love.

DON JOSÉ

Carmen!	Carmen!

CARMEN

Mon officier n'est pas un capitaine;	My officer is not a captain,
Pas même un lieutenant,	not even a lieutenant,
Il n'est que brigadier;	he's only a corporal;
Mais c'est assez pour une Bohémienne,	but that's enough for a gypsy,
Et je daigne m'en contenter!	and I deign to be content with him!

DON JOSÉ

Carmen, je suis comme un homme ivre;   Carmen, I am like a drunken man;
Si je cède, si je me livre,   if I yield, if I surrender,
Ta promesse, tu la tiendras?   your promise, you will keep it?
Ah! si je t'aime, Carmen,   Ah! if I love you, Carmen,
Carmen, tu m'aimeras?   Carmen, you will love me?

CARMEN

Oui.   Yes.

DON JOSÉ

Chez Lillas Pastia,   At Lillas Pastia's,

(He loosens the cord that binds Carmen's hands.)

CARMEN

Nous danserons . . .   We'll dance . . .

DON JOSÉ

Tu le promets!   You promise!

CARMEN

. . . la Séguedille   . . . the Seguedilla

DON JOSÉ

Carmen, . . .   Carmen, . . .

CARMEN

En buvant du Manzanilla.   and drink Manzanilla.

DON JOSÉ

. . . Tu le promets!   . . . You promise!

CARMEN

Près des remparts de Séville,   Near to the ramparts of Seville,
Chez mon ami Lillas Pastia,   at the tavern of my friend Lillas Pastia,
Nous danserons la Séguidille   We'll dance the Seguidilla
Et boirons du Manzanilla: and drink Manzanilla:
Tra la la la la la la la la la la.   Tra la la la la la la la la la la.

—HENRI MEILHAC AND
LUDOVIC HALÉVY

In 1872, Georges Bizet was invited to compose an opera in collaboration with librettists Henri Meilhac and Ludovic Halévy for the Opéra-Comique in Paris. Bizet proposed basing it on Prosper Mérimée's 1845 novel that depicts the free love and violent death of Carmen, a Gypsy in Spain who consorts with thieves and works at a cigarette factory. The setting and main character were exotic—usually a good selling point for an opera—but the risqué subject matter and modern-day realism met resistance from the opera house's directors, who were well aware of their audience's conservative tastes. Although Bizet prevailed, resistance continued from management, singers, orchestra, and—after the premiere on March 3, 1875—audience members and critics. The production was successful enough to complete its first run, closing the following February after forty-eight performances, but Bizet had died of a heart attack in June. In Vienna later in 1875, a production that featured recitatives by Ernest Guiraud in place of the original spoken dialogue (traditional in *opéras comiques*) was a triumph, and soon *Carmen* became one of the most popular operas of all time.

The story hinges on a pair of love triangles. Don José, a peasant who has become a corporal in the army, is faithfully loved by Micaëla, a young woman from his village. Yet he falls in love with Carmen, whose overt sexuality and carefree manner make her both enticing and dangerous, and he eventually joins the gang of smugglers to which she belongs. Uninterested in being faithful to one man, Carmen tires of Don José and takes up with the famous bullfighter Escamillo. When Don José begs her to return, Carmen throws at his feet the ring he had given her, and he kills her. By this time, it was common for operas to end with the death of the female lead, as in Verdi's *La Traviata* (NAWM 127) and Wagner's *Tristan und Isolde* (NAWM 128), but in *Carmen* that death acquires disturbing overtones, as if the work's creators meant to suggest that Carmen offers too great a threat to society for Don José to allow her to live.

The scene included here is a seduction in which Carmen at first seems to be in the subordinate position but soon makes it clear that she is totally in control. She has been arrested for fighting with a fellow worker and has been left in the custody of Don José, who is under orders to take her to prison. Although commanded not to speak, she sings a song about a tavern where she plans to go and enjoy the pleasures of drinking and dancing the *seguidilla*, a Spanish dance in moderately quick triple time. Her song is framed by a refrain (measures 13–30) that she repeats several times throughout the scene, using it like a hook and line to reel in her prey. During the verse (measures 37–81), Carmen explains that she has just sent her lover packing and is looking for a new one. Then she repeats her refrain with an implicit invitation for Don José to join her. In recitative, Don José tells her to be quiet (measure 102), but instead she becomes more suggestive, hinting that she knows he loves her and that she might love him in return. In her next refrain, a step lower and with new words, she promises to be content with Don José (measure 125). He is intoxicated and responds in impassioned recitative in which he asks her to promise to love him. As the orchestra returns to the music that began her verse (measure 148), she says "yes," and he loosens the cord around her hands, but she continues as if she is promising just to dance and drink with him. Finally, she repeats her refrain in its original key (measure 162), now including him in her plans. She later makes her escape, leaving him to be captured and imprisoned for letting her go.

Carmen's exotic allure and seductive power are clearly conveyed in the music. Her song is itself a seguidilla. The orchestra imitates the pluck-and-strum accompaniment of a Spanish guitar, Carmen adds the cadential melismas typical of seguidillas, and the harmony includes Phrygian cadences that were associated with Spanish flamenco music, marked by a descending half step in the bass (as at measures 23–25). The refrain portrays Carmen as both slippery and entrancing, in part through the harmony, which begins as if in F♯ major, moves by half step to an E-minor seventh chord, cadences on D major, continues around the circle of fifths to C major, and finally slips down chromatically to close on B minor, the "real" key of the song. Each turn is unexpected yet pleasing, and Carmen remains hard to pin down—all elements of a well-executed seduction. The verse centers on D, the relative major, but both harmony and melody emphasize half-step motion, adapted from the flamenco cadence (already introduced) and made into a central idea of the song. Half-step relationships also suffuse the harmonic plan of the following dialogue, as Carmen slips down to D♭ major (measure 108) and repeats her refrain a half step lower. Don José's passionate outburst then slips back up from B♭ minor to B major (measures 141–48). Her enticing half steps have won him over, and he is lost in her charms.

MODEST MUSORGSKY (1839–1881)

Boris Godunov: Coronation Scene

Opera

1868–69, REV. 1871–74

130

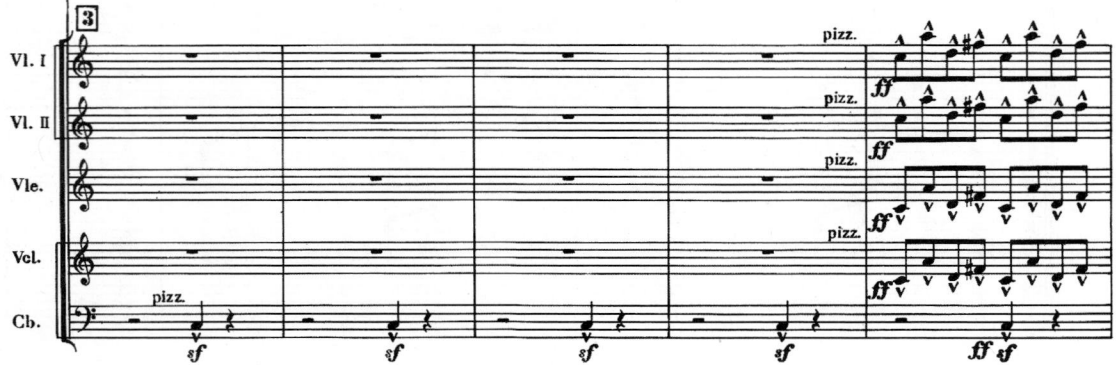

Великий колокольный звон на сцене
A great peal of bells on stage.

С Красного крыльца начинается торжественное шествие бояр к Успенскому собору: впереди рынды, стрельцы, боярские дети;
далее князь Шуйский с венцом Мономаха на падушке; за ним бояре, Щелкалов с царским посохом, и.т.д...

From the Great Staircase boyars in solemn procession start towards the Cathedral of the Assumption; in front are guards, Streltsy, and boyar children; then comes Shuisky, carrying the crown of Monomach on a cushion. Behind him boyars, Shchelkalov carrying the Imperial sceptre, etc.

91

Колокольный звон на сцене.
A peal of bells on stage.

Бояре. С паперти собора, народу,
Bovars. *From the Cathedral porch, to
the crowd:*

Да
All
Es

Be- ли- чай ца- ря Бо- ри- са и
Let all hail the Tsar Bo- ris, and re-
Ru- fet all: Es le- be der Zar Bo-

Be- ли- чай ца- ря Бо- ри- са и
Let all hail the Tsar Bo- ris, and re-
Ru- fet all: Es le- be der Zar Bo-

Суматоха; борьба приставов с народом.
Tumult. The police struggle with the crowd.

Boris comes out of the cathedral and proceeds towards the palace.

Бори́с выхо́дит из собо́ра и направля́ется к терема́м.

Modest Musorgsky adapted the libretto for his opera *Boris Godunov* from the play by Aleksander Pushkin (1799–1837), Russia's most renowned poet and playwright. The historical drama relates the life of Boris Godunov, who was named tsar (emperor) despite a rumor that he caused the murder of the child who was heir to the throne. A young monk poses as the true heir and leads a popular rebellion. Boris is undone by his own weakness and by the loss of the public support that had initially sustained him. After composing the first version, in seven scenes, in 1868–1869, Musorgsky offered the opera to the Mariinsky Theater in St. Petersburg, but it was rejected because there was no leading female role. He then revised both text and music, adding a female love interest for the young pretender, writing new scenes, and deleting others to produce an opera with a prologue and four acts. After further revisions, the vocal score was published in January 1874, and later that month, the opera was finally premiered at the Mariinsky Theater. Although panned by many critics, it won success with the public and has become the most popular Russian opera.

The Coronation Scene is the second scene in both the original and the final versions of the opera. As church bells peal, the people and the nobles gather at the Kremlin in Moscow for Boris's coronation and salute him in song. Boris wins their support through his humility before God and his invitation to the people to share in the coronation banquet, leading them to repeat their praise with even greater enthusiasm.

Musorgsky's ideal of opera, nurtured in discussions with composer-critic César Cui and the other composers in the group known as the Mighty Handful (Mily Balakirev, Aleksander Borodin, and Nikolay Rimsky-Korsakov), was a sensitive musical treatment of a well-crafted play. To achieve this, he set most of the words syllabically and placed the natural speech accents on strong beats and often on higher pitches. His vocal lines sometimes resemble liturgical recitation on one or two notes (see measures 40–42 and 94–97) or operatic recitative (measures 134–36). But most often, as in Boris's speeches (measures 114–31 and 137–43), Musorgsky composes fluid arioso lines that feature elements adapted from Russian folk songs: relatively narrow range; repetition of short melodic or rhythmic motives; and phrases that usually first rise and then more slowly sink down to cadence.

Like other Russian composers, Musorgsky organized his music and created dramatic effects through the repetition and accumulation of single impressions, rather than by thematic development to a climax. Typical of Musorgsky's approach, the music in *Boris Godunov* is built from large blocks of material, each relatively consistent in style and figuration, but strongly contrasting with its neighbors. The Coronation Scene opens with the brass section playing two alternating dominant seventh chords with roots a tritone apart, on A♭ and D. These chords are then overlaid with ostinatos in winds and strings that gradually increase their pace to a climax. This entire passage repeats, accompanied by the pealing of bells (measure 21). There follows a rapid kaleidoscope of different ideas (at measure 40): Prince Shuisky's cheer for the new tsar, rapid scales upwards, and more slowly descending chords. The bells stop, and the people sing their praises with a folk song, one of the few genuine folk melodies Musorgsky ever used (measure 50). The tune is developed in the orchestra (measure 62), contrasted with other ideas (measure 83 and 91), and then repeated with greater intensity (measure 99), culminating in cries of "Slava!" (Glory!). Boris voices his doubts, prays, and speaks to the crowd. He is answered by new cries of "Slava!," a varied reprise of earlier material, and a glorious coda to end the scene.

Among Musorgsky's most significant contributions to the development of music was his treatment of harmony, which drew on the innovations of Liszt and influenced many later French and Russian composers. His music is tonal, but his chords and chord progressions are often novel, straying far from common practice. The tritone-related dominant seventh chords at the beginning of the scene share the common tones C and G♭/F♯, and indeed it is C, repeated insistently in the bass, that turns out to be the principal key of the entire scene. When Prince Shuisky hails Boris, the chords in the brass are E major, C major, A major, and E major (at concert pitch, notated in measures 40–42 a fifth higher for the horns in F and a whole step higher for the trumpet in B♭). Like the preceding dominant seventh chords, these chords do not function as part of a normal harmonic progression, but simply decorate the common tone they share, the E that repeats in the voice. The rushing scales and falling chords in measures 42–48 alternate between the notes of the D♭ major and C major scales, juxtaposing different pitch collections in a manner that would later become characteristic of the music of Debussy, Stravinsky, and many twentieth-century composers. The harmonization of the folk song at measure 50 includes the first functional progressions in the scene, and even this leads to a static alternation of two chords in the middle section (measure 83). Throughout, Musorgsky uses harmony as an expressive device and as a way to characterize his varied blocks of material, establishing tonal centers as much by assertion or repetition as by harmonic motion.

For years, *Boris Godunov* was performed most often in a revised version by Nikolay Rimsky-Korsakov, who "corrected" what he saw as Musorgsky's technical shortcomings. By the 1920s, Musorgsky's reputation had changed from that of a self-taught amateur to that of a pioneer of modernist techniques, and a new edition of the opera was published that restored his original music. In performances since the 1970s, editions based on Musorgsky's versions have largely replaced the version by Rimsky-Korsakov. The edition printed here was published in 1975 and based primarily on Musorgsky's revised autograph score, although it incorporates some elements from the first version in the scenes shared by both.

ARTHUR SULLIVAN (1842–1900)

The Pirates of Penzance: Act II, No. 17, *When the foeman bares his steel*

Operetta (comic opera)

1879

CD 10|12

From W. S. Gilbert and Arthur Sullivan, *The Pirates of Penzance, or The Slave of Duty*, ed. Bryceson Treharne (New York: G. Schirmer, n.d.), 119–37.

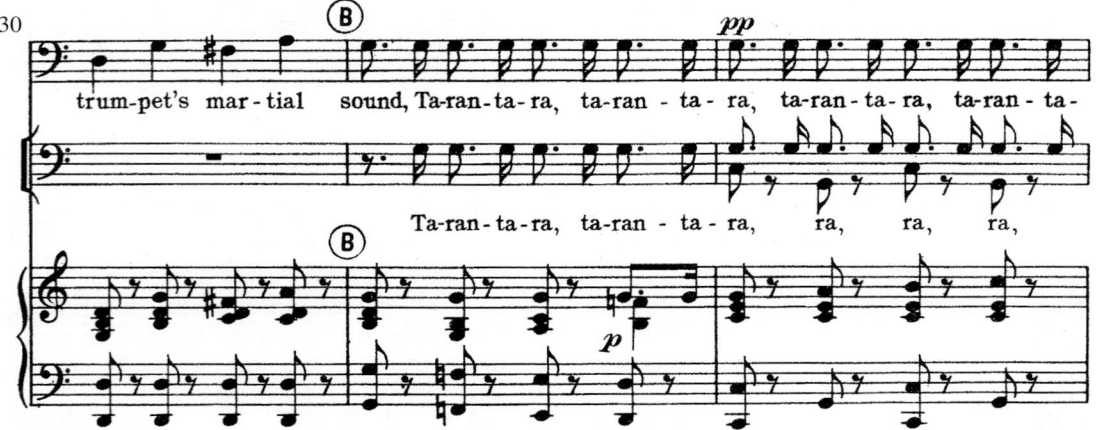

(*Exeunt Police. Mabel tears herself from Fred., and exits R., followed by her sisters, consoling her. The Major-General and others follow the police off L. Fred. remains alone.*)

The Pirates of Penzance, or The Slave of Duty was the third operetta W. S. Gilbert (librettist) and Arthur Sullivan (composer) created on commission from impresario Richard D'Oyly Carte, after *The Sorcerer* and *H.M.S. Pinafore*. Because *Pinafore* had been staged in pirated versions in the United States, earning nothing for its creators or for D'Oyly Carte, the team premiered *Pirates* not in London but in New York on December 31, 1879. A partial premiere the day before in Paignton, Devonshire secured copyright throughout the United Kingdom and Europe. Sullivan's habit was to delay beginning work on an operetta until it was almost too late, and then to put in eighteen-hour days until the piece was completed and rehearsals could begin. He had partly completed work on *Pirates* before sailing with Gilbert and the rest of the company to New York, but realized en route that he had left his draft back in London. He then had to reconstruct the music from memory, and he finished scoring it in New York. As was their standard practice, Gilbert directed the staging, Sullivan conducted, and the overture was written just before the premiere. Despite the team's efforts, pirated productions sprang up quickly, a sign of the operetta's tremendous popularity. The London premiere came on April 3, 1880, followed by a run of 363 performances.

The convoluted plot satirizes grand opera with ridiculous situations and plot twists. Frederick was apprenticed to a pirate because his nurse Ruth misheard his father's request to apprentice him to a *pilot* (which in the nineteenth century meant the helmsman of a ship, not an aviator). Now Frederick is twenty-one and no longer an apprentice, and he tells the pirates that it is his duty to bring them to justice. He encounters a bevy of beautiful maidens, all daughters of Major-General Stanley, and falls in love with Mabel. The pirates capture the maidens and vow to marry them at once (any other agenda would have offended Victorian sensibilities). The Major-General enters and falsely claims to be an orphan, and the sympathetic pirates, who are orphans themselves, let his daughters go. In the second act, Frederick prepares to lead the police against the pirates, but the Pirate King and Ruth arrive and tell him that he is obligated to continue his apprenticeship until his twenty-first *birthday*, and because he was born on February 29, that will not occur for another sixty-three years. A slave to duty, he sadly bids goodbye to Mabel and rejoins the pirates. In the final battle, the pirates triumph until the police sergeant demands they yield in Queen Victoria's name, and as loyal Englishmen, they all do. Ruth reveals that the pirates are actually noblemen gone wrong. They are forgiven, and all ends happily as the Major-General consents to their marrying his daughters.

The chorus and ensemble included here exemplifies the rich comedy of both Gilbert and Sullivan. Many operatic conventions are evoked, but all go curiously astray. The police march in to receive the blessing of the Major-General and his daughters before going off to fight the pirates. The sergeant admits that they are scared and are merely keeping up appearances—true of many soldiers, but not something operatic male choruses were expected to acknowledge. Sullivan composes their tune in dotted rhythms to create a martial effect, but Gilbert directs them to pretend their clubs are trumpets, so that they sing "Tarantara!" like boys playing soldiers. Sullivan extends this figure at great length, creating humor through exaggeration. When Mabel charges them to go and become heroes with a stirring melody modeled on grand opera, she dwells at length on their likely deaths in battle (measure 40). The sergeant mildly comments that, however well meant, her words are not likely to cheer his nervous men (measure 57), a reasonable observation of the sort that audience members must often willingly suppress in order to accept the usual histrionics of tragic opera. Sullivan leads the harmony into distant keys, from the opening C major through E♭, to the remote key of G♭ for further "encouragement" from Mabel's sister Edith (measure 74), and finally back to the tonic. Sullivan's wit is evident when he reveals (at measure 103) that despite their greatly dissimilar styles and sentiments, Mabel's song and the sergeant's melody fit together in perfect counterpoint. Here, Sullivan is spoofing the operatic convention that in an ensemble, everyone onstage must eventually sing together (apparently, whether they agree or not). The Major-General commands the police to be on their way (measure 126), but they, in typical operatic form, say "Yes, yes, we go!" without budging, just as many operatic characters spend a whole aria saying they are about to rush off before they actually do. The Major-General complains, the maidens salute them ("At last they really, really go!"), and finally the police depart. Through the entire scene, the libretto mocks the standard situations of opera, from gender roles to appeals to glory, and the music slyly evokes and deflates standard styles from martial to dramatic.

— dense harmonies
— metrical complexity
— intellectual intensity
— 3rds used as transformation
"developing variation"
— rhythmic complexity

JOHANNES BRAHMS (1833–1897) *Passacaglia*

Symphony No. 4 in E Minor, Op. 98: Fourth movement, Allegro energico e passionato

Symphony
1884–85

— organicism
— sense of unity + structure between movements
same themes in different movements
— three part exposition *fanfare fanfare fanfare*

A ~ B ~ C CL ; AX

sesquitertia — 4:3

CD 10|18   CD 5|52

Allegro energico e passionato

2 Flöten	
2 Oboen	
2 Klarinetten in A	
2 Fagotte	
Kontrafagott	
4 Hörner in E 1./2. / in C 3./4.	
2 Trompeten in E	
3 Posaunen 1./2. / 3.	
Pauken in G.H.E	
1. Violine	
2. Violine	
Bratsche	
Violoncell	
Kontrabaß	

Allegro energico e passionato

perfectionist — craft

From Johannes Brahms, *Sämtliche Werke*, vol. 2, *Symphonien für Orchester II*, ed. Hans Gál (Leipzig: Breitkopf & Härtel, 1926), 154–84. Used by permission.

studied older composers like Bach, Beethoven

Development

Coda/Finale

Johannes Brahms wrote his Symphony No. 4 in E Minor in 1884–85. It was premiered in October 1885 by the court orchestra at Meiningen in Germany, conducted by Brahms himself, and was an immediate success. Brahms and the orchestra went on tour together with the piece throughout western Germany and the Netherlands before it was published in 1886.

By the 1880s, Brahms was well off, with more income from performances, sales of his works, and investments than he needed for his modest lifestyle. He was in a position to compose when and what he wished, rather than serving a patron or writing music for a wide public. In this symphony, he sought to write a masterpiece for the ages, combining elements from the nineteenth-century symphonic tradition and the more distant past in a unified vision that was distinctly his own. This combination of influences is exemplified in the finale, which draws from music spanning the previous two hundred years yet ends up sounding like pure Brahms.

The finale is a chaconne or passacaglia, a Baroque form consisting of a series of variations over a repeating bass line in triple meter. Brahms was familiar with chaconnes by several Baroque composers and used some of them as models for this movement. The key of E minor and some aspects of both the theme and certain variations appear to stem from Dieterich Buxtehude's Ciaccona in E Minor for organ. The idea of returning to or echoing earlier variations (described below) may derive in part from François Couperin's Rondeau-Passacaille from the Eighth Ordre (harpsichord suite), a work Brahms edited for the Couperin complete works edition. According to a friend's recollection, Brahms adapted the bass ostinato in this movement from the final chorus of J. S. Bach's cantata *Nach dir, Herr, verlanget mich*, BWV 150:

Bach's four-measure ostinato:

Brahms's eight-measure theme:

Both motives have a similar rising scalar contour culminating in a descending octave leap, but Brahms introduces a chromatic passing tone and stretches the theme out to double its length, ending back on the tonic. His finale consists of thirty-one variations on this eight-measure theme, varying both the theme itself and the figurations that accompany it, and ends with a substantial coda.

Another apparent model is Bach's chaconne finale from Partita No. 2 in D Minor for Solo Violin, BWV 1004, which Brahms had transcribed in 1877 as a left-hand exercise for piano. Both finales are in a minor key with a middle section in the parallel major; many variations in both are grouped in pairs; and the return to minor is signaled with a reappearance of the opening idea and texture. There are even details of figuration that the two pieces share, all characteristic of Baroque music: sarabande rhythm, stressing the second beat with a dotted quarter note followed by an eighth note (variations 5–7, measures 33–56); eighth-note figures that begin just after rather than on the beat (variation 6, measure 41); dotted rhythms (variation 8, measure 57); and *bariolage,* a figuration in which the violinist alternates rapidly between strings, playing a repeated note on one and a moving line on the other (variations 9–10, measures 65–80).

But all is not Baroque. By ending with a set of variations, unusual for a symphony finale, Brahms recalls Beethoven's *Eroica* Symphony, the most famous previous symphony to end with a variations movement. In both finales, the bass line is first presented in the upper and middle registers, only later being placed in the bass; in the Brahms, the theme is in the top voice in variations 1–2, is in the middle for variations 3–4, and arrives in the bass only with variation 5. Several other variations also place the theme in the middle or upper registers. Each time, Brahms takes the opportunity to introduce new harmonic progressions, avoiding the harmonic monotony that might otherwise ensue from so many repetitions of the same sequence of chords. Indeed, several variations strongly hint at C major, the key of the third movement and an important secondary key in the first two movements.

Another similarity to the *Eroica* finale is that Brahms groups variations into large sections that suggest aspects of sonata form. There are five main sections:

1. Variations 1–12 (measures 1–96) serve as an exposition.
2. The next four variations (13–16, measures 97–128) constitute an interlude in $\frac{3}{2}$ meter, moving to the parallel major and concluding with two chorale-like variations that feature trombones and horns, an effect reminiscent of Schumann's Third Symphony finale.
3. Variation 17 (measure 129) recalls the opening of the movement, initiating a series of variations that resemble a development section, revisiting and reworking rhythmic and melodic motives from the first several variations.
4. The fourth section then serves as a recapitulation. Variations 24–27 (measures 185–216) are varied restatements of variations 1–4, decorated with the two-against-three rhythmic patterns that are practically a Brahms trademark. Variations 28–29 (measures 217–32) are more distant relatives of variation 6, and variations 30–31 (measures 233–52) introduce falling chains of thirds, a direct reference to the first theme of the first movement.
5. Like the *Eroica* finale, Brahms's finale ends with a faster coda (measure 253) that begins with a recollection of the movement's opening; develops the thematic material in a new way, finally freed of the theme's recurring eight-measure phrases; and builds excitement to a stirring close.

Throughout, Brahms constantly varies the theme itself through figuration and registral placement and by giving each variation a distinctive type of material in the other voices. Yet almost everything new is an extension of something we have heard before, all ultimately deriving from the ideas presented at the very beginning. Arnold Schoenberg called this process of continuously building on germinal motives *developing variation,* and it is characteristic of Brahms.

In contrast to Wagner, Brahms had a reputation as a conservative. But his harmonies and the links he created between movements were quite up to date, and it was novel indeed to synthesize these elements with an old form like the chaconne and to blend elements borrowed from music across a two-hundred-year span. In his awareness of the past and his ability to create something new and highly individual in response, Brahms was a quintessentially modern composer and an inspiration for many in the twentieth century.

Richard Strauss (1864–1949)

Don Quixote, Op. 35: Themes and Variations 1–2

Symphonic poem

1897

133

CD 10|25 CD 5|59

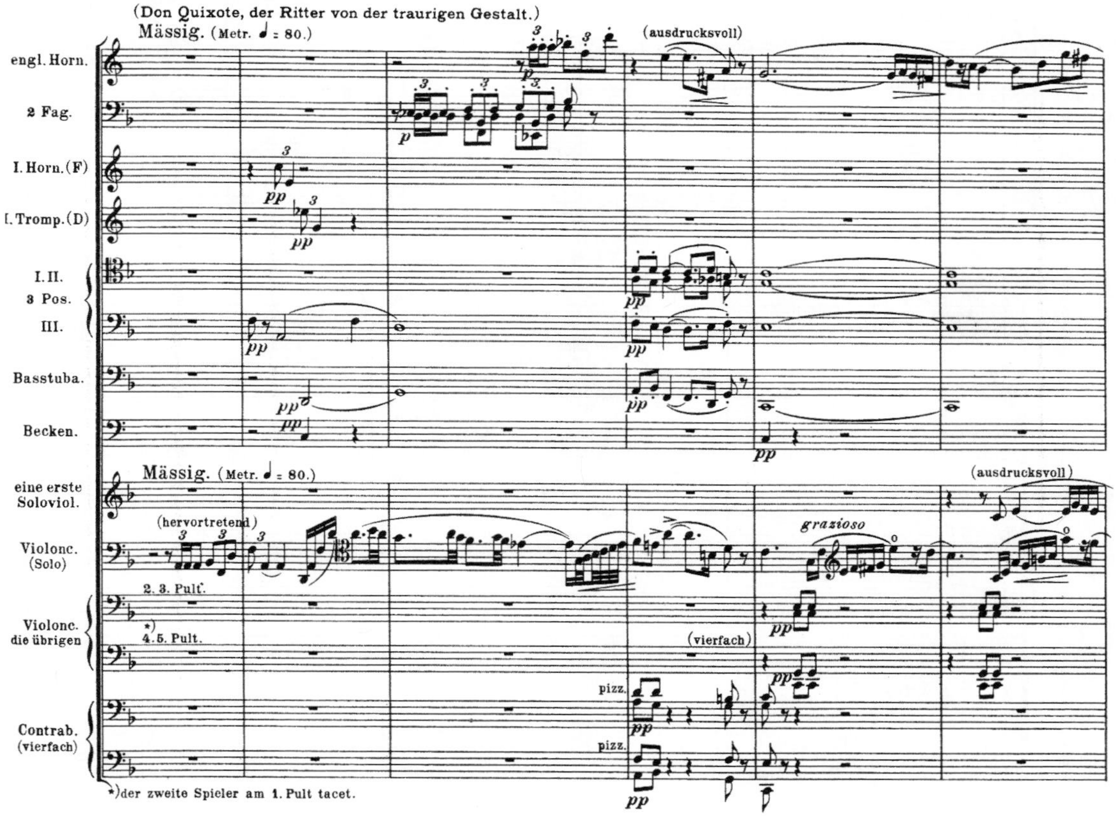

From Richard Strauss, *Don Quixote* (Munich: Jos. Aibl, 1898). Reprinted in Richard Strauss, *Tone Poems: Series I, Don Juan, Tod und Verklärung, Don Quixote* (New York: Dover, 1979), 215–28. Dover Publications, Inc.

*) alle in den Bläsern als 𝆑 notirten Stellen sind mit Zungenschlag auszuführen.

116

Richard Strauss composed his symphonic poem *Don Quixote* in 1897, and it was premiered in March the following year. The work is an instrumental dramatization of Miguel de Cervantes's picaresque novel of 1605 about a bungling hero, Don

Quixote, who imagines himself a knight in the days of chivalry; his horse, Rosinante; and his servant, Sancho Panza, who plays the role of squire to Don Quixote. The music closely follows the events of the novel, depicting them in clever, sometimes literal ways. In one adventure, Don Quixote imagines fighting giants, but they are actually windmills, and in another a flock of sheep appears to Don Quixote as an army that he must battle in order to defend a weaker brigade. In the continuum of symphonic poems from representational to philosophical, *Don Quixote* is the former, offering a strong contrast to the less overtly descriptive music of *Also sprach Zarathustra*, written the year before.

After a prologue (not included here), Strauss presents the two principal themes—the first on Don Quixote, the second on Sancho Panza—in two separate sections. In *Don Quixote, der Ritter von der traurigen Gestalt* (Don Quixote, the Knight of the Sorrowful Countenance), the solo cello states the knight's theme in D minor, echoed and joined by solo violin and English horn. The theme soars, then gradually sinks, then soars again, in a musical analogy to Don Quixote's ever-frustrated but always renewed idealism. Then bass clarinet and tenor tuba present Sancho Panza's theme in F major, using a turning gesture and wide leaps to suggest the lumbering, roly-poly servant on his donkey. These ideas alternate with a variety of motives in the solo viola that suggest Don Quixote's horse Rosinante. Ten "fantastic" variations and an Epilogue make up the remainder of the piece.

The association of the themes with particular solo instruments gives the musical texture a transparent clarity. The variations do not preserve a melody, harmonic progression, or form. Instead, the themes of the two main characters appear within new musical contexts and are subjected to transformations in which the head of a theme usually leads to a new melodic continuation. This method suggests an interaction of the main characters with a series of incidents. Combining a program with solo instruments and variations structure, the piece is an amalgamation of genres, including elements of concerto and variations as well as symphonic poem.

The first variation is built on a scaffolding supplied by transformations of the two main themes in their characteristic instruments. We overhear an abstract and sometimes abstruse conversation between cello and bass clarinet. This leads to the tilting with windmills (measures 60–78). Their creaking blades are suggested by fast repeated notes played *col legno* (with the wood of the bow) in the orchestral cellos and staccato in the flutes and piccolo, and their slow but relentless turning, represented by a repeated downward arpeggiation by thirds, knocks Don Quixote off his horse (measures 71–72). He picks himself up, remounts, and goes on to the next adventure.

In the second variation of the knight's theme, figures in the strings portray Don Quixote's attempts to be bold and heroic, but his efforts are immediately ridiculed by the winds' mocking transformation of the Sancho theme. This variation depicts the encounter with the sheep (beginning at measure 101), with flutter-tonguing (rapid tongue motions while otherwise playing normally) in the brass and winds to imitate the bleating of the sheep. Here Strauss anticipates a technique that Arnold Schoenberg called *Klangfarbenmelodie*, in which instruments maintaining constant pitches drop in and out of an orchestral texture, creating a melody of tone colors.

(Schoenberg experimented with this method in *Farben* [Colors], which he later called *Summer Morning by a Lake*, the third of his Five Orchestral Pieces, Op. 16, of 1909.) Strauss's changing colors transport us into a dream world, where the normal dimensions of melody and harmony no longer pertain. Naturally, the sheep win the "battle," but once again Don Quixote reasserts his heroism and is ready for another trial. "Fantastic" is an apt word for these variations, where familiar themes and relationships lose their normal thread and footing.

Amy Marcy Beach (1867–1944)

Piano Quintet in F-sharp Minor, Op. 67: Third movement, Allegro agitato

Piano quintet

1907

CD 10|31

From Mrs. H. H. A. Beach, *Quintet in F-sharp minor for Pianoforte, 2 Violins, Viola and Violoncello, Op. 67* (Boston, Leipzig, New York: Arthur P. Schmidt, 1909; repr. New York: Da Capo Press, 1979), 30–47. Copyright 1909, A. P. Schmidt, Evanston, Illinois. Copyright renewed. Reprinted by Da Capo Press, Inc.

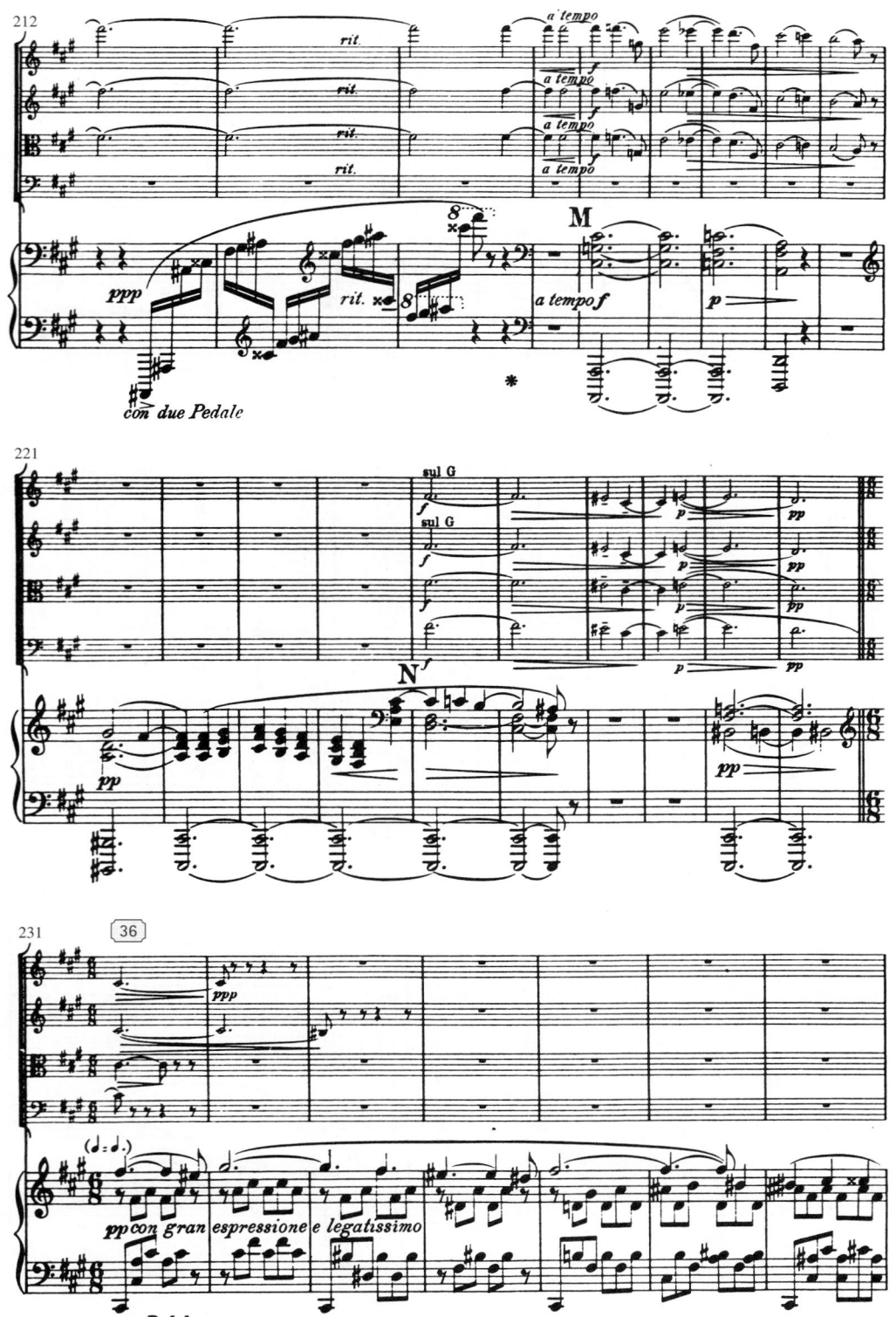

Amy Marcy Beach wrote her Quintet for Piano and Strings between 1905 and 1907 and first performed it with the Hoffman Quartet in Boston on February 27, 1908. It was unanimously praised by the critics; one called it "truly substantial, free, variously imagined and restlessly expressive music" and "truly modern." It was published the following year, under the name Beach always used: "Mrs. H. H. A. Beach," a title that signaled her social standing as the wife of a wealthy physician. Indeed, she was able to achieve what she did, as a woman in a field dominated by men, in part because she did not have to earn a living and could devote herself to composition, with her husband's encouragement.

Beach's inspiration for writing her quintet was Brahms's Piano Quintet in F Minor, Op. 34, which she had performed in 1900 with the Kneisel Quartet, then the leading string quartet in the United States. She used the second theme of Brahms's finale as a starting point. In each of her three movements, Beach's first theme is adapted from Brahms's theme, and her themes are then related to each other through thematic transformation. The theme in the finale is the most distantly related to Brahms's (shared tones are marked with an x):

Brahms, Piano Quintet in F Minor, Op. 34, fourth movement

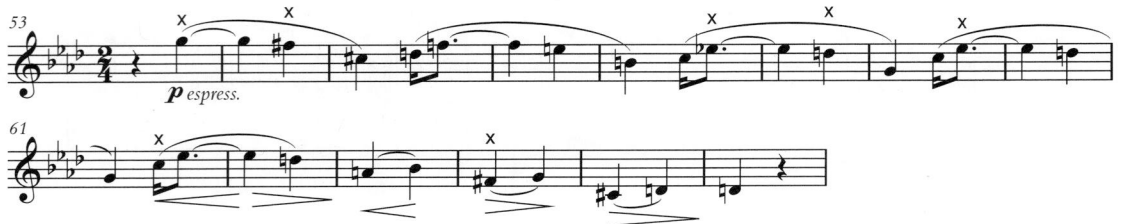

Beach, Piano Quintet, third movement

In Beach's finale, her individual voice emerges forcefully. The movement's rich harmony, rooted in chromatic progressions common in the late nineteenth century, ventures into unusual inversions, augmented triads, and colorful non-chord tones. The rhapsodic sweep and brilliant piano writing are reminiscent of Chopin and Liszt (see NAWM 118 and 119) and resemble those of her younger contemporary Rachmaninov (see NAWM 139). The most prominent gestures in the movement are the augmented second of the main theme and the upward leap of the minor ninth in its second phrase (see measures 18–21).

The form of the movement is a modified sonata form, as charted below:

Section:	Exposition							Development			
Music:	Intro	1T	Tr	2T				(1T)	Intro	fugato	(1st mvt)
				a	a'	b	a				
Key:	f♯			mod	A		to V of f♯	f♯, mod	f♯		
Measure:	1	13	32	60	76	92	108	132	164	176	208

Section:	Recapitulation					Coda
Music:	2T				1T	(from 1T)
	a	a'	b	a		
Key:	f♯					f♯
Measure:	231	247	263	279	303	311

The exposition begins with a dramatic introduction that dwells on an augmented triad. The first theme, begun by the first violin and completed by the piano, starts to destabilize the tonic key of F♯ minor even before it is firmly established. The transition (measure 32) restates the theme a major third lower in the unison strings against rapid chromatic filigree and chordal passages in the piano and culminates in a varied recollection of the introduction (measure 50)—a most unusual way to effect a modulation. In accordance with the standard sonata form, the second theme appears in the relative major, but the A major triad itself occurs only rarely amid the highly chromatic harmony. The theme is in AA'BA form and has the character of a nocturne, progressing slowly from lyricism to drama.

The first theme quietly returns to begin the development and leads to yet another varied restatement of the introduction (measure 164). Tremolo strings then play a fugato on the first theme that is—surprisingly—in the tonic. This leads to a stirring climax on a diminished seventh chord, and another surprise— a recollection of the Adagio introduction from the first movement, including that movement's main theme (at measure 215). The development has dwelt so much on the first theme and on F♯ minor that to repeat it would be redundant, so the recapitulation begins with the second theme in the tonic, now introduced by the piano. The movement ends with a brief final statement of the first theme and a Presto coda that recalls both that theme and the first movement.

There are other ways to read the form of the finale: as a sonata form without development, interpreting measures 132–207 as a varied recapitulation of the first theme and transition; or as a sonata-rondo form with the statements of the second theme treated as episodes. Such ambiguity of form in a movement clearly based on the sonata principle is typical of works composed during the latter nineteenth and early twentieth centuries, when devising a novel variant of sonata form was almost as important as inventing original and appealing themes.

JOHN PHILIP SOUSA (1854–1932)

The Stars and Stripes Forever

March

1897

135

From John Philip Sousa, *The Stars and Stripes Forever* (Cincinnati: John Church, 1897). Reprinted in John Philip Sousa, *Sousa's Great Marches in Piano Transcription*, ed. Lester S. Levy (New York: Dover, 1975), 68–71. Dover Publications, Inc.

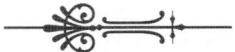

John Philip Sousa joined the United States Marine Band at age thirteen as an apprentice, left several years later to pursue a freelance career as performer and composer, and returned at age twenty-five as conductor. After leading the Marine Band (known as "The President's Own") to national prominence through touring, he founded his own band in 1892 and reigned for the next four decades as the most famous band conductor and composer of all time. Although he composed in a wide variety of genres, he is best remembered for his marches, which earned him the nickname "The March King."

The Stars and Stripes Forever (1897) is a perfect example of Sousa's mature march style: strong contrasts between sections are complemented by contrasting materials within each section, producing the great variety within a simple form that became part of Sousa's appeal. The form of this particular piece can be diagrammed as follows:

Section:	March							Trio		Break Strain	Trio	
	Intro	‖:	A	:‖:	B	:‖		C	‖:	D		C	:‖
Key:	E♭							A♭					
Measure:	1		5		21			37		69		93	

The march begins with a four-bar introduction, featuring unharmonized octaves, followed by two repeated sixteen-bar strains, the first sprightly and the second featuring a noble-sounding tune played *fortissimo*. Sousa then modulates to the key a fourth higher for the lyrical thirty-two bar section called the trio.

Earlier marches were meant for parade use and typically would have continued with several additional strains and a *da capo* return to allow for the continual recycling of musical materials as the band moved past its audience. Sousa's Band, however, was a concert organization and rarely took part in parades. As a result, his mature marches have a linear form and highlight what the composer called "the story-telling quality" of the piece. Like other nineteenth-century instrumental works, going back to Beethoven's symphonies, Sousa's marches emphasize the end of the piece rather than its beginning, which Sousa accomplished by following the trio with a sudden change in dynamic, texture, and instrumentation to create a contrasting section commonly referred to as the *break strain*. It is also called the *dogfight*, referring to the composer's frequent practice of alternating short statements between high and low instruments as if they were dueling back and forth. The break strain is the most chromatic section of the march. The rest of the march alternates between the break strain and the trio, repeated as a unit.

In order to avoid simple repetition and to increase the sense of a continuing narrative, Sousa adds new countermelodies for each pass through the trio, first in the piccolos and then in the low brass. These countermelodies are not included in the sheet music shown here, which was intended for home performance by amateur pianists, but are included in the parts. In the nineteenth century, band marches were rarely published in score but were available in piano transcription or as a set of parts.

Given Sousa's position as a composer, performer, and businessman, it is not surprising that his pieces were often performed—even by him—in ways differing from the published sheet music. By changing instrumentation, articulations, and dynamics, the Sousa Band was able to surprise audiences with novel effects. The result is a piece simple enough for an amateur pianist, challenging enough for a professional band, and interesting enough for audiences. Indeed, Sousa found *The Stars and Stripes Forever* so flexible that in response to the Spanish-American War he set it with words for the musical pageant *Trooping of the Colors* in 1898, and published it as a song. *The Stars and Stripes Forever* was also the last work he conducted, at a rehearsal shortly before his death. It has been suggested that this march may have sold more copies in sheet music than any other piece.

SCOTT JOPLIN (1867/8–1917)

Maple Leaf Rag

Piano rag
1899

[Joplin recording] CD 10|43

[Morton recording] CD 10|47

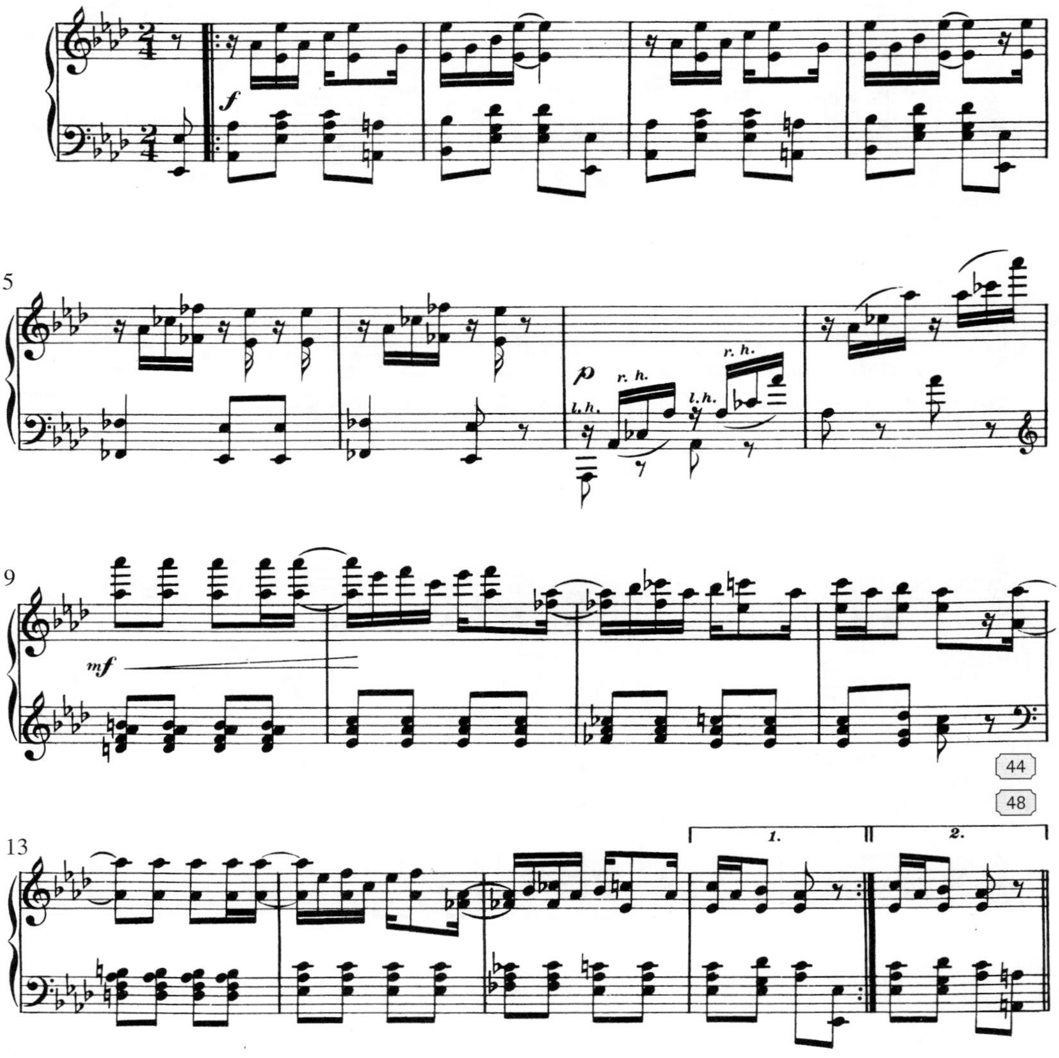

From Scott Joplin, *Maple Leaf Rag* (Sedalia, Mo: John Stark & Son, 1899). Reprinted in Scott Joplin, *Complete Piano Works*, ed. Vera Brodsky Lawrence (New York: The New York Public Library, 1971), 26–28. Used by permission.

Scott Joplin named his *Maple Leaf Rag* after the Maple Leaf Club in Sedalia, Missouri, where he performed regularly as a pianist in the late 1890s. Instead of selling the piece outright to a publisher, as was a frequent practice of composers at the time, he negotiated with his publisher, John Stark, for a royalty of one cent per copy. The first year only about four hundred copies were sold, but eventually buyers took home more than a million copies, making it the most famous piano rag in history and the first piece by an African American to sell so well. Although ragtime was a type of popular music, Joplin intended his rags as classical works, equivalent to other stylized dances, such as Chopin's mazurkas and waltzes (compare NAWM 117).

The form of a rag is like that of a march, with two repeated sixteen-measure strains followed by a trio, usually in a key a fourth higher, that features two more strains. *Maple Leaf Rag* is unusual in that it lacks the typical four-measure introduction, repeats the first strain once again after the second strain and before the trio, and returns to the original key in the last strain. Thus its form is AABBACCDD, in which the C strain is in the subdominant D♭ major and the others in the tonic A♭ major. The contrasts of melody and figuration between and within strains are strong, as in Sousa's march (NAWM 135), but the logical form and several recurring rhythmic figures lend the piece a satisfying unity.

In a rag, the left-hand accompaniment keeps a steady beat in eighth notes while the right hand plays syncopated figures above it. The most common accompanimental pattern for rags is the alternation of a bass octave on the beat with chords on the offbeats, as at measures 17 and 49, but *Maple Leaf Rag* also includes other patterns, like those at measures 1 and 9. Throughout the rag, the syncopations in the right hand vary tremendously, with well over a dozen different possible combinations of rhythms within a measure. Longer or accented notes often fall on the sixteenth note just before or just after the beat. These constantly changing rhythms give the music much of its energy. But the harmony is also colorful, with chromatic passing tones, lowered sixth chords (measure 5), changes of mode (to minor in measure 7), diminished seventh chords (measure 9), ninth chords (measures 31 and 49), and other effects. All strains but the first begin away from the tonic chord, and all cadences involve some chromaticism, providing momentum toward resolution.

The accompanying recording includes two performances. The first is by Scott Joplin himself, recorded on a player piano roll in April 1916. Player pianos literally play themselves, with an internal mechanism that depresses the keys. As a paper roll passes over a metal cylinder that has a small hole for each key on the piano keyboard, a suction pump draws in air wherever a hole is cut in the paper, and a mechanical mechanism presses the corresponding key, sounding that note. Many famous pianists—including several composers, such as Joplin—recorded music this way. Piano rolls were one form in which music was sold in the late nineteenth and early twentieth centuries, and they helped to popularize Joplin's music. His roll gives us a good sense of his playing: steady, clear, and not too fast (he often admonished players not to play ragtime fast). He adds notes and flourishes here and there, especially to the bass line.

The second performance is by Jelly Roll Morton (1890–1941), recorded in June 1938. Morton was one of the pioneers of jazz, and his playing shows the characteristics of the early New Orleans style. While Joplin played the piece more or less as notated (as a classical piece would be played), Morton renders the sixteenth notes in the swinging style associated with jazz, in which the notes on the beat (here, on each eighth note) are elongated and those on the offbeats shortened, creating a rhythm like triplets alternating eighth and sixteenth notes. Moreover, he freely changes the material, adding an introduction (based on the second half of the first strain), adding new syncopations, and altering some passages almost beyond recognition. He also omits the repetitions of the first two strains, to keep the piece under the three- to four-minute limit for 78-rpm records.

GUSTAV MAHLER (1860–1911)

Kindertotenlieder: No. 1, *Nun will die Sonn' so hell aufgeh'n*

Orchestral song cycle

1901

CD 10|51   CD 5|65

Langsam und schwermütig; nicht schleppend.

2 Flöten.

1 Oboe. *klagend*

2 Clarinetten in B.

Baß-Clarinette in B.

2 Fagotte. II.

Horn I in F. *sempre p*

Horn II in F.

Harfe.

Glockenspiel.

Violine I.

Violine II.

Viola.

Singstimme.

Nun will die

Violoncell.

Baß.

Langsam und schwermütig; nicht schleppend.

From Gustav Mahler, *Songs of a Wayfarer* and *Kindertotenlieder* in full score (New York: Dover), 59–73.
Used by permission of Dover Publications, Inc.

Das Unglück ge- schah nur mir al- lein!

Crazy intervals!

Nun will die Sonn' so hell aufgeh'n,	Now will the sun so brightly rise
Als sei kein Unglück die Nacht gescheh'n!	as if no misfortune had happened during the night!
Das Unglück geschah nur mir allein!	The misfortune happened to me alone!
Die Sonne, sie scheinet allgemein!	The sun, it shines on everyone!
Du musst nicht die Nacht in dir verschränken,	You must not enfold the night within you,
Musst sie ins ew'ge Licht versenken!	You must immerse it in everlasting light!
Ein Lämplein verlosch in meinem Zelt!	A little lamp went out in my tent!
Heil sei dem Freudenlicht der Welt!	Hail to the joy-light of the world!

—FRIEDRICH RÜCKERT

Gustav Mahler's *Kindertotenlieder* (Songs on the Death of Children) is a cycle of five songs for solo voice and orchestra on poems by Friedrich Rückert about the deaths of children and the feelings of grieving parents. Rückert wrote the poems after his own two children died from scarlet fever, but when Mahler wrote the first three songs in the cycle during a two-week period in the summer of 1901, including the song shown here, he was unmarried and childless. He was attracted to the poems because of the intense emotions they conveyed, the painful irony of a parent mourning a child instead of the other way around, and perhaps the coincidence that Rückert's son was named Ernst, the name of Mahler's beloved younger brother, who died at age thirteen. By the time Mahler finished the cycle in 1904, he was married and a father, and his wife Alma later recalled that she thought he was tempting fate by continuing to work on these songs. The cycle was first performed in Vienna in January 1905.

In the first song, *Nun will die Sonn' so hell aufgeh'n,* Rückert's text is not comforting, but bitterly ironic. The speaker's child has died during the night, but the sun shines anyway as if nothing had happened; the sorrow is his alone, and neither the world nor the sun seems to care.

Mahler's setting heightens these ironies. The opening duet of horn and oboe sounds stark, its bare harmonic fourths and octaves empty. The apparently joyful words "Now will the sun so brightly rise" are set to a mournful descending melody composed primarily of half-steps, an emblem of sadness since the Renaissance madrigal, and accompanied by half-step motives in horn and bassoon. Yet for the next line, which tells of the misfortune that occurred during the night, the music slowly shifts to major through a rising chromatic melody, and the cadence is in a radiant D major. The misalignment of mood between text and music makes clear that the sun is not a source of joy for the poet today, but an uncaring and even mocking observer.

An orchestral interlude leads the music back to minor for the second couplet (at measure 22). Here the music varies what we have already heard, but the mismatch of mood is gone; the poet's sense of being alone with his misfortune is clearly etched by the mournful melody, and the bright D-major cadence is perfectly suited to the sentiment that the sun shines on everyone, although the poet is left to feel even more alone in his misery.

The music sounds like it will repeat once more (measures 41–47), but instead the singer inverts the melody and heads in a new direction (at measure 47). This third couplet is the only one in the poem not to mention misfortune or the sun directly, so Mahler gives it new music, developing the half-step motive, chromatic motion, and other ideas already heard. The words suggest a path out of despair— you must not give in to darkness by holding it in yourself, but must bathe it in endless light—but the music reaches a new height of dissonance, chromaticism, and intensity, suggesting that such advice could not be followed easily, if at all.

The final couplet (measure 67) returns to the music of the first couplet, with intensified emphasis on melodic seconds through rhythmic diminution. Here, though, the major-mode cadence in the voice is followed by another cadential phrase, repeating the words "to the joy-light of the world!" to mournful music first heard in the orchestra (compare measures 79–82 with measures 17–20) and closing in a poignant D minor.

The very simplicity of this music makes it even more affecting. The form is a modified AABA song form, yet the changing relationship between music and text along with subtle variations in the music keep it fresh. The contrasts between D minor and D major and between diatonic and chromatic passages are again simple, but wonderfully effective and typical of Mahler. The sparse use of instruments creates a transparent sound, yet the delicate counterpoint is suffused with chromaticism and dissonance to convey the sense of loss and hurt so poignantly articulated in the text.

Claude Debussy (1862–1918)

Nocturnes: No. 1, *Nuages* (Clouds)

Symphonic poem

1897–99

138

CD 10|59 CD 5|73

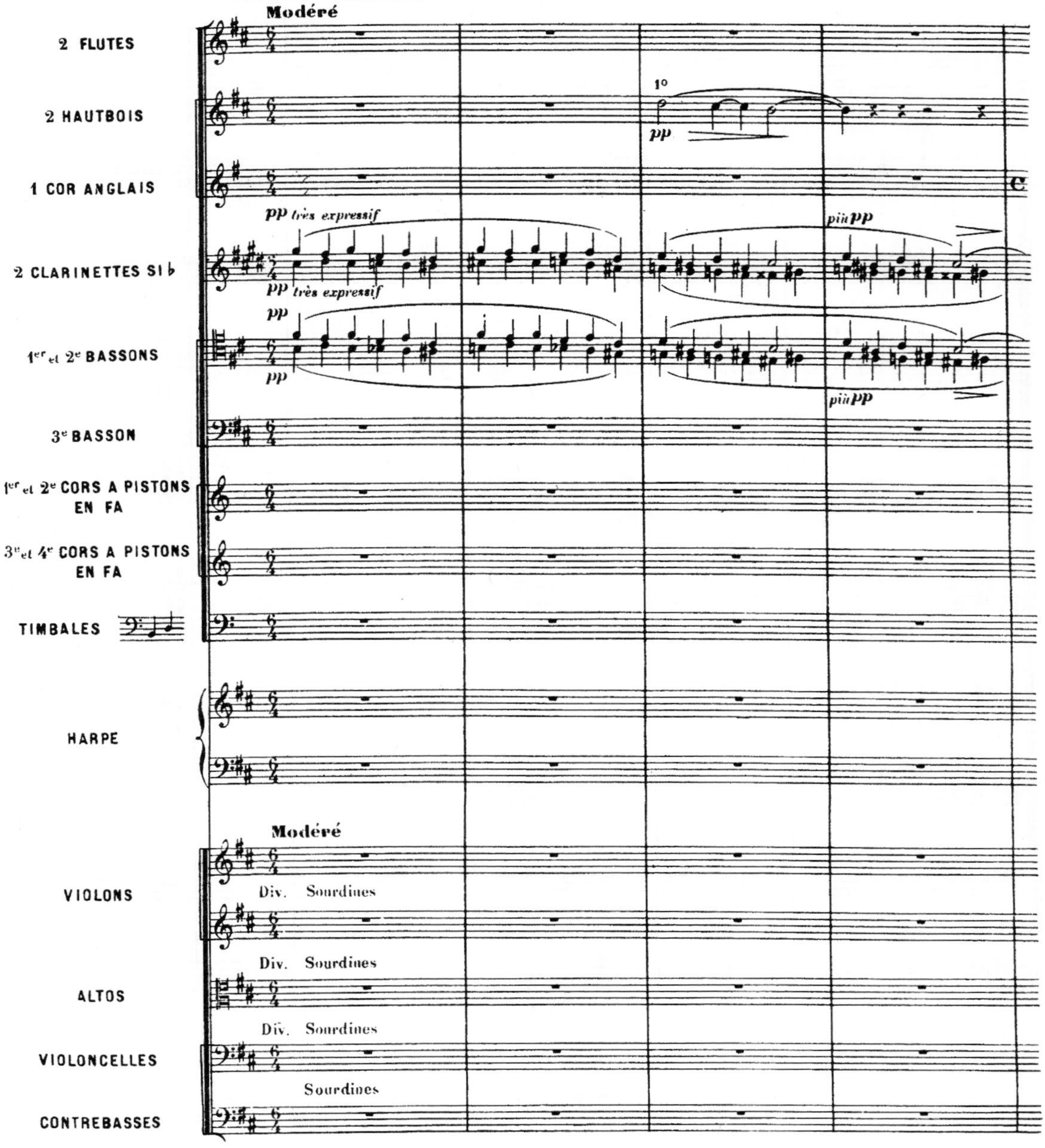

From Claude Debussy, *Nocturnes*, ed. Clinton F. Nieweg (New York: E. F. Kalmus, 1990, 2004), 2–18.

Claude Debussy began his three *Nocturnes* as a set of pieces for solo violin and orchestra for violinist Eugène Ysaÿe, but soon recast them as symphonic poems for orchestra alone. They took him almost three years to complete (1897–99), between work on other projects. The name *Nocturnes* was meant not to evoke the genre Chopin had helped to popularize (see NAWM 118), but to suggest musical pictures of nighttime scenes: *Nuages* (Clouds), evoking shifting clouds; *Fêtes* (Festivals), depicting evening festivities; and *Sirènes* (Sirens), bringing to life the Sirens of ancient Greece with a wordless women's chorus behind the orchestra. The first two movements were performed in 1900, and the complete piece was published later that year.

Like all of Debussy's orchestral music, *Nuages* is a play of musical images, each characterized by instrumental color, motive, pitch collection, rhythm, and register. In the course of the movement, images are juxtaposed, superimposed, repeated, and altered, creating a kind of musical experience that seems almost visual, rather than following the older literary or rhetorical model of music that presents, develops, and recapitulates themes. *Nuages* consists of three sections in a modified ABA' form, with the A section (measures 1–63) far longer than the others (measures 64–79 and 80–102 respectively).

The opening image, a pattern of alternating fifths and thirds adapted from a song by Musorgsky, suggests movement without a strong sense of direction, an apt musical representation of slowly moving clouds. It changes almost every time it recurs: the winds are replaced by strings (measure 11), the oscillations by parallel ninth chords (measure 14) or triads (measure 29), the open fifths and thirds by full triads (measure 21) or seventh chords (measure 43, joined by pizzicato offbeats), and so on. In the brief A' section the pattern is heard only in fragments (measures 94–97), as if the clouds were scattering.

Juxtaposed with or superimposed upon the opening image is a motive in the English horn, set off in a meter of its own ($\frac{4}{4}$ against $\frac{6}{4}$ in the other instruments), that quickly rises and slowly descends through a portion of the octatonic scale, spanning a tritone (measures 5–8). Unlike the constantly changing clouds, this figure changes little. The final notes are sometimes omitted or repeated, but the motive is otherwise the same at each appearance, never developed, transposed, or played by another instrument, and the English horn never plays anything else. After most statements, the horns answer with a tritone (as at measure 23) or another brief gesture, drawing their notes from the same octatonic scale as the English horn (or, in the A' section, from a whole-tone scale). At the end, the final notes of the English horn motive echo a couple of times, and then it disappears.

The shifting cloud and steady English horn ideas are interspersed with contrasting episodes: a chordal idea in the strings (measures 15–20) and a unison melody, perhaps derived from the cloud figure, that gradually rises in sequence and crescendos (measures 33–42). The middle section has a more exotic source: Debussy heard a *gamelan*, a Javanese orchestra made up mainly of gongs and percussion, at the Paris Exposition in 1889. He simulated the gamelan texture in

Nuages by giving the flute and harp a simple pentatonic tune, analogous to Javanese themes, while the other instruments supply a static background.

As in works by Musorgsky (see NAWM 130) and Fauré, chords in *Nuages* are not used to shape a phrase by tension and release. Instead, each chord is conceived as a sonorous unit in a phrase whose structure is determined more by melodic shape or color than by harmonic movement. Oscillating chords, parallel triads and ninth chords, and sustained chords all serve to create distinctive musical images. However, such a procedure does not necessarily negate tonality, which Debussy maintains in *Nuages* through pedal points and frequent returns to the primary chords of B minor, the key of the A sections.

Often, Debussy uses different pitch collections to distinguish blocks of sound from one another as they are juxtaposed. The opening cloud figure features a B-minor scale tinged with chromaticism, which contrasts with the octatonic scale in the English horn motive and its accompanying chords. The B section inhabits a contrasting tonal world centered on the D♯ Dorian scale (measures 64–68).

Debussy's writing for orchestra is full of striking touches, including the identification of the English horn with a single motive, the use of the horns for only brief gestures, and the bell-like combination of flute in unison with harp. The strings are muted and divided (the violins in as many as twelve parts, the violas and cellos in two), giving a rich but distant sound, and independent lines for solo violin and viola add contrasting colors. Very soft timpani rolls, barely heard near the beginning and end of the piece, create a sense of vibrant stillness.

139

Sergei Rachmaninov (1873–1943)

Prelude in G Minor, Op. 23, No. 5

Piano prelude

1901

CD 10|67

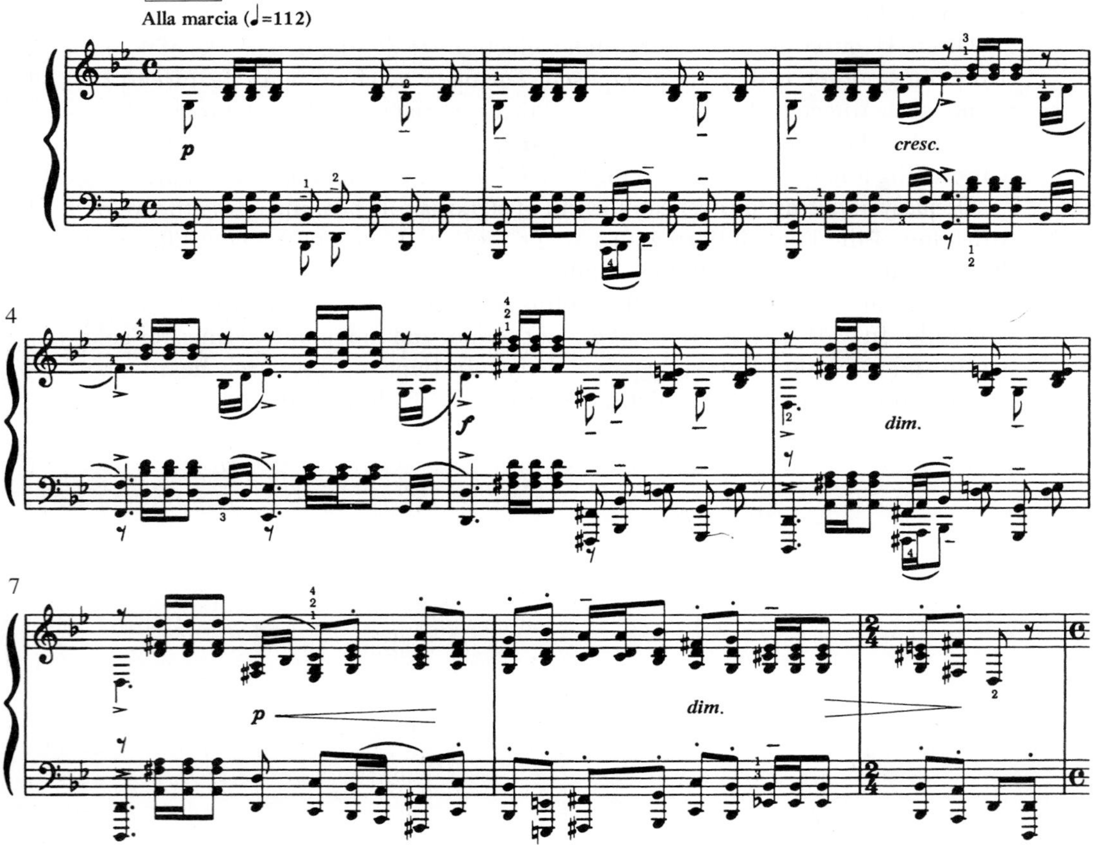

From Sergei Rachmaninoff, *Prelude, Opus 3, No. 2 in C-sharp Minor; Ten Preludes, Opus 23*, ed. Ruth Laredo (New York: C. F. Peters, 1985), 24–29.

Sergei Rachmaninov composed his Prelude in G Minor in 1901 as a freestanding work, then in 1903 added nine more and published them as his Ten Preludes, Op. 23. Later, he wrote thirteen more preludes for his Op. 32 (1910). These two collections, together with the C♯-minor prelude of 1892, constituted a complete set of twenty-four preludes in every major and minor key, following the model of Chopin's Preludes, Op. 28, and of Bach's *Well-Tempered Clavier*. Yet because they were initially conceived individually, Rachmaninov's preludes are longer than those of Chopin and Bach and are rarely played as a group.

The form of the Prelude in G Minor is relatively simple: ABA Coda, with the A section itself in aaba song form. Yet almost every time an idea repeats, Rachmaninov introduces new variants, maintaining interest through constant if subtle changes:

Section:	A				B			A				Coda
Figure:	a	a'	b	a''	c	c'	trans (a)	a'''	a''''	b	a'''''	(from a)
Harmony:	i		mod	i	V			i	iv	mod	i	
Measure:	1	10	17	25	35	42	50	54	58	64	72	82

The two main sections differ greatly in character. The A theme is marchlike, with repeated sixteenth notes on the offbeats suggesting drumrolls, and builds to a powerful climax. The B theme is lyrical and passionate, over rolling arpeggiations in the accompaniment. Such stark contrasts of material and such strongly etched emotions are quintessential Rachmaninov.

Rachmaninov was not the innovator in harmony that his contemporaries Strauss, Debussy, Scriabin, and Schoenberg were. But he developed a highly individual and recognizable style within the musical language of Romanticism, which is perhaps an even more difficult feat. One element that set him apart was his gift for creating melodies that sounded familiar yet fresh, moving in unexpected ways yet always sounding right in retrospect. The opening melody, in the bass, is little more than an arpeggiated G-minor triad followed by an embellished stepwise descent from G to D, but its striking rhythm and the sixteenth-note figures that decorate its main notes make it unique and memorable. The middle-section theme hovers around A, straining to rise and sinking back twice, then climbs almost an octave before falling back into place again. Subtle connections link this theme to that of the first section, including a prominent diminished fourth between F♯ and B♭ (compare measures 36 and 5) and another bass stepwise descent from G to D (measures 39–40). The second time through (measure 42), a countermelody appears in the tenor, pressing upward and heightening the sense of yearning.

Another factor in Rachmaninov's individual style was his use of innovative textures on the piano, such as the figuration in the A section, where both hands move constantly back and forth between melody and accompaniment and between higher and lower registers. Even the treatment of harmony is unusual. The music never leaves the key of G minor; instead, Rachmaninov introduces motion up the circle of fifths (measures 17–21) to suggest a modulation within the A section, then focuses on the dominant seventh chord in the B section, in both cases relying on the major thirds in the chords to create a sense of contrast with the prevailing minor of the opening theme.

The performance on the accompanying recording is by Rachmaninov himself, recorded in April 1920 on a piano roll that, when replayed on an Ampico reproducing piano, reproduces not only the notes themselves (like the recording of Scott Joplin in NAWM 136) but also the pedaling, the dynamic level, and the emphasis the pianist gave to each note. Recordings of this sort had advantages over audio records of the time because they could go beyond the three- to four-minute limit for 78-rpm records, could be corrected by the artist, and could sound truer than any record because they were played on actual pianos. Rachmaninov's piano roll shows his dynamic playing, his variety of touch, his use of the pedal, and the fluctuating tempo that was part of the Romantic performing aesthetic. Arpeggiated chords in the middle section and an added note at the end suggest the freedom Romantic pianists took with music, especially their own.

140

Alexander Scriabin (1872–1915)

Vers la flamme, Op. 72

Tone poem for piano

1914

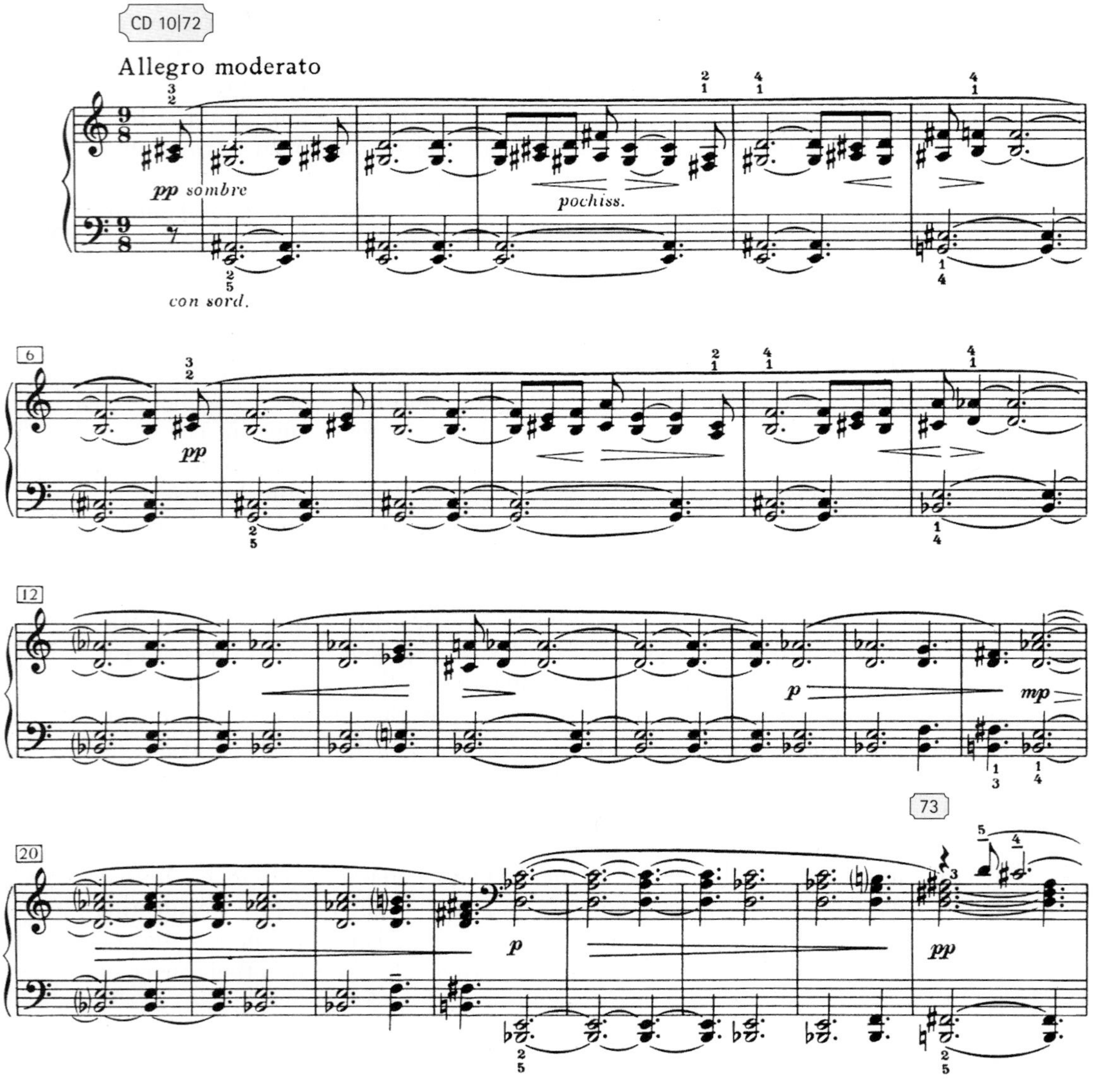

Alexander Scriabin composed *Vers la flamme* (Toward the Flame) in early 1914, conceiving it first as an orchestral work, and then as a sonata, before settling on the novel genre of a tone poem for piano, in emulation of the symphonic poem. The title suggests a journey toward enlightenment or even immolation, without specifying the course of events. Accordingly, the piece presents a series of abstract ideas, gradually increasing in activity and dynamic level and expanding upward in register until it reaches a transcendent climax at the end.

There are two main thematic ideas that define the form, which may be called theme A (measures 1–6) and theme B (measures 27–34). Theme A always involves two voices moving together in counterpoint, and theme B is a single melody. Both begin with repeated neighbor-note motion, then reach upward, fall back, and rise again, an apt image for the sense of striving implied by the piece's title and over-all shape. The piece unfolds as a series of textures, delineating four large sections that place the two thematic elements in new contexts:

Section	Measure	Texture	Theme
1	1	Block chords under melodies	A
	27		B
2	41	Stratified layers, oscillating bass and middle voice in 5 against 9	half-step motive from B
	65	Stratified layers, oscillating middle voice, arpeggios in bass	half-step motive from B, later part of A (measures 70, 74)
3	77	Rapid triplets over chords	A'
	81	Rapid triplets over leaping bass	B (repeats at measure 89)
	95	Rapid triplets alternating with tremolos/high pulsed chords	transition
4	107	Tremolos and high pulsed chords	A
	125		B (beginning only)

The work is not tonal in a conventional sense. Rather, a referential sonority of two interlocked tritones announced at the beginning, E–A♯–G♯–D, often embellished with C♯ or F♯, serves as a kind of tonic chord, transposed and varied over the course of the movement. Variants appear at measures 28, 41, 65, 77, 95, 107, and 125. Several of these substitute B for A♯ or include both, thereby creating a sonority that resembles a dominant seventh chord with added notes. At the end the D is raised to D♯ (measure 125), resolving any remaining tension in a climactic apotheosis marked by the widest range and highest pitches of the whole movement. Although theme B appears in a new transposition each time, theme A returns in sections 3 and 4 at its original pitch, creating a sense of stability in the second half of the piece akin to a return to the tonic in a piece of tonal music.

Scriabin's use of harmonic relationships by thirds in this piece is characteristic of his work in general. Theme A is almost entirely octatonic (excepting only the F♯), and Scriabin treats it in sequence by minor third (measures 1–12). Theme B highlights a chord of stacked thirds (B–D–F♯–A♯–C♯) that moves by minor third as well (measures 29–32). Other passages also feature movement by major third (see the bass line in measures 41–64) or minor third (measures 68–77). Most chords have four or more notes, and the final sonority has six, combining traditional tertian structure in the lower notes with stacks of fourths in the upper register. The many dissonances do not require resolution; instead, as in the music of Musorgsky (NAWM 130) or Debussy (NAWM 138), they provide harmonic color that serves to distinguish one block of ideas from another, while the movement from one complex chord to the next conveys a sense of harmonic progression.

A virtuoso showpiece, *Vers la flamme* poses numerous difficulties for the performer, including rhythms of five against nine (see the passages beginning at measures 41 and 81) and rapid leaps around the keyboard. At the end, Scriabin requires three staves to notate his massive sonorities (measure 125).

ARNOLD SCHOENBERG (1874–1951)

Pierrot lunaire, Op. 21: Excerpts

Melodrama (song cycle) for speaker and chamber ensemble

1912

(a) No. 8: *Nacht* (Night)

Und vom Him — mel er — denwärts sen_ken sich mit schwe — renSchwin — gen

un — — sichtbar die Un — ge_tü — me auf die Men — — schen_

her — — zen nie — der... fin — _stre,schwar — _ze

sehr große Pause, aber quasi im Takt, dann folgt:
Gebet an Pierrot.
Klavier, Klarinette in A.

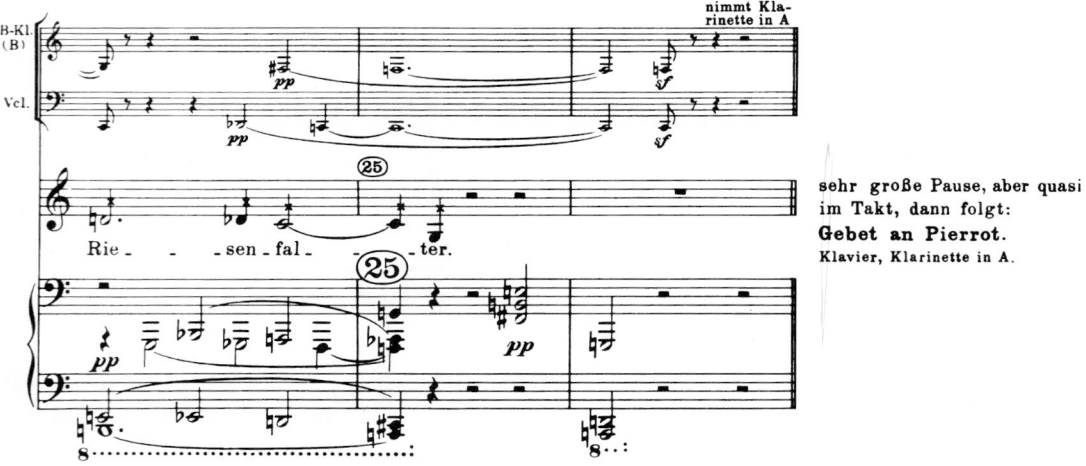

(b) No. 13: *Enthauptung* (Beheading)

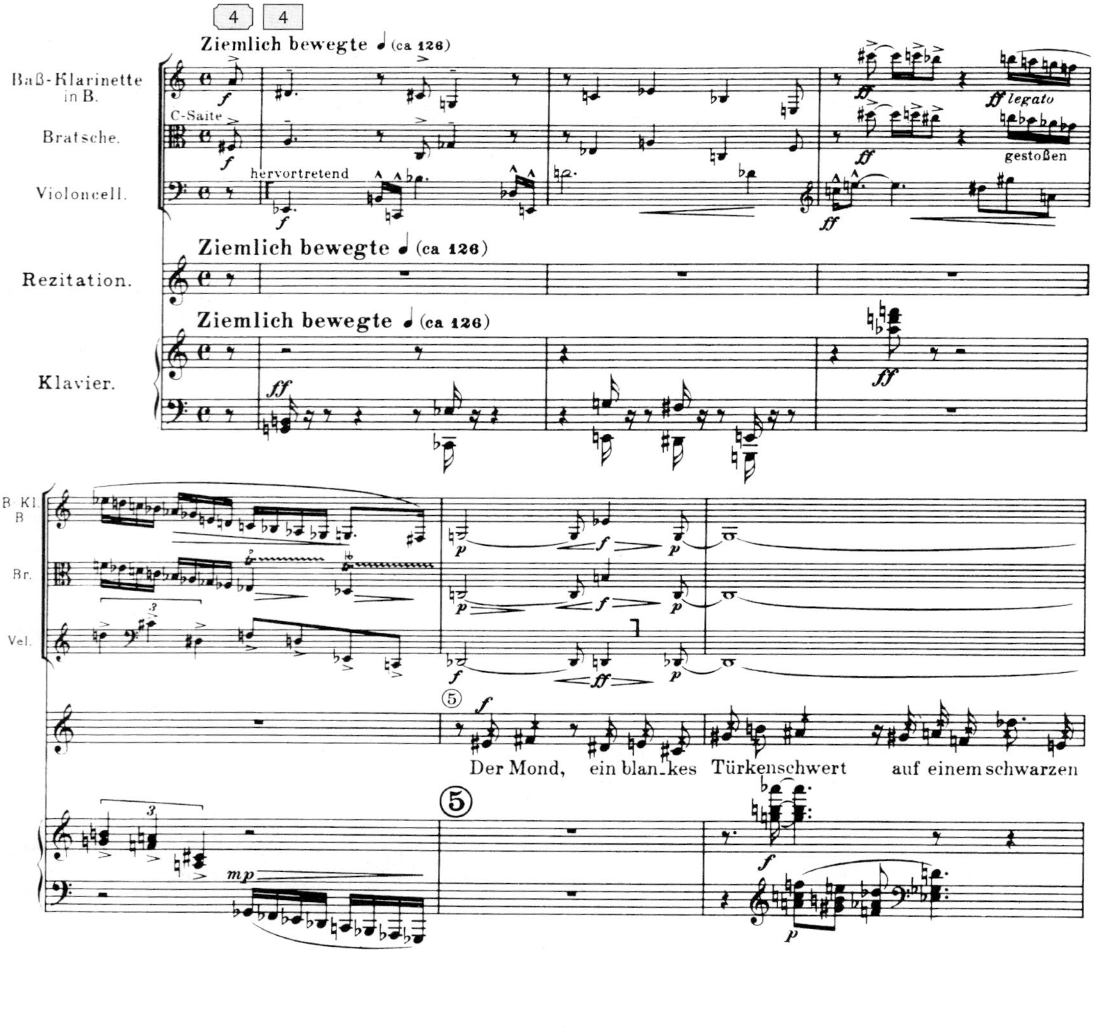

folgt: **Die Kreuze**
unmittelbar anschließend.
Klavier (anfangs allein) später
dazu Flöte, Klar. (A), Geige, Vcl.

⌐ ⌐ bedeutet Hauptstimme.

NACHT

Finstre, schwarze Riesenfalter
Töteten der Sonne Glanz.
Ein geschloßnes Zauberbuch,
Ruht der Horizont—verschwiegen.

Aus dem Qualm verlorner Tiefen
Steigt ein Duft, Erinnrung mordend!
Finstre, schwarze Riesenfalter
Töteten der Sonne Glanz.

Und vom Himmel erdenwärts
Senken sich mit schweren Schwingen
Unsichtbar die Ungetüme
Auf die Menschenherzen nieder . . .
Finstre, schwarze Riesenfalter.

ENTHAUPTUNG

Der Mond, ein blankes Türkenschwert,
Auf einen schwarzen Seidenkissen,
Gespenstisch groß—dräut er hinab
Durch schmerzensdunkle Nacht.

Pierrot irrt ohne Rast umher
Und starrt empor in Todesängsten
Zum Mond, dem blanken Türkenschwert
Auf einem schwarzen Seidenkissen.

Es schlottern unter ihm die Knie,
Ohnmächtig bricht er jäh zusammen.
Er wähnt: es sause strafend schon
Auf seinen Sündenhals hernieder
Der Mond, das blanke Türkenschwert.

NIGHT

Dark black giant moths
killed the radiance of the sun.
A sealed book of magic,
the horizon rests, keeping silence.

From the vapor of forgotten depths
rises a fragrance, killing memory!
Dark black giant moths
killed the radiance of the sun.

And from heaven earthwards
they sink with ponderous oscillations,
invisible monsters,
down to the hearts of men . . .
Dark black giant moths.

BEHEADING

The moon, a polished scimitar
on a black silken cushion,
ghostly vast, menaces downwards
through pain-dark night.

Pierrot wanders about, restless,
and stares on high in mortal terror
at the moon, the polished scimitar
on a black silken cushion.

His knees knock together under him;
swooning, he suddenly collapses.
He imagines: in punishment, it is already
rushing down on his guilty neck,
the moon, the polished scimitar.

—ALBERT GIRAUD, TRANSLATED FROM
THE FRENCH BY O. ERICH HARTLEBEN

Arnold Schoenberg wrote *Pierrot lunaire* in the spring of 1912, after moving from Vienna to Berlin with his family the previous fall. The full title of this cycle of songs translates as "Three times seven poems from Albert Giraud's *Pierrot lunaire.*" He composed it at the request of Albertine Zehme, an actress who asked for a piano accompaniment over which she could recite the poetry. As Schoenberg worked on it, he added other instruments, and the result was a piece scored for a speaker and five musicians, some of whom doubled on a second instrument: flute (piccolo), clarinet (bass clarinet), violin (viola), cello, and piano. By using a different combination of instruments for every song in the cycle, Schoenberg achieves a maximum variety of color. Throughout the cycle, the voice declaims the text in what Schoenberg called *Sprechstimme* (speaking voice), following the notated rhythm exactly but only approximating the written pitches in gliding tones of speech. He indicated this effect—an innovative synthesis of melodrama and song—with an x through the stem of each note. Schoenberg conducted the premiere with Zehme in October 1912, and then they took the work on tour through Germany and Austria. It was well received and helped to establish his reputation as a leading modernist composer of his generation. When *Pierrot lunaire* was published in 1914, Schoenberg designated it Opus 21, the same number as there are songs in the cycle.

For his text, Schoenberg selected poems from a collection by Albert Giraud, a Belgian symbolist poet, translated into German by O. Erich Hartleben. Giraud imagined Pierrot, the stock comic character from the improvised theatrical tradition of *commedia dell'arte*, pursued by fantastic, threatening visions of the moon. The extreme situations and vivid images prompted Schoenberg to use an intense and dissonant musical language in the instruments, heightened by the eerie effect of the gliding, inexact pitches in the voice. Just as certain expressionist painters, such as Oskar Kokoschka and Egon Schiele, distorted representations of real objects to reflect their feelings about their surroundings and themselves, so Schoenberg used exaggerated graphic images and speech inflections in this work to express the feelings conveyed in the poetry.

The poems in the cycle are unrhymed but follow a strict form: each is thirteen lines long, divided in two quatrains and a quintain, and uses the first two lines as a refrain, repeating them as lines 7–8 and stating line 1 again as line 13. In most of the songs, Schoenberg reflected this form by including instrumental interludes after each quatrain and by highlighting repeated lines of text with an allusion to their original music at the same pitch level.

Pierrot lunaire is *atonal*, meaning that no pitch serves as a tonal center. Instead, Schoenberg relies on motivic development to give his music coherence and shape, using the method he called *developing variation*, presenting a basic idea at the outset and then continuously drawing out new variants of that idea. Many of the songs evoke old forms or genres or rely on traditional techniques—such as canons—to ensure unity and give the listener something familiar to grasp.

In No. 8, *Nacht* (Night), Pierrot sees giant black moths casting gloom over the world, shutting out the sun. The basic motive, a rising minor third followed by a descending major third, reappears constantly in various note values throughout the parts, often overlapping itself. At the beginning, for example, the first three notes, *E'–G'–E♭'*, form a statement of the motive, but the second note initiates another statement (*G'–B♭'–G♭'*), whose second note in turn initiates another (*B♭'–D♭–A'*), and so on, until six intertwined statements appear in the first three measures. (Note that the bass clarinet in B♭ sounds a major ninth lower than written.) This three-note motive suffuses the entire piece, in various transformations including inversion and retrograde, and its omnipresence creates a fitting musical image of Pierrot's obsession with the giant moths. At one point (measure 10), the voice stops speaking and sings the motive. Even the motive's shape, in original form or inverted, suggests the wings of the moths.

Schoenberg calls this song a *passacaglia*, a set of variations over a repeated bass, but it is an unusual one. The bass ostinato consists of the basic motive on E (E–G–E♭) followed by a chromatic descent. The ostinato is first stated in measures 4–6 by the bass clarinet and imitated at one-measure intervals by the cello and the two hands on the piano. It reappears varied over ten more times, usually in the piano left hand, returning with particular prominence at measures 11, 16, 23 (in the voice), and 24 to mark the refrains and musical interludes. At the end (measures 24–25), the original complex of overlapping statements of the basic motive (from measures 1–3) repeats at pitch, modified to include the chromatic descent that characterizes the bass ostinato. Despite the atonal harmonies, this frequent repetition of the passacaglia ostinato and its opening notes E–G–E♭ creates a sense of tonal location, allowing Schoenberg to establish a home region, depart from it, and return at significant points and at the end, just as in tonal music.

In No. 13, *Enthauptung* (Beheading), Pierrot imagines that he is beheaded by the moonbeam for his crimes. The first five measures encapsulate the poem and include a cascade of notes in the bass clarinet and viola—using both whole-tone scales one after the other—that illustrates the sweep of the scimitar. The next ten measures depict the atmosphere of the moonlit night and Pierrot scurrying to avoid the moonbeam. Even though it may appear to the listener that thematic development has been abandoned for free improvisation shaped by the text, the ideas presented at the outset return frequently in new guises. Augmented chords in the piano move in parallel in a rhythm and melodic contour taken from the cello and piano parts in the opening measures to evoke the image of Pierrot's knees knocking together (measure 17). The song ends with the downward runs played by viola and bass clarinet in measures 3–4, at the same pitch level but this time in the piano, while the other instruments play glissandos. An Epilogue recalls the music of No. 7, *Der kranke Mond* (The Sick Moon).

On the accompanying recording, the vocalist renders the Sprechstimme by touching or approximating each pitch, then slowly gliding to the next one, varying the timbre of her voice in an exaggerated manner to convey the changing moods and images of the text. Schoenberg calls for some special playing techniques; for example, in *Nacht*, the cello bows overs the bridge (*am Steg*, measure 10), producing a thin metallic sound, or plays harmonics (*Flag.* for *flageolet*, measure 11), and the bass clarinet uses flutter-tonguing (measure 13). In some passages, such as the opening of *Enthauptung*, Schoenberg uses brackets to indicate the leading voice, or *Hauptstimme* (here, the cello).

Arnold Schoenberg (1874–1951)

142

Piano Suite, Op. 25: Excerpts

Suite

1921–23

(a) Prelude

CD 11|8 CD 6|8

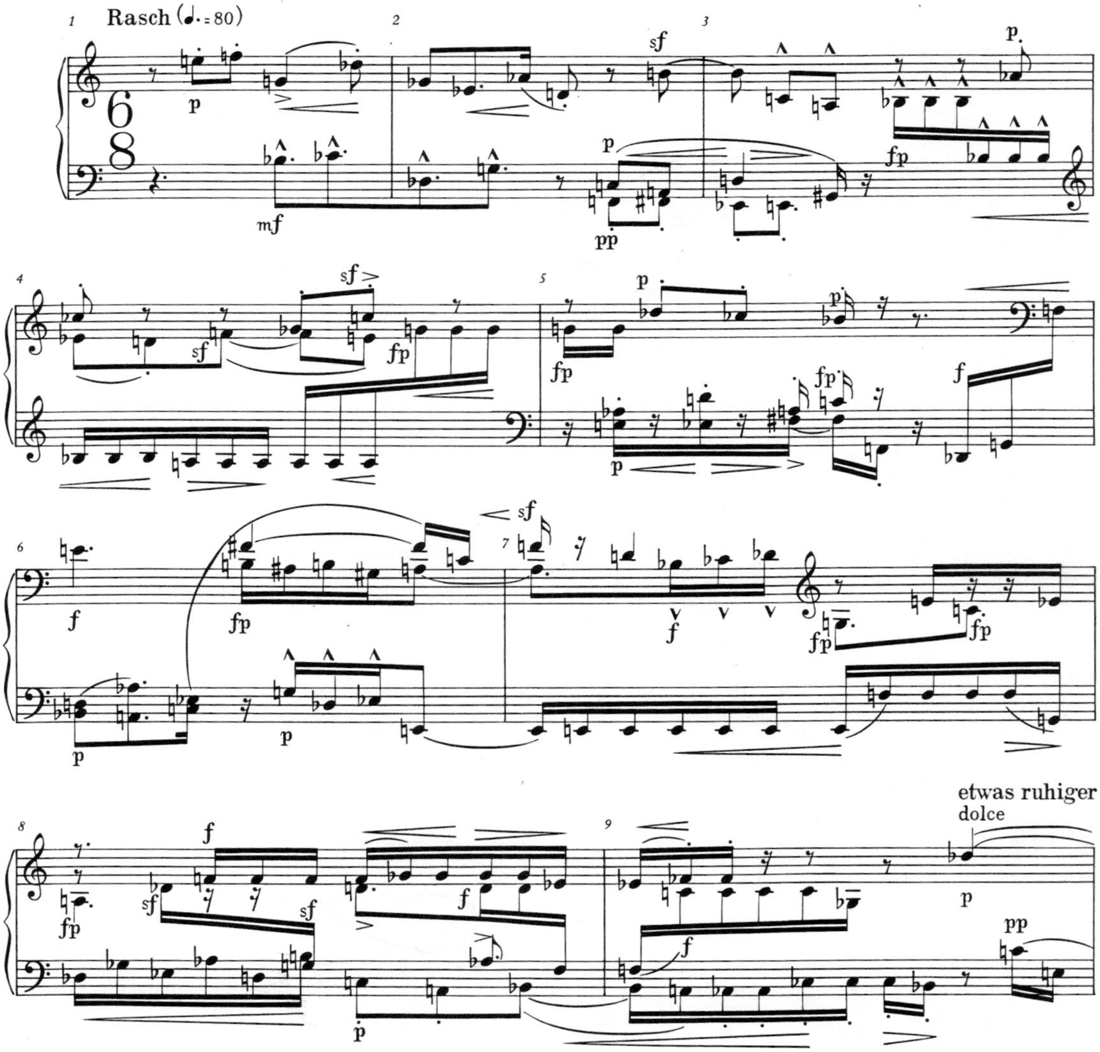

From Arnold Schoenberg, *Complete Works*, part 2, *Klavier- und Orgelmusik*, ser. A, vol. 4, *Werke für Klavier zu zwei Händen*, ed. Eduard Steuermann and Reinhold Brinkmann (Mainz: B. Schott's Söhne, and Vienna: Universal Edition, 1968), 44–45 and 54–56.

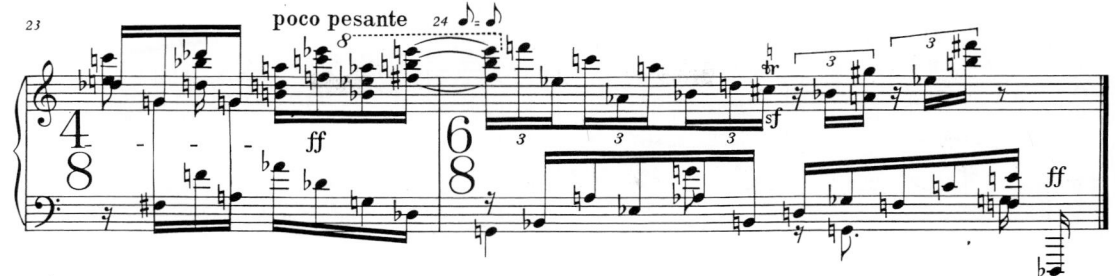

(b) Minuet and Trio

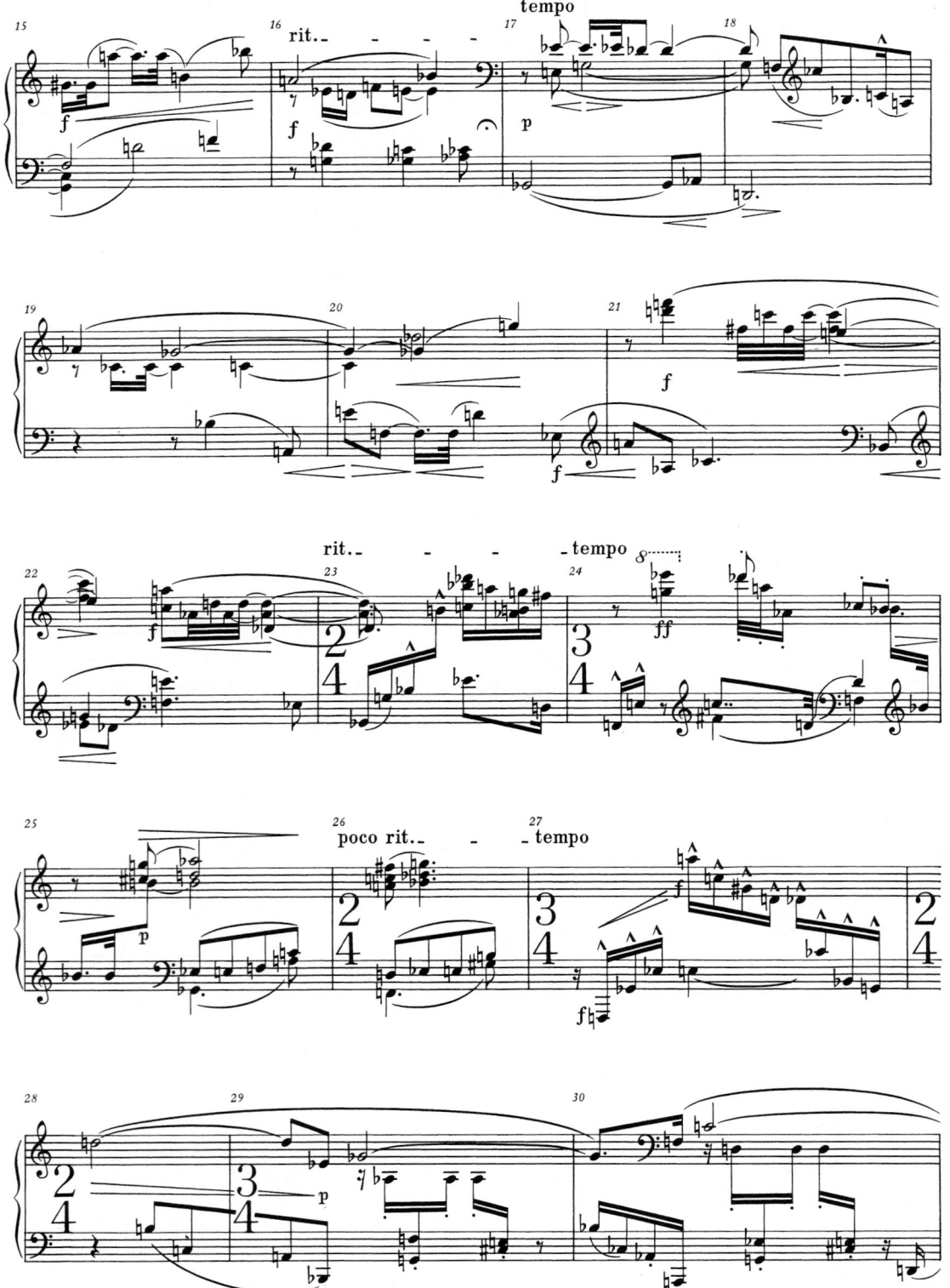

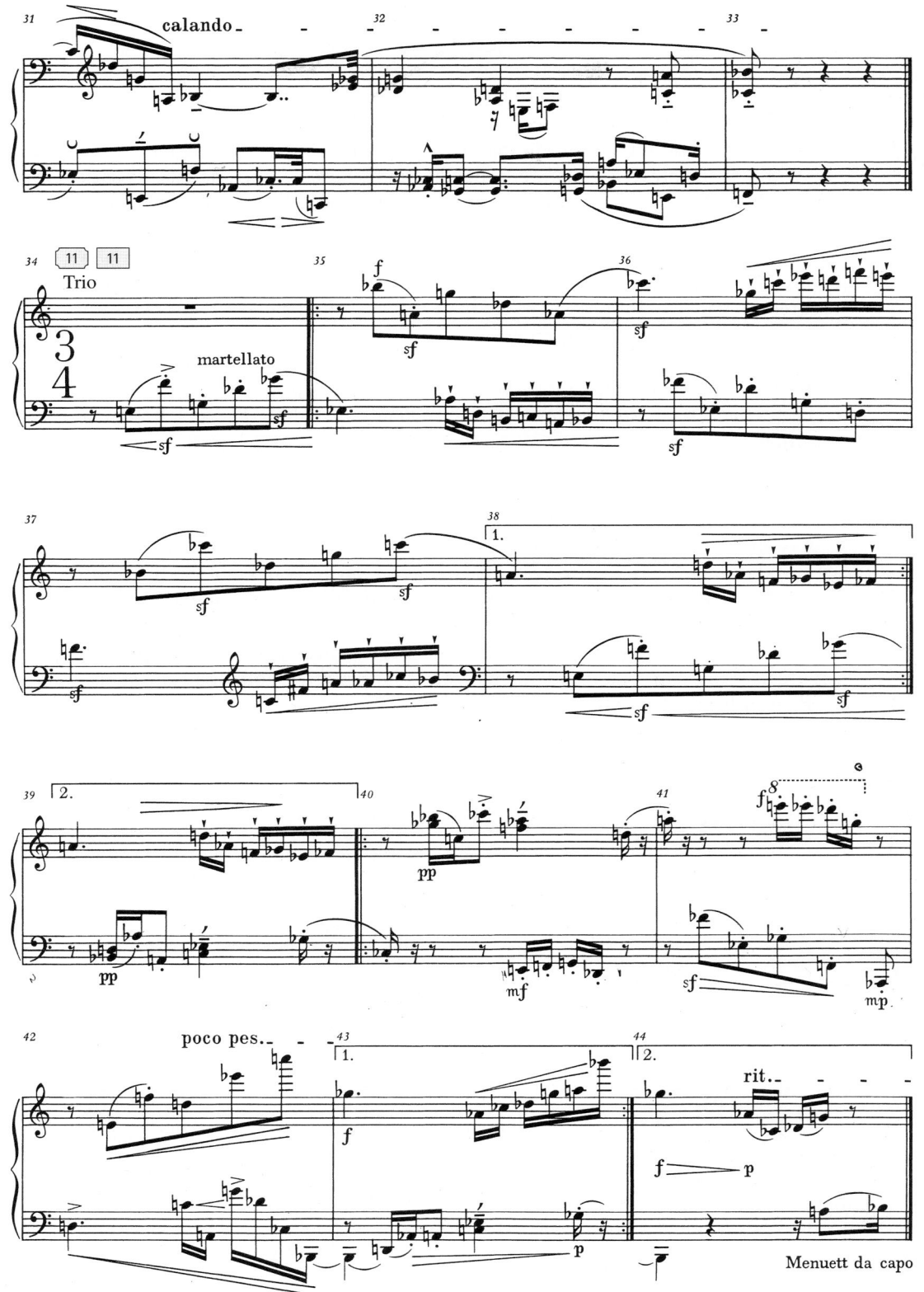

Menuett da capo

In the late 1910s, Schoenberg became preoccupied with how to recreate what he called "the structural functions of tonality" in his atonal music. In *Pierrot lunaire* (NAWM 141), he created a sense of tonal location by presenting an idea at a certain pitch level and restating it later at the same pitch level (or octave equivalent), paralleling a fundamental procedure of tonal music: the establishment of a tonic, departure from it, and return to it. But he had no analogue to the function of a dominant chord as the opposite pole of the tonic nor an analogue to harmonic progression and resolution, and so could not create extended forms without relying on a text to give a work coherence.

He found the solution in the *twelve-tone method,* which he codified in his Piano Suite. The Prelude was the first twelve-tone piece he composed, in July 1921, and he began the Intermezzo the same month. In February and March 1923, he added the other movements—Gavotte, Musette, Minuet and Trio, and Gigue—to create a suite of dances on the Baroque model. By this time, always obsessed with numbers, Schoenberg was publishing one opus a year, whose number usually matched the year of publication; the Piano Suite, Op. 25, was issued in June 1925.

A twelve-tone *row,* or *series,* consists of all twelve notes of the chromatic scale arranged in an order that provides the sequence of intervals and motives the composer wishes to use. By including all twelve notes, the row avoids emphasizing any one as the tonal center. Instead, the row itself functions as a kind of tonal region, and its transformations (described below) serve as contrasting regions. Typically, a piece uses the same row throughout, creating both motivic and tonal consistency; the row for the Piano Suite is shown in the example below.

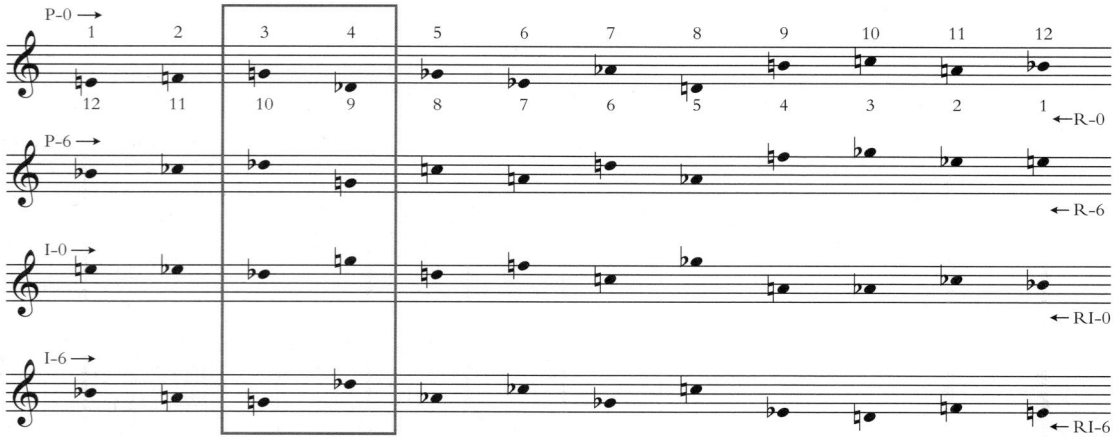

A row can be presented in its original, or *prime*, form but also in *inversion* (upside down), *retrograde* (backward), or *retrograde inversion* (upside down and backward), and each of these forms may appear in any of twelve possible transpositions. In the Piano Suite, Schoenberg used only two transpositions of each form, as shown in the example: P-0, the untransposed prime form beginning on E; P-6, the prime form transposed up six semitones; I-0, the inversion beginning on E; I-6, the inversion transposed up six semitones; and their retrogrades, R-0, R-6, RI-0, and RI-6 respectively. He had designed the row so that each of these transpositions begins on E and ends on B♭ or the reverse, and that each prime or inverted form has the tritone G–D♭ in notes 3 and 4 (shown by the box in the example). These shared characteristics relate these row forms to each other and distinguish them from all other possible transpositions of the row. In Schoenberg's mind, the use of these eight row forms exclusively was analogous to establishing a key in tonal music, and by using the same eight in each movement he preserved that consistency throughout the suite, just as all the dances in a Baroque suite are usually in the same key. Indeed, in a sketch, he designated P-0 "tonic" and P-6 "dominant," showing that he was thinking of analogies to functional tonality.

Schoenberg often broke the series into smaller units that he used to form motives and chords. Here the most frequent division is into three segments of four notes, called *tetrachords*. The first four notes of R-0, B♭–A–C–B♮, form the letters B–A–C–H in German nomenclature, a salute to the composer whose suites Schoenberg meant to emulate. Variants of this distinctive motive pervade the entire suite, linking Schoenberg's music intimately to Bach's.

The opening passages of the movements included here illustrate Schoenberg's procedures. At the start of the Prelude, P-0 is in the right hand as a melody (measures 1–3) and P-6 accompanies in the left hand, with the second tetrachord (C–A–D–G♯), stated simultaneously with the third (F–F♯–E♭–E). (Enharmonic notes are considered the same, so G♯ and A♭ are used interchangeably, as are G♭ and F♯.) The pickup to measure 4 begins a statement of I-6, with the first tetrachord in the lowest contrapuntal voice (B♭–A–G–D♭, completed on the second beat of measure 5), the second tetrachord in the top voice (A♭–C♭–G♭–C♮), and the third tetrachord in the middle. R-6 follows in measure 5, with the three tetrachords similarly layered in counterpoint (the G and D♭ overlap with the previous row), and then a brief rest marks a cadence. In Schoenberg's analogy, the first phrase moved from "tonic" (P-0) to "dominant" (R-6, the retrograde of P-6).

As the work proceeds, it can be a challenge to locate and identify the rows. Since Schoenberg consistently divides the row into tetrachords, the best strategy is to find one of the tetrachords, figure out what row form it is from, and then search for the other tetrachords from that row form nearby. For instance, the D♭–G–F–E from the end of measure 5 to the downbeat of measure 6 is from R-0, and the other tetrachords of that row appear in the next eight notes. It can be ambiguous whether a retrograde form is being used, because sometimes the order of notes within a tetrachord is reversed or otherwise changed.

The Prelude is somewhat free-form, in the tradition of the Baroque prelude (see NAWM 78a for an example). But the Minuet and Trio follows a strict dance form, and it is intriguing to see the ways that Schoenberg has reflected the traditional genre in his new language. It is typical of a trio to be lighter in texture than the minuet that frames it, and that is true here. Schoenberg uses two-part counterpoint in the Trio: P-0 in the left hand (measure 34) is imitated in inversion by I-6 in the right hand, followed by I-0 in the left hand (measure 36) and P-6 in the right. These four measures repeat, and a similar canon constitutes the second half of the Trio. The result cunningly evokes both the spirit of a Bach invention, through a little canon in inversion, and the two-measure phrasing and binary form of a minuet.

At the beginning of the Minuet, the periodic phrasing and the lilting, dance-like rhythms are apparent even without looking for the rows. Each measure-long unit in the right hand is set off from the next by a brief rest. The second two-measure phrase echoes the rhythmic and melodic motives of the first, forming an antecedent-consequent pair. Both of these two-measure phrases end with an allusion to leading-tone motion at a cadence; the fact that the second ends a fifth lower than the first is a reference to the dominant-tonic relationships of traditional tonality. When we do look for the rows, we find that the first two measures present P-0, using the first tetrachord (E–F–G–Db) in the left hand as an accompaniment to the other two, which occupy one measure each; measures 3–4 present I-6 in a similar arrangement, with some internal reordering of notes within the tetrachords.

The presentation of one complete row statement every two measures creates a kind of harmonic rhythm. Schoenberg then picks up the pace, completing the next three row statements in four beats (P-6), three beats (I-0), and two beats (P-0) respectively, before settling down to one row statement per measure until the repeat mark at the end of the first section. Once again, rhythmic and motivic repetition on the surface, such as the sequences in measures 5–6 and measures 9–10, articulate the changes of row form. This twelve-tone rhythm is quite a close analogy to the use of chord progressions in tonal music to establish the meter and phrasing through harmonic motion. Thus in many ways, Schoenberg's complex twelve-tone method provided the tools he needed for recreating the functions of tonality in a musical language that did not define a central pitch.

The Minuet follows the standard rounded binary form, except that the second section is not repeated. The first five measures of the second section offer contrasting material derived from the first measure of the movement, then a varied restatement of the first section begins at measure 17. At first it is quite distant, but by measure 21 the motives from measures 5–8 are readily apparent, and measures 29–31 repeat the end of the first section almost exactly. Throughout, Schoenberg marks the ends of important subsections with ritardandos, making it easy to see how he himself envisioned the formal divisions. A brief coda in measures 32–33 ends the Minuet with the same two row forms with which it began, P-0 in the right hand and I-6 in the left, providing an analogy in twelve-tone terms to the closure granted by a V-I cadence at the end of a tonal work.

The question almost everyone asks about twelve-tone music is "Can you really hear the rows?" One response is to note that the piece can be perfectly coherent even without recognizing a single row form. The inverted canon of the Trio and the antecedent-consequent phrasing and sequences in the Minuet are evident in the musical contours, without tracing the exact intervals or pitches. In Schoenberg's music, it is less important to hear and identify entire rows than to recognize the motives he draws from the row, like the tetrachords in the Piano Suite, and perhaps to be aware of the harmonic rhythm marked off by successive segments of music containing all twelve tones. These are things listeners can train themselves to hear and performers can quickly locate in the score and represent in performance, without doing a complete analysis of the rows.

Schoenberg meticulously marked the dynamics, articulation, phrasing, and tempo fluctuations, knowing that in such an unfamiliar idiom the performer would have difficulty making choices in such matters without guidance. In some places, such as measure 22 of the Prelude and measures 2 and 4 of the Minuet, he used marks derived from poetry to indicate notes that should be stressed ($'$) or left unstressed ($\smile$) in cases where his intended accentuation contradicts the regular meter.

ALBAN BERG (1885–1935)

Wozzeck, Op. 7: Act III, Scene 3

Opera

1917–22

143

*) Triller ohne Nachschlag

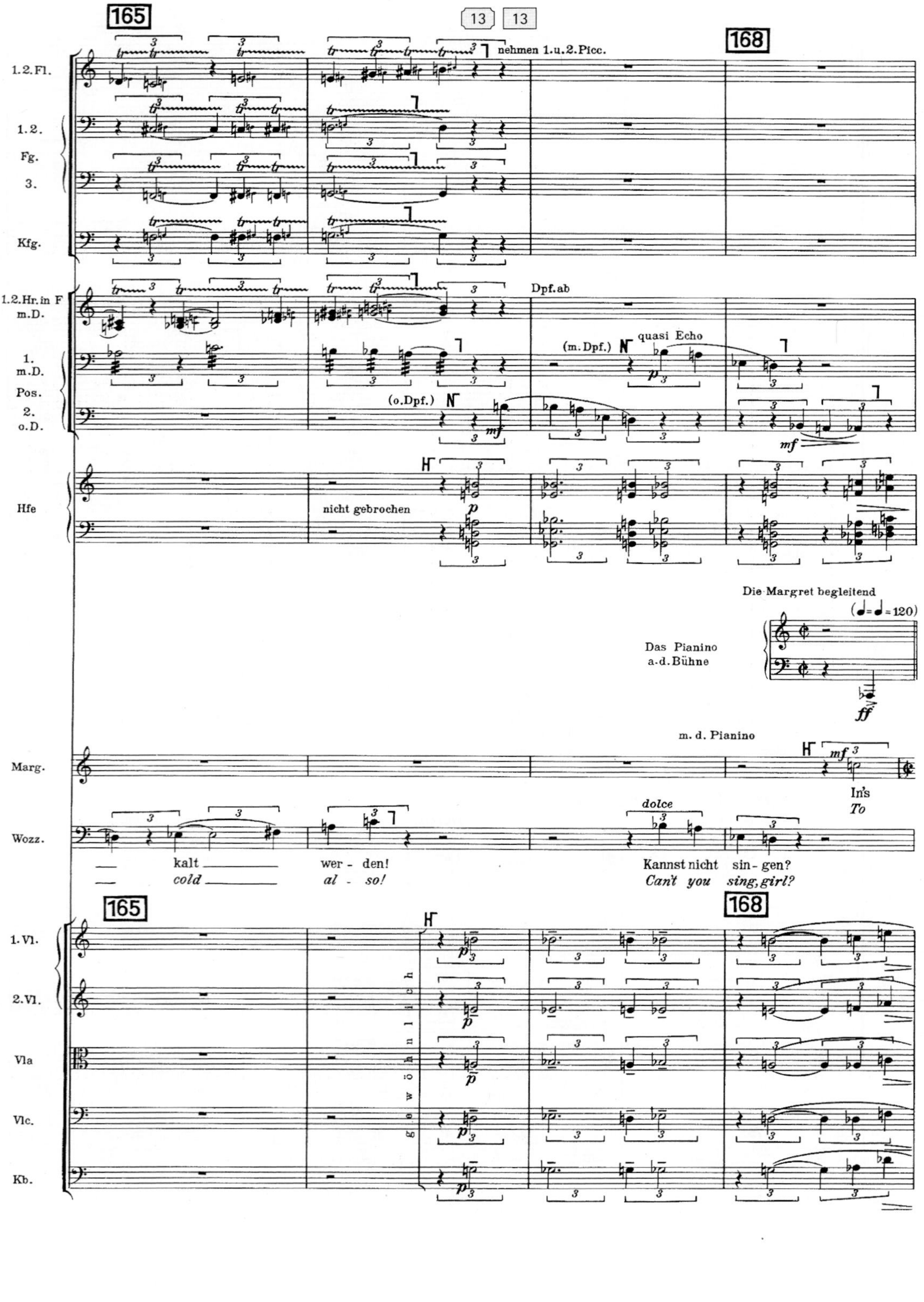
165
13 13
168
1.2. Fl.
nehmen 1.u.2.Picc.
1.2. Fg. 3.
Kfg.
1.2.Hr. in F m.D.
Dpf.ab
1. m.D. Pos. 2. o.D.
(m.Dpf.)
quasi Echo
(o.Dpf.)
Hfe
nicht gebrochen
Die Margret begleitend
Das Pianino a.d. Bühne
m. d. Pianino
Marg.
In's
To
dolce
Wozz.
kalt
cold
wer - den!
al - so!
Kannst nicht sin - gen?
Can't you sing, girl?
165
168
1. Vl.
2. Vl.
Vla
Vlc.
Kb.
gewöhnlich

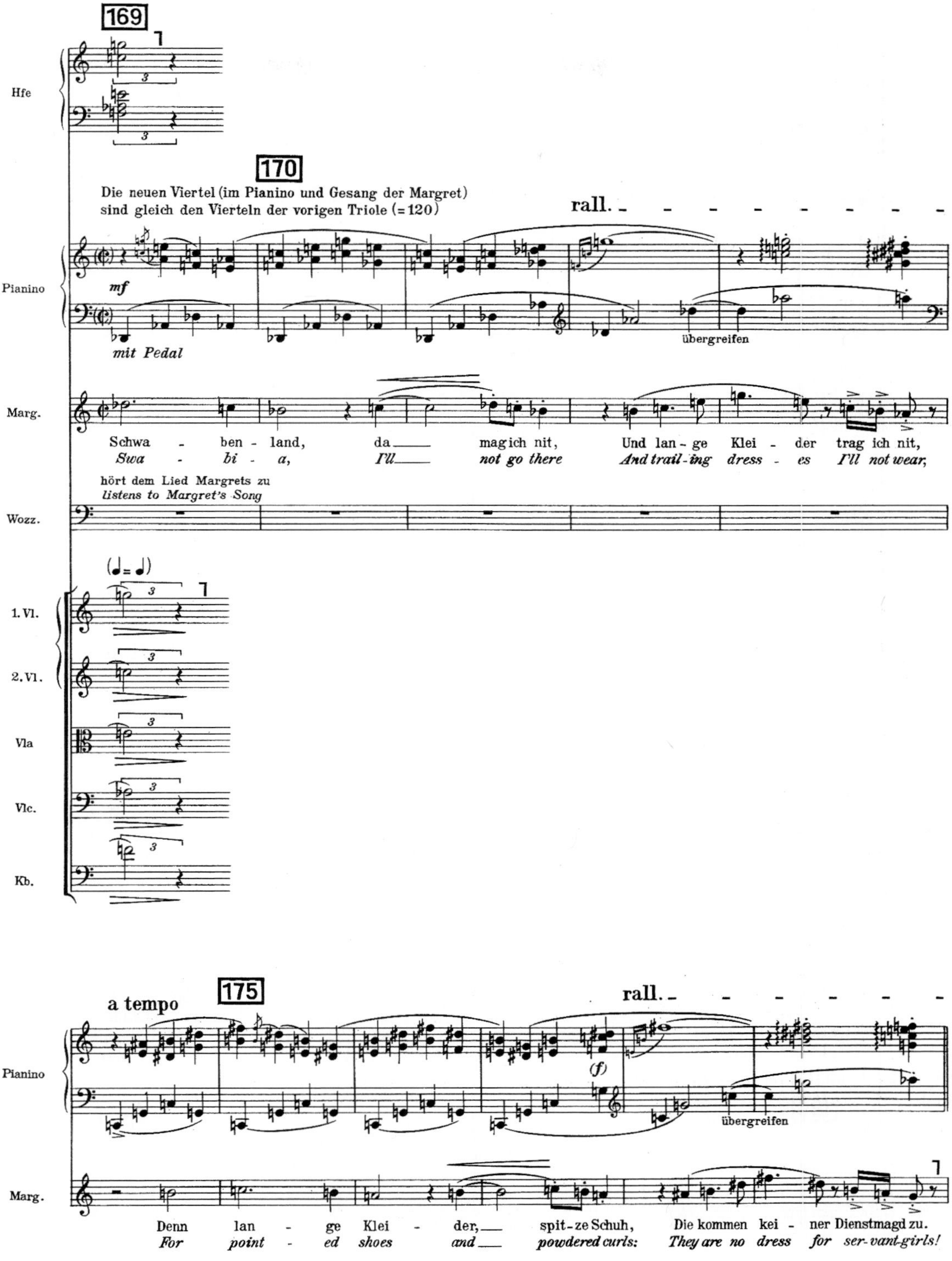
169
Hfe
170
Die neuen Viertel (im Pianino und Gesang der Margret) sind gleich den Vierteln der vorigen Triole (=120)
rall.
Pianino
mf
mit Pedal
übergreifen
Marg.
Schwa - ben - land, da mag ich nit, Und lan - ge Klei - der trag ich nit,
Swa - bi - a, I'll not go there And trail - ing dress - es I'll not wear,
hört dem Lied Margrets zu
listens to Margret's Song
Wozz.
1. Vl.
2. Vl.
Vla
Vlc.
Kb.
a tempo
175
rall.
Pianino
(f)
übergreifen
Marg.
Denn lan - ge Klei - der, spit - ze Schuh, Die kommen kei - ner Dienstmagd zu.
For point - ed shoes and powdered curls: They are no dress for ser - vant-girls!

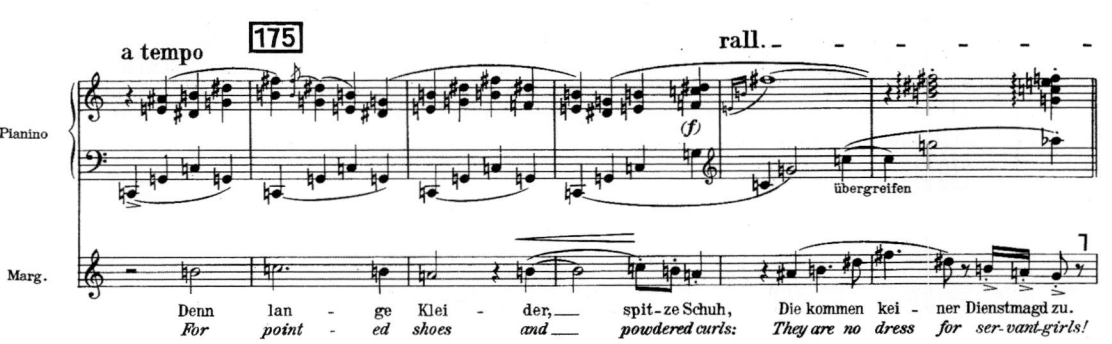

plötzlich noch langsamer (♩=80)

190
195
1. Fg.
Kfg.
Es stellen sich Leute um Margret u. Wozzeck
People gather round Margret and Wozzeck
Marg.
Frei - lich Blut.
Sure-ly blood!
Wozz.
Blut? Blut?
Blood? Blood?
Ich glaub; ich hab' mich
I think I must have
Solo Vla
gewöhnl. gestr.
1. Solo Vlc.
(col legno gestr.)
2. Solo
gewöhnl. gestr.
(col legno gestr.)
Solo Kb.
200
1.2.3.4. Kl. in B
a 4
Bkl. in B
1. Fg. 2.3.
a 2
Kfg.
den Tonfall Wozzecks parodierend
imitating Wozzeck's tone of voice
Marg.
Wie kommt's denn zum El - - len-bo-gen?
How comes it then on your el-bow?
Wozz.
geschnit-ten, da an der rech - ten Hand
I've cut it some-time on my right hand
Ich hab's
I've wiped
Solo Vla
1. Solo Vlc. 2. Solo
Solo Kb.

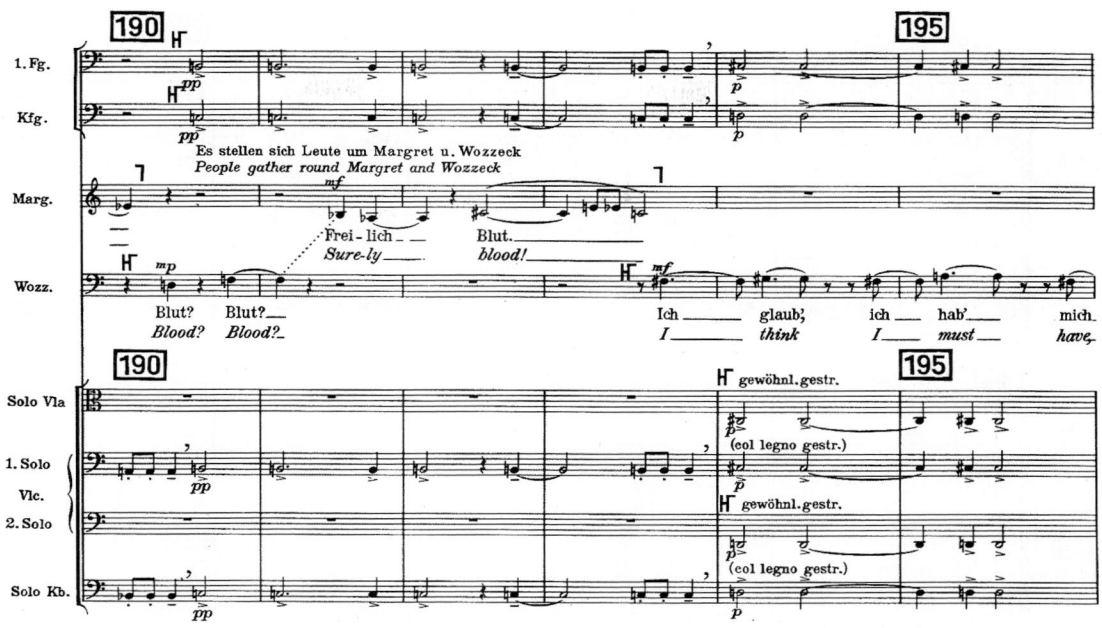

*If the Chorus encounters insuperable difficulties with pitch, their entrances can be
  sounded by the onstage piano (audible only to the singers).

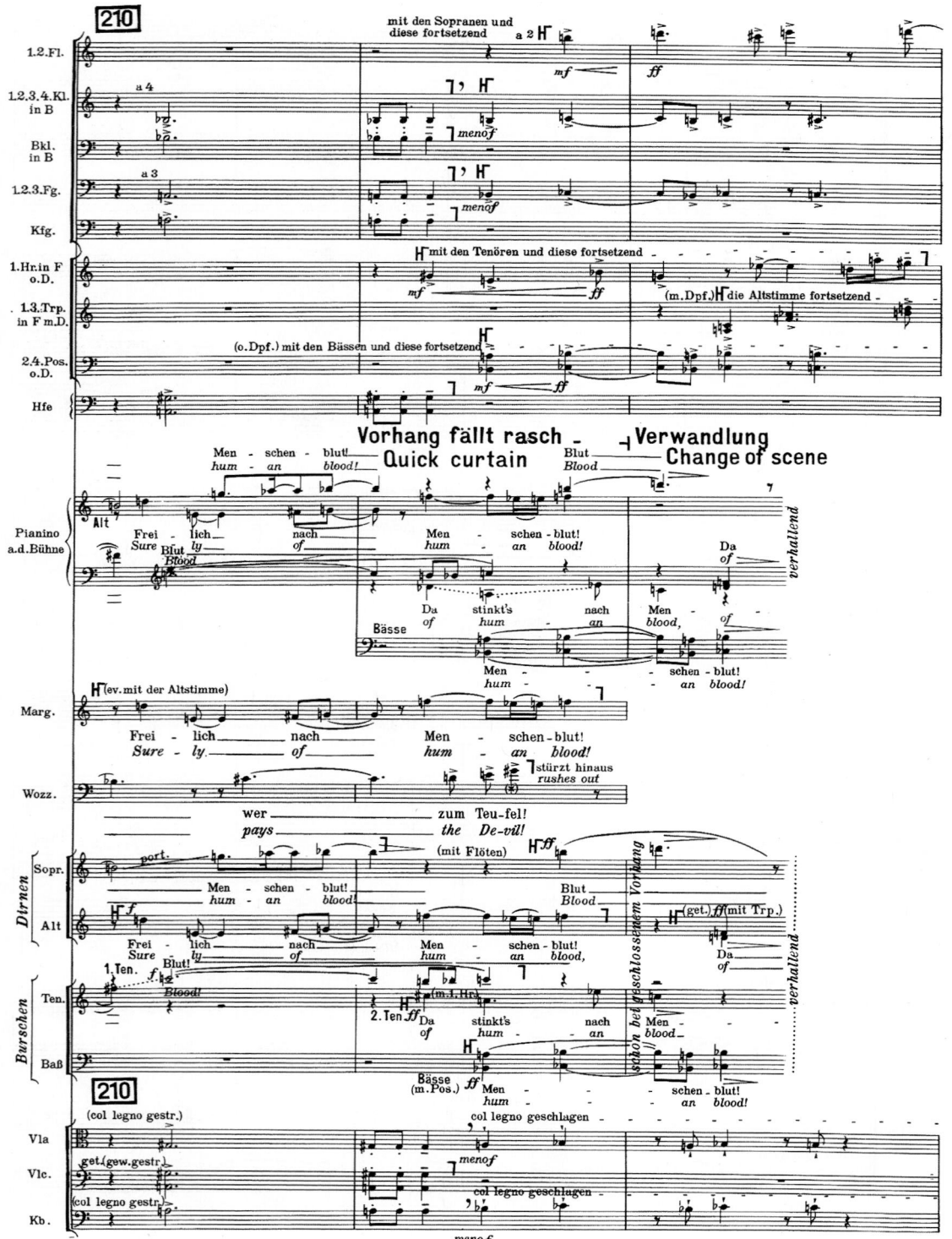

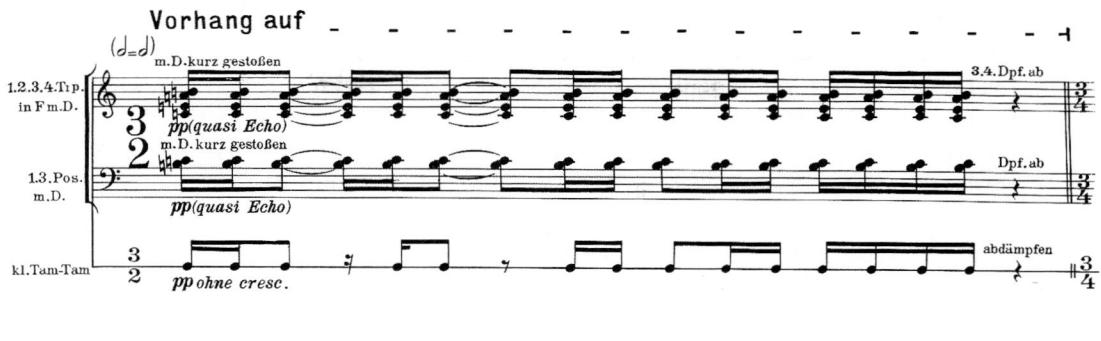

In 1824, Johann Christian Woyzeck was executed for killing the woman he lived with, although many believed he was innocent by reason of insanity. A young doctor and writer, Georg Büchner (1813–1837) wrote a play based on the incident, casting the central figure as a poor soldier who is a powerless victim of circumstances, but Büchner died before finishing it. Decades later, Büchner's play was assembled by a literary scholar (who misread the y as a z and transcribed the name as *Wozzeck*). This version was published in 1879 and, finally, staged in 1913. Alban Berg saw the Vienna production the next year and immediately decided to set the play as an opera, adapting his libretto from the original text and reordering some of the scenes. His own service in the Austrian military during World War I gave him a sense of Wozzeck's life as a soldier and provided details for the opera. He completed the music in 1922 and had the vocal score printed in order to stimulate interest. The work was finally premiered in 1925 at the Berlin State Opera, to excellent reviews. Within a few years it became established as one of the most successful modern operas and by far the most popular atonal opera.

The story centers on Franz Wozzeck, a poor soldier, who is mocked by his Captain, has apocalyptic visions, and submits to a Doctor's experiments in order to earn extra money. (The poor characters all have names, but the well-to-do ones have only titles, a symbol of the power they wield in Wozzeck's world.) Wozzeck has a child with his common-law wife Marie, but with his many part-time jobs he has little time for them. When the Drum Major woos Marie, she gives in to his attentions. Wozzeck learns of their affair, and, driven mad by despair, he kills her and then accidentally drowns while seeking to hide the bloody knife. In the heartbreaking final scene, their orphaned child rides his hobby horse, not comprehending what has happened, while other children run to look at Marie's body.

Berg laid out the libretto in three acts with five scenes each. In addition to using leitmotives throughout the opera, he composed each scene as a traditional musical form. These forms help to describe the characters and convey the dramatic situation, but they also show Berg's interest in reflecting on the music of the past, a common theme of modernist composers. The first act introduces the characters, with a Baroque suite to suggest the Captain's devotion to convention; a rhapsody for Wozzeck's visions; a march and lullaby as Marie glimpses the Drum Major and sings to her child; a passacaglia for the Doctor's fixation on his experiments; and a rondo as the Drum Major repeatedly tries to seduce Marie and finally succeeds. The second act is a symphony in five movements, portraying the dramatic developments through a sonata-form movement, a fantasia and fugue, a ternary slow movement, a scherzo, and a rondo, as Wozzeck learns of the affair, ineffectually fights for Marie, and sinks into despair. The third act is a series of six inventions, each on a single element—a theme, a single note, a rhythmic pattern, a chord, a key, and a duration—suggesting Wozzeck's obsessions. The music in each act is continuous, with linking orchestral interludes between scenes. The longest interlude, before the last scene, is like a symphonic Adagio that sums up the tragedy.

The scene included here is the invention on a rhythm. Wozzeck sits in a tavern, having just murdered Marie in the previous scene. An onstage piano, mistuned to suggest the sound of a cheap barroom piano, introduces the rhythmic pattern—a series of eight durations—in the form of a fast polka. Throughout the scene, the rhythmic pattern repeats incessantly, in its original values, in augmentation, and in diminution, and in both instruments and voices, often in more than one form at a time. Berg indicates every instance with the sign of an H attached to a bracket, a symbol Schoenberg had invented to designate the main melodic line (H standing for *Hauptstimme*, main voice) but used here to indicate the main rhythm (*Hauptrhythmus*). These constant repetitions envelop Wozzeck, symbolizing his obsession with his guilt.

Wozzeck picks up the rhythm as he watches the dancers (measures 130–41), then briefly frees himself from it by singing a folk song, using a tune from Marie's Act I lullaby (at measure 145). He asks Marie's friend Margret to dance with him, then sits down with her on his lap and asks her to sing a song. But there is no respite for him—even her song is in the obsessive rhythm of the scene (measures 168–79). She notices blood on his hand, singing again in that rhythm (measures 185–93). As others gather around them, Wozzeck says he must have cut himself, but she points out the blood on his elbow and says it smells of human blood, and the others agree. By this point all of them, Wozzeck included, are singing only in the scene's main rhythm, as the orchestra plays its own statements. Surrounded by the emblem of his guilt, Wozzeck flees in a frenzy.

Berg's music is atonal (not twelve-tone), but he frequently imitates the styles and textures of tonal music, as in the triadic accompaniment to the piano polka; the prominent fourths, triadic shapes, and melodic sequences of Wozzeck's imitation folk song; and the rocking accompaniment, balanced phrases, and arching lines of the popular-style song Margret sings. By constantly using familiar elements like these, Berg makes his music both dramatically effective and accessible to a wide range of listeners.

It can be difficult for singers to find their pitches in atonal music. Sometimes the pitches of the vocal lines are contained in the harmonies that accompany them, as in Wozzeck's folksong at measure 145, but that is not always the case. Berg recognized the difficulty, and in measures 202–12 he provided an optional part for the onstage piano that includes a transcription of the parts for the Chorus. This part may be played—audible only to the singers—if they need assistance in finding their pitches.

ANTON WEBERN (1883–1945)

Symphony, Op. 21: First movement, Ruhig schreitend

Symphony

1927–28

*)*Klingt wie notiert*
Sounds as notated (i.e., not transposed)

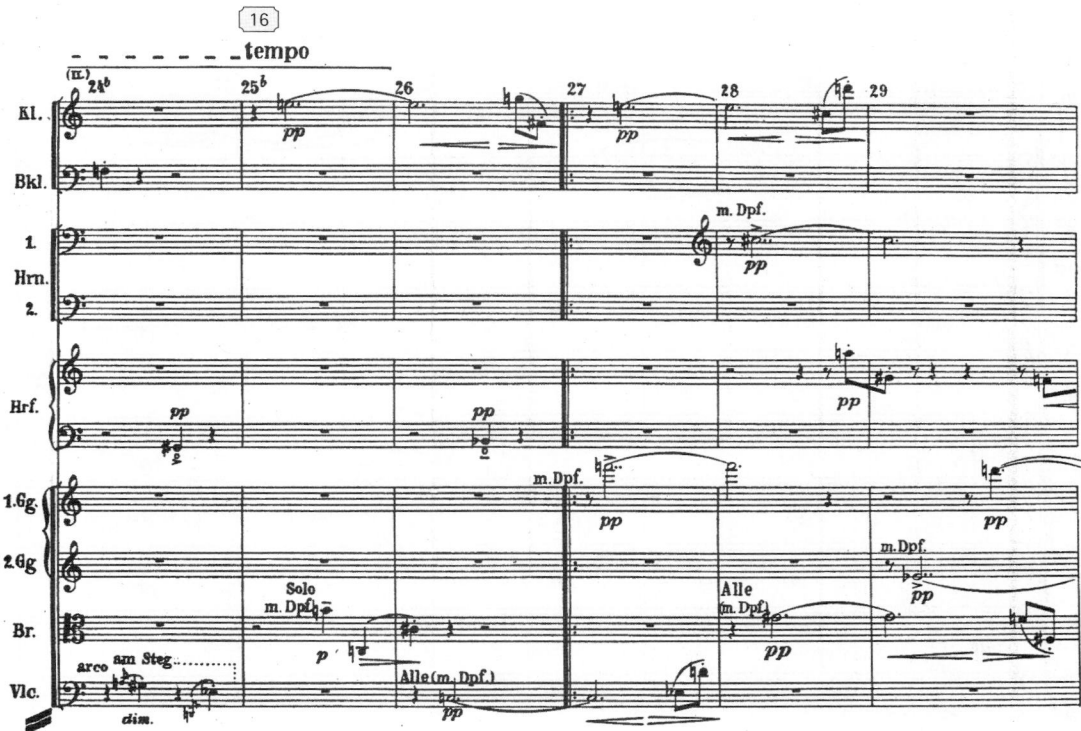

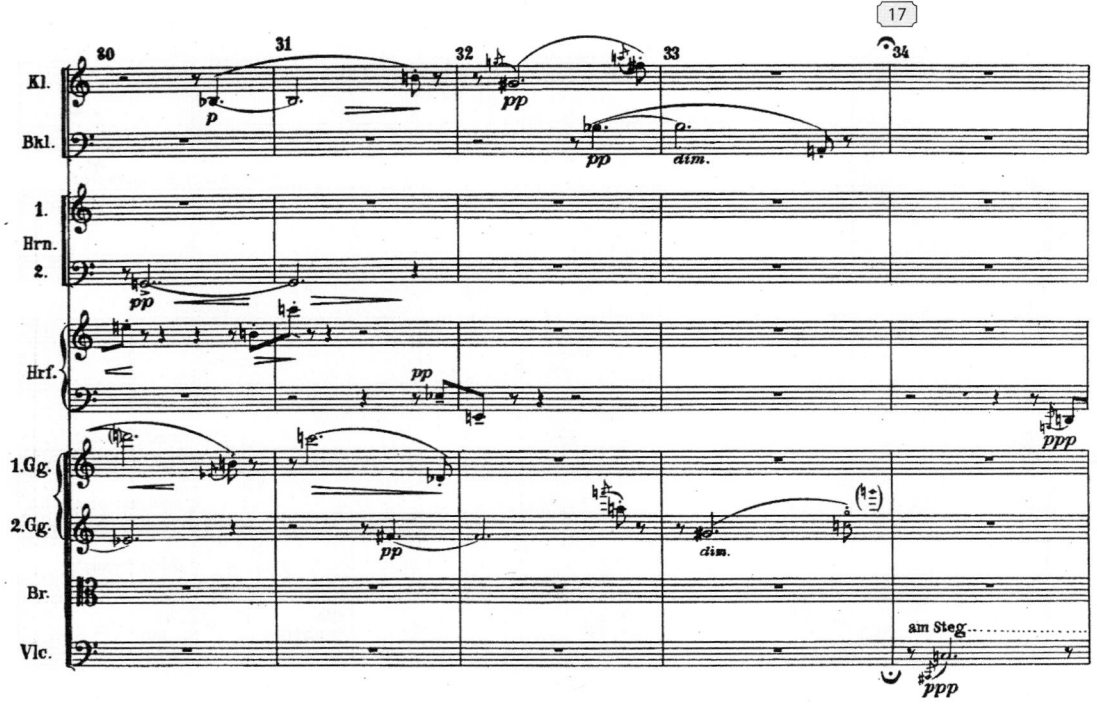

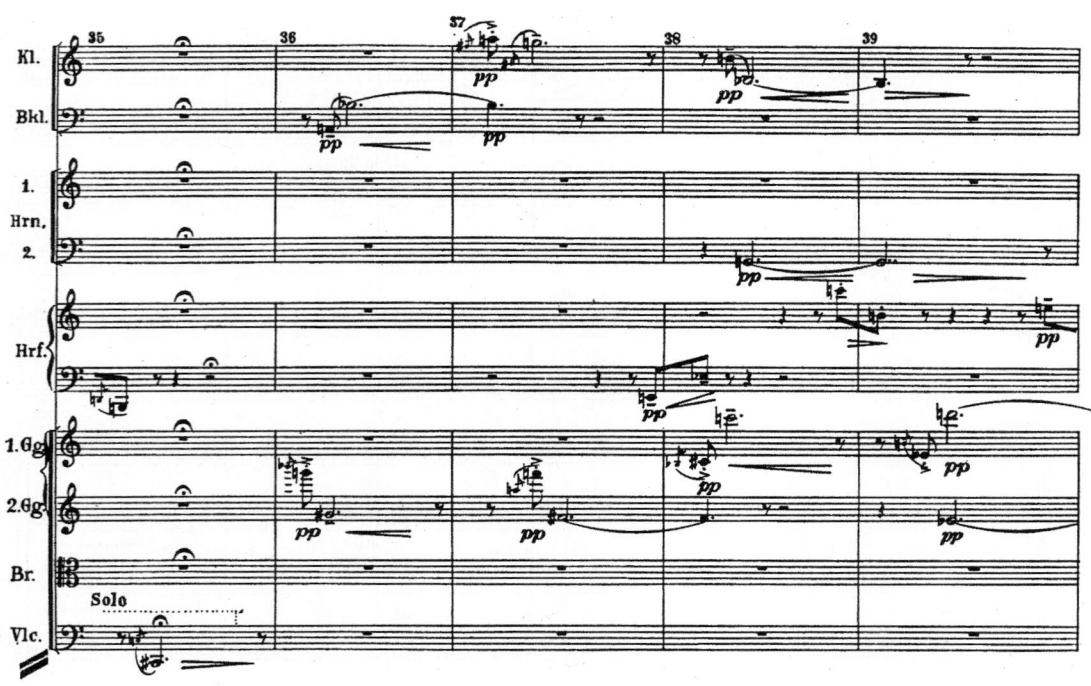

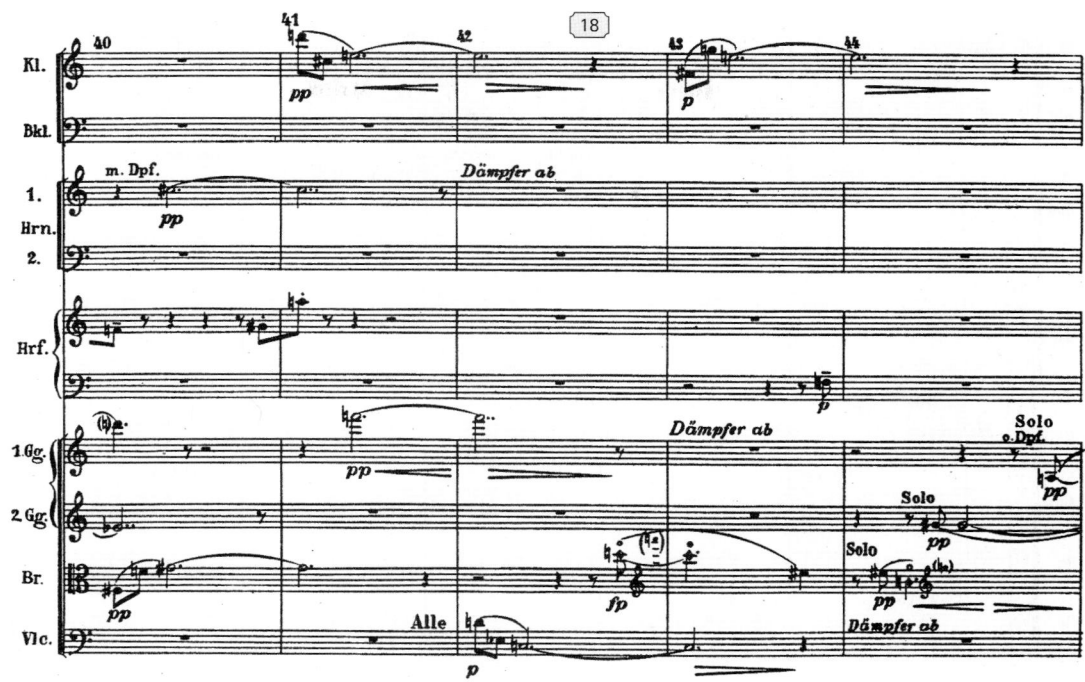

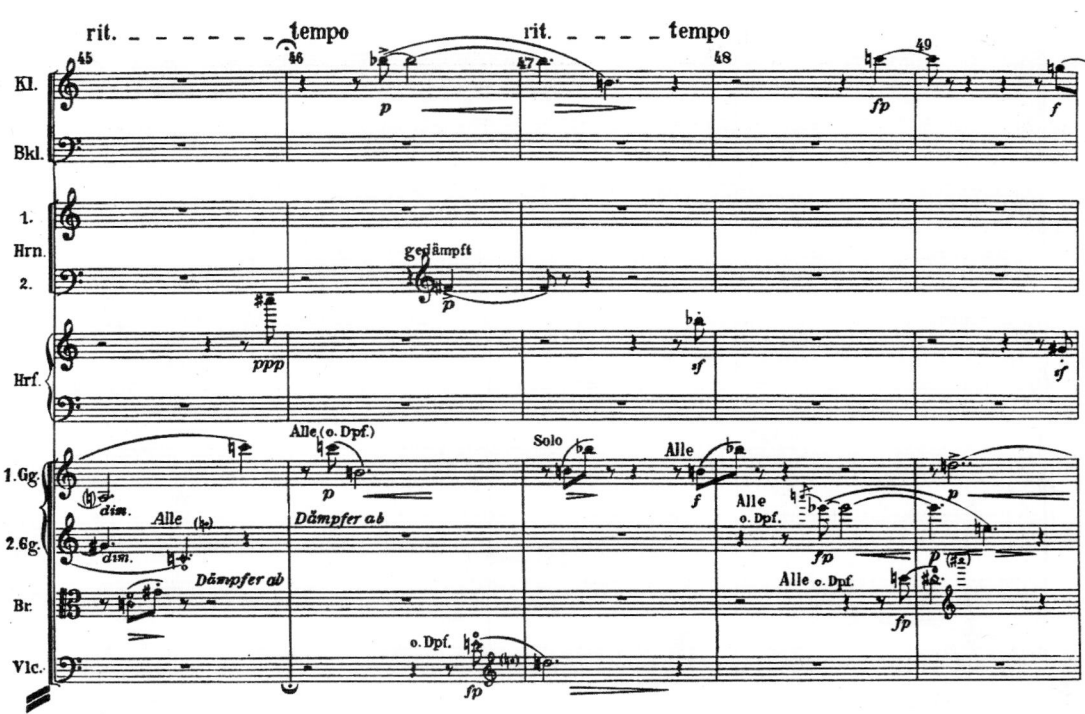

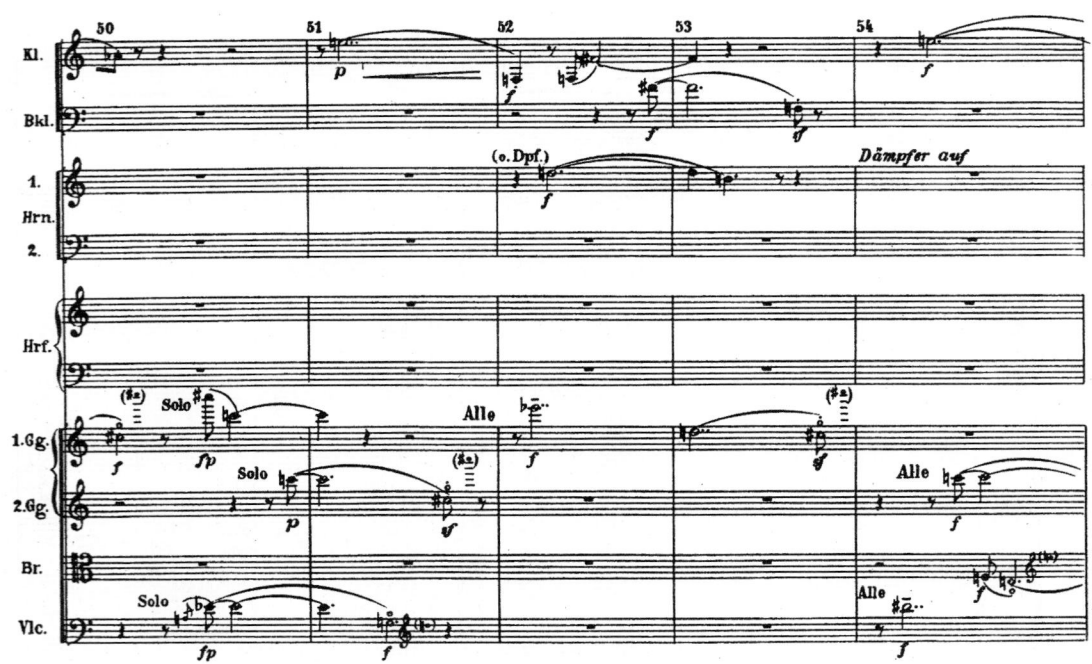

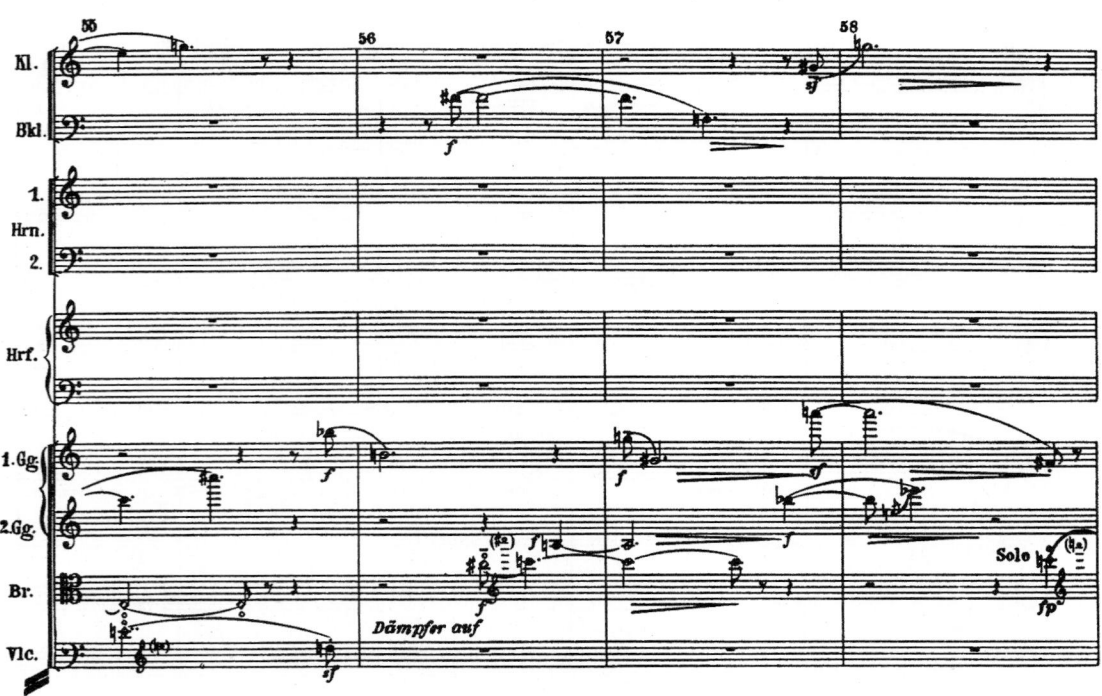

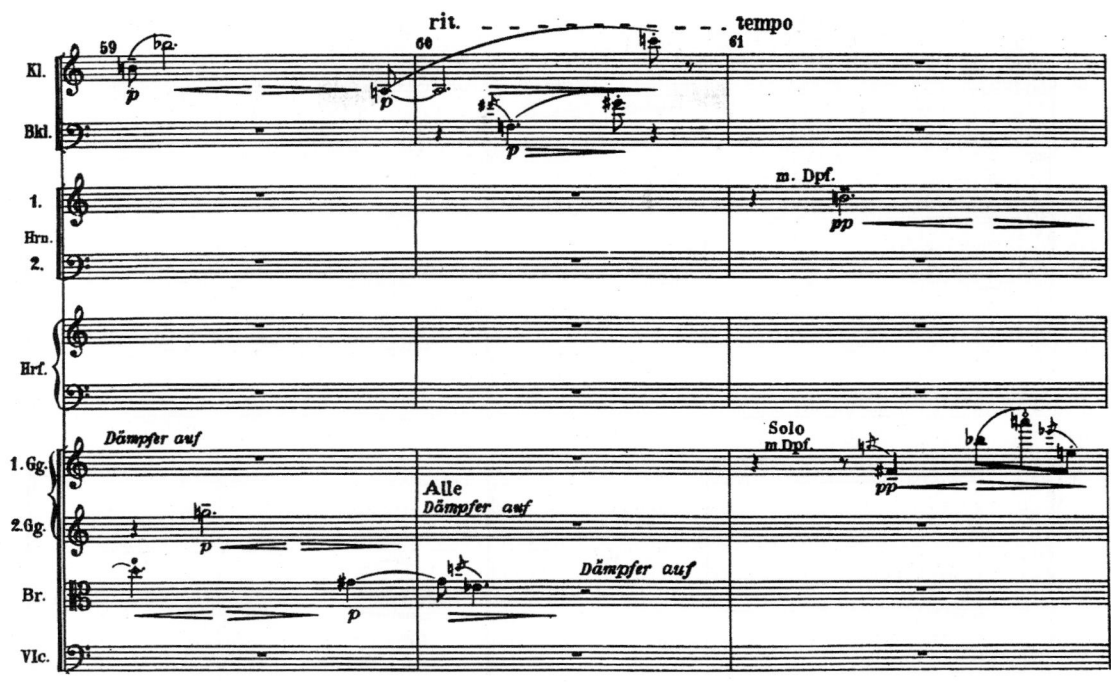

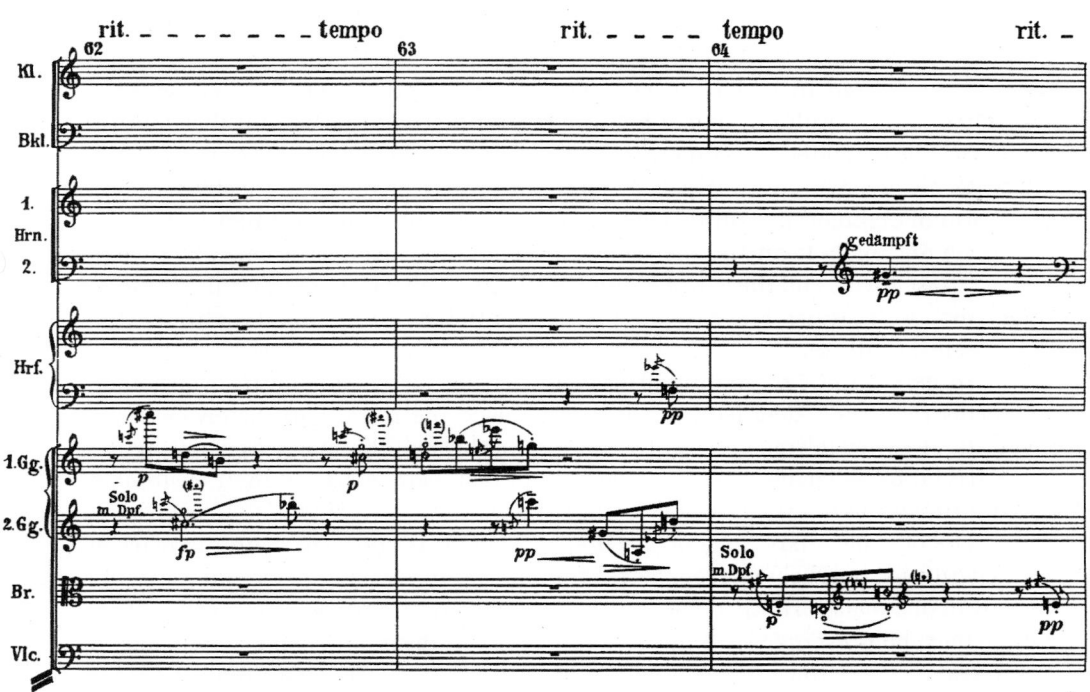

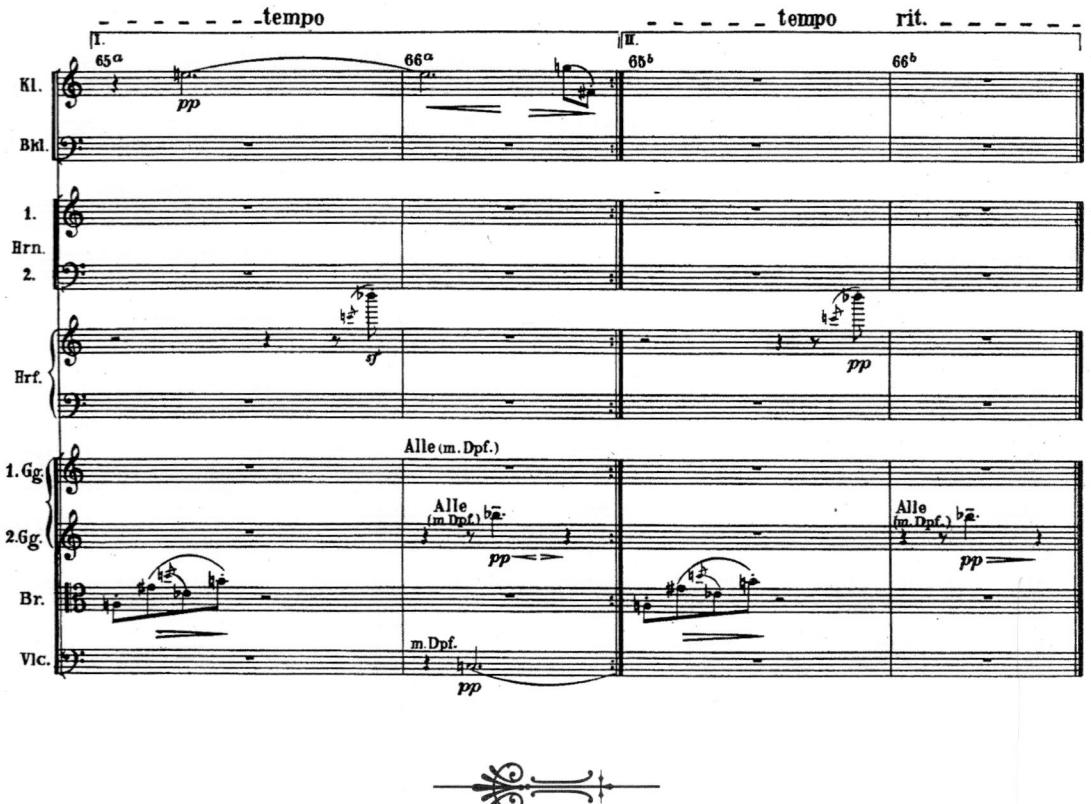

After a decade in which he composed only songs, Anton Webern adopted Schoenberg's twelve-tone method in the mid-1920s, finding in it the solution to writing extended instrumental works in an atonal language. The second such work was his Symphony, Op. 21, scored for a small chamber orchestra in emulation of eighteenth-century symphonies. It has only two movements, the first based on sonata form and the second a theme with seven variations. By invoking these forms and the genre of the symphony, Webern sought to link his modernist twelve-tone language to the conventional forms and tonality of the classical tradition.

To gain an understanding of how he remade past elements in twelve-tone terms requires a detailed look at how he used the rows. Fortunately, Webern made it easier to trace the twelve-tone rows through the music by notating the clarinet, bass clarinet, and horns at actual pitch (rather than in their customary transpositions).

The overall binary form of the first movement is apparent from the marked repetitions, but Webern reconceives the exposition, development, and recapitulation of sonata form in a new way. In the exposition, instead of two contrasting themes, he presents two simultaneous canons in inversion, using statements of his twelve-tone row in the canonic voices (see HWM, p. 818, for a simplified score that shows the beginnings of the canons). Thus he substitutes the Renaissance texture of imitative polyphony for the melody-and-accompaniment texture typical of classical symphonies. However, rather than present any of the canonic voices in a single instrument, he makes the change of instrumental timbre itself part of the melody, an effect Schoenberg called *Klangfarbenmelodie* (tone-color-melody).

The leading voice of the first canon begins in horn 2, continues in the clarinet, and concludes the first row statement in the cello, with each instrument stating one tetrachord (four-note segment) from the row (P–0), as shown here:

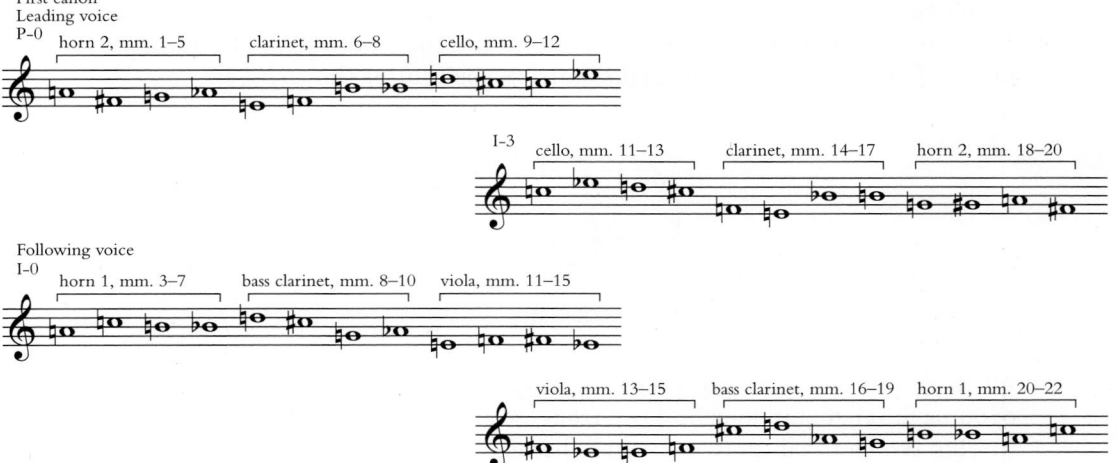

The last two notes of the row overlap with I-3, an inverted statement of the row, which moves from cello back to clarinet and horn 2, as shown in the example. Webern has so designed the row that this inversion results in the same sequence of tetrachords (allowing for internal reordering of notes) but in reverse order, a symmetry highlighted by the symmetry of timbres.

The following voice of the canon, an inversion of the first voice that starts on the same note (I-0) exactly two measures later, traces a similar path from horn 1 to bass clarinet to viola, then back again, using the same kinds of timbres as the leading voice and in the same order (brass, single-reed wind, and string instrument), as shown in the example. The symmetries of timbre and tetrachord echo a symmetry in the row itself: its transposed retrograde R-6 is the same as P-0, making the row a virtual palindrome (something that is the same backward as it is forward, like "Able was I ere I saw Elba").

The first canon exhibits the short phrases and frequent rests typical of Webern's music. The second canon is even more short-breathed, with sometimes just one note in an instrument. The result is a succession of tiny points, or wisps, of sound, a texture described as *pointillism* that is often the most immediately recognizable aspect of a Webern score. The leading voice in the second canon begins in the harp (measure 2), then moves through plucked and bowed cello (measures 3–5), violin 2 (measure 6), harp (measures 7–8), horn 2 (measures 9–10), harp (measures 11–12, overlapping with a new row statement), horn 2 (measures 12–13), violin 1 (14–15), harp (measure 16), viola (measures 16–17, overlapping with another row statement), and so on. Meanwhile, the following voice, in inversion, begins two measures later and traces a similar path through harp, viola, violin 1, and so on. The use of so many timbres in each canonic voice and the appearance of notes from more than one canonic line in each instrument combine to make the canons very difficult to hear.

In the exposition, the somewhat more lyrical first canon serves as "first theme," and the more rapidly changing and pointillistic second canon serves as "second theme." The sense of a "home key" is created by registration, another source of symmetry. Except for E♭/D♯, which can appear in the octave either just above or just below middle C, every other note of the chromatic scale appears in one, and only one, octave during the entire exposition, as shown here:

All these pitches taken together form a symmetrical arrangement around the opening *a*, ranging in fourths down from the *e♭'* above it or up from the *d♯* below it. This symmetrical array is possible because of the strict canon in inversion, equally spaced around the central pitch *a*. The recurrence of these specific pitches throughout the exposition provides a very strong sense of location, although A does not function as a traditional tonic.

The recapitulation reprises the same row forms in the same order as the exposition, but the surface looks and sounds very different, making it hard to hear the return. The recapitulation begins on the last eighth note of measure 42 (highlighted with a *forte-piano* marking), with a statement of the pitches from the first canon's leading voice in viola (through measure 45), cello (measures 46–47), violin 1 (last eighth of measure 47 through measure 53), and again viola (measures 54–55) and violin 1 (measures 55–58). (Some notes in the strings are written as harmonics, and Webern indicates the sounding pitch in small notes.) The following voice of the canon appears exactly two measures later, as it did in the exposition, moving from violin 1 to viola, clarinet, cello, viola, and back to clarinet. The second canon can be traced in similar fashion, beginning with the harp notes in measures 43 and 45.

In the recapitulation, the pitches are again symmetrical, in an arrangement shown here:

Some pitches are in the same octave as in the exposition, others one to three octaves higher, and the axis of symmetry is now eb''. This recapitulation resembles traditional ones by restating the material from the exposition, but it does so in a novel way.

The relatively brief development is a palindrome, providing another kind of symmetry. It begins with the clarinet in measure 25b and concludes with the clarinet in measures 43–44, overlapping the beginning of the recapitulation, and measures 34–35 form its center point. The development and recapitulation repeat as a unit, as in many early symphonies (see NAWM 100).

All these canons, symmetries, and palindromes may be difficult or even impossible to hear, reflecting Webern's interest in structural devices that are not necessarily audible. He absorbed this interest, along with his fondness for canons, from his studies of medieval and Renaissance music as a doctoral student of musicology at the University of Vienna. More audible is the subtle progress of the composite rhythm (the rhythm of all parts taken together), which begins by repeating a gentle syncopated figure (quarter note, half note, quarter note) in almost every measure, then gradually introduces an articulation on every quarter note (measure 13), then increases the pace to use eighth notes in the development, and uses more continuous eighth notes in the recapitulation. Webern did not want his performers to analyze the row structure; instead, he insisted that performers should focus on the musical surface—making each note as expressive as an entire phrase of a Romantic symphony—and he believed that the music's coherence would be clear.

145

Igor Stravinsky (1882–1971)

The Rite of Spring: Excerpts

Ballet

1911–13

(a) *Danse des adolescentes* (Dance of the Adolescent Girls)

CD 11|19 CD 6|15

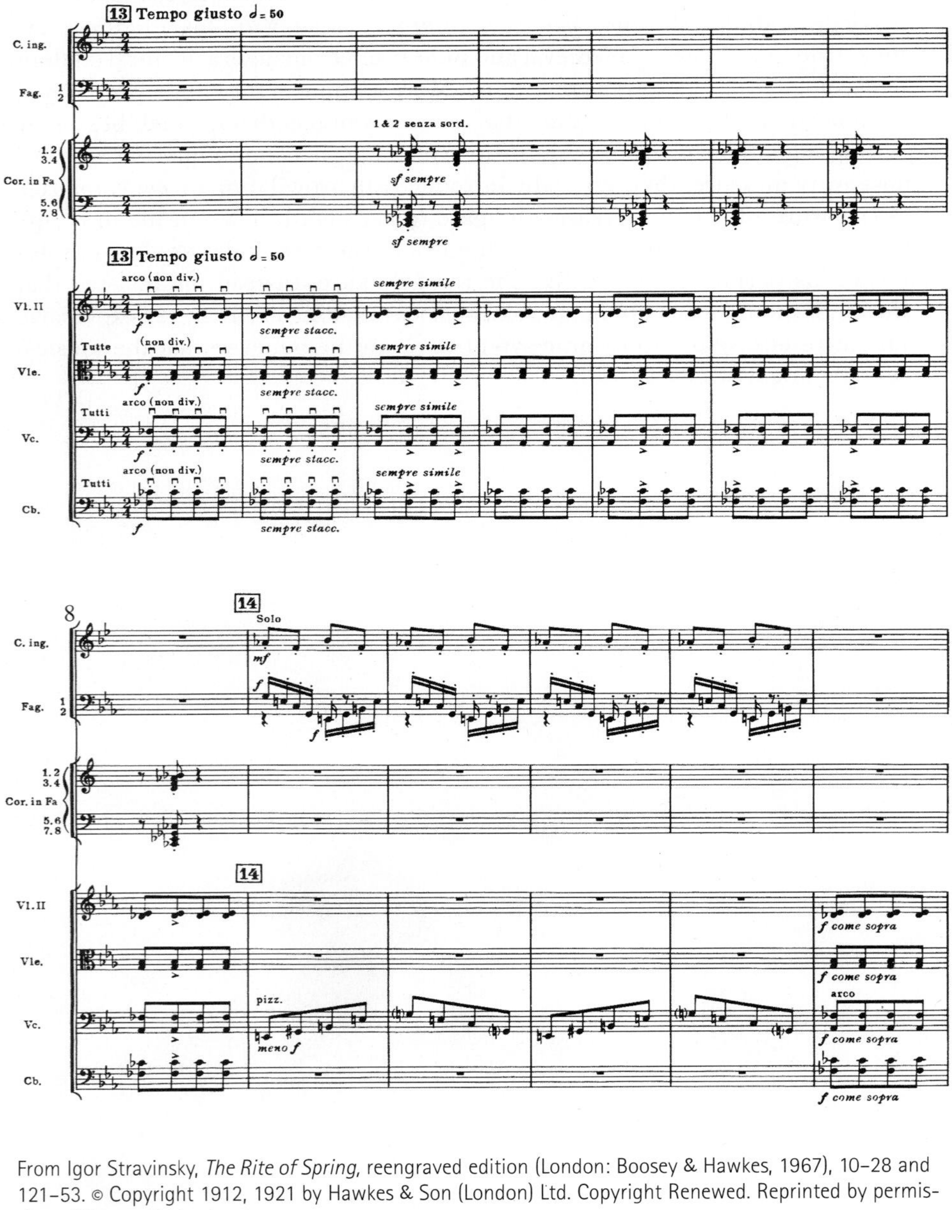

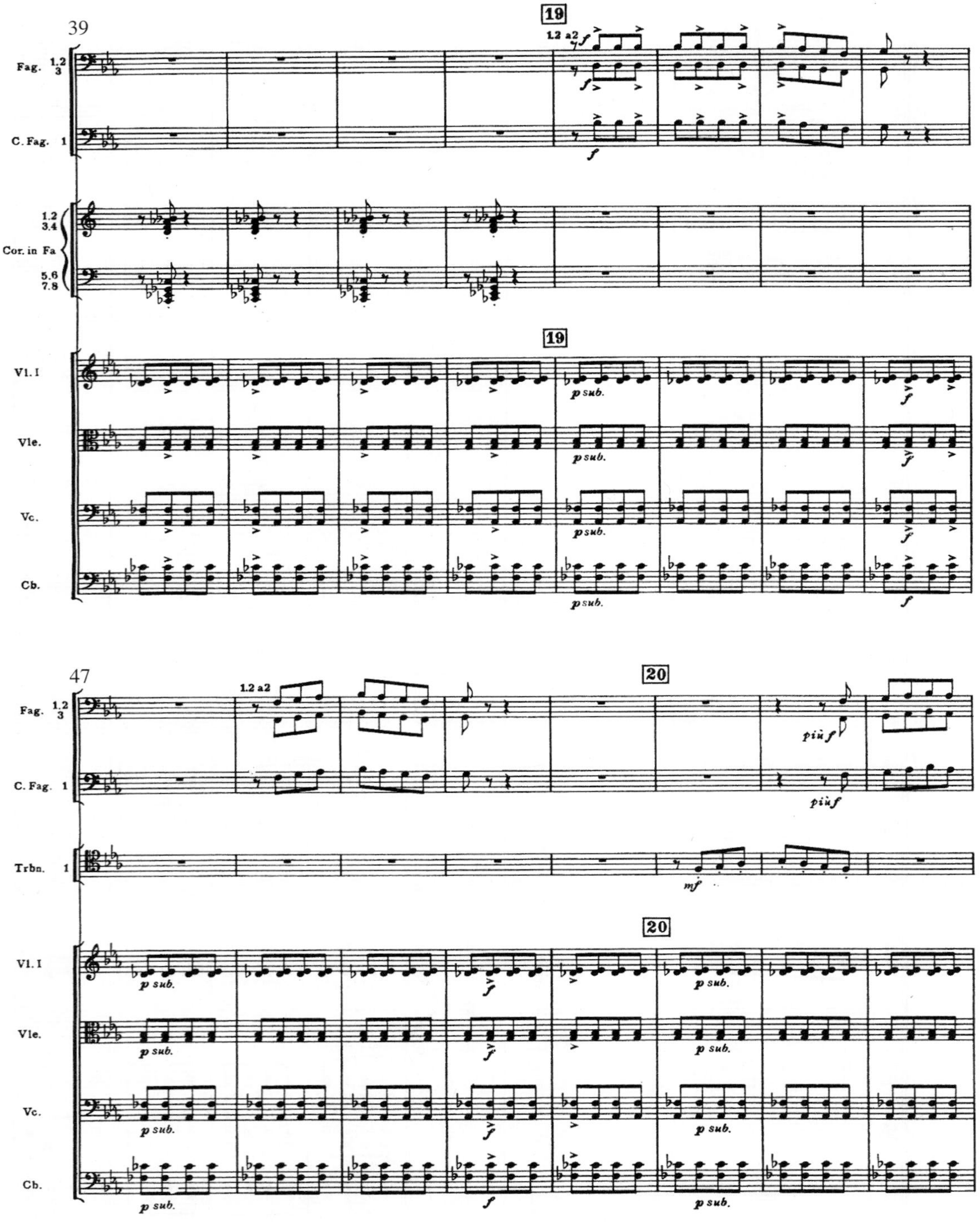

39
19
1.2 a2
Fag. 1.2 3
C. Fag. 1
Cor. in Fa 1.2 3.4 5.6 7.8
Vl. I
Vle.
Vc.
Cb.
p sub.
47
20
piú f
Trbn. 1
mf

(b) *Danse sacrale* (Sacrificial Dance)

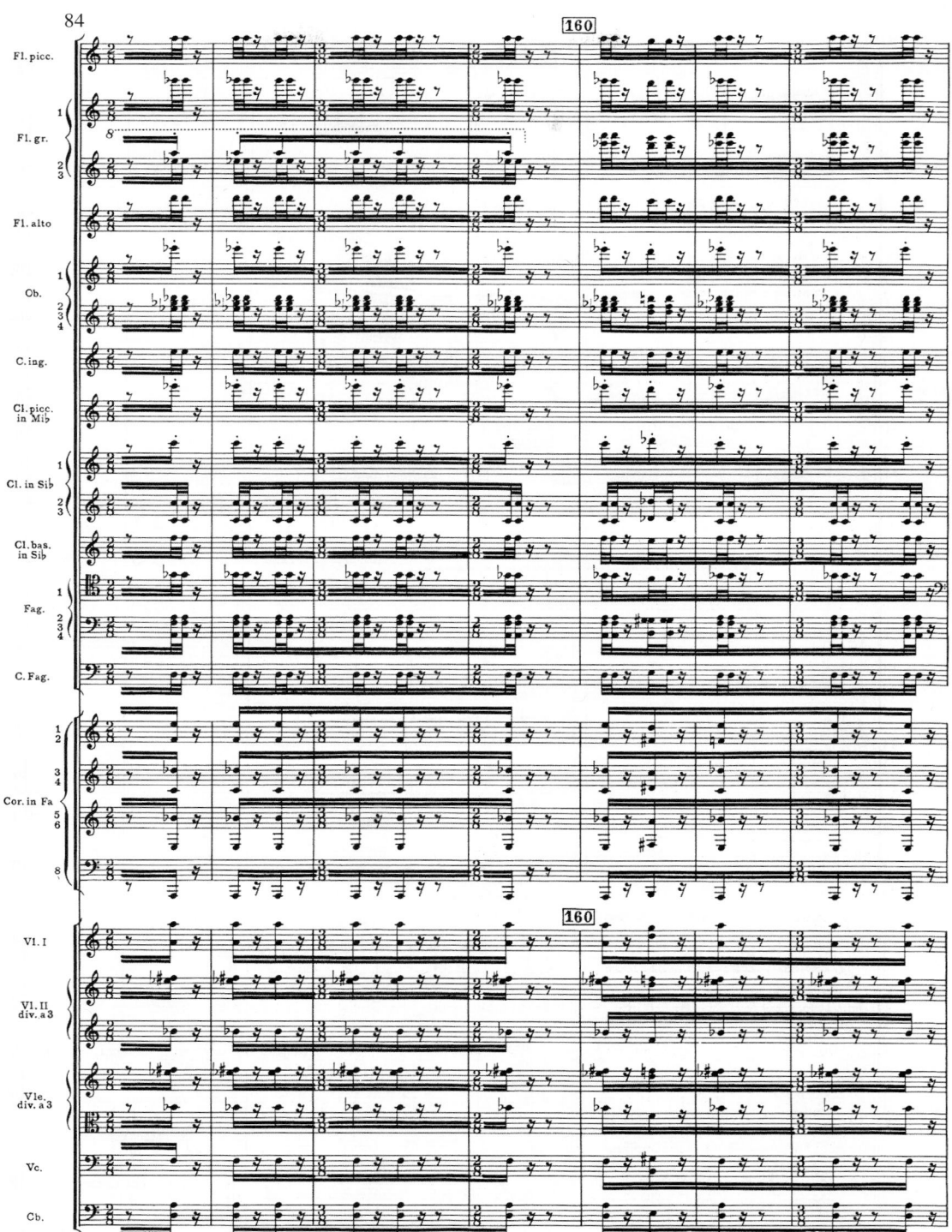

The Rite of Spring was the third ballet Igor Stravinsky wrote for the Ballets Russes (Russian Ballet) in Paris, following his phenomenally successful *Firebird* (1910) and *Petrushka* (1911). The company's impresario, Serge Diaghilev, sought in his productions to fuse the arts in collaborative works drawing on Russian culture. Stravinsky first conceived of *The Rite of Spring* in 1910, imagining a pagan ritual in prehistoric Russia in which a young girl is chosen to dance herself to death as a sacrifice to the god of Spring. He worked out the scenario for the ballet with Nikolai Roerich, an artist and expert on the ancient Slavs.

The goal of the collaborators was not to tell a story, as in previous ballets, but to show a ritual on stage, invoking the spirit of primitive life as a balm for the ills of modern urban society. Roerich designed the sets and costumes, working from Russian peasant designs. Choreographer Vaclav Nijinsky invented deliberately awkward movements for the dancers, the opposite of the refined, graceful motions of traditional ballet. For the music, Stravinsky drew from folk songs, as was his practice, but invented an anti-Romantic, dissonant, and sometimes shocking musical language to suggest primitivism.

At the premiere in May 1913, the audience protested in one of the most notorious scandals in music history (see HWM, p. 824, for Stravinsky's account). Their outrage was aimed more at the choreography than at the music, which was a great success when performed as a concert work in Moscow and Paris in 1914. Ironically, this composition that Stravinsky intended as part of a collective artwork has rarely been performed as a ballet since, and instead it became one of the most popular and frequently played orchestral works of the twentieth century.

After an Introduction, the curtain rises on the *Danse des adolescentes* (Dance of the Adolescent Girls). The strings, using double stops and downbows on every chord, reiterate a sonority that includes all seven notes of an A♭ harmonic minor scale. The dissonance is intense, but there is no expectation of resolution; the chord is simply a musical object, one of many that Stravinsky juxtaposes throughout the piece, and the striking dissonance evokes a primal feeling. The barring is regular, but because each chord in the first two measures is played in exactly the same manner there is no clear indication of the meter. An unusual pattern of accents, reinforced by eight horns, destroys any feeling of metrical regularity. The effect of the unpredictable accents is to reduce meter to mere pulsation on every eighth note, strongly conveying the idea of primitivism by emphasizing pulse, the most elemental aspect of rhythm.

This texture suddenly breaks off, and we hear another: an ostinato in the English horn, a four-note figure common in Slavic folk music, over arpeggiated triads in bassoons and cellos. Although this sounds quite different from what precedes it, there is more continuity between these blocks than may be apparent, for all the pitches of the preceding chord appear here as well, with only two new ones (one new note, *c*, and one octave doubling, low *G*). Such combinations of contrast with continuity are typical of Stravinsky's music and occur throughout *The Rite of Spring*.

The pounding chords resume, with an abbreviated form of the accent pattern (measures 13–16 repeat measures 2–5). At measure 17, the English horn ostinato appears over the chords, and other ideas are added, creating a texture of superimposed layers that is characteristic of the entire ballet. Typically, each idea is given its own timbre or group of timbres as well as a unique figuration. The chords break off but the ostinato continues as new ideas are superimposed. Often, blocks of sound are juxtaposed in close succession: for instance, a fanfare figure of stacked fifths in the brass and clarinets at measure 26, repeated in measures 28 and 29, alternates with an embellished running idea in flutes and violin I in measures 27 and 30–33, while the other parts play ostinatos. In the original choreography, many of these alternating ideas accompanied motions by different groups of dancers on stage, and the effect is strongly visual, like cross-cutting between shots in a film or music video. The music moves forward by layering, juxtaposing, and alternating ideas in this fashion rather than through motivic development or any of the other sophisticated means of traditional classical music; this is another emblem of the primitive.

The pounding chords return (measure 35), then grow suddenly quieter. Here Stravinsky at last introduces a melody based on a Russian folk tune (bassoons, measure 43), repeating and varying it several times. After a sudden pause (measures 70–71), the English horn ostinato returns, now passed back and forth among other instruments, and it remains a constant presence through the end of the dance. Material heard earlier sometimes returns in new guises (compare measures 78–81 to measures 9–12; measures 99–106 to measures 18–22; and the rhythm in the clarinets at measures 133–40 to the opening rhythm in the horns). But from measure 83 to the end, Stravinsky gradually increases the intensity by building up layers of activity. The leading melody in this section is a folklike tune introduced by solo horn and immediately varied by the flute (measures 89–96). Another folklike melody briefly joins it, presented in cellos and in parallel thirds by the trumpets (measure 119). Then the texture thins suddenly and gradually builds again, adding layer on layer and crescendoing until the next dance suddenly begins. This pattern of building intensity by repeating and overlaying ideas is characteristic of *The Rite of Spring* and appears in almost every dance.

Stravinsky was a master of orchestration, often using special instrumental effects. In *The Rite of Spring*, he includes the unusual timbres of instruments like the low alto flute, the high clarinet, and the trumpet in D, and devices such as mutes and flutter-tonguing. Frequent staccatos and detached playing produce a dry sound, quite far from the lush orchestral sounds of most Romantic composers. Additionally, Stravinsky often divided complex figures between instruments to make them easier to execute, like the piccolo figuration in measures 27–33. At measures 78–81, the violas play a harmonic glissando, moving the finger up and down the C string (without pressing it against the fingerboard) to obtain different notes from the harmonic series, a technique Stravinsky learned from his teacher, Rimsky-Korsakov.

The last dance in *The Rite of Spring* is *Danse sacrale*, the sacrificial dance of the chosen one. Here Stravinsky uses two techniques to undermine meter and reduce rhythm to pulsation: constant changes of meter, as at the beginning, and repeating chords interspersed with rests in unpredictable ways (beginning at measure 34).

The dissonant chords, unexpected accents, and loud dynamics convey an atmosphere of violence appropriate to the disturbing events on stage.

The opening section, A, repeats its main idea (measures 2–5) many times, sometimes alternated with other figures of a similar character (as at measures 11–12 and 16). A new section, B (measure 34), begins softly with pulsing chords interrupted by frequent rests; adds a chromatic idea above the chords (measures 47–48); builds to a frightening climax (measures 91–92); then suddenly returns to its opening dynamic level and gradually builds again. The A section returns, transposed down a semitone (measure 116). Then a new section, C, begins (measure 149), signaled by heavy percussion and a whole-tone tune introduced by the horns (measure 154), soon transformed into a folklike melody (measures 160–71). The opening of section A briefly interrupts (measures 174–80). Finally, ideas from A return over an A–C–A–C ostinato in the bass (at measure 203), the music builds to a final climax, and the chosen one collapses to rising chromatic scales in the flutes.

Throughout the ballet, Stravinsky elevates rhythm and tone color to a position equal to pitch and motive as determinants of the form, shape, and progress of the music. His prominent use of ostinatos, changing meters, unpredictable rests and attacks, rhythm and melody reduced to their elements, juxtaposed blocks of sound, layering, discontinuity, and motives identified with specific timbres all had a significant impact on later composers, making *The Rite of Spring* one of the most influential pieces of music ever written.

Igor Stravinsky (1882–1971)

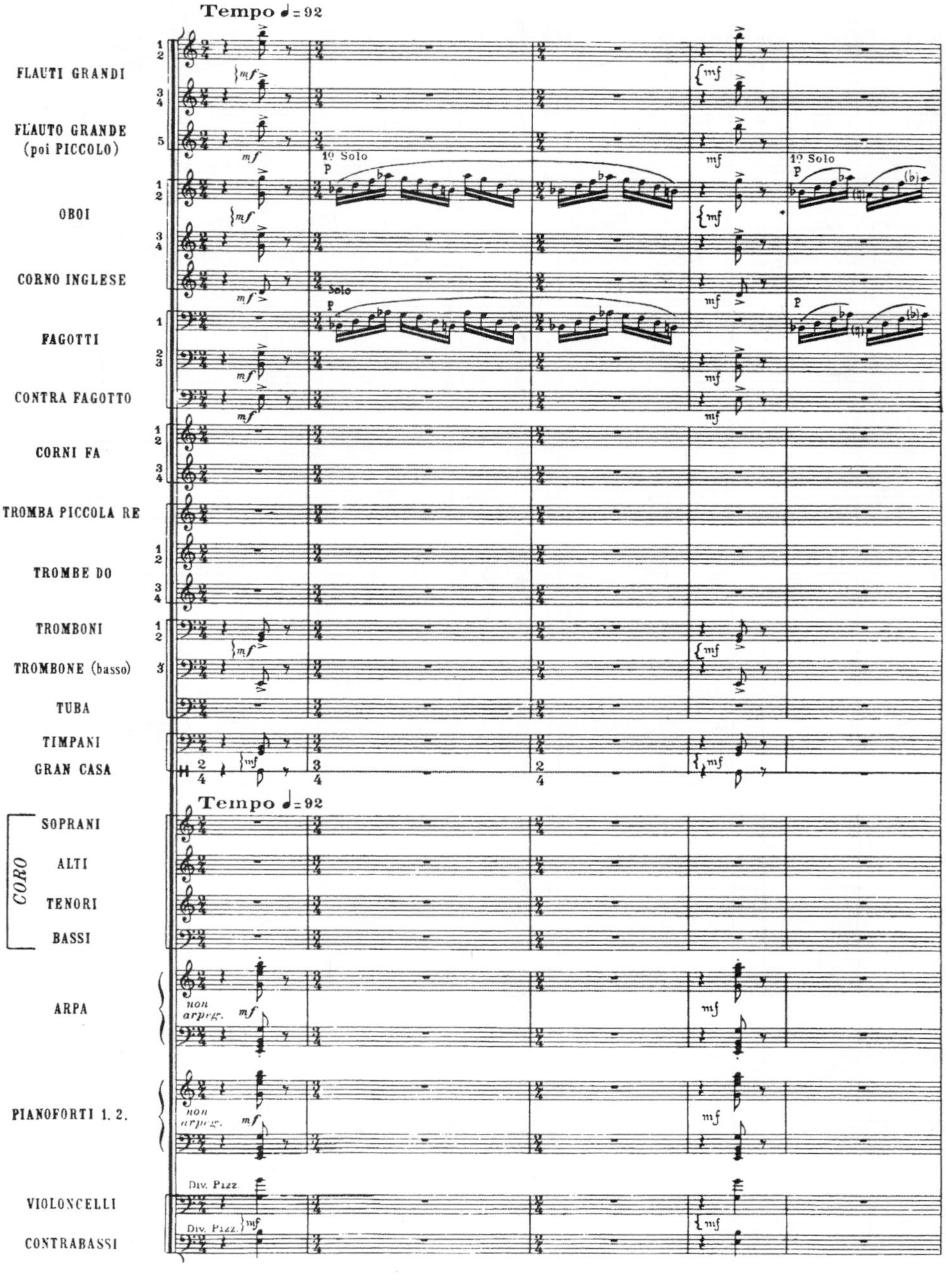

Symphony of Psalms: First movement

Choral symphony

1930

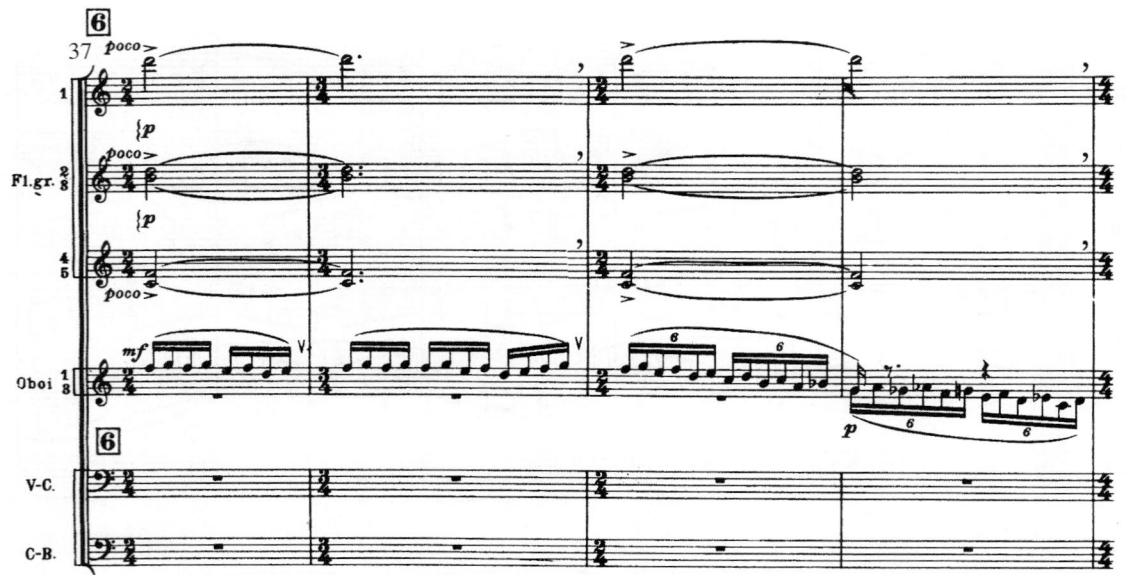

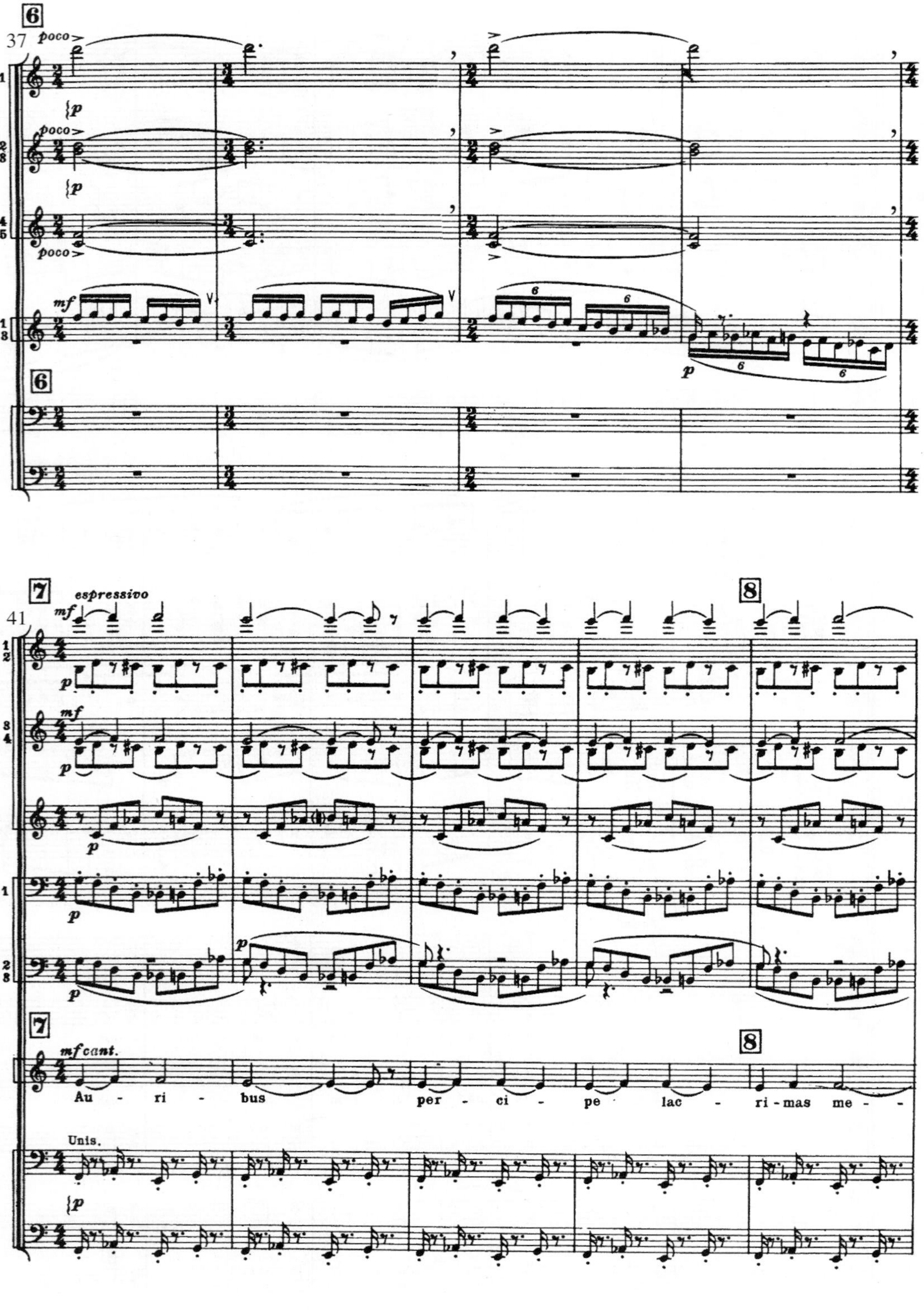
6
37
poco
Fl.gr.
Oboi
V-C.
C-B.
7
41
espressivo
8
Oboi
C.I.
Fag.
A.
mf cant.
Au - ri - bus per - ci - pe lac - ri - mas me - -
Unis.
V-C.
C-B.

Exaudi orationem meam, Domine, et deprecationem meam:	Hear my prayer, Lord, and my supplication:
auribus percipe lacrimas meas.	give ear to my tears.
Ne sileas.	Do not keep silence.
Quoniam advena ego sum apud te et peregrinus, sicut omnes patres mei.	For I am a stranger to you and a wanderer, like all my fathers.
Remitte mihi, ut refrigerer prius quam abeam et amplius non ero.	Pardon me, that I may be refreshed before I depart and am no more.

—PSALM 38:13–14 (39:12–13)

In late 1929, Serge Koussevitzky, conductor of the Boston Symphony Orchestra, commissioned Stravinsky to compose a symphonic piece for the fiftieth anniversary of the Orchestra, occurring the following year. Stravinsky's response was *Symphony of Psalms*, a three-movement work that set three Latin psalms, combining orchestra with chorus. The first movement uses the last two verses of Psalm 38 in the Latin Vulgate Bible (Psalm 39 in the Protestant numbering).

In this work and others during his neoclassical period (1920–51), Stravinsky applied the trademarks of his mature style, developed in *The Rite of Spring* (NAWM 145), to pieces that echoed the styles, genres, and forms of music from the eighteenth century or earlier. Such works were no longer nationalist, like the early ballets, but were intended as universal statements. Stravinskian traits abound. Just in the opening measures, we hear sudden discontinuities and juxtapositions of material; rapid changes of meter; and unpredictable rhythms and rests that tend to emphasize elemental pulsation rather than meter. Later passages use ostinatos and superimpose multiple layers (as in measures 26–36). Yet the music is less dissonant than the *Rite*, and there are frequent references to the language and styles of the past, including many triads and diatonic scales, an imitation of liturgical chant in the vocal lines, and the fugue in the second movement.

After an introduction, there are two main musical ideas that alternate, A and B, and a contrasting middle section, C:

Music:	Intro	A	trans	B1	B2	trans	B1'	A'	C	A''	B1''	B2'	Cadence
Measure:	1	15	18	26	33	37	41	49	53	65	68	72	75

Considering only the portion with text (measures 26–78), the form might be described as an arch, with C at the center. Theme A is associated with the most direct appeals to God, at "Ne sileas" (Do not keep silence) and "Remitte mihi" (Pardon me), and section C with the psalmist's description of himself as a wanderer. The juxtaposition of contrasting blocks of material, common in Musorgsky (see NAWM 130) and other Russian composers as well as in Stravinsky's early ballets, is here used no longer as a national characteristic but as a device to articulate an abstract form.

One of the most important aspects of neoclassical music is that it is *neotonal*, establishing a tonal center not through traditional harmony but through repetition and assertion. At the beginning of the first movement, an E-minor chord, repeated irregularly over the next several measures, creates a center on E, but the prominence of G in the chord (G occurs in four octaves, and E in only the lower and uppermost octaves) suggests that the G will be important as well. The A sections are primarily diatonic, using the notes of the E Phrygian scale and sustaining a drone E in the bass. The B sections are largely octatonic, offering a tonal contrast while (at least in the B1 sections) featuring G–B–E sonorities on the downbeats. The transitions and the first B2 section hint strongly at G as an alternate center, and in the closing cadence (measures 74–78) the bass marches down stepwise from E to G while the voices rise from E through F to G. The way Stravinsky juxtaposes E and G as two rival centers, then leads the music from the former rival to the latter, is a novel reinterpretation of traditional tonality, the sort of reinvention of past conventions that is at the heart of neoclassicism.

Béla Bartók (1881–1945)

Music for Strings, Percussion and Celesta: Third movement, Adagio

Symphonic suite

1936

From Béla Bartók, *Music for String Instruments, Percussion and Celesta* (New York: Boosey & Hawkes, 1939), 66–94. © Copyright 1937 for the USA by Boosey & Hawkes, Inc. Copyright Renewed. Reprinted by permission of Boosey & Hawkes, Inc. All rights reserved. Used in the territory of the world excluding the United States by permission of European American Music Distributors Corporation, sole Canadian agent for Universal Edition.

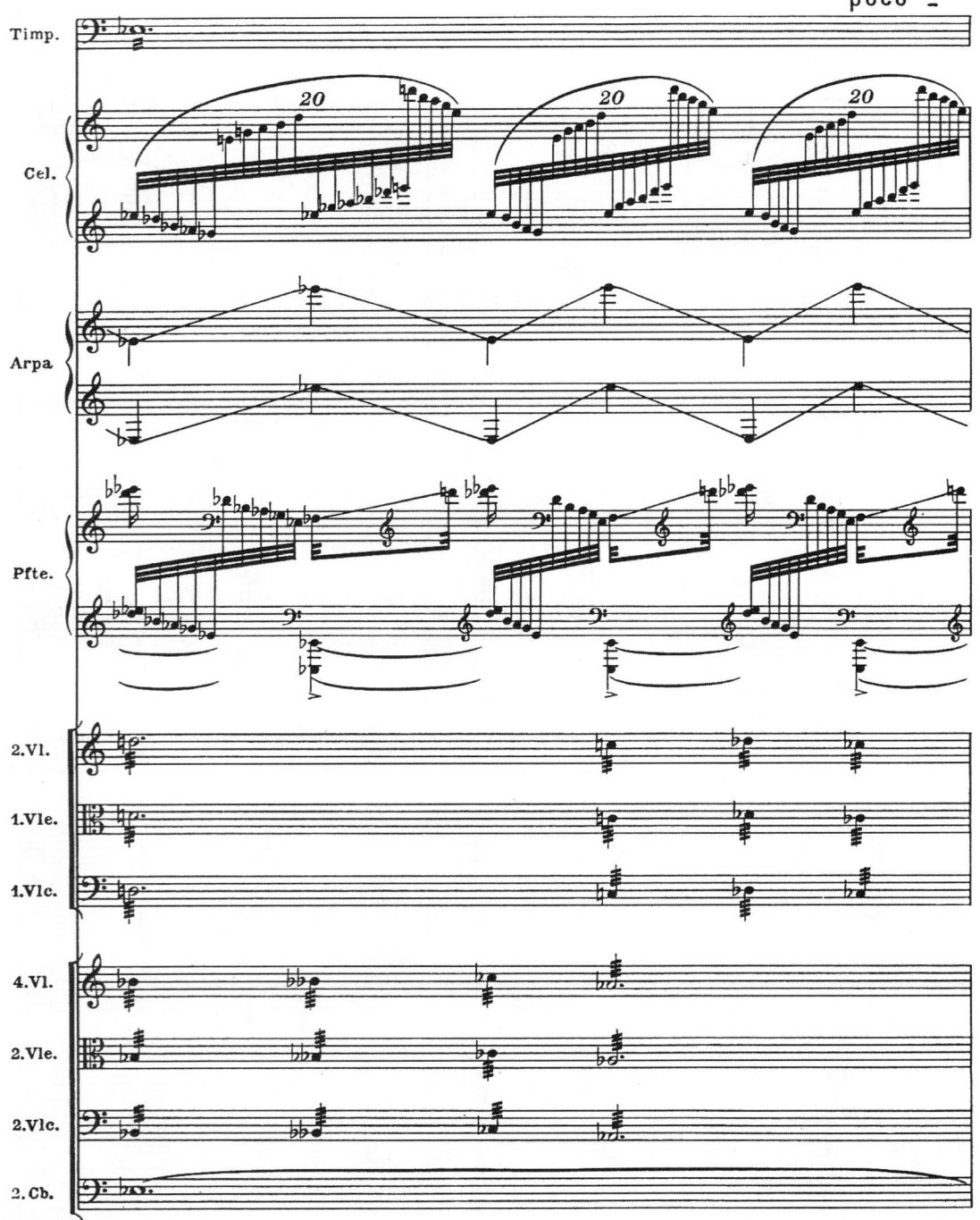

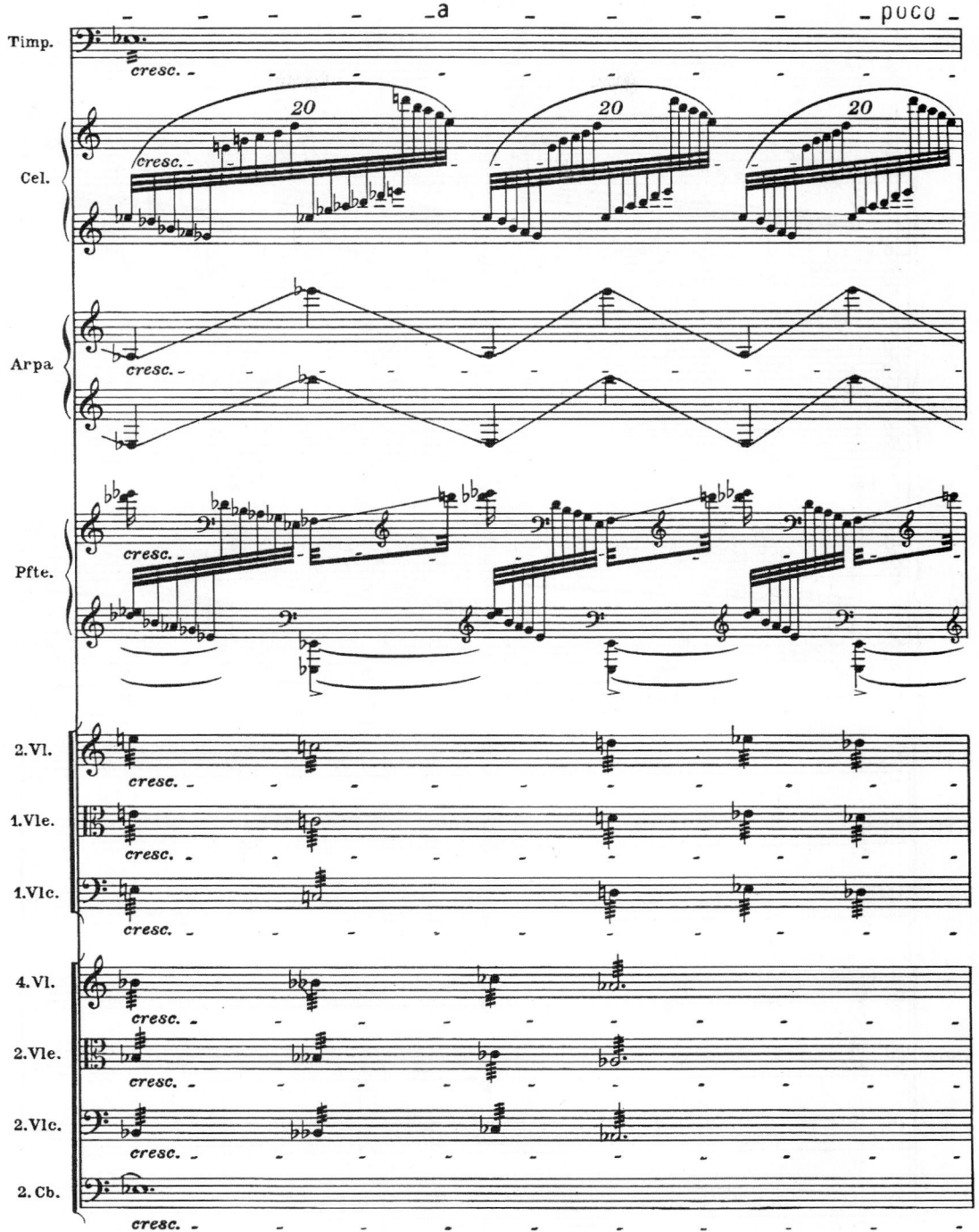

*) kleineres Instrument mit höherem Ton / *instrument plus petit au son plus clair*
   smaller cymbal with higher tone

*) kleineres Instrument / *instrument plus petit*
   smaller cymbals

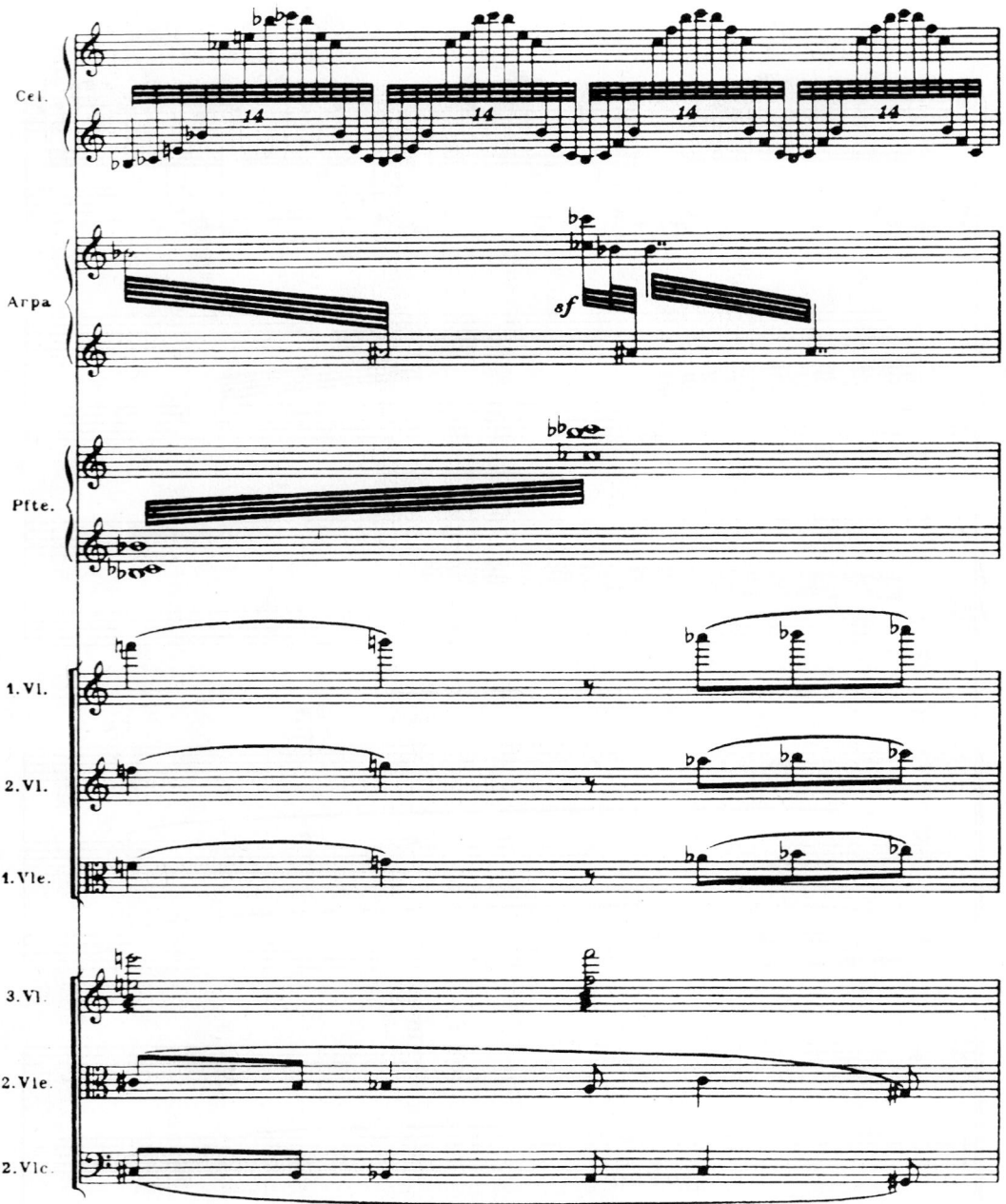

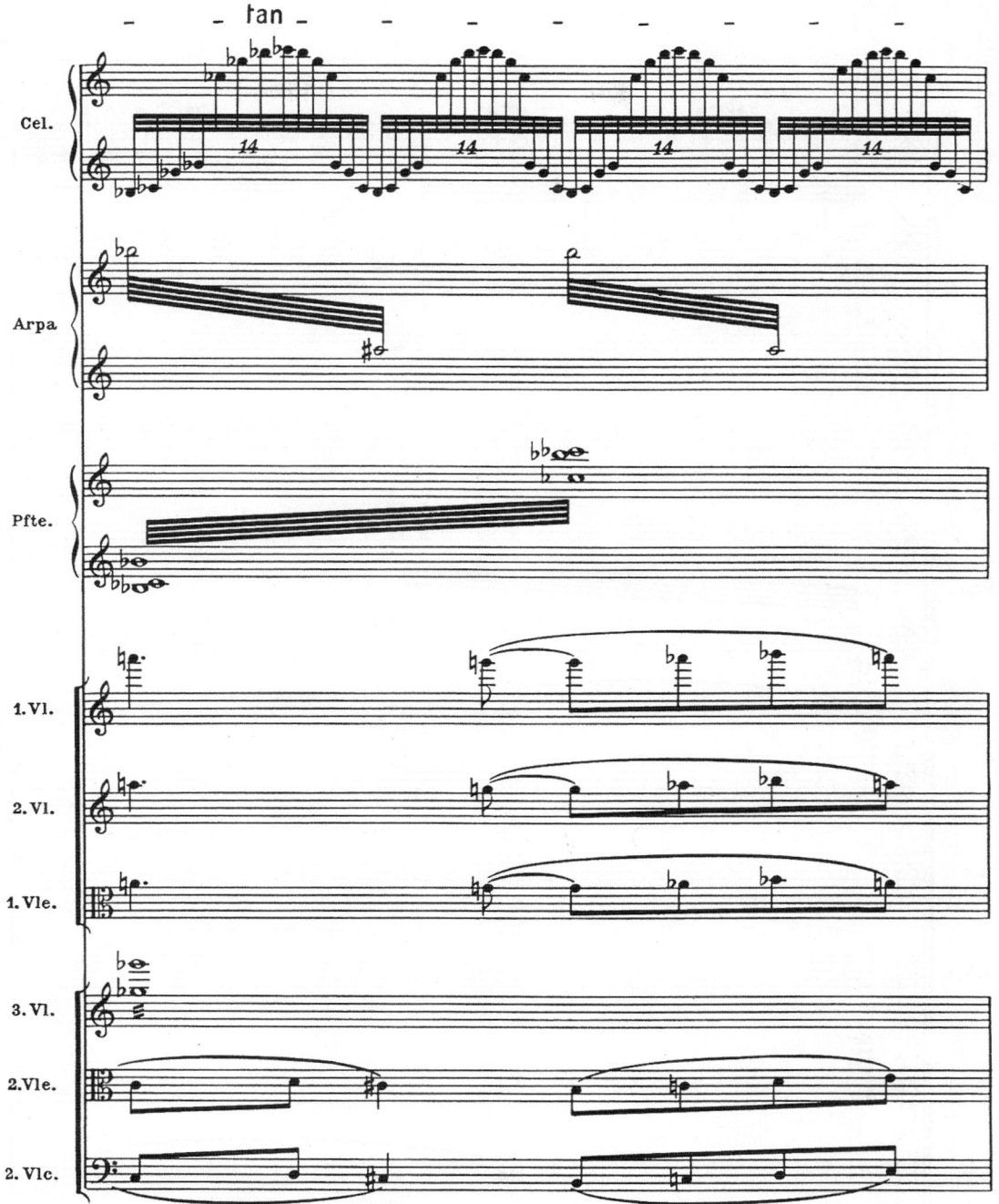

Durée d'exécution: - A ca 1' 45"
(Timings)

A - B	„	1' 12"
B - C	„	55"
C - D	„	57"
D - E	„	58"
E -	„	48"
	ca	6' 35"

Béla Bartók wrote *Music for Strings, Percussion and Celesta* in the summer of 1936 for the Basel Chamber Orchestra and its conductor, Paul Sacher. Bartók's concept for the piece was so clear in his mind that he wrote it out from the start in full score, rather than beginning with a reduced score as composers usually do for orchestral works. It was premiered the next January in Basel, Switzerland, to such great applause that the orchestra played the fourth movement again as an encore.

The work has four movements: a slow fugue, a fast sonata form, a slow arch form, and a rondo finale. The fugue theme is recalled in each later movement. The movements are also linked by a symmetrical scheme of tonal centers—A for the outer movements, with the notes a minor third above (C) and below (F♯) serving as centers for the second and third movements respectively. Like *Symphony of Psalms* (NAWM 146), the piece is neotonal, rather than based on traditional harmony. In each movement, the note a tritone away from the tonal center serves as an opposite pole. Another symmetrical aspect of the music is the layout of the orchestra itself: the strings are divided into two halves (violins 1 and 2, viola 1, cello 1, and bass 1 on the left, curving from front to back, with the others on the right in a mirror arrangement), and the piano, harp, celesta, and percussion are in the middle.

The slow movement, included here, exhibits symmetries on both a minute and a large scale. The opening xylophone solo is a palindrome centered on the first beat of measure 3, that is, the rhythm from that beat is the same going in either direction. The form is also palindromic (though not exactly so), punctuated by the four phrases of the fugue theme (FT) from the first movement:

Section:	A	FT1	B	FT2	C	FT3	B'	FT4	A'
Measure:	1	19	20	34	35	60	63	74	75

The A section is marked by four striking sounds: the xylophone, which repeats a single pitch (f'''); glissandos on the timpani between F♯ and C, the two tonal poles of the movement; low string tremolos on C and F♯; and figures in violas and violins that snake through chromatic space. After the first phrase of the fugue appears (in viola 1 and cello 1 at measure 19), two solo violins and celesta share the B theme, accompanied by an eerie background of trills in the strings and parallel major sevenths articulated by the piano, violin glissandos, and string tremolos.

After another fugue segment, the C section begins with glissandos and two mutually exclusive pentatonic scales played rapidly in the harp, piano, and celesta, over which a twisting theme in parallel octave tremolos gradually rises. This texture has become known as Bartók's "night music," named for the movement *Musiques nocturnes* in his piano suite *Out of Doors* (1926). The twisting theme builds to a climax as celesta, harp, and piano drop out. At the peak, the last segment of the twisting theme is transformed into a transposed, modified retrograde: omitting the bracketed notes, A–A♯–[D♯]–E♯–[F♯]–E–G (violin 1, measures 44–45) becomes C–A–B♭–E♭–D (measure 46). This new motive is itself heard in retrograde in alternation with its original form (measures 48 and 50) or in counterpoint with it (measures 51–53), as if to emphasize the symmetries. The new motive suffuses the texture, imitated in every instrument. Then, as the third phrase of the fugue theme enters (violin 3 and viola 2, measures 60–63), we may hear a hidden connection: the new motive turns out to derive from the last five notes of this phrase of the fugue theme, changing the whole steps into larger intervals (compare D–C–D♭–C♭–B♭ in measures 61–63, from the fugue theme, with the new motive C–A–B♭–E♭–D in measure 46).

A modified reprise of the B theme follows, treated in canon at the tritone and accompanied by a texture reminiscent of the first half of the C section, with tremolos and arpeggios in piano, harp, and celesta and violin tremolos in a high register. The last phrase of the fugue theme appears in piano and celesta, and an abbreviated recollection of the A section closes the movement.

Bartók drew on folk music, not just as a way to evoke a national or folklike style, but as a source of ideas for renewing modern music. That is evident in this movement, which does not sound folklike in the least but draws many elements from folk styles. The string melodies in the A sections borrow their short on-beat accents (as in measure 6) from a rhythm common in Hungarian folk tunes, and take their rapid, snaking figuration (as in measures 7–8) from the ornate, partly chromatic vocal ornaments of Serbo-Croatian folk songs. The B section and the climax of the C section (measures 45–59) both—in different ways—echo a technique of Bulgarian dance orchestras, in which instruments play in octaves against drones and a chordal tapestry of sound is produced by plucked instruments. In the latter passage, the $\frac{5}{4}$ meter suggests the Bulgarian dance rhythm of 2 + 3 (the *paidushko*). Thus, in this movement, and throughout *Music for Strings, Percussion and Celesta*, Bartók has fully assimilated elements of folk music into one of his most original works of art music.

This piece is highly individual in style, form, and even genre. It is clearly related to the four-movement symphony but differentiated from the symphony by its movement structure and prominent percussion and keyboard parts. Paradoxically, such a high degree of individuality is typical of the twentieth century, when composers sought both to follow in the footsteps of the classical masters of the past and to stake out new territory, forging distinctive identities for themselves and for each new piece.

CHARLES IVES (1874–1954)

General William Booth Enters into Heaven

Song

1914

148

CD 11|42 CD 6|25

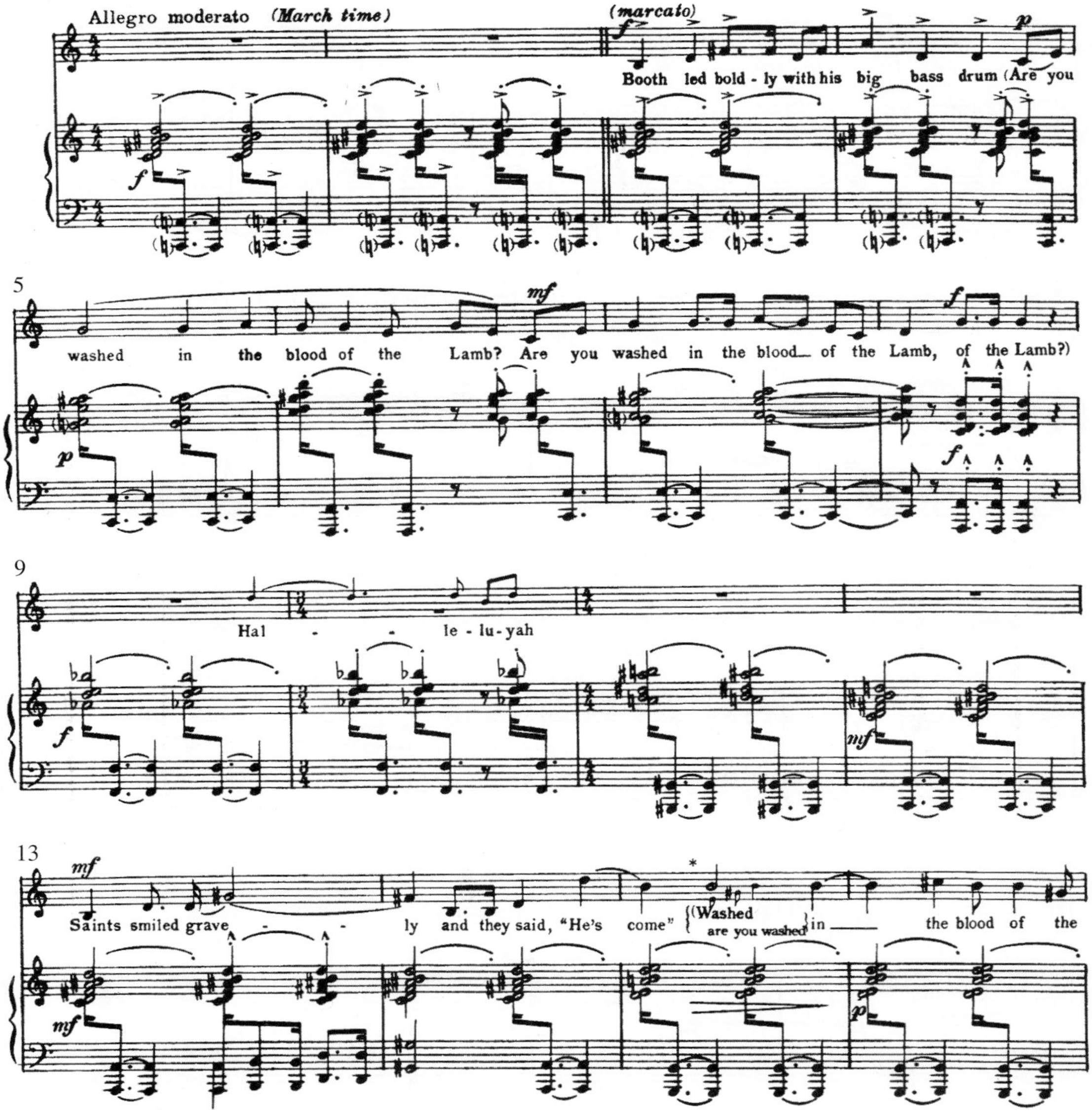

*Both small and large notes in voice part are sung if there is a chorus.

From Charles Ives, *Nineteen Songs* (Bryn Mawr, Pa.: Theodore Presser, 1935), 2–7. Reprinted by permission of Theodore Presser.

Charles Ives found the poem *General William Booth Enters into Heaven* by American poet Vachel Lindsay (1879–1931) in a 1914 review of Lindsay's first book of poetry. There was probably no poet better suited for Ives's musical idiom than Lindsay, who infused his poems (and his onstage readings of them) with the rhythms and performing styles of hymns, vaudeville, and ragtime. Ives based his song on only the extracts printed in the review: the first, second, and fourth stanzas of the seven-stanza poem. The song remained unpublished until 1935, when Henry Cowell produced nineteen of Ives's songs as an issue of *New Music,* a quarterly journal of works by modern composers.

Lindsay wrote the poem on the death of William Booth, evangelist and founder of the Salvation Army, whom Lindsay pictures entering Heaven beating a bass drum at the head of an army of the souls he had saved. Appropriately, Lindsay drew inspiration from a gospel hymn, indicating that the poem was "to be sung to the tune of 'The Blood of the Lamb.'" He quoted the hymn's refrain line frequently ("Are you washed in the blood of the Lamb?"), and for the other lines he used the hymn's accent pattern of three stressed, three unstressed, and three stressed syllables.

Ives's setting is an art song in the classical tradition, but he incorporates elements from the band music and popular songs of the American vernacular tradition, from Protestant hymnody, and from the experimental music in which he was a pioneer. At the opening, he evokes Booth's bass drum through his technique of imitating drumbeats as dissonant chords on the piano, an experiment from his teen years; the bass notes arrive after the rest of the chord, just as on a bass drum the resonance of the drum head is heard just after the sound of the initial impact. The rhythm here is the "street beat" (measures 1–2), the pattern drummers use to keep marchers moving in step and one of the first things Ives would have learned as a drummer in his father's band. Ives based the vocal melody on motives paraphrased from the hymn "There Is a Fountain Filled with Blood," whose imagery closely matches that of the hymn Lindsay used.

In the second section of the song (measures 19–39), Lindsay describes Booth's followers, and Ives gives each group a different musical characterization, using ostinatos, parallel dissonant chords, and other modernist sounds. At each appearance of the refrain line "(Are you washed in the blood of the Lamb?)," Ives presents a new paraphrase of "There Is a Fountain."

When the marchers arrive at the center of Heaven—depicted as a "mighty courthouse square" like those in county seats across America—Ives suggests the milling crowd through a rising and falling whole-tone scale in the voice and repeating ostinatos in the piano (measures 40–51). At the line "Big-voiced lassies made their banjos bang" (measures 52–55), the piano paraphrases *Oh, Dem Golden Slippers* by James A. Bland, a minstrel song about going to Heaven whose second verse begins "Oh my ole banjo." Later Ives adds a bugle call for the line "Loons with trumpets blowed a blare," and a hint of the hymn "Onward, Upward" where the words of Lindsay's poem almost quote it (measures 70–74). All these elements show Ives's affectionate, good-humored approach to depicting the motley crowd, although both Lindsay's poem and Ives's song are entirely serious.

When Jesus appears at the court house door and blesses the marchers, Ives states most of "There Is a Fountain," slightly reworked, in the piano (measures 82–88), accompanying a repeating motive in the voice that depicts the crowd still circling around the square. This is the first mostly diatonic passage in the song, and its slow, soft, dignified character reflects Jesus' serenity. Booth does not see Jesus at first (he was blind when he died), and continues to lead the march even as he and all the marchers are cleansed and healed by Jesus' blessing. At the climactic moment of transformations, over the drum pattern in the piano, the singer presents the complete verse of "There Is a Fountain," set awkwardly to Lindsay's words as if to express the force of will it took Booth to motivate his followers. This moment is the culmination of the drama in Lindsay's poem and also of the thematic process of the whole song, a gradual emergence of the hymn tune as the principal theme. The song is thus an example of *cumulative form*, the form Ives used most often, in which the main theme is heard first in fragments and paraphrases and appears complete only at the end.

In the final measures, the action stops, and the closing refrain is set twice, over soft arpeggiated chords and then in the four-part harmony of Protestant hymns. The stark contrasts of style seen here and throughout the song are typical of Ives, who used them to articulate his cumulative form and for expressive purposes, just as Mozart used contrasting styles in his music (see the commentaries for NAWM 105 and 107). In this context, the use of a familiar style amid so many novel sounds suggests the humble devotion of a hymn, and thus brings the message of the song home. The moment quickly passes, and the parade fades away in the distance.

After writing this song, Ives sketched an arrangement for unison choir and chamber orchestra. When he published the song more than twenty years after writing it, he included a number of passages in small notes, indicating that they should be sung if the piece was performed by a choir, and these are sometimes included even when it is sung by a soloist.

BESSIE SMITH (1894–1937)

Back Water Blues

Blues

1927

1. When it rains five days and the skies turn dark at night,
    When it rains five days and the skies turn dark at night,
    Then trouble's takin' place in the lowlands at night.

2. I woke up this mornin', can't even get out of my door.
    I woke up this mornin', can't even get out of my door.
    That's enough trouble to make a poor girl wonder where she want to go.

3. Then they rowed a little boat about five miles 'cross the farm.
    Then they rowed a little boat about five miles 'cross the farm.
    I packed all my clothes, throwed them in and they rowed me along.

4. When it thunders and lightnin', and the wind begins to blow,
    When it thunders and lightnin', and the wind begins to blow,
    There's thousands of people ain't got no place to go.

5. Then I went and stood upon some high old lonesome hill.
    Then I went and stood upon some high old lonesome hill.
    Then looked down on the house where I used to live.

6. Back-water blues done caused me to pack my things and go.
    Back-water blues done caused me to pack my things and go.
    'Cause my house fell down and I can't live there no more.

7. (Moan . . .) I can't move no more,
    (Moan . . .) I can't move no more,
    There ain't no place for a poor old girl to go.

Bessie Smith, known as the "Empress of the Blues," wrote both lyrics and music
for her hit song *Back Water Blues.* Columbia Records marketed Smith's recording,
made on February 2, 1927, as a response to a flood in Mississippi in April of 1927,
and it became one of her best-known records. She had written the song several
months earlier after a flood on Christmas Day, 1926, in Nashville, where she sang
in a show a few days after the flood.

Smith constructed the song in conventional blues form. Each of the seven stanzas shares the same AAB poetic form: the second line repeats the first line intact,
followed by a new line of poetry with the same end rhyme. The rhyme is often a
near-rhyme, as in the pairing of "go" with "more" in the last two verses; the quality of the vowel is always more important than the ending consonants. The last line
of each stanza either completes the thought begun by the first or packs a surprise
by offering new information, as in the sixth verse.

Each stanza follows the form of a twelve-bar blues, with four measures for each
line of poetry and a general harmonic pattern of tonic chords in the first phrase,
subdominant to tonic in the second, and dominant to tonic in the third. After a
brief piano introduction, Smith settles into the tonic for four measures, with the
piano moving to the subdominant in the second measure, as sometimes occurs in
the form. The next four-measure phrase begins on the subdominant, moving
back to the tonic after two measures. For the final line of the stanza, in measures
9–12 of the blues pattern, Smith moves to the dominant for a measure, then to the
subdominant (with added ninth and seventh) before moving back to the tonic for
the final two measures. Here, as in many blues, the voice begins just before the
first measure of each phrase and cadences on the third measure, allowing space in
the third and fourth measures for the pianist to respond in an evocation of the
call-and-response structure typical of African-American group singing.

The twelve-bar blues is a flexible harmonic pattern, used as a general framework. Exact adherence to the chords specified here is not crucial; rather, it is the
combination of the harmonic framework, use of blue notes (flatted thirds and
sevenths, sometimes also flatted fifths), poetic structure, and general mood that
together give life to the blues.

The sheet music included here is merely an approximation for the performance, as Smith's recording reveals. Many blues were performed and recorded

before they were written down in notation, and there are elements of the performance that the notation is not well equipped to capture. Smith sings a somewhat different melody for each verse, emphasizing the blue notes and altering the rhythm to fit the words of each stanza while following the same basic melodic shape. Pianist James P. Johnson, famed as an exponent of the stride piano style, reponds to Smith's phrases with improvised additions of his own. Some of his figurations respond to the text, as when during the fourth stanza he produces a dramatic, downward skipping bass line to imitate the thunder, lightning, and blowing wind. His rocking accompaniment in the left hand throughout most of the song seems to suggest a reassurance that time and life go on and the flood will subside.

KING OLIVER [JOE OLIVER] (1885–1938)

West End Blues, as performed by Louis Armstrong and His Hot Five

Blues

RECORDED 1928

150

(a) Original sheet music [not on recording]

way   to the West End,   And there's where troub-les will be – gin;
way   to the West End,   To   lose   those ug – ly West End blues,

Chorus
p-f

My   man,   my dan,   low down,   Mean houn'   In

town   with   my   best friend,____ run-nin' a – roun'   Soon the

un – der-tak – er man, gon – na knock u – pon his   door,

(b) Transcription of recording by Louis Armstrong and His Hot Five

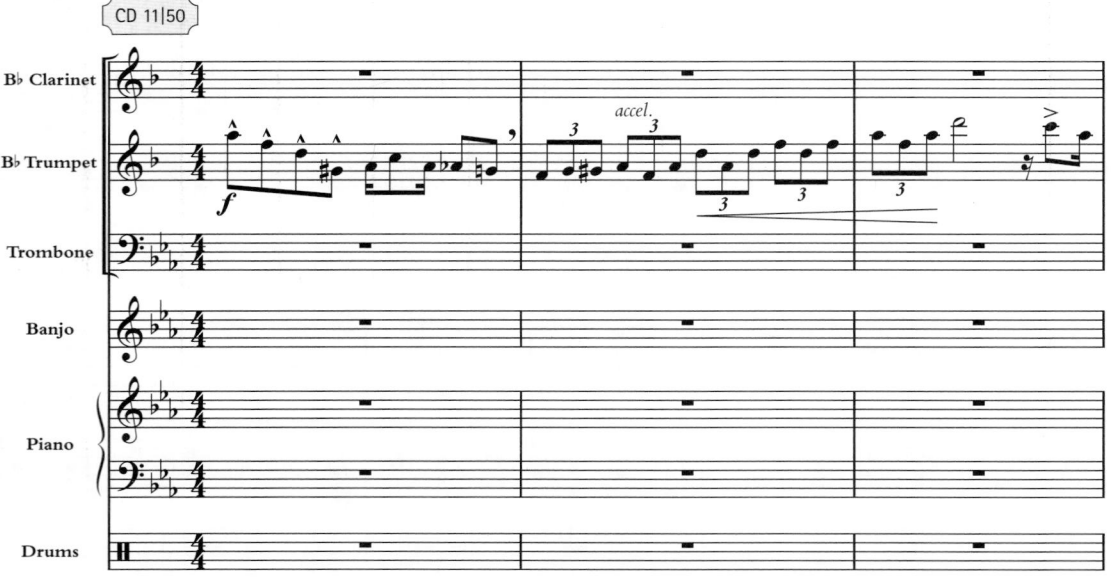

Transcription from Joe "King" Oliver and Clarence Williams, *West End Blues: As Recorded by Louis Armstrong and His Hot Five, 1928,* transcribed by Randy Sandke, ed. David N. Baker. International copyright secured. All rights reserved. Used by permission of Hal Leonard Corp.

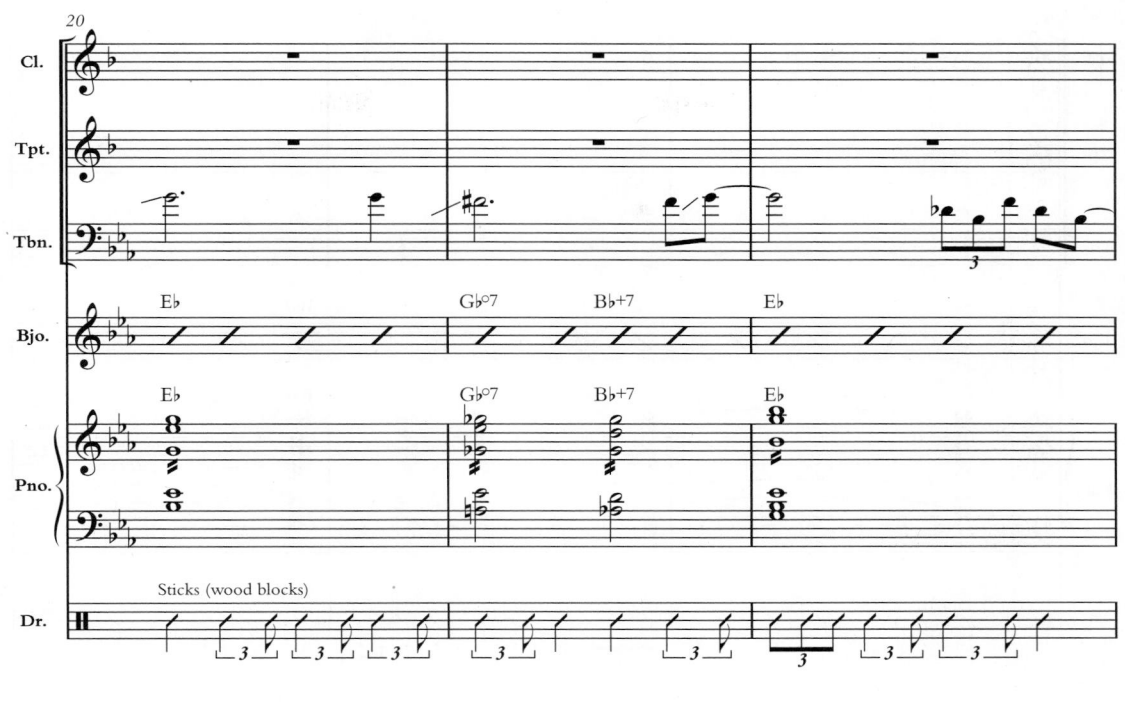

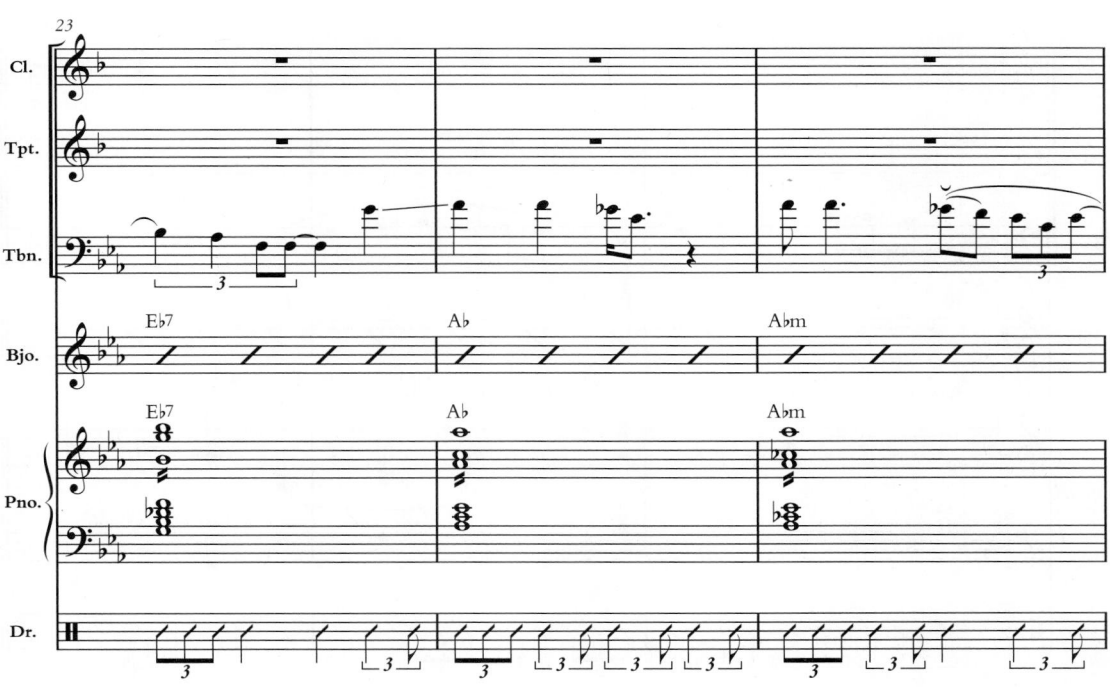

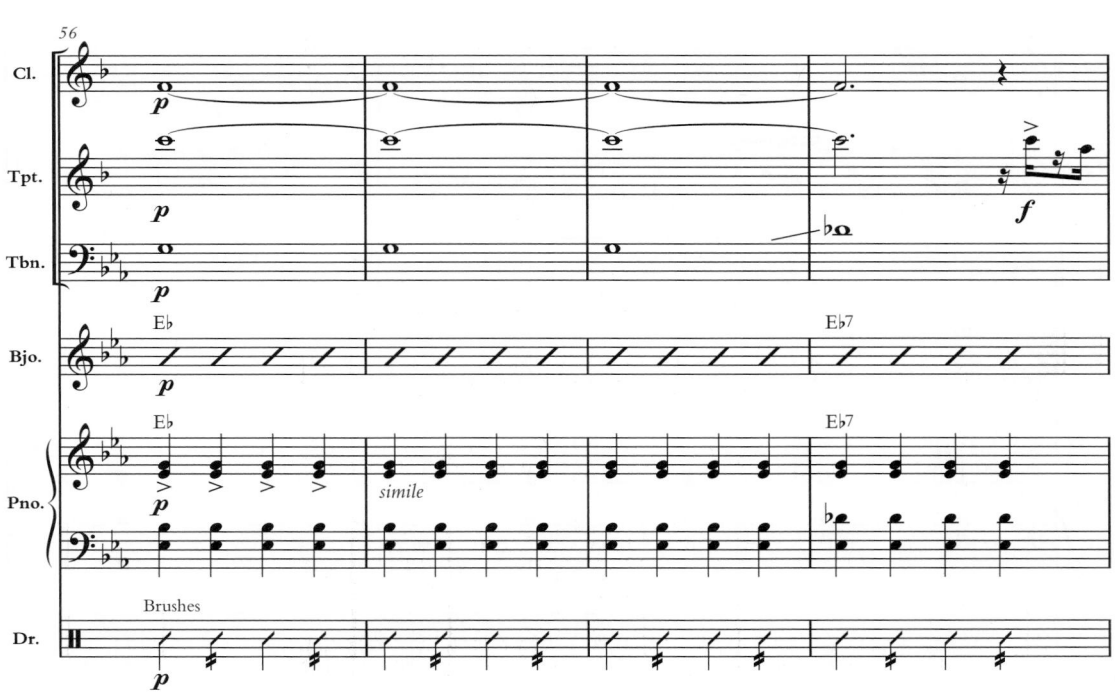

In the period between the two world wars, jazz and other types of popular music were sold both as recordings by star performers and as sheet music for amateurs to play at home or for other musicians to use in their own performances. These two versions of *West End Blues* illustrate the difference between the two formats, as well as the ways jazz performers used the songs they played as the basis for improvisation.

NAWM 150a shows the sheet music for *West End Blues* as written and published in 1928 by Joe "King" Oliver (music) and Clarence Williams (lyrics). Typical of the popular songs in sheet music of the time, this song begins with a brief piano introduction and is laid out in verse-refrain form. The two bars leading into the first verse are labeled "Vamp," an instruction to the accompanist to keep repeating these measures until the singer joins in. The music for the verse is built over one complete statement of a twelve-bar blues progression (compare NAWM 149). The refrain, to be sung after each verse, presents two successive statements of the twelve-bar blues. Each time through the twelve-bar progression, Oliver writes a different melody and varies the harmony slightly, creating greater variety. The rhythm often features dotted eighths and sixteenths, a written approximation to the swinging rhythms typical of jazz, in which even eighth notes are played in a uneven pattern alternating long and short notes.

The same year Oliver and Williams wrote *West End Blues*, Louis Armstrong and His Hot Five—with Armstrong on trumpet backed by Jimmy Strong on clarinet, Fred Robinson on trombone, Earl Hines on piano, Mancy Cara on banjo, and Zutty Singleton on drums—recorded an instrumental version for OKeh Records in Chicago. This recording is on the accompanying CD set, and it is transcribed in NAWM 150b.

In place of the piano introduction, the recorded version begins with a virtuosic solo by Armstrong. The recorded version has no verse-refrain structure; it has, instead, five statements of the twelve-bar blues pattern, in which members of the group take turn playing solos that are either improvised or in the style of improvisation. In jazz parlance, each such statement is called a *chorus* (derived from, but different from, the alternate term for the refrain of a popular song).

The entire ensemble plays the first chorus together, with Armstrong taking the melody—a flexible, freely decorated version of the vocal melody of the original song's verse. The second chorus features Robinson on trombone, beginning with the opening notes of the chorus and then introducing new variations. He is backed by the rhythm section of piano, banjo, and drum set, here played mostly on wood blocks. The third rendition of the blues progression features the clarinet alternating in call and response with Armstrong, who puts down his trumpet and sings in a novelty vocal style that he had made popular: he "scats," singing nonsense syllables to an improvised melody, making his voice sound like an instrument. Hines solos on the piano in the fourth chorus, alternating between elaborate figurations in the right hand and syncopated chordal decorations of the melody. The entire ensemble returns for the fifth and final chorus. Once again,

Armstrong takes the lead, holding a single high pitch for four measures before filling the next four bars with a virtuosic burst of inventive improvisation. The performance ends with a brief cadential tag.

This recording of *West End Blues* exemplifies two of Armstrong's innovative techniques that were seminal to the development of jazz. The first was scat singing, which allowed a voice to imitate an instrument. Scat remains an important technique for jazz singers. Armstrong also quickly became known as an outstanding soloist and paved the way for dynamic, improvised jazz solos, a crucial element of jazz's musical language.

151

GEORGE GERSHWIN (1898–1937)

I Got Rhythm, from *Girl Crazy*

Broadway show song

1930

CD 11|55 CD 6|32

[Instrumental Introduction]

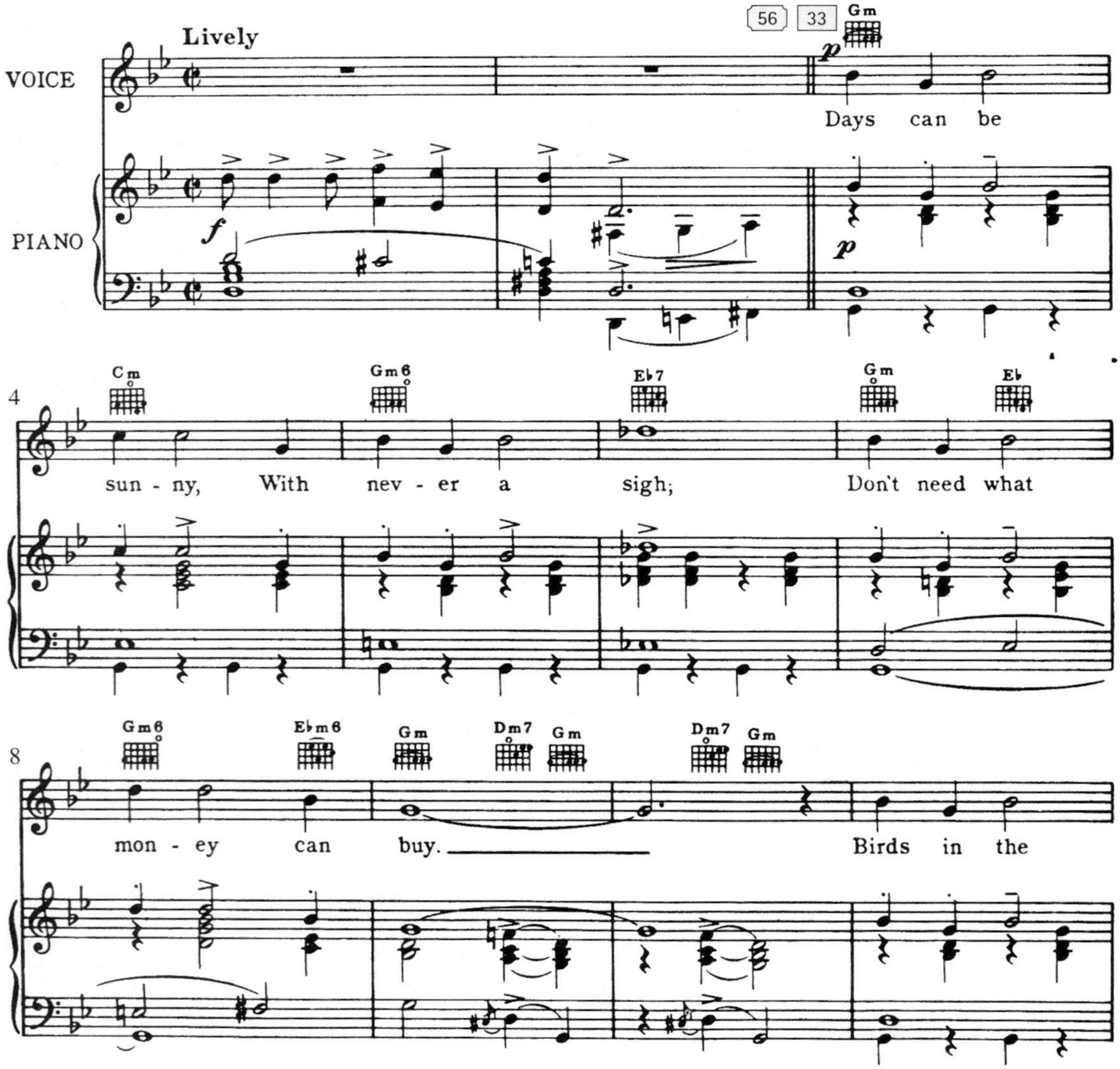
Lively
VOICE
PIANO
56
33
Gm
Days can be
4
Cm
Gm6
Eb7
Gm
Eb
sun - ny, With nev - er a sigh; Don't need what
8
Gm6
Ebm6
Gm
Dm7
Gm
Dm7
Gm
mon - ey can buy. Birds in the

George Gershwin composed *I Got Rhythm*, with lyrics by his brother Ira, for the Broadway musical *Girl Crazy*, which premiered on October 14, 1930, at the Alvin Theater. George typically composed the melody first, and Ira then fitted it with lyrics, the practice also of several other Tin Pan Alley and Broadway songwriting teams. The show introduced Ginger Rogers and Ethel Merman, who became stars on Broadway and in the movies. Merman debuted *I Got Rhythm* in the role of Frisco Kate and later recorded the song in the version heard on the accompanying recordings. The song was published in 1930 in the version reproduced here, arranged with piano accompaniment and with guitar chords and fingerings.

Gershwin laid out *I Got Rhythm* in standard Tin Pan Alley form: verse plus thirty-two-bar chorus with phrases in an AABA' pattern (plus a two-bar tag). Following the trend at the time, the work has only one verse, and the main emphasis in the song is on the chorus, which is immediately repeated. To provide a clear contrast of mood and style, Gershwin set the verse and chorus in different keys. The verse begins in G minor, but modulates to the relative major, B♭, which remains the key area of the A sections of the chorus. The B section of the chorus, called the "bridge," shifts to the mediant, D major, and then travels down the circle of fifths to get back to B♭ in the final A section of the chorus. Ira's lyrics are fresh, modern, optimistic, and slangy, as they are in most of his songs; the opening phrase, for example, is not "I've got" or "I have," but the grammatically incorrect yet catchy "I got." Ira matches George's heavily syncopated rhythm with a punchy text that allows every syllable to be stressed (as in the first four measures of the chorus).

I Got Rhythm was an immediate popular hit, and not only in its original form. Instrumental versions based on the song's chorus began to appear, and soon this song became a jazz standard. However, in jazz performances of the song, it is not the melody that is the focus; rather, jazz performers have valued the harmony, which provided the framework for their improvisations. The "changes" (the jazz term for a specific harmonic progression) of this song became the basis for so many new jazz tunes in the following decades that this particular chord progression came to be known simply as "rhythm changes" (short for "the *I Got Rhythm* changes"). NAWM 152, Duke Ellington's *Cotton Tail*, is one example of a new jazz tune built over this harmonic progression.

Typically, the scores of Tin Pan Alley songs and indeed of most popular songs are merely guidelines for performance. The two-measure introduction can be repeated indefinitely as a vamp to set the stage for the singer. In Merman's recording, the band plays the entire melody of the chorus before returning to the two opening measures as written. Merman then enters with the verse, and follows with the chorus. The recording captures Merman's trademark nasal, chest-voiced performing style, nearly spoken delivery, and textual additions, such as interpolating the words "hanging 'round my front or back door" in the final statement of the chorus. The performance concludes with Merman's signature flourish: punching the final note of the chorus up a fifth and holding it for several measures as the orchestra finishes the melody.

DUKE ELLINGTON (1899–1974)

Cotton Tail

Jazz composition (contrafact)

1940

Duke Ellington, *Cotton Tail,* as recorded by Duke Ellington and His Orchestra on May 4, 1940. Transcribed by David Berger, edited by Brian Almeter.

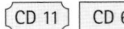

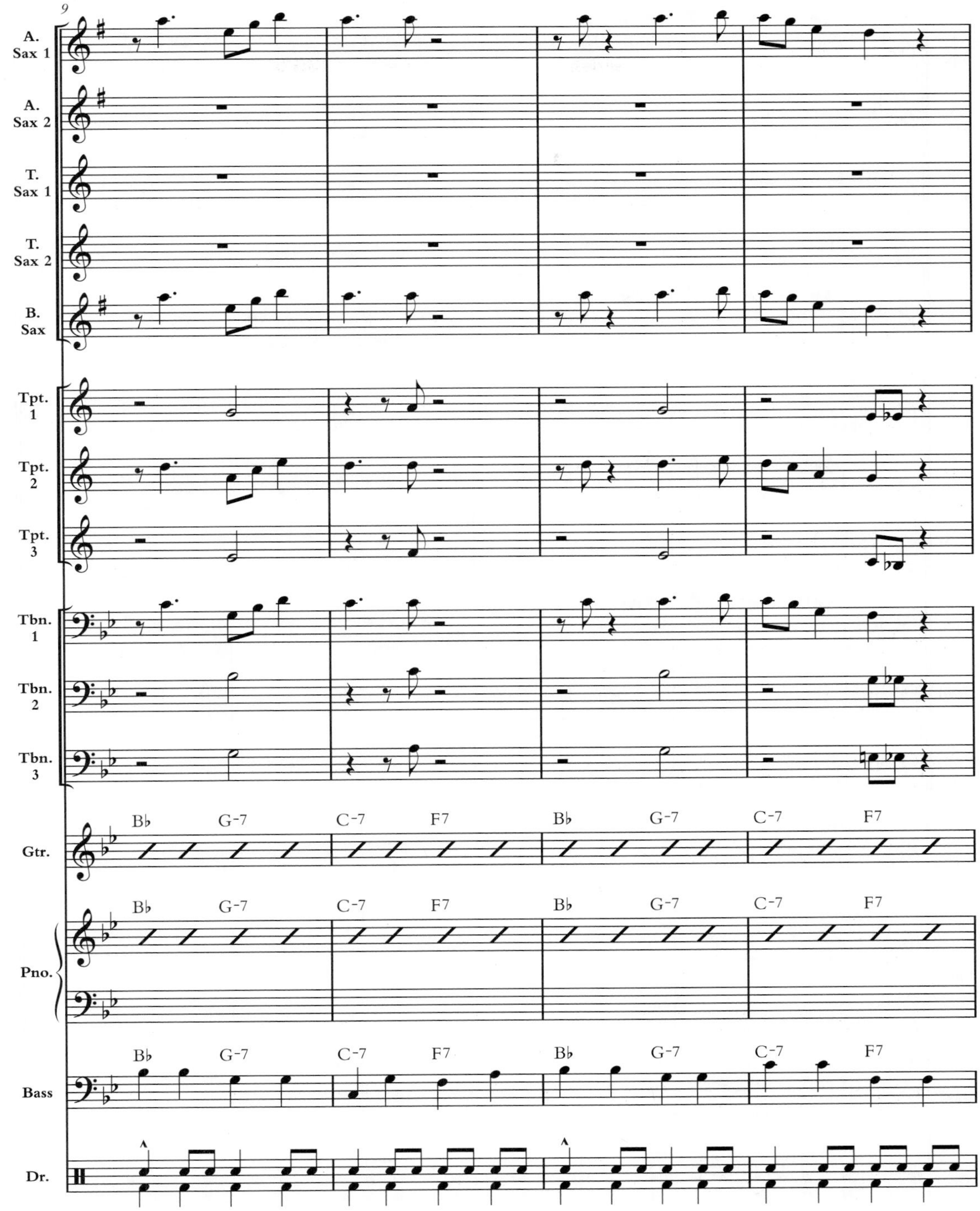
9
A. Sax 1
A. Sax 2
T. Sax 1
T. Sax 2
B. Sax
Tpt. 1
Tpt. 2
Tpt. 3
Tbn. 1
Tbn. 2
Tbn. 3
Gtr.
Pno.
Bass
Dr.
B♭ G-7 C-7 F7 B♭ G-7 C-7 F7

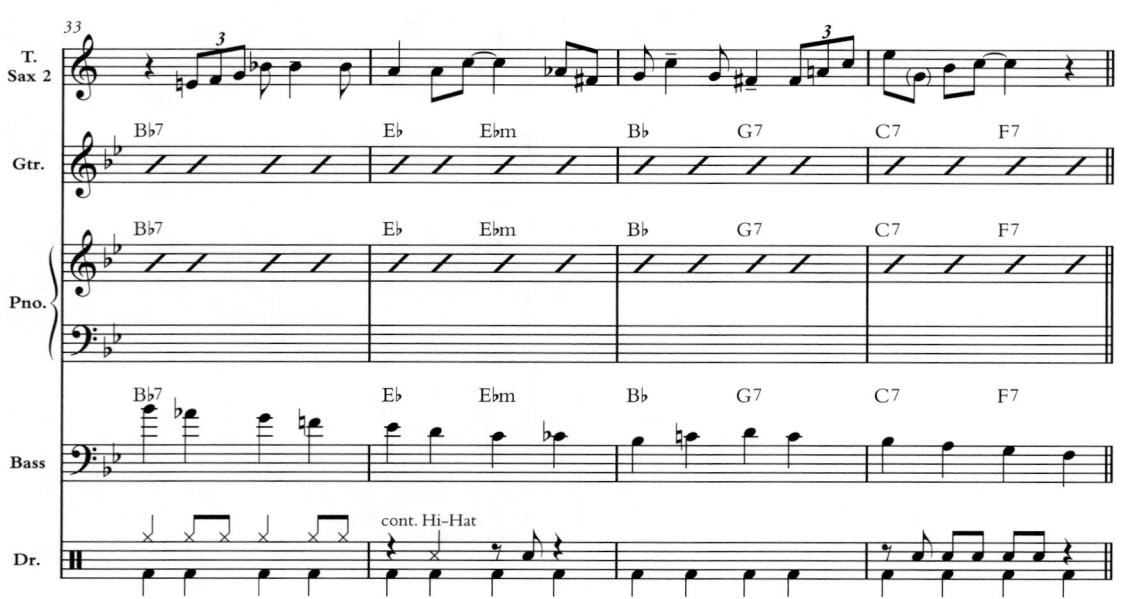

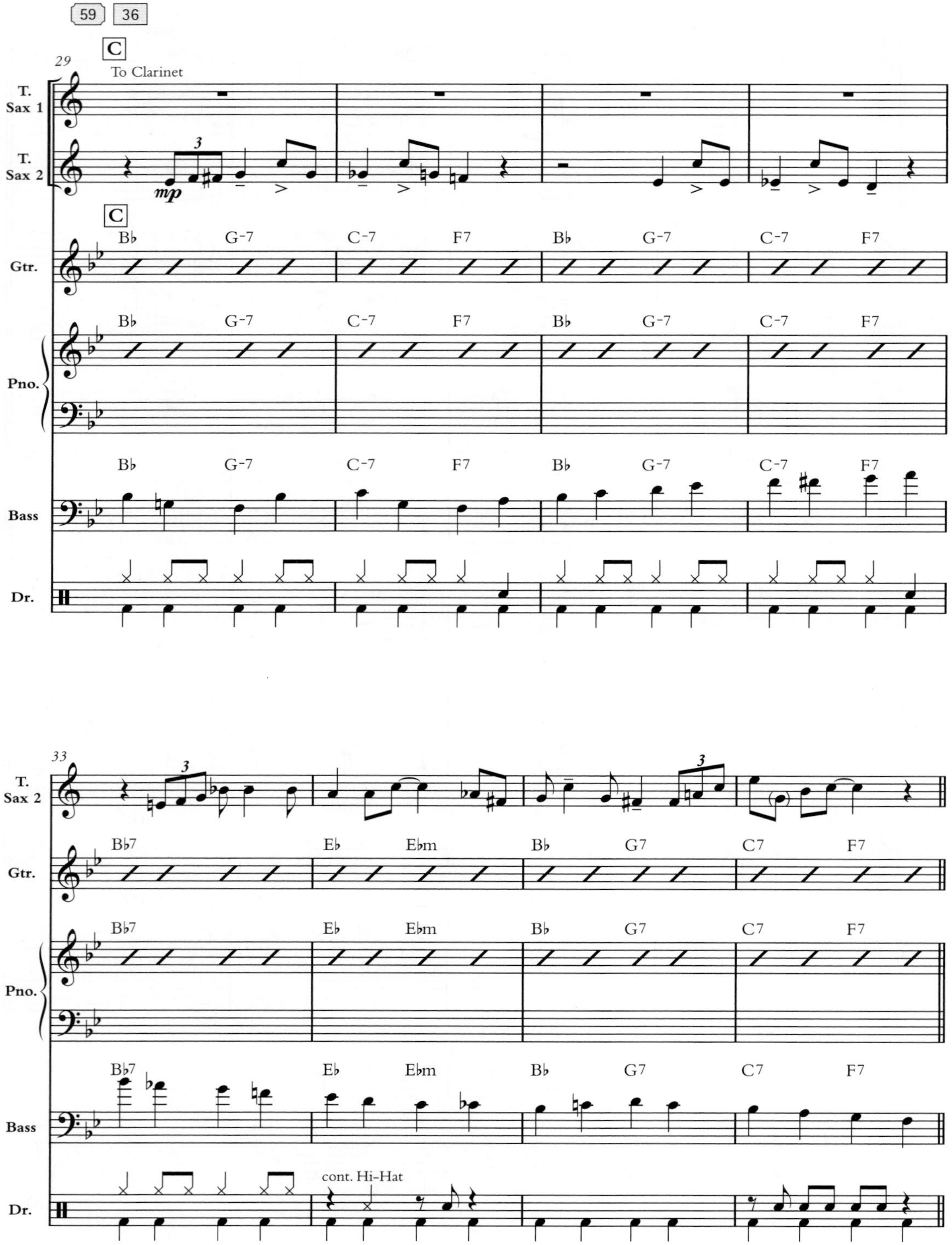
59
36
C
29
To Clarinet
T. Sax 1
T. Sax 2
3
mp
C
Gtr.
Pno.
Bass
Dr.
Bb G-7 C-7 F7 Bb G-7 C-7 F7
33
T. Sax 2
3
Bb7 Eb Ebm Bb G7 C7 F7
cont. Hi-Hat

152 **DUKE ELLINGTON** *Cotton Tail*

60
37
E
61
To Tenor
T. Sax 1
T. Sax 2
E
B♭ G-7 C-7 F7 B♭ G-7 C-7 F7 B♭
Gtr.
Pno.
B♭ B♭ B♭ B♭
Bass
Dr.

Growl
65
T. Sax 2
G-7 C-7 F7 B♭ G-7 B♭
Gtr.
Pno.
B♭ B♭ B♭ B♭
Bass
Dr.

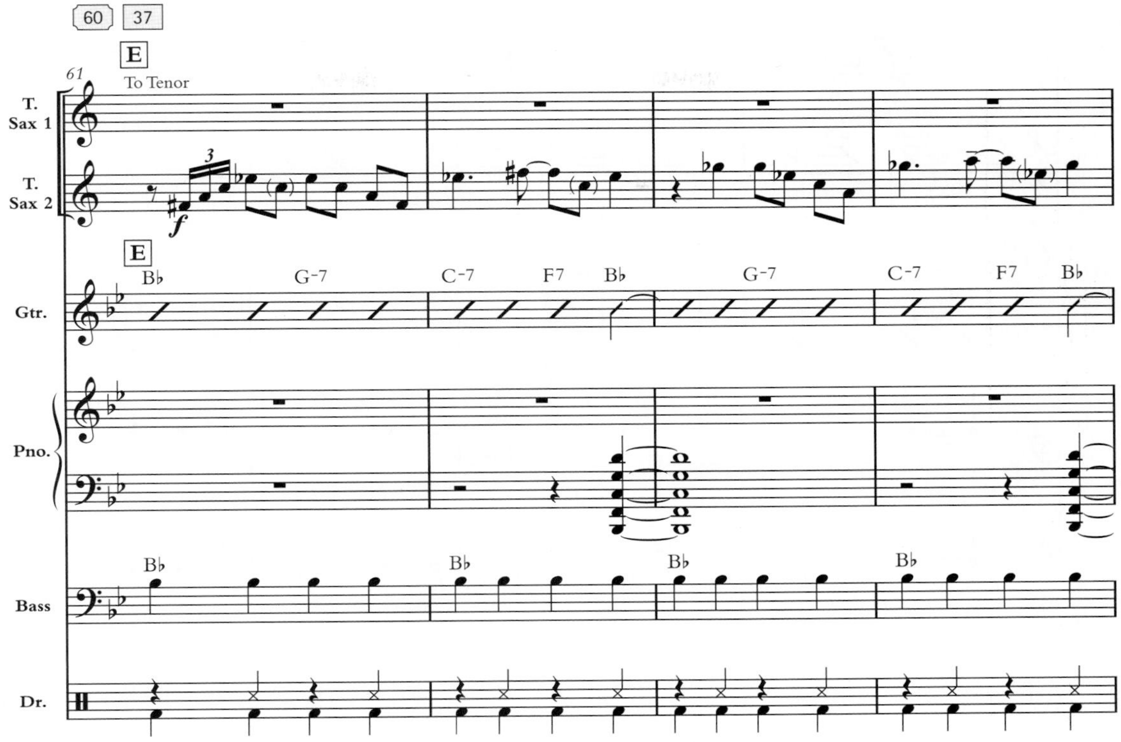

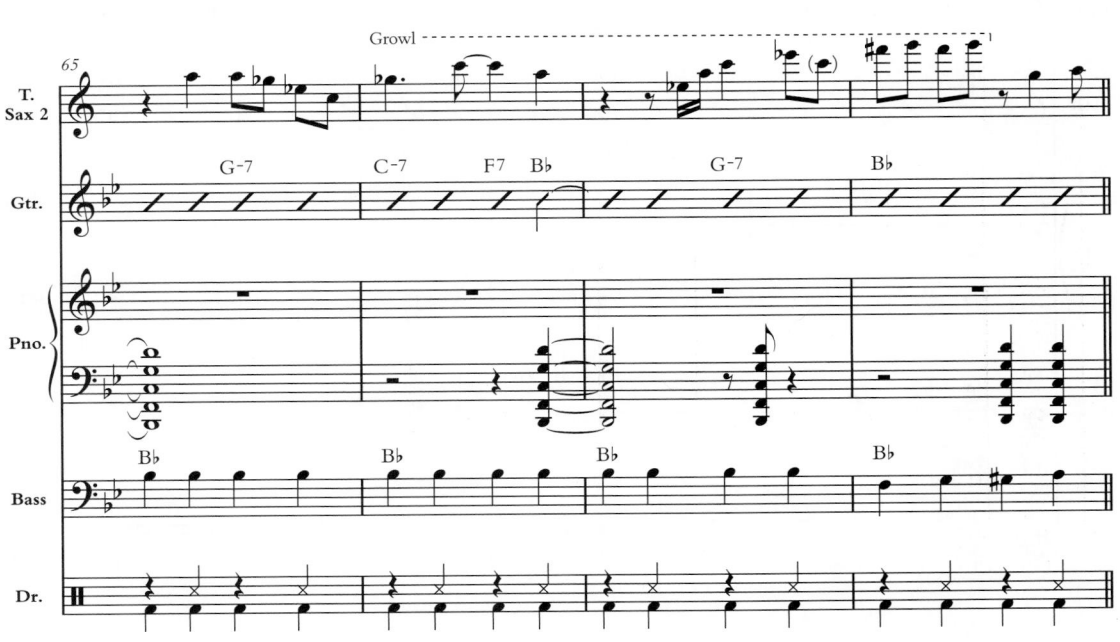

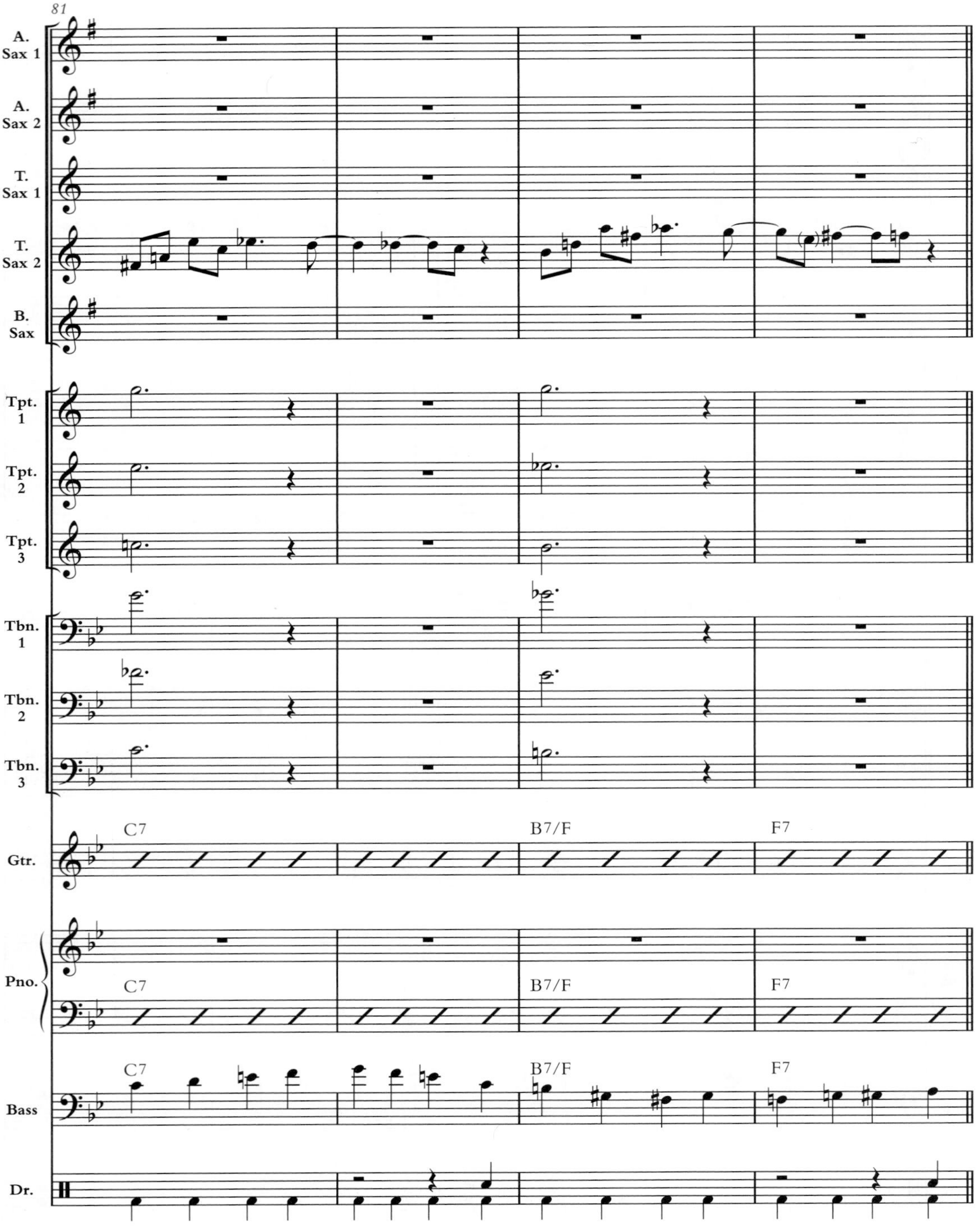
81
A. Sax 1
A. Sax 2
T. Sax 1
T. Sax 2
B. Sax
Tpt. 1
Tpt. 2
Tpt. 3
Tbn. 1
Tbn. 2
Tbn. 3
Gtr.
Pno.
Bass
Dr.
C7
B7/F
F7

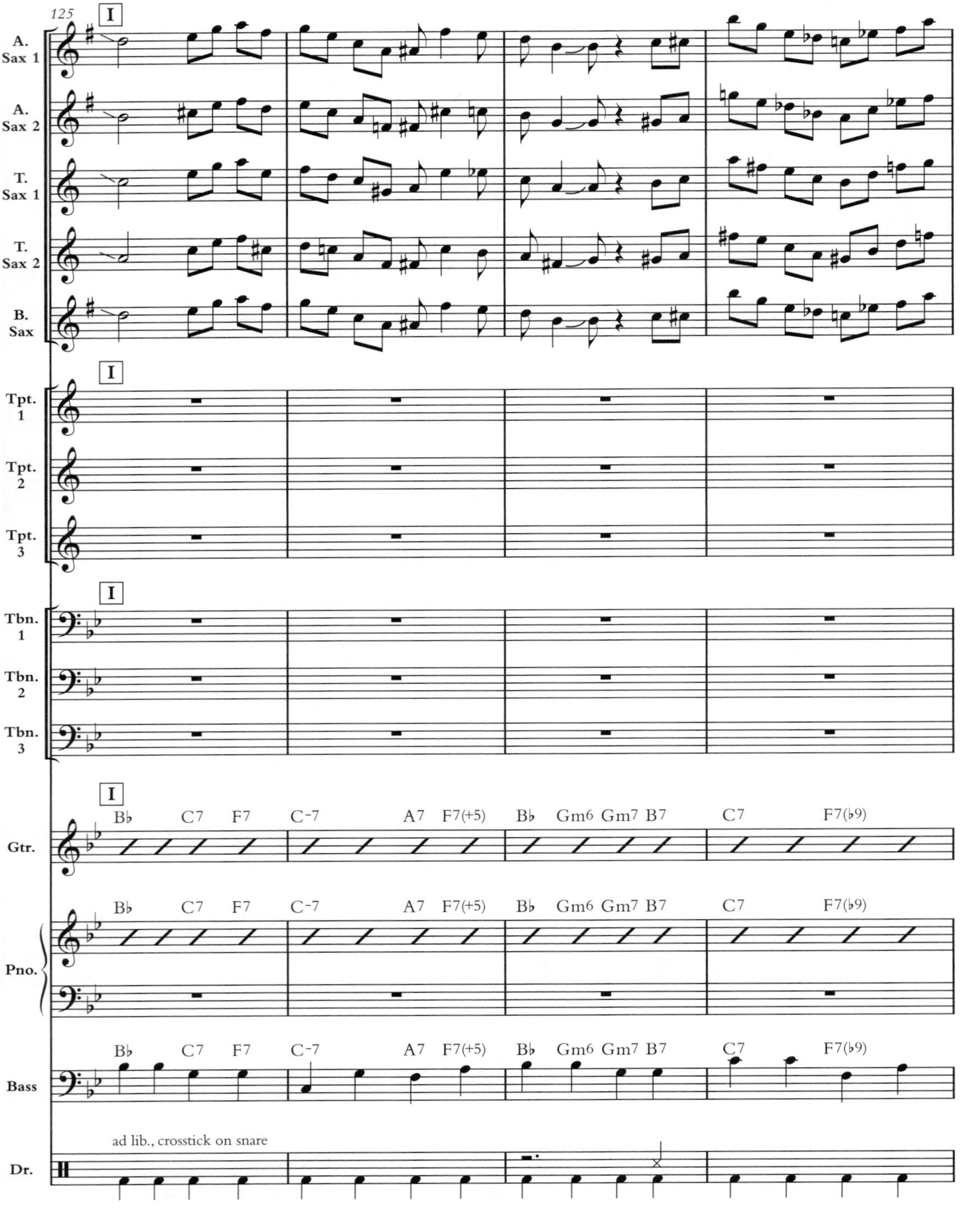
125
I
A. Sax 1
A. Sax 2
T. Sax 1
T. Sax 2
B. Sax
Tpt. 1
Tpt. 2
Tpt. 3
Tbn. 1
Tbn. 2
Tbn. 3
Gtr.
Pno.
Bass
Dr.
B♭ C7 F7 C-7 A7 F7(+5) B♭ Gm6 Gm7 B7 C7 F7(♭9)
ad lib., crosstick on snare

Throughout his career as a band leader and composer, Duke Ellington hired performers more for their individual sounds than for their ability to blend seamlessly into the ensemble, and he wrote music to showcase their particular abilities. In *Cotton Tail*, composed in 1940, Ellington took advantage of the talents of two new members of his band: virtuoso bassist Jimmy Blanton and tenor saxophonist Ben Webster.

Cotton Tail is a *contrafact*, a new tune composed over a harmonic progression borrowed from another song. Ellington composed a new melody (measures 1–28) to be played over the harmonic progression from the chorus of George Gershwin's *I Got Rhythm* (NAWM 151). Using a familiar harmonic progression was convenient, since players already knew the harmonies and could therefore extemporize with confidence, but adding a new tune and giving it a new name meant that no royalties had to be paid for recording or playing the original song. The harmonic progression from *I Got Rhythm* was used for more contrafacts than any other except the blues, in part because its structure provided interesting possibilities: the A phrases changed chords every half-measure, while the B section lingered on each chord for two measures, offering a strong contrast between rapid and slow harmonic rhythm (the pace of the harmonic progression). Ellington follows Gershwin's harmonies in general outline, but makes many small changes. For example, in measure 5, he underpins the unexpected E natural (equivalent to F♭, the flatted fifth) in the melody with a B♭⁷ chord with flatted fifth, enriched from a simple tonic B♭ major chord in the original. Later there are several passages in which the harmony is colored by substitute chords, though the overall structure of the progression is maintained.

After the opening statement of the new tune to Gershwin's progression (with its last eight-bar phrase shortened to four bars, measures 25–28), each subsequent statement, or chorus, of the AABA harmonic pattern is given different orchestration. The first two choruses (at measures 29 and 61) feature Ben Webster's blistering, agile solo on tenor sax, punctuated at times by chords from the band. The third chorus (measure 93) is divided into smaller units: the brass and rhythm sections play the first two A sections; Harry Carney on baritone sax takes the B section (measure 109); and Ellington himself rounds out the final A' with a brief piano solo. The fourth chorus (measure 125) features the reed section (saxophonists Webster, Carney, Barney Bigard, Otto Hardwick, and Johnny Hodges) in block chords. The fifth and final chorus (measure 157) is again divided. The first two A sections feature a trademark Ellington technique: brass and reed sections trading short, repeated melodic statements known as *riffs*, in call-and-response style. The entire band plays the B section, and the final A section returns to the tune from the beginning of the piece, with both reed and brass instruments playing the melody.

The accompanying CDs include the first recording of *Cotton Tail*, made on May 4, 1940, and featuring all the original musicians. The score shown here is a transcription from that recording. Thanks to rapid dissemination of the record, Webster's impressive solo became so associated with the tune that later musicians—and even Webster himself—refrained from improvising during the choruses and simply reproduced the solo note for note. In this way, recordings came to preserve performances, even improvised ones, in a form as permanent as notation.

PAUL HINDEMITH (1895–1963)

Un cygne, from *Six Chansons*

Choral partsong

1939

CD 11|64

From Paul Hindemith, *Sämtliche Werke*, vol. 7, no. 5, *Chorwerke a cappella*, ed. Alfred Rubeli (Mainz:
B. Schott's Söhne, 1989), 38–39 © 1943, 1971 Schott Music International. © Renewed. All Rights Reserved.
Used by permission of European American Music Distributors, LLC, sole U.S. and Canadian agent for
Schott Music International. English rhymed, singing translation by Elaine de Sinçay. For a more literal
translation, see p. 1057.

Un cygne avance sur l'eau
tout entouré de lui-même,
comme un glissant tableau;
ainsi à certains instants
un être que l'on aime
est tout en espace mouvant.

A swan advances on the water
completely surrounded by itself,
like a gliding tableau;
in the same way, at certain times,
a being whom one loves
is entirely a moving space.

Il se rapproche, doublé,
comme ce cygne qui nage
sur notre âme troublée . . .
qui à cet être ajoute
la tremblante image
de bonheur et de doute.

And draws near, doubled,
like this swan who swims
on our troubled soul . . .
which adds to this being
the trembling image
of happiness and of doubt.

—Rainer Maria Rilke

Fleeing persecution from the Nazi government, Paul Hindemith left Germany in 1938. Before settling in the United States in 1940, he resided in Switzerland, where he met Georges Haenni, founder of the Sion Conservatory and director of the Chanson Valaisanne, a local amateur chorus. Haenni introduced Hindemith to a collection of French poems by the prominent German poet Rainer Maria Rilke, who had once visited Villais and penned the poems in gratitude for the Swiss hospitality. Responding in kind, Hindemith selected six of Rilke's poems and composed the *Six Chansons* for a cappella chorus, dedicating the work to Haenni and the Chanson Valaisanne. According to Haenni, Hindemith completed all six pieces in a single day.

Un cygne (A Swan), the second chanson of the set, presents its text syllabically, with sensitive declamation, and in a mostly chordal texture, like a chanson of four centuries earlier (compare NAWM 54). The poem is in two stanzas, each divided in half by the rhyme scheme (aba cbc) and by punctuation. In the first stanza, the two halves are entirely distinct: the first describes the swan, and the second uses it as a metaphor for the person one loves. But in the second stanza, the images start to blend, and the line between swan and person blurs.

Hindemith follows Rilke's structure, presenting two distinct sets of ideas in the first half of the piece, and then interweaving them in the second. The opening phrase depicts the placid motion of the gliding swan with a repeated B in the soprano, inflected by a single half-step rise to C, over descending parallel fourth chords in the other voices. Like the swan on the water, the music combines stillness with movement. The next two phrases vary this idea, first with ascending chords over a repeated note in the bass (at measure 2), then with the opening melody back in the soprano above descending parallel triads (at measure 4), and the first section cadences on a B major triad (at measure 5). The second section begins with a brief point of imitation between tenor and sopranos (measures 5–7), as the music briefly becomes more active. At the mention of the loved one, a chordal texture returns with a new pair of phrases (measures 7–11), marked by a surprising turn to an Eb major triad (at the word *aime*, "loves") and a cadence on an open fifth E and B to close the first half.

For the first two lines of the second stanza, Hindemith returns to material from the first section, repeating and varying the opening motive in tenor and bass while the soprano varies its second phrase (compare measures 11–14 with 2–3). When the text refers to "our troubled soul," the music again becomes more active. Like an expanding wedge, the outer parts move outwards from a unison E, rising and falling a ninth as the choir swells to *forte* for the brief climax of the work (measures 14–16). The final section (beginning in measure 18) reprises the opening phrase (the swan's theme) and then the music first associated with the loved one (compare measures 19–22 with 8–11), linking the two thematic ideas in the same way that the text links the "being one loves" with the "trembling image of happiness and of doubt" suggested by the swan.

The harmony includes fourth chords, triads, open fifths and octaves, and dissonances of a second or seventh, all common devices for Hindemith. These are arranged in phrases according to Hindemith's theory of "harmonic fluctuation," in which relatively consonant chords move toward greater dissonance and then gradually or suddenly back to consonance. Although the piece does not use the procedures of traditional tonality, E emerges as a tonal center, suggested by the emphasis on its dominant B in the first section and confirmed by cadences at the ends of both stanzas. Poignant cross-relations are frequent, such as between C and C♯ in measure 4, D♯ and D in measure 5, and F and F♯ in measure 6, and culminating in the surprising turns to E♭ at measures 9 and 20.

Because Hindemith composed these chansons for amateur choirs, they are well suited to amateur performance. The vocal range of each part lies comfortably within the interval of a tenth, and the individual lines predominantly move by step or repeat a single pitch. The harmonic language, with its shifts from triads to dissonances, still provides a significant performance challenge, but Hindemith carefully includes pitch references for even the strongest harmonic clashes. After coming to the United States, Hindemith frequently toured college campuses as a guest conductor. In this capacity, he directed numerous performances of *Six Chansons* with college choral ensembles. Today, the work remains a standard in the twentieth-century choral repertory.

Dmitri Shostakovich (1906–1975)

Symphony No. 5, Op. 47: Second movement, Allegretto

Symphony

1937

154

CD 11|66

From Dmitri Shostakovich, *Sobranie Sochinenij* [Collected Works], vol. 3 (Moscow: Izdatelstvo Muzika, 1980), 52–82.

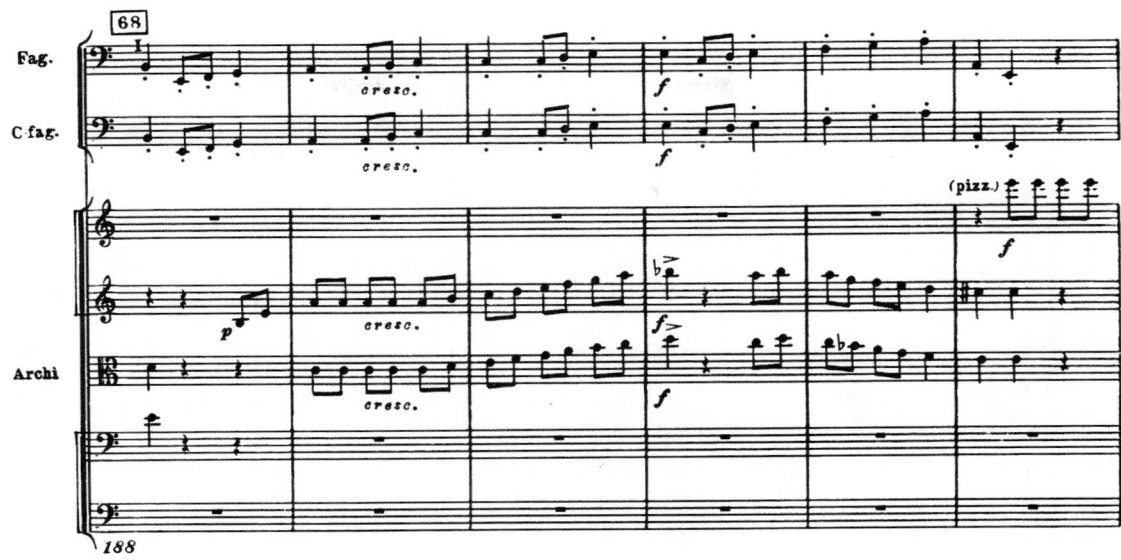

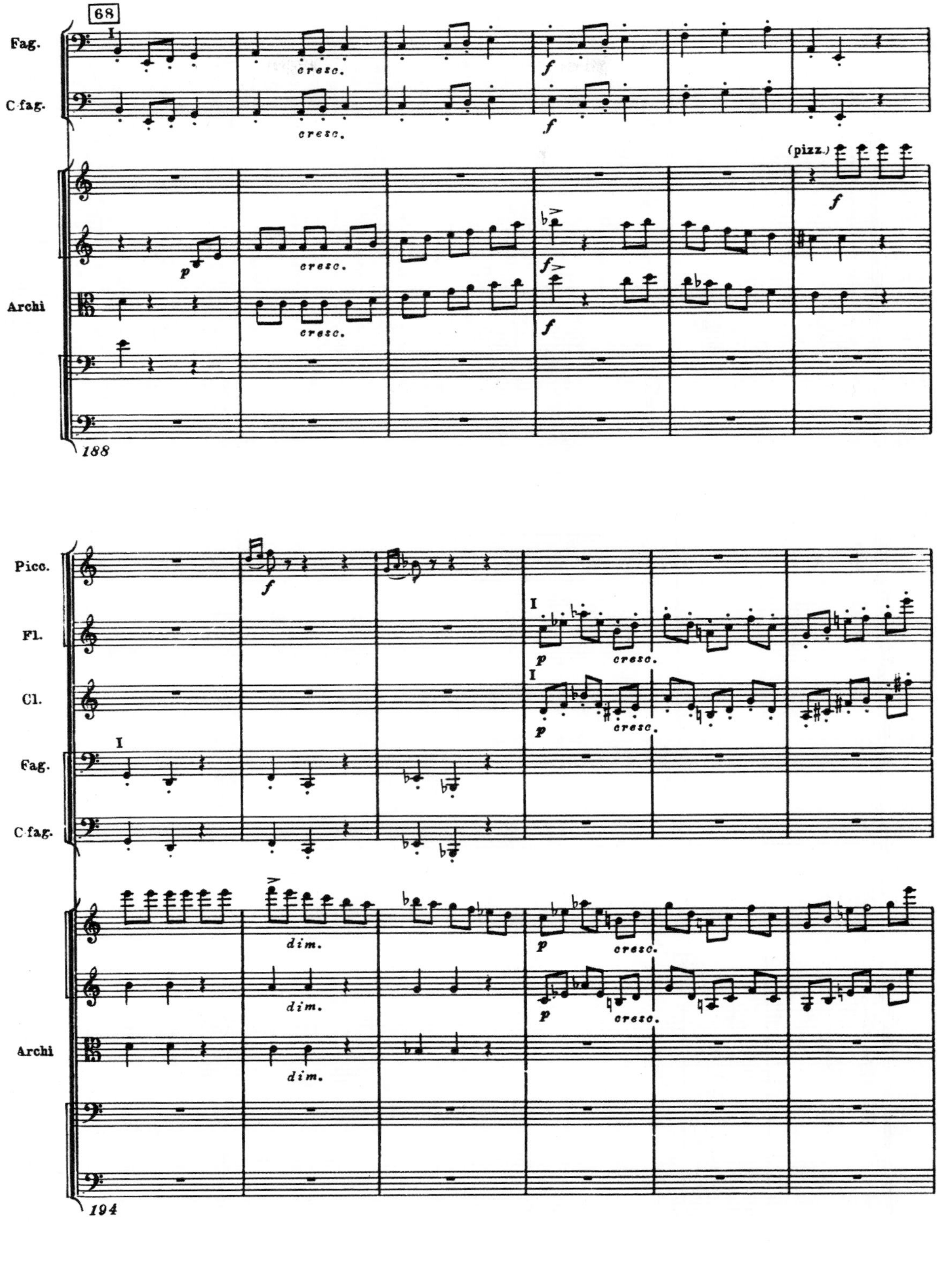
68
Fag.
C.fag.
Archi
I
cresc.
f
(pizz.)
p
188
Picc.
Fl.
Cl.
dim.
194

208

Dmitri Shostakovich earned international recognition at the age of nineteen with performances of his First Symphony (1926) and enjoyed celebrity status in the Soviet Union throughout the next decade. Thus he was stunned when in 1936 the Communist Party newspaper *Pravda*, at the instigation of Soviet dictator Joseph Stalin, suddenly denounced the modernist compositional style of his opera *Lady Macbeth of the Mtsensk District*. Unsure of his future in a time of political purges, Shostakovich shelved his already completed but thoroughly modernist Fourth Symphony and composed his Fifth Symphony in a more moderate idiom. His desire to regain state approval was encapsulated in a critic's description of the piece as "a Soviet artist's reply to just criticism." The work was premiered on November 21, 1937, in Leningrad (now St. Petersburg) by the Leningrad Philharmonic, conducted by Evgeny Mravinsky. The reception by the audience was overwhelming, and Shostakovich was once again viewed favorably by the communist regime.

Compared to many of his earlier works, the Fifth Symphony represents a retrenchment of style, with simpler formal procedures and more direct expression. While this change in approach may be linked to political pressures, it also represents a new idea that Shostakovich had been developing, inspired by studies of Mahler. The symphony, set in a classical four-movement structure, evokes the heroic spirit of the orchestral works of Beethoven and Tchaikovsky.

The second movement, marked Allegretto, is a scherzo in the style of an Austrian Ländler (as are several of Mahler's scherzos). For the most part, Shostakovich follows the form of the dance movement in a classical symphony, as can be observed in the diagram below. The overall form is ternary (Scherzo-Trio-Scherzo), with a trio in written-out binary form (i.e., with the repetitions written out and slightly varied rather than marked with repeat signs) and a scherzo in modified binary form.

Section:	Scherzo							Trio				Scherzo							Coda
Music:	A			B		B'		C	C'	D	D'	A'			B''		B'		
	a	b	a'	c	d	c'	d	e	e'	f	f'	a''	b'	a'''	c''	d'	c'	d	e''
Key:	a			c	F	c	F	C				a			c#	F#	c	F	a
Measure:	1	11	29	45	56	64	75	87	103	119	138	157	167	185	201	212	220	231	241

(Note that the measure numbers in this score are below the bottom staff rather than above the top staff as usual.)

Mahler's influence can be heard in the orchestration, the jarring contrasts of mood, the occasionally satirical tone, and the use of counterpoint. The vigorous, rather awkward, and tonally ambiguous melody in the low strings at the beginning of the movement introduces a number of motives that will be incorporated in later thematic ideas, such as the rising scale and the repeated notes. The horns (measure 11) usher in a new, playful or even sarcastic tune played primarily in the E-flat clarinet. The upper woodwinds present another idea with repeated notes (measure 20), and the bassoon follows with an extended solo. In Mahleresque fashion, the bassoon melody obscures the return of the opening low string theme at measure 29, and suggestions of the woodwind figures appear in the violins at measure 37. Thus the first part of the scherzo continually presents and develops ideas, yet it still hints at the structure one would expect at the beginning of a scherzo: a musical period that is stated (measures 1–28) and repeated (measures 29–44), constituting the first half of a binary form.

An abrupt shift to C minor marks the beginning of the second part of the scherzo (measure 45). Two divergent ideas are presented and then repeated: a crude waltz and a boisterous march (at measure 56). The first of these incorporates two $\frac{4}{4}$ measures that comically offset the established triple meter, and the second, with blaring horns, suggests a military fanfare. In the repetition of the waltz, the winds and strings reverse roles. Although the two halves of the scherzo differ in mood and melodic content, several recurring motives link them together. One notable example is the trilled figure in measures 14–15, which returns prominently in measures 52–54.

For those who know of and sympathize with Shostakovich's political situation at the time he wrote this symphony, the comic touches here—such as the rowdy fanfare—may suggest that he was mocking the government that threatened to censor him. Yet the circumstances were far too dangerous for anyone to mock Stalin, and we should be cautious about reading into the music meanings the composer may not have intended. More likely, Shostakovich was emulating the jesting, ironic tone of Mahler's scherzos, and leaving it to the listener to decide what the music might mean.

The trio begins with an elegant waltz tune played by a solo violin and accompanied by a harp and pizzicato cello. In the repetition of this sixteen-measure tune by the flute, the delicate mood is enhanced by glissandos in the harp and low strings. Unison strings rudely interrupt with the second half of the trio (at measure 119), which shifts briefly to B major for a phrase from the waltz theme (measures 129–33). On the repetition, the unison figure is given to the woodwinds.

Shostakovich continues to reverse the roles of winds and strings at the reprise of the scherzo. The opening bass melody is now in bassoon and contrabassoon, and pizzicato strings play the themes first introduced by horns and woodwinds. In a nod from one Fifth Symphony to another, Shostakovich's distinctive timbre of bassoon with pizzicato strings recalls the corresponding section in the scherzo of Beethoven's Symphony No. 5. The second part of the scherzo begins a half-step higher than it was originally presented, in C♯ minor, and the march tune, now in F♯ major, is given to the trumpets. Order is restored with the repetition, as the original key areas return and the horns play the march theme one last time. The coda opens with a brief recollection of the trio melody, which is abruptly and forcibly brought to a final cadence.

Although the overall harmonic scheme of the movement is traditional (A minor, with the relative major C in the trio), Shostakovich's harmony is full of modern elements. Alongside the occasional dominant-tonic cadence, there are many moments when the harmony takes an unexpected turn, lurching onto a new chord or into a new key with little or no preparation. Examples include the abrupt shifts of key mentioned above and, on a more local level, the succession in the C-major trio theme of A major, G major, F minor, and G minor chords leading right back to C major (measures 97–102). Ultimately, the tonal centers seem more often asserted than established, as if this were neotonal music pretending to be tonal—an apt metaphor for a modernist composer trying to conform to the restrictions imposed by a totalitarian state.

In writing for orchestra, Shostakovich had an array of outstanding musicians available to him in the Soviet Union, which is reflected in his virtuoso treatment of all sections, including the percussion. With its technical demands and wide range of emotions, this symphony remains popular with audiences and continues to test the limits of modern professional orchestras.

SILVESTRE REVUELTAS (1899–1940)

Sensemayá

Symphonic poem

1937–38

155

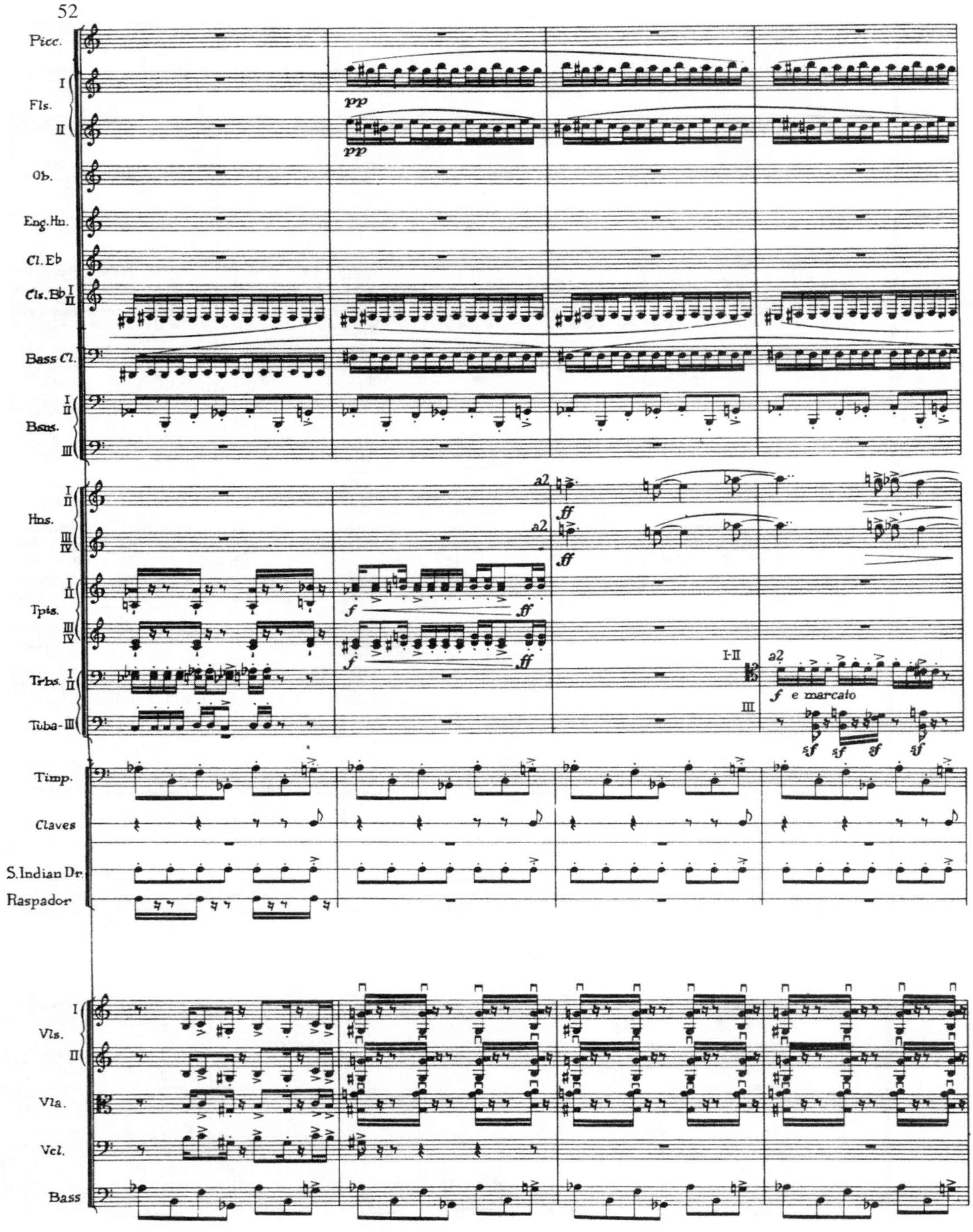
52
Picc.
I
Fls.
II
pp
pp
Ob.
Eng. Hn.
Cl. E♭
Cls. B♭ I II
Bass Cl.
I II
Bsns.
III
I II
Hns.
III IV
a2
ff
a2
ff
I II
Tpts.
III IV
f
ff
f
ff
Trbs. I II
I-II
a2
f e marcato
Tuba-III
III
sf
sf
sf
sf
Timp.
Claves
S. Indian Dr.
Raspador
I
Vls.
II
Vla.
Vcl.
Bass

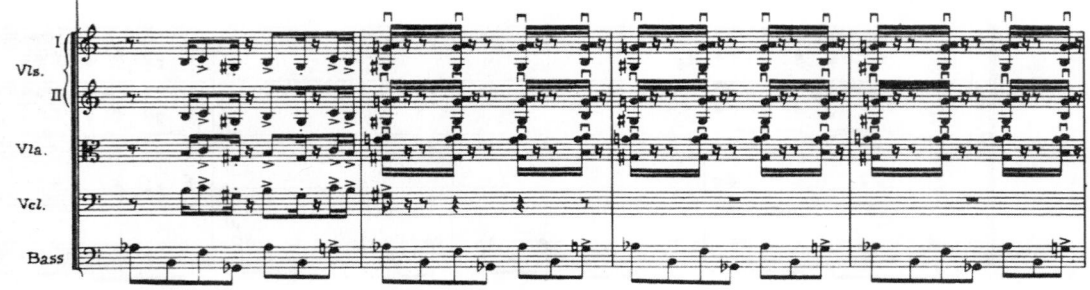

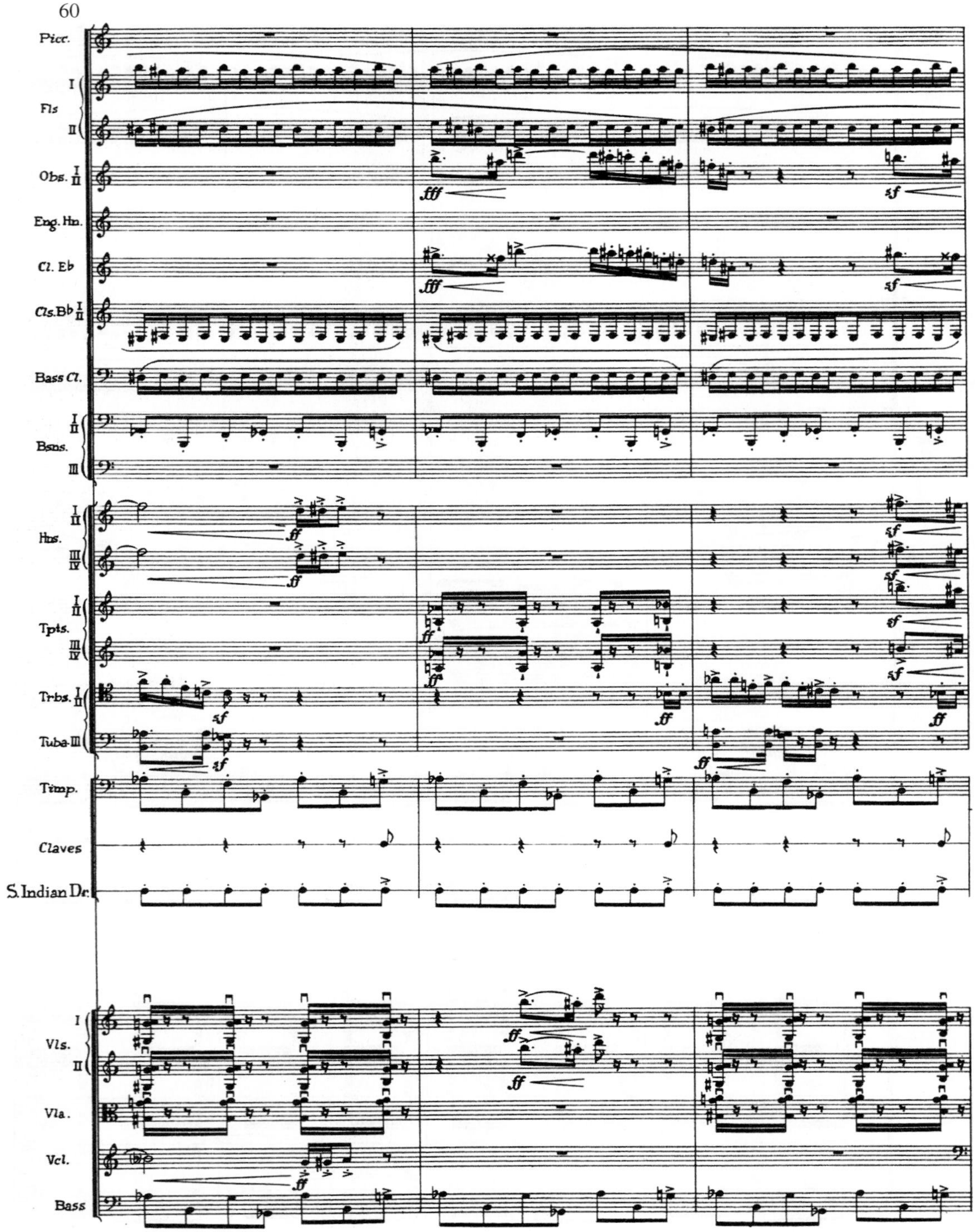
60
Picc.
Fls I II
Obs. I II
Eng. Hn.
Cl. Eb
Cls. Bb I II
Bass Cl.
Bsns. I II III
Hns. I II III IV
Tpts. I II III IV
Trbs. I II
Tuba-III
Timp.
Claves
S. Indian Dr.
Vls. I II
Vla.
Vcl.
Bass
fff
sf
ff

CD 11 · CD 6

*Violins divided in 4. Half play tremolo; half, sostenuto cantabile.

**Half of the cellos tremolo sul ponticello; half, natural and cantabile.

Mexico City, **March 6, 1938**

score autographed by J.P. Bruno

Silvestre Revueltas composed *Sensemayá* for chamber ensemble in 1937, then reworked it for large orchestra the next year. The work is based on a poem by Cuban poet Nicolás Guillén that reenacts a magical rite of the African-Cuban Mayombe sect. The ritual centers around a large figure, carried by a skilled dancer, that represents a snake—a symbol of threat—and during the ritual the snake is symbolically killed. The word *sensemayá*, which repeats throughout the poem, may stand for the snake or for the ritual; it apparently is a combination of *sensa*, a Bantu word for "Providence," and *Yemenyá*, an Afro-Cuban goddess whose name comes from the Yoruba language of west Africa. As composer Ricardo Zohn-Muldoon has demonstrated, Revueltas apparently set the text of the poem to music and then used the resulting melody throughout the piece, accompanied by other ideas and interspersed with interludes. The result is literally a song without words for orchestra.

According to Zohn-Muldoon's analysis, the piece falls into four large sections, following the course of the poem:

Measure	Section	Poem	Text/Thematic Material
1	1	(Introduction)	"Sen-se-ma-yá" rhythm (throughout section 1)
9			Snake theme
45		Stanza 1	Incantation: "¡Mayombe-bombe-mayombe!"
55		Stanza 2	Description of snake
65		Stanza 3	Incantation: "¡Mayombe-bombe-mayombe!"
68		Stanza 4	How to kill the snake
76		(Interlude)	Theme of man
88	2	(Interlude)	Altered "sen-se-ma-yá" rhythm
93		Stanza 5	Confrontation with the snake
100	3	(Interlude)	Material from section 1 introduction, with interjections
119			Continues, with theme of man
133		Stanza 6	Describes dead snake
142		(Interlude)	Striking the snake
145			Snake's dying convulsions
150	4	(Interlude)	Material from section 1
154		Stanza 7	Incantation "¡Mayombe-bombe-mayombe!" and narration of death *plus* snake theme *plus* theme of man

At the beginning of the work, a repeating pattern in the percussion of alternating eighth notes and eighth rests in $\frac{7}{8}$ meter suggests the word "sen-se-ma-yá" (measure 1), which continues throughout the first section. Revueltas overlays this pattern with ostinatos in the bass clarinet and bassoon, later joined or replaced by other instruments. A theme representing the snake enters in the tuba (measures 9–20), is completed by the horn, and is repeated twice in other instruments.

After this introduction, the ostinatos continue underneath the first four stanzas of the poem. The strings state the melody for the first stanza, a repeated incantation "¡Mayombe-bombe-mayombé!" (measures 46–49), interleaved with elements from the snake theme and other ideas. The melody for the second stanza, describing the snake, appears in trombones I and II (measures 55–65). The strings return with the third stanza, a repetition of the first, and then the trombones state the fourth, describing how to kill the snake, using material from the second stanza. The first large section concludes with an interlude that presents a new theme representing man (i.e., humanity; trumpet, E♭ clarinet, and flute, measures 76–84), as the string incantation joins the other ostinatos. The music fades, perhaps to represent the act of sneaking up quietly on the snake.

The loud, exciting, and relatively brief second section (measures 89–99) depicts the confrontation with the snake suggested by the fifth stanza of the poem, altering the "sen-se-ma-yá" rhythm and setting the rhythm and accents of the text in the trombones (with a new meter of $\frac{9}{8}$).

The third section begins as if it were a return to the first, but the musical flow is frequently interrupted by single measures of $\frac{7}{16}$, with rapid sixteenth-note figures (as at measures 106 and 110) suggesting the struggle between human and snake. The theme of man reappears in this context (measure 119). Then the trombones state the melody for the poem's sixth stanza (measures 133–42), which describes what the dead snake will no longer be able to do: eat, whistle, walk, run, watch, drink, breathe, or bite. The following interlude pictures the violent blows to the snake (measure 142) and the writhing snake's death-agony (measure 145).

The final section is a celebratory postlude, setting the final stanza of the poem. That stanza joins the incantation of the first stanza (violin II and viola, measures 154–56) to a narration of the snake's death (violin I and winds, measures 160–67). The themes of the snake and of man are heard again as well, along with numerous ostinati, in a climactic conclusion of overwhelming power.

As in most program music, knowing the relationship of the music to the poem that inspired it helps us follow the succession of events and understand why the piece takes the shape it does. Yet the work also makes sense in more abstract musical terms, presenting, layering, and juxtaposing a variety of ideas in a logical manner. Each of the ostinatos and melodies appears at only one pitch level, creating a sense of tonal location and lending coherence to the work even though a tonal center is not firmly established.

The emphasis on winds, brass, and percussion in this piece, along with the driving rhythm and alternating blocks of sound, shows the influence of Stravinsky, especially *The Rite of Spring*. The percussion features several Cuban or Mexican instruments, including *claves* (resonant short wooden sticks), *raspador* (a rasp or scraper), Indian drum, tom-toms (small tuned drums), and gourd.

RUTH CRAWFORD SEEGER (1901–1953)

String Quartet 1931: Fourth movement, Allegro possibile

String Quartet

1931

CD 11|83   CD 6|50

Allegro possibile

From Ruth Crawford, *String Quartet, 1931* (Bryn Mawr, Pa.: Merion Music, 1941), 16–22. © 1941 by Merion Music, Inc./Theodore Presser, Inc. Reprinted by permission of Theodore Presser. Accidentals apply only to the notes directly following. For example, the fourth note in the fifth measure is D♮, not D♭, and the last note in the sixth measure is B♮, not B♭.

Ruth Crawford composed her String Quartet in 1931 during a year in Berlin and Paris on a Guggenheim Fellowship, the first awarded to a woman. Over the previous year, she had assisted her composition teacher Charles Seeger (whom she later married in 1932 after her return from Europe) in developing ideas of dissonant counterpoint for an unpublished book manuscript, and many of those ideas appear in her quartet. She saw his and her own work as representative of an American tradition in modern music, independent of the European modernists. Accordingly, while in Europe she studied with no one, avoided contact with Schoenberg (who was in Berlin), and met only briefly with Berg and Bartók. Her String Quartet was given the subtitle "1931" when it was published ten years later in *New Music*, a quarterly periodical of new scores by "ultramodern" composers, published by Henry Cowell.

The String Quartet is full of new ideas. Although it consists of four movements in a familiar order—fast, scherzo-like, slow, and fast—each movement is based on a different set of devices, most of which had never been tried in a quartet. The first movement is built on a counterpoint of almost wholly independent melodies. The second movement develops a three-note motive through constant shifts of accent and implied meter. In the third movement, all four instruments play almost constantly but swell to dynamic peaks at different times, and those peaks are heard as a kind of melody passed among the instruments.

The finale, included here, is the most systematic: a palindrome, whose second half is an exact retrograde of the first, transposed up a half step. (The pivot point is at measures 58–59, with the transposition beginning at the second eighth note of measure 60.) The texture consists of two contrapuntal lines. In the first half of the piece, the first violin plays one note, then two, then three, increasing the number of notes in succession to twenty-one, while getting gradually softer. The pitches and rhythms are freely chosen. Meanwhile the other three instruments, muted and playing in octaves, interject phrases of twenty notes, then nineteen, then eighteen, reducing the number of notes to one, while getting gradually louder. In contrast to the varied durations and freely chosen pitches of the first violin line, the lower instruments play only eighth notes (sometimes sustaining the last note in a phrase) and use pitches generated by permutations of a ten-note series. The result is a paradigm of apposition: one line (in the violin) of free notes and rhythms, unmuted, that gradually decrescendoes through phrases that grow ever longer, and a second line (in the other instruments) of even notes and rhythms, that gradually crescendoes through phrases that grow ever shorter. After both lines arrive at their last note in measure 57, they sustain it at a soft dynamic level through the pivot point, and then everything reverses.

The series in the lower line is handled in an innovative manner. Rather than invert or retrograde the series, as in the twelve-tone music of Schoenberg, Berg, and Webern, Crawford permutes it through a process called *rotation*, taking the first note and moving it to the end, then doing this again with the second note, and so on:

```
D   E   F   E♭  F♯  A   A♭  G   D♭  C
    E   F   E♭  F♯  A   A♭  G   D♭  C   D
        F   E♭  F♯  A   A♭  G   D♭  C   D   E
            E♭  F♯  A   A♭  G   D♭  C   D   E   F
                F♯  A   A♭  G   D♭  C   D   E   F   E♭    etc.
```

The first phrase, with twenty notes, has the first two statements of this series (measures 3–5), the next phrase has all but the last note of the next two statements (adding up to nineteen notes, in measures 7–9), and so on, until the series has been stated ten times in all possible rotations, ending with the second eighth note of measure 21. At this point, the entire process unfolds again, with the series transposed up a whole step (one note is missing in one of the rotations—can you find it?). After the second set of ten rotations is complete, the series returns in its original form and transposition (measures 47–54), and the process halts at the pivot point of the palindrome on what would be the first note of the next rotation.

This movement is unique in Crawford's output—no other piece works like this—and is therefore characteristic of Crawford, whose every piece is unique in its language and musical devices. The movement's intense conflicts between elements, such as the opposition in almost every parameter between the two contrapuntal lines, is also typical of her music. Such opposition introduces difficulties for the players in coordinating their parts, which is heightened here by an emphasis on duration and pulse, tending to obscure meter. The slurring in the lower line, which freely alternates groups of four, two, and three notes, also works against the meter, creating a free, rhapsodic interplay of opposing forces—the very embodiment of her and Seeger's notion of dissonant counterpoint.

Aaron Copland (1900–1990)

Appalachian Spring, Excerpt: Variations on *'Tis the Gift to Be Simple*

Ballet suite

1943–44, orchestrated 1945

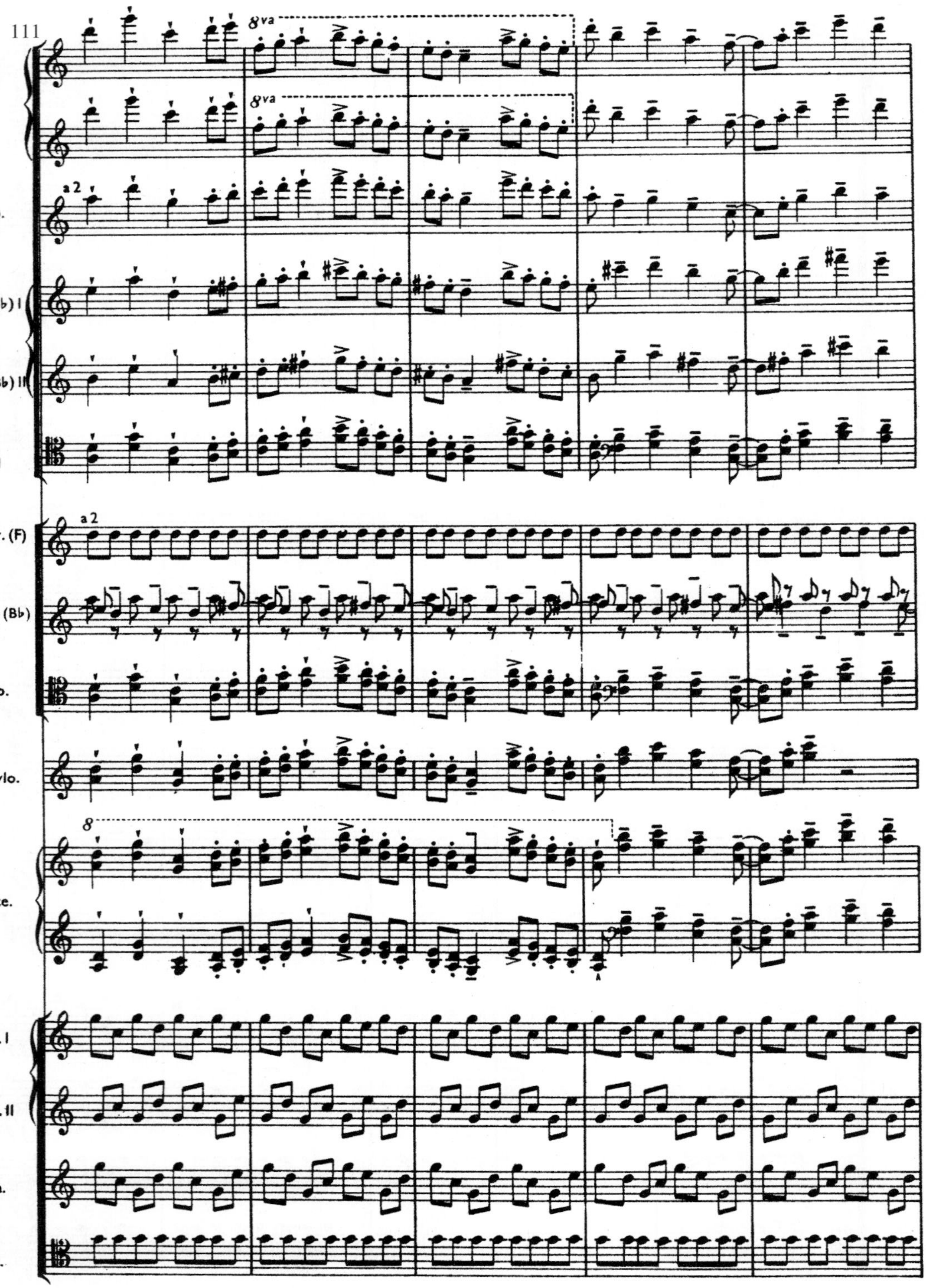
111
8va
a 2
I.
Fl.
II.
Ob.
I. II
(in B♭) I
Cl.
(in B♭) II
Fg.
I. II
Cor. (F)
I. II
Tr. (B♭)
I. II
Trb.
I. II
Xylo.
Pfte.
Vl. I
Vl. II
Vla.
Vc.

★ Shaker melody "The gift to be simple"

Modern dancer and choreographer Martha Graham used Aaron Copland's dissonant and rhythmically complex *Piano Variations* (1930) as the music for a solo dance in 1931, and the result was so successful that the composer and choreographer looked for an opportunity to collaborate. Their chance came in 1942, when Elizabeth Sprague Coolidge, a prominent patron of modern music, commissioned three ballet scores for Graham, including one from Copland. Graham devised the scenario, which went through many changes even after Copland had begun composing the music. The final version of the ballet centers around a couple about to be married in rural nineteenth-century Pennsylvania, who are feted by a minister and neighbors on the completion of their farmhouse.

In accordance with the commission, Copland scored the original ballet for a chamber ensemble of thirteen instruments. He called the piece simply "Ballet for Martha" while working on it, and only when he arrived in Washington, D.C., for the October 30, 1944, premiere did he learn the title she had given the work, *Appalachian Spring*. He was later amused how often people said to him, "When I listen to that ballet of yours, I can just *feel* spring and *see* the Appalachians," since neither was in his mind as he composed. The ballet was a great success, and the music won Copland the Pulitzer Prize and the New York Music Critics' Circle Award. He later arranged the piece as a suite for full orchestra, premiered on October 4, 1945, in New York, and in that form it has become his most widely known work.

During the 1930s, Copland turned from the astringent modernism typified by the *Piano Variations* to a deliberately simpler, more accessible style, seeking to appeal to a broader public. Without leaving behind the dissonance, counterpoint, motivic unity, and juxtaposed blocks of sound that had marked his modernist works, he incorporated diatonic melodies and harmonies, transparent textures, and recognizable allusions to familiar types and styles of music, including some direct quotations of folk or popular songs. His new style is exemplified in *Appalachian Spring*, which evokes country fiddling, dancing, and singing and captures the spirit of rural America.

In the Allegro and Presto sections that begin the excerpt included here, the shifting meters, offbeat accents, and sudden changes of texture show Stravinsky's influence (see NAWM 145 and 146). But the predominantly diatonic melodies and harmonies, syncopation, and guitarlike chords give it a flavor of American folk music. Many passages vertically combine consonant and dissonant notes of the diatonic scale in a technique that has been called *pandiatonicism*. The rapid melodic figuration of the Presto (measure 18 of the excerpt) suggests country fiddling, while counterpoint (as at measures 35–38, 61–65, and 74–87) and motivic links between the Allegro and Presto (the figure from measures 5–6 recurs throughout the Presto) show the heritage of the European classical tradition.

At the Meno mosso (measure 138 of the excerpt), leaps of fourths and fifths in the violin and oboe solos and wide spacing of the chords suggest a sparsely populated landscape. This texture, together with diatonic melodies and lightly dissonant diatonic chords, established a distinctive sound that has been used ever since to depict the open spaces and rugged people of frontier America. A recollection of the opening passage of the ballet ("As at first," measure 151) includes the ballet's characteristic sound, superimposed tonic and dominant or tonic and subdominant triads (measures 152–55 and 158–61, respectively).

At the Doppio movimento (Double time, measure 171), Copland begins a set of variations on the Shaker hymn *Simple Gifts*, by Elder Joseph Brackett (1797–1882):

The Shakers were a religious sect who practiced celibacy and lived communally, raising their own food and making virtually everything they used themselves. Their hymns were used in religious services, sung in unaccompanied unison while most of the congregation danced. Copland discovered the tune in a published collection of Shaker hymns and thought it ideally suited Graham's scenario because of its links to dance and to rural America, although the people in her ballet were not Shaker (and there were never Shaker settlements in rural Pennsylvania).

Copland's approach to varying this monophonic hymn tune is to change the melody relatively little, but to place it in a series of contrasting settings. The one alteration he consistently makes is in the phrasing, treating the first two notes of the hymn's final phrase as if they were the last two notes of the third phrase and thereby emphasizing the long note on "turn" in measure 13 of the tune. The first variation, in A♭ major, is for clarinet, accompanied quite simply by irregularly alternating dominant and tonic sustained tones in flutes and harp. The second variation (measure 191) has a similar texture, a step lower, with the melody in the oboe, paralleled by bassoon a tenth lower, and accompanied by brass and other winds. The third variation gives the melody, half as fast, to trombones and violas, who are later joined in canon by the horns and first violins, but omits the second half of the tune (measures 207–33). The melody passes to the trumpet and to C major in the fourth variation (measure 240), accompanied by trombone, doubled by winds in the third phrase, and joined for the second and fourth phrases by violins and violas fiddling in rapid scales. The final variation presents the two halves of the tune in reverse order: the opening motive in bassoon (measure 272) turns out to be a counterpoint to the second half of the melody in the clarinet, and then the entire orchestra proclaims the first half of the theme over a slowly descending bass (measure 288).

WILLIAM GRANT STILL (1895–1978)

Afro-American Symphony (Symphony No. 1):
First movement, Moderato assai

Symphony

1930

*) with nails, and close to the sounding board.

9 allegro ♩ = 160
72
Fl's. 1 2
Picc.
Oboi 1 2
Clar's. in Bb 1 2 3
Bass Clar.
Bassoons 1 2
Horns in F 1 2 3 4
Tpts. in Bb 1 2 3
Trb.-ni 1 2 3
Tuba
Timp.
Sn. Dr.
Cymb.s
Harp
Vl. I.
Vl. II.
Viola
Vc.
Bass
a 2
staccatiss.
mf (Harmon mutes)
f stacc.
Ab-Bb-Eb
Allegro ♩ = 160
pizz.
9

82
Fl's. 1 2
Picc.
Oboi 1 2
a2
Clar's. in Bb 1 2 3
mf stacc.
Bass Clar.
f stacc.
B'ss'ns. 1 2
mf stacc.
Horns in F 1 2 3 4
Tpt's. in Bb 1 2 3
Harmon mute
Trb.-ni 1 2 3
Tuba
Timp.
Sn. Dr. B. D.
Damped Cymb.
Cymb.
Harp
Vl. I.
arco
Vl. II.
arco
Vla.
arco
Vc.
arco
Bass
arco
f stacc.

92

104

*) The dotted 8ths and 16ths should be played as though written as follows:

126
rit.
13 Meno
Fl's.
Oboi
E.H.
Clar's. in Bb
Bass Clar.
Solo
mf tenute
B'ss'ns.
Horns.
Tpt's. in Bb
stacc.
Tr-b.-ni.
mf Harmon mutes
Timp.
Sm. Cymb.
W. Br.
Harp
Solo
Meno
Vl. I.
unis.
gliss.
div.
Vl. II.
arco
Vla.
Vc.
Bass
pizz.
arco
13

William Grant Still composed his *Afro-American Symphony* in 1930. When it was premiered in 1931 by the Rochester Philharmonic Orchestra conducted by Howard Hanson, it became the first symphony by a black composer to be performed by a major orchestra. Other black composers followed in Still's wake, including Florence Price, whose Symphony in E Minor was played by the Chicago Symphony Orchestra in 1933, and William Dawson, whose *Negro Folk Symphony* was premiered by the Philadelphia Orchestra in 1934. As a pathbreaker—and one of the most prolific American composers of his era—Still became known as the dean of African-American composers. His symphony was published in 1935, and he later revised it in 1969, having written four more symphonies in the interim.

The *Afro-American Symphony* has the traditional four movements, with a sonata-form first movement, a slow movement, a scherzo, and a fast finale. The movements are not explicitly programmatic, but each is a character sketch that is also linked to verses from a poem by Paul Laurence Dunbar (1872–1906), who wrote about African-American life in the South, using folk materials and dialects. Originally Still also gave each movement a subtitle appropriate to its content: *Longings; Sorrows; Humor;* and *Aspirations.*

The first movement blends sonata form with an archlike ABCBA form, since the two main themes appear in reverse order in the recapitulation. The movement opens with a brief introductory melody in the English horn, followed by a first theme in the trumpet in the form of a twelve-bar blues in A♭ (measures 7–18; see the blues in NAWM 149 and 150). In addition to the blues melody (in classic AAB form) and harmonic progression, many other elements reflect characteristic features of African-American music. Syncopations appear in both melody and accompaniment, and phrases often end just before rather than on a strong beat. The call-and-response structure of African-American song is echoed in the frequent interjections by other instruments between the short phrases of melody. Lowered fifth, third, and seventh scale degrees in the melody (as in measures 2–4 and 15–16) imitate blue notes, as do chords that include both major and minor thirds (measures 4–5 and 7). Instrumental timbres are varied and often unusual, including groupings and sounds typical of jazz bands: trumpets and trombones with Harmon mutes, which give a distant, pinched, metallic sound (measures 6–8); steady taps on the bass drum and dampened strikes on the cymbal; winds and brass used in groups of similar sound, like sections in a jazz band, and voiced in chords of four notes (as in measures 7–10); and, later in the movement, a vibraphone (see especially measures 133–35).

The first theme repeats in the clarinet with interjections from other winds, accompanied by strings playing *col legno* (with the wood of the bow) to create a percussive effect. Then the transition begins (measure 33), developing motives from the first theme, as is typical of European symphonies. The second theme (measures 45–67), in the surprising key of G major (a half step below the tonic A♭, rather than the expected dominant, E♭), has the pentatonic contours and melancholy air of a spiritual, which along with blues and jazz was the type of music most widely identified with African Americans. The theme is in ABA' form, beginning in the oboe and moving in turn to violins, flutes, cello, and harp. Once again, interjections by other instruments between phrases of the oboe theme suggests the call-and-response of African-American song.

As the second theme concludes, the tempo picks up and the development section begins (measure 68). As in the earlier transition, here the procedures are those of a European sonata-form movement, fragmenting and developing elements from both themes and from the opening English horn melody. After calm is restored, the recapitulation brings back the two main themes in reverse order (measures 104 and 114 respectively), the second in the tonic A♭ minor and the first in A♭ major, with almost no transition between them. This time, the first theme appears in swinging rhythms (alternating long and short notes) rather than even ones; because Still knew that some orchestral musicians might not know what was intended, he marked in a note (at measure 116) that the dotted-eighth-sixteenth rhythms should be played like triplets, the usual ratio of swing. A brief coda (measures 128–36) brings the movement to a close with a reminiscence of the introduction, emphasizing the archlike structure of the entire movement.

The combination of blues and spiritual is appropriate to the sense of longing Still sought to capture in the movement, and to the verses of Dunbar he linked to it:

'All my life long twell de night has pas'
Let de wo'k come ez it will,
So dat I fin' you, my honey, at last,
Somewhaih des ovah de hill.'

To a listener today, the way Still uses the orchestra in the *Afro-American Symphony* can sound like movie music. This is neither coincidence nor a sign of unoriginality; in 1934, Still moved to Los Angeles, where he composed for films while continuing to write concert music in classical forms. The manner in which he integrated the string sounds of the symphonic orchestra with the distinctive wind and brass sounds of the jazz orchestra helped to define a style that many other composers and arrangers used for films and popular music.

159

Charlie Parker (1920–1955) and Dizzy Gillespie (1917–1993)

Anthropology

Bebop tune and solo

1945

(a) Lead sheet

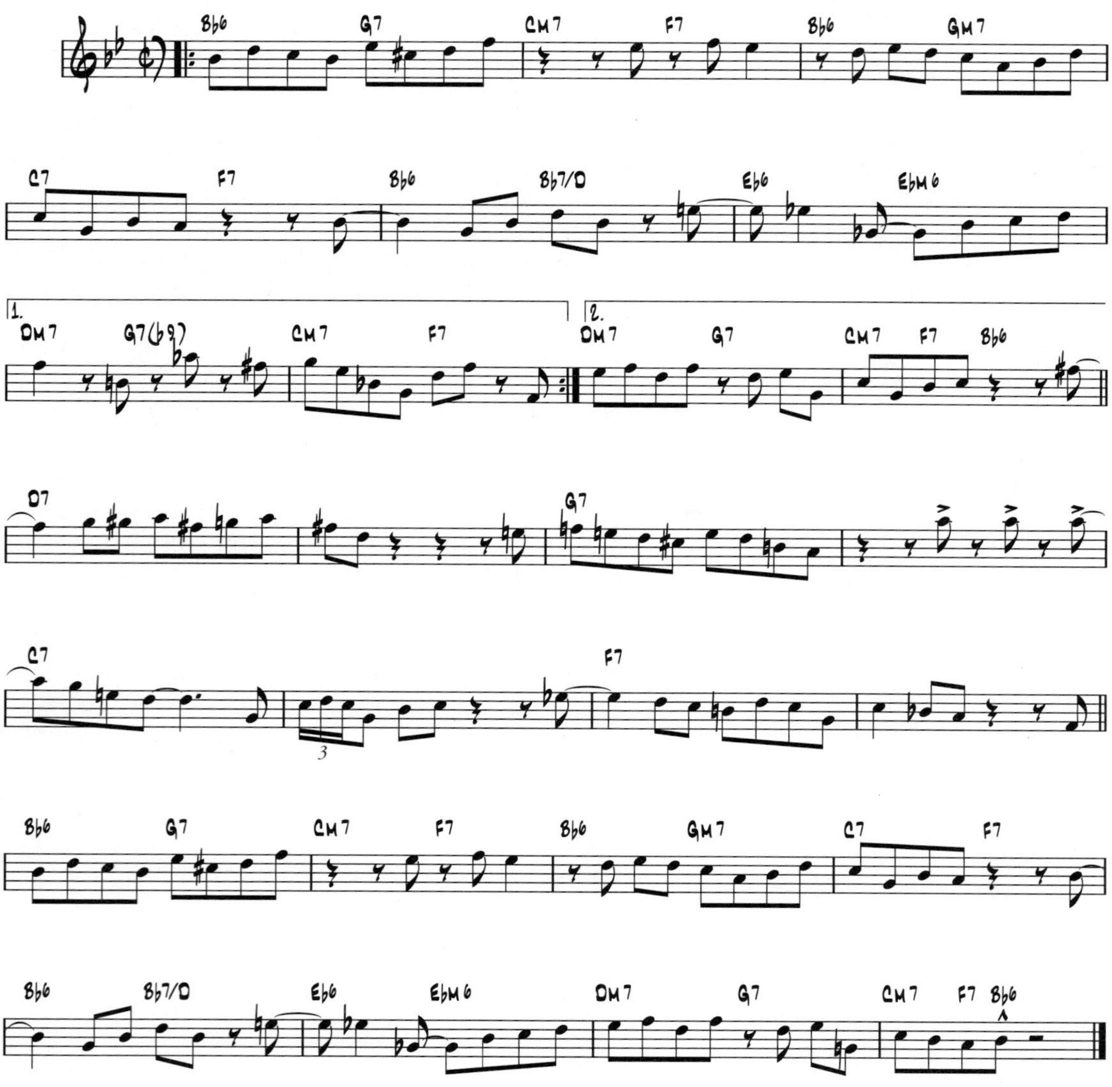

(b) Transcription of Charlie Parker's solo (transposed an octave lower)

[12] [74] [Dizzy Gillespie's solo]

[13] [Bud Powell's solo]

[14] [Trading fours with drummer]

[15] [Head]

Anthropology is one of dozens of mid-1940s collaborations between Charlie "Bird" Parker and John Birks "Dizzy" Gillespie. The two met in Kansas City, Parker's home town, when Gillespie was on tour with Cab Calloway's big band. In the early 1940s, Parker, Gillespie, and other young jazz virtuosos convened in New York City clubs such as Minton's Playhouse and Monroe's Uptown House to play and improvise together in lengthy after-hours sessions. Out of these jam sessions grew a new musical language known as *bebop*, featuring breakneck speeds, complex chord changes, and angular melodies.

Like many bebop compositions, *Anthropology* is a contrafact—a new tune composed over a harmonic progression borrowed from another song. Specifically, like Duke Ellington's *Cotton Tail* (NAWM 152), it is a contrafact on "rhythm changes," jazz musicians' term for the chord progression from the chorus of George Gershwin's *I Got Rhythm* (NAWM 151). Contrafacts were a major source for new bebop compositions because they constituted a common language for jazz musicians, could easily be molded into a new tune for a last-minute recording session, and did not require payment of royalties to the composer of the original tune. Contrafacts were especially important for Parker: new tunes built over the blues, rhythm changes, and the standard *Honeysuckle Rose* account for much of Parker's output.

The version of *Anthropology* that is included on the accompanying recording is from a live broadcast made on March 31, 1951, and released on LP as *Summit Meeting at Birdland.* The players were all stars, with Parker on alto saxophone and Gillespie on trumpet supported by a rhythm section made up of Bud Powell on piano, Tommy Potter on bass, and Roy Haynes on drums.

The tune begins with the *head*, a lead melody in AABA form played in unison or octaves by the melody instruments at the beginning and end of the song. The musicians play from a lead sheet, shown here as NAWM 159a, that includes only the head and the chord changes. Everything else is improvised or worked out by ear in rehearsal. In this performance, after the head, Parker plays a solo that fills up three choruses (statements of the AABA harmonic progression), shown here in transcription as NAWM 159b. (The transcription includes the head; the solo begins at measure 29.) Gillespie then solos for three choruses, followed by Powell on piano for two. For the next two choruses, Parker and Gillespie "trade fours" with Haynes, alternating four measures of melody instrument with four measures of drum solo for each eight-measure phrase. The song ends as it began, with Parker and Gillespie leading the way in another statement of the head.

The musicians play at a blistering pace that is characteristic of bebop. The many syncopations (as in measures 8–10) and sudden rests keep the rhythm fresh and surprising. The convoluted, highly decorated melody is also typical of bebop: both the head and Parker's solo are full of chromatic notes, and the melody is dissonant with the underlying harmony almost as often as it is consonant. The solos do not offer variations on the tune, but spin out a constant variety of new ideas that fit within the harmonic progression. The virtuosity is astonishing, as the performers meant it to be. With bebop, jazz came to be recognized as an art music worthy of the same intent listening as classical music.

OLIVIER MESSIAEN (1908–1992)

Quartet for the End of Time: First movement, *Liturgie de cristal*

Quartet for violin, clarinet, violoncello, and piano

1940–41

From Olivier Messiaen, *Quatuor pour la fin du temps* (Paris: Durand, 1942), 1–6.

Olivier Messiaen wrote his *Quartet for the End of Time* during World War II in the winter of 1940–41 while interned at a prisoner-of-war camp in Silesia. He had been captured by the Germans the previous May as he was serving in the French army. He wrote the piece for performance by himself as pianist, together with a violinist, clarinetist, and cellist who were also imprisoned there. They gave the work its first performance in the camp, in the middle of winter, for their fellow prisoners.

The title refers to the biblical prophecy of the Apocalypse, which will bring the end of time as a progression of finite moments and the beginning of eternity. The score, published in 1942 after Messiaen had been released from captivity, carries the inscription, "In homage to the Angel of the Apocalypse, who raises his hand to the heavens and says, 'There will be no more Time.'" Four of the eight movements are for all four players, but the third is for clarinet alone, the fourth omits piano, the fifth is for cello and piano, and the eighth is for violin and piano.

The quartet is a study of time—measured, finite time, and timelessness, or eternity. Although the quartet lacks a text, it is a piece of sacred music, as is a great deal of Messiaen's output. Religion is not so much on the surface of his compositions as it is the motivation and goal for his creative effort.

The first movement, *Liturgie de cristal* (Crystal Liturgy), included here, conveys a sense of ecstatic contemplation of the passage of time. The clarinet and violin each play stylized birdcalls (of the blackbird and nightingale respectively), a type of melody that Messiaen often used to suggest nature as a divine gift. The figures do not develop, but change in unpredictable ways. Like the birds they imitate, each instrument sticks to its own repertoire of sounds. The rhythm is also that of nature, having a pulse but no clear meter.

The cello and piano lay out complex patterns of duration and pitch that repeat in cycles. The cello constantly repeats a five-note sequence (C–E–D–F♯–B♭) in high harmonics (see below), using a pattern of fifteen durations. New statements of the pattern begin on the second quarter note of measure 8, the last eighth of measure 13, and so on, every five-and-a-half measures. These melodic and rhythmic cycles are like the *color* (repeating melody) and *talea* (repeating rhythm) of fourteenth-century isorhythm (see NAWM 24 and 25). The durational pattern Messiaen has chosen here combines two *non-retrogradable rhythms*, his term for rhythms that are palindromes, the same forward and backward: the first three notes (respectively 4, 3, and 4 eighth notes in duration) and the remaining twelve (which form the pattern 4–1–1–3–1–1–1–1–3–1–1–4, again counting eighth notes). Such rhythms remain the same whichever direction time runs, and thus suggest the unchangeable, the divine, and the eternal.

The cycles in the piano are more complex, with a series of twenty-nine chords overlapping a rhythmic pattern of seventeen durations. The rhythmic cycle begins again on the downbeat of measure 6 and every thirteen beats thereafter. The second statement of the chord cycle begins on the last eighth note of measure 8, with different rhythms because of the new alignment with the durational pattern. It would take twenty-nine repetitions of the rhythmic pattern and seventeen repetitions of the chord cycle, or a total of 377 beats, to return to the original alignment, and a total of 12,441 beats (4147 measures) if the cello pattern is taken into account. Perhaps Messiaen meant this to imply a very long cycle, of which we hear only a part, as a metaphor for time everlasting, during which we each exist for only a moment.

The combination of the repeating cycles with variable alignment and freer repetition and variation in the violin and clarinet creates music that combines constancy and change. This presentation of ideas is typical of Messiaen, whose works embody a kind of meditation on a few materials that parallels meditative prayer.

The cello harmonics are played on the instrument's highest string, tuned to the A just below middle C. While the index finger of the left hand presses the string against the fingerboard to select the pitch, the smallest finger lightly touches the string at a spot a fourth higher (indicated by a diamond-shaped note), which produces a harmonic two octaves higher than the notated pitch. The ethereal sound, in the same range as the high birdcalls in the violin, lends height and depth to the scene suggested in the music.

BENJAMIN BRITTEN (1913–1976)

Peter Grimes: Act III, Scene 2, *To hell with all your mercy!*

Opera

1944–45

BALSTRODE: *(Crossing to lift Peter up)* Come on, I'll help you with the boat.
ELLEN: No!
BALSTRODE: Sail out till you lose sight of the Moot Hall. Then sink the boat. D'you hear? Sink her. Goodbye Peter.

There is a crunch of shingle as Balstrode leads Peter down to his boat, and helps him push it out. After a short pause, he returns, takes Ellen by the arm, and leads her away.

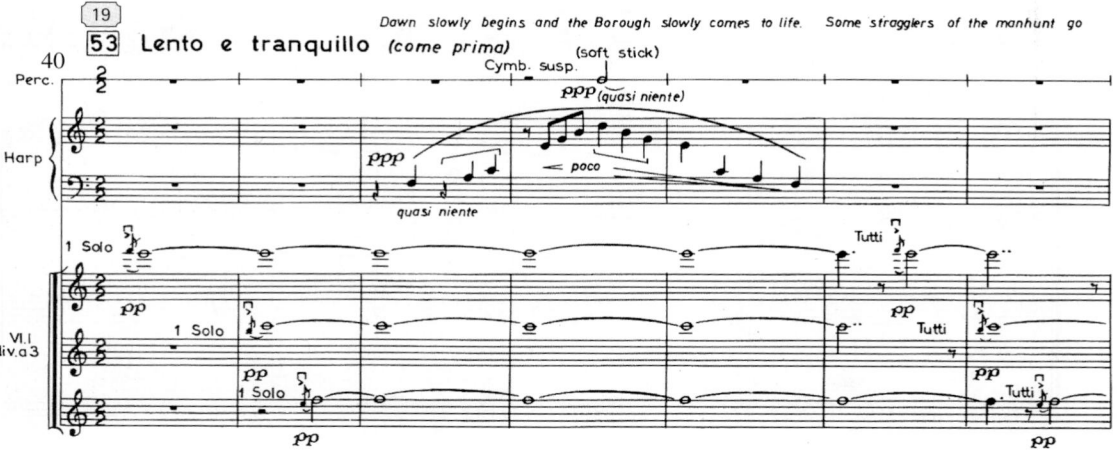

across the street to their houses. Shutters are drawn back.

The stage is now filled with people singing at their daily work.

End of Opera

Benjamin Britten took his character Peter Grimes from *The Borough* (1810), a narrative poem by English poet George Crabbe about the people of Aldeburgh, a coastal town in Suffolk near Britten's childhood home. The story of Grimes, a fisherman who beat his apprentices, lost them in accidents, and went mad, might seem an unpromising plot for an opera. But for Britten and his life partner, tenor Peter Pears, Grimes's life as an outcast paralleled their own lives as pacifists, as conscientious objectors to all wars (including World War II, then raging), and as homosexuals, hated beyond reason by a society that could not accept them as they were. Grimes himself was neither a pacifist nor a homosexual, nor even a very sympathetic character. Instead, the focus of the libretto, written by Montagu Slater from the scenario Britten and Pears had conceived, was on the crowd's persecution of Grimes simply for being different, and on the way his internalization of their hatred leads to his destruction.

Britten composed the music between January 1944 and February 1945, assisted by a commission from the Koussevitzky Musical Foundation. *Peter Grimes* was premiered at Sadler's Wells Theatre in London on June 7, 1945, just a month after the war ended in Europe, with Pears in the title role. The opera's powerful message about the relationship between the individual and the state resonated deeply in the postwar world, and its emotional, accessible music established Britten's and Pears's reputations as the leading English composer and tenor of their time, respectively. The opera was soon staged throughout Europe and North America and has become one of the most popular postwar operas.

The opera begins with a prologue, an inquest into the death of Peter's apprentice on a fishing trip when they ran out of drinking water. Although Peter is exonerated, the townspeople blame him for the boy's death, and he is advised not to take on another apprentice unless he can get a woman to look after the boy. One solution would be to marry Mrs. Ellen Orford, a widowed schoolmistress and one of the few people friendly to Peter. But Grimes is not ready to marry Ellen, even though he is in love with her, because he feels he must prove himself to the town first by making lots of money. Knowing that Peter cannot handle his boat by himself, Ned Keene, the apothecary, finds him a new boy from the workhouse. Ellen is sympathetic to the boy, but when she discovers a bruise on him, she reproaches Peter for his temper. Peter strikes her and forces the boy to leave with him. This moment, when Peter accepts the town's brutalized image of him, is the crux of the drama, and it begins the downward spiral. Propelled by rumors that he is mistreating the boy, the townspeople come looking for Peter and his apprentice, only to find Peter's home, an old upturned boat beside a cliff, neatly kept but unoccupied. They do not know that their coming spurred Peter to hurry down to his boat and set out to sea, and on the way the boy slipped and fell into a chasm. After a few days with no sign of the boy, rumors fly and the townspeople again come after Peter, unaware that they themselves caused the boy's death. Ellen and the retired merchant skipper Balstrode, who has supported Peter in the past, encounter him wandering in the fog, overcome by grief and stress. Ellen wants to comfort him, but Balstrode advises him to take his boat out to sea and sink with it, which Peter proceeds to do.

The excerpt included here, from the very end of the opera, begins as the off-stage chorus of townspeople repeatedly calls Peter's name, and he answers them in a florid and meandering recitative. This tragic scene eloquently displays the remarkable dramatic effects that Britten creates from simple means. Here, the only accompaniment to the chorus's calls and Peter's raving is the foghorn, on the tonal center of E♭. The rest of the scene recalls earlier music, as is appropriate to the final moments of a tragedy. When Peter cries out, "To hell with all your mercy! To hell with your revenge, And God have mercy upon you!," he echoes the motive introduced at the crucial scene when he hit Ellen, to the words "And God have mercy upon me!," which has pervaded the opera ever since. When Ellen comes to take him home, Peter does not respond to her directly, but recalls his song from Act I when he imagined finding a safe harbor in her love (measures 22–37 of this excerpt). When Balstrode helps Peter cast off, there is no music at all; here, Britten recognized that silence is more meaningful.

At the end, what remains are the sea and the townspeople, equally indifferent to Peter's fate. Britten captures that indifference through bitonality, returning to earlier music associated with sea and town, in two simultaneous keys, like two mutually indifferent planes of sound. The calm sea is depicted by sustained tones (e''', c''', and f'') in the upper strings decorated with grace notes, like flecks on the surface, with occasional waves suggested by arpeggiated thirds in harp and clarinet that encompass all the notes of the C-major scale, and a haunting melody in the flute (measures 52–59). Against this backdrop and supported by chords in the brass, the townspeople sing in A major (starting at measure 64) a song in hymn style about their daily routines, first heard at the opening of Act I. Between verses, someone mentions a report of a sinking boat (measures 84–89), but it is dismissed as a rumor (measures 105–9)—ironically, the only one in the opera that is true. The townspeople sing the final verse of their hymn, about the ceaseless, unpitying motions of the tide, this time inverting the second half of the melody into a majestic descent, and the curtain slowly falls.

The performance on the accompanying recording is conducted by Britten himself, with Peter Pears as Peter Grimes. Since Britten wrote this and most of his tenor parts for Pears, the music is ideally suited for Pears's reedy, flexible voice.

Samuel Barber (1910–1981)

Hermit Songs, Op. 29: No. 8, *The Monk and His Cat*

Song cycle

1952–53

162

** Notes marked(—) in these two measures should be slightly longer, pochissimo rubato; also on the fourth page.

Samuel Barber wrote his *Hermit Songs* between November 1952 and January 1953, on a commission from the Elizabeth Sprague Coolidge Foundation. Inspired by a trip to Ireland the previous summer, he chose ten short anonymous texts, written between the eighth and thirteenth centuries by Irish monks and scholars and translated into modern English by a number of poets. Varying from religious visions to sly observations about monastic life, these short poems or fragments, most written in the margins of manuscripts the monks were preparing, are windows into their world. The song cycle was premiered on October 30, 1953, by soprano Leontyne Price with Barber at the piano, at the Library of Congress in Washington, D.C. Barber dedicated the song included here to Isabelle Vengerova, his piano teacher at the Curtis Institute in Philadelphia.

The Monk and His Cat, with a text translated by W. H. Auden, celebrates the happy life of scholar and cat, contentedly living together while each focuses on his own work, theology and mouse control respectively. Several musical devices depict the medieval monk: melodic open fifths in the piano left hand (for instance, between the last five notes in measure 1), suggesting the open harmonies of medieval music; parallel fifths as in medieval organum (the left hand in measures 8–9); a slowly moving chantlike melody in the piano (measures 1–5, returning at measures 16 and 39); and a later, more rapid line in the voice that alternates groups of twos and threes (as in chant) while hovering around a reciting tone (measures 29–37). The cat, meanwhile, is evoked by half steps and whole steps that resolve outward chromatically to thirds (as in measures 6–9), as though the cat himself is walking on the keys; and by sudden, loud, brief chords surrounded by rests (measures 12 and 22–23), to suggest the cat pouncing on a mouse.

The form is simple yet subtle, interweaving looks at the monk and the cat. The poem is in five sentences, each punctuated in the middle, like a psalm verse (compare NAWM 4a), with the first sentence (or verse) repeated at the end of the song. Some verses vary the opening phrase (A), and most are separated from the next by the catlike dissonances (B). But others introduce contrasting material, often changing midway to mark the two halves of the sentence (designated as a and b below). The result is a sort of rondo form:

Verse:	1		2a	2b		3		4a	4b	5	1		1a	
Music:	A	B	C1(~B)	C2	B	A'	B	D1	D2	E	A	B	A''	B
Key:	F							A		F♯	F			
Measure:	1	6	8		12	14	16	20	22	24	28	39	44	46	50

Barber used traditional techniques in his music (rather than inventing a new musical language as Schoenberg and other modernists did), but he gives each element a novel twist to create an individual sound. Although the song is clearly in F major, the harmony is suffused with gentle dissonances, consonant chords are rare, and the excursions to A major and F♯ major are unusual. The meter and rhythm are especially notable. In this as in all the songs of the set, Barber omits the time signature and freely changes the number of beats per measure to follow the accents of the text. The piano shifts from $\frac{9}{8}$ to $\frac{6}{8}$, $\frac{3}{4}$, $\frac{5}{8}$, and even $\frac{11}{8}$ over the course of the song. The vocal melody often contradicts the implied meter in the piano; for instance, in measures 2–4, each measure in the voice seems to suggest a $\frac{4}{4}$ measure beginning on the second eighth. These syncopations against the piano, augmented by the marked rubato in measures 3 and 4, create an agile, flexible line well suited both to the rhythm of the words and to the image of the cat. An appreciation of the vocal line's subtle beauty is heightened by the realization that it is a decorated paraphrase of the piano's chantlike melody, paralleling the latter a fourth higher:

Barber's ability to create fresh-sounding music from traditional elements has endeared him to audiences and performers alike. *Hermit Songs* has become a staple of the vocal repertoire, often performed in student recitals. The songs are tuneful yet present many performing problems, especially in rhythm and coordination between voice and piano. Echoing the spirit of this song, this commentary is dedicated to my cats Diego, Arthur, and Xander, who helped to write this book by sitting on the manuscript and stealing my pencils.

GEORGE CRUMB (B. 1929)

Black Angels: Thirteen Images from the Dark Land: Images 4 and 5

Electric string quartet

1970

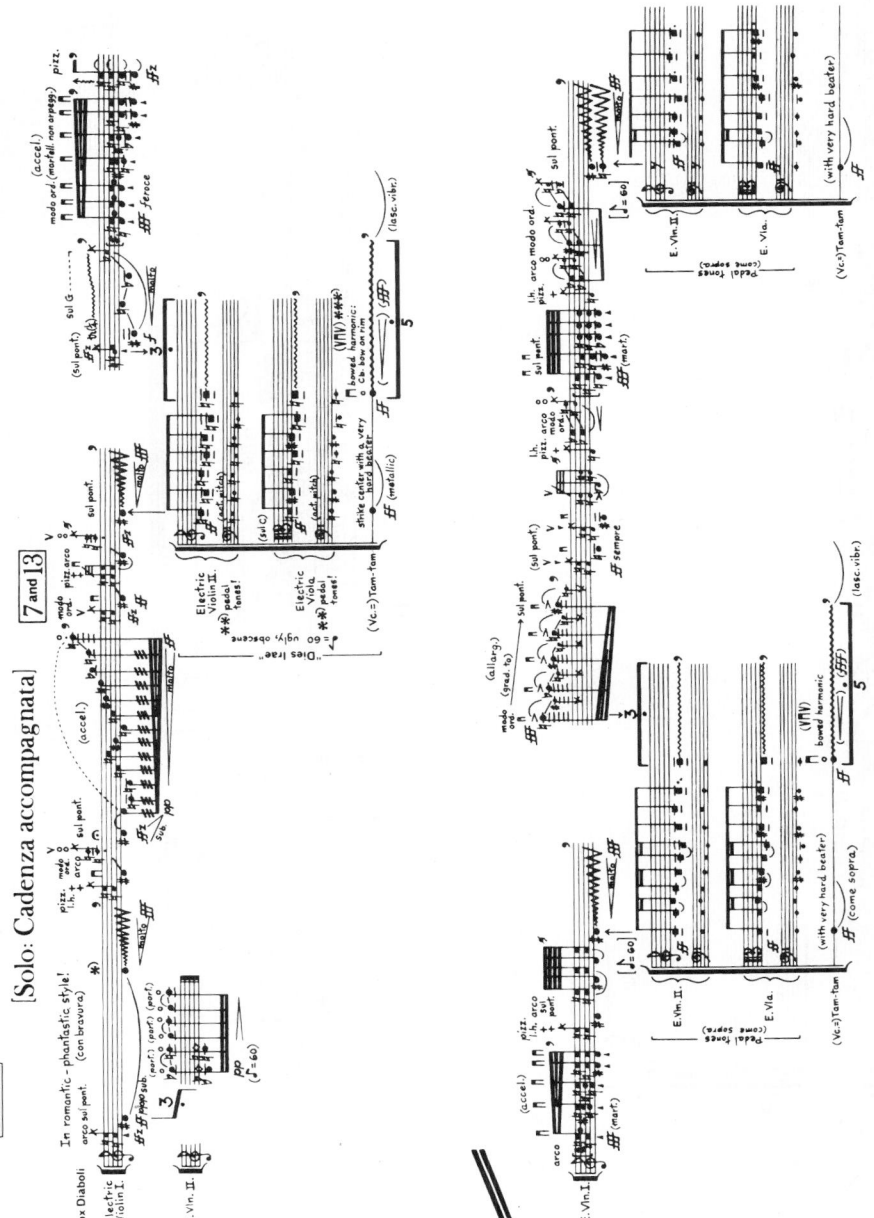

(a) Image 4: *Devil–Music*

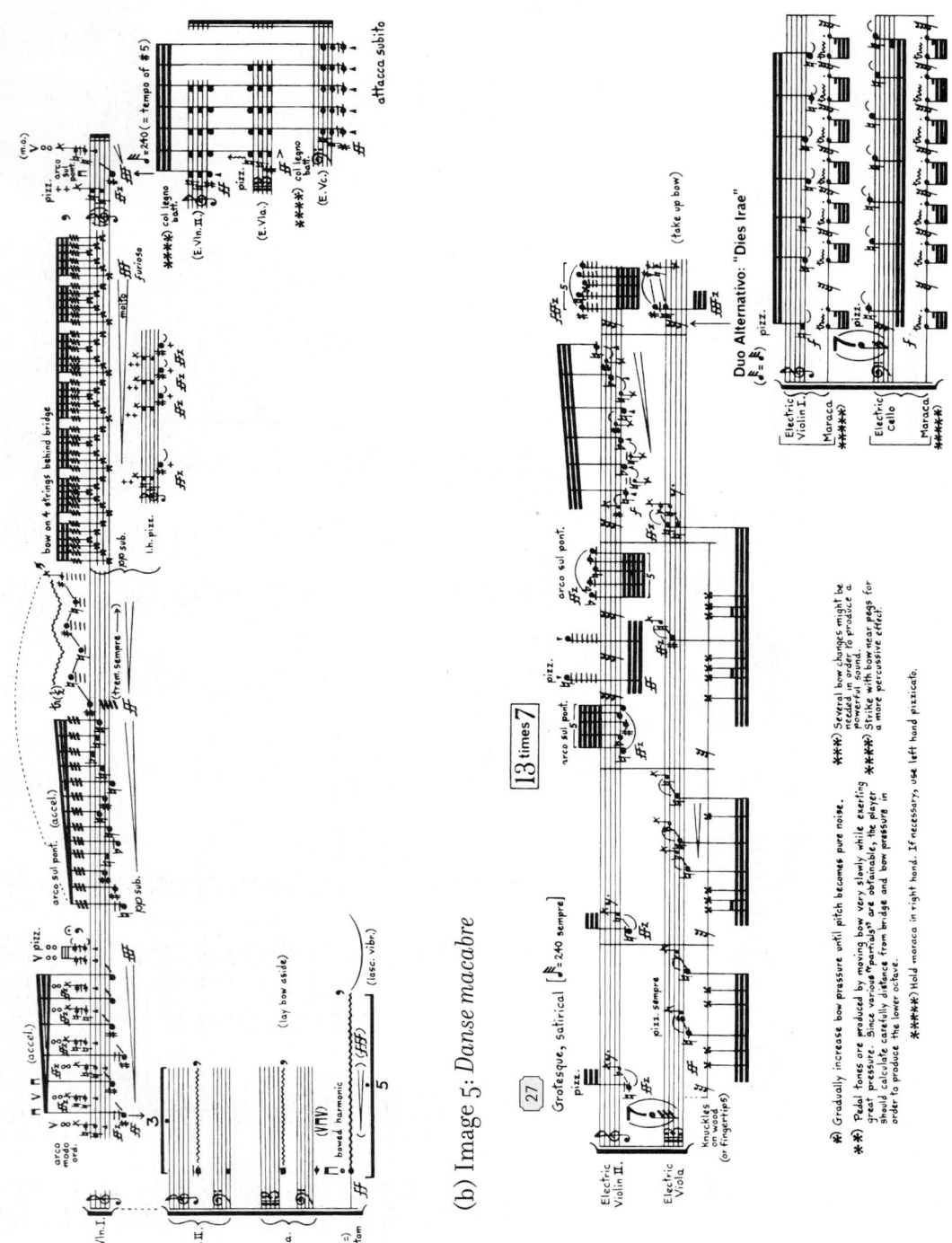

(b) Image 5: *Danse macabre*

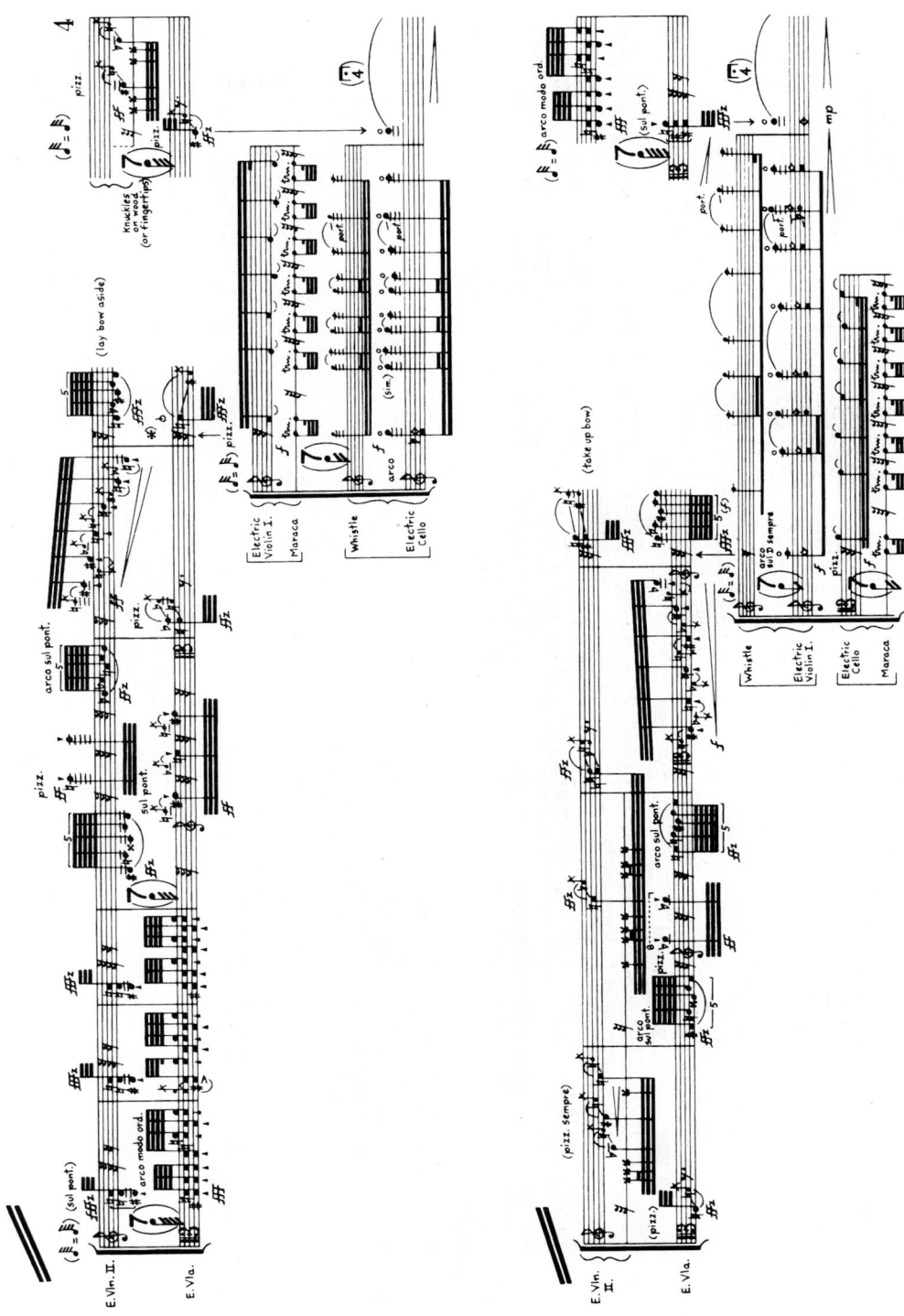

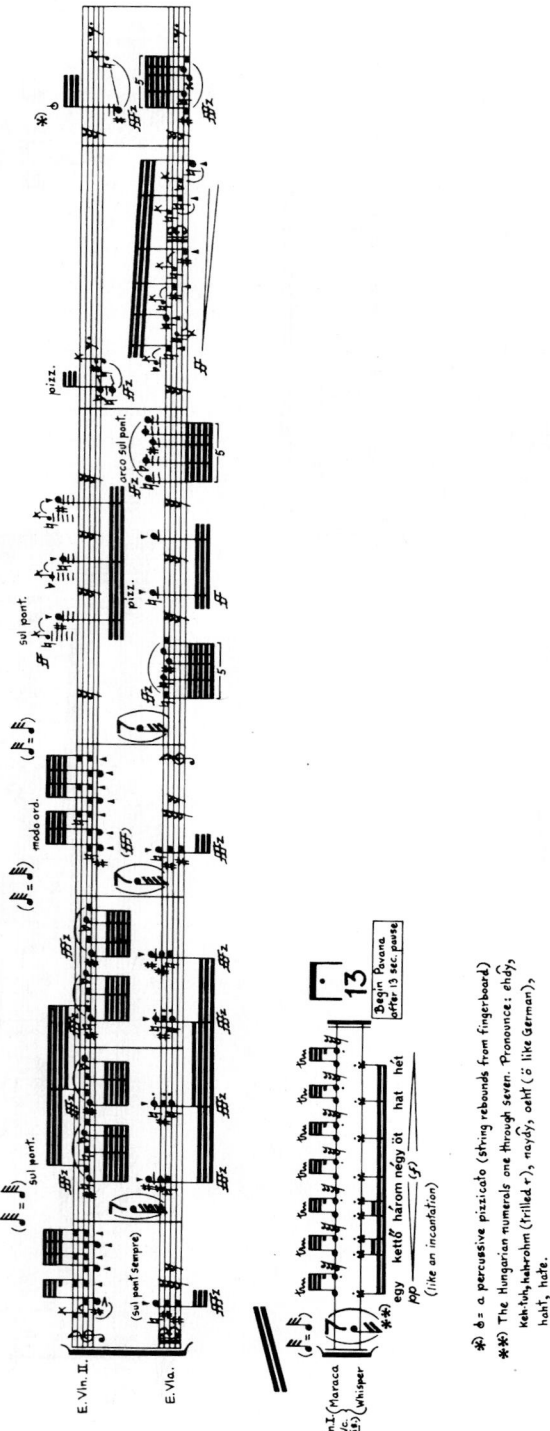

The late 1960s and early 1970s were turbulent years in the history of the United States. The Vietnam War and other issues were vehemently debated, especially on college campuses. George Crumb, a professor at the University of Pennsylvania, was deeply affected by this strife, as were many of his artist colleagues across the country. For a commission from the University of Michigan, Crumb composed *Black Angels* in 1970, inscribing at the end of the score "in tempore belli" (in time of war). The work is both a protest of the Vietnam War and a reaction to the troubled world of the late 1960s. The premiere by the Stanley Quartet in Ann Arbor, Michigan, on October 23, 1970, received a standing ovation.

A black angel is a conventional image used by painters to represent a fallen angel. According to the composer, the work represents three stages in the journey of the soul: fall from grace (the section marked "Departure," including Images 1–5), spiritual annihilation ("Absence," Images 6–9), and redemption ("Return," Images 10–13). The subtitle *Thirteen Images from the Dark Land* suggests the pervasive numerology underlying this work. The score contains numerous references to the numbers 7 and 13, which Crumb characterized as "fateful numbers"—numbers that are considered to be lucky or unlucky. These numbers affect duration, pitch, harmony, and melody. Several of the movements, for example, are based on a prominent chord with $d\sharp'–a'–e''$; counting downward in semitones from the e'', these pitches represent the numbers 0–7–13. At the conclusion of the work, Crumb duly noted: "finished on Friday the Thirteenth, March 1970."

Crumb creates a surrealistic, dreamlike character through his imaginative use of color. An electronically amplified string quartet can produce a variety of unique sounds, and Crumb explores unusual means of bowing, such as striking the strings near the pegs with the bow, holding the bow underhand in the manner of viol players, and bowing between the left-hand fingers and the pegs, along with glissandos, *sul ponticello* (on the bridge, creating a thin, metallic sound), and percussive pizzicato. In addition, the performers are asked to play a variety of percussion instruments, including maracas, tam-tams, and water-tuned crystal glasses, and to make vocal sounds, such as clicking, whistling, whispering, and chanting. The spoken words involve ritualistic counting focusing on the numbers seven and thirteen in German, French, Russian, Hungarian, Japanese, and Swahili. These effects are not mere striving for novelty; the composer employed them to create a nightmarish atmosphere as a substrate for his poetic message.

Image 4, *Devil-Music*, and Image 5, *Danse macabre*, should be considered as a pair. There is no break between them, they share a common theme, and they have similar structures. Indeed, one can hear *Devil-Music* as an improvisatory introduction to *Danse macabre*. The titles of both movements refer to medieval artworks in which the devil is shown playing the violin and leading various dancing figures to their deaths. These images were also treated in two celebrated compositions from the nineteenth century, Franz Liszt's *Totentanz* for piano and orchestra, and Camille Saint-Saëns's *Danse macabre* for violin and orchestra. The titles of both can be translated as "dance of death." Images 4 and 5 share several characteristics with these orchestral works. As in *Totentanz*, Death is associated with the Gregorian chant melody from the Requiem Mass, *Dies irae*, first used with such association in the finale of Berlioz's *Symphonie fantastique* (NAWM 121). As in Saint-Saëns's *Danse macabre*, Death plays the violin, and the tritone involving an open string is emphasized. For Saint-Saëns, the sound of open strings and a tritone represented the devil tuning his violin. In the medieval era, the tritone was called *diabolus in musica* (devil in music).

In both Images 4 and 5, the first three phrases of *Dies irae* alternate with contrasting material. In *Devil-Music* the principal line, labeled *Vox Diaboli* (devil's voice), features an intense solo cadenza for the first violinist. Virtuosic effects include triple-stopped chords, pizzicato notes plucked by the left hand (normally used only for fingering), and harmonics. In several instances, the soloist is instructed to press on the bow until "pitch becomes pure noise." Throughout the cadenza, perfect fifths and diminished fifths can be heard, often incorporating open strings; the $d\sharp'$–a'–e'' sonority, which uses two open strings (a' and e''), predominates. Interspersed in the brief breaks of the cadenza are the phrases of the *Dies irae* played by the second violin and viola in pedal tones—pitches an octave lower than notated (and lower than the instruments can normally play), produced by moving the bow slowly while exerting great pressure. The cellist accompanies with the tam-tam. For the final cadence, all of the instruments present a version of the principal three-note chord. The bottom three string parts employ the percussive effects of pizzicato or *col legno* (hitting the strings with the wood side of the bow).

Danse macabre alternates material played by the second violin and viola with the phases of the *Dies irae* in the first violin and cello. The second violin and viola lines rely heavily on pizzicato and other unusual effects, such as tapping on the viola with knuckles. Embedded in the second and fourth statements of these two instruments are brief quotations from Saint-Saëns's *Danse macabre*. The *Dies irae* is also presented with unusual timbres, involving pizzicato, harmonics, maracas, and whistling. At the conclusion of this Image, the first violinist and cellist whisper the numbers one through seven in Hungarian.

A performance of *Black Angels* demands considerable technical skills, creativity, and theatricality. Because a string quartet plays without a conductor, Crumb requires each performer to play from the score (rather than from a single part, as customary) so that the coordination of the parts is every player's responsibility. As an aid to the musicians, Crumb simplified the notation by omitting unnecessary rests, and he created oversized scores that can be read easily from a distance (but which had to be reduced to fit into a book this size). The score is in his own neat, very distinctive handwriting. In addition to numerous explanations and suggestions, Crumb includes a chart showing a preferred arrangement of percussion instruments. This work has become a staple in the repertory of several young professional quartets, including the Concord String Quartet heard in the recording.

Milton Babbitt (b. 1916)

Philomel: Section I

Monodrama for soprano, recorded soprano, and synthesized sound

1964

164

CD 12|28 CD 6|79

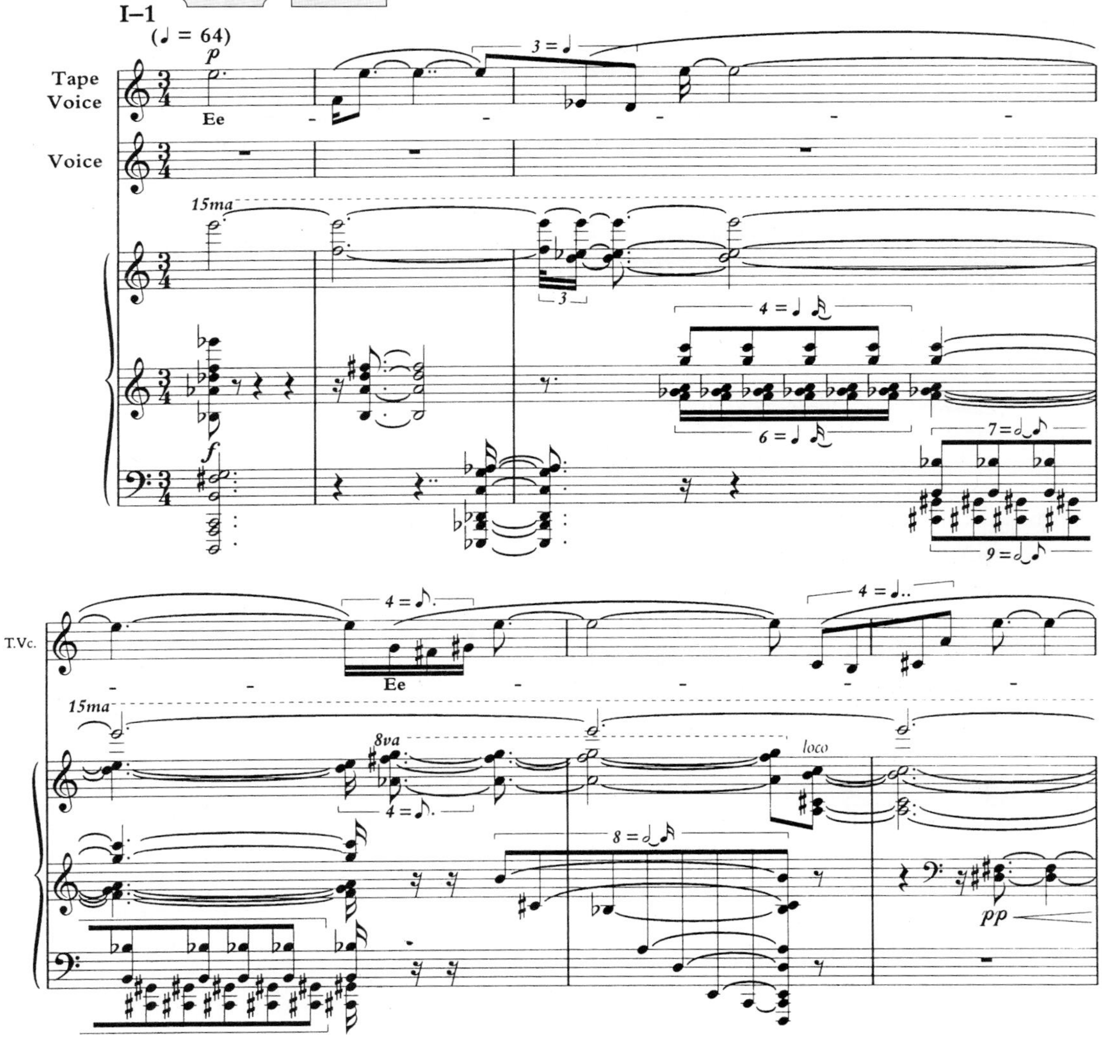

 Accidentals affect only those notes they immediately precede, with the exception of tied notes.

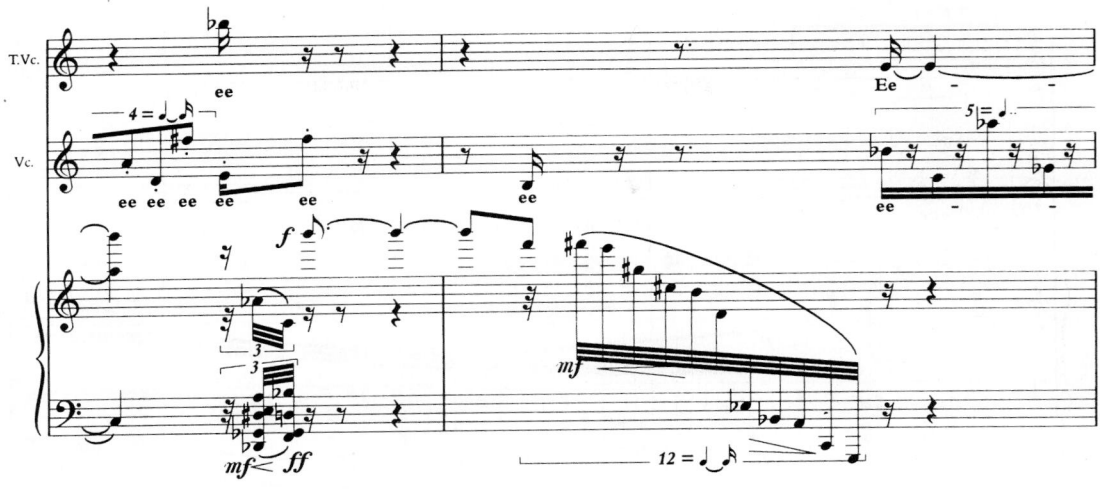

164 MILTON BABBITT *Philomel*

INTERLUDE (Tape)

Not true tears — Not true trees —

CD 12 CD 6

INTERLUDE

INTERLUDE

TAPE VOICE: **Pillowing melody, honey unheard —**

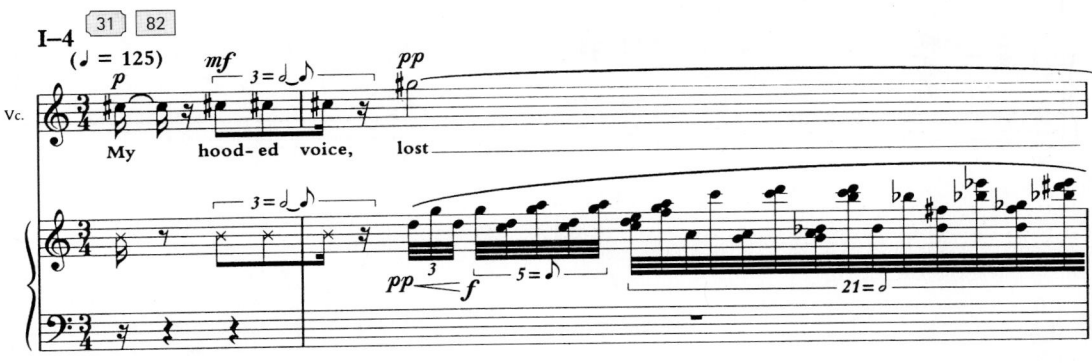

164 **MILTON BABBITT** *Philomel*

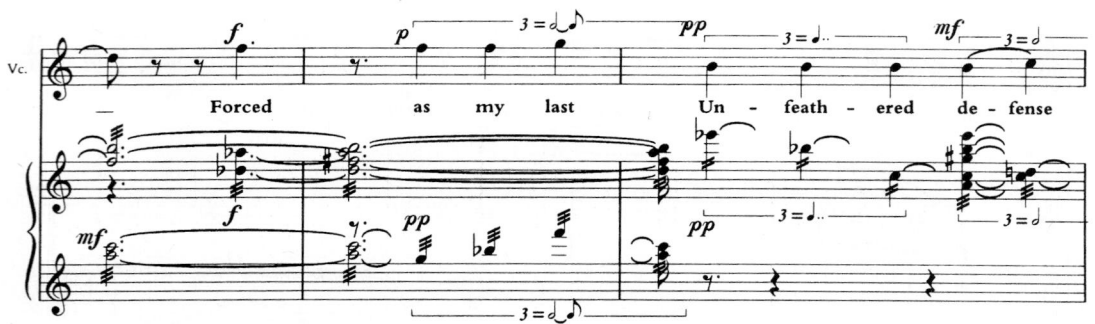

Forced as my last Un-feath-ered de-fense

Fast - tang - led _____ in lust Of these woods so dense.

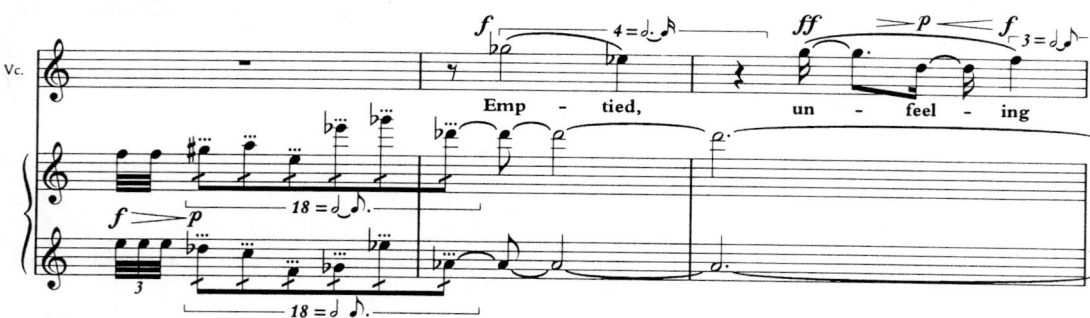

Emp - tied, un - feel - ing

and un - filled ___ By trees here where no birds ___

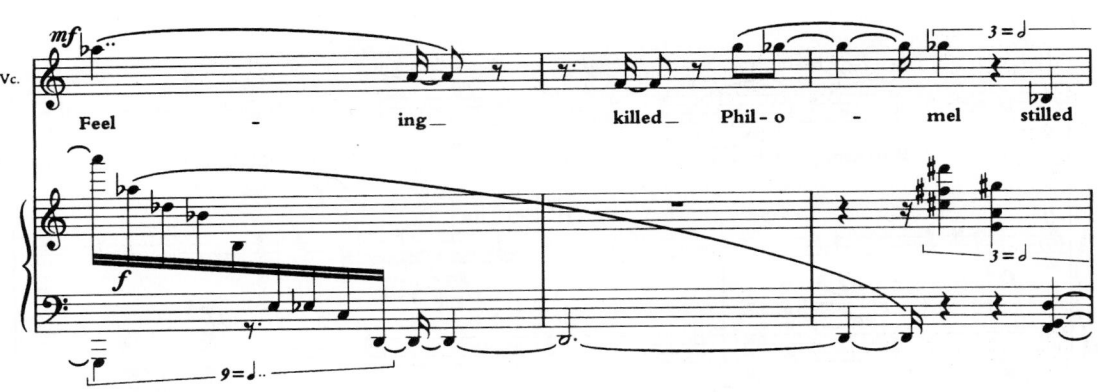

INTERLUDE

TAPE VOICE: Feeling killed, Philomel stilled, Her honey unfulfilled.

TAPE

(Recorded Soprano)
(Eeeeeeeeeeeeeeeeee)

PHILOMEL

Eeeeeeeeeeeeeeeeeee!
Eeeeeeeeeeeeeeeeeee!
Feeeeeeeeeeeeeeeeee!
I feel
Feel a million trees
And the heat of trees

TAPE

Not true trees—

PHILOMEL

Feel a million tears

TAPE

Not true tears—
Not true trees—

PHILOMEL

Is it Tereus I feel?

TAPE

Not Tereus: not a true Tereus—

PHILOMEL

Feel a million filaments;
Fear the tearing, the feeling
Trees, of ephemeral leaves
Trees tear,
And I bear
Families of tears
I feel a million Philomels

TAPE

Trees filled with mellowing
Felonous fame—

PHILOMEL

I feel trees in my hair
And on the ground,
Honeymelons fouling
My knees and feet
Soundlessly in my

Flight through the forest;
I founder in quiet.
Here I find only
Miles of felted silence
Unwinding behind me,
Lost, lost in the wooded night.

TAPE

Pillowing melody,
Honey unheard—

PHILOMEL

My hooded voice, lost
Lost, as my first
Unhoneyed tongue;
Forced, as my last
Unfeathered defense
Fast-tangled in lust
Of these woods so dense.
Emptied, unfeeling and unfilled
By trees here where no birds have
    trilled—
Feeling killed
Philomel stilled
Her honey unfulfilled.

TAPE

Feeling killed
Philomel stilled
Her honey unfulfilled

PHILOMEL

What is that sound?
A voice found?
Broken, the bound
Of silence, beyond
Violence of human sound,
As if a new self
Could be founded on sound.
The trees are astounded!

PHILOMEL AND TAPE
(simultaneously)
What is this humming?
I am becoming
My own song . . .

—JOHN HOLLANDER

Milton Babbitt's *Philomel* was commissioned by the Ford Foundation for the soprano Bethany Beardslee and premiered by her in 1964. Probably Babbitt's most popular work, it combines live performance with prerecorded tape and synthesized sounds. The soprano soloist is heard against a tape that incorporates an altered recording of her own voice, a kind of distorted echo, together with electronic sounds. The "score" shown here includes the complete part for voice and—with exceptions—a total representation of the rhythmic and pitch content of the synthesized and recorded accompaniment in all those sections of the work in which the singer participates. The exceptions occur when, to avoid notational complexity, the rhythmic representation is only closely approximate, and registral relations are simplified. Such a score is unusual for electronic music, in which "composition" typically happens on tape rather than on paper, but is useful for the singer. The tape interludes, in which the singer does not participate, are not notated.

The poem, written expressly for this setting by John Hollander, is based on a fable by Ovid (*Metamorphoses* 6:412–674). Procne, wife of Tereus, king of Thrace, is eager to see her sister, Philomela, after an absence of many years, and sends Tereus to fetch her. On the return trip Tereus rapes Philomela in a Thracian wood and cuts out her tongue to prevent disclosure, but his guilt is exposed nevertheless by a tapestry in which Philomela weaves her story. Procne, horrified, avenges herself against her husband by killing their son and feeding Tereus from the butchered corpse. In a rage, Tereus pursues the two sisters, but before he can catch them the gods transform him into a hoopoe bird, Procne into a swallow, and Philomela into a nightingale. In the metamorphosis Philomela regains her voice. The sung text begins at this point.

Babbitt's composition, like John Hollander's poem, is in three sections. In the first, excerpted here, Philomel screams as she recalls the pain of violation; dazed, she expresses her feelings in vivid but incoherent images. She runs through the forest in fear and confusion. In Section 2, Philomel seeks answers about her predicament from a thrush, a hawk, an owl, and a gull. In the third section, she sings a strophic lament, joined in refrains by her taped voice.

The taped voice often answers the soloist by distorting her line or, speaking, comments like a Greek chorus. Every detail in the vocal sections was worked out in serial terms. The vocal sections alternate with unnotated synthesized and tape interludes that are more freely composed.

The vocal melody is extremely disjunct, with leaps of major sevenths, ninths, and even elevenths. Some of the notes are sung in Sprechstimme, marked by an X instead of a notehead, and expressive glissandos punctuate some phrases. The pitch-class E, the first note sung by the taped voice, is central to the construction of the opening passage. The twelve-tone row is stated, then transposed, in such a way that E becomes successively the first, second, third, fourth, and fifth pitch-class in the row. With each unfolding of the row, the taped voice claims more of the row's pitch-classes up to E—in the second measure two, in the third three, and so on. The accompaniment each time claims the remainder of the row or aggregate (the twelve pitch-classes of the chromatic scale). The first sonority, as the taped soprano screams "Eeeeeee" on E, contains all twelve pitch-classes and covers a seven-octave span. Subsequent simultaneities are less populated, with increasingly arpeggiated and pointillistic unfoldings of the row. The high E is heard as a steady pedal note through the first eight measures. When Philomel's natural voice enters, it begins on F, and E is now the last member of the row, appearing as the highest note in the accompaniment in measure 9.

Like Schoenberg in *Pierrot lunaire*, Babbitt tore some leaves from the book of the sixteenth-century madrigalists. The pitch E for the scream is a madrigalian conceit, as are the synthesized trills on the word "trilled." But he went beyond the madrigalists in the second section of the poem, where, instead of bird imitations, he introduced recorded birdsong.

This work is extraordinarily difficult to perform. The score and tape can be rented from the publisher; since the tape uses Bethany Beardslee's voice, most sopranos try to match her sound, though some have made their own tape. The piece requires a singer with perfect pitch, outstanding command of rhythm, and total control of dynamic contrasts. It exemplifies the trend among some composers in the 1960s to write music only for the very best performers and to challenge their abilities to the utmost.

KRZYSZTOF PENDERECKI (B. 1933)

Threnody: To the Victims of Hiroshima

Tone poem for string orchestra

1960

165

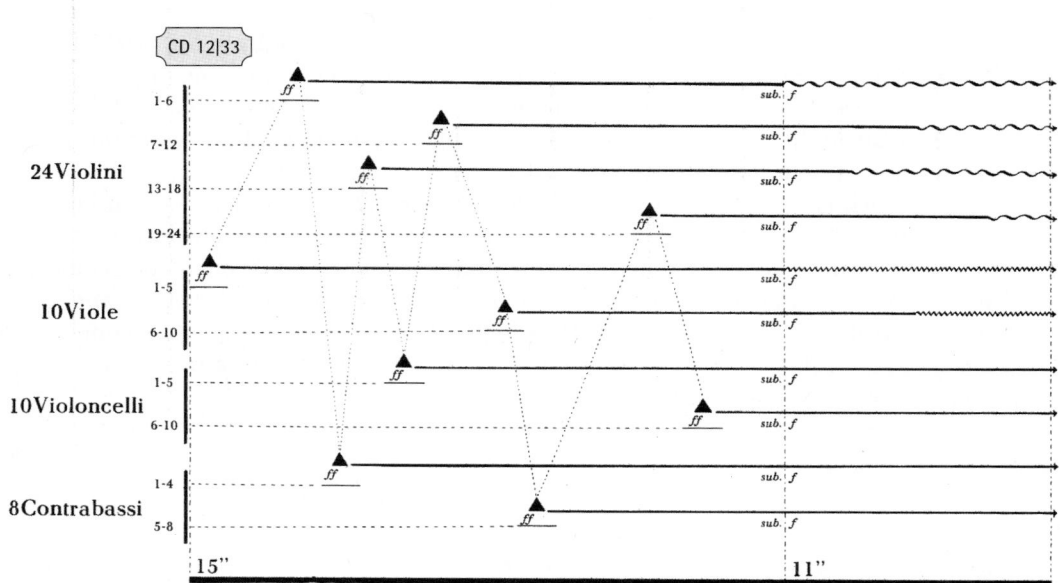

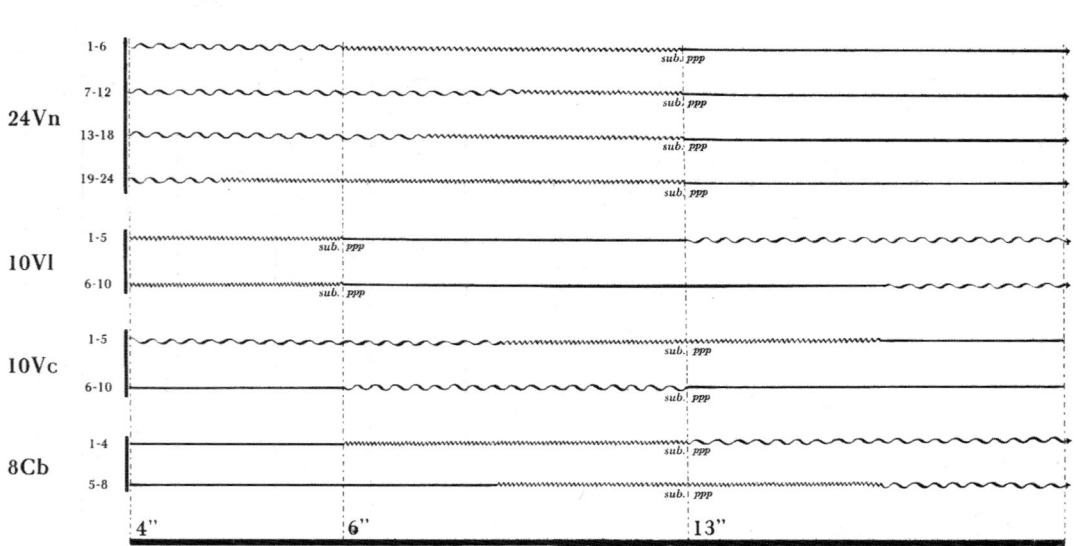

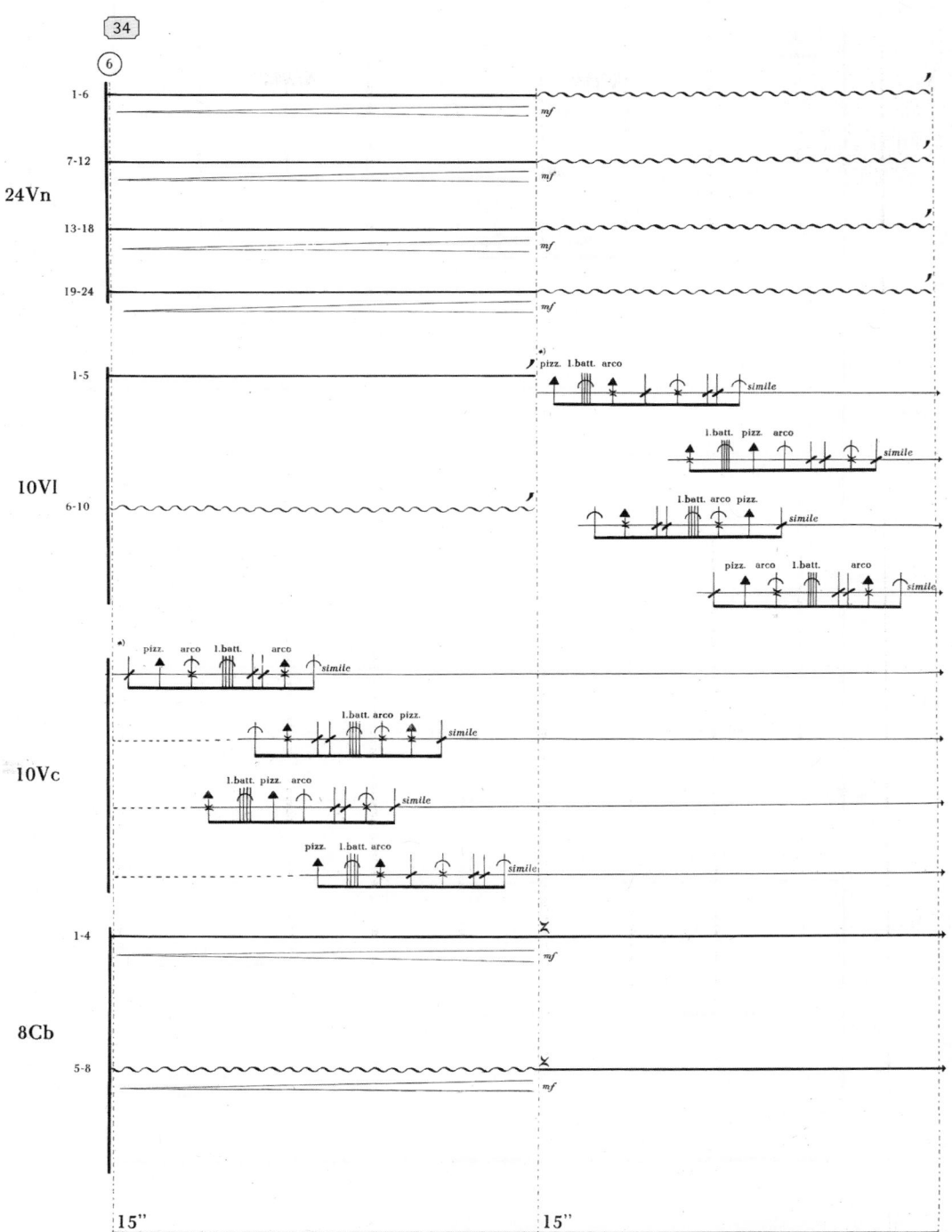

*) Each instrumentalist chooses one of the four given groups and
executes it (within a fixed space of time) as rapidly as possible.

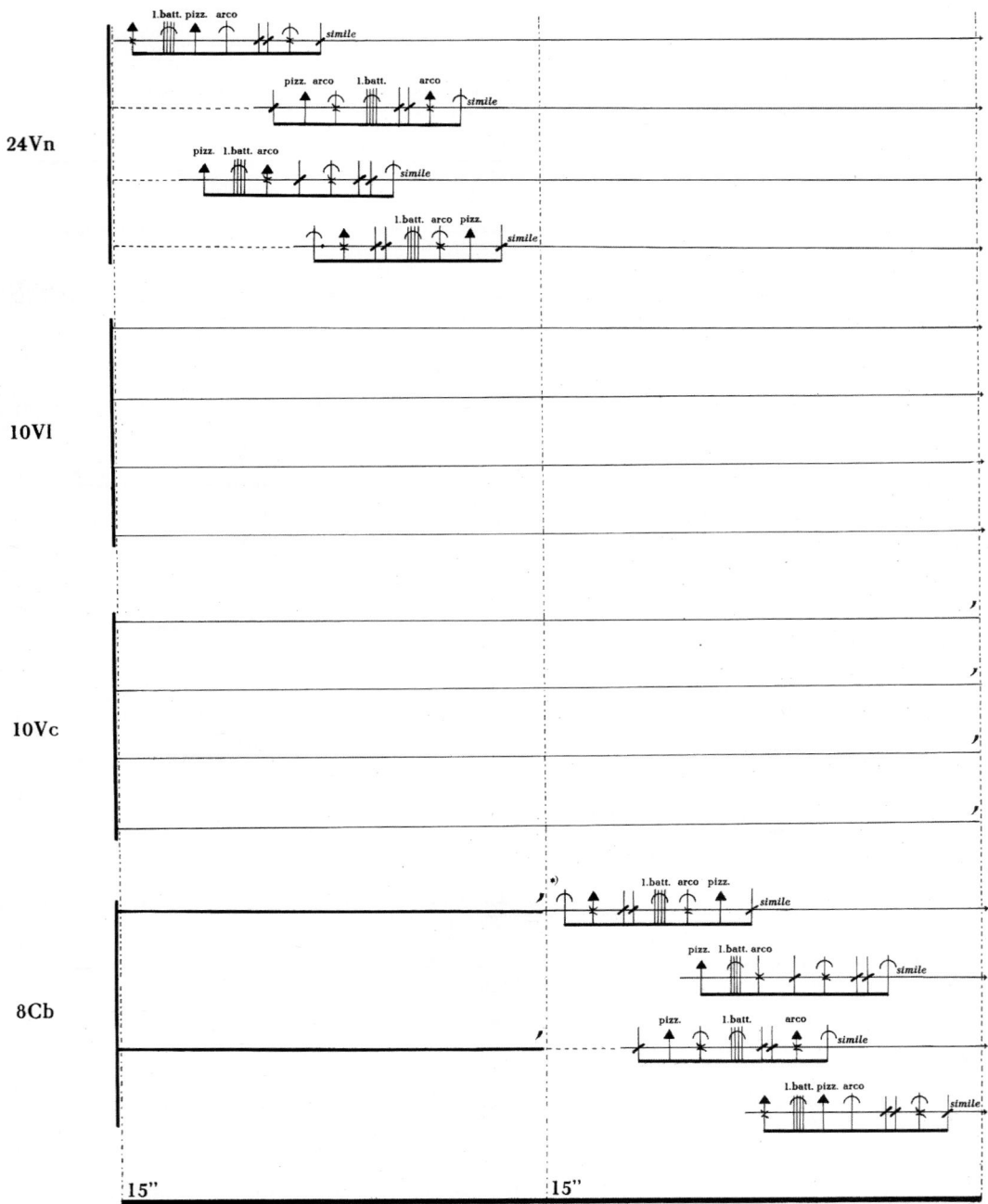

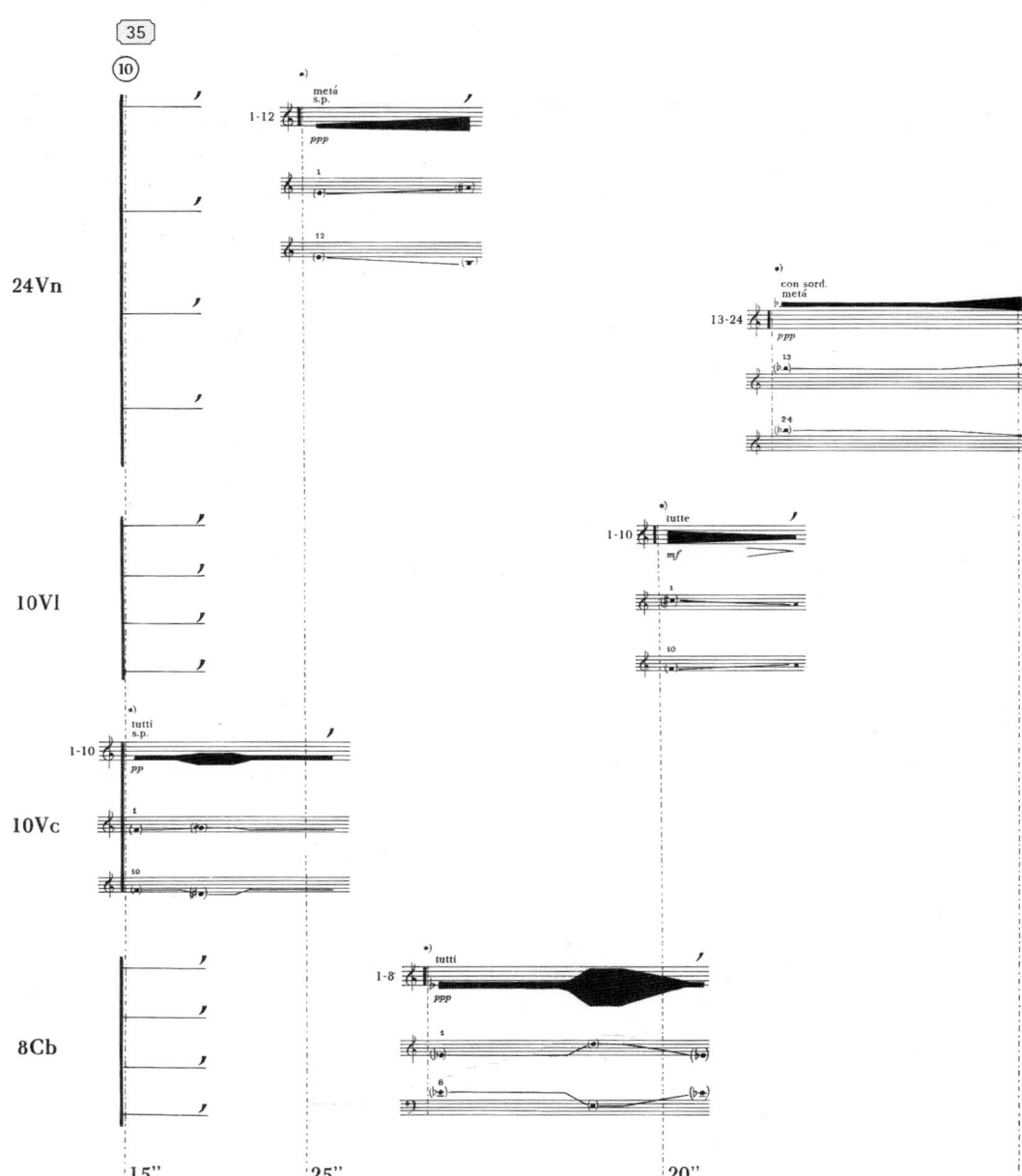

*) Exact notation is given in the parts.

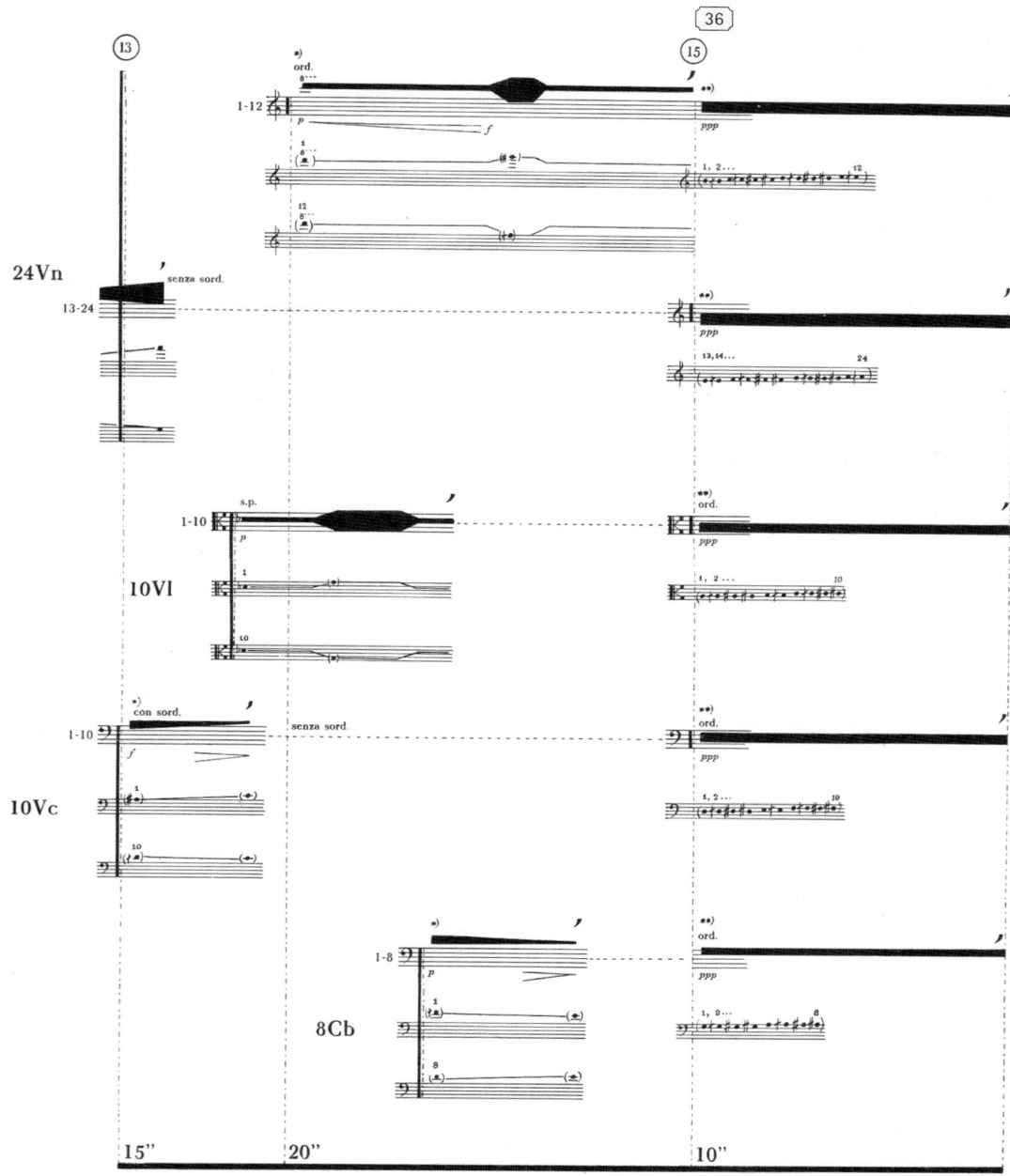

*) See previous note.

**) Each instrumentalist plays the tone allocated to his instrument, so that the whole
quarter-tone scale between the indicated lowest and highest tones sounds simultaneously.

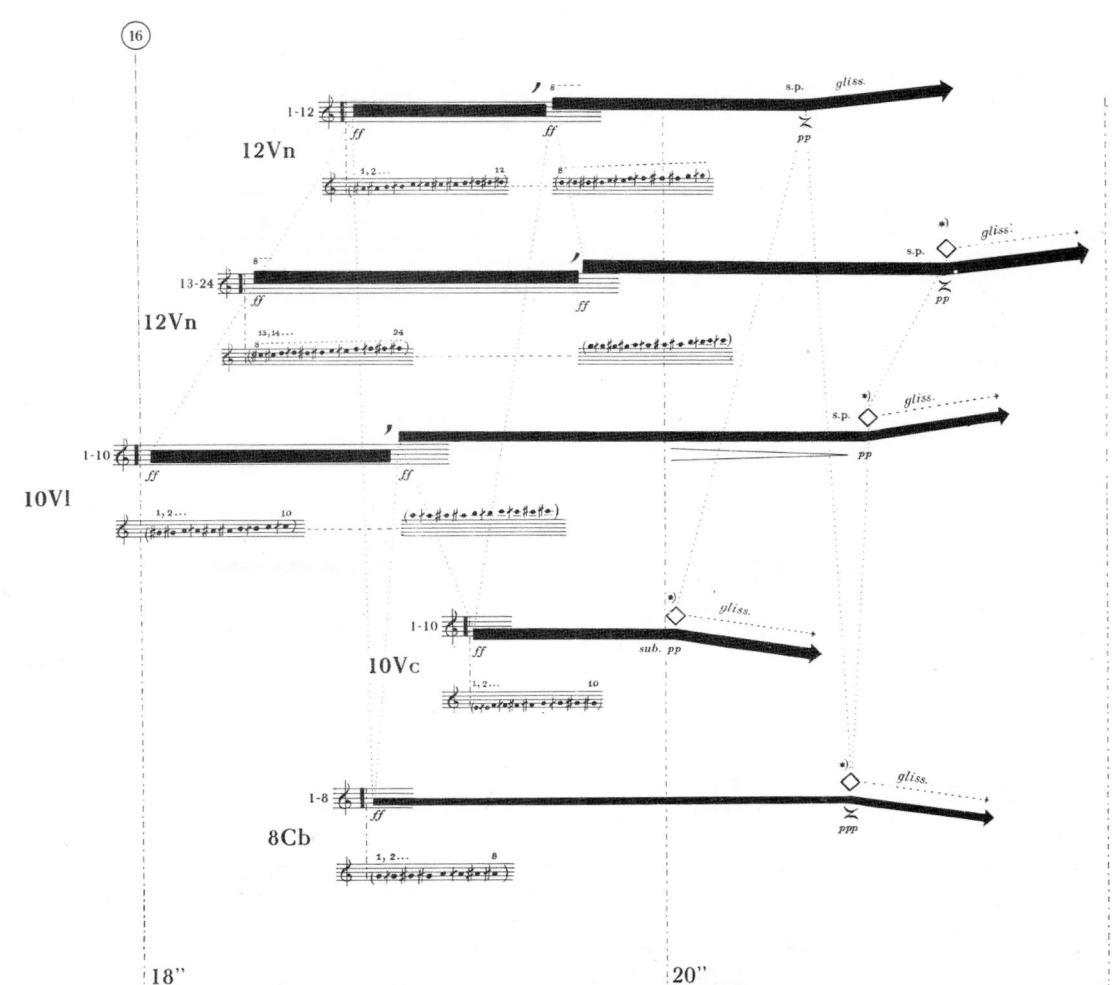

*) Harmonics

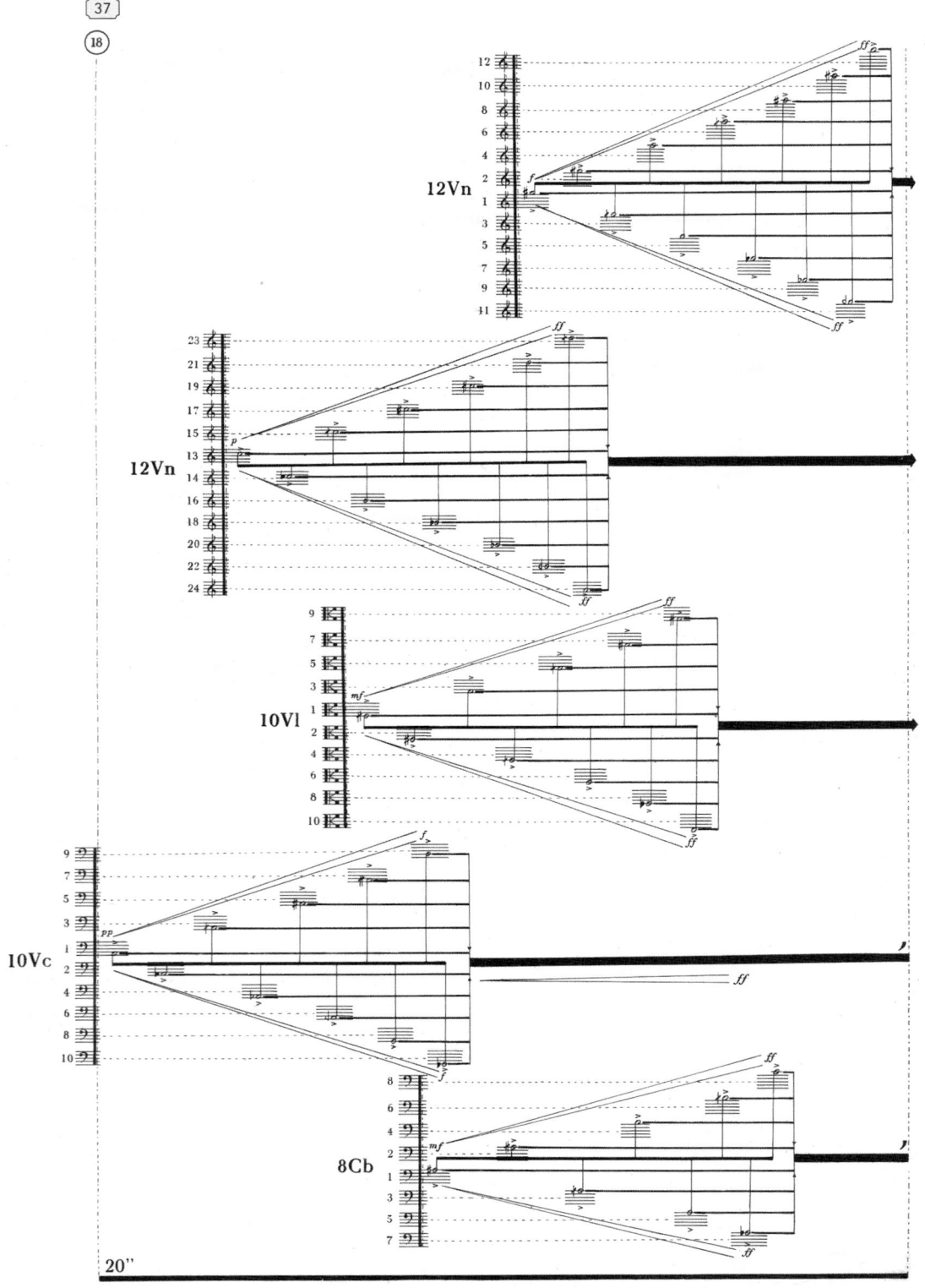

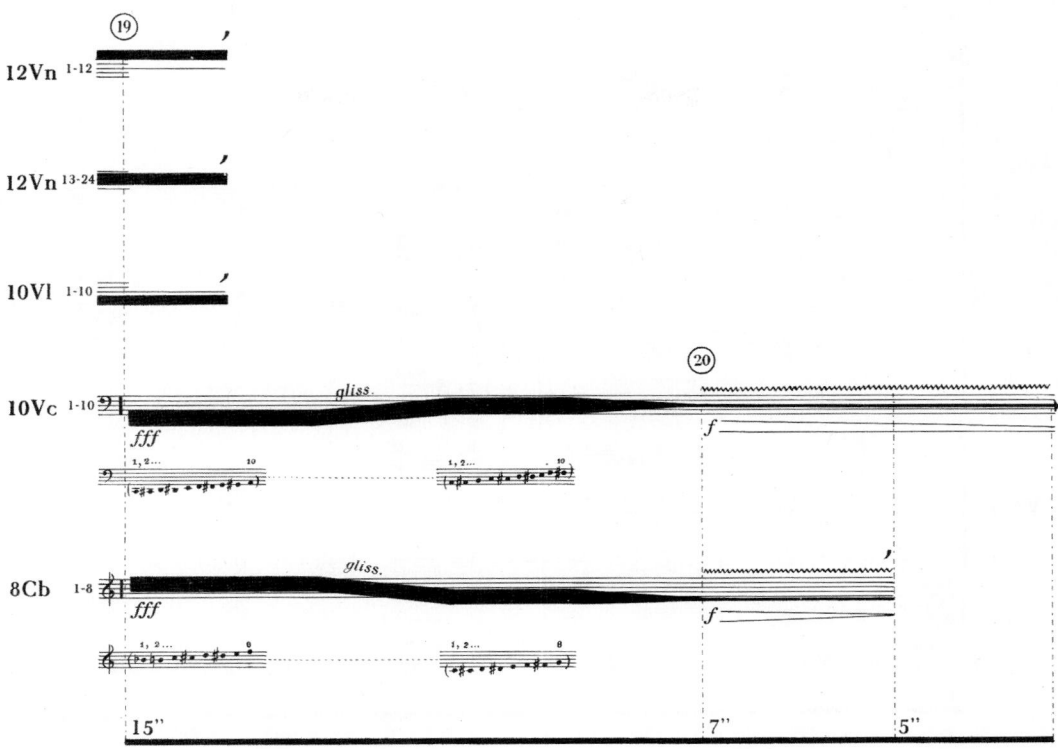

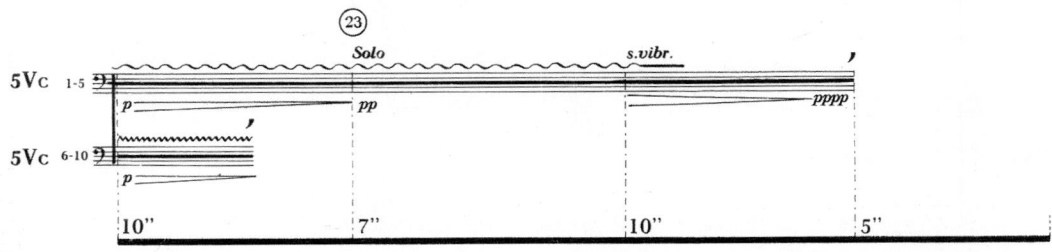

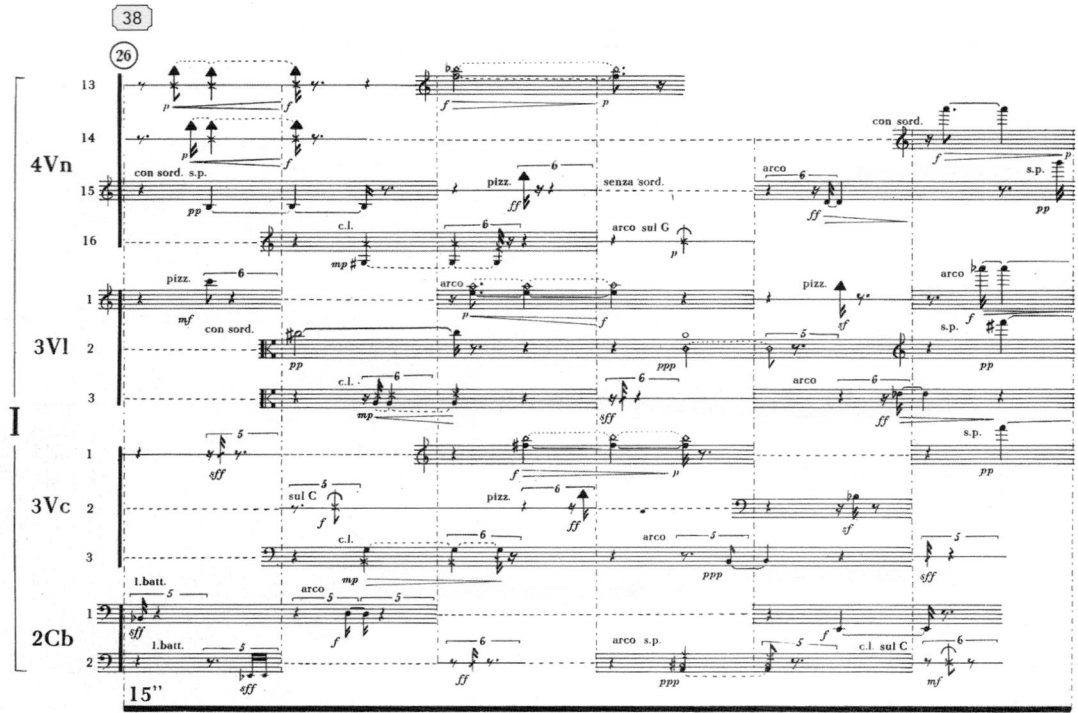

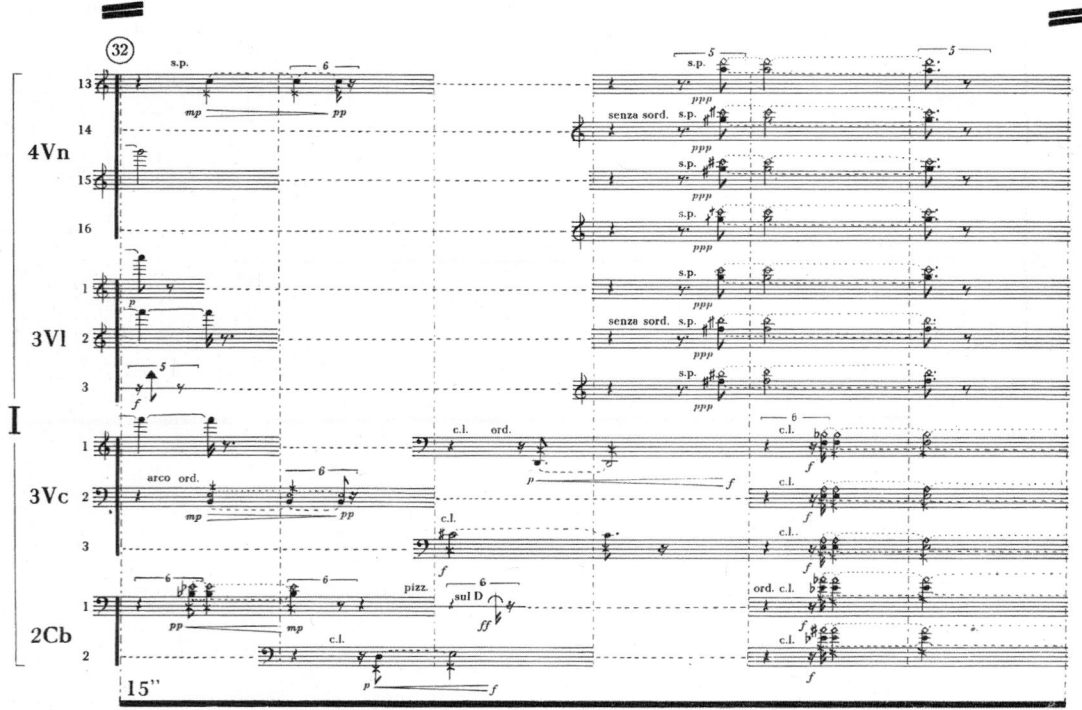

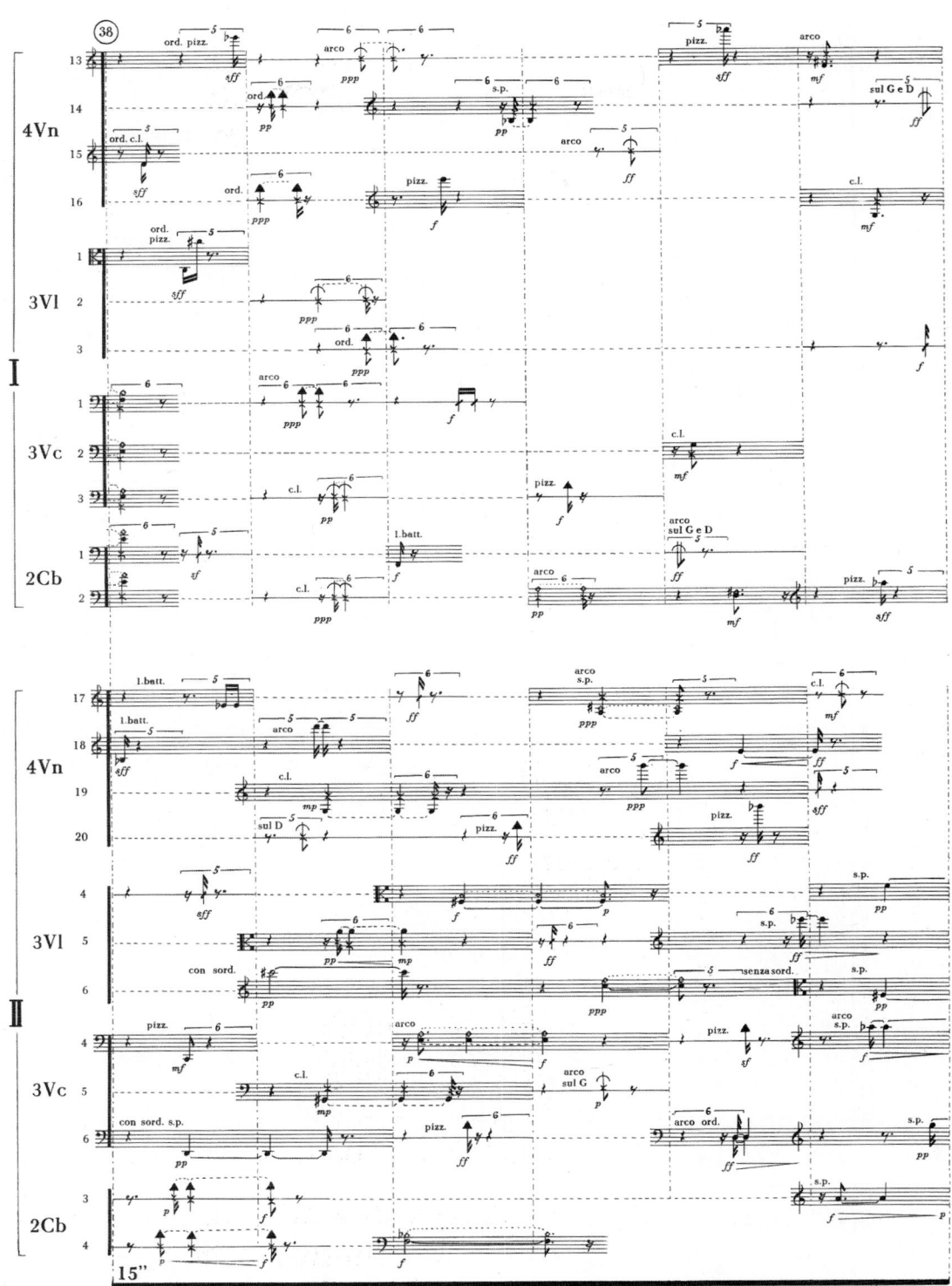

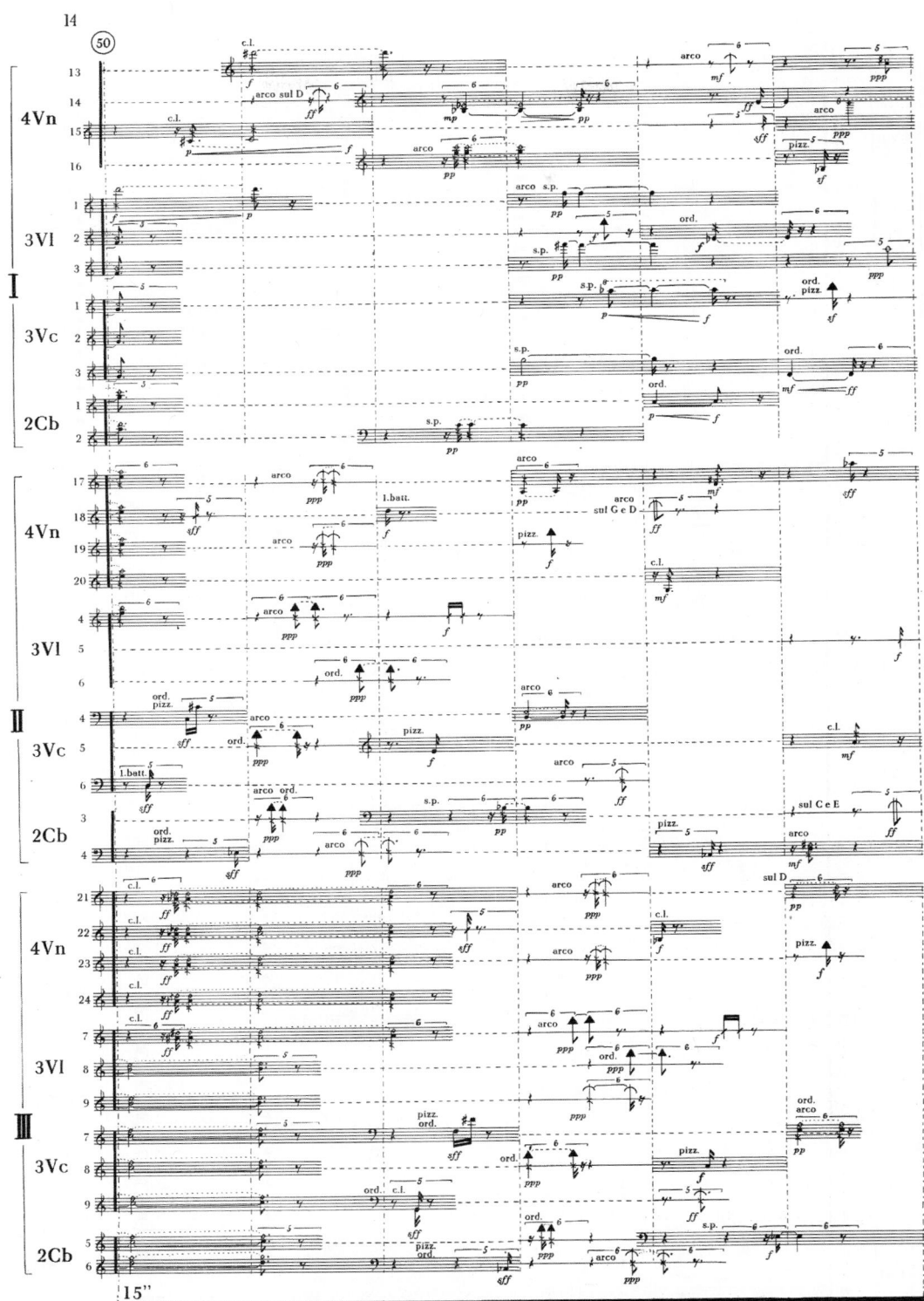

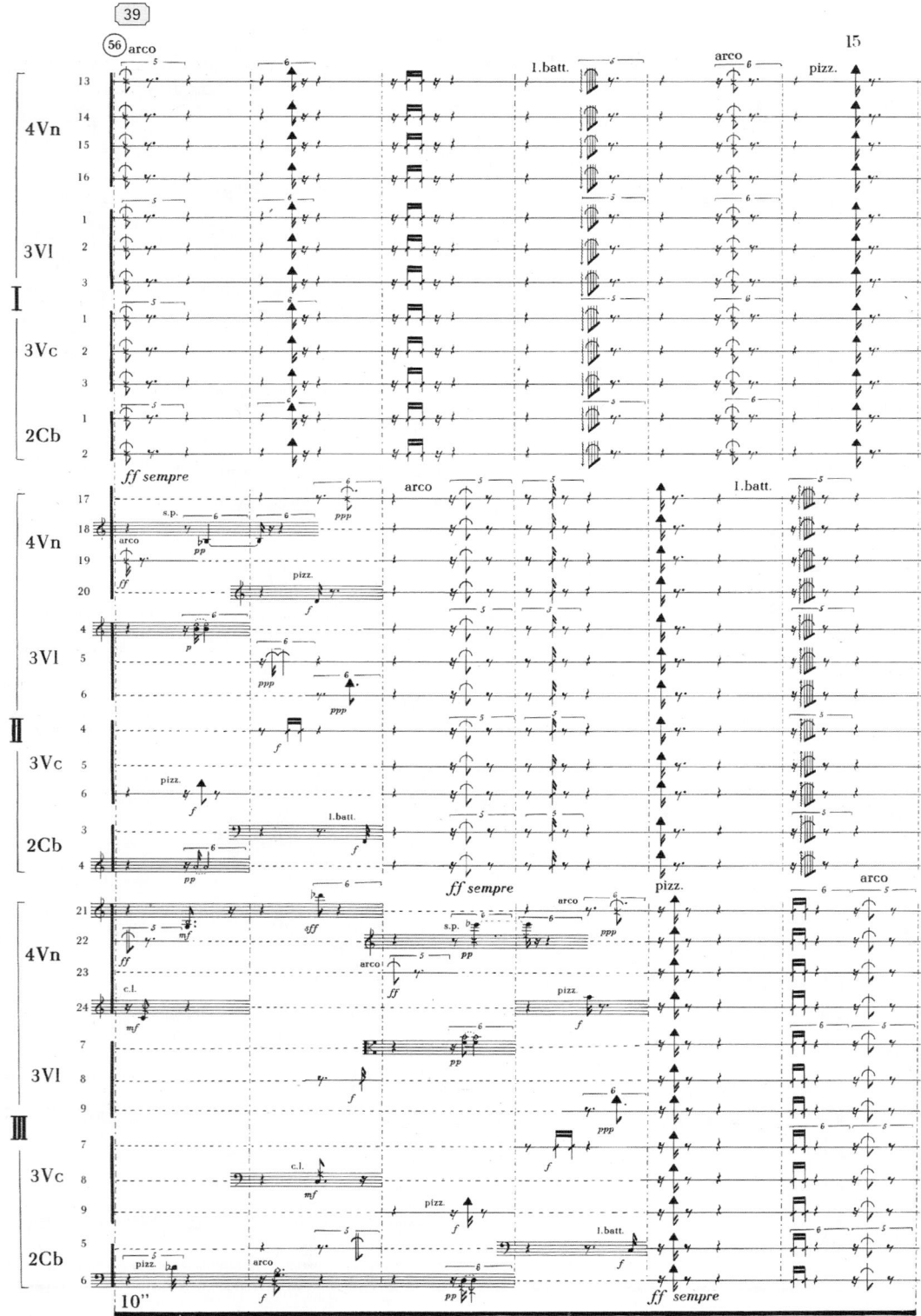

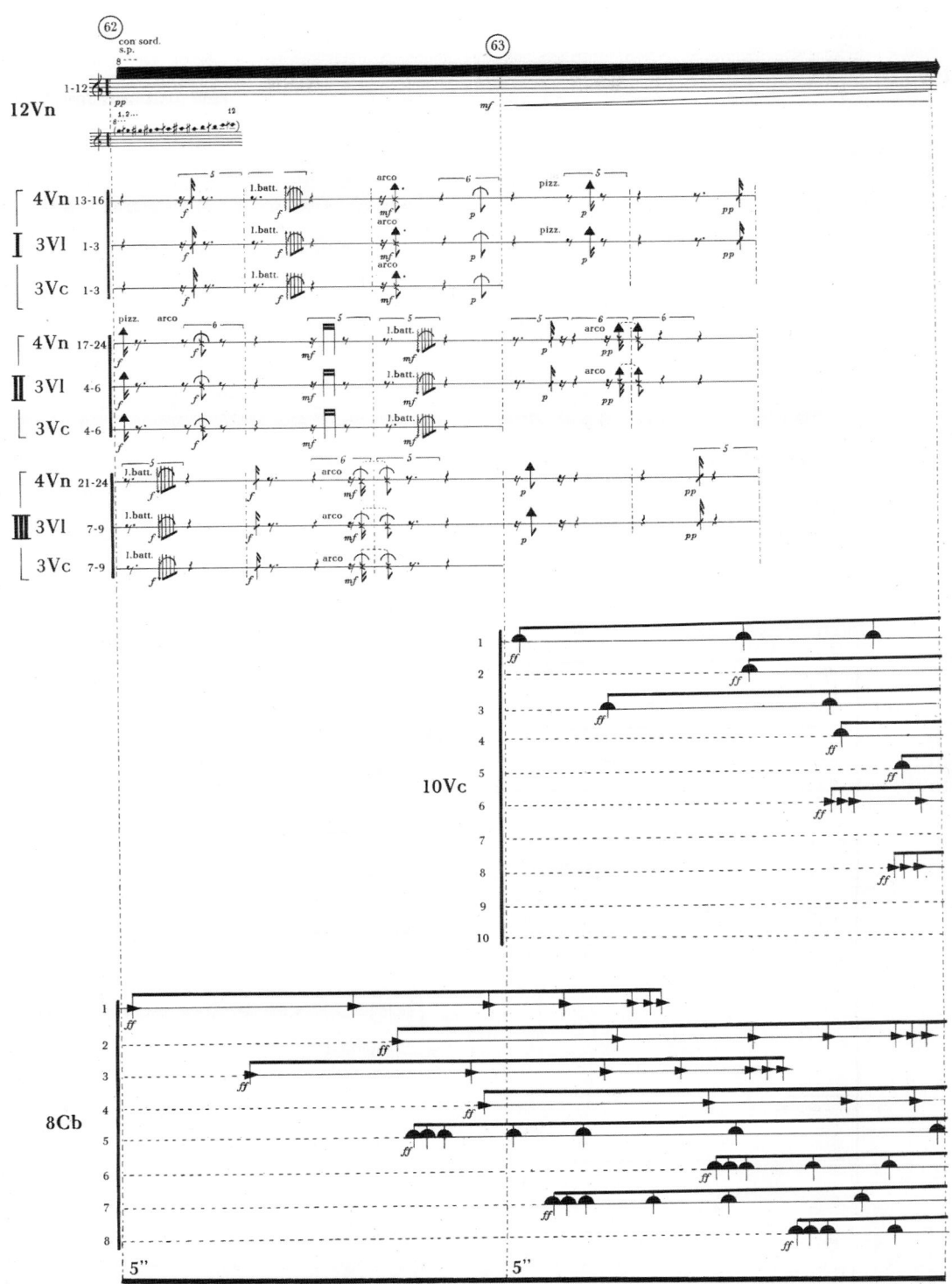

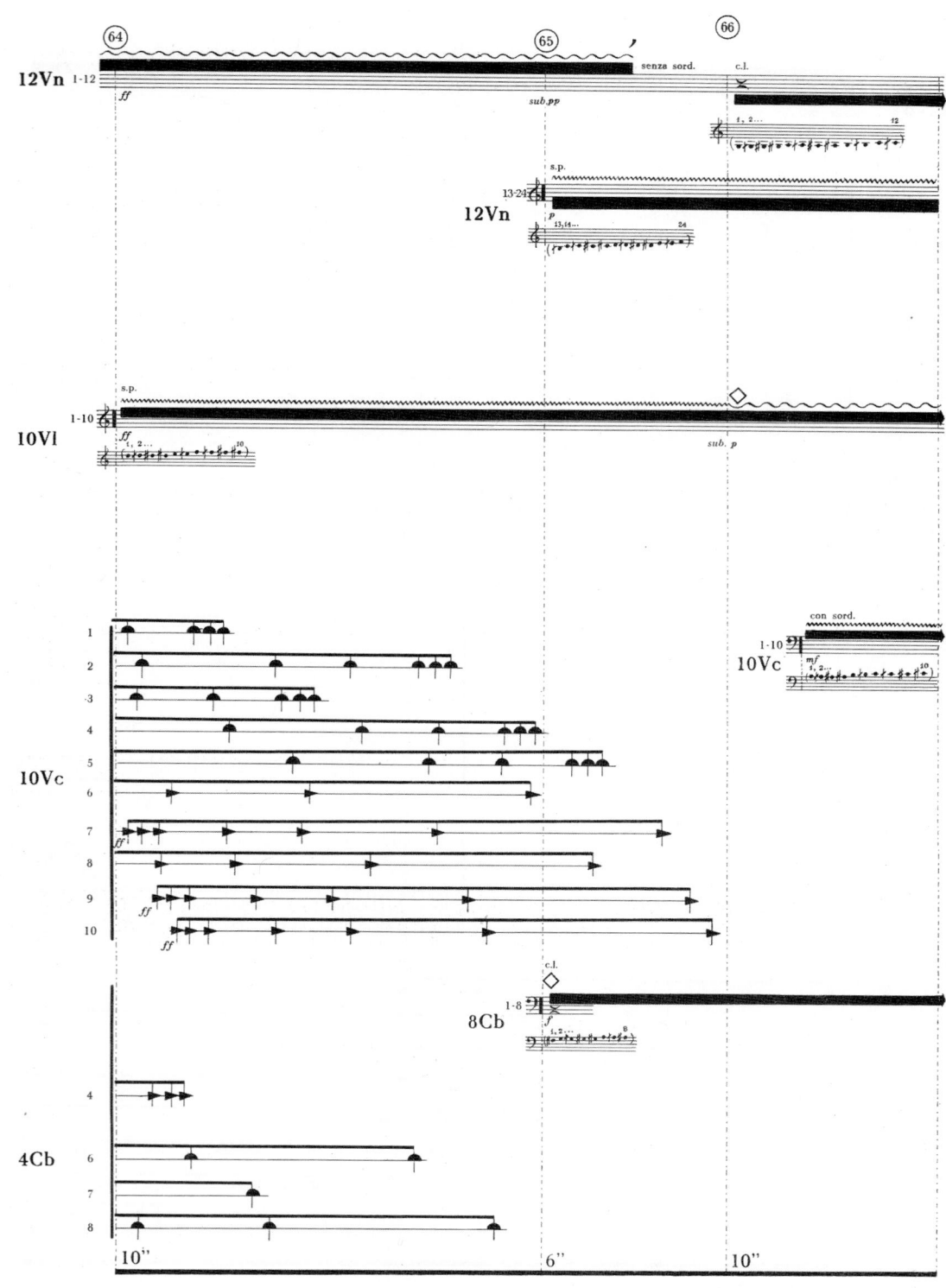

67
68
69
senza trem.
12Vn 1-12
ff
sub pp
13-24
12Vn
pp
10Vl 1-10
f
senza trem.
s.p.
p
10Vc 1-10
sub p
pp
8Cb 1-8
senza trem.
sub.p
arco
s.p.
mf
sub pp
6"
8"
10"
70
s.p.
ord.
s.t.
tutti
archi
fff
pppp
24Vn 1-24
10Vl 1-10
10Vc 1-10
8Cb 1-8
30"

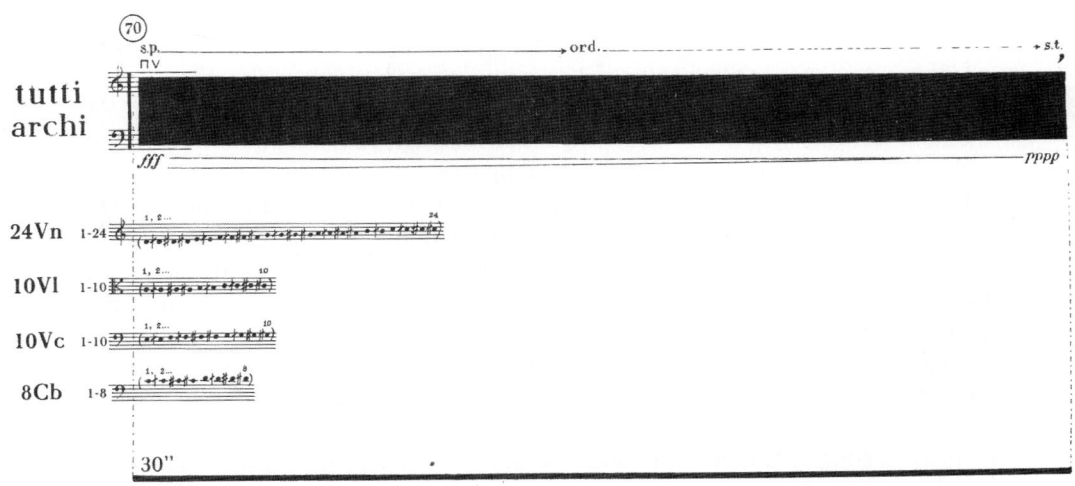

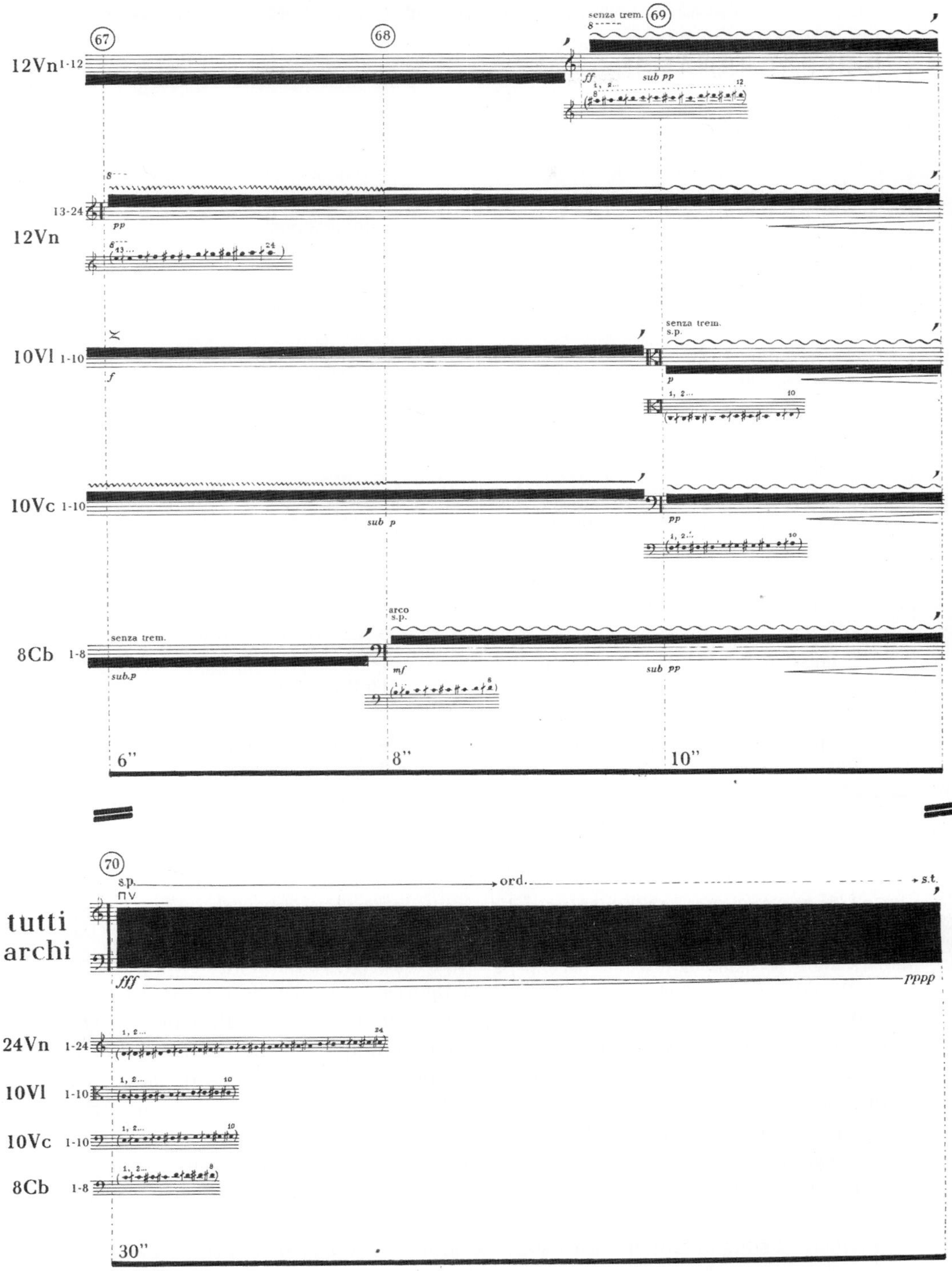

GUIDE TO NOTATION

s. p. = sul ponticello [bow on the bridge]
s. t. = sul tasto [bow above the fingerboard]
c. l. = col legno [bow with the wood of the bow]

l. batt. = col legno battuto [strike the string with the wood of the bow]
ord. = ordinario [in an ordinary manner, canceling any of the above indications]

$\dagger$ = raised by $\frac{1}{4}$ tone

$\ddagger$ = raised by $\frac{3}{4}$ tone

$\flat$ = lowered by $\frac{1}{4}$ tone

$\backslash$ = lowered by $\frac{3}{4}$ tone

t = highest note of the instrument (indefinite pitch)

$\uparrow$ = play between bridge and tailpiece

$\text{\Barpeggio}$ = arpeggio on 4 strings behind the bridge

$\top$ = play on tailpiece (arco) [bowed]

$\uparrow$ = play on bridge

f = percussion effect: strike the upper sounding board of the violin with the nut [of the bow] or the fingertips

$\sqcap\vee$ = several irregular changes of bow direction in succession

$\sim\sim$ = molto vibrato

$\sim\!\!\sim$ = very slow vibrato with a $\frac{1}{4}$ tone frequency difference produced by sliding the finger

$\times$ = very rapid non-rhythmical tremolo

Polish composer Krzysztof Penderecki (pronounced KZHISH-toff pen-de-RETS-ki) is one of the most recognized and influential figures of the post–World War II generation. With the liberalization of communism after the end of Stalinism in 1956, Penderecki began to explore new compositional techniques and styles. International attention quickly focused on him when he composed a series of sensational works, including *Threnody*. After winning the UNESCO Prize of the International Composers Jury in 1961, this work, for string orchestra, premiered to great acclaim later that year at the Warsaw Autumn Festival, and it remains his most famous piece.

Penderecki initially conceived of the composition as an abstract work, calling it *8'37"*, a name derived from its performance length. The change of title to *Threnody* (a song of lamentation) with the subtitle *To the Victims of Hiroshima* gave the piece a powerful image and message. For contemporary audiences, it not only depicted a horrific event of the recent past—the destruction of a Japanese city by the first atomic bomb used in war—but also suggested the imminent future in the aftermath of a possible World War III.

Traditional concepts of melody, harmony, and meter are absent in this work. Instead, Penderecki creates a sense of form by moving through several sections of diverse sounds. *Threnody* is written for 52 strings: 24 violins, 10 violas, 10 cellos, and 8 double basses. Each performer is given a unique part, often requiring the use of unusual performance techniques and notation (explained in the chart on the facing page). These distinctive timbres help to delineate five large sections, some of which overlap:

Section	Measure	Sounds
1	1	high pitched dissonant clusters
2	6	varied texture of multiple sound effects in rapid succession
3	10	sustained tones and quarter-tone clusters linked with glissandos
4	26	isolated pitches and various sound effects, in canon
5	56	unison sound effects and clusters that lead to the final climactic chord

The sound effects and sustained tone clusters in section 5 recall the sounds of sections 2 and 3, a relationship that is reinforced by parallel climaxes in measures 19 and 70. Based on this sense of return, it is possible to view the entire work as a modified ABA' structure, with the first three sections as the initial A.

Section 1 immediately establishes the mood of the work. Ten groups of four to six instruments enter in quick succession, alternating relatively high and low instruments. Each performer is instructed to play the highest note possible on the instrument; since the highest note differs from player to player, the result is intense high-pitch clusters that suggest screaming. Beginning in measure 2, the sound is varied through dynamic changes and the addition of two kinds of vibrato (variations in pitch)—one rapid, the other wide and slow.

Several unusual effects are featured in section 2. Penderecki requires seven different sounds, including striking the soundboard of the instrument with the hand or bow and bowing on the strings between the bridge and tailpiece (which produces very high but indeterminate notes on these short lengths of string). These sounds are arranged in four patterns, and the performers are instructed to choose one pattern and play it repeatedly as fast as possible, entering in imitative fashion by section (first cellos, then violas, violins, and contrabasses). The resultant effect has been likened to the sound of static from a shortwave radio.

In section 3, Penderecki divides the strings into the five groups of a traditional string orchestra. For the first time, sustained pitches are heard in the middle-to-lower registers, as the various groups swell with glissando effects between unisons and quarter-tone clusters. The score is written in a graphic notation that conveys the effect of a thickening and narrowing band of sound; the individual parts are shown in standard notation (with glissandos and the signs for quarter-tones). Two further variants of the clusters occur in this section. At measure 15, clusters in each group crescendo before dissolving with upward or downward glissandos. At measure 18, the clusters are formed as each successive instrument in a group enters on a note a quarter-tone higher or lower than is already sounding, and the sound crescendos into a climax at measure 19, before resolving to a solo cello in measure 23.

Section 4 presents the most complex passage of the composition. Penderecki divides the ensemble into three orchestras and initiates what can be analyzed as a three-part canon. Each orchestra has twelve independent parts playing a variety of sounds, pitches, and even rhythmic gestures with traditional notation. The entrance of Orchestra II at measure 38 is at the same pitch level as Orchestra I, but the registers are inverted. Orchestra I begins with a B♭ followed by two E♭s in the double-basses; at the entrance of Orchestra II, these pitches appear in the violins, with the other material similarly reversed. Orchestra III, which enters at measure 44, omits the first four measures of the material and transposes the remaining pitches either up a fourth or down a fifth. The material of all three orchestras begins to appear in retrograde with reverse registers after their seventeenth measure.

The final section begins at measure 56, as each of the three orchestras in succession turns to playing the sound effects from section 2, but now all at the same time. At measure 62, the first 12 violins, absent for section 4, return with a sustained quarter-tone cluster, supported by the lower strings bowing over their tail-pieces and bridges. Gradually returning to the five-part division of the strings, Penderecki soon has all groups playing sustained quarter-tone clusters with vibrato. At measure 70, the instruments converge, and each performer sounds a different pitch in a stunning pitch cluster of 52 quarter tones, played *fortississimo*. This remarkable chord is sustained for thirty seconds, gradually diminishing in volume as the players move from playing *sul ponticello* (over the bridge, producing a metallic sound) to *ordinario* (normal playing) to *sul tasto* (over the fingerboard for a rich, somewhat hollow sound). The chord then fades to nothing, bringing the piece to a silent and somber close.

For this work, Penderecki employed an effective notation (shown on page 1298) that communicates complex effects in relatively simple terms. He incorporated features of traditional notation to denote specific pitches and rhythms when needed. The standard symbol for glissandos, a diagonal line, is the basis for notating shifting tone clusters, which is readily understood by string players. To indicate specific quarter-tone pitches, Penderecki used variants of the symbols for sharps and flats, and for vibrato he simply added a wavy line. For some of the unusual performance techniques, such as playing behind the bridge, Penderecki developed images that can easily be linked to those effects. For example, a small arch suggests the bridge, and four lines represent the four strings. Professional performers would have little difficulty memorizing these symbols.

Since measure lengths in this work are defined in seconds rather than beats (except in section 4), the primary roles of the conductor are to keep time and give cues. Some conductors use a stopwatch in order to be as precise as possible, but others treat time more freely. The recording accompanying this anthology maintains a fairly strict time, but many performances are longer than the indicated eight minutes and twenty-six seconds. Indeed, one of the recordings with Penderecki himself conducting extends to nine minutes and forty-five seconds.

JOHN CAGE (1912–1992)

Music of Changes: Book I

Chance composition for piano

1951

Music of Changes was one of the first pieces in which John Cage explored the possibility of determining aspects of the music by chance operations. He composed the work in four sections he called "books." Book I, included here, was composed in May 1951 and premiered that August by pianist David Tudor at the University of Colorado in Boulder; the other three books were completed later that year, and Tudor premiered the entire work in New York in January 1952.

The form of the piece was designed in advance. Cage used forms based on duration, particularly what he sometimes called square-root form, in which the large-scale divisions of the work as a whole are reflected within each unit; for example, a simple version might have seven units of seven measures each. *Music of Changes* is far more complex, with a structure of durations based on a total of 29⅝ durational units, each 29⅝ measures long. Both the piece as a whole and each unit are divided into segments defined by the ratios 3–5–6¾–6¾–5–3⅛. Book I contains the first three units (measures 1–30, 31–60, and 61–90); in each, the last measure is only ⅝ as long as the others, for a total of 29⅝ measures. The divisions within each unit—of 3, 5, 6¾, 6¾, 5, and 3⅛ measures respectively—can be seen in the score, delineated by indications of tempo (see the tempo markings in the first unit, at measures 4, 9, 15, 22, and 27) and by changes of musical material and density.

Once Cage designed the durational structure, he filled it using chance operations. The title of the work refers to the ancient Chinese book *I-Ching* (Book of Changes), which contains a method for consulting an oracle by tossing coins six times to determine an answer from a list of sixty-four possible outcomes. For *Music of Changes*, Cage set up a series of charts, each with sixty-four elements that he chose using the same system. One chart determined how many events would occur during a particular segment; another determined the tempo (there were thirty-two tempos and thirty-two blanks, which if chosen maintained the previous tempo). Then there were eight charts each for sounds, dynamics (including accents), and durations. In the charts for sounds, half the possibilities were silences; the rest ranged from single notes to chords to "constellations" (several quick notes in a row) to noises (such as striking or slamming the lid of the keyboard). All these sounds were also designed in advance, so that only their selection for a particular position was determined by chance.

The result, as Cage noted, is a piece whose sequence of sounds is determined neither by the taste or psychology of the composer, nor by the traditions of past music. Neither the composer, the performer, nor the listener needs to make any value judgments, and no message is being communicated. The sounds are simply themselves, to be appreciated for their own sake.

The notation (in Cage's own distinctive handwriting) is unusual, but what the performer plays is completely determined. The "beat" set by the tempo is the quarter note, or one-fourth of a measure, shown by a line (2.5 centimeters long in the original score, here reduced). The notation is proportional: a note's place in time is shown precisely by its position in the measure, reading the length of the measure as an exact timeline. Diamond-shaped notes indicate keys (sometimes a single key, sometimes a range of keys, as at the beginning) that are depressed silently to raise the dampers, which are then kept off the strings by the sostenuto (sustain) pedal (marked with a dash-and-dot line under the notes), so that the strings resonate with harmonics generated by other notes. Other indications include using the damper pedal (marked with a solid line under the notes) and *una corda* pedal (which shifts the hammers to strike one instead of three strings for each note, marked with a dashed line, as in measures 33–34) and releasing a key to stop the tone (a plus above the note). Full of unusual techniques and rhythms, the piece is quite difficult to play, but the performer can take comfort from Cage's comment about this and other pieces generated by chance: "A 'mistake' is beside the point, for once anything happens it authentically is."

KAREL HUSA (B. 1921)

Music for Prague 1968: First movement, Introduction
and Fanfare, Adagio—Allegro

Concert band suite

1968

From Karel Husa, *Music for Prague 1968* (New York: Associated Music Publishers, 1969), 4–30. Copyright
© 1969 (Renewed) by Associated Music Publishers, Inc. (BMI). International copyright secured. All rights
reserved. Reprinted by permission of Associated Music Publishers, Inc. (BMI).

* † = quartertone higher(valid for the following note only).

39
Picc.
Fls. 1 2
Obs. 1 2
E. H.
Bns. 1 2
Cbn.
E♭ Cl.
B♭ Cls. 1 2 3
A. Cl.
B. Cl.
Cb. Cl.
A. Saxs. 1 2
T. Sax.
Bar. Sax.
B. Sax.
Tpts. 1 2 3 4
ff
Hns. 1 2 3 4
open
ff brassy
f
Tbns. 1 2 3
Bar. 1 2
Tuba
St. B.
Mar.
Vib.
Timp.
Perc.
Tam-t.
sm.
m.
l.
let vibrate

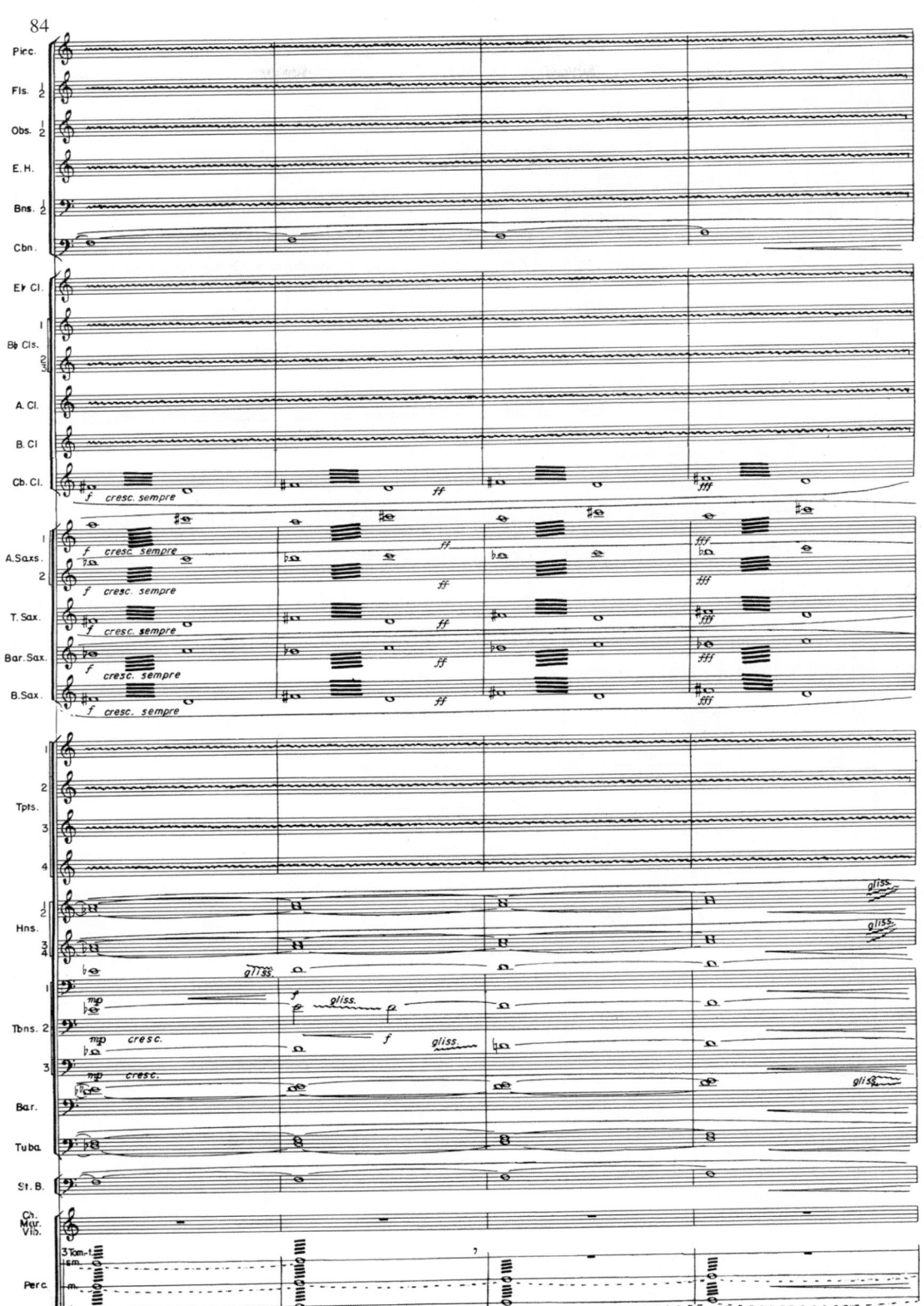

In the twentieth century, band conductors sought to develop a repertoire of music for band and for wind ensemble that attained the same seriousness and level of artistry as the masterpieces of orchestral music, going beyond the marches, medleys, arrangements, and solo display pieces traditionally played by bands. Over the century, a repertoire of classics for band developed, and one of its central pieces is Karel Husa's *Music for Prague 1968.* Commissioned by the Ithaca College Concert Band and composed during the summer and fall of 1968, the work was premiered on January 31, 1969, at the Music Educators National Conference in Washington, D.C., and has been performed over eight thousand times since then. In 1970, Husa rescored the piece for orchestra, and it has been played many times in that form as well.

Husa was born in Prague, Czechoslovakia (now in the Czech Republic), and educated there and in Paris. Stranded in France when the communists assumed power in his native country in 1948, he came to the United States to teach at Cornell University in 1954 and became a naturalized American citizen in 1959. He was inspired to write *Music for Prague 1968* by the events of August 1968, when Soviet tanks rolled into Prague to overthrow the liberal communist government of Alexander Dubček and reassert Soviet control. The piece is in four movements: Introduction and Fanfare; Aria; Interlude (for percussion alone); and Toccata and Chorale.

The central thematic idea of the piece is the first phrase from a fifteenth-century Czech chorale tune, previously used by Czech composer Bedřich Smetana in his tone poems *Tábor* and *Blaník,* the last two movements of *Má vlast* (My Country, ca. 1872–79). The chorale "You Who Are God's Warriors" was a song of the Hussites, followers of religious reformer Jan Hus (ca. 1369–1415), whose fortress at Tábor became a symbol of Czech resistance to outside oppression. Legend held that in times of need, the Hussite warriors would ride out of their hiding places to save the Czech nation. By using the chorale, Husa invoked the legend, surely appropriate during the crisis in 1968. But he also alluded to the first great Czech nationalist composer and to music almost every Czech would know.

In an apt metaphor for the gathering of the warriors, Smetana's *Tábor* develops the theme in fragments before stating it whole at the end, making it an early example of cumulative form (see Ives's *General William Booth,* NAWM 148). *Music for Prague 1968* is also in cumulative form, both as a four-movement work and in the first movement. The whole chorale phrase, shown in the example on the next page, appears only at the end of the last movement, having been developed over the course of the entire piece. In the first movement, the first two measures of the tune soar triumphantly in the brass near the end of the movement (measures 74–76), and reappear soon afterward in the timpani, now with the first three notes of the third measure as well (measures 90–94). The last few notes continue, unable to complete the phrase, as the music dwindles away, waiting for the finale to gather the complete band of warriors in full force.

At the beginning of the movement, the timpani softly presents fragments of the chorale: the first measure in the right rhythm (measure 1), but the second distorted intervallically, so that the rising whole step and falling major third (D–E–C) become a rising half step and falling whole tone (D–E♭–C♯), as shown in the example below. The timpani persists with these ideas throughout the slow introduction. Then at the start of the fanfare (measure 35), the trumpets take up the notes from the timpani to create a four-note idea (D–E♭–D♭–C), ultimately derived from the chorale. This motive becomes the main material for the fanfare, presented in retrograde, inverted, and permuted forms as well as in its original form. Development of this motive builds to the climactic presentation of the first two measures of the chorale. In the second movement, the fanfare motive (transposed) and its retrograde become segments of the twelve-tone row that underlies the entire movement. Meanwhile, the piccolo and flute solos that dominate the introduction of the first movement are suffused with ideas drawn from the chorale or the fanfare figure, and a three-chord motive (measures 3–4) that becomes important in this and later movements is also related to the fanfare figure. All these relationships are also shown in the example. Thus, most of the motivic material in the piece ultimately derives from the chorale theme, symbolizing the reliance of the Czech people on their historical traditions of resistance.

First phrase of chorale

Distorted from in timpani

Fanfare figure

Twelve-tone row (second movement)

fanfare figure   retrograde

Piccolo line and three–chord motive

2 Picc.   fanfare figure

pp

from chorale (intervals enlarged)   Cl., Fl., Hns.

combines   fanfare figure

inversion

In addition to using developing variation and twelve-tone procedures, Husa draws on other modern methods in some passages. Instruments often have contradictory dynamics, so that chords change as they sound (as at measures 3–4), and at times dynamics themselves become a virtual melody (see clarinet 1, measures 10–14). The brass use a variety of mutes to create different colors, and the alto saxophone plays quarter tones (measures 33–34). In order to achieve maximum density at the climax (measures 81–87), Husa uses indeterminate notation, instructing the winds to play notes "at random," fast, loud, and staccato, and the trumpets to repeat a note "freely and irregularly." The effect is overwhelming, and the passage is easier to perform than it would be if each note were written out.

Such a piece is as intricately worked out as an orchestral composition by Webern or Bartók (compare NAWM 144 and 147) and is a far cry from the light entertainment music that dominated the band repertoire before World War II. It also resembles orchestral music in offering a profound emotional experience that is appropriate to its program. From quiet stillness, the Adagio introduction slowly gathers force through dissonant chords and a slow development of ideas, then the Allegro fanfare builds layers and density to a visceral climax of rage and defiance before it gradually calms. Over the course of all four movements, Husa touches a wide range of emotions ranging from grief to exhilaration. The work ends with the chorale as a commitment that, however long it takes, the Czech people will be free.

JOHN ADAMS (B. 1947)

Phrygian Gates: Excerpt

For piano

1977–78

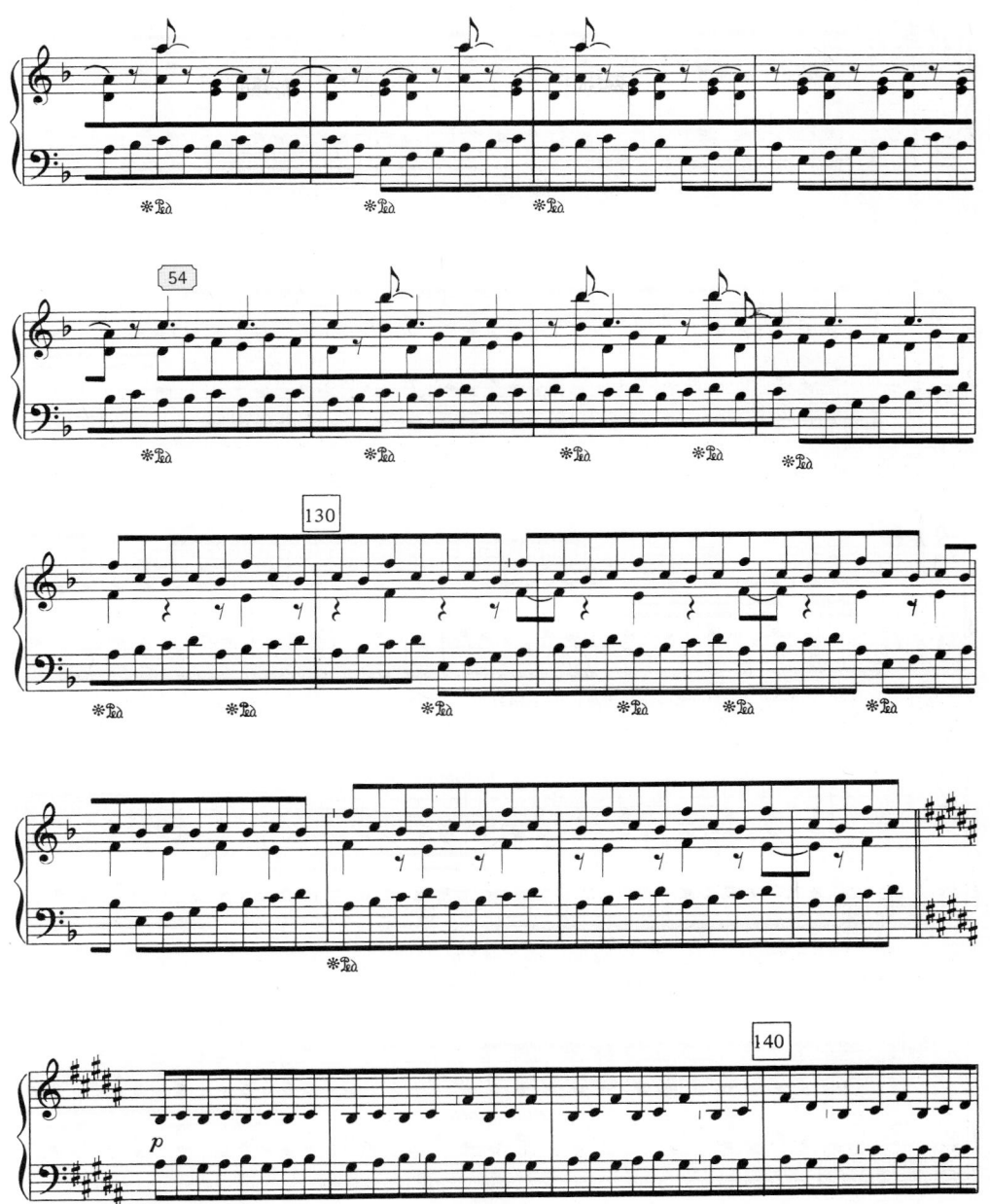

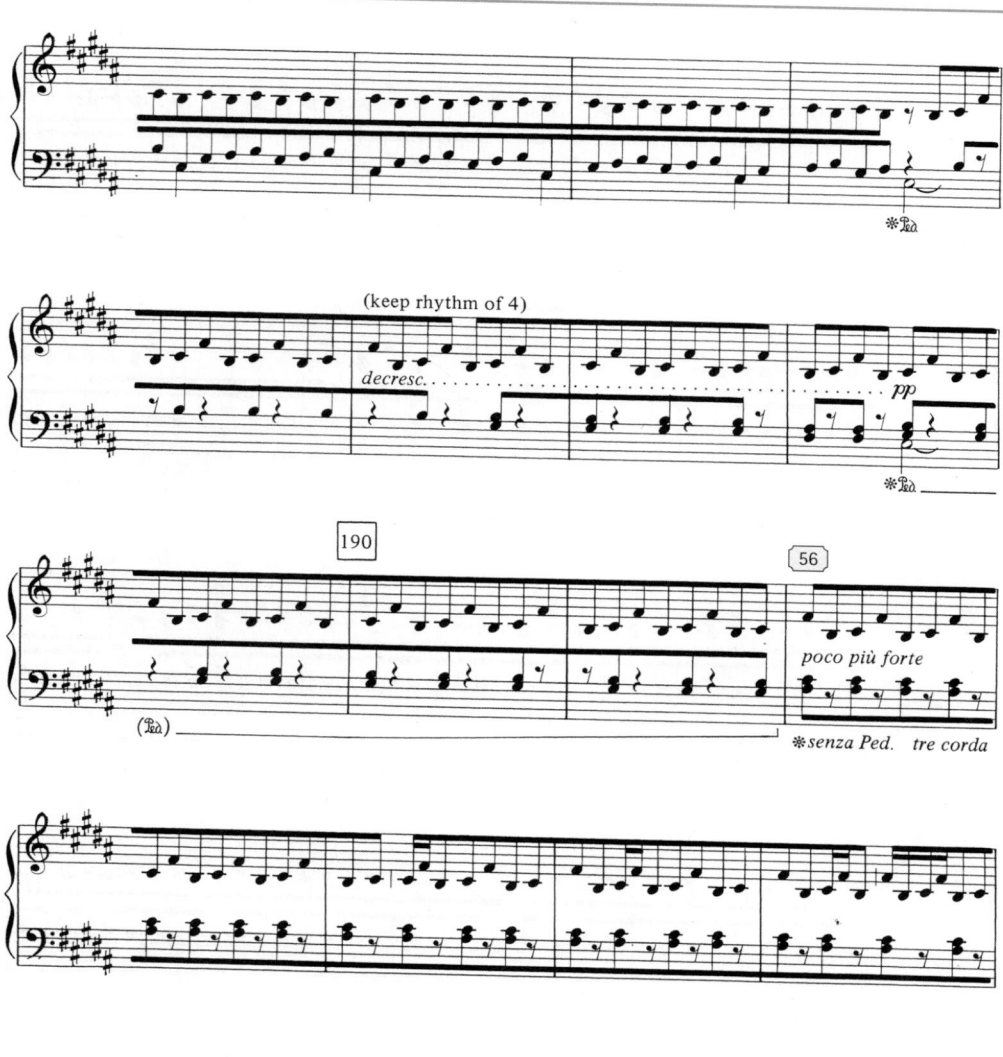

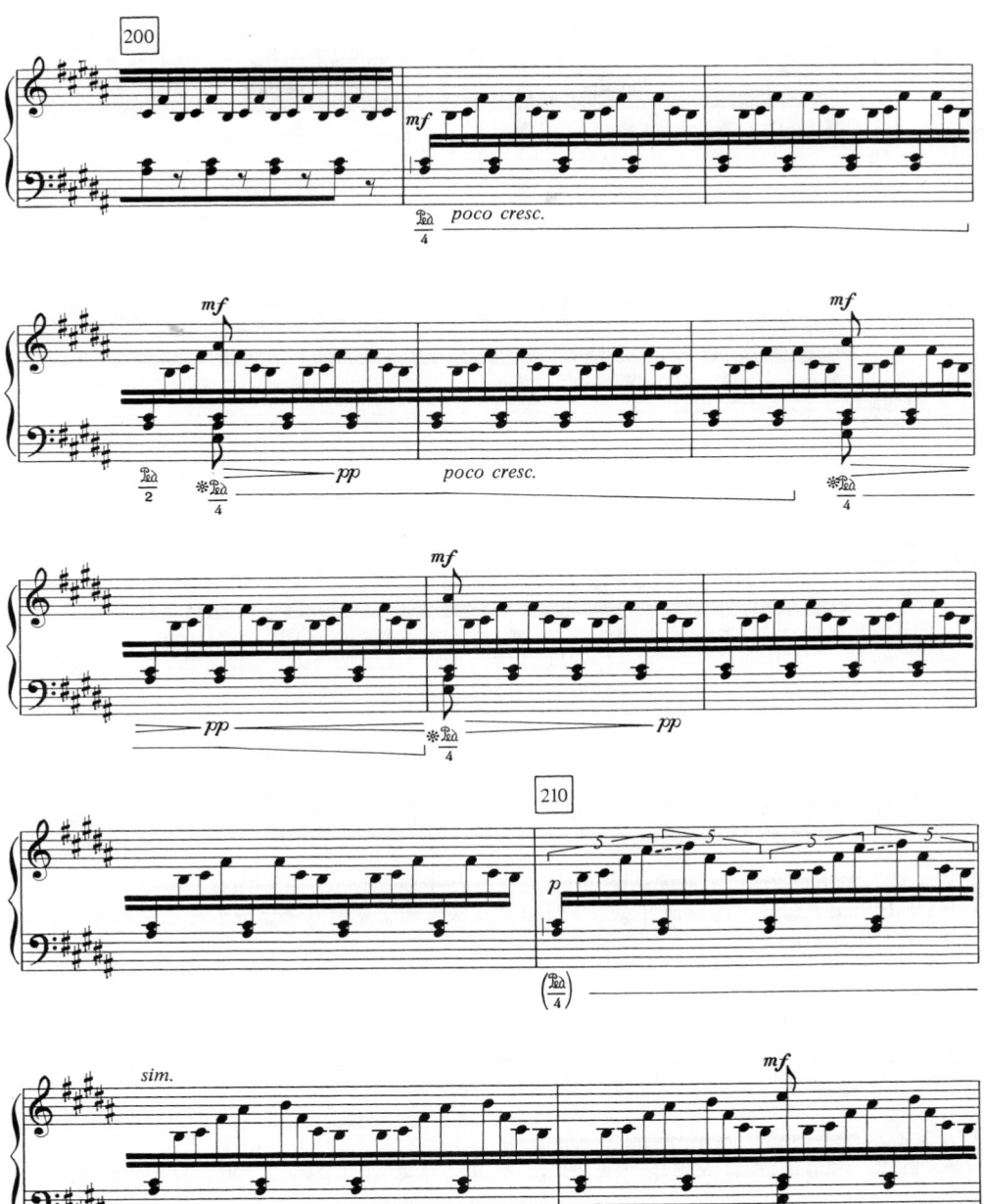

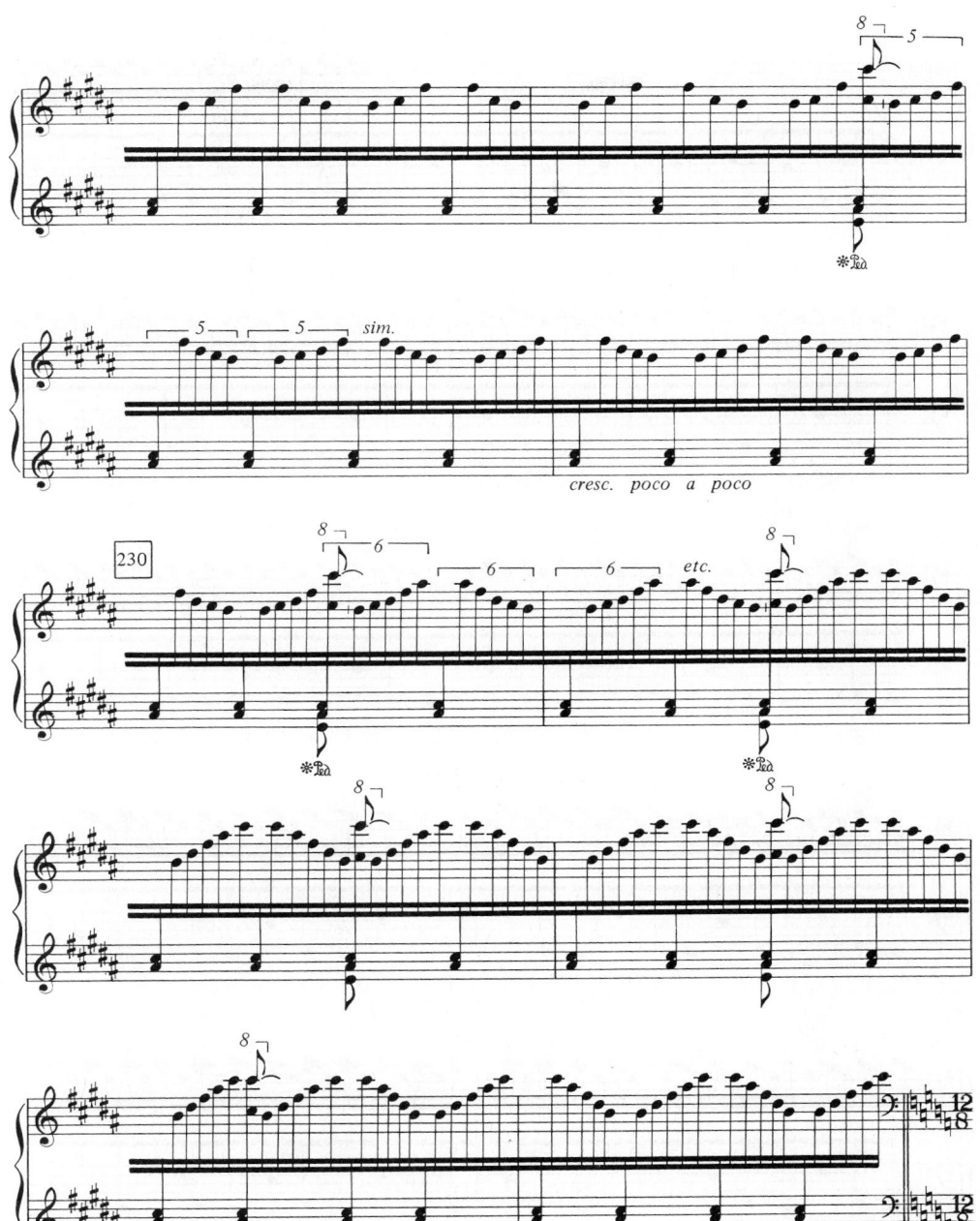

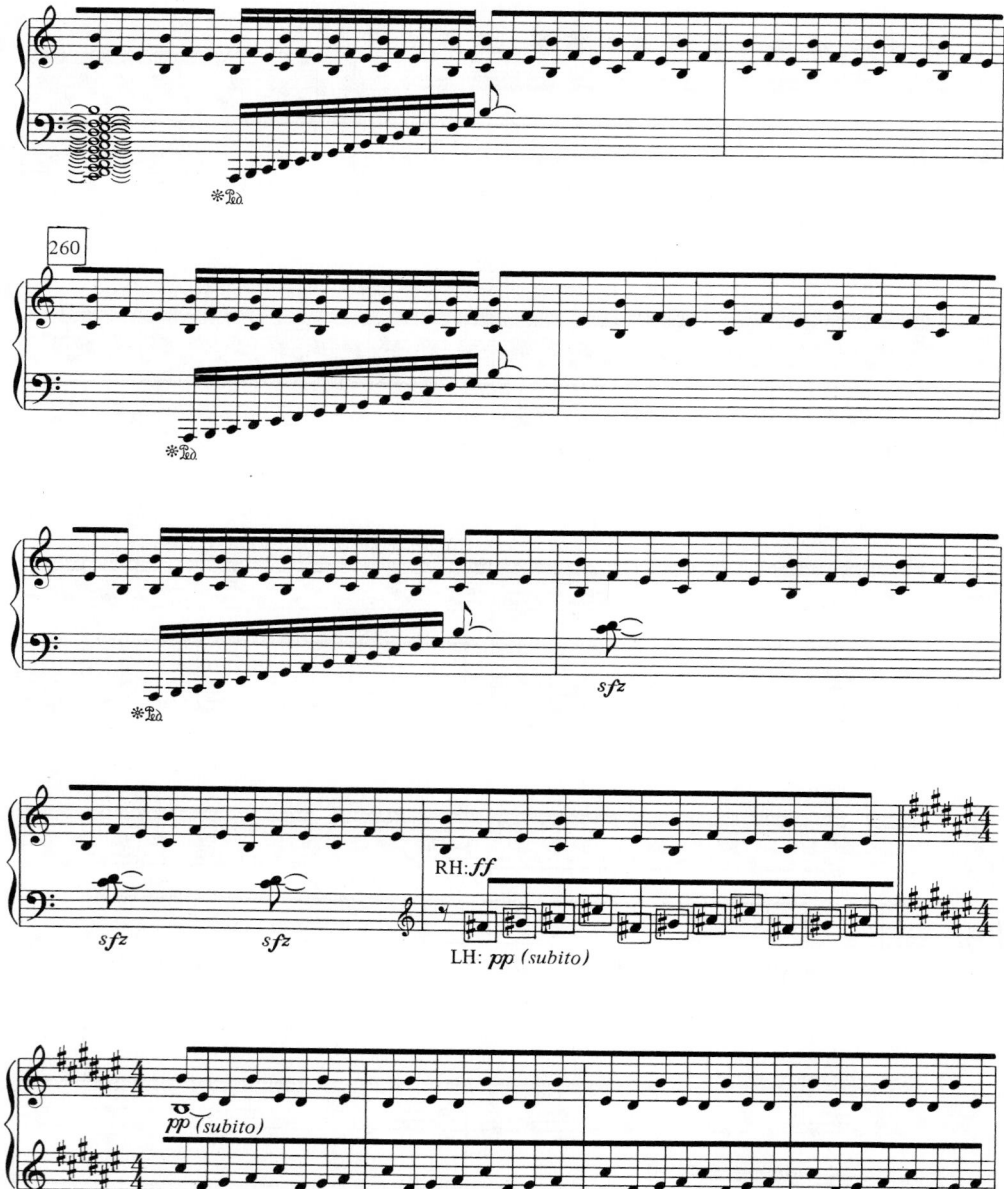

Inspired by the music of Steve Reich and Philip Glass, John Adams began to experiment with minimalism in the mid-1970s. His first major composition in this new language was *Phrygian Gates*, premiered by Mack McCray on March 17, 1978, at Hellman Hall in San Francisco. With this work, Adams began to define a distinctive new voice in the minimalist tradition. While adopting basic techniques of earlier minimalists, including constant pulsation and repetition of simple rhythmic and melodic material, he enriched the sound with more rapid changes, harmonic variety, and emotional surges. Along with several other composers, Adams helped transform minimalism from its origins as an avant-garde aesthetic into a style that appealed to a broad public.

Reflecting Adams's new fascination with minimalist techniques, this twenty-four-minute movement for solo piano relies almost entirely on rapid repetitive figuration or alternating chords. Because of the constant use of the damper pedal, the notes of each figuration blend into a single chord, so that the listener experiences a kaleidoscope of pandiatonic harmonies. At some points Adams calls for the pedal to be pressed only halfway (as at measure 57) or a quarter of the normal amount (measure 85) to produce different levels of blurring. The only contrast to these waves of motion is a middle section entitled "A System of Weights and Measures" (measures 640–808), which consists of changing sustained chords.

During the movement, the pitch content undergoes a number of changes from one diatonic collection to another (the first occurs at measure 114). Adams calls the points of change "gates," a term borrowed from electronic music, referring to switches that regulate the flow of electrical current. Moving through the circle of fifths, Adams explores seven tonal centers: A, E, B, F♯, C♯, G♯, and D♯. These pitch centers correspond to the notes of the A Lydian mode, which is also the first pitch collection in the piece. For each tonal center, Adams begins with the pitch content of the Lydian mode on that note and then changes to the Phrygian mode. There is no modulation, just abrupt and often dramatic changes of modes. These changes give the work its title.

The excerpt included here (measures 1–269) features five distinct pitch areas separated by four gates. The pitch content of each area is as follows:

Measures	Mode	Pitches
1–113	A Lydian	A B C♯ D♯ E F♯ G♯
114–136	A Phrygian	A B♭ C D E F G
137–235	E Lydian	E F♯ G♯ A♯ B C♯ D♯
236–265	E Phrygian	E F G A B C D
266–333	B Lydian	B C♯ D♯ E♯ F♯ G♯ A♯

As evident from the measure numbers, Adams gives more time to the Lydian sections initially. However, as the movement progresses, he reverses the proportions, and the Phrygian sections gradually become dominant. Throughout the work Adams changes dynamics, registers, figurations, and harmony to articulate structural points and to heighten the emotional impact. For Adams, the Lydian and Phrygian modes not only provide pitch content, but also suggest moods based on their roles in the music of ancient Greece, where Lydian was seen as light and sensual, and Phrygian as volatile and unstable. (Of course, the Lydian and Phrygian scales Adams used are those of Western medieval and Renaissance music, which are not the same as the Lydian and Phrygian scales of ancient Greece; see HWM, pp. 18–20.)

The opening A Lydian and A Phrygian sections establish Adams's distinctive approach. The movement begins with repetitions of E, the only pitch other than A that is common to A Lydian and A Phrygian and the only pitch present in all of the first four tonal areas. During the opening section, Adams gradually adds the pitches of the A Lydian mode, saving A for last (measure 57). Newly added notes are readily audible to the listener and often highlighted in the notation. A few B♭s appear in measures 63–64 and 71–73, set off in boxes, foreshadowing the mode change to come. At the first gate (measure 114), the pitch content changes to A Phrygian, and all seven notes of the new mode are heard within the first three beats. The arrival of the first gate coincides with a *forte* dynamic marking, the culmination of a gradual increase in dynamics since measure 1.

The E Lydian and E Phrygian sections are given a similar dynamic contour. The E Lydian section begins with a drop in dynamics to *piano* (measure 137), and the dynamics eventually crescendo to *fff* at the arrival of the third gate (measure 236). The drama of this moment is further enhanced by a sudden shift to the lower registers. Other changes, some subtle and some pronounced, appear during this portion of the work. Syncopations enliven the sound after measure 150. Sixteenth notes are introduced in measure 194, and rhythmic values continue to speed up, leading to measure 210 with twenty notes and measure 231 with twenty-four. The number of different pitches sounding in a measure also gradually increases. At measure 236, just after the third gate, there are only five pitches (counting notes in different octaves as different pitches); by measure 255, there are twenty-two.

One critic, observing the frequency of change and the variety of sounds in Adams's works, described him as "a minimalist bored with minimalism." *Phrygian Gates* supports this view, with the ever-increasing activity culminating in the coda, where the final two modes alternate in a rapid fashion. Adams has likened the overall sound of this piece to that of the rippling of waveforms (some waves are tranquil and others violent, as in a white-water expedition). He treats each hand in a wave-like manner that coordinates with the movement of the other. One of the challenges facing a performer is maintaining evenness between the two hands and among the individual pitches. A performance of this work takes considerable physical endurance, an ability to sustain long arches of sound, and a wide range of musical expression.

ELLEN TAAFFE ZWILICH (B. 1939)

Symphony No. 1: First movement

Symphony

1982

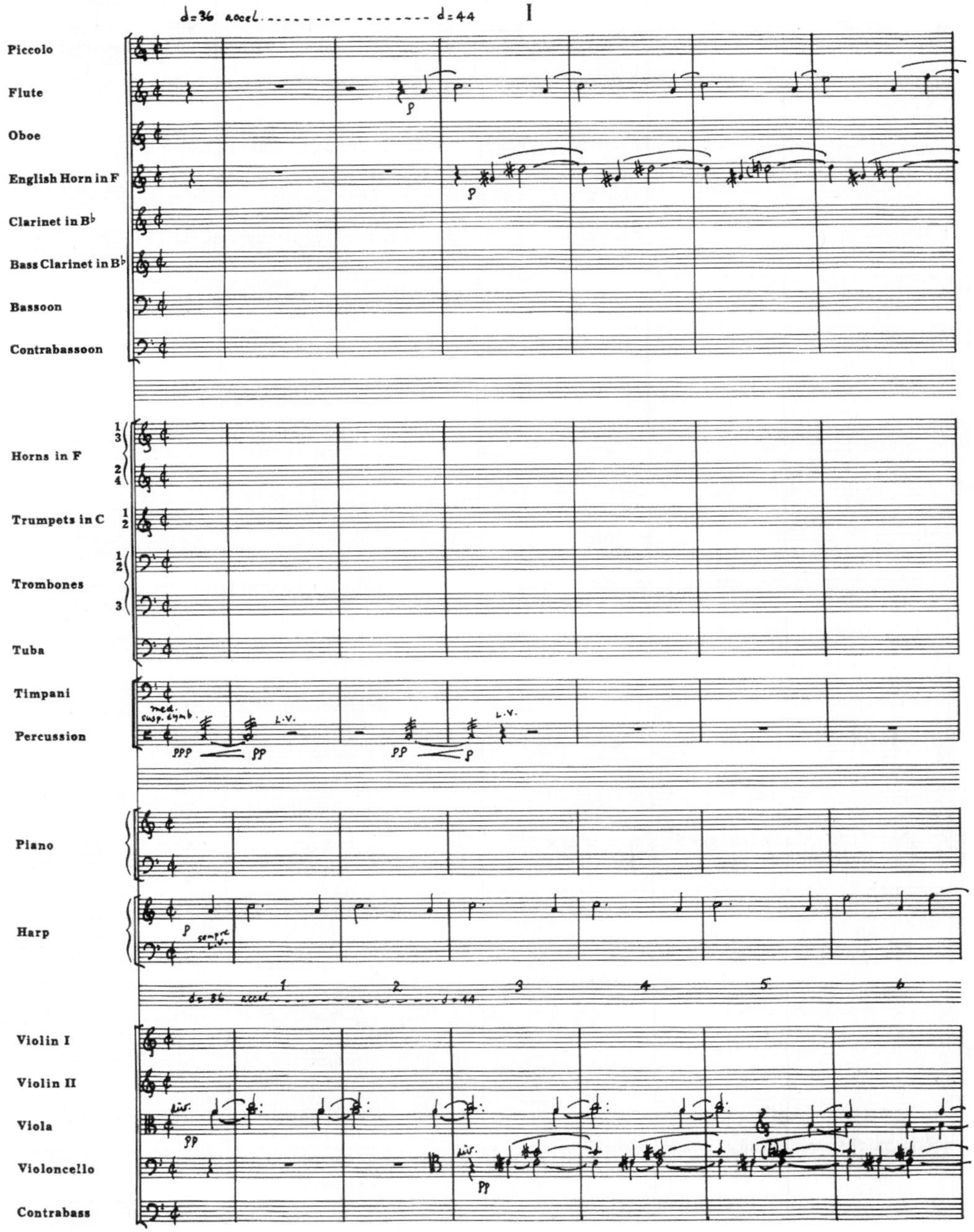

From Ellen Taaffe Zwilich, *Symphony No. 1 (Three Movements for Orchestra)* (Newton, Mass.: Margun Music, 1983), 3–51.

* arpeggio always before the beat, highest note on the beat

Ellen Taaffe Zwilich's Symphony No. 1 (originally titled *Three Movements for Orchestra*) was commissioned by the American Composers Orchestra and the National Endowment for the Arts and also supported by the Guggenheim Foundation. It was premiered at Lincoln Center in New York on May 5, 1982, by the American Composers Orchestra, conducted by Gunther Schuller. The work was well received by the audience and praised by reviewers, and the following year it earned Zwilich the Pulitzer Prize in Music, the first ever awarded to a woman.

Almost all the material in the first movement evolves from the opening fifteen measures, in a process of *developing variation.* The term was coined by Arnold Schoenberg more than fifty years earlier to describe procedures of constant development he found in Bach and Brahms and adopted in his own music. Zwilich's work descends from the same tradition. Yet where Schoenberg used complex ideas and developed them rapidly, Zwilich uses relatively simple elements, develops them gradually, and repeats material more often than Schoenberg does, making her music easier to follow. Although the piece is not tonal in a traditional sense, it uses familiar harmonic materials, including tonal centers, prominent thirds and fifths, and occasional triads. Zwilich frequently uses gestures reminiscent of the expressive sweep of Romantic symphonies. Certain moments, such as the E-major triad and passionate melody at measure 13, sound almost like Mahler.

The piece opens with a threefold rising minor third, *a'–c'*, played *accelerando* (with gradually increasing tempo). This motive establishes A as the tonal center for the movement. The third is answered by a rising fifth, *c♯'–g♯'*, introducing notes that both form 014 sets with the initial third (G♯–A–C, and A–C–C♯). This set, containing both a minor and a major third as well as a half step, becomes the central material for the movement, appearing in a variety of guises. One such guise, combining two overlapping 014 sets, is the motive C–E♭–B–D, which appears at measures 8–11 in the winds. (The C–E♭ is in English horn and clarinet, both of which are transposing instruments, whose parts are notated respectively a fifth higher and a whole step higher than they sound.) Other melodies derived from 014 sets appear in the violins at measures 9–10 (*g–(a)–b♭–b♭'–g♯*) and at measures 13–14 (*b'''–c'''–b''–e♭'''–c'''–d'''–c♯''*). Thus, each of the principal ideas in the movement can trace its ancestry back to the opening gestures, giving the music coherence at the same time it embraces constant change. All these ideas recur throughout the movement, in new variations; the last melody, for instance, impassioned when first heard, reappears in a calm and contemplative mood near the end, transposed and slower in the cellos (measures 227–33).

The opening motto is heard several times in the first section, each time associated with an accelerando, as the tempo gradually increases. This process leads to the central part of the movement, an Allegro (measure 78). Its theme begins *a–c'–c♯''*, another instance of the 014 set, and secondary ideas introduced at measures 100 and 114 also draw on the set. The Allegro builds to a climax at measures 128–31, then subsides to a pause, and material returns in a new order (compare measures 143–93 to measures 99–123, 78–85, 110–15, and 92–98). The final section (measures 199–243) returns to a slow tempo and to ideas from the first section, now in a much sparser texture, and gradually calms to a close.

ARVO PÄRT (B. 1935)

Seven Magnificat Antiphons: Excerpts

Choral antiphons

1988, REVISED 1991

(a) No. 1: *O Weisheit*

CD 12|65

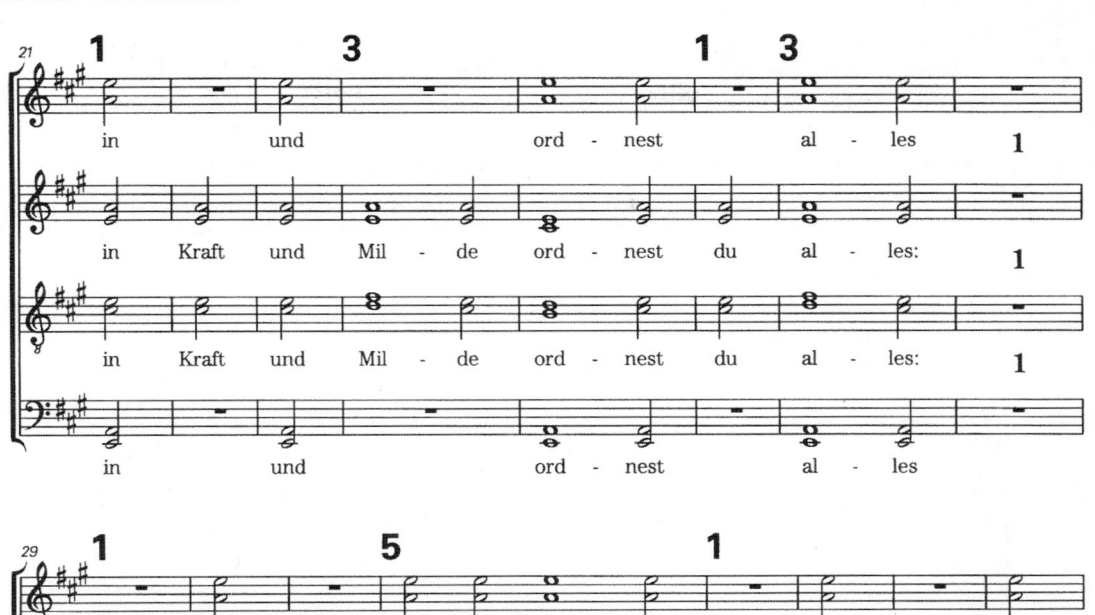

O Weisheit, hervorgegangen aus dem
    Munde des Höchsten,
die Welt umspannst du von einem Ende
    zum andern,
in Kraft und Milde ordnest du alles:

o komm und offenbare uns den Weg der
    Weisheit und der Einsicht.

O Wisdom, sprung forth from the mouth
    of the most high,
you embrace the world from one end to
    the other,
in strength and mildness you put
    everything in order;
O come and reveal to us the way of
    wisdom and understanding.

(b) No. 6: *O König aller Völker*

O König aller Völker,
ihre Erwartung end Sehnsucht,
Schlußstein, der den Bau zusammenhält:

o komm und errette den Menschen, den
  du aus Erde gebildet!

O king of all peoples,
their expectation and longing;
keystone, which holds the building
  together:

O come and redeem mankind, whom
  you have fashioned out of clay!

Arvo Pärt left his native Estonia (then a constituent republic of the Soviet Union) in 1980 and settled in Berlin, seeking greater international opportunities. In 1988, he wrote *Seven Magnificat Antiphons*, his first major choral work in German, the language of his adoptive country. The texts are translations of the Latin antiphons that are sung just before and after the Magnificat in Vespers services on the seven evenings immediately preceding Christmas Eve. These seven antiphons, one for each evening's service, are known as the "O Antiphons" because they all begin with the exclamation "O" and conclude with a line beginning "O come," appropriate for the season of Advent. The work is dedicated to the RIAS-Kammerchor, the chamber choir of RIAS (Radio in the American Sector).

The *Magnificat Antiphons* exemplify Pärt's distinctive *tintinnabuli* style (named after the Latin word for ringing bells), which he devised in the mid-1970s after studying Gregorian chant and early polyphony. In this technique, one voice presents a diatonic melody that generally moves by step around a central pitch, and the other voices sound notes of the tonic triad that are determined by a preset system. The two movements included here demonstrate different ways of applying this simple method.

The text of *O Weisheit* is set syllabically and homophonically. Measure lines are used to indicate lengths of individual words but do not suggest a meter. One-syllable words are set with half notes, but longer words are set with a whole note on the syllable that receives the greatest stress. Throughout, the soprano and bass sing every other word, regardless of syllable lengths or declamation, and a three-beat measure of rests follows every comma.

The principal melody appears in the tenor, where it is doubled in parallel thirds. The tenors reiterate a C♯ and E for each half note, and alternate moving up and down a step for whole notes. The entire melodic range remains within the span of a third. The other voices of the ensemble derive their pitches from the A-major triad. The bass and soprano lines are limited to E and A, arranged as a perfect fourth or fifth. The repetition of these open harmonies at irregular intervals suggests the ringing of a bell. The upper and lower alto lines sing the two pitches from the A-major triad that are higher than and closest to the notes of the comparable tenor lines. For the most part, the altos remain on *e'* and *a'*, but when the tenors descend to *b* and *d'*, the altos move down to a *c♯'* and *e'*.

As a result of this simple construction, the movement has only six different harmonies; the tenors and altos sound a first-inversion A-major triad on each half note and alternate two four-note dissonant diatonic sonorities on the whole notes, and each of these three chords may either sound alone or be accompanied by the notes in the bass and soprano. This simplicity, coupled with the sustained quiet dynamics, effectively supports the antiphon's plea for wisdom and understanding. The movement recalls the recitation of prayers in Gregorian chant and the sonorities of early polyphony. In the process, Pärt also foreshadows the principal tonal centers of the work as a whole. The first two chords contain all the pitches that will serve as tonal centers for the seven movements: A–F♯–C♯–A–E–D–A.

O König aller Völker employs tintinnabuli techniques in a different manner. The texture is divided into three distinct parts. The sopranos sing with half notes and whole notes, following a pattern similar to that observed in *O Weisheit*, although some single-syllable words at the beginning of phrases receive whole notes. The tenors and basses sing the same rhythmic values as the sopranos, but in diminution. The third line is provided by the altos, who chant independently on D in quarter notes.

The principal melody is sung by the second tenor and the second soprano in a canon in augmentation. As in *O Weisheit*, the melody moves primarily by step within a limited range. The other voices draw their pitches from the D-minor triad in a predetermined manner. The first soprano always sings the pitch from the D-minor triad that is above and closest to the note of the second soprano. The bass and first tenor are given pitches that are second closest to those of the second tenor, respectively below and above it. In the first measure, for example, the second tenor and second soprano are on A. The closest higher pitch to A in the D-minor triad is D, which is sung by the first soprano. The second closest higher pitch is an F, heard in the first tenor. The second closest pitch below A in the D-minor triad is D, which is given to the bass.

In *O König aller Völker*, because of the shifting relationship between the voices, harmonies are more varied than in *O Weisheit*, dissonances are more prevalent, and there are no rests in all voices at once—a note is always sounding in at least one voice. The recited D in the alto line also builds in intensity. Initially, it echoes the text as presented in the lower voices, but as the dynamics climb, the alto line pushes forward so that it must repeat the line "o komm und errette den Menschen" (O come and redeem mankind) twice before the work comes to a dramatic fortissimo close.

The utmost simplicity of Pärt's music makes it rewarding and approachable for choirs and audiences alike, yet the frequent small changes maintain interest. The rhythmic complexities of *O König aller Völker* present some challenges to performers. Traditional beating patterns from the conductor cannot be applied, since there are three different rhythmic notations in the score. The unifying factor in these lines is the beat, indicated as a quarter note.

Sofia Gubaidulina (b. 1931)

Rejoice! Sonata for Violin and Violoncello: Fifth movement, *Listen to the still small voice within*

171

Sonata

1981

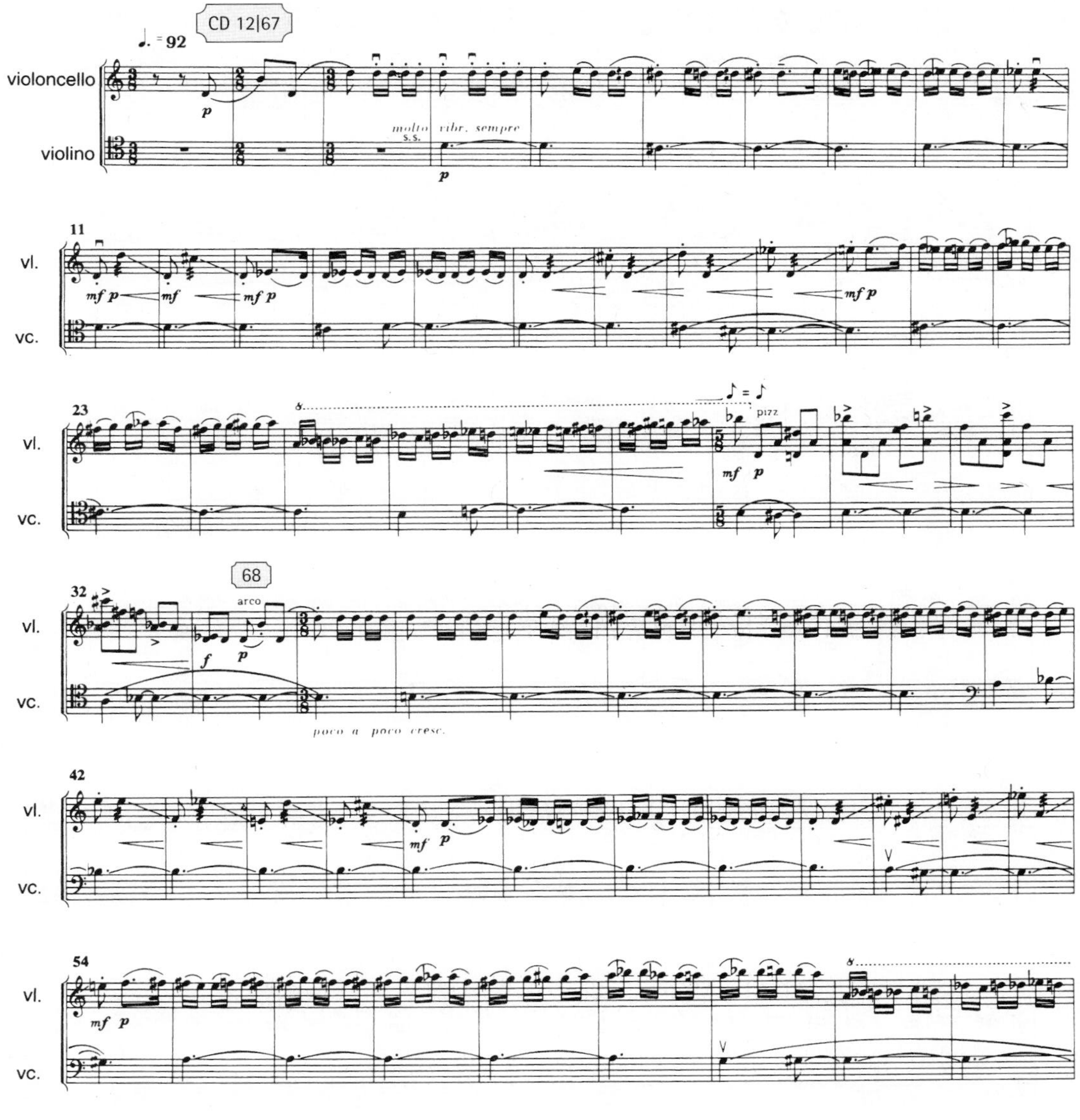

Sofia Gubaidulina was born in the Tatar Republic, an autonomous region in central Russia, four hundred miles east of Moscow. Her childhood there, together with her combined Tatar, Russian, Polish, and Jewish heritage, led to a profound interest in blending sounds and influences. As she once said, "I am the place where East and West meet." Her sensitivity to sound is reflected in *Rejoice!*, a duo sonata for violin and cello that is a study in chromaticism, glissandos, tremolos, and harmonics. The piece also reflects her interest in spirituality, which put her at odds with the Soviet authorities. Like many of her works, this sonata was first performed outside the Soviet Union; it was premiered in Kuhmo, Finland, in 1988, seven years after she composed it. The quotations heading the movements are from the spiritual lessons of the Ukrainian philosopher Grigory Skovoroda (1722–1794).

In the fifth movement, *Listen to the still small voice within*, Gubaidulina introduces a sequence of gestures, then offers three variations on the same series of ideas. There are four principal motives in the violin: a leaping and pulsing figure, A (measures 1–5); a neighbor-note figure, B (measures 5–10); a tremolo glissando, C (measures 10–13); and a pizzicato jumping figure, D (measures 29–33). All of them suggest a tonal center on the note D, which is often the lowest or most frequently repeated note in the phrase. The cello, playing with intense vibrato throughout, traces a slowly moving, mostly chromatic line that gradually winds down two octaves from *d'* to *D* over the course of the piece, confirming D as the tonal center.

Figure A remains essentially the same at each appearance, serving to introduce each main section (at measures 1, 33, 70, and 122). Figure D undergoes extension but is also otherwise unchanged, closing off each section but the last. But figures B and C are constantly changing. In the first section, B appears in three variants—in the upper octave (measures 5–10), in the lower octave (measures 13–16), and climbing into the stratosphere (measures 20–28)—and C in two, either falling (measures 10–13) or rising (measures 16–20). Neither ever returns in exactly the same form. In the second section, B is lengthened at each occurrence, and in later sections it ranges widely, adding large leaps alongside its original stepwise motion (see at measures 93–104 and 151–74). C is transformed even more radically, as the glissandos morph into diatonic scales (measures 80–93), arpeggios (measures 104–7, 134–38, and 142–46), and rising and falling waves of glissandos (175–81).

Near the end, soon after the cello descends to *D♯*, its lowest note so far, the violin soars up to *c♯''''*, where it becomes transfixed (measure 194). The cello finally finds its voice, moving around chromatically and then rising repeatedly in a glissando from low *E♭* to a natural harmonic on the C string. Gubaidulina commented about this sonata that the transition from normal sound to harmonics was a metaphor for transfiguration, a "transition to another plane of existence," representing both the "voice within" of the movement's title and the emerging joy suggested by the title of the entire sonata. After the cello touches its low D *col legno* (with the wood of the bow), the piece ends with high natural harmonics in both instruments, sounding an inverted F♯-major triad.

Most of the notation is traditional, but at the end several new signs are used. The notation for the violin in measure 198—featuring stems without noteheads and beams that are not parallel, but gradually merge together—is used to indicate that the player repeats the same note while gradually slowing down from sixteenth notes to eighths (and even slower, as signaled by the widening distance between the stems). The wavy beams in measures 206 and 219 indicate wide vibrato, a fast rocking of the finger against the fingerboard that changes the pitch slightly. Measure 219 calls for each player to repeat a pattern, without coordinating it with the other player, for about ten seconds, until both performers stop at the same time.

BRIGHT SHENG (B. 1955)

Seven Tunes Heard in China: No. 1, *Seasons*

For solo cello

1955

Bright Sheng was born in Shanghai, China, and worked in the Qinghai province near Tibet for seven years during the Cultural Revolution (1966–76), China's repressive mass mobilization, when young intellectuals were exiled to rural areas to work beside and be "reeducated" by the peasants. When the universities finally reopened in 1978, Sheng was one of the first music students accepted at the Shanghai Conservatory, and four years later he came to the United States. Conversant in both Chinese traditional music and Western classical music, he has synthesized the two traditions in many works. His *Seven Tunes Heard in China* for solo cello was commissioned by the Pacific Symphony on behalf of a patron, George Cheng, and was dedicated to his wife, Arlene Cheng. Sheng wrote the piece for cellist Yo-Yo Ma, who premiered it at Cheng Hall at the University of California, Irvine, in 1995.

In this suite, Sheng combines features of the Bach cello suites, including dancelike rhythms, double stops, motivic repetition, sequences, and simulated polyphony, with the character and style of Chinese music. Each of the seven movements presents a melody Sheng heard in a different province in China, and the ornamentation, glissandos, and free treatment of meter suggest a Chinese performance style. During the course of the suite, the cello imitates the sounds of several Chinese string, wind, and percussion instruments, including the two-stringed bowed *erhu* and the plucked *qin*.

The first movement, *Seasons*, freely treats a melody from the Qinghai province. The tune contains several short melodic ideas that are highly rhythmic, suggesting the playful nature of the song text:

> Spring is coming,
> Narcissi are blooming,
> The maiden is out from her boudoir seeking,
> My love boy, lend me a hand, please.

The opening three measures establish A as the initial tonal center and present two of the recurring motives—the rising fourths followed by descending motion in measure 1 and the repeated pentatonic idea in measures 2–3. The next three measures complete the principal theme, rising to a high vibrato note followed by two mostly pentatonic phrases, and closing with a scalar descent. The remainder of the movement develops these motives.

Numerous characteristics of Chinese music appear in the melody, including quick ornamental turns, slides between pitches, and long held notes that crescendo with an intense vibrato (measures 4 and 16). Yet Sheng also develops motivic ideas in a traditional Western manner. In measures 7–11, the repeated motive with its alternating registers and double stops suggests two-part imitative counterpoint in the manner of J. S. Bach, culminating in a cadence on A in measure 12. The tonal center starts to wander with a move to E♭ in measure 13, and simulated imitation in measures 14–15 suggests polytonality, as motivic statements alternate centers on B♭ and E (measures 14–15). A varied statement of the second phrase of the theme, transposed up a fifth (beginning in the last beat of measure 15), leads to more quasi-polytonal alternations that highlight tritone transpositions between E and B♭ (measures 17–20 and 23–26) and A and E♭ (measures 21–22). The movement comes to a quiet close on an E♭, a tritone away from the tonal center at the beginning.

A performance of this work requires experience with both Western and Asian music. Yo-Yo Ma, heard on the accompanying recording, is ideally suited to these needs, combining mastery of the Bach cello suites with understanding of Chinese instruments and performance manners. He also edited the published score of the work. Indications of fingerings are not abundant, but his suggestion that the first measure should be played primarily with one finger establishes a technique that can be applied to the entire movement.

INSTRUMENT NAMES AND ABBREVIATIONS

The following tables set forth the English, Italian, German, and French names used for the various musical instruments in these scores, and their respective abbreviations.

WOODWINDS

English	*Italian*	*German*	*French*
Piccolo (Picc.)	Flauto piccolo (Fl. Picc.); Ottavino (Ott.)	Kleine Flöte (kl. Fl.)	Petite flûte
Flute (Fl.)	Flauto (Fl.), pl. Flauti; Flauto grande (Fl. gr.)	Flöte (Fl.), pl. Flöten; Große Flöte (gr. Fl.)	Flûte (Fl.)
Alto flute	Flauto alto (Fl. alto); Flauto contralto (fl.c-alto)	Altflöte	Flûte en sol
Oboe (Ob.)	Oboe (Ob.)	Hoboe (Hb.); Oboe (Ob.), pl. Oboen	Hautbois (Hb.)
English horn (E.H.)	Corno inglese (C. ing., Cor. ingl., C.i.)	Englisches Horn (engl. Horn)	Cor anglais (C.A.)
Sopranino clarinet	Clarinetto piccolo (clar. picc.)		
Clarinet (C., Cl., Clt., Clar.)	Clarinetto (Cl., Clar.), pl. Clarinetti	Klarinette (Kl., Klar.), pl. Klarinetten; Clarinette (Cl.)	Clarinette (Cl.)
Alto clarinet (A. Cl.)			
Bass clarinet (B. Cl.)	Clarinetto basso (Cl. b., Cl. bas., Cl. basso, Clar. basso)	Bass Klarinette (Bkl.), Bassclarinette (Basscl.)	Clarinette basse (Cl. bs.)
Contrabass clarinet (Cb. Cl.)			
Saxophone (Sax.) [alto, tenor, baritone, bass]	Sassofone	Saxophon	Saxophone
Bassoon (Bsn., Bssn.)	Fagotto (Fag., Fg.), pl. Fagotti	Fagott (Fag., Fg.), pl. Fagotte	Basson (Bssn., Bon.)
Contrabassoon (C. Bsn.); Double bassoon (D. Bsn.)	Contrafagotto (Cfg., C. Fag., Cont. F.)	Kontrafagott (Kfg.)	Contrebasson (C. bssn.)

BRASS

English	Italian	German	French
Horn, French horn (Hr., Hn.)	Corno (Cor., C., Cr.), pl. Corni	Horn (Hr.), pl. Hörner (Hrn.)	Cor; Cor à pistons
Trumpet (Tpt., Trpt., Trp., Tr.)	Tromba (Tr., Trb.), pl. Trombe (Trbe., Tbe.); Clarino, pl. Clarini	Trompete (Tr., Trp., Tromp.), pl. Trompeten	Trompette (Tr.)
Piccolo trumpet	Tromba piccola (Tr. picc.)		
Bass trumpet	Tromba bassa (Tr. bas.)		
Cornet	Cornetta	Kornett	Cornet à pistons (C. à p., Pist.)
Trombone (Tr., Tbe., Trb., Trm., Trbe.) [alto, tenor, bass]	Trombone (Trbn.), pl. Tromboni (Tbni., Trbni., Trni.)	Posaune (Ps., Pos.), pl. Posaunen	Trombone (Tr.)
Contrabass trombone	Cimbasso (Cimb.)		
Baritone horn (Baritone, Bar.)			
Tenor tuba		Tenortuba	
Tuba (Tb.)	Tuba (Tb., Tba.)	Tuba (Tb.); Basstuba (Btb.)	Tuba (Tb.)

STRINGS

English	Italian	German	French
Violin (V., Vl., Vn., Vln., Vi.)	Violino (V., Vl., Vn., Vln., Viol.), pl. Violini (Vni.); Viola da braccio	Violine (V., Vl., Vln., Viol.), pl. Violinen; Geige (Gg.), pl. Geigen	Violon (V., Vl., Vln., Von.)
Viola (Va., Vl., pl. Vas.)	Viola (Va., Vla., Vl.) pl. Viole (Vle.)	Bratsche (Br.), pl. Bratschen	Alto (A., Alt.)
Violoncello, Cello (Vcl., Vc.)	Violoncello (Vc., Vcl., Vcll., Vcllo.), pl. Violoncelli	Violoncell (Vc., Vcl.), pl. Violoncelli	Violoncelle (Vc., Velle., Vcelle.)
Double bass (D. Bs.); String bass; Bass viol	Contrabasso (Cb., C. B.), pl. Contrabassi or Bassi (C. Bassi, Bi.); Violon, violone [may also designate or include cello or bass viola da gamba]	Kontrabass (Kb.), pl. Kontrabässe; Bass	Contrebasse (C. B.)
Viola da gamba; Viol; Gamba	Viola da gamba	Gambe	Viole

PERCUSSION

English	Italian	German	French
Percussion (Perc.)	Percussione	Schlagzeug (Schlag.)	Batterie (Batt.)
Timpani (Timp.); Kettledrums (K. D.)	Timpani (Timp., Tp.)	Pauken (Pk.)	Timbales (Timb.)
Snare drum (S. D., Sn. Dr.)	Tamburo piccolo (Tamb. picc.); Tamburo militare (Tamb. milit.)	Kleine Trommel (Kl. Tr.)	Caisse claire (C. cl.); Tambour militaire (Tamb. milit.)
Tenor drum	Cassa rullante	Rührtrommel	Caisse roulante
Indian drum			
Tom-tom			
Bass drum (B. drum, Bass dr., Bs. Dr.)	Gran cassa (Gr. Cassa, Gr. C., G. C.)	Große Trommel (Gr. Tr.)	Grosse caisse (Gr. c.)
Tambourine (Tamb.)	Tamburino (Tamb.)	Schellentrommel, Tamburin	Tambour de Basque (T. de B., Tamb. de Basque)
Cymbals (Cym., Cymb.)	Piatti (P., Ptti., Piat.)	Becken (Beck.)	Cymbales (Cym.)
Suspended cymbal (Sus. cym., Susp. cymb.)			
Sizzle cymbal (Sizz. cym.)			
Tam-Tam (Tam-T.); Gong	Tam-Tam (Tam-T.)	Tam-Tam	Tam-Tam
Triangle (Trgl., Tri.)	Triangolo (Trgl.)	Triangel (Trgl.)	Triangle (Triang.)
Glockenspiel (Glocken.)	Campanelli (Cmp.)	Glockenspiel (Glsp.)	Carillon
Bells; Tubular bells (Tub. bells); Chimes	Campane (Cmp.)	Glocken	Cloches
Antique Cymbals	Crotali, Piatti antichi	Antiken Zimbeln	Cymbales antiques (Cym. ant.)
Xylophone (Xyl., Xylo.)	Xilofono	Xylophon (Xyl.)	Xylophone
Vibraphone			
Marimba			
Claves			
Raspador			
Gourd			
Maraca			

OTHER INSTRUMENTS

English	Italian	German	French
Harp (Hp., Hrp.)	Arpa (A., Arp.)	Harfe (Hrf.)	Harpe (Hp.)
Piano	Pianoforte (P.-f., Pft., Pfte.)	Klavier	Piano
Celesta (Cel.)	Celesta		Céleste
Harpsichord	Cembalo (Cemb.); Clavicembalo	Cembalo	Clavecin
Organ (Org.)	Organo (Org.) [Organo di legno is an organ with wooden pipes]	Orgel	Orgue
Guitar	Chitarra	Gitarre (Git.)	Guitare
Lute	Lauto, leuto, liuto	Laute	Luth
Theorbo	Teorba; Chitarrone	Theorb; Chitarron	Téorbe
Archlute	Arcileuto	Erzlaute	Archiluth
Banjo			

Transposing instruments and timpani tunings are indicated using the following pitch names:

English	C	D	E♭	E	F	G	A	B♭	B
Italian	Do	Re	Mi♭	Mi	Fa	Sol	La	Si♭	Si
French	Ut	Ré	Mi♭	Mi	Fa	Sol	La	Si♭	Si
German	C	D	Es	E	F	G	A	B	H

For transposing instruments, if the music is written in C major, it will sound in the designated key; thus "in A" means that a notated C will sound as A, and every notated pitch will sound a minor third lower than written. Horns, clarinets in B♭ and A, and trumpets in B♭ sound lower than written; clarinets in D and E♭ and trumpets in D and F sound higher than written. English horns are in F, sounding a fifth lower than written; alto flutes are in G, sounding a fourth lower.

GLOSSARY OF SCORE AND PERFORMANCE INDICATIONS

For a glossary of general music terms, see *A History of Western Music*, 7th ed.

a, à The phrases *a 2 (à 2), a 3 (à 3)*, etc. indicate that the part is to be played in unison by 2, 3 (etc.) players, or that the group is to divide into 2, 3 (etc.) different parts (which meaning holds is usually obvious from the context); when a simple number (1., 2., etc.) is placed over a part, it indicates that only the first (second, etc.) player in that group should play.

A Alto.

a piacere As you please; the execution of the passage is left to the performer's discretion.

a tempo At the (basic) tempo.

ab Off; *Dämpfer ab*, remove mute.

abdämpfen Damp; stop from vibrating.

aber But.

accelerando (accel., acceler.) Growing faster.

accompagnamento Accompanying; in a keyboard concerto, this indicates a passage in which the keyboard accompanies the orchestra rather than taking the lead as the soloist.

accompagnato Accompanied.

ad libitum (ad lib.) An indication giving the performer liberty; for example, to vary from strict tempo, to include or omit the part of some voice or instrument, or to include a cadenza of one's own invention.

adagio Slow, leisurely.

affettuoso Tender; with feeling.

affrettando Hurrying; hurried.

agitato Agitated, excited.

al fine Until the end; until the *fine* marking.

alla marcia Like a march; in march tempo.

allargando (allarg.) Growing broader or slower.

alle All; tutti.

allegretto A moderately fast tempo, between allegro and andante.

allegro A rapid tempo, between allegretto and presto.

allegro assai Very fast.

allegro di molto Very rapid tempo.

allegro possibile As fast as possible.

alto, Alt (A) The deeper of the two main divisions of women's (or boys') voices; in vocal music in four or more parts, a part above the tenor and below the highest voice.

altri The others; used to designate the other players in an orchestral section when one or more players in the section are given separate parts.

am Frosch At the frog; play with the part of the bow nearest the player's hand (the *frog* of the bow).

am Griffbrett On a string instrument, bow near, or over, the fingerboard; *sul tasto*.

am Steg On a string instrument, bow over or very near the bridge, producing a thin, metallic sound; *sul ponticello*.

ancora meno Still less.

andante A moderately slow tempo, between adagio and allegretto, about walking speed.

andantino A tempo slightly faster than andante.

anima Spirit, animation.

animato, animé Animated.

appassionato Impassioned; passionate.

archi Strings, the string section of the orchestra.

arco Played with the bow; used to mark a return to bowing after a pizzicato passage.

ardente Ardent, passionate.

armonioso Harmonious.

arpeggiando, arpeggiato (arpeg.) Arpeggiated; played in harp style, sounding the notes of the chord in quick succession rather than simultaneously.

assai Very.

auf On; *Dämpfer auf*, put mute in place.

auf dem On the (as in *auf dem G*, on the G string).

auf dem Theater, wie vom Lande her In the theater or backstage (rather than in the orchestra pit), as if from the land.

auf der Bühne (a.d. Bühne) On stage.

Ausdruck Expression.

ausdrucklos Expressionless.

ausdrucksvoll Full of expression.

avec With

avec une émotion naissante With new feeling.

avec une joie voilée With veiled joy.

B Bass.

bacchetta (bacch.) Drumstick.

bacchetta di legno (bacch. di legno) Wooden drumstick.

bacchetta di triangolo (bacch. di Triang.) Metal stick used to play the triangle.

baguettes Drumsticks.

baguettes d'éponge Sponge-headed drumsticks.

bass, basso, Baß (B); pl. bassi, Bässe A low male voice, or the lowest part in a vocal or instrumental work.

bedeutet Means, indicates.

begleitend Accompanying; indicates that another part has the leading voice in the texture.

Begleitung Accompaniment.

ben Very, well.

bewegt, bewegte Agitated.

bewegter More agitated.

bien Very, well.

Bläsern The wind and brass instruments.

bravura Skill, virtuosity.

breit Broad, broadly.

breiter More broadly.

brillante Brilliant, showy.

brio Spirit, vivacity.

brushes Play with wire brushes rather than drumsticks.

Bühne Stage.

cadenza A short or extended passage for solo instrument or voice in free, improvisatory style, at or just before or after a cadence.

calando Diminishing in volume and speed.

cambiare l'arco ad lib. Change bow direction as necessary; used to indicate that on a sustained tone the entire section should not bow simultaneously.

campana in aria On a brass instrument, play with the bell raised to achieve an especially prominent tone.

cantabile (cant., cantab.) In a singing style.

cantando Singing; in a singing manner.

cantando la melodia Emphasize the melody as if singing it.

canto Voice.

Chor Chorus.

Chorauszug Transcription of the chorus parts, used for rehearsal or for cues during performance.

chorus (1) Group of singers, normally several on each part. (2) In a popular song, the refrain.

col, colla, coll' With the.

col canto, colla voce, colla parte With the voice or solo part; indicates that the accompaniment is to follow the solo part in tempo and expression.

col legno, col ligno (c.l.) With the wood of the bow.

col legno battuto (col legno batt., l. batt.) Striking the strings with the wood of the bow.

come prima (come Ima), come sopra As at first, as above, as previously.

comme Like, as.

comme une fanfare Like a fanfare.

comme un oiseau Like a birdcall.

comodo Comfortable, easy.

con With.

con due Pedale In piano music, indicates that both the damper pedal (see *pedal*) and the *una corda* pedal are to be depressed.

coperto, coperti Of a drum, covered with a cloth to muffle the sound.

coro Chorus.

crescendo (cresc., cres.) Increasing in volume.

cuivré On a horn, play with a loud, brassy tone.

da capo (D.C.) Repeat from the beginning, usually up to the indication *Fine* (end).

daher Therefore, hence.

dal segno Repeat from the sign, usually up to the indication *Fine* (end).

damp Muffle, silence; stop from vibrating.

damped Of a cymbal, muffled as soon as it is struck.

Dämpfer (Dpf.) Mute.

dann Then.

das, der, die The.

de plus en plus More and more, gradually.

declamato Sung in declamatory fashion.

decrescendo (decresc., decres.) Decreasing in volume.

delicato Delicate, soft.

delicatissimo (delicatiss.) Very delicate.

descendez le "la" un demi-ton plus bas
Tune the A string a semitone lower.
détaché With a broad, vigorous bow stroke, each note bowed singly.
deutlich Distinctly.
di Of.
diese This.
diminuendo (dim., dimin.) Decreasing in volume.
distinto Distinctly.
divisi, divise (div.) Divided; indicates that the group should be divided into two or more parts to perform the passage in question.
dolce Gentle, soft.
dolcissimo (dolciss.) Very gentle.
dolente Sorrowful.
Doppelgriff Double stop; on string instruments, playing two strings at once
doppelt so schnell Twice as fast.
doppio movimento Twice as fast.
drängend Pressing on.
dreifach Divided in three parts.

e And.
echo tone, Echoton Like an echo.
éclatant Sparkling, brilliant.
egualmente Equally.
ein, eine One; a.
elegante Elegant.
en In.
en dehors Emphasized, prominent.
enchaînez Play the next movement without a break.
encore Still, yet (as in *encore plus lent,* still more slowly).
Ende des zweiten Aufzuges End of Act II.
energico Energetic.
enveloppé de pedale Veiled or enveloped by the pedal.
environ About.
erschütterung A violent shaking, deep emotion.
erst, erste First.
espressione (espress.) Expression.
espressivo (espress., espr.) Expressive, expressively.
et And.
etwas Somewhat, rather.
eventuell nur eine (event. nur eine) If necessary, only one player.
expressif (express.) Expressive.

f Forte.
facilité Designates a simpler or less difficult alternative passage.
feroce Ferocious.

ff Fortissimo.
fff Fortississimo.
fine End, close.
Flageolet (Flag.) Harmonic.
flautando (flaut.) On a string instrument, producing a flute-like tone by bowing lightly and swiftly above the fingerboard.
flüchtig Fleeting, transient.
flutter-tongue, Flatterzunge (fl. t., Flttzg.) Very fast tonguing technique for wind and brass intruments, producing a rapid trill-like sound.
folgt There follows.
forte (f) Loud.
forte-piano (fp) Loud, then immediately soft on the same note.
fortissimo (ff) Very loud.
fortississimo (fff) Extremely loud.
fortsetzend Continuing.
forza Force.
forzando, forzato (fz) Play with a strong accent.
fp Forte-piano; loud, then immediately soft.
frog The part of the bow nearest the player's hand, used to tighten the bowhairs.
fuoco Fire, spirit.
furioso Furious, furiously.
fz Forzando, forzato.

gebrochen Broken, arpeggiated.
gedämpft Muted; for a horn, stopped by inserting the right hand in the bell.
gedehnt Held back; slow and restrained.
gehende Moderate tempo, walking speed; andante.
gemächlich Comfortable.
Generalpause (G.P.) Rest for the complete ensemble.
geschlagen Struck.
geschwind Rapid, swift.
gesprochen Spoken.
gesteigert Intensified.
gestopft Stopped; for the notes of a horn obtained by placing the hand in the bell.
gestoßen Detached, not legato.
gestrichen (gestr.) Bowed.
gesungen Sung.
geteilt (get.) Divided, divisi; indicates that the group should be divided into two or more parts to perform the passage in question.
gewöhnlich (gew., gewöhnl.) Usual, customary; used to cancel an indication to play in an unusual manner, such as *am Steg* or *col legno.*
giocoso Jesting, playful.
giusto Moderate.
gleichmässig Equal.

gleichsam versuchend, eine Begleitung für das Lied Wozzecks zu finden As if seeking to devise an accompaniment for Wozzeck's song.

gli altri The others; used to designate the other players in an orchestral section when one or more players in the section are given separate parts.

glissando (gliss.) Rapidly gliding over strings or keys, producing a fast scale on a harp or piano or a fast continuous slide on string instruments, timpani, or trombone.

G.P. *Generalpause*; rest in all parts.

gran, grande Great, large.

grandioso Grandiose; grandly.

grazia Grace; gracefulness.

grazioso Graceful.

Griffbrett Fingerboard of a string instrument.

groß, große Large, big.

H *Hauptstimme* or *Hauptrhythmus*.

Halt Stop, hold.

Harmon mute Mute for trumpet or trombone that can be adjusted or covered with the hand to allow different amounts of air through, producing a more or less distant sound.

harmonic (harm.) A flute-like sound produced on a string instrument by lightly touching the string with the finger instead of pressing down on the string (natural harmonic), or by stopping the string with one finger and lightly touching the string at another point, usually a perfect fourth higher (artificial harmonic).

Hauptrhythmus Principal rhythm; the main rhythmic pattern.

Hauptstimme Principal voice; the most important part in the texture.

Hauptzeitmass Original tempo.

hervor Given prominence.

hervortretend Prominent; coming to the fore.

Holzbläser Woodwinds.

hörbar Audible.

il The.

il primo tempo Resume the original tempo.

im Tempo, im Zeitmaß In tempo.

immer Always.

impetuoso Impetuous, violent.

in Used for indicating transposing instruments or changes of pitch. An instrument *in* C sounds as written, but one designated as in another key sounds in that key when its notated part is in C major; thus a clarinet *in* A

will sound an A when it plays a C. See the chart of pitch names, p. 1430.

in tempo Resume the previous tempo; used after a ritardando or other variation in tempo.

innig Sincere, tender, fervent.

klagend Lamenting.

klangvoll Sonorous, full-sounding.

klingen lassen Let ring; allow to sound.

klingt wie notiert Sounds as written, meaning that the score shows the sounding pitches for transposing instruments (like horn in F or clarinet in A) as a convenience to the score-reader; the normal transpositions appear in the parts from which the instruments play.

kräftig Stong, forceful.

kriegerisch Martial, warlike.

kurz Short.

kurzer Shorter.

L Left; play with the left hand.

la The.

laissez vibrer, lascia vibrare (lasc. vibr., l.v.) Let vibrate; an indication to the player of a harp, cymbal, etc., that the sound must not be damped.

langsam Slow, slowly.

langsamer Slower.

languendo Languishing, weakening.

largamente Broadly.

larghetto Slightly faster than largo.

largo A very slow tempo.

lebhaft Lively.

lebhafter More lively.

legatissimo Very legato.

legato Performed without any perceptible interruption between notes; the opposite of staccato.

leggiero, leggieramente (legg.) Light and graceful.

leggierissimo (leggeriss.) Very light and graceful.

leggio (legg.) Music stand; in an orchestral score, *legg. 5.6.* indicates the players at the fifth and sixth stands in the section (normally there are two players at each stand in the string sections).

legno, ligno The wood of the bow.

leidenschaftlich Passionate, vehement.

lent Slow, slowly.

lento A slow tempo, between andante and largo.

l.h. Left hand; play with the left hand.

ligato Legato.

loco To be played where written; cancels an *octava* sign.

lumineux Luminous, brilliant.

l.v. Let vibrate; *laisser vibrer, lascia vibrare.*

ma But.

ma non troppo But not too much.

maestoso Majestic; stately.

maggiore In the major mode; used to mark a change to or section in the parallel or relative major.

main droite (m.d.) Play with the right hand.

main gauche (m.g.) Play with the left hand.

mais But.

malinconico Melancholy, dejected.

mano destra (m.d.) Play with the right hand.

mano sinistra (m.s.) Play with the left hand.

marcatissimo (marcatiss.) With very marked emphasis.

marcato (marc.) Marked, with emphasis.

marcato il basso Emphasize the bass line.

marcia March.

marqué Marked, with emphasis.

martellato Hammered.

marziale In martial (military) style; march-like.

mässig Moderate.

m.d. *Main droite, mano destra*; play with the right hand.

m.D. *Mit Dämpfer*; with mute.

m.d. Pianino *Mit dem Pianino*; with the upright piano.

melodrama, Melodram Style of theatrical presentation that features spoken words over continuous music.

meno Less.

meno mosso Less fast.

menuetto, Menuett Minuet.

metronome marking (Metr., M.M.) Indicates metronome setting for the correct tempo, in beats per minute.

mezza voce Half-voice; with half the voice power.

mezzo forte (*mf*) Moderately loud.

mezzo piano (*mp*) Moderately soft.

mf Mezzo forte.

m.g. *Main gauche*; play with the left hand.

minore In the minor mode; used to mark a change to or section in the parallel or relative minor.

misterioso Mysteriously.

misurato Measured; moderate.

mit (m.) With.

M.M. Metronome marking; followed by

metronome setting for the correct tempo, in beats per minute.

moderato, modéré At a moderate tempo.

modo ordinario (modo ord.) In an ordinary fashion; cancels a previous indication to play in an unusual manner, such as *sul ponticello.*

molto Very, much.

morendo Dying away; becoming very soft.

mosso Rapid; with movement.

moto Motion.

mp Mezzo piano.

muta in Change the tuning of the instrument as specified; or change to another instrument as specified.

m.s. *Mano sinistra*; play with the left hand.

N⌐ *Nebenstimme.*

Nachschlag Auxiliary note at the end of a trill.

naturale (nat.) Natural; used to cancel a previous indication for an unusual technique (such as *coperto* for a drummer), or to indicate a natural harmonic on an open string.

Nebenstimme The second most important voice in the texture; compare *Hauptstimme.*

nehmen (nimmt) Take; used to indicate a change of instrument, as from flute to piccolo.

neue New.

nicht Not.

nicht zu Not too.

nimmt Takes; used to indicate a change of instrument, as from bass clarinet to clarinet.

noch Still, yet.

non Not.

non troppo, non tanto Not too much.

Noten Notes.

o. *Ohne*; without.

obligato, obbligato A line that must be played; often indicates a featured solo part, or a part that might otherwise play with the bass.

octava (okt., 8va, 8.) Octave; *8va alto* means an octave higher, *8va basso* or *Okt. tiefer* an octave lower. If not otherwise qualified, the notes marked should be played an octave higher than written if *8va* is written above the affected notes, or an octave lower if written below them.

offen Open; cancels *gedämpft.*

ohne (o.) Without.

open (1) In brass instruments, the opposite of muted. (2) In string instruments, refers to the unstopped string (i.e., sounding at its full length).

ordinario, ordinairement, ordinèrement (ord.) In the usual way; cancels an instruction to play in some special manner, such as *sul ponticello.*

ossia Or rather; used to indicate an alternate reading of a passage.

otto Imi Vni Eight first violins.

ouvert Open.

p Piano (the dynamic level); soft.

parte Part; *colla parte* means that the accompaniment is to follow the voice parts.

passionato Passionate, impassioned.

passione Passion.

pause Rest.

pavillon en l'air (pav. en l'air) Bell in the air; sign for horn players to lift their bells to direct the sound forward.

pedal, pedale (ped., P.) In piano music, indicates that the damper pedal should be depressed; an asterisk indicates the point of release (brackets below the music are also used to indicate pedalling).

perdendosi Gradually dying away.

pesante Heavy.

peu Little, a little.

Pianino Upright piano.

pianissimo (*pp*) Very soft.

pianississimo (*ppp*) Extremely soft; *pppp* indicates a still softer dynamic.

piano (*p*) Soft.

più More.

più mosso, più moto Faster.

più voce Full voice; cancels a previous marking of *mezza voce.*

pizzicato (pizz.) On a string instrument, plucked with the finger instead of played with the bow; compare *arco.*

plötzlich Sudden, suddenly, immediately.

plunger A kind of mute for brass instruments used in jazz to create a wah-wah effect.

plus More.

pochissimo (pochiss.) Very little.

poco, un poco Little, a little.

poco a poco Little by little.

ponticello (pont.) The bridge of a string instrument.

portamento Fast slide between notes.

portato Performance manner between legato and staccato.

possibile Possible, as much as possible.

pp Pianissimo.

ppp Pianississimo.

près de la table On the harp, pluck the strings near the soundboard, producing a metallic sound.

presto A very quick tempo (faster than allegro).

prima, primo (Imo) First, as in first bassoon part.

pult Music stand. There are normally two string players per stand in an orchestra; 2 *Pult.* means "second stand" (i.e., second two players in the section), and *der zweite Spieler am 1. Pult* means "the second player at the first stand."

pultweise geteilt Divided by stand, so one player at each stand takes one of the two parts.

quasi Almost, as if.

quasi Arpa Like a harp.

quasi in den Tanz einfallend As if joining in the dance.

quasi niente Almost nothing, i.e., as softly as possible.

R Right; play with right hand.

rallentando (rall., rallent.) Growing slower.

rapido Fast.

rasch Fast.

rascher Faster.

recitative, recitativo, Rezitativ (recit.) A vocal style designed to imitate and emphasize the natural inflections of speech.

Rezitation Reciting voice.

r.h., R.H. Right hand; play with the right hand.

risoluto Resolute.

ritardando (rit., ritard.) Gradually slackening in speed.

ritenuto (riten.) Holding back.

ritmato, ritmico Rhythmic.

rubato A certain elasticity and flexibility of tempo, speeding up and slowing down the performance of written music.

ruhig Calm.

ruhiger Calmer; more calmly.

rythmé Rhythmic.

S Soprano.

Saite String; e.g., C-Saite means C-string.

sans Without.

scherzando (scherz.) Playfully; jesting.

schleppend Dragging.

schnell Fast.

schon Already.

schon bei geschlossenem Vorhang verhaltend Stop when the curtain closes.

Schwammschlägel Sponge-headed drumstick.

schwerer Heavier.

schwermütig Dejected, sad.

secco Dry.

segno Sign; especially one indicating the beginning of a section to be repeated.

segue (1) Continue in the same manner; (2) continue to the next movement without pausing.

sehr Very.

semplice Simple, in a simple manner.

sempre Always, continually.

senza Without.

sforzando, sforzato (*sfz*, *sf*) With sudden emphasis.

sforzando-piano (*sfp*) Sforzando, then suddenly soft.

simile Likewise; continue in a similar manner.

sino al, sin al Until, up to (usually followed by a new tempo marking, or by a dotted line indicating a terminal point).

Singstimme Singing voice; vocal line.

smorzando (smorz.) Getting slower, as if dying away.

soft stick Use padded or sponge drumstick.

solo (pl. soli) (1) To be played by one performer. (2) Indicates the most prominent part in an ensemble texture.

sombre Dark, somber.

son Sound.

son fluté, vers la pointe On a string instrument, played near the tip of the bow, producing a flute-like sound.

sonore Sonorous, with full tone.

sopra Above; in piano music, used to indicate that one hand must reach over the other.

soprano, Sopran (Sop., S) The voice with the highest range.

sordino (sord., pl. sordini) Mute.

sostenuto (sost.) Sustained.

sotto voce In an undertone, subdued, under the breath.

sourdine (sourd.) Mute.

soutenu Sustained.

Spieler Player.

spirito Spirited, lively.

spiritoso Humorous.

sprezando Becoming more distant.

staccato (stacc.) Detached, separated; held for less than the full notated duration.

staccatissimo Very staccato.

Steigerung Growing intensity.

stem in, stem out On a Harmon mute, indi-cates whether the stem of the plunger is pushed in, cutting off most of the air flow, or pulled out, allowing more air through.

Stimme Voice.

Streicher Strings, the string section of the orchestra.

straight mute Conical mute for brass instruments, placed in the bell and held there by cork strips that allow some air through.

strepitoso Noisy, boisterous.

stretto In a nonfugal composition, indicates an increase in speed.

Strich Stroke of the bow; *mit breitem Strich*, with broad bowstrokes.

stringendo (string.) Quickening.

subito (sub.) Suddenly, immediately.

sul On the (as in *sul G.* on the G string).

sul ponticello (sul pont., s.p.) On a string instrument, bow over or very near the bridge; this emphasizes the higher harmonics to produce a thin, metallic sound.

sul tasto (s.t.) On a string instrument, bow near, or over, the fingerboard; this minimizes the harmonics to produce a flute-like, ethereal sound.

sur On.

sur la touche On a string instrument, bow near, or over, the fingerboard; *sul tasto*.

T Tenor.

tacet Be silent; refrain from playing.

Takt Bar, beat.

tanto So much.

tasto Fingerboard of a string instrument.

tempo The speed or relative pace of the music.

tempo blues In the tempo of a blues.

tempo di marcia March tempo.

tempo giusto Moderate or appropriate tempo.

tempo primo (tempo I, tempo Io) At the original tempo.

teneramente Tenderly.

tenor, tenore (T., ten.) High male voice or part; in choral music, the second voice from the bottom of the texture.

tenuto (ten.) Held, sustained.

tiefer Lower.

touche Fingerboard or fret (of a string instrument).

tr Trill.

tranquillo Quiet, calm.

tre corde, tre corda Three strings; cancels *una corda* marking.

tremolo (trem) On string instruments, a quick reiteration of the same tone, produced by a rapid up-and-down movement of the bow.

tremulo Trill; *tremulo nell' A la mi re*, trill on A above middle C.

très Very.

trill (*tr*) The rapid alternation of a given note with the note above it. In a drum part it indicates rapid alternating strokes with two drumsticks.

Triller ohne Nachschlag Trills without final auxiliary or grace note.

Trio Second or middle section of a minuet and trio, a scherzo, a march, or a rag.

Triole Triplets.

troppo Too much.

tumultueuse Tumultuous.

tutta forza Full force.

tutti, tutte Literally, "all"; usually means all the instruments in a given category as distinct from a solo part; cancels the designation *solo*.

tutto fortissimo possibile As loudly as possible.

übergreifen Reach over; in piano music, indicates that one hand should reach over the other.

übertönend Drowning out.

übrigen The others, the remaining; used to designate the other players in an orchestral section when one or more players in the section are given separate parts.

un, una, une One; a.

un poco, un peu A little.

una corda One string; tells the player of a grand piano to depress the left pedal, which shifts the hammer mechanism over so that only one string is struck for each note (rather than three or two).

und (u.) And.

unison (unis.) The same notes or melody played by several instruments at the same pitch. Often used to emphasize that a phrase is not to be divided among several players.

unite, uniti Unison.

unmittelbar anschließend Immediately following.

Unterbrechung Interruption, suspension.

vamp Brief introduction which may be repeated ad libitum until the singer begins.

veloce Fast.

velocissimo Very fast.

verhalten Restrained, held back.

verklingen lassen Let the sound die away; do not damp.

verstimmt Out of tune; *ein verstimmtes Pianino*, an out-of-tune upright piano.

Verwandlung Change of scene.

vibrato (vib., vibr.) Slight fluctuation of pitch around a sustained tone.

vierfach Divided in four parts.

Viertel Quarter note; *die neuen Viertel . . . sind gleich den Vierteln der vorigen Triole*, the new quarter note is equivalent to the quarter notes in the preceding triplets.

vigoroso Vigorous, strong.

vivace Quick, lively.

vivo Lively.

voce Voice.

volante Literally, "flying"; play swiftly and lightly.

Vorhang auf Curtain up.

Vorhang fällt, Vorhang zu Curtain down.

voriges, vorigen Preceding.

vorwärts Forward, onward.

weg Away; *Dämpfer weg*, remove mutes.

werdend Becoming.

wieder Again.

womöglich If possible.

zart Tenderly, delicately.

Zeitmaß Tempo

ziemlich Rather, fairly.

zu 2 Same as *a 2*.

Zungenschlag Tonguing; flutter-tonguing.

zurückhaltend Slackening in speed.

zurückkehrend zum Returning to, going back to.

INDEX OF COMPOSERS

INDEX OF TITLES

INDEX OF FORMS AND GENRES